797,885 Books

are available to read at

Forgotten Books

www.ForgottenBooks.com

Forgotten Books' App
Available for mobile, tablet & eReader

ISBN 978-1-330-47146-3
PIBN 10066177

This book is a reproduction of an important historical work. Forgotten Books uses state-of-the-art technology to digitally reconstruct the work, preserving the original format whilst repairing imperfections present in the aged copy. In rare cases, an imperfection in the original, such as a blemish or missing page, may be replicated in our edition. We do, however, repair the vast majority of imperfections successfully; any imperfections that remain are intentionally left to preserve the state of such historical works.

Forgotten Books is a registered trademark of FB &c Ltd.
Copyright © 2017 FB &c Ltd.
FB &c Ltd, Dalton House, 60 Windsor Avenue, London, SW19 2RR.
Company number 08720141. Registered in England and Wales.

For support please visit www.forgottenbooks.com

1 MONTH OF FREE READING

at

www.ForgottenBooks.com

By purchasing this book you are eligible for one month membership to ForgottenBooks.com, giving you unlimited access to our entire collection of over 700,000 titles via our web site and mobile apps.

To claim your free month visit:

www.forgottenbooks.com/free66177

* Offer is valid for 45 days from date of purchase. Terms and conditions apply.

English
Français
Deutsche
Italiano
Español
Português

www.forgottenbooks.com

Mythology Photography **Fiction**
Fishing Christianity **Art** Cooking
Essays Buddhism Freemasonry
Medicine **Biology** Music **Ancient Egypt** Evolution Carpentry Physics
Dance Geology **Mathematics** Fitness
Shakespeare **Folklore** Yoga Marketing
Confidence Immortality Biographies
Poetry **Psychology** Witchcraft
Electronics Chemistry History **Law**
Accounting **Philosophy** Anthropology
Alchemy Drama Quantum Mechanics
Atheism Sexual Health **Ancient History**
Entrepreneurship Languages Sport
Paleontology Needlework Islam
Metaphysics Investment Archaeology
Parenting Statistics Criminology
Motivational

BELTANE
THE SMITH

A Romance of the Greenwood

By JEFFERY FARNOL

AUTHOR OF
"The Money Moon," "The Broad Highway,"
"The Amateur Gentleman," Etc.

With Frontispiece
By ARTHUR E. BECHER

A. L. BURT COMPANY

Publishers   New York

Published by Arrangement with LITTLE, BROWN & COMPANY

Copyright, 1915,
BY LITTLE, BROWN, AND COMPANY.

All rights reserved.

Published, November, 1915
Reprinted, December, 1915

TO
FREDERICK HUGHSON HAWLEY
TO WHOM BELTANE IS NO STRANGER
I DEDICATE THIS ROMANCE

Jeffery Farnol

London, August, 1915.

BELTANE THE SMITH

CHAPTER I

HOW BELTANE LIVED WITHIN THE GREENWOOD

In a glade of the forest, yet not so far but that one might hear the chime of bells stealing across the valley from the great minster of Mortain on a still evening, dwelt Beltane the Smith.

Alone he lived in the shadow of the great trees, happy when the piping of the birds was in his ears, and joying to listen to the plash and murmur of the brook that ran merrily beside his hut; or pausing 'twixt the strokes of his ponderous hammer to catch its never failing music.

A mighty man was Beltane the Smith, despite his youth already great of stature and comely of feature. Much knew he of woodcraft, of the growth of herb and tree and flower, of beast and bird, and how to tell each by its cry or song or flight; he knew the ways of fish in the streams, and could tell the course of the stars in the heavens; versed was he likewise in the ancient wisdoms and philosophies, both Latin and Greek, having learned all these things from him whom men called Ambrose the Hermit. But of men and cities he knew little, and of women and the ways of women, less than nothing, for of these matters Ambrose spake not.

Thus, being grown from youth to manhood, for that a man must needs live, Beltane builded him a hut beside the brook, and set up an anvil thereby whereon he beat out bill-hooks and axe-heads and such implements as the charcoal-burners and they that lived within the green had need of.

Oft-times, of an evening, he would seek out the hermit Ambrose, and they would talk together of many things, but seldom of men and cities, and never of women and the ways of women. Once, therefore, wondering, Beltane had said:

"My father, amongst all these matters you speak never of women and the ways of women, though history is full of their doings, and all poets sing praise of their wondrous beauty, as this Helena of Troy, whom men called 'Desire of the World.'"

But Ambrose sighed and shook his head, saying:

"Art thou indeed a man, so soon, my Beltane?" and so sat watching him awhile. Anon he rose and striding to and fro spake sudden and passionate on this wise: "Beltane, I tell thee the beauty of women is an evil thing, a lure to wreck the souls of men. By woman came sin into the world, by her beauty she blinds the eyes of men to truth and honour, leading them into all manner of wantonness whereby their very manhood is destroyed. This Helen of Troy, of whom ye speak, was nought but a vile adulteress, with a heart false and foul, by whose sin many died and Troy town was utterly destroyed."

"Alas!" sighed Beltane, "that one so fair should be a thing so evil!"

Thereafter he went his way, very sad and thoughtful, and that night, lying upon his bed, he heard the voices of the trees sighing and murmuring one to another like souls that sorrowed for sin's sake, and broken dreams and ideals.

"Alas! that one so fair should be a thing so evil!" But, above the whispers of the trees, loud and insistent rose the merry chatter of the brook speaking to him of many things; of life, and the lust of life; the pomp and stir of cities; the sound of song and laughter; of women and the beauty of women, and of the sweet, mad wonder of love. Of all these things the brook sang in the darkness, and Beltane sighed, and sighing, fell asleep.

How He Lived in the Greenwood 3

Thus lived my Beltane in the woodland, ranging the forest with eye quick to see the beauty of earth and sky, and ear open to the thousand voices around him; or, busied at his anvil, hearkening to the wondrous tales of travel and strange adventure told by wandering knight and man-at-arms the while, with skilful hand, he mended broken mail or dented casque; and thereafter, upon the mossy sward, would make trial of their strength and valour, whereby he both took and gave right lusty knocks; or again, when work failed, he would lie upon the grass, chin on fist, poring over some ancient legend, or sit with brush and colours illuminating on vellum, wherein right cunning was he. Now it chanced that as he sat thus, brush in hand, upon a certain fair afternoon, he suddenly espied one who stood watching him from the shade of a tree, near by. A very tall man he was, long and lean and grim of aspect, with a mouth wry-twisted by reason of an ancient sword-cut, and yet, withal, he had a jovial eye. But now, seeing himself observed, he shook his grizzled head and sighed. Whereat said Beltane, busied with his brush again:

"Good sir, pray what's amiss?"

"The world, youth, the world—'tis all amiss. Yet mark me! here sit you a-dabbing colour with a little brush!"

Answered Beltane:

"An so ye seek to do your duty as regardfully as I now daub this colour, messire, in so much shall the world be bettered."

"My duty, youth," quoth the stranger, rasping a hand across his grizzled chin, "my duty? Ha, 'tis well said, so needs must I now fight with thee."

"Fight with me!" says Beltane, his keen gaze upon the speaker.

"Aye, verily!" nodded the stranger, and, forthwith, laying by his long cloak, he showed two swords whose broad blades glittered, red and evil, in the sunset.

"But," says Beltane, shaking his head, "I have no quarrel with thee, good fellow."

"Quarrel?" exclaimed the stranger, "no quarrel, quotha? What matter for that? Surely you would not forego a good bout for so small a matter? Doth a man eat only when famishing, or drink but to quench his thirst? Out upon thee, messire smith!"

"But sir," said Beltane, bending to his brush again, "an I should fight with thee, where would be the reason?"

"Nowhere, youth, since fighting is ever at odds with reason; yet for such unreasonable reasons do reasoning men fight."

"None the less, I will not fight thee," answered Beltane, deftly touching in the wing of an archangel, "so let there be an end on't."

"End forsooth, we have not yet begun! An you must have a quarrel, right fully will I provoke thee, since fight with thee I must, it being so my duty —"

"How thy duty?"

"I am so commanded."

"By whom?"

"By one who, being dead, yet liveth. Nay, ask no names, yet mark me this — the world's amiss, boy. Pentavalon groans beneath a black usurper's heel, all the sins of hell are loose, murder and riot, lust and rapine. March you eastward but a day through the forest yonder and you shall see the trees bear strange fruit in our country. The world's amiss, messire, yet here sit you wasting your days, a foolish brush stuck in thy fist. So am I come, nor will I go hence until I have tried thy mettle."

Quoth Beltane, shaking his head, intent upon his work:

"You speak me riddles, sir."

"Yet can I speak thee to the point and so it be thy wish, as thus — now mark me, boy! Thou art a fool, a dog, a fatuous ass, a slave, a nincompoop, a cowardly boy, and as such — mark me again! — now do I spit at thee!"

Hereupon Beltane, having finished the archangel's wing, laid by his brush and, with thoughtful mien, arose, and being upon his feet, turned him, swift and sudden, and caught the stranger in a fierce and cunning wrestling

How He Lived in the Greenwood 5

grip, and forthwith threw him upon his back. Whereat this strange man, sitting cross-legged upon the sward, smiled his wry and twisted smile and looked upon Beltane with bright, approving eye.

"A pretty spirit!" he nodded. "'Tis a sweet and gentle youth all good beef and bone; a little green as yet, perchance, but 'tis no matter. A mighty arm, a noble thigh, and shoulders — body o' me! But 'tis in the breed. Young sir, by these same signs and portents my soul is uplifted and hope singeth a new song within me!" So saying, the stranger sprang nimbly to his feet and catching up one of the swords took it by the blade and gave its massy hilt to Beltane's hand. Said he:

"Look well upon this blade, young sir; in duchy, kingdom or county you shall not find its match, nor the like of the terrible hand that bore it. Time was when this good steel — mark how it glitters yet! — struck deep for liberty and justice and all fair things, before whose might oppression quailed and hung its head, and in whose shadow peace and mercy rested. 'Twas long ago, but this good steel is bright and undimmed as ever. Ha! mark it, boy — those eyes o' thine shall ne'er behold its equal!"

So Beltane took hold upon the great sword, felt the spring and balance of the blade and viewed it up from glittering point to plain and simple cross-guard. And thus, graven deep within the broad steel he read this word:

RESURGAM.

"Ha!" cried the stranger, "see you the legend, good youth? Speak me now what it doth signify."

And Beltane answered:

"'I shall arise!'"

"'Arise' good boy, aye, verily, mark me that. 'Tis a fair thought, look you, and the motto of a great and noble house, and, by the Rood, I think, likewise a prophecy!" Thus speaking the stranger stooped, and taking up the other sword faced Beltane therewith, saying in soft and wheedling tones: "Come now, let us fight together thou and I, and deny me not, lest,— mark me this well, youth,— lest I spit at thee again."

Then he raised his sword, and smote Beltane with the flat of it, and the blow stung, wherefore Beltane instinctively swung his weapon and thrilled with sudden unknown joy at the clash of steel on steel; and so they engaged.

And there, within the leafy solitude, Beltane and the stranger fought together. The long blades whirled and flashed and rang upon the stillness; and ever, as they fought, the stranger smiled his wry smile, mocking and gibing at him, whereat Beltane's mouth grew the grimmer and his blows the heavier, yet wherever he struck, there already was the stranger's blade to meet him, whereat the stranger laughed fierce and loud, taunting him on this wise:

"How now, thou dauber of colours, betake thee to thy little brush, belike it shall serve thee better! Aye me, betake thee to thy little brush, 'twere better fitted to thee than a noble sword, thou daubing boy!"

Now did my Beltane wax wroth indeed and smote amain until his breath grew short and thick, but ever steel rang on steel, and ever the stranger laughed and gibed until Beltane's strokes grew slower: — then, with a sudden fierce shout, did the stranger beset my Beltane with strokes so swift and strong, now to right of him, now to left, that the very air seemed full of flaming, whirling steel, and, in that moment, as Beltane gave back, the stranger smote thrice in as many moments with the flat of his blade, once upon the crown, once upon the shoulder, and once upon the thigh. Fierce eyed and scant of breath, Beltane redoubled his blows, striving to beat his mocker to the earth, whereat he but laughed again, saying:

"Look to thy long legs, dullard!" and forthwith smote Beltane upon the leg. "Now thine arm, slothful boy — thy left arm!" and he smote Beltane upon the arm. "Now thy sconce, boy, thy mazzard, thy sleepy, golden head!" and straightway he smote him on the head, and,

How He Lived in the Greenwood 7

thereafter, with sudden, cunning stroke, beat the great sword from Beltane's grip, and so, laughing yet, paused and stood leaning upon his own long weapon.

But Beltane stood with bent head, hurt in his pride, angry and beyond all thought amazed; yet, being humbled most of all he kept his gaze bent earthwards and spake no word.

Now hereupon the stranger grew solemn likewise and looked at Beltane with kindly, approving eyes.

"Nay, indeed," quoth he, "be not abashed, good youth; take it not amiss that I have worsted thee. 'Tis true, had I been so minded I might have cut thee into gobbets no larger than thy little brush, but then, body o' me! I have lived by stroke of sword from my youth up and have fought in divers wars and countries, so take it not to heart, good youth!" With the word he nodded and, stooping, took up the sword, and, thereafter, cast his cloak about him, whereat Beltane lifted his head and spake:

"Art going, sir? Wilt not try me once again? Methinks I might do a little better this time, an so God wills."

"Aye, so thou shalt, sweet youth," cried the stranger, clapping him upon the shoulder, "yet not now, for I must begone, yet shall I return."

"Then I pray you leave with me the sword till you be come again."

"The sword — ha! doth thy soul cleave unto it so soon, my good, sweet boy? Leave the sword, quotha? Aye, truly — some day. But for the nonce — no, no, thy hand is not fitted to bear it yet, nor worthy such a blade, but some day, belike — who knows? Fare thee well, sweet youth, I come again to-morrow."

And so the tall, grim stranger turned him about, smiling his wry smile, and strode away through the green. Then Beltane went back, minded to finish his painting, but the colours had lost their charm for him, moreover, the light was failing. Wherefore he put brushes and colours aside, and, stripping, plunged into the cool, sweet waters of a certain quiet pool, and so, much heartened and refreshed thereby, went betimes to bed. But now he thought no more of women and the ways of women, but rather of this stranger man, of his wry smile and of his wondrous sword-play; and bethinking him of the great sword, he yearned after it, as only youth may yearn, and so, sighing, fell asleep. And in his dreams all night was the rushing thunder of many fierce feet and the roaring din of bitter fight and conflict.

Up to an elbow sprang Beltane to find the sun new risen, filling his humble chamber with its golden glory, and, in this radiance, upon the open threshold, the tall, grim figure of the stranger.

"Messire," quoth Beltane, rubbing sleepy eyes, "you wake betimes, meseemeth."

"Aye, sluggard boy; there is work to do betwixt us."

"How so, sir?"

"My time in the greenwood groweth short; within the week I must away, for there are wars and rumours of wars upon the borders."

Quoth Beltane, wondering:

"War and conflict have been within my dreams all night!"

"Dreams, boy! I tell thee the time groweth ripe for action — and, mark me this! wherein, perchance, thou too shalt share, yet much have I to teach thee first, so rise, slug-a-bed, rise!"

Now when Beltane was risen and clad he folded his arms across his broad chest and stared upon the stranger with grave, deep-searching eyes.

"Who art thou?" he questioned, "and what would you here again?"

"As to thy first question, sir smith, 'tis no matter for that, but as for thy second, to-day am I come to teach thee the use and manage of horse and lance, it being so my duty."

"And wherefore thy duty?"

"For that I am so commanded."

"By whom?"

"By one who yet liveth, being dead."

Now Beltane frowned at this, and shook his head, saying:

"More riddles, messire? Yet now will I speak thee plain, as thus: I am a smith, and have no lust to strife or knightly deeds, nor will I e'er attempt them, for strife begetteth bitter strife and war is an evil thing. 'They that trust to the sword shall perish by the sword,' 'tis so written, and is, meseemeth, a faithful saying. This sorry world hath known over much of war and hate, of strife and bloodshed, so shall these my hands go innocent of more."

Then indeed did the stranger stare with jaws agape for wonder at my Beltane's saying, and, so staring, turned him to the door and back again, and fain would speak, yet could not for a while. Then:

"Besotted boy!" he cried. "O craven youth! O babe! O suckling! Was it for this thou wert begot? Hast thou no bowels, no blood, no manhood? Forsooth, and must I spit on thee indeed?"

"And so it be thy will, messire," said Beltane, steady-eyed.

But as they stood thus, Beltane with arms yet crossed, his lips up-curving at the other's fierce amaze, the stranger grim-faced and frowning, came a shadow athwart the level glory of the sun, and, turning, Beltane beheld the hermit Ambrose, tall and spare beneath his tattered gown, bareheaded and bare of foot, whose eyes were bright and quick, despite the snow of hair and beard, and in whose gentle face and humble mien was yet a high and noble look at odds with his lowly guise and tattered vesture; at sight of whom the grim-faced stranger, of a sudden, bowed his grizzled head and sank upon his knee.

"Lord!" he said, and kissed the hermit's long, coarse robe. Whereon the hermit bent and touched him with a gentle hand.

"*Benedicite*, my son!" said he. "Go you, and leave us together a while."

Forthwith the stranger rose from his knee and went out into the glory of the morning. Then the hermit came to Beltane and set his two hands upon his mighty shoulders and spake to him very gently, on this wise:

"Thou knowest, my Beltane, how all thy days I have taught thee to love all fair, and sweet, and noble things, for they are of God. 'Twere a fair thought, now, to live out thy life here, within these calm, leafy solitudes — but better death by the sword for some high, unselfish purpose, than to live out a life of ease, safe and cloistered all thy days. To live for thine own ends —'tis human; to die for some great cause, for liberty, or for another's good — that, my son, were God-like. And there was a Man of Sorrows Whose word was this, that He came 'not to bring peace on this earth, but a sword.' For good cannot outface evil but strife must needs follow. Behold now here another sword, my Beltane; keep it henceforth so long as thou keep honour." So saying, Ambrose the Hermit took from beneath his habit that for which Beltane had yearned, that same great blade whereon whose steel was graven the legend:

> RESURGAM.

So Ambrose put the sword in Beltane's hand, saying:

"Be terrible, my son, that evil may flee before thee, learn to be strong that thou may'st be merciful." Then the hermit stretched forth his hands and blessed my Beltane, and turned about, and so was gone.

But Beltane stood awhile to swing the great blade lightly to and fro and to stare upon it with shining eyes. Then, having hid it within his bed, he went forth into the glade. And here he presently beheld a great grey horse tethered to a tree hard by, a mettled steed that tossed its noble head and snuffed the fragrant air of morning, pawing at the earth with impatient hoof. Now, as he stood gazing, came the stranger and touched him on the arm.

"Messire," said he, "try an thou canst back the steed yonder."

How He Lived in the Greenwood

Beltane smiled, for he had loved horses all his days, and loosing the horse, led it out into the open and would have mounted, but the spirited beast, knowing him not, reared and plunged and strove to break the grip upon the bridle, but the grip was strong and compelling; then Beltane soothed him with gentle voice and hand, and, of a sudden, vaulted lightly into the saddle, and being there, felt the great beast rear under him, and, laughing joyously, struck him with open palm and set off at a thunderous gallop. Away, away they sped up the sunny glade, past oak and beech and elm, through light and shadow, until before them showed a tree of vast girth and mighty spread of branches. Now would Beltane have reined aside, but the great horse, ears flat and eyes rolling, held blindly on. Then Beltane frowned and leaning forward, seized the bridle close beside the bit, and gripping it so, put forth his strength. Slowly, slowly the great, fierce head was drawn low and lower, the foam-flecked jaws gaped wide, but Beltane's grip grew ever the fiercer until, snorting, panting, wild-eyed, the great grey horse faltered in his stride, checked his pace, slipped, stumbled, and so stood quivering in the shade of the tree. Thereafter Beltane turned him and, galloping back, drew rein where the stranger sat, cross-legged, watching him with his wry smile.

"Aye," he nodded, "we shall make of thee a horseman yet. But as to lance now, and armour —"

Quoth Beltane, smiling:

"Good sir, I am a smith, and in my time have mended many a suit of mail, aye, and made them too, though 'twas but to try my hand. As for a lance, I have oft tilted at the ring astride a forest pony, and betimes, have run a course with wandering men-at-arms."

"Say you so, boy?" said the stranger, and rising, took from behind a tree a long and heavy lance and thrust it into Beltane's grip; then, drawing his sword, he set it upright in the sward, and upon the hilt he put his cap, saying:

"Ride back up the glade, and try an thou canst pick

up my cap on thy point, at a gallop." So Beltane rode up the glade and wheeling at a distance, came galloping down with levelled lance, and thundered by with the cap fluttering from his lance point.

"Art less of a dullard than I thought thee," said the stranger, taking back his cap, "though, mark me boy, 'tis another matter to ride against a man fully armed and equipped, lance to lance and shield to shield, than to charge a harmless, ancient leathern cap. Still, art less of a dullard than I thought thee. But there is the sword, now — with the sword thou art indeed but a sorry fool! Go fetch the sword and I will e'en belabor thee again."

So Beltane, lighting down from the horse that reared and plunged no more, went and fetched the great sword; and when they had laid their jerkins by (for the sun was hot) they faced each other, foot to foot and eye to eye. Then once again the long blades whirled and flew and rang together, and once again the stranger laughed and gibed and struck my Beltane how and where he would, nor gave him stay or respite till Beltane's mighty arm grew aweary and his shoulder ached and burned; then, when he recked not of it, the stranger, with the same cunning stroke, beat the sword from Beltane's hand, and laughed aloud and wagged his head, saying:

"Art faint, boy, and scant o' breath already? Methinks we ne'er shall make of thee a lusty sworder!" But beholding Beltane's flushing cheek and drooping eye, reached out and clapped him on the shoulder.

"Go to!" cried he, "art young and all unlearned as yet — heed not my gibes and quirks, 'tis ever so my custom when steel is ringing, and mark me, I do think it a good custom, as apt to put a man off his ward and flurry him in his stroke. Never despair, youth, for I tell thee, north and south, and east and west my name is known, nor shall you find in any duchy, kingdom or county, a sworder such as I. For, mark me now! your knight and man-at-arms, trusting to his armour, doth use his sword but to thrust and smite. But — and mark me again, boy! a man

How He Lived in the Greenwood 13

cannot go ever in his armour, nor yet be sure when foes are nigh, and, at all times, 'tis well to make thy weapon both sword and shield; 'tis a goodly art, indeed I think a pretty one. Come now, take up thy sword and I will teach thee all my strokes and show thee how 'tis done."

Thus then, this stranger dwelt the week with Beltane in the greenwood, teaching him, day by day, tricks of sword and much martial lore beside. And, day by day, a friendship waxed and grew betwixt them so that upon the seventh morning, as they broke their fast together, Beltane's heart was heavy and his look downcast; whereat the stranger spake him thus:

"Whence thy dole, good youth?"

"For that to-day needs must I part with thee."

"And thy friends are few, belike?"

"None, messire," answered Beltane, sighing.

"Aye me! And yet 'tis well enough, for — mark me, youth! — friends be ofttimes a mixed blessing. As for me, 'tis true I am thy friend and so shall ever be, so long as you shall bear yon goodly blade."

"And wherefore?" questioned Beltane.

"Moreover thou art my scholar, and like, perchance, to prove thyself, some day, a notable sworder and a sweet and doughty fighter, belike."

"Yet hast never spoken me thy name, messire."

"Why, hast questioned me but once, and then thou wert something of a blockhead dreamer, methought. But now, messire Beltane, since thou would'st know — Benedict of Bourne am I called."

Now hereupon Beltane rose and stood upon his feet, staring wide-eyed at this grim-faced stranger who, with milk-bowl at lip, paused to smile his wry smile. "Aha!" said he, "hast heard such a name ere now, even here in the greenwood?"

"Sir," answered Beltane, "betimes I have talked with soldiers and men-at-arms, so do I know thee for that same great knight who, of all the nobles of Pentavalon, doth yet withstand the great Duke Ivo —"

"Call you that black usurper 'great,' youth? Body o' me! I knew a greater, once, methinks!"

"Aye," nodded Beltane, "there was him men called 'Beltane the Strong.'"

"Ha!" quoth Sir Benedict, setting down his milk-bowl, "what know you of Duke Beltane?"

"Nought but that he was a great and lusty fighter who yet loved peace and mercy, but truth and justice most of all."

"And to-day," sighed Sir Benedict, "to-day we have Black Ivo! Aye me! these be sorry days for Pentavalon. 'Tis said he woos the young Duchess yonder. Hast ever seen Helen of Mortain, sir smith?"

"Nay, but I've heard tell that she is wondrous fair."

"Hum!" quoth Sir Benedict, "I love not your red-haired spit-fires. Methinks, an Ivo win her, she'll lead him how she will, or be broke in the adventure — a malison upon him, be it how it may!"

So, having presently made an end of eating, Sir Benedict arose and forthwith donned quilted gambeson, and thereafter his hauberk of bright mail and plain surcoat, and buckling his sword about him, strode into the glade where stood the great grey horse. Now, being mounted, Sir Benedict stayed awhile to look down at Beltane, whiles Beltane looked up at him.

"Messire Beltane," said he, pointing to his scarred cheek, "you look upon my scar, I think?"

Quoth Beltane, flushing hot:

"Nay, sir; in truth, not I."

"Why look now, sweet youth, 'tis a scar that likes me well, though 'twas in no battle I took it, yet none the less, I would not be without it. By this I may be known among a thousand. 'Benedict o' the Mark,' some call me, and 'tis, methinks, as fair a name as any. But look now, and mark me this well, Beltane,— should any come to thee within the green, by day or night, and say to thee, 'Benedict o' the Mark bids thee arise and follow,'— then follow, messire, and so, peradventure, thou shalt arise indeed. Dost mark me well, youth?"

"Aye, Sir Benedict."

"Heigho!" sighed Sir Benedict, "thou'rt a fair sized babe to bear within a cloak, and thou hast been baptized in blood ere now — and there be more riddles for thee, boy, and so, until we meet, fare thee well, messire Beltane!"

So saying, Sir Benedict of Bourne smiled his twisted smile and, wheeling his horse, rode away down the glade, his mail glistening in the early light and his lance point winking and twinkling amid the green.

CHAPTER II

HOW BELTANE HAD WORD WITH THE DUKE, BLACK IVO

Now it fell out upon a day, that as Beltane strode the forest ways, there met him a fine cavalcade, gay with the stir of broidered petticoat and ermined mantle; and, pausing beneath a tree, he stood to hearken to the soft, sweet voices of the ladies and to gaze enraptured upon their varied beauty. Foremost of all rode a man richly habited, a man of great strength and breadth of shoulder, and of a bearing high and arrogant. His face, framed in long black hair that curled to meet his shoulder, was of a dark and swarthy hue, fierce looking and masterful by reason of prominent chin and high-arched nose, and of his thin-lipped, relentless mouth. Black were his eyes and bold; now staring bright and wide, now glittering 'twixt heavy, narrowed lids; yet when he smiled they glittered brightest, and his lips showed moistly red. Beside him rode a lady of a wondrous dark beauty, sleepy eyed and languid; yet her glance was quick to meet the Duke's bold look, and, 'neath her mantle, her fingers met, once in a while, and clung with his, what time his red lips would smile; but, for the most part, his brow was gloomy and he fingered his chin as one in thought.

As he paced along upon his richly caparisoned steed, pinching at his long, blue-shaven chin with supple fingers, his heavy brows drawn low, of a sudden his narrowed lids widened and his eyes gleamed bright and black as they beheld my Beltane standing in the shade of the tree.

"Aha!" said he, drawing rein, "what insolent, long-legged rogue art thou, to stand gaping at thy betters?"

And Beltane answered:

How He Had Word with the Duke 17

"No rogue, messire, but an honest man, I pray God, whom folk call Beltane the Smith."

The staring eyes grew suddenly narrow, the scarlet mouth curled in a slow smile, and the tall man spake, yet with his gaze bent ever upon Beltane:

"Fair lords," he said, "and you, most sweet and gentle ladies, our sport hath been but poor, hitherto — methinks I can show you a better, 'tis a game we play full oft in my country. Would that our gracious lady of Mortain were here, nor had balked us of her wilful company. Ho! Gefroi!" he called, "come you and break me the back of this 'honest' rogue." And straightway came one from the rear, where rode the servants and men-at-arms, a great, bronzed fellow, bearded to the eyes of him, loosing his sword-belt as he came; who, having tossed aside cap and pourpoint, strode toward Beltane, his eyes quick and bright, his teeth agleam through the hair of his beard.

"Come, thou forest rogue," said he, "my lord Duke loveth not to wait for man or maid, so — have at thee!"

Great he looked and tall as Beltane's self, a hairy man of mighty girth with muscles that swelled on arm and breast and rippled upon his back. Thus, as he stood and laughed, grimly confident and determined, not a few were they who sighed for Beltane for his youth's sake, and because of his golden curls and gentle eyes, for this Gefroi was accounted a very strong man, and a matchless wrestler withal.

"'Tis a fair match, how think you, Sir Jocelyn?" said the Duke, and turned him to one who rode at his elbow; a youthful, slender figure with long curled hair and sleepy eyes, "a fair match, Sir Jocelyn?"

"In very sooth, sweet my lord, gramercy and by your gracious leave — not so," sighed Sir Jocelyn. "This Gefroi o' thine is a rare breaker of necks and hath o'erthrown all the wrestlers in the three duchies; a man is he, set in his strength and experienced, but this forester, tall though he be, is but a beardless youth."

The Duke smiled his slow smile, his curving nostrils

quivered and were still, and he glanced toward Sir Jocelyn through veiling lids.   Quoth he:

"Art, rather, for a game of ball, messire, or a song upon a lute?" So saying he turned and signed to Gefroi with his finger; as for Sir Jocelyn, he only curled a lock of his long hair, and hummed beneath his breath.

Now Beltane, misliking the matter, would fain have gone upon his way, but wheresoever he turned, there Gefroi was also, barring his path, wherefore Beltane's eye kindled and he raised his staff threateningly.

"Fellow," quoth he, "stand from my way, lest I mischief thee."

But Gefroi only laughed and looked to his lord, who, beckoning an archer, bid him lay an arrow to his string.

"Shoot me the cowardly rogue so soon as he turn his back," said he, whereat Gefroi laughed again, wagging his head.

"Come, forest knave," quoth he, "I know a trick to snap thy neck so sweetly shalt never know, I warrant thee. Come, 'twill take but a moment, and my lord begins to lack of patience."

So Beltane laid by his staff, and tightening his girdle, faced the hairy Gefroi; and there befell that, the which, though you shall find no mention of it in any chronicle, came much to be talked of thereafter; so that a ballade was writ of it the which beginneth thus:

> ' Beltane wrestled in the green
>   With a mighty man,
> A goodlier bout was never seen
>   Since the world began.'

While Beltane was tightening his girdle, swift and sudden Gefroi closed, pinning his arms in a cunning hold, and thrice he swung my Beltane from his feet so that many clapped their hands the while the squires and men-at-arms shouted lustily. Only Sir Jocelyn curled the lock of hair upon his finger and was silent.

To him quoth my lord Duke, smiling:

How He Had Word with the Duke 19

"Messire, an you be in a mind to wager now, I will lay you this my roan stallion 'gainst that suit of triple mail you won at Dunismere joust, that Gefroi breaks thy forester's back within two falls — how say you?"

"Sweet my lord, it liketh me beyond telling, thy roan is a peerless beast!" sighed Sir Jocelyn, and so fell once more to humming his song beneath his breath.

Now Beltane had wrestled oft with strangers in the greenwood and had learned many cunning and desperate holds; moreover, he had learned to bide his time; thus, though Gefroi's iron muscles yet pinned his arms, he waited, calm-eyed but with every nerve a-quiver, for that moment when Gefroi's vicious grip should slacken.

To and fro the wrestlers swayed, knee to knee and breast to breast, fierce and silent and grim. As hath been said, this Gefroi was a very cunning fellow, and once and twice, he put forth all his strength seeking to use a certain cruel trick whereby many a goodly man had died ere now; but once, and twice, the hold was foiled, yet feebly and as though by chance, and Gefroi wondered; a third time he essayed it therefore, but, in that moment, sudden and fierce and strong, Beltane twisted in his loosened grasp, found at last the deadly hold he sought, and Gefroi wondered no more, for about him was a painful grip that grew ever tighter and more relentless. Now Gefroi's breath grew short and laboured, the muscles stood out on his writhing body in knotted cords, but ever that cruel grip grew more deadly, crushing his spirit and robbing him of his wonted strength. And those about them watched that mighty struggle, hushed for wonder of it; even Sir Jocelyn had forgot his lock of hair, and hummed no more.

For, desperately though he fought and struggled, they saw Gefroi's great body was bending slowly backward; his eyes stared up, wild and bloodshot, into the fierce, set face above him; swaying now, he saw the wide ring of faces, the quiver of leaves and the blue beyond, all a-swim through the mist of Beltane's yellow hair, and then, writhing in his anguish, he turned and buried his teeth in Beltane's naked arm, and with a cunning twist, broke from that deadly grip and staggered free.

Straightway the air was full of shouts and cries, some praising, some condemning, while Gefroi stood with hanging arms and panted. But Beltane looking upon his hurt, laughed, short and fierce, and as Gefroi came upon him, stooped and caught him below the loins. Then Beltane the strong, the mighty, put forth his strength and, whirling Gefroi aloft, hurled him backwards over his shoulder. So Gefroi the wrestler fell, and lay with hairy arms widetossed as one that is dead, and for a space no man spake for the wonder of it.

"By all the Saints, but 'twas a mighty throw!" sighed Sir Jocelyn, "though alack! sweet my lord, 'twould almost seem my forester hath something spoiled thy wrestler!"

"And is the roan stallion thine," frowned the Duke, "and to none would I lose him with a fairer grace, for 'twas a good bout as I foretold: yet, by the head of St. Martin! meseemeth yon carrion might have done me better!" So saying, my lord Duke gave his horse the spur and, as he passed the prostrate form of Gefroi, leaned him down and smote the wrestler thrice with the whip he held and so rode on, bidding his followers let him lie.

But Sir Jocelyn paused to look down at Beltane, who was setting his dress in order.

"Sir forester, thou hast a mighty arm," quoth he, "and thy face liketh me well. Here's for thee," and tossing a purse to Beltane's feet, he rode upon his way.

So the gay cavalcade passed 'neath the leafy arches, with the jingle of bridle and stirrup and the sound of jest and laughter, and was presently lost amid the green; only Gefroi the wrestler lay there upon his back and groaned. Then came Beltane and knelt and took his heavy head upon his knee, whereat Gefroi opened his eyes and groaned again.

"Good fellow," said Beltane, "I had not meant to throw thee so heavily —"

"Nay, forester, would it had been a little harder, for a ruined man am I this day."

"How so — have you not life?"

"I would 'twere death. And I bit you — in the arm, I mind me?"

"Aye, 'twas in the arm."

"For that am I heartily sorry, forester. But when a man seeth fame and fortune slipping from him — aye, and his honour, I had nigh forgot that — fame and fortune and honour, so small a thing as a bite may be forgiven?"

"I forgive thee — full and freely."

"Spoke like an honest forester," said Gefroi, and groaned again. "The favour of a lord is a slippery thing — much like an eel — quick to wriggle away. An hour agone my lord Duke held me in much esteem, while now? And he struck me! On the face, here!" Slowly Gefroi got him upon his feet, and having donned cap and pourpoint, shook his head and sighed; quoth he:

"Alack! 'tis a ruined man am I this day! Would I had broken thy neck, or thou, mine — and so, God den to ye, forester!" Then Gefroi the wrestler turned and plodded on his way, walking slow and with drooping head as one who knoweth not whither he goes, or careth. Now, as he watched, Beltane bethought him of the purse and taking it up, ran after Gefroi and thrust it into his hand.

"'Twill help thee to find a new service, mayhap." So saying my Beltane turned upon his heel and strode away, while Gefroi stood staring wide-eyed long after Beltane was vanished amid the trees.

So thus it was that Beltane looked his first upon Duke Ivo of Pentavalon, and thus did he overthrow Gefroi the famous wrestler. And because of this, many were they, knights and nobles and esquires, who sought out Beltane's lonely hut beside the brook, with offers of service, or to try a fall with him. But at their offers Beltane laughed and shook his head, and all who came to wrestle he threw upon their backs. And thus my Beltane dwelt within the greenwood, waxing mightier day by day.

CHAPTER III

HOW LOVE CAME TO BELTANE IN THE GREENWOOD

UPON a day Beltane stood at his forge fashioning an axe-head. And, having tempered it thereafter in the brook, he laid it by, and straightening his back, strode forth into the glade all ignorant of the eyes that watched him curiously through the leaves. And presently as he stood, his broad back set to the bole of a tree, his blue eyes lifted heavenwards brimful of dreams, he brake forth into a song he had made, lying sleepless upon his bed to do it.

Tall and stately were the trees, towering aloft, nodding slumberously in the gentle wind; fair were the flowers lifting glad faces to their sun-father and filling the air with their languorous perfume; yet naught was there so comely to look upon as Beltane the Smith, standing bare-armed in his might, his golden hair crisp-curled and his lifted eyes a-dream. Merrily the brook laughed and sang among the willows, leaping in rainbow-hues over its pebbly bed; sweet piped the birds in brake and thicket, yet of all their music none was there so good to hear as the rich tones of Beltane the Smith.

So thought the Duchess Helen of Mortain where she sat upon her white palfrey screened by the thick-budded foliage, seeing nought but this golden-locked singer whose voice thrilled strangely in her ears. And who so good a judge as Helen the Beautiful, whose lovers were beyond count, knights and nobles and princelings, ever kneeling at her haughty feet, ever sighing forth vows of service and adoration, in whose honour many a stout lance had shivered, and many a knightly act been wrought? Wherefore I say, who so good a judge as the Duchess Helen of Mortain? Thus Beltane the maker of verses, all ignorant that any heard save the birds in the brake, sang of the glories of the forest-lands. Sang how the flowers, feeling the first sweet promise of spring stirring within them, awoke; and lo! the frost was gone, the warm sun they had dreamed of through the long winter was come back, the time of their waiting passed away. So, timidly, slowly, they stole forth from the dark, unveiling their beauties to their lord the sun and filling the world with the fragrance of their worship.

Somewhat of all this sang Beltane, whiles the Duchess Helen gazed upon him wide-eyed and wondering.

Could this be Beltane the Smith, this tall, gentle-eyed youth, this soft-voiced singer of dreams? Could this indeed be the mighty wrestler of whom she had heard so many tales of late, how that he lived an anchorite, deep hidden in the green, hating the pomp and turmoil of cities, and contemning women and all their ways?

Now, bethinking her of all this, the Duchess frowned for that he was such a goodly man and so comely to look on, and frowning, mused, white chin on white fist. Then she smiled, as one that hath a bright thought, and straightway loosed the golden fillet that bound her glowing tresses so that they fell about her in all their glory, rippling far down her broidered habit. Then, the song being ended, forth from her cover rode the lady of Mortain, and coming close where Beltane leaned him in the shade of the tree, paused of a sudden, and started as one that is surprised, and Beltane turning, found her beside him, yet spake not nor moved.

Breathless and as one entranced he gazed upon her; saw how her long hair glowed a wondrous red 'neath the kisses of the dying sun; saw how her purpled gown, belted at the slender waist, clung about the beauties of her shapely body; saw how the little shoe peeped forth from the perfumed mystery of its folds, and so stood speechless, bound by the spell of her beauty. Wherefore, at length, she spake to him, low and sweet and humble, on this wise:

"Art thou he whom men call Beltane the Smith?"

He answered, gazing at her lowered lashes:

"I am Beltane the Smith."

For a space she sat grave and silent, then looked at him with eyes that laughed 'neath level brows to see the wonder in his gaze. But anon she falls a-sighing, and braided a tress of hair 'twixt white fingers ere she spoke:

"'Tis said of thee that thou art a hermit and live alone within these solitudes. And yet — meseemeth — thine eyes are not a hermit's eyes, messire!"

Quoth Beltane, with flushing cheek and eyes abased:

"Yet do I live alone, lady."

"Nor are thy ways and speech the ways of common smith, messire."

"Yet smith am I in sooth, lady, and therewithal content."

Now did she look on him 'neath drooping lash, sweet-eyed and languorous, and shook her head, and sighed.

"Alas, messire, methinks then perchance it may be true that thou, for all thy youth, and despite thine eyes, art a mocker of love, a despiser of women? And yet — nay — sure 'tis not so?"

Then did Beltane the strong come nigh to fear, by reason of her fair womanhood, and looked from her to earth, from earth to sky, and, when he would have answered, fell a-stammering, abashed by her wondrous beauty.

"Nay lady, indeed — indeed I know of women nought — nought of myself, but I have heard tell that they be — light-minded, using their beauty but to lure the souls of men from high and noble things — making of love a jest — a sport and pastime —"

But now the Duchess laughed, very soft and sweeter, far, to Beltane's thinking than the rippling music of any brook, soever.

"Aye me, messire anchorite," said she smiling yet, "whence had you this poor folly?"

Quoth Beltane gravely:

"Lady, 'twas from one beyond all thought wise and learned. A most holy hermit —"

"A hermit!" says she, merry-eyed, "then, an he told thee this, needs must he be old, and cold, and withered, and beyond the age of love, knowing nought of women save what memory doth haunt his evil past. But young art thou and strong, and should love come to thee — as come, methinks, it may, hearken to no voice but the pleading of thine own true heart. Messire," she sighed, "art very blind, methinks, for you sing the wonders of these forest-lands, yet in thy song is never a word of love! O blind! O blind! for I tell thee nought exists in this great world but by love. Behold now, these sighing trees love their lord the sun, and, through the drear winter, wait his coming with wide-stretched, yearning arms, crying aloud to him in every shuddering blast the tale of their great longing. And, after some while, he comes, and at his advent they clothe themselves anew in all their beauty, and with his warm breath thrilling through each fibre, put forth their buds, singing through all their myriad leaves the song of their rejoicing. Something the like of this, messire, is the love a woman beareth to a man, the which, until he hath felt it trembling in his heart, he hath not known the joy of living."

But Beltane answered, smiling a little as one that gloried in his freedom:

"No woman hath ever touched my heart, yet have I lived nor found it lonely, hitherto."

But hereupon, resting her white fingers on his arm, she leaned nearer to him so that he felt her breath warm upon his cheek, and there stole to him the faint, sweet perfume of her hair.

"Beware, O scorner of women! for I tell thee that ere much time hath passed thou shalt know love — aye, in such fashion as few men know — wherefore I say — beware, Beltane!"

But Beltane the strong, the mighty, shook his head and smiled.

"Nay," quoth he, "a man's heart may be set on other things, flowers may seem to him fairer than the fairest women, and the wind in trees sweeter to him than their voices."

Now as she hearkened, the Duchess Helen grew angry, yet straightway, she dissembled, looking upon him 'neath drooping lashes. Soft and tender-eyed and sighing, she answered:

"Ah, Beltane! how unworthy are such things of a man's love! For if he pluck them, that he may lay these flowers upon his heart, lo! they fade and wither, and their beauty and fragrance is but a memory. Ah, Beltane, when next ye sing, choose you a worthier theme."

"Of what shall I sing?" said Beltane.

Very soft she answered, and with eyes abased:

"Think on what I have told thee, and sing — of love."

And so she sighed, and looked on him once, then wheeled her palfrey, and was gone up the glade; but Beltane, as he watched her go, was seized of a sudden impulse and overtook her, running.

"Beseech thee," cried he, barring her path, "tell me thy name!"

Then Helen the Beautiful, the wilful, laughed and swerved her palfrey, minded to leave him so; but Beltane sprang and caught the bridle.

"Tell me thy name," said he again.

"Let me go!"

"Thy name, tell me thy name."

But the Duchess laughed again, and thinking to escape him, smote her horse so that it started and reared; once it plunged, and twice, and so stood trembling with Beltane's hand upon the bridle; wherefore a sudden anger came upon her, and, bending her black brows, she raised her jewelled riding-rod threateningly. But Beltane only smiled and shook his head, saying:

"Unless I know thy name thou shalt not fare forth of the greenwood."

So the proud lady of Mortain looked down upon Beltane in amaze, for there was none in all the Duchy, knight, noble or princeling, who dared gainsay her lightest word; wherefore, I say, she stared upon this bold forest knave with his golden hair and gentle eyes, his curved lips and square chin; and in eyes and mouth and chin was a look of masterfulness, challenging, commanding. And, meeting that look, her heart leapt most strangely with sudden, sweet thrill, so that she lowered her gaze lest he should see, and when she spake her voice was low and very sweet:

"Tell me I pray, why seek you my name, and wherefore?"

Quoth Beltane, soft and slow as one that dreams:

"I have seen thine eyes look at me from the flowers, ere now, have heard thy laughter in the brook, and found thy beauty in all fair things: methinks thy name should be a most sweet name."

Now was it upon her lips to tell him what he asked, but, being a woman, she held her peace for very contrariness, and blushing beneath his gaze, looked down and cried aloud, and pointed to a grub that crawled upon her habit. So Beltane loosed the bridle, and in that moment, she laughed for very triumph and was off, galloping 'neath the trees. Yet, as she went, she turned and called to him, and the word she called was:—

"Helen!"

CHAPTER IV

OF THE LOVE AND THE GRIEF OF HELEN THE PROUD

LONG stood Beltane where she had left him, the soft shadows of night deepening about him, dreaming ever of her beauty, of her wondrous hair, and of the little foot that had peeped forth at him 'neath her habit, and, full of these thoughts, for once he was deaf to the soft voices of the trees nor heard the merry chatter of the brook. But later, upon his bed he lay awake full long and must needs remember yet another Helen, with the same wondrous hair and eyes of mystery, for whose sake men had died and a noble city burned; and, hereupon, his heart grew strangely heavy and cold with an unknown dread.

Days came and went, and labouring at the forge or lying out in the sunshine gazing wistfully beyond the swaying tree-tops, Beltane would oft start and turn his head, fancying the rustle of her garments in his ears, or her voice calling to him from some flowery thicket; and the wind in the trees whispered "Helen!" and the brook sang of Helen, and Helen was in his thoughts continually.

Thus my Beltane forgot his loves the flowers, and sang no more the wonders of the forest-lands.

And oft-times the Duchess, seated in state within her great hall of Mortain looking down upon her knights and nobles, would sigh, for none was there so noble of form nor so comely as Beltane the Smith. Hereupon her white brow would grow troubled and, turning from them all, she would gaze with deep, unfathomable eyes, away across the valley to where, amid the mystery of the trees, Beltane had his lonely dwelling.

Wherefore it was, that, looking up one evening from

Of the Love and Grief of Helen

where he sat busied with brush and colours upon a border of wondrous design, Beltane beheld her of whom he was dreaming; and she, standing tall and fair before him, saw that in his look the which set her heart a-fluttering at her white breast most strangely; yet, fearing she should betray aught of it, she laughed gaily and mocked him, as is the way of women, saying:

"Well, thou despiser of Love, I hearkened vainly for thy new song as I rode hither through the green."

Red grew my Beltane's cheek and he looked not to her as he answered:

"Lady, I have no new song."

"Why then, is thy lesson yet unlearned?" said she. "Have ye no love but for birds and flowers?" and her red lip curled scornfully.

Quoth Beltane:

"Is there aught more worthy?"

"O Beltane!" she sighed, "art then so simple that such will aye content thee; doth not thy heart hunger and cry within thee for aught beside?"

Then Beltane bowed his head, and fumbled with his brush and dropped it, and ere he could reach it she had set her foot upon it; thus it chanced that his hand came upon her foot, and feeling it beneath his fingers, he started and drew away, whereat she laughed low and sweet, saying:

"Alack, and doth my foot affright thee? And yet 'tis none so fierce and none so large that thou shouldst fear it thus, messire — thou who art so tall and strong, and a mighty wrestler withal!"

Now, looking up, he saw her lips curved and scarlet, and her eyes brimful of laughter, and fain would he have taken up the brush yet dared not. Therefore, very humbly, she stooped and lifting the brush put it in his hand. Then, trembling 'neath the touch of her soft fingers, Beltane rose up, and that which he had hidden deep within his heart brake from him.

"Helen!" he whispered, "O Helen, thou art so wondrous fair and belike of high estate, but as for me, I am but what I am. Behold me," he cried, stretching wide his arms, "I am but Beltane the Smith; who is there to love such as I? See, my hands be hard and rough, and would but bruise where they should caress, these arms be unfitted for soft embracements. O lady, who is there to love Beltane the Smith?"

Now the Duchess Helen laughed within herself for very triumph, yet her bosom thrilled and hurried with her breathing, her cheek grew red and her eyes bright and tender, wherefore she stooped low to cull a flower ere she answered.

"Beltane," she sighed, "Beltane, women are not as thy flowers, that embraces, even such as thine, would crush them."

But Beltane stooped his head that he might not behold the lure and beauty of her, and clenched his hands hard and fierce and thereafter spake:

"Thou art so wondrous fair," said he again, "and belike of noble birth, but — as for me, I am a smith!"

Awhile she stood, turning the flower in gentle fingers yet looking upon him in his might and goodly youth, beholding his averted face with its strong, sweet mouth and masterful chin, its curved nostrils and the dreaming passion of his eyes, and when she spake her voice was soft and very sweet.

"Above all, thou art — a man, messire!"

Then did my Beltane lift his head and saw how the colour was deepened in her cheek and how her tender eyes drooped before his.

"Tell me," he said, "is there ever a woman to love such a man? Is there ever a woman who would leave the hum and glitter of cities to walk with such as I in the shadow of these forest-lands? Speak, Oh speak I do beseech thee!" Thus said he and stopped, waiting her answer.

"Nay, Beltane," she whispered, "let thine own heart speak me this."

All blithe and glorious grew the world about him as he

Of the Love and Grief of Helen

stooped and caught her in his arms, lifting her high against his heart. And, in this moment, he forgot the teaching of Ambrose the Hermit, forgot all things under heaven, save the glory of her beauty, the drooping languor of her eyes and the sweet, moist tremor of her mouth. And so he kissed her, murmuring 'twixt his kisses:

"Fairer art thou than all the flowers, O my love, and sweeter thy breath than the breath of flowers!"

Thus Helen the Proud, the Beautiful, yielded her lips to his, and in all the world for her was nought save the deep, soft voice of Beltane, and his eyes, and the new, sweet ecstasy that thrilled within her. Surely nowhere in all the world was there such another man as this, so strong and gentle, so meet for love and yet so virginal. Surely life might be very fair here in the green solitudes, aye, surely, surely —

Soft with distance came the peal of bells, stealing across the valley from the great minster in Mortain, and, with the sound, memory waked, and she bethought her of all those knights and nobles who lived but to do her will and pleasure, of Mortain and the glory of it; and so she sighed and stirred, and, looking at Beltane, sighed again. Quoth she:

"Is this great love I foretold come upon thee, Beltane?"

And Beltane answered:

"Truly a man hath not lived until he hath felt a woman's kisses upon his lips!"

"And thou wilt flout poor Love no more?"

"Nay," he answered, smiling, "'tis part of me, and must be so henceforth — forever!"

But now she sighed again, and trembled in his arms and clasped him close, as one beset by sudden fear, while ever soft with distance came the silvery voices of the bells, low yet insistent, sweet yet commanding; wherefore she, sighing, put him from her.

"Why then," said she, with drooping head, "fare thee well, messire. Nay, see you not? Methinks my task is done. And it hath been a — pleasing task, this — of teaching thee to love — O, would you had not learned so soon! Fare thee well, Beltane!"

But Beltane looked upon her as one in deep amaze, his arms fell from her and he stepped back and so stood very still and, as he gazed, a growing horror dawned within his eyes.

"What art thou?" he whispered.

"Nay, Beltane," she murmured, "ah — look not so!"

"Who art thou — and what?" he said.

"Nay, did I not tell thee at the first? I am Helen — hast thou not known? I am Helen — Helen of Mortain."

"Thou — thou art the Duchess Helen?" said Beltane with stiffening lips, "thou the Duchess and I — a smith!" and he laughed, short and fierce, and would have turned from her but she stayed him with quivering hands.

"And — did'st not know?" she questioned hurriedly, "methought it was no secret — I would have told thee ere this had I known. Nay — look not so, Beltane — thou dost love me yet — nay, I do know it!" and she strove to smile, but with lips that quivered strangely.

"Aye, I love thee, Helen of Mortain — though there be many fair lords to do that! But, as for me — I am only a smith, and as a smith greatly would I despise thee. Yet may this not be, for as my body is great, so is my love. Go, therefore, thy work here is done, go — get thee to thy knightly lovers, wed this Duke who seeks thee — do aught you will but go, leave me to my hammers and these green solitudes."

So spake he, and turning, strode away, looking not back to where she stood leaning one white hand against a tree. Once she called to him but he heeded not, walking ever with bowed head and hearing only the tumult within him and the throbbing of his wounded heart. And now, in his pain needs must he think of yet another Helen and of the blood and agony of blazing Troy town, and lifting up his hands to heaven he cried aloud:

"Alas! that one so fair should be a thing so evil!"

All in haste Beltane came to his lonely hut and taking

Of the Love and Grief of Helen 33

thence his cloak and great sword, he seized upon his mightiest hammer and beat down the roof of the hut and drave in the walls of it; thereafter he hove the hammer into the pool, together with his anvil and rack of tools and so, setting the sword in his girdle and the cloak about him, turned away and plunged into the deeper shadows of the forest.

But, ever soft and faint with distance, the silvery voices of the bells stole upon the warm, stilly air, speaking of pomp and state, of pride and circumstance, but now these seemed but empty things, and the Duchess Helen stood long with bent head and hands that strove to shut the sounds away. But in the end she turned, slow-footed amid the gathering shadows and followed whither they called.

* * * *

But that night, sitting in state within her great hall of Mortain, the Duchess Helen sighed deep and oft, scarce heeding the courtesies addressed to her and little the whispered homage of her guest Duke Ivo, he, the proudest and most potent of all her many wooers; yet to-night her cheek burned beneath his close regard and her woman's flesh rebelled at his contact as had never been aforetime. Thus, of a sudden, though the meal was scarce begun, she arose and stepped down from the dais, and when her wondering ladies would have followed forbade them with a gesture. And so, walking proud and tall, she passed out before them, whereat Duke Ivo's black brow grew the blacker, and he stared before him with narrowed eyes, beholding which, the faces of my lady's counsellors waxed anxious and long; only Winfrida, chiefest of the ladies, watched the Duke 'neath drooping lids and with a smile upon her full, red lips.

Now the Duchess, being come to her chamber, lifted her hands and tore the ducal circlet from her brow and cast it from her, and, thereafter, laid by her rings and jewels, and coming to the open casement fell there upon her knees and reached forth her pale hands to where, across the valley, the dark forest stretched away, ghostly and unreal, 'neath the moon.

"My beloved!" she whispered, "O my beloved!" And the gentle night-wind bore her secret in its embrace away across the valley to the dim solitudes of the woods. "Beltane!" she sighed, "love hath come into mine heart even as it came to thee, when I recked not of it. My beloved — O my beloved!" Anon she rose and stood awhile with head bowed as one that dreams, and of a sudden her cheek glowed warmly red, her breath caught and she gazed upon the moon with eyes of yearning tenderness; thereafter she laughed, soft and happily and, snatching up a cloak, set it about her and fled from the chamber. So, swift and light of foot, she sped by hidden ways until she came where old Godric, her chief huntsman, busied himself trimming the shaft of a boar-spear, who, beholding his lady, rose up in amaze.

"Godric," said she, white hands upon his arm, "thou didst love me or ever I could walk?"

"Aye, verily thou hast said, dear my lady."

"Love you me yet?"

"Truly thou knowest that I love thee."

"Thou hast heard, Godric, how that my counsellors have long desired me to wed with Duke Ivo, and do yet await my answer to his suit — nay hearken! So to-night shall my mind be known in the matter once and for all! Come, my Godric, arm you and saddle two horses — come!"

"Nay, sweet my lady, what would ye?"

"Fly hence with thee, my Godric! Come — the horses!"

"Fly from Mortain, and thou the Duchess? Nay, dear lady, 'tis madness, bethink thee! O dear my Mistress — O little Helen that I have cherished all thy days, bethink thee — do not this thing —"

"Godric, did not the Duke, my father, strictly charge thee to follow ever my call?"

"Aye, my lady."

"Then follow now!" And so she turned and beckoned, and Godric perforce followed after.

Hand in hand they went a-down the winding stair, down to the great, dim courtyard that whispered to their tread. And, thereafter, mounting in haste, the Duchess galloped from Mortain, unheeding stern old Godric by her side and with never a look behind, dreaming ever of Beltane with cheeks that crimsoned 'neath her hood.

Fast and faster she rode 'neath the pale moon, her eyes ever gazing towards the gloom of the forest, her heart throbbing quick as the hoof-beats of her horse. So at last, being come to that glade whereby Beltane had his dwelling, she lighted down, and bidding Godric wait, stole forward alone.

Autumn was at hand, and here and there the fallen leaves rustled sadly under foot while the trees sighed and mourned together for that the flowers so soon must wither and die. But in the heart of the Duchess Helen, Spring was come, and all things spake to her of coming joys undreamed till now as she hasted on, flitting through the pallid moonbeams that, falling athwart rugged bole and far-flung branch, splashed the gloom with radiant light. Once she paused to listen, but heard nought save the murmur of the brook and the faint stirring of leaves. And now, clear and strong the tender radiance fell athwart the lonely habitation and her heart leapt at the sight, her eyes grew moist and tender and she hurried forward with flying steps, then — beholding the ruin of thatch and wall, she stopped and stood aghast, gazing wide-eyed and with her heart numb in her bosom. Then she shivered, her proud head drooped and a great sob brake from her, for that she knew she was come too late, her dreams of wandering with Beltane through sunny glades were nought but dreams after all. Beltane the Smith was gone!

Then a great loneliness and desolation came upon her and, sinking down at the foot of that tree whereby he had been wont to lean so often, her yearning arms crept about its rugged bole and she lay there in the passion of her grief weeping long and bitterly.

But the gentle trees ceased mourning over their own coming sorrow in wonder at the sight, and bending their heads together, seemed to whisper one to the other saying:

"He is gone, Beltane the Smith is gone!"

CHAPTER V

WHICH TELLS OF THE STORY OF AMBROSE THE HERMIT

DEEP, deep within the green twilight of the woods Ambrose the Hermit had builded him a hut; had built and framed it of rude stones and thatched it with grass and mosses. And from the door of the hut he had formed likewise a path strewn thick with jagged stones and sharp flints, a cruel track, the which, winding away through the green, led to where upon a gentle eminence stood a wooden cross most artfully wrought and carven by the hermit's skilled and loving fingers.

Morning and evening, winter and summer it was his custom ever to tread this painful way, wetting the stones with the blood of his atonement.

Now upon a certain rosy dawn, ere yet the sun was up, Beltane standing amid the leaves, saw the hermit issue forth of the hut and, with bowed head and folded hands, set out upon his appointed way. The cruel stones grew red beneath his feet yet he faltered not nor stayed until, being come to the cross, he kneeled there and, with gaunt arms upraised, prayed long and fervently so that the tears of his passion streamed down his furrowed cheeks and wetted the snow of his beard.

In a while, having made an end, he arose and being come to his hut once more, he of a sudden espied Beltane standing amid the leaves; and because he was so fair and goodly to look upon in his youth and might, the pale cheek of the hermit flushed and a glow leapt within his sunken eyes, and lifting up his hand, he blessed him.

"Welcome to this my solitude, my son," quoth he, " and wherefore hast thou tarried in thy coming? I have watched for thee these many days. Come, sit you here beside me in this blessed sun and tell me of thy latter doings."

But the eyes of Beltane were sad and his tongue unready, so that he stammered in his speech, looking ever upon the ground; then, suddenly up-starting to his feet, he strode before the hut, while Ambrose the wise looked, and saw, yet spake not. So, presently, Beltane paused, and looking him within the eyes spake hurriedly on this wise:

"Most holy father, thou knowest how I have lived within the greenwood all my days nor found it lonely, for I did love it so, that I had thought to die here likewise when my time should come. Yet now do I know that this shall never be — to-day I go hence."

"Wherefore, my son?"

"There is come a strange restlessness upon me, a riot and fever of the blood whereby I am filled with dreams and strange desires. I would go forth into the great world of men and cities, to take my rightful place therein, for until a man hath loved and joyed and sorrowed with his fellows, he knoweth nought of life."

"Perchance, my son, this is but the tide of youthful blood that tingles in thy veins? Or is it that thou hast looked of late within a woman's eyes?"

Then Beltane kneeled him at the feet of Ambrose and hid his face betwixt his knees, as he had been wont to do whiles yet a little child.

"Father," he murmured, "thou hast said." Now looking down upon this golden head, Ambrose sighed and drew the long curls through his fingers with a wondrous gentleness.

"Tell me of thy love, Beltane," said he.

Forthwith, starting to his feet, Beltane answered:

"'Tis many long and weary months, my father, and yet doth seem but yesterday. She came to me riding upon a milk-white steed. At first methought her of the fairy kind thither drawn by my poor singing, yet, when I looked on her again, I knew her to be woman. And she was fair —

O very fair, my father. I may not tell her beauty for 'twas compounded of all beauteous things, of the snow of lilies, the breath of flowers, the gleam of stars on moving waters, the music of streams, the murmur of wind in trees — I cannot tell thee more but that there is a flame doth hide within her hair, and for her eyes — O methinks 'tis for her eyes I do love her most — love her? Aye, my body doth burn and thrill with love — alas, poor fool, alas it should be so! But, for that she is proud and of an high estate, for that I am I, a poor worker of iron whom men call Beltane the Smith, fit but to sigh and sigh and forever sigh, to dream of her and nothing more — so must I go hence, leaving the sweet silence of the woods for the strife and noise of cities, learning to share the burdens of my fellows. See you not, my father, see you not the way of it?" So spake Beltane, hot and passionate, striding to and fro upon the sward, while Ambrose sat with bitterness in his heart but with eyes ineffably gentle.

"And is this love of thine so hopeless, my Beltane?"

"Beyond all thought; she is the Duchess Helen of Mortain!"

Now for a while the hermit spake not, sitting chin in hand as one who halts betwixt two courses.

"'Tis strange," he said at length, "and passing strange! Yet, since 'tis she, and she so much above thee, wherefore would ye leave the tender twilight of these forests?"

Quoth Beltane, sighing:

"My father, I tell thee these woods be full of love and her. She looketh at me from the flowers and stealeth to me in their fragrance; the very brooks do babble of her beauty; each leaf doth find a little voice to whisper of her, and everywhere is love and love and love — so needs must I away."

"And think you so to escape this love, my Beltane, and the pain of it?"

"Nay my father, that were thing impossible for it

doth fill the universe, so must I needs remember it with every breath I draw, but in the griefs and sorrows of others I may, perchance, learn to bear mine own, silent and patiently, as a man should."

Then Ambrose sighed, and beckoning Beltane to his knee, laid his hands upon his shoulders and looked deep within his eyes.

"Beltane my son," said he, "I have known thee from thy youth up and well do I know thou canst not lie, for thy heart is pure as yet and uncorrupt. But now is the thing I feared come upon thee — ah, Beltane, hast thou forgot all I have told thee of women and the ways of women, how that their white bodies are filled with all manner of wantonness, their hands strong in lures and enticements? A woman in her beauty is a fair thing to the eyes of a man, yet I tell thee Beltane, they be snares of the devil, setting father 'gainst son and — brother 'gainst brother, whereby come unnatural murders and bloody wars."

"And yet, needs must I love her still, my father!"

"Aye, 'tis so," sighed Ambrose, "'tis ever so, and as for thee, well do I know the blood within thee for a hot, wild blood — and thou art young, and so it is I fear for thee."

But, looking up, Beltane shook his head and answered:

"Holy father, thou art wise and wondrous learned in the reading of books and in the ancient wisdoms and philosophies, yet methinks this love is a thing no book can teach thee, a truth a man must needs find out for himself."

"And think you I know nought of love, Beltane, the pain and joy of it — and the shame? Thou seest me a poor old man and feeble, bent with years and suffering, one who but waiteth for the time when my grievous sin shall be atoned for and God, in His sweet clemency, shall ease me of this burden of life. Yet do I tell thee there was a time when this frail body was strong and tall, wellnigh, as thine own, when this white hair was thick and black, and these dim eyes bold and fearless even as thine.

Ah, Beltane, well do I know women and the ways of women! Come, sit you beside me and, because thou art fain to go into the world and play thy man's part, so now will I tell thee that the which I had thought to bear with me to the grave."

Then Ambrose the Hermit, leaning his head upon his hand, began to speak on this wise:

"Upon a time were two brothers, nobles of a great house and following, each alike lovers of peace yet each terrible in war; the name of the one was Johan and of the other Beltane. Now Beltane, being elder, was Duke of that country, and the country maintained peace within its borders and the people thereof waxed rich and happy. And because these twain loved each other passing well the way of the one was ever the way of the other so that they dwelt together in a wondrous amity, and as their hearts were pure and strong so waxed they in body so that there was none could cope with them at hand-strokes nor bear up against the might of their lances, and O, methinks in all this fair world nought was there fairer than the love of these two brethren!

"Now it befell, upon a day, that they set out with a goodly company to attend a tourney in a certain town whither, likewise, were come many knights of renown, nobles and princes beyond count eager to prove their prowess, thither drawn by the fame of that fair lady who was to be Queen of Beauty. All lips spake of her and the wonder of her charms, how that a man could not look within her eyes but must needs fall into a passion of love for her. But the brethren smiled and paid small heed and so, together, journeyed to the city. The day of the joust being come, forth they rode into the lists, side by side, each in his triple mail and ponderous helm, alike at all points save for the golden circlet upon Duke Beltane's shining casque. And there befell, that day, a mighty shivering of lances and many a knightly deed was wrought. But, for these brethren there was none of all these knights and nobles who might abide their onset; all day long they together maintained the lists till there none remained to cope with them, wherefore the marshal would have had them run a course together for proof which was the mightier. But Beltane smiled and shook his head saying, 'Nay, it is not meet that brother strive with brother!' And Johan said: 'Since the day doth rest with us, we will share the glory together.' So, amid the acclaim of voice and trumpet, side by side they came to make obeisance to the Queen of Beauty, and gazing upon her, they saw that she was indeed of a wondrous beauty. Now in her hand she held the crown that should reward the victor, yet because they were two, she knew not whom to choose, wherefore she laughed, and brake the crown asunder and gave to each a half with many fair words and gentle sayings. But, alas, my son! from that hour her beauty came betwixt these brethren, veiling their hearts one from the other. So they tarried awhile in that fair city, yet companied together no more, for each was fain to walk apart, dreaming of this woman and the beauty of her, and each by stealth wooed her to wife. At last, upon an evening, came Johan to his brother and taking from his bosom the half of the crown he had won, kissed it and gave it to Beltane, saying: 'The half of a crown availeth no man, take therefore my half and join it with thine, for well do I know thy heart, my brother — and thou art the elder, and Duke; go therefore and woo this lady to wife, and God speed thee, my lord.' But Beltane said: 'Shame were it in me to take advantage of my years thus; doth age or rank make a man's love more worthy? So, get thee to thy wooing, my brother, and heaven's blessing on thee.' Then grew Johan full of joy, saying: 'So be it, dear my brother, but an I come not to thee within three days at sunset, then shalt know that my wooing hath not prospered.' Upon the third day, therefore, Beltane the Duke girded on his armour and made ready to ride unto his own demesne, yet tarried until sunset, according to his word. But his brother Johan came not. Therefore he, in turn, rode upon his wooing and came unto the lady's presence in hauberk of mail, and thus ungently clad wooed her as one in haste to be gone, telling her that this world was no place for a man to sigh out his days at a woman's feet, and bidding her answer him 'Yea' or 'Nay' and let him be gone to his duty. And she, whom so many had wooed on bended knee, spake him 'Yea'— for that a woman's ways be beyond all knowledge — and therewith gave her beauty to his keeping. So, forthwith were they wed, with much pomp and circumstance, and so he brought her to his Duchy with great joy and acclaim. Then would Johan have departed over seas, but Beltane ever dissuaded him, and fain these brethren would have loved each other as they had done aforetime, yet was the beauty of this woman ever betwixt them. Now, within that year, came news of fire and sword upon the border, of cruel rape and murder, so Beltane sent forth his brother Johan with an army to drive back the invaders, and himself abode in his great castle, happy in the love of his fair, young wife. But the war went ill, tidings came that Johan his brother was beaten back with much loss and he himself sore wounded. Therefore the Duke made ready to set forth at the head of a veteran company, but ere he rode a son was born to him, so needs must he come to his wife in his armour, and beholding the child, kissed him. Thereafter Duke Beltane rode to the war with a glad heart, and fell upon his enemies and scattered them, and pursued them far and smote them even to their own gates. But in the hour of his triumph he fell, by treachery, into the hands of his cruelest enemy, how it mattereth not, and for a space was lost to sight and memory. But as for Johan, the Duke's brother, he lay long sick of his wounds, so came the Duchess and ministered to him; and she was fair, and passing fair, and he was young. And when his strength was come again, each day was Johan minded to ride forth and seek the Duke his brother — but he was young, and she passing fair, wherefore he tarried still, bound by the lure of her beauty. And, upon a soft and stilly eve as they walked together in the garden, she wooed Johan with tender look and word, and wreathed her white arms about him and gave to his her mouth. And, in that moment came one, fierce and wild of aspect, in dinted casque and rusty mail who stood and watched — ah God!"

Here, for a while, the hermit Ambrose stayed his tale, and Beltane saw his brow was moist and that his thin hands clenched and wrung each other.

"So thus, my son, came Duke Beltane home again, he and his esquire Sir Benedict of Bourne alone of all his company, each alike worn with hardship and spent with wounds. But now was the Duke stricken of a greater pain and leaned him upon the shoulder of his esquire, faint and sick of soul, and knew an anguish deeper than any flesh may know. Then, of a sudden, madness came upon him and, breaking from the mailed arms that held him, he came hot-foot to the courtyard and to the hall beyond, hurling aside all such as sought to stay him and so reached at last my lady's bower, his mailed feet ringing upon the stones. And, looking up, the Duchess saw and cried aloud and stood, thereafter, pale and speechless and wide of eye, while Johan's cheek grew red and in his look was shame. Then the Duke put up his vizor and, when he spake, his voice was harsh and strange: 'Greeting, good brother!' said he, 'go now, I pray you, get you horse and armour and wait me in the courtyard, yet first must I greet this my lady wife.' So Johan turned, with hanging head, and went slow-footed from the chamber. Then said the Duke, laughing in his madness, 'Behold, lady, the power of a woman's beauty, for I loved a noble brother once, a spotless knight whose honour reached high as heaven, but thou hast made of him a something foul and base, traitor to me and to his own sweet name, and 'tis for this I will requite thee!' But the Duchess spake not, nor blenched even when the dagger gleamed to strike — O sweet God of mercy, to strike! But, in that moment, came Benedict of Bourne and leapt betwixt and took the blow upon his cheek, and, stanching the blood within his tattered war-cloak, cried: 'Lord Duke, because I love thee,

ne'er shalt thou do this thing until thou first slay me!'
A while the Duke stood in amaze, then turned and strode
away down the great stair, and coming to the courtyard,
beheld his brother Johan armed at all points and mounted,
and with another horse equipped near by. So the Duke
laughed and closed his vizor and his laughter boomed
hollow within his rusty casque, and, leaping to the saddle,
rode to the end of the great tilt-yard, and, wheeling,
couched his lance. So these brethren, who had loved each
other so well, spurred upon each other with levelled lances
but, or ever the shock came — O my son, my son! — Johan
rose high in his stirrups and cried aloud the battle-cry of
his house 'Arise! Arise! I shall arise!' and with the
cry, tossed aside his lance lest he might harm the Duke his
brother — O sweet clemency of Christ! — and crashed to
earth — and lay there — very still and silent. Then the
Duke dismounted and, watched by pale-faced esquires and
men-at-arms, came and knelt beside his brother, and laid
aside his brother's riven helm and, beholding his comely
features torn and marred and his golden hair all hatefully
bedabbled, felt his heart burst in sunder, and he groaned,
and rising to stumbling feet came to his horse and
mounted and rode away 'neath grim portcullis and over
echoing drawbridge, yet, whithersoever he looked, he saw
only his brother's dead face, pale and bloody. And fain
he would have prayed but could not, and so he came
into the forest. All day long he rode beneath the trees
careless of his going, conscious only that Benedict of
Bourne rode behind with his bloody war-cloak wrapped
about him. But on rode the Duke with hanging head and
listless hands for before his haggard eyes was ever the
pale, dead face of Johan his brother. Now, as the moon
rose, they came to a brook that whispered soft-voiced amid
the shadows and here his war-horse stayed to drink.
Then came Sir Benedict of Bourne beside him, 'Lord
Duke,' said he, 'what hast thou in thy mind to do?' 'I
know not,' said the Duke, 'though methinks 'twere sweet
to die.' 'Then what of the babe, lord Duke?' and, speak-

ing, Sir Benedict drew aside his cloak and showed the babe asleep beneath. But, looking upon its innocence, the Duke cried out and hid his face, for the babe's golden curls were dabbled with the blood from Sir Benedict's wound and looked even as had the face of the dead Johan. Yet, in a while, the Duke reached out and took the child and setting it against his breast, turned his horse. Said Sir Benedict: 'Whither do we ride, lord Duke?' Then spake the Duke on this wise: 'Sir Benedict, Duke Beltane is no more, the stroke that slew my brother Johan killed Duke Beltane also. But as for you, get you to Pentavalon and say the Duke is dead, in proof whereof take you this my ring and so, farewell.' Then, my Beltane, God guiding me, I brought thee to these solitudes, for I am he that was the Duke Beltane, and thou art my son indeed."

CHAPTER VI

HOW BELTANE FARED FORTH OF THE GREEN

Thus spake the hermit Ambrose and, having made an end, sat thereafter with his head bowed upon his hands, while Beltane stood wide-eyed yet seeing not, and with lips apart yet dumb by reason of the wonder of it; therefore, in a while, the hermit spake again:

"Thus did we live together, thou and I, dear son, and I loved thee well, my Beltane: with each succeeding day I loved thee better, for as thine understanding grew, so grew my love for thee. Therefore, so soon as thou wert of an age, set in thy strength and able to thine own support, I tore myself from thy sweet fellowship and lived alone lest, having thee, I might come nigh to happiness."

Then Beltane sank upon his knees and caught the hermit's wasted hands and kissed them oft, saying:

"Much hast thou suffered, O my father, but now am I come to thee again and, knowing all things, here will I bide and leave thee nevermore." Now in the hermit's pale cheek came a faint and sudden glow, and in his eyes a light not of the sun.

"Bethink thee, boy," said he, "the blood within thy veins is noble. For, since thou art my son, so, an thou dost leave me and seek thy destiny thou shalt, perchance, be Duke of Pentavalon — an God will it so."

But Beltane shook his head. Quoth he:

"My father, I am a smith, and smith am I content to be since thou, lord Duke, art my father. So now will I abide with thee and love and honour thee, and be thy son indeed."

Then rose the hermit Ambrose to his feet and spake with eyes uplifted:

"Now glory be to God, Who, in His mercy, hath made of thee a man, my Beltane, clean of soul and innocent, yet strong of arm to lift and succour the distressed, and therefore it is that you to-day must leave me, my well-beloved, for there be those whose need of thee is greater even than mine."

"Nay, dear my father, how may this be?"

Now hereupon Ambrose the Hermit stood awhile with bent head, and spake not, only he sighed full oft and wrung his hands.

"I thought but of myself!" he groaned, "great sorrow is oft-times greatly selfish. Alas, my son — twenty weary years have I lived here suing God's forgiveness, and for twenty bitter years Pentavalon hath groaned 'neath shameful wrong — and death in many hateful shapes. O God have mercy on a sinner who thought but on himself! List, my son, O list! On a day, as I kneeled before yon cross, came one in knightly armour and upon his face, 'neath the links of his camail, I saw a great scar — the scar this hand had wrought. And, even as I knew Sir Benedict, in that same moment he knew me, and gave a joyous cry and came and fell upon his knee and kissed my hand, as of old. Thereafter we talked, and he told me many a woeful tale of Pentavalon and of its misery. How, when I was gone, rose bitter fight and faction, barons and knights striving together which should be Duke. In the midst of the which disorders came one, from beyond seas, whom men called Ivo, who by might of sword and cunning tongue made himself Duke in my place. Sir Benedict told of a fierce and iron rule, of the pillage and ravishment of town and city, of outrage and injustice, of rack and flame and gibbet — of a people groaning 'neath a thousand cruel wrongs. Then, indeed, did I see that my one great sin a thousand other sins had bred, and was I full of bitter sorrow and anguish. And, in my anguish, I thought on thee, and sent to thee Sir Benedict, and watched thee wrestle, and at stroke of sword, and praised God for thy goodly might and strength. For O, dear my

How Beltane Fared Forth 49

son, meseemeth that God hath raised thee up to succour these afflicted, to shield the weak and helpless — hath made thee great and mightier than most to smite Evil that it may flee before thee. So in thee shall my youth be renewed, and my sins, peradventure, purged away."

"Father!" said Beltane rising, his blue eyes wide, his strong hands a-tremble, "O my father!" Then Ambrose clasped those quivering hands and kissed those wide and troubled eyes and spake thereafter, slow and soft:

"Now shall I live henceforth in thee, my son, glorying in thy deeds hereafter. And if thou must needs — bleed, then shall my heart bleed with thee, or if thou meet with death, my Beltane, then shall this heart of mine die with thee."

Thus speaking, the hermit drew the sword from Beltane's girdle and held the great blade towards heaven.

"Behold, my son," said he, "the motto of our house, 'I will arise!' So now shalt thou arise indeed that thy destiny may be fulfilled. Take hold upon thy manhood, my well-beloved, get thee to woeful Pentavalon and, beholding its sorrows, seek how they may be assuaged. Now my Beltane, all is said — when wilt thou leave thy father?"

Quoth Beltane, gathering his cloak about him:

"An so it be thy wish, my father, then will I go this hour."

Then Ambrose brought Beltane into his humble dwelling where was a coffer wrought by his own skilful fingers; and from this coffer he drew forth a suit of triple mail, wondrously fashioned, beholding the which, Beltane's eyes glistened because of the excellence of its craftsmanship.

"Behold!" quoth the hermit, "'tis an armour worthy of a king, light is it, yet marvellous strong, and hath been well tried in many a desperate affray. 'Tis twenty years since these limbs bore it, yet see — I have kept it bright from rust lest, peradventure, Pentavalon should need thee to raise again the battle cry of thy house and lead her men to war. And, alas dear son, that day is now! Pentavalon calls to thee from out the gloom of dungeon, from the anguish of flame, and rack, and gibbet — from blood-soaked hearth and shameful grave she calls thee — so, my Beltane, come and let me arm thee."

And there, within his little hut, the hermit Ambrose, Duke of Pentavalon that was, girt the armour upon Beltane the mighty, Duke of Pentavalon to be, if so God willed; first the gambeson of stuffed and quilted leather, and, thereafter, coifed hauberk and chausses, with wide sword-belt clamped with broad plates of silver and studs of gold, until my Beltane stood up armed in shining mail from head to foot. Then brought Ambrose a wallet, wherein were six gold pieces, and put it in his hand, saying:

"These have I kept against this day, my Beltane. Take them to aid thee on thy journey, for the county of Bourne lieth far to the south."

"Do I then journey to Bourne, my father?"

"Aye, to Sir Benedict, who yet doth hold the great keep of Thrasfordham. Many sieges hath he withstood, and daily men flee to him — stricken men, runaway serfs, and outlaws from the green, all such masterless men as lie in fear of their lives."

Said Beltane, slow and thoughtful:

"There be many outlaws within the green, wild men and sturdy fighters as I've heard. Hath Sir Benedict many men, my father?"

"Alas! a pitiful few, and Black Ivo can muster bows and lances by the ten thousand —"

"Yet doth Sir Benedict withstand them all, my father!"

"Yet must he keep ever within Bourne, Beltane. All Pentavalon, save Bourne, lieth 'neath Ivo's iron foot, ruled by his fierce nobles, and they be strong and many, 'gainst whom Sir Benedict is helpless in the field. 'Tis but five years agone since Ivo gave up fair Belsaye town to ravishment and pillage, and thereafter, builded him a mighty gallows over against it and hanged many men thereon."

Now hereupon, of a sudden, Beltane clenched his hands and fell upon his knees.

"Father," said he, "Pentavalon indeed doth cry, so must I now arise and go unto her. Give me thy blessing that I may go."

Then the hermit laid his hands upon Beltane's golden head and blessed him, and whispered awhile in passionate prayer. Thereafter Beltane arose and, together, they came out into the sunshine.

"South and by west must you march, dear son, and God, methinks, shall go beside thee, for thy feet shall tread a path where Death shall lie in wait for thee. Let thine eyes be watchful therefore, and thine ears quick to hear. Hearken you to all men, yet speak you few words and soft. But, when you act, let your deeds shout unto heaven, that all Pentavalon may know a man is come to lead them who fears only God. And so, my Beltane, fare-thee-well! Come, kiss me, boy; our next kiss, perchance — shall be in heaven."

And thus they kissed, and looked within each other's eyes; then Beltane turned him, swift and sudden, and strode upon his way. But, in a little, looking back, he saw his father, kneeling before the cross, with long, gaunt arms upraised to heaven.

CHAPTER VII

HOW BELTANE TALKED. WITH ONE HIGHT GILES BRABBLE-COMBE, WHO WAS A NOTABLE AND LEARNED ARCHER

THE morning was yet young when my Beltane fared forth into the world, a joyous, golden morning trilling with the glad song of birds and rich with a thousand dewy scents; a fair, sweet, joyous world it was indeed, whose glories, stealing in at eye and ear, filled him with their gladness. On strode my Beltane by rippling brook and sleepy pool, with step swift and light and eyes wide and shining, threading an unerring course as only a forester might; now crossing some broad and sunny glade where dawn yet lingered in rosy mist, anon plunging into the green twilight of dell and dingle, through tangled brush and scented bracken gemmed yet with dewy fire, by marsh and swamp and lichened rock, until he came out upon the forest road, that great road laid by the iron men of Rome, but now little better than a grassy track, yet here and there, with mossy stone set up to the glory of proud emperor and hardy centurion long since dust and ashes; a rutted track, indeed, but leading ever on, 'neath mighty trees, over hill and dale towards the blue mystery beyond.

Now, in a while, being come to the brow of a hill, needs must my Beltane pause to look back upon the woodlands he had loved so well and, sighing, he stretched his arms thitherward; and lo! out of the soft twilight of the green, stole a gentle wind full of the scent of root and herb and the fresh, sweet smell of earth, a cool, soft wind that stirred the golden hair at his temples, like a caress, and so — was gone. For a while he stood thus, gazing towards where he knew his father yet knelt in prayer for him, then turned he slowly, and went his appointed way.

How Beltane Talked with One Giles 53

Thus did Beltane bid farewell to the greenwood and to woodland things, and thus did the green spirit of the woods send forth a gentle wind to kiss him on the brow ere he went out into the world of men and cities.

Now, after some while, as he walked, Beltane was aware of the silvery tinkle of bells and, therewith, a full, sweet voice upraised in song, and the song was right merry and the words likewise:

> "O ne'er shall my lust for the bowl decline,
> Nor my love for my good long bow;
> For as bow to the shaft and as bowl to the wine,
> Is a maid to a man, I trow."

Looking about, Beltane saw the singer, a comely fellow whose long legs bestrode a plump ass; a lusty man he was, clad in shirt of mail and with a feather of green brooched to his escalloped hood; a long-bow hung at his back together with a quiver of arrows, while at his thigh swung a heavy, broad-bladed sword. Now he, espying Beltane amid the leaves, brought the ass to a sudden halt and clapped hand to the pommel of his sword.

"How now, Goliath!" cried he. "*Pax vobiscum*, and likewise *benedicite!* Come ye in peace, forsooth, or is it to be *bellum internecinum?* Though, by St. Giles, which is my patron saint, I care not how it be, for mark ye, *vacuus cantat coram latrone viator*, Sir Goliath, the which in the vulgar tongue signifieth that he who travels with an empty purse laughs before the footpad — moreover, I have a sword!"

But Beltane laughed, saying:

"I have no lust to thy purse, most learned bowman, or indeed to aught of thine unless it be thy company."

"My company?" quoth the bowman, looking Beltane up and down with merry blue eyes, "why now do I know thee for a fellow of rare good judgment, for my company is of the best, in that I have a tongue which loveth to wag in jape or song. Heard ye how the birds and I were a-carolling? A right blithesome morn, methinks, what with my song, and the birds' song, and this poor ass's bells — aye, and the flowers a-peep from the bank yonder. God give ye joy of it, tall brother, as he doth me and this goodly ass betwixt my knees, patient beast."

Now leaning on his quarter-staff Beltane smiled and said:

"How came ye by that same ass, master bowman?"

"Well — I met a monk!" quoth the fellow with a gleam of white teeth. "O! a ponderous monk, brother, of most mighty girth of belly! Now, as ye see, though this ass be sleek and fat as an abbot, she is something small. 'And shall so small a thing needs bear so great a mountain o' flesh?' says I (much moved at the sight, brother). 'No, by the blessed bones of St. Giles (which is my patron saint, brother), so thereafter (by dint of a little persuasion, brother) my mountainous monk, to ease the poor beast's back, presently got him down and I, forthwith, got up — as being more in proportion to her weight, sweet beast! O! surely ne'er saw I fairer morn than this, and never, in so fair a morn, saw I fairer man than thou, Sir Forester, nor taller, and I have seen many men in my day. Wherefore an so ye will, let us company together what time we may; 'tis a solitary road, and the tongue is a rare shortener of distance."

So Beltane strode on beside this garrulous bowman, hearkening to his merry talk, yet himself speaking short and to the point as was ever his custom; as thus:

BOWMAN. "How do men call thee, tall brother?"

BELTANE. "Beltane."

BOWMAN. "Ha! 'Tis a good name, forsooth I've heard worse — and yet, forsooth, I've heard better. Yet 'tis a fairish name —'twill serve. As for me, Giles Brabblecombe o' the Hills men call me, for 'twas in the hill country I was born thirty odd years agone. Since then twelve sieges have I seen with skirmishes and onfalls thrice as many. Death have I beheld in many and divers shapes and in experience of wounds and dangers am rich, though,

How Beltane Talked with One Giles

by St. Giles (my patron saint), in little else. Yet do I love life the better, therefore, and I have read that ' to despise gold is to be rich.' "

BELTANE. " Do all bowmen read, then? "

BOWMAN. " Why look ye, brother, I am not what I was aforetime — *non sum qualis eram* — I was bred a shaveling, a mumbler, a be-gowned do-nothing — brother, I was a monk, but the flesh and the devil made of me a bowman, heigho — so wags the world! Though methinks I am a better bowman than ever I was a monk, having got me some repute with this my bow."

BELTANE (shaking his head). " Methinks thy choice was but a sorry one for —"

BOWMAN (laughing). " Choice quotha! 'Twas no choice, 'twas forced upon me, *vi et armis*. I should be chanting prime or matins at this very hour but for this tongue o' mine, God bless it! For, when it should have been droning psalms, it was forever lilting forth some blithesome melody, some merry song of eyes and lips and stolen kisses. In such sort that the good brethren were wont to gather round and, listening,— sigh! Whereof it chanced I was, one night, by order of the holy Prior, drubbed forth of the sacred precincts. So brother Anselm became Giles o' the Bow — the kind Saints be praised, in especial holy Saint Giles (which is my patron saint!). For, heed me — better the blue sky and the sweet, strong wind than the gloom and silence of a cloister. I had rather hide this sconce of mine in a hood of mail than in the mitre of a lord bishop — *nolo episcopare*, good brother! Thus am I a fighter, and a good fighter, and a wise fighter, having learned 'tis better to live to fight than to fight to live."

BELTANE. " And for whom do ye fight? "

BOWMAN. " For him that pays most, *pecuniae obediunt omnia*, brother."

BELTANE (frowning). " Money? And nought beside? "

BOWMAN (staring). " As what, brother? "

BELTANE. "The justice of the cause wherefore ye fight."

BOWMAN. "Justice quotha — cause! O innocent brother, what have such matters to do with such as I? See you now, such lieth the case. You, let us say, being a baron (and therefore noble!) have a mind to a certain other baron's castle, or wife, or both — (the which is more usual) wherefore ye come to me, who am but a plain bowman knowing nought of the case, and you chaffer with me for the use of this my body for so much money, and thereafter I shoot my best on thy behalf as in mine honour bound. Thus have I fought both for and against Black Ivo throughout the length and breadth of his Duchy of Pentavalon. If ye be minded to sell that long sword o' thine, to none better market could ye come, for there be ever work for such about Black Ivo."

BELTANE. "Aye, 'tis so I hear."

BOWMAN. "Nor shall ye anywhere find a doughtier fighter than Duke Ivo, nor a leader quicker to spy out the vantage of position and attack."

BELTANE. "Is he so lusty a man-at-arms?"

BOWMAN. "With lance, axe, or sword he hath no match. I have seen him lead a charge. I have watched him fight afoot. I have stormed behind him through a breach, and I know of none dare cope with him — unless it be Sir Pertolepe the Red."

BELTANE. "Hast ne'er heard tell, then, of Benedict of Bourne?"

BOWMAN (clapping hand to thigh). "Now by the blood and bones of St. Giles 'tis so! Out o' the mouth of a babe and suckling am I corrected! Verily if there be one to front Black Ivo 'tis Benedict o' the Mark. To behold these two at handstrokes — with axes — ha, there would be a sweet affray indeed — a sight for the eyes of holy archangels! Dost know aught of Sir Benedict, O Innocence?"

BELTANE. "I have seen him."

BOWMAN. "Then, my soft and gentle dove-like youth,

How Beltane Talked with One Giles

get thee to thy marrow-bones and pray that kind heaven shall make thee more his like, for in his shoes doth stand a man — a knight — a very paladin!"

BELTANE. "Who fighteth not for — hire, Sir Bowman!"

BOWMAN. "Yet who hireth to fight, Sir Dove-eyed Giant, for I have fought for him, ere now, within his great keep of Thrasfordham within Bourne. But, an ye seek employ, his is but a poor service, where a man shall come by harder knocks than good broad pieces."

BELTANE. "And yet, 'spite thy cunning and all thy warring, thy purse goeth empty!"

BOWMAN. "My purse, Sir Dove? Aye, I told thee so for that I am by nature cautious — *sicut mos est nobis!* But thy dove's eyes are honest eyes, so now shall you know that hid within the lining of this my left boot be eighty and nine gold pieces, and in my right a ring with stones of price, and, moreover, here behold a goodly chain."

So saying, the bowman drew from his bosom a gold chain, thick and long and heavy, and held it up in the sunlight.

"I got this, Sir Dove, together with the ring and divers other toys, at the storming of Belsaye, five years agone. Aha! a right good town is Belsaye, and growing rich and fat against another plucking."

"And how came Belsaye to be stormed?"

Quoth Giles the Bowman, eying his golden chain:

"My lord Duke Ivo had a mind to a certain lady, who was yet but a merchant's daughter, look ye. But she was young and wondrous fair, for Duke Ivo hath a quick eye and rare judgment in such pretty matters. But she (and she but a merchant's daughter!) took it ill, and when Duke Ivo's messengers came to bear her to his presence, she whined and struggled, as is ever woman's way, and thereafter in the open street snatched a dagger and thereupon, before her father's very eye did slay herself (and she but a merchant's daughter!), whereat some hot-head plucked out sword and other citizens likewise, and of my lord Duke's messengers there none escaped save one and he sore wounded. So Belsaye city shut its gates 'gainst my lord Duke and set out fighting-hoards upon its walls. Yet my lord Duke battered and breached it, for few can match him in a siege, and stormed it within three days. And, by Saint Giles, though he lost the merchant's daughter methinks he lacked not at all, for the women of Belsaye are wondrous fair."

The rising sun made a glory all about them, pouring his beams 'twixt mighty trees whose knotted, far-flung branches dappled the way here and there with shadow; but now Beltane saw nought of it by reason that he walked with head a-droop and eyes that stared earthward; moreover his hands were clenched and his lips close and grim-set. As for Giles o' the Bow, he chirrupped merrily to the ass, and whistled full melodiously, mocking a blackbird that piped amid the green. Yet in a while he turned to stare at Beltane rubbing at his square, shaven chin with strong, brown fingers.

"Forsooth," quoth he, nodding, "thou'rt a lusty fellow, Sir Gentleness, by the teeth of St. Giles, which is my patron saint, ne'er saw I a goodlier spread of shoulder nor such a proper length of arm to twirl an axe withal, and thy legs like me well — hast the makings of a right lusty man-at-arms in thee, despite thy soft and peaceful look!"

"Yet a lover of peace am I!" said Beltane, his head yet drooping.

"Peace, quotha — peace? Ha? by all the holy saints — peace! A soft word! A woman's word! A word smacking of babes and milk! Out upon thee, what hath a man with such an arm — aye, and legs — to do with peace? An you would now, I could bring ye to good service 'neath Duke Ivo's banner. 'Tis said he hath sworn, this year, to burn Thrasfordham keep, to hang Benedict o' the Mark and lay waste to Bourne. Aha! you shall see good fighting 'neath Ivo's banner, Sir Dove!"

Then Beltane raised his head and spake, swift and sudden, on this wise:

"An I must fight, the which God forbid, yet once this my sword is drawn ne'er shall it rest till I lie dead or Black Ivo is no more."

Then did the archer stare upon my Beltane in amaze with eyes full wide and mouth agape, nor spake he for awhile, then:

"Black Ivo — thou!" he cried, and laughed amain. "Go to, my tender youth," said he, "methinks a lute were better fitted to thy hand than that great sword o' thine." Now beholding Beltane's gloomy face, he smiled within his hand, yet eyed him thoughtfully thereafter, and so they went with never a word betwixt them. But, in a while, the archer fell to snuffing the air, and clapped Beltane upon the shoulder.

"Aha!" quoth he, "methinks we reach the fair Duchy of Pentavalon; smell ye aught, brother?" And now, indeed, Beltane became aware of a cold wind, foul and noisome, a deadly, clammy air breathing of things corrupt, chilling the flesh with swift unthinking dread; and, halting in disgust, he looked about him left and right.

"Above — above!" cried Giles o' the Bow, "this is Sir Pertolepe's country — look you heavenward, Sir Innocence!"

Then, lifting his eyes to the shivering leaves overhead, Beltane of a sudden espied a naked foot — a down-curving, claw-like thing, shrivelled and hideous, and, glancing higher yet, beheld a sight to blast the sun from heaven: now staring up at the contorted horror of this shrivelled thing that once had lived and laughed, Beltane let fall his staff and, being suddenly sick and faint, sank upon his knees and, covering his eyes, crouched there in the grass the while that grisly, silent thing swayed to and fro above him in the gentle wind of morning and the cord whereby it hung creaked faintly.

"How now — how now!" cried Giles; "do ye blench before this churlish carrion? Aha! ye shall see the trees bear many such hereabouts. Get up, my qualmish, maid-like youth; he ne'er shall injure thee nor any man again — save by the nose — faugh! Rise, rise and let us be gone."

So, presently Beltane, shivering, got him to his feet and looking up, pale-faced, beheld upon the ragged breast a parchment with this legend in fair, good writing:

HE KILLED A DEER

Then spake Beltane 'twixt pallid lips:
"And do they hang men for killing deer in this country?"
"'Aye, forsooth, and very properly, for, heed me, your ragged rogues be a plenty, but a stag is a noble creature and something scarcer — moreover they be the Duke's."
"By whose order was this done?"
"Why, the parchment beareth the badge of Sir Pertolepe, called the Red. But look you, Sir Innocent, no man may kill a deer unless he be of gentle blood."
"And wherefore?"
"'Tis so the law!"
"And who made the law?"
"Why — as to that," quoth Giles, rubbing his chin, "as to that — what matters it to you or me? Pah! come away lest I stifle!"

But now, even as they stood thus, out of the green came a cry, hoarse at first but rising ever higher until it seemed to fill the world about and set the very leaves a-quiver. Once it came, and twice, and so — was gone. Then Beltane trembling, stooped and caught up his long quarter-staff, and seized the bowman in a shaking hand that yet was strong, and dragging him from the ass all in a moment, plunged into the underbrush whence the cry had come. And, in a while, they beheld a cottage upon whose threshold a child lay — not asleep, yet very still; and beyond the cottage, his back to a tree, a great hairy fellow, quarter-staff in hand, made play against five others whose steel caps and ringed hauberks glittered in the sun. Close

How Beltane Talked with One Giles

and ever closer they beset the hairy man who, bleeding at the shoulder, yet swung his heavy staff; but ever the glittering pike-heads thrust more close. Beside the man a woman crouched, young and of comely seeming, despite wild hair and garments torn and wrenched, who of a sudden, with another loud cry, leapt before the hairy man covering him with her clinging body and, in that moment, her scream died to a choking gasp and she sank huddled 'neath a pike-thrust. Then Beltane leapt, the great sword flashing in his grasp, and smote the smiter and set his feet upon the writhing body and smote amain with terrible arm, and his laughter rang out fierce and wild. So for a space, sword clashed with pike, but ever Beltane, laughing loud, drave them before him till but two remained and they writhing upon the sward. Then Beltane turned to see Giles o' the Bow, who leaned against a tree near by, wide-eyed and pale.

"Look!" he cried, pointing with quivering finger, "one dead and one sore hurt — Saint Giles save us, what have ye done? These be Sir Pertolepe's foresters — behold his badge!"

But Beltane laughed, fierce-eyed.

"How, bowman, dost blench before a badge, then? I was too meek and gentle for thee ere this, but now, if thou'rt afraid — get you gone!"

"Art surely mad!" quoth Giles. "The saints be my witness here was no act of mine!" So saying he turned away and hasted swift-footed through the green. Now when the bowman was gone, Beltane turned him to the hairy man who yet kneeled beside the body of the woman. Said he:

"Good fellow, is there aught I may do for thee?"

"Wife and child — and dead!" the man muttered, "child and wife — and dead! A week ago, my brother — and now, the child, and then the wife! Child and wife and brother — and dead!" Then Beltane came, minded to aid him with the woman, but the hairy man sprang before her, swinging his great staff and muttering in his beard;

therefore Beltane, sick at heart, turned him away. And, in a while, being come to the road once more, he became aware that he yet grasped his sword and beheld its bright steel dimmed here and there with blood, and, as he gazed, his brow grew dark and troubled.

" 'Tis thus have I made beginning," he sighed, " so now, God aiding me, ne'er will I rest 'till peace be come again and tyranny made an end of!"

Then, very solemnly, did my Beltane kneel him beside the way and lifting the cross hilt of his sword to heaven kissed it, and thereafter rose. And so, having cleansed the steel within the earth, he sheathed the long blade and went, slow-footed, upon his way.

CHAPTER VIII

HOW BELTANE HELD DISCOURSE WITH A BLACK FRIAR

THE sun was high, and by his shadow Beltane judged it the noon hour; very hot and very still it was, for the wind had died and leaf and twig hung motionless as though asleep. And presently as he went, a sound stole upon the stillness, a sound soft and beyond all things pleasant to hear, the murmurous ripple of running water near by. Going aside into the green therefore, Beltane came unto a brook, and here, screened from the sun 'neath shady willows, he laid him down to drink, and to bathe face and hands in the cool water.

Now as he lay thus, staring sad-eyed into the hurrying waters of the brook, there came to him the clicking of sandalled feet, and glancing up, he beheld one clad as a black friar. A fat man he was, jolly of figure and mightily round; his nose was bulbous and he had a drooping lip.

"Peace be unto thee, my son!" quoth he, breathing short and loud, "an evil day for a fat man who hath been most basely bereft of a goodly ass — holy Saint Dunstan, how I gasp!" and putting back the cowl from his tonsured crown, he puffed out his cheeks and mopped his face. "Hearkee now, good youth, hath there passed thee by ever a ribald in an escalloped hood — an unhallowed, long-legged, scurvy archer knave astride a fair white ass, my son?"

"Truly," nodded Beltane, "we parted company scarce an hour since."

The friar sat him down in the shade of the willows and sighing, mopped his face again; quoth he:

"Now may the curse of Saint Augustine, Saint Benedict, Saint Cuthbert and Saint Dominic light upon him for a lewd fellow, a clapper-claw, a thieving dog who hath no regard for Holy Church — forsooth a most vicious rogue, *monstrum nulla virtute redemptum a vitiis!*"

"Good friar, thy tongue is something harsh, methinks. Here be four saints with as many curses, and all for one small ass!"

The friar puffed out his cheeks and sighed:

"'Twas a goodly ass, my son, a fair and gentle beast and of an easy gait, and I am one that loveth not to trip it in the dust. Moreover 'twas the property of Holy Church! To take from thy fellow is evil, to steal from thy lord is worse, but to ravish from Holy Church — *per de* 'tis sacrilege, 'tis foul blasphemy thrice — aye thirty times damned and beyond all hope of redemption! So now do I consign yon archer-knave to the lowest pit of Acheron — *damnatus est*, amen! Yet, my son, here — by the mercy of heaven is a treasure the rogue hath overlooked, a pasty most rarely seasoned that I had this day from my lord's own table. 'Tis something small for two, alack and yet — stay — who comes?"

Now, lifting his head, Beltane beheld a man, bent and ragged who crept towards them on a stick; his face, low-stooped, was hid 'neath long and matted hair, but his tatters plainly showed the hideous nakedness of limbs pinched and shrunken by famine, while about his neck was a heavy iron collar such as all serfs must needs wear. Being come near he paused, leaning upon his staff, and cried out in a strange, cracked voice:

"O ye that are strong and may see the blessed sun, show pity on one that is feeble and walketh ever in the dark!"

And now, beneath the tangled hair, Beltane beheld a livid face in whose pale oval, the eyeless sockets glowed fierce and red; moreover he saw that the man's right arm was but a mutilated stump, whereat Beltane shivered and, bowing his head upon his hands, closed his eyes.

"Oho!" cried the friar, "and is it thou, Simon? Trouble ye the world yet, child of Satan?"

Hereupon the blind man fell upon his knees.

Discourse with a Black Friar

"Holy father," he groaned, clasping his withered arms upon his gaunt breast, "good Friar Gui I die of hunger; aid me lest I perish. 'Tis true I am outlaw and no man may minister unto me, yet be merciful, give me to eat — O gentle Christ, aid me —"

"How!" cried the friar, "dare ye speak that name, ye that are breaker of laws human and divine, ye that are murderer, dare ye lift those bloody hands to heaven?"

"Holy sir," quoth Beltane, "he hath but one; I pray you now give him to eat."

"Feed an outlaw! Art mad, young sir? Feed a murderer, a rogue banned by Holy Church, a serf that hath raised hand 'gainst his lord? He should have hanged when the witch his daughter burned, but that Sir Pertolepe, with most rare mercy, gave to the rogue his life."

"But," sighed Beltane, "left him to starve —'tis a death full as sure yet slower, methinks. Come, let us feed him."

"I tell thee, fond youth, he is excommunicate. Wouldst have me contravene the order of Holy Church? Go to!"

Then my Beltane put his hand within his pouch and taking thence a gold piece held it out upon his palm; said he:

"Friar, I will buy the half of thy pasty of thee!" Hereupon Friar Gui stared from the gold to the pasty, and back again.

"So much!" quoth he, round-eyed. "Forsooth 'tis a noble pasty and yet — nay, nay, tempt me not — *retro Sathanas!*" and closing his eyes he crossed himself. Then Beltane took out other two gold pieces and set them in the blind man's bony hand, saying:

"Take these three gold pieces and buy you food, and thereafter —"

"Gold!" cried the blind man, "gold! Now the Saints keep and bless thee, young sir, sweet Jesu love thee ever!" and fain would he have knelt to kiss my Beltane's feet. But Beltane raised him up with gentle hand, speaking him kindly, as thus:

"Tell now, I pray you, how came ye to slay?"

"Stay! stay!" cried Friar Gui, "bethink thee, goo[d] youth — so much gold, 'tis a very fortune! With s[o] much, masses might be sung for his wretched soul; give [it] therefore to Holy Church, so shall he, peradventure, at[-]tain Paradise."

"Not so," answered Beltane, "I had rather he, of surety, attain a full belly, Sir Friar." Then, turning h[is] back upon the friar, Beltane questioned the blind ma[n] again, as thus:

"Tell me, an ye will, how ye came to shed blood?" an[d] the outlaw, kneeling at Beltane's feet answered with bowe[d] head:

"Noble sir, I had a daughter and she was young an[d] fair, therefore came my lord Pertolepe's chief verderer t[o] bear her to my lord. But she cried to me and I, forgettin[g] my duty to my lord, took my quarter-staff and, se[r]f though I was, smote the chief verderer that he died there[-]after, but, ere he died, he named my daughter witch. An[d] when they had burned her, they put out mine eyes, an[d] cut off my hand, and made of me an outlaw. So is my si[n] very heavy upon me."

Now when the man had made an end, Beltane stoo[d] silent awhile, then, reaching down, he aided the blind ma[n] to his feet.

"Go you to Mortain," said he, "seek out the herm[it] Ambrose that liveth in Holy Cross Thicket; with him sha[ll] you find refuge, and he, methinks, will surely win thy so[ul] to heaven."

So the blind man blessed my Beltane and turning, cre[pt] upon his solitary way.

"Youth," said the friar, frowning up into Beltan[e's] gentle eyes, "thou hast this day put thy soul [in] jeopardy — the Church doth frown upon this t[hy] deed!"

"And yet, most reverend sir, God's sun doth shi[ne] upon this my body!"

FRIAR. "He who aideth an evil-doer is enemy to t[he] good!"

Discourse with a Black Friar 67

BELTANE. "Yet he who seeketh to do good to evil that good may follow, doeth no evil to good."

FRIAR. "Ha! thou art a menace to the state —"

BELTANE. "So shall I be, I pray God, the whiles this state continue!"

FRIAR. "Thou art either rogue or fool!"

BELTANE. "Well, thou hast thy choice."

FRIAR. "Alack! this sorry world is full of rogues and fools and —"

BELTANE. "And friars!"

FRIAR. "Who seek the salvation of this wretched world."

BELTANE. "As how?"

FRIAR. "Forsooth we meditate and pray —"

BELTANE. "And eat!"

FRIAR. "Aye verily, we do a little in that way as the custom is, for your reverent eater begetteth a devout pray-er. The which mindeth me I grow an hungered, yet will I forego appetite and yield thee this fair pasty for but two of thy gold pieces. And, look ye, 'tis a noble pasty I had this day from my lord Pertolepe's own table."

BELTANE. "That same lord that showed mercy on yonder poor maimed wretch? Know you him?"

FRIAR. "In very sooth, and 'tis a potent lord that holdeth me in some esteem, a most Christian knight —"

BELTANE. "That ravisheth the defenceless! Whose hands be foul with the blood of innocence —"

FRIAR. "How — how? 'Tis a godly lord who giveth bounteously to Holy Church —"

BELTANE. "Who stealeth from the poor —"

FRIAR. "Stealeth! Holy Saint Dunstan, dare ye speak thus of so great a lord — a son of the Church, a companion of our noble Duke? Steal, forsooth! The poor have nought to steal!"

BELTANE. "They have their lives."

FRIAR. "Not so, they and their lives are their lord's, 'tis so the law and —"

BELTANE. "Whence came this law?"

FRIAR. "It came, youth — it came — aye, of God!"

BELTANE. "Say rather of the devil!"

FRIAR. "Holy Saint Michael —'tis a blasphemous youth! Never heard ears the like o' this —"

BELTANE. "Whence cometh poverty and famine?"

FRIAR. "'Tis a necessary evil! Doth it not say in Holy Writ, 'the poor ye have always with you'?"

BELTANE. "Aye, so shall ye ever — until the laws be amended. So needs must men starve and starve —"

FRIAR. "There be worse things! And these serfs be born to starve, bred up to it, and 'tis better to starve here than to perish hereafter, better to purge the soul by lack of meat than to make of it a fetter of the soul!"

"Excellently said, holy sir!" quoth Beltane, stooping of a sudden. "But for this pasty now, 'tis a somewhat solid fetter, meseemeth, so now do I free thee of it — thus!" So saying, my Beltane dropped the pasty into the deeper waters of the brook and, thereafter, took up his staff. "Sir Friar," said he, "behold to-day is thy soul purged of a pasty against the day of judgment!"

Then Beltane went on beside the rippling waters of the brook, but above its plash and murmur rose the deep-toned maledictions of Friar Gui.

CHAPTER IX

WHEREIN IS SOME ACCOUNT OF THE PHILOSOPHY OF FOLLY
AND THE WISDOM OF A FOOL

As the day advanced the sun grew ever hotter; birds chirped drowsily from hedge and thicket, and the warm, still air was full of the slumberous drone of a myriad unseen wings. Therefore Beltane sought the deeper shade of the woods and, risking the chance of roving thief or lurking foot-pad, followed a devious course by reason of the underbrush.

Now as he walked him thus, within the cool, green twilight, watchful of eye and with heavy quarter-staff poised upon his shoulder, he presently heard the music of a pipe now very mournful and sweet, anon breaking into a merry lilt full of rippling trills and soft, bubbling notes most pleasant to be heard. Wherefore he went aside and thus, led by the music, beheld a jester in his motley lying a-sprawl beneath a tree. A long-legged knave was he, pinched and something doleful of visage yet with quick bright eyes that laughed 'neath sombre brows, and a wide, up-curving mouth; upon his escalloped cape and flaunting cock's-comb were many little bells that rang a silvery chime as, up-starting to his elbow, he greeted my Beltane thus:

"Hail, noble, youthful Sir, and of thy sweet and gracious courtesy I pray you mark me this — the sun is hot, my belly lacketh, and thou art a fool!"

"And wherefore?" questioned Beltane, leaning him upon his quarter-staff.

"For three rarely reasonable reasons, sweet sir, as thus: — item, for that the sun burneth, item, my belly is

empty, and item, thou, lured by this my foolish
hither come to folly. So I, a fool, do greet t
and welcome thee to this my palace of ease and p
where, an ye be minded to list to the folly of
foolish fool, I will, with foolish jape and quip, b
mind to mirth and jollity, for thou art a sad
thinks, and something melancholic!"

Quoth Beltane, sighing:

"'Tis a sad world and very sorrowful!"

"Nay —'tis a sweet world and very joyful —
as have eyes to see withal!"

"To see?" quoth Beltane, frowning, "this
I seen a dead man a-swing on a tree, a babe de
its cradle, and a woman die upon a spear! All
I breathed an air befouled by nameless evil; whit
I go needs must I walk 'twixt Murder and Sham

"Then look ever before thee, so shalt see neit

"Yet will they be there!"

"Yet doth the sun shine in high heaven, so n
things be till God and the saints shall mend them
thou must needs be doleful, go make thee trouble
own but leave the woes of this wide world to Go

"Nay," said Beltane, shaking his head, "ho
leave these things to thee and me?"

"Why then methinks the world must wag a
Yet must we repine therefore? Out upon thee fc
long-legged, doleful wight. Now harkee! Her
a fool, mark these bells! And a hungry fool!
less fool! A fool who hath, this day, been dr
of my lord's presence with blows and cruel strij
wherefore? 'Twas for setting a bird free of i
small matter methinks — though there be bi
birds, but mum for that! Yet do I grieve and
fore, O doleful long-shanks? Not so — fie on'
away my sorrows through the music of this my
and, lying here, set my wits a-dancing and lo! I
a king, a very god! I create me a world wherei
hunger nor stripes, a world of joy and lau

blessed within his dreams, even a fool may walk with gods and juggle with the stars!"

"Aye," nodded Beltane, "but how when he awake?"

"Why then, messire," laughed the fellow, leaping nimbly to his feet, "why then doth he ask alms of thee, as thus: Prithee most noble messire, of thy bounty show kindness to a fool that lacks everything but wit. So give, messire, give and spare not, so may thy lady prove kind, thy wooing prosper and love strengthen thee."

Now when the jester spake of love, my Beltane must needs sigh amain and shake a doleful head.

"Alas!" said he, "within my life shall be no place for love, methinks."

"Heigho!" sighed the jester, "thy very look doth proclaim thee lover, and 'tis well, for love maketh the fool wise and the wise fool, it changeth saints into rogues and rogues into saints, it teacheth the strong man gentleness and maketh the gentle strong. 'Tis sweeter than honey yet bitter as gall — Love! ah, love can drag a man to hell or lift him high as heaven!"

"Aye verily," sighed Beltane, "I once did dream of such a love, but now am I awake, nor will I dream of love again, nor rest whiles Lust and Cruelty rule this sorrowful Duchy —"

"Ha, what would ye then, fond youth?"

"I am come to smite them hence," said Beltane, clenching mighty fists.

"How?" cried the jester, wide of eye. "Alone?"

"Nay, methinks God goeth with me. Moreover, I have this sword!" and speaking, Beltane touched the hilt of the great blade at his side.

"What — a sword!" scoffed the jester, "think ye to mend the woes of thy fellows with a sword? Go to, thou grave-visaged, youthful fool! I tell thee, 'tis only humour and good fellowship can mend this wretched world, and there is nought so lacking in humour as a sword — unless it be your prating priest or mumbling monk. A pope in cap and bells, now — aha, there would be a world indeed, a world of joy and laughter! No more gloom, no more bans and damnings of Holy Church, no more groaning and snivelling in damp cloister and mildewed chapel, no more burnings and hangings and rackings —"

"Yet," said Beltane, shaking his head, "yet would kings and dukes remain, Christian knights and godly lords to burn and hang and rack the defenceless."

"Aye, Sir Gravity," nodded the jester, "but the Church is paramount ever; set the pope a-blowing of tunes upon a reed and kings would lay by their sceptres and pipe too and, finding no time or lust for warring, so strife would end, swords rust and wit grow keen. And wit, look you, biteth sharper than sword, laughter is more enduring than blows, and he who smiteth, smiteth only for lack of wit. So, an you would have a happy world, lay by that great sword and betake thee to a little pipe, teach men to laugh and so forget their woes. Learn wisdom of a fool, as thus: 'Tis better to live and laugh and beget thy kind than to perish by the sword or to dangle from a tree. Here now is advice, and in this advice thy life, thus in giving thee advice so do I give thee thy life. And I am hungry. And in thy purse is money wherewith even a fool might come by food. And youth is generous! And thou art very young! Come, sweet youthful messire, how much for thy life — and a fool's advice?"

Then Beltane smiled, and taking out one of his three remaining gold pieces, put it in the jester's hand.

"Fare thee well, good fool," said he, "I leave thee to thy dreams; God send they be ever fair —"

"Gold!" cried the jester, spinning the coin upon his thumb, "ha, now do I dream indeed; may thy waking be ever as joyous. Farewell to thee, thou kind, sweet, youthful fool, and if thou must hang some day on a tree, may every leaf voice small prayers for thy gentle soul!"

So saying, the jester nodded, waved aloft his bauble, and skipped away among the trees. But as Beltane went, pondering the jester's saying, the drowsy stillness was shivered by a sudden, loud cry, followed thereafter by a

The Philosophy of Folly

clamour of fierce shouting; therefore Beltane paused and turning, beheld the jester himself who ran very fleetly, yet with three lusty fellows in close pursuit.

"Messire," panted the jester, wild of eye and with a trickle of blood upon his pallid face, "O sweet sir — let them not slay me!"

Now while he spake, and being yet some way off, he tripped and fell, and, as he lay thus the foremost of his pursuers, a powerful, red-faced man, leapt towards him, whirling up his quarter-staff to smite; but, in that moment, Beltane leapt also and took the blow upon his staff and swung it aloft, yet stayed the blow, and, bestriding the prostrate jester, spake soft and gentle, on this wise:

"Greeting to thee, forest fellow! Thy red face liketh me well, let us talk together."

But, hereupon, as the red-faced man fell back, staring in amaze, there came his two companions, albeit panting and short of breath.

"What, Roger," cried one, "doth this fellow withstand thee?"

But Roger only growled, whiles Beltane smiled upon the three, gentle-eyed, but with heavy quarter-staff poised lightly in practised hand; quoth he:

"How now, would ye harm the fool? 'Tis a goodly fool forsooth, yet with legs scarce so nimble as his wit, and a tongue — ha, a golden tongue to win all men to humour and good fellowship —"

"Enough!" growled red-faced Roger, "Sir Pertolepe's foresters we be, give us yon scurvy fool then, that we may hang him out of hand."

"Nay," answered Beltane, "first let us reason together, let us hark to the wisdom of Folly and grow wise —"

"Ha, Roger!" cried one of the men, "tap me this tall rogue on his golden mazzard!"

"Or," said Beltane, "the fool shall charm thy souls to kindliness with his pipe —"

"Ho, Roger!" cried the second forester, "split me this tall talker's yellow sconce, now!"

serve the devil?"

"Devil? Ha, what talk be this? We serve no devil!"

"Aye," nodded Beltane, "though they call him Pertolepe the Red, hereabouts."

"Devil!" cried Black Roger aghast. And, falling back a step he gaped in amaze from Beltane to his gaping fellows. "Devil, forsooth!" he gasped, "aha, I've seen many a man hang for less than this —"

"True," sighed Beltane, "men hang for small matters here in Pentavalon, and to hang is an evil death, methinks!"

"So, so!" nodded Black Roger, grim-smiling, "I've watched them kick a fair good while, betimes!"

"Ah!" cried Beltane, his eyes widening, "those hands of thine, belike, have hanged a man ere this?"

"Aye, many a score. Oho! folk know Black Roger's name hereabouts. I carry ever a noose at my girdle here — behold it!" and he showed a coil of rope that swung at his belt.

Now looking from the man's grim features to this murderous cord, Beltane blenched and shivered, whereat Black Roger laughed aloud, and pointed a scornful finger.

"Look'ee, 'tis fair, good rope this, and well-tried, and shall bear even thy great carcase sweetly — aye, sweetly —"

"How — would'st hang me also?" said Beltane faintly, and the heavy quarter-staff sagged in his loosened grip.

"Hang thee — aye. Thou didst withstand us with this fool, thou hast dared miscall our lord — we be all witnesses to it. So now will we —"

But swift as lightning-flash, Beltane's long quarter-staff whirled and fell, and, for all his hood of mail, Black Roger threw wide his arms and, staggering, fell upon his face

The Philosophy of Folly 75

and so lay; then, fierce and grim, he had leapt upon the other two, and the air was full of the rattle and thud of vicious blows. But these foresters were right lusty fellows and they, together, beset my Beltane so furiously, right and left, that he perforce gave back 'neath their swift and grievous blows and, being overmatched, turned and betook him to his heels, whereat they, incontinent, pursued with loud gibes and fierce laughter. But on ran Beltane up the glade very fleetly yet watchful of eye, until, seeing one had outstripped his fellow, he checked his going somewhat, stumbling as one that is spent, whereat the forester shouted the louder and came on amain. Then did my cunning Beltane leap aside and, leaping, turned and smote the fellow clean and true upon the crown, and, laughing to see him fall, ran in upon the other forester with whirling quarter-staff. Now this fellow seeing himself stand alone, stayed not to abide the onset, but turning about, made off into the green. Then Beltane leaned him, panting, upon his staff, what time the fallen man got him unsteadily to his legs and limped after his comrade; as for the jester, he was gone long since; only Black Roger lay upon his face and groaned faintly, ever and anon. Wherefore came Beltane and stood above him as one in thought and, seeing him begin to stir, took from him his sword and coil of rope and loosing off his sword-belt, therewith bound his hands fast together and so, dragged him 'neath a tree that stood hard by. Thus when at last Black Roger opened his eyes, he beheld Beltane standing above him and in his hand the deadly rope. Now, looking from this to the desolation about him, Black Roger shivered, and gazing up into the stern face above, his florid cheek grew pale.

"Master," said he hoarsely, "what would ye?"

"I would do to thee as thou hast done to others."

"Hang me?"

"Aye!" quoth Beltane, and setting the noose about his neck, cast the rope across a branch.

"Master, how shall my death profit thee?"

"The world shall be the better, and thy soul know less of sin, mayhap."

"Master," said Black Roger, stooping to wipe sweat from his face with fettered hands, "I have store of money set by —"

But Beltane laughed with pallid lips, and, pulling upon the rope, dragged Black Roger, choking, to his feet.

"Master," he gasped, "show a little mercy —"

"Hast ever shown mercy to any man — speak me true!"

"Alack! — no, master! And yet —"

"How then shall ye expect mercy? Thou hast burnt and hanged and ravished the defenceless, so now shall be an end of it for thee, yet — O mark me this, thy name shall live on accursed in memory long after thou'rt but poor dust."

"Aye, there be many alive to curse Black Roger living, and many dead to curse me when I'm dead; poor Roger's soul shall find small mercy hereafter, methinks — ha, I never thought on this!"

"Thou had'st a mother —"

"Aye, but they burned her for a witch when I was but a lad. As for me, 'tis true I've hanged men, yet I was my lord's chief verderer and did but as my lord commanded."

"A man hath choice of good or evil."

"Aye. So now, an I must die — I must, but O master, say a prayer for me — my sins lie very heavy —"

But Beltane, trembling, pulled upon the rope and swung Black Roger writhing in mid-air; then, of a sudden, loosing the rope, the forester fell and, while he lay gasping, Beltane stooped and loosed the rope from his neck.

"What now?" groaned the forester, wild-eyed, "Sweet Jesu — ah, torture me not!"

"Take back thy life," said Beltane, "and I pray God that henceforth thou shalt make of it better use, and live to aid thy fellows, so shall they, mayhap, some day come to bless thy memory."

The Philosophy of Folly

Then Black Roger, coming feebly to his knees, looked about him as one that wakes upon a new world, and lifted wide eyes from green earth to cloudless sky.

"To live!" quoth he, "to live!" And so, with sudden gesture, stooped his head to hide his face 'neath twitching fingers.

Hereupon Beltane smiled, gentle-eyed, yet spake not, and, turning, caught up his staff and went softly upon his way, leaving Black Roger the forester yet upon his knees.

CHAPTER X

HOW BELTANE MADE COMRADE ONE BLACK ROGER THAT WAS A HANGMAN

THE sun was low what time Beltane came to a shrine that stood beside the way, where was a grot built by some pious soul for the rest and refreshment of wearied travellers; and here also was a crystal spring the which, bubbling up, fell with a musical plash into the basin hollowed within the rock by those same kindly hands. Here Beltane stayed and, when he had drunk his fill, laid him down in the grateful shade and setting his cloak beneath his head, despite his hunger, presently fell asleep. When he awoke the sun was down and the world was become a place of mystery and glooming shadow; a bird called plaintively afar off in the dusk, the spring bubbled softly near by, but save for this a deep silence brooded over all things; above the gloom of the trees the sky was clear, where bats wheeled and hovered, and beyond the purple upland an orbed moon was rising.

Now as Beltane breathed the cool, sweet air of evening and looked about him drowsily, he suddenly espied a shadow within the shadows, a dim figure — yet formidable and full of menace, and he started up, weapon in fist, whereupon the threatening figure stirred and spake:

"Master —'tis I!" said a voice. Then Beltane came forth of the grot and stared upon Black Roger, grave-eyed.

"O Hangman," said he, "where is thy noose?"

But Roger quailed and hung his head, and spake with eyes abased:

"Master, I burned it, together with my badge of service."

"And what would ye here?"

"Sir, I am a masterless man henceforth, for an I hang not men for Sir Pertolepe, so will Sir Pertolepe assuredly hang me."

"And fear ye death?"

"Messire, I — have hanged many men and — there were women also! I have cut me a tally here on my belt, see — there be many notches — and every notch a life. So now for every life these hands have taken do I vow to save a life an it may be so, and for every life saved would I cut away a notch until my belt be smooth again and my soul the lighter."

"Why come ye to me, Black Roger?"

"For that this day, at dire peril, I saw thee save a fool, Master. So now am I come to thee to be thy man henceforth, to follow and serve thee while life remain."

"Why look now," quoth Beltane, "mine shall be a hard service and a dangerous, for I have mighty wrongs to set aright."

"Ha! belike thou art under some vow also, master?"

"Aye, verily, nor will I rest until it be accomplished or I am slain. For mark this, lonely am I, with enemies a many and strong, yet because of my vow needs must I smite them hence or perish in the adventure. Thus, he that companies me must go ever by desperate ways, and 'tis like enough Death shall meet him in the road."

"Master," quoth Black Roger, "this day have ye shown me death yet given me new life, so beseech thee let me serve thee henceforth and aid thee in this thy vow."

Now hereupon Beltane smiled and reached forth his hand; then Black Roger falling upon his knee, touched the hand to lip, and forehead and heart, taking him for his lord henceforth, and spake the oath of fealty: but when he would have risen, Beltane stayed him:

"What, Black Roger, thou hast sworn fealty and obedience to me — now swear me this to God: — to hold ever, and abide by, thy word: to shew mercy to the distressed and to shield the helpless at all times!"

And when he had sworn, Black Roger rose bright-eyed and eager.

"Lord," said he, "whither do we go?"

"Now," quoth Beltane, "shew me where I may eat, for I have a mighty hunger."

"Forsooth," quoth Roger, scratching his chin, "Shallowford village lieth but a bowshot through the brush yonder — yet, forsooth, a man shall eat little there, methinks, these days."

"Why so?"

"For that 'twas burned down, scarce a week agone —"

"Burned! — and wherefore?"

"Lord Pertolepe fell out with his neighbour Sir Gilles of Brandonmere — upon the matter of some wench, methinks it was — wherefore came Sir Gilles' men by night and burned down Shallowford with twenty hunting dogs of Sir Pertolepe's that chanced to be there: whereupon my lord waxed mighty wroth and, gathering his company, came into the demesne of Sir Gilles and burned down divers manors and hung certain rogues and destroyed two villages — in quittance."

"Ah — and what of the village folk?"

"My lord, they were but serfs for the most part, but — for Sir Pertolepe's dogs — twenty and two — and roasted alive, poor beasts!"

But here Black Roger checked both speech and stride, all at once, and stood with quarter-staff poised as from the depth of the wood came the sound of voices and fierce laughter.

"Come away, master," he whispered, "these should be Sir Pertolepe's men, methinks."

But Beltane shook his head:

"I'm fain to see why they laugh," said he, and speaking, stole forward soft-footed amid the shadows; and so presently parting the leaves, looked down into an open dell or dingle full of the light of the rising moon; light that glinted upon the steel caps and hauberks of some score men, who leaned upon pike or gisarm about one who

sat upon a fallen tree — and Beltane saw that this was
Giles the Bowman. But the arms of Giles were bound
behind his back, about his neck hung a noose, and his
face showed white and pallid 'neath the moon, as, lifting
up his head, he began to sing:

> "O ne'er shall my lust for the bowl decline,
> Nor my love for my good long bow;
> For as bow to the shaft and as bowl to the wine,
> Is a —"

The rich voice was strangled to a gasping sob as the
rope was tightened suddenly about the singer's brawny
throat and he was swung, kicking, into the air amid the
hoarse gibes and laughter of the men-at-arms. But, grim
and silent, Beltane leaped down among them, his long
blade glittering in the moonlight, and before the mighty
sweep of it they fell back, crowding upon each other and
confused; then Beltane, turning, cut asunder the cord and
Giles Brabblecombe fell and lay 'neath the shade of the
tree, wheezing and whimpering in the grass.

And now with a clamour of cries and fierce rallying
shouts, the men-at-arms, seeing Beltane stand alone, set
themselves in array and began to close in upon him. But
Beltane, facing them in the tender moonlight, set the point
of his sword to earth and reached out his mailed hand in
salutation.

"Greeting, brothers!" said he, "why seek ye the death
of this our brother? Come now, suffer him to go his
ways in peace, and God's blessing on ye, one and all."

Now at this some laughed and some growled, and one
stood forth before his fellows staring upon Beltane 'neath
close-drawn, grizzled brows:

"'Tis a rogue, and shall dance for us upon a string!"
laughed he.

"And this tall fellow with him!" said another.

"Aye, aye, let us hang 'em together," cried others.

"Stay!" said Beltane, "behold here money; so now
will I ransom this man's life of ye. Here be two pieces

of gold, 'tis my all — yet take them and yield me his life!"

Hereupon the men fell to muttering together doubtfully, but in this moment the grizzled man of a sudden raised a knotted fist and shook it in the air.

"Ha!" cried he, pointing to Beltane, "look ye, Cuthbert, Rollo — see ye not 'tis him we seek? Mark ye the size of him, his long sword and belt of silver —'tis he that came upon us in the green this day and slew our comrade Michael. Come now, let us hang him forthwith and share his money betwixt us after."

Then my Beltane sighed amain, and sighing, unsheathed his dagger.

"Alas!" said he, " and must we shed each other's blood forsooth? Come then, let us slay each other, and may Christ have pity on our souls!"

Thus saying, he glanced up at the pale splendour of the moon, and round him on the encircling shadows of the woods dense and black beneath the myriad leaves, and so, quick-eyed and poised for action, waited for the rush.

And, even as they came upon him, he sprang aside where the gloom lay blackest, and they being many and the clearing small, they hampered each other and fell into confusion; and, in that moment, Beltane leapt among them and smote, and smote again, now in the moonlight, now in shadow; leaping quick-footed from the thrust of sword and pike, crouching 'neath the heavy swing of axe and gisarm; and ever his terrible blade darted with deadly, point or fell with deep-biting edge. Hands gripped at him from the gloom, arms strove to clasp him, but his dagger-hand was swift and strong. Pike heads leapt at him and were smitten away, axe and gisarm struck, yet found him not, and ever, as he leapt, he smote. And now in his ears were cries and groans and other hateful sounds, and to his nostrils came a reek of sweating flesh and the scent of trampled grass; while the moon's tender light showed faces wild and fierce, that came and went, now here — now there; it glinted on head-piece and ringed mail, and flashed back from whirling steel — a round, placid moon that seemed, all at once, to burst asunder and vanish, smitten into nothingness. He was down — beaten to his knee, deafened and half blind, but struggling to his feet he staggered out from the friendly shadow of the trees, out into the open. A sword, hard-driven, bent and snapped short upon his triple mail, the blow of a gisarm half stunned him, a goring pike-thrust drove him reeling back, yet, ringed in by death, he thrust and smote with failing arm. Axe and pike, sword and gisarm hedged him in nearer and nearer, his sword grew suddenly heavy and beyond his strength to wield, but stumbling, slipping, dazed and with eyes a-swim, he raised the great blade aloft, and lifting drooping head, cried aloud the battle-cry of his house — high and clear it rang above the din:

"Arise! Arise! I will arise!"

And even in that moment came one in answer to the cry, one that leapt to his right hand, a wild man and hairy who plied a gleaming axe and, 'twixt each stroke, seemed, from hairy throat, to echo back the cry:

"Arise! Arise!"

And now upon his left was Black Roger, fierce-eyed behind his buckler. Thereafter a voice hailed them as from far away, a sweet, deep voice, cheery and familiar as one heard aforetime in a dream, and betwixt every sentence came the twang of swift-drawn bow-string.

"O tall brother, fall back! O gentle paladin, O fair flower of lusty fighters, fall back and leave the rest to our comrades, to me and my good bow, here!"

So, dazed and breathless, came Beltane on stumbling feet and leaned him gasping in the shadow of a great tree whereby stood Giles o' the Bow with arrows planted upright in the sod before him, the which he snatched and loosed so fast 'twas a wonder to behold. Of a sudden he uttered a shout and, setting by his bow, drew sword, and leaping from the shadow, was gone.

But, as for Beltane, he leaned a while against the tree as one who is very faint; yet soon, lifting heavy head, wondered at the hush of all things, and looking toward the clearing saw it empty and himself alone; therefore turned he thitherwards. Now as he went he stumbled and his foot struck a something soft and yielding that rolled before him in the shadow out — out into the full brilliance of the moon, and looking down, he beheld a mangled head that stared up at him wide-eyed and with mouth agape. Then Beltane let fall his reeking sword and staggering out into the light, saw his bright mail befouled with clotted blood, and of a sudden the world went black about him and he fell and lay with his face among the trampled grass.

In a while he groaned and opened his eyes to find Black Roger bathing his face what time Giles o' the Bow held wine to his lips, while at his feet, a wild figure grim and ragged, stood a tall, hairy man leaning upon a blood-stained axe.

"Aha!" cried the bowman. "Come now, my lovely fighter, my gentle giant, sup this —'tis life, and here behold a venison steak fit for Duke Ivo's self, come —"

"Nay, first," says Beltane, sitting up, "are there many hurt?"

"Aye, never fear for that, my blood-thirsty dove, they be all most completely dead save one, and he sore wounded, *laus Deo, amen!*"

"Dead!" cried Beltane, shivering, "dead, say you?"

"Aye, Sir Paladin, all sweetly asleep in Abraham's bosom. We three here accounted for some few betwixt us, the rest fell 'neath that great blade o' thine. O sweet Saint Giles! ne'er saw I such sword-work — point and edge, sa-ha! And I called thee — dove! — aye 'dove' it was, I mind me. O blind and worse than blind! But *experientia docet*, tall brother!"

Now hereupon Beltane bowed his head and clasping his hands, wrung them.

"Sweet Jesu forgive me!" he cried, "I had not meant to slay so many!"

Then he arose and went apart and, kneeling among the shadows, prayed long and fervently.

CHAPTER XI

WHICH TELLS HOW THREE MIGHTY MEN SWARE FEALTY TO BELTANE: AND HOW GOOD FRIAR MARTIN DIGGED A GRAVE IN THE WILD

Now when Beltane's mighty hunger was assuaged he sat — his aching head yet ringing with the blow — and stared up at the moon, sad and wistful-eyed as one full of heaviness the while Black Roger standing beside him gazed askance at the archer who sat near by whistling softly and busied with certain arrows, cleaning and trimming them ere he set them back in his quiver. And presently Black Roger spake softly, low-stooping to Beltane's ear:

"Lord, we have saved the life of yon prating archer-fellow, and behold my belt lacketh for one notch, which is well. So come, let us go our ways, thou and I, for I love not your talkers, and this fellow hath overmuch to say."

But now, ere Beltane could make reply, came the hairy man — but behold his rags had given place to fair garments of tanned leather (albeit something small) together with steel cap and shirt of ringed mail, and, about his middle, a broad belt where swung a heavy sword; being come to Beltane he paused leaning upon his axe, and gazed upon him fierce-eyed:

"Messire," said he, "who ye are I know not, what ye are I care not, for art quick of foot and mighty of arm, and when ye fight, cry a point of war, a battle-shout I knew aforetime ere they enslaved and made of me a serf — and thus it is I would follow thee."

Quoth Beltane, his aching head upon his hand:

"Whither?"

"To death if needs be, for a man must die soon or late, yet die but once whether it be by the steel, or flame, or rope. So what matter the way of it, if I may stand with this my axe face to face with Gilles of Brandonmere, or Red Pertolepe of Garthlaxton Keep: 'twas for this I followed his foresters."

"Who and whence are you?"

"Walkyn o' the Dene they call me hereabouts — though I had another name once — but 'twas long ago, when I marched, a lad, 'neath the banner of Beltane the Strong!"

"What talk be this?" grunted Black Roger, threatening of mien, "my lord and I be under a vow and must begone, and want no runaway serf crawling at our heels!"

"Ha!" quoth Walkyn, "spake I to thee, hangman? Forsooth, well do I know thee, Roger the Black: come ye into the glade yonder, so will I split thy black poll for thee — thou surly dog!"

Forth leapt Black Roger's sword, back swung Walkyn's glittering axe, but Beltane was between, and, as they stood thus came Giles o' the Bow:

"Oho!" he laughed, "must ye be at it yet? Have we not together slain of Sir Pertolepe's foresters a round score? —"

"'Twas but nineteen!" growled Roger, frowning at Walkyn.

"So will I make of this hangman the twentieth!" said Walkyn, frowning at Roger.

"'Tis a sweet thought," laughed the archer, "to it, lads, and slay each other as soon as ye may, and my blessings on ye. As for us, Sir Paladin, let us away — 'tis true we together might give check to an army, yet, minding Sir Pertolepe's nineteen foresters, 'twere wiser to hie us from Sir Pertolepe's country for the nonce: so march, tall brother — march!"

"Ha!" snarled Walkyn, "fear ye Red Pertolepe yet, bowman? Well, we want ye not, my lord and I, he hath a sword and I an axe — they shall suffice us, mayhap, an Pertolepe come. So hie thee hence with the hangman and save thy rogue's skin."

"And may ye dangle in a noose yet for a prating do-nothing!" growled Roger.

"Oho!" laughed Giles, with a flash of white teeth, "a hangman and a serf — must I slay both?" But, ere he could draw sword, came a voice from the shadows near by — a deep voice, clear and very sweet:

"Oh, children," said the voice, "oh, children of God, put up your steel and pray for one whose white soul doth mount e'en now to heaven!" and forth into the light came one clad as a white friar — a tall man and slender, and upon his shoulder he bare a mattock that gleamed beneath the moon. His coarse, white robe, frayed and worn, was stained with earth and the green of grass, and was splashed, here and there, with a darker stain; pale was he, and hollow-cheeked, but with eyes that gleamed 'neath black brows and with chin long and purposeful. Now at sight of him, fierce-eyed Walkyn cried aloud and flung aside his axe and, falling on his knees, caught the friar's threadbare robe and kissed it.

"Good brother!" he groaned, "O, gentle brother Martin, pity me!"

"What, Walkyn?" quoth the friar. "What do ye thus equipped and so far from home?"

"Home have I none, henceforth, O my father."

"Ah! What then of thy wife, Truda — of thy little son?"

"Dead, my father. Red Pertolepe's men slew them this day within the green. So, when I had buried them, I took my axe and left them with God: yet shall my soul go lonely, methinks, until my time be come."

Then Friar Martin reached out his hand and laid it upon Walkyn's bowed head; and, though the hand was hard and toil-worn, the touch of it was ineffably gentle, and he spake with eyes upraised to heaven:

"O Christ of Pity, look down upon this stricken soul, be Thou his stay and comfort. Teach him, in his grief and sorrow, to pity the woes of others, that, in comforting his fellows, he may himself find comfort."

Now when the prayer was ended he turned and looked upon the others, and, beholding Beltane in his might and glittering mail, he spake, saluting him as one of rank.

"Sir Knight," said he, "do these men follow thee?"

"Aye, verily," cried the archer, "that do I in sooth — *Verbum sat sapienti* — good friar."

"Not so," growled Roger, "'tis but a pestilent archer that seeketh but base hire. I only am my lord's man, sworn to aid him in his vow."

"I also," quoth Walkyn, "an so my lord wills?"

"So shall it be," sighed Beltane, his hand upon his throbbing brow.

"And what have ye in mind to do?"

"Forsooth," cried Giles, "to fight, good friar, *manibus pedibusque.*"

"To obey my lord," said Roger, "and speak good Saxon English."

"To adventure my body in battle with joyful heart," quoth Walkyn.

"To make an end of tyranny!" sighed Beltane.

"Alas!" said the friar, "within this doleful Duchy be tyrants a many, and ye are but four, meseemeth; yet if within your hearts be room for pity — follow me, and I will show you a sight, mayhap shall nerve you strong as giants. Come!"

So Beltane followed the white friar with the three upon his heels who wrangled now no more; and in a while the friar paused beside a new-digged grave.

"Behold," said he, "the bed where we, each one, must sleep some day, and yet 'tis cold and hard, methinks, for one so young and tender!" So saying he sighed, and turning, brought them to a hut near by, an humble dwelling of mud and wattles, dim-lighted by a glimmering rush. But, being come within the hut Beltane stayed of a sudden and held his breath, staring wide-eyed at that which lay so still: then, baring his head, sank upon his knees.

She lay outstretched upon a bed of fern, and looked as

How Three Men Sware Fealty 89

one that sleeps save for the deathly pallor of her cheek and still and pulseless bosom: and she was young, and of a wondrous, gentle beauty.

"Behold," said the friar, "but one short hour agone this was alive — a child of God, pure of heart and undefiled. These gentle hands lie stilled forever: this sweet, white body (O shame of men!) blasted by brutality, maimed and torn — is nought but piteous clay to moulder in the year. Yet doth her radiant soul lie on the breast of God forever, since she, for honour, died the death — Behold!" So saying, the friar with sudden hand laid bare the still and marble bosom; and, beholding the red horror wrought there by cruel steel, Beltane rose up, and taking off his cloak, therewith reverently covered the pale, dead beauty of her, and so stood awhile with eyes close shut and spake, soft-voiced and slow, 'twixt pallid lips:

"How — came this — thing?"

"She was captive to Sir Pertolepe, by him taken in a raid, and he would have had her to his will: yet, by aid of my lord's jester, she escaped and fled hither. But Sir Pertolepe's foresters pursued and took her and — so is she dead: may God requite them!"

"Amen!" quoth Giles o' the Bow, hoarse-voiced, "so do they all lie dead within the green!"

"Save one!" said Roger.

"But he sore wounded!" quoth Walkyn.

"How!" cried the friar aghast, "have ye indeed slain Sir Pertolepe's foresters?"

"Nineteen!" nodded Roger, grimly.

"Alas!" cried the friar, "may God save the poor folk hereabouts, for now will Sir Pertolepe wreak vengeance dire upon them."

"Then," said Beltane, "then must I have word with Sir Pertolepe."

Now when he said this, Black Roger stared agape and even the archer's tongue failed him for once; but Walkyn smiled and gripped his axe.

"Art mad, tall brother!" cried Giles at length, "Sir Pertolepe would hang thee out of hand, or throw thee to his dogs!"

"Lord," said Roger, "Sir Pertolepe hath ten score men-at-arms in Garthlaxton, beside bowmen and foresters."

"There should be good work for mine axe!" smiled Walkyn.

"None the less must I speak with him," said Beltane, and turned him to the door.

"Then will I die with thee, lord," growled Roger.

"So will I come and watch thee die — hangman, and loose a shaft or two on mine own account!"

But now, of a sudden, Walkyn raised a warning hand.

"Hark!" said he: and, in a while, as they listened, upon the stillness came a rustle of leaves and thereafter a creeping step drawing slowly nearer: then swift and soft-treading, Walkyn stole out into the shadows.

Very soon he returned, leading a woman, pale and baggard, who clasped a babe within her threadbare cloak; her eyes were red and sore with much weeping and upon the threshold she paused as one in sudden fear, but espying the friar, she uttered a cry:

"O Father Martin — good father — pray, pray for the soul of him who is father to my child, but who at dawn must die with many others upon my lord Duke's great gallows!"

"Alas!" cried the friar, wringing his hands, "what news is this?"

"O good friar," sobbed the woman, "my lord's hand hath been so heavy upon us of late — so heavy: and there came messengers from Thrasfordham in Bourne bidding us thither with fair promises: — and my father, being head of our village, hearkened to them and we made ready to cross into Bourne. But my lord came upon us and burned our village of Shallowford and lashed my father with whips and thereafter hanged him, and took my man and many others and cast them into the great dungeon at

Belsaye — and with the dawn they must hang upon the Duke's great gallows."

So she ended and stood weeping as one that is hopeless and weary. But of a sudden she screamed and pointed at Black Roger with her finger:

" 'Tis Roger!" she cried, " 'tis Black Roger, that slew my father!"

Then Roger the Black groaned and hid his face within his arm and shrank before the woman's outstretched finger and, groaning, cowered to his knees; whereupon the archer turned his back and spat upon the floor while Walkyn glared and fingered his great axe: but in this moment my Beltane came beside him and laid his hand on Roger's stooping shoulder.

"Nay," said he, "this is my friend henceforth, a man among men, who liveth to do great things as thus: To-night he will give back to thee the father of thy child, and break open the dungeon of Belsaye!"

Thus spake my Beltane while all stared at his saying and held their peace because of their amaze: only Black Roger turned of a sudden and caught his hand and kissed it savagely.

"Sir," said the woman, peering up in Beltane's face, "Lord — ah, would ye mock the weak and helpless —"

"Nay," said Beltane gently, "as God seeth me, to-night the prisoners shall go free, or this man and I die with them. So now be comforted — go you to Bourne, to Sir Benedict within Thrasfordham Keep, and say you come from Beltane, Duke of Pentavalon, who swore thee, by the honour of the Duke Beltane his father, that never again shall a man hang from the great gallows of Black Ivo the usurper — from this night it shall cease to be!"

Now would the woman have knelt and kissed his hand, but Beltane smiled and brought her to the door. Then, wondering and amazed, she made her obeisance to Beltane and with her babe clasped to her bosom went forth into the night. Thereafter Beltane turned and looked grave-eyed upon the three.

"My masters," quoth he, "ye have heard my words, how this night I go to take down Black Ivo's great gallows. Come ye with me? Aye or no?"

"Aye, lord!" cried the three in one acclaim.

"Do ye then stand with me henceforth 'gainst Black Ivo and all his might? Aye or no?"

"Aye, lord!" cried they again.

Then Beltane smiled and drew his sword and came to them, the great blade gleaming in his hand.

"'Tis well!" said he, "but first come now and lay your hands here upon my sword and swear me this, each one,— To follow ever where I shall lead, to abide henceforth in brotherhood together, to smite evil within you and without, to be pitiful to the weak, and to honour God at all times."

Then did the three, being upon their knees, lay their hands upon the sword and swear the oath as Beltane commanded; now came the white friar and stared upon the sword and beholding the motto graven in the steel, lifted up his hand to heaven and cried aloud:—

"Now greeting and fair greeting to thee, lord Duke, may thy body be strong for war and thy head wise in the council, for Pentavalon hath dire need of thee, Beltane, son of Duke Beltane the Strong. Moreover I was sent to thee by Sir Benedict of Bourne who bids thee 'Arise and follow' for that the time is at hand."

"How," cried Beltane, "art thou indeed from Sir Benedict?"

"Even so, lord. In Thrasfordham be seven hundred chosen men-at-arms, and within Bourne, mayhap a thousand more. It is become a haven for those that flee from tyranny and bitter wrong. As for me, I journey where I will within the Duchy, serving the poor and ministering to the broken-hearted, and everywhere is black sin and suffering and death. So now in the name of these oppressed do I give thee welcome to this thy sorrowful Duchy, and may God make of thee Duke indeed!"

Quoth Beltane:

"Duke am I in blood and Duke will I yet be in very sooth an God so will it." Then turning to the three, who stood hearkening open-mouthed and wide of eye, he smiled and reached to them his hand.

"Good friends," said he, "knowing nought of me yet were ye willing to follow my fortunes. For this do I thank ye one and all, and so shall my fortune, high or low, be thine, henceforth. To-day is Ivo Duke, and I thy companion-in-arms, no more, no less — this, I pray you all, remember."

So saying, Beltane sheathed his sword and beholding Friar Martin on his knees beside that muffled figure, he knelt also, and the three with him. Thereafter at a sign from the friar, Beltane stooped and raised this slender, shrouded figure in his arms and reverently bore it out into the shadows.

And there, all in the tender radiance of the moon, they buried her whose name they never knew, and stood a while in silence. Then, pointing to the new-turned earth, Friar Martin spake soft-voiced:

"Lo, here — in but a little time, wild flowers shall bloom above her — yet none purer or sweeter than she! In a little shall the grass be green again, and she sleep here forgot by all — save God! And God, my brothers, is a gentle God and very pitiful — so now do we leave her in God's abiding care."

And presently they turned, soft-footed, and went upon their way leaving the place to solitude.

But from the vault of heaven the stars looked down upon that lonely grave like the watching eyes of holy angels.

CHAPTER XII

WHICH TELLS HOW DUKE IVO'S GREAT GALLOWS CEASED TO BE

SCARCE a mile without the walls of the fair city of Belsaye my lord Duke had builded him a great gallows, had set it high upon a hill for all the world to see; from whose lofty cross-beams five score rogues had hanged ere now, had writhed and kicked their lives away and rotted there in company, that all the world might know how potent was the anger of my lord Duke Ivo.

Day in, day out, from rosy morn till dewy eve, it frowned upon Belsaye, a thing of doom whose grim sight should warn rebellious townsfolk to dutiful submission; by night it loomed, a dim-seen, brooding horror, whose loathsome reek should mind them how all rogues must end that dared lift hand or voice against my lord Duke, or those proud barons, lords, and knights who, by his pleasure, held their fiefs with rights of justice, the high, the middle and the low.

Day in, day out, the men of Belsaye eyed it askance 'neath scowling brows and, by night, many a clenched hand was shaken and many a whispered malediction sped, toward that thing of doom that menaced them from the dark.

To-night the moon was full, and thus, following Friar Martin's bony outstretched finger, Beltane of a sudden espied afar the Duke's great gallows, rising grisly and stark against the moon's round splendour. So for a space, standing yet within the shade of the woods, Beltane stared fierce-eyed, the while Giles, with Roger at his elbow, pointed out divers shapes that dangled high in air, at sight of which the friar knelt with bowed head and lips that moved in prayer: and Walkyn, scowling, muttered in his beard.

"Messire," said the archer, "my lord Duke's gallows is great and very strong, and we but five all told!"

"I have mine axe!" quoth Walkyn.

"Had we fifty axes we scarce should bring it down ere dawn: moreover, the night is very still and sounds carry far—"

"Nathless," quoth Roger, "to-night we surely shall destroy it—my lord hath said so."

"Aye—but how?" questioned Giles. "In Belsaye is that pale fox Sir Gui of Allerdale with many trusty men-at-arms to hold the town for Black Ivo and teach Belsaye its duty: how may we destroy my lord Duke's gallows 'neath the very beards of my lord Duke's garrison, wilt tell me that, my good, Black Rogerkin?"

"Aye," nodded Roger, "that will I—when I have asked my lord." So saying, he came and touched Beltane and humbly put the question.

Then, with his gaze yet upon the gallows, Beltane sighed and answered:

"There hath been no rain for weeks, look you: the underbrush is dry, methinks, and should burn well!"

"Aye, for sure," said Roger, "we shall burn Black Ivo's gallows to ashes, bowman, and a good end 'twill be."

"By fire!" cried the archer, aghast, "but lord, so soon as they shall see the flames, Sir Gui and his men will sally out upon us!"

"Nay," said Beltane, "for we shall sally in."

"Into Belsaye, mean you, lord?"

"Certes," answered Beltane, "how else may we break open the dungeon? The night is young yet, but we have much to do—follow!" So saying, Beltane turned and keeping ever within the shadow of the trees, set off towards that distant hill where stood the gallows, black against the moon.

Swiftly they went and for the most part in silence, for Beltane's mind was busied upon many matters.

So betimes they climbed the hill and stood at last beneath the gallows, and, glancing up, Beltane beheld noisome shapes, black and shrivelled, that once had lived and laughed. Forthwith he drew his sword and fell to cutting down the brush, whereat friar Martin, girding up his frock, took Walkyn's sword and fell to likewise.

Now, as Beltane laboured thus, he was suddenly aware of a wild and ragged figure, the which started up before him as if from the very ground. An old man he was, bent with years, yet with eyes that burned fierce and undimmed 'neath hoary brows, and shrivelled hands that gripped upon a rusty sword.

"Who are ye," he cried, harsh-voiced, "who are ye that disturb this woeful place? 'Tis here that men are dragged to die — and, being dead, do hang i' the air to rot and rot — and thereby hangs a tale of wolves that howl and birds that shriek, aha! — carrion crows and hook-billed kites —, they be well gorged since Ivo came. 'Caw!' they cry, 'caw!'— soft child's flesh and the flesh of tender maids — aha! — I know — I've watched — I've seen! Ah! since my lord Duke Beltane died, what sights these eyes have seen!"

"Old man," quoth Beltane, bending near, "who art thou?"

"I am the ghost that haunts this place, but, ages since, I was Sir Robert Bellesme of Garthlaxton Keep. But my wife they slew, my daughter ravished from me — and my son — Ah! Christ — my son! They hanged him here — yonder he hung, and I, his father, watched him die. But, by night, when all was still, I crept hither and found a hole to shelter me. And here I stayed to watch over him — my son who hung so quiet and so still. And the rough wind buffeted him, the cruel rain lashed him, and the hot sun scorched him, but still he hung there, so high! — so high! Yet I waited, for the strongest rope will break in time. And upon a moony night, he fell, and I gathered him in my arms, close here against my

How Ivo's Gallows Ceased to Be 97

heart, and buried him — where none can know — save God. Many others have I buried also, for the strongest cords must break in time! And folk do say the devil bears them hence, since none are ever found — but I know where they lie — six hundred and seventy and nine — I know — these hands have buried them and I have kept a tally. Ah! — but you, gentle youth, what would ye here?"

"Burn down the gallows," said Beltane, "'tis an accursed thing, so shall it shame earth and heaven no longer."

"How! — how!" cried the ancient man, letting fall his rusty sword, "Destroy Black Ivo's gibbet? Dare ye — dare ye such a thing indeed? Are there men with souls unconquered yet? Methought all such were old, or dead, or fled away — dare ye this, youth?"

"Aye," nodded Beltane. "Watch now!" and hereupon he, together with the others, fell to hewing down the dry brush with might and main, and piling it about the gibbet's massy beams, while the ancient man, perched upon a rock hard by, watched them 'neath his shaggy brows and laughed soft and shrill.

"Aha!" he cried, "the fire ye kindle here shall set the Duchy in a flame mayhap, to burn Black Ivo with Gui of Allerdale and Red Pertolepe — mayhap! For them, fire on earth and flame in hell — aha! To burn the gibbet! 'tis well bethought: so shall carrion kite and jay go light-bellied hereabouts, mayhap, oho! 'Caw,' they shall cry, 'Caw — give us to eat — fair white flesh!' Yet how may they eat when the gallows is no more?"

Thus spake he with shrill laughter while Beltane laboured until the sweat ran from him, while Walkyn's great axe flashed and fell near by and steel glittered among the underbrush that clothed the slopes of the hill.

Very soon they had stacked great piles of kindling about the gallows' weather-beaten timbers — twigs below, faggots above — cunningly ordered and higher than Beltane's head. Now as Beltane leaned upon his sword to wipe the sweat from his eyes, came Roger and Walkyn yet panting from their labour.

"Master," said Roger, "they should burn well, I trow, and yet —"

"And yet," quoth Walkyn, "these beams be thick: methinks, when the others go, one man should stay to tend the fires until the flame gets fair hold —"

"And that man I!" said Roger.

"No, no," frowned Walkyn, "an one of us must die, it shall be me —"

But now came the ancient man, leaning upon his ancient weapon.

"No, children," said he, "'tis for age to die — death is sweet to the old and weary: so will I tend the fire. Yet, beseech thee, grant me this: that these my hands shall fire the gallows whereon they hanged my son, long ago: young was he, and tall — scarce yet a man — they hanged him yonder, so high — so high — so far beyond my care: and the carrion birds — kites, see you, and crows — and the wind and rain and dark — Ah, God! my son! I am but an old man and feeble, yet, beseech thee, let this be the hand to fire Black Ivo's gibbet!"

Then Beltane took from his pouch flint and steel and tinder and gave them to the old man's trembling fingers as Giles o' the Bow came running with the stalwart friar behind him.

So, while the five stood hushed and wide of eye, the old man knelt before them in his rags and struck flint to steel. Once he struck, and twice — and behold a spark that leapt to a small flame that died to a glow; but now, flat upon his belly lay Giles and, pursing his lips, puffed and blew until the glow brightened, spread, and burst into a crackling flame that leapt from twig to twig. And when the fire waxed hot, Beltane took thence a glowing brand, and, coming to the other great pile, fired it therewith. Up rose the flames high and higher until they began to lick, pale-tongued, about the gibbet's two great supporting timbers, and ever as they rose, Walkyn and Roger, Giles and the

How Ivo's Gallows Ceased to Be

friar, laboured amain, stacking logs near by wherewith to feed the fires.

"Enough," said Beltane at last, "it shall suffice, methinks."

"Suffice?" cried the old man, his eyes bright in the ruddy glow, "aye, it shall suffice, sweet boy. See — see, the timbers catch e'en now. Ha! burn, good fire — eat, hungry flame! O, happy sight — would my dear son were here — they hanged his fair young body, but his soul — Ha, his soul! O souls of hanged men — O spirits of the dead, come about me, ye ghosts of murdered youth, come and behold the gibbet burn whereon ye died. What — are ye there, amid the smoke, so soon? Come then, let us dance together and trip it lightly to and fro — merrily, merrily! Hey boy, so ho then — so ho, and away we go!" Hereupon, tossing up gaunt arms, the old man fell to dancing and capering amid the sparks and rolling smoke, filling the air with wild talk and gabbling high-pitched laughter that rose above the roar of the fires. And so in a while Beltane, sighing, turned and led the way down the hill towards the glooming shadow of the woods; but ever as they went the flames waxed fiercer behind them and the madman's laughter shrilled upon the air.

Swift-footed they plunged into the underbrush and thus hidden began to close in upon Belsaye town. And of a sudden they heard a cry, and thereafter the shattering blare of a trumpet upon the walls. And now from within the waking city rose a confused sound, a hum that grew louder and ever more loud, pierced by shout and trumpet-blast while high above this growing clamour the tocsin pealed alarm.

Thus, in a while the trembling citizens of Belsaye, starting from their slumber, stared in pallid amaze beholding afar a great and fiery gibbet whose flames, leaping heavenward, seemed to quench the moon.

CHAPTER XIII

HOW THEY BRAKE OPE THE DUNGEON OF BELSAYE

BEING yet in the shade of the woods, Beltane paused, hearkening to the distant uproar of Belsaye town and watching the torches that hovered upon its walls and the cressets that glowed on tower and bartizan.

"Messire Beltane," quoth the friar, setting his rumpled frock in order, "are ye minded still to adventure breaking ope the dungeon of Belsaye?"

"Aye, verily!" nodded Beltane. "Know you the city, good friar?"

"That do I, my brother: every lane and street, every hole and corner of it — 'twas there I first drew breath. A fair, rich city, freed by charter long ago — but now, alas, its freedom snatched away, its ancient charter gone, it bleeds 'neath a pale-checked tyrant's sway — a pallid man who laughs soft-voiced to see men die, and smiles upon their anguish. O Belsaye, grievous are thy wrongs since Ivo came five years agone and gave thee up to pillage and to ravishment. O hateful day! O day of shame! What sights I saw — what sounds I heard — man-groans and screams of women to rend high heaven and shake the throne of God, methinks. I see — I hear them yet, and must forever. Jesu, pity!" and leaning against a tree near by, the stalwart friar shivered violently and hid his eyes.

"Why, good brother Martin," said Beltane, setting an arm about him, "doth memory pain thee so, indeed? good Brother Martin, be comforted —"

"Nay, nay — 'tis past, but — O my son, I — had a sister!" said the good friar, and groaned. Yet in a while he raised his head and spake again: "And when Duke Ivo had wrought his will upon the city, he builded the great gibbet yonder and hanged it full with men cheek by jowl, and left Sir Gui the cruel with ten score chosen men for garrison. But the men of Belsaye have stubborn memories; Sir Gui and his butchers slumber in a false security, for stern men are they and strong, and wait but God's appointed time. Pray God that time be soon!"

"Amen!" said Beltane. Now, even as he spake came the sound of a distant tucket, the great gates of Belsaye swung wide, and forth rode a company of men-at-arms, their bascinets agleam 'neath the moon.

"Now!" spake the friar, "and you are for Belsaye, my brother, follow me; I know a way — albeit a moist way and something evil — but an you will follow,— come!"

So saying Friar Martin set off among the trees, and Beltane, beckoning to the others, followed close. Fast strode the friar, his white robe fluttering on before, through moonlight and shadow, until they reached a brook or freshet that ran bubbling betwixt flowery banks; beside this strode the tall friar, following its winding course, until before them, amid the shadow — yet darker than the shadow — loomed high an embattled flanking tower of the walls of Belsaye town; but ever before them flitted the friar's white gown, on and on until the freshet became a slow-moving river, barring their advance — a broad river that whispered among the reeds on the one side and lapped against rugged wall on the other.

Here the friar stayed to glance from gloomy wall and turret to fast waning moon on their left, then, girding up his gown, he stepped down into the reeds, and a moment later they saw him — to their amaze — fording the river that flowed scarce knee deep.

So, heedfully, Beltane followed, and, stepping into the water found his feet upon a narrow causeway cunningly devised. Thus, slowly and carefully, because of the flowing of the water, they came betimes to where the friar waited in the shadow of the massy wall; yet, even as they came near, the friar waved his arm, stooped — and was gone; whereon my Beltane stared amazed and the three muttered uneasily behind him. But, coming nearer, Beltane espied above the hurrying waters the curve of an arch or tunnel, and pointing it to the others, took a great breath and, stooping beneath the water, stumbled on and on until it shallowed, and he was free to breathe again.

On he went, through water now breast-high, with slimy walls above him and around, seeing naught by reason of the pitchy blackness, and hearing only the smothered splash of those behind, and gasping breaths that boomed hollow in the dark. Yet presently he saw a gleam before him that broadened with each step, and, of a sudden, was out beneath the sky — a narrow strip wherein stars twinkled, and so beheld again friar Martin's white frock flitting on, ghostlike, before. In a while he brought them to a slimy stair, and climbing this, with ever growing caution, they found themselves at last beneath the frowning shadow of the citadel within the walls of Belsaye town. Now, looking north, Beltane beheld afar a fiery gallows that flamed to heaven, and from the town thitherward came a confused hum of the multitude who watched; but hereabouts the town seemed all deserted.

"The dungeons lie beneath our feet," whispered Friar Martin. "Come!"

So, keeping ever in the shadow of the great square keep, they went on, soft-treading and alert of eye till, being come to the angle of the wall, the friar stayed of a sudden and raised a warning hand. Then came Beltane with Walkyn close behind, and peering over the friar's broad shoulders, they beheld a sentinel who stood with his back to them, leaning on his spear, to watch the burning gallows, his chain-mail agleam and his head-piece glittering as he stirred lazily in time to the merry lilt he sang softly.

Then, or ever Beltane could stay him, Walkyn o' the Dene laid by his axe, and, his soaked shoes soundless upon the stones, began to steal upon the unconscious singer, who yet lolled upon his spear some thirty paces away. With great body bowed forward and hairy fingers crooked, Walkyn stole upon him; six paces he went, ten — twenty — twenty-five — the soldier ceased his humming, stood erect and turned about; and Walkyn leapt — bore him backward down into the shadow — a shadow wherein their bodies writhed and twisted silently awhile. When Walkyn rose out of the shadow and beckoned them on.

So, following ever the friar's lead, they came to a narrow doorway that gave upon a small guard-room lighted by a smoking torch socketed to the wall. The place was empty, save for a medley of arms stacked in corners, wherefore, treading cautiously, the friar led them a-down a narrow passage and so to a second and larger chamber where burned a fire of logs. Upon the walls hung shining head-pieces; cloaks and mantles lay where they had been flung on bench and floor, but none was there to give them let or hindrance. Then Friar Martin took a torch that smoked near by, and, crossing to the hearth, reached down a massy key from the wall, and with this in his hand, came to a door half hidden in a corner, beyond which were steps that wound downwards into the dark, a darkness close and dank, and heavy with corruption.

But on went the friar — his torch lighting the way — down and ever down until they trod a narrow way 'twixt reeking walls, where breathed an air so close and foul the very torch languished. At length the friar stopped before a mighty door, thick-banded with iron bars and with massy bolts, and while Beltane held the torch, he fitted key to lock and thereafter the great door swung on screaming hinge and showed a dungeon beyond — a place foul and noisome, where divers pale-faced wretches lay or crouched, blinking in the torch's glare.

"What?" cried one, coming to his feet, a squat broad-shouldered man — "be this the dawn so soon? Well, we be ready, better to hang i' the clean air than rot in a dungeon, say I. So we be ready, eh, my brothers?"

But now, some groaned and wept and others laughed, while yet others got them to their knees, bowed of head and silent. Then went in the friar to them and laid his hands upon the squat man's shoulder and spake him gently.

"And is it Osric," said he. "Day is not yet, my son, nor with the day shalt thou die nor any here, an ye be silent all and follow where we lead, soft-footed, so will we bring you to God's good world again. Rise, then, each one, speak nothing, but follow!"

So then did these men, snatched of a sudden from the horror of death to the hope of new life, follow on stumbling feet, out from the noisome gloom of the dungeon, out from the clammy air breathing of death, up the narrow winding stair; and with each step came strength and manhood. Thus as they strode forth of the frowning keep, each man bore sword or gisarm. So, with breath in check, but hearts high-beating, they came one and all, to where the slimy stair led down into the gloom. Yet here Friar Martin paused, sighing, to look behind, whence rose the distant hum of those thronging townsfolk who yet crowded wall and street and market square to watch the gallows burn.

"Now sweet Christ shield ye, good people of Belsaye!" he sighed.

"What mean ye, my brother?" questioned Beltane.

"Alas! my son," groaned the friar, "I needs must think upon the coming day and of the vengeance of Sir Gui for this our work!"

"His vengeance, friar?"

"There will be torture and death busy hereabouts tomorrow, my son, for, the prisoners being gone, so will Sir Gui vent his anger on the townsfolk—'tis ever his custom—"

"Ha!" quoth my Beltane, knitting his brows, "I had not thought on this!"—and with the word, he turned him back, drawing on his hood of mail.

"Come, lord," whispered Black Roger in his ear, "let us be going while yet we may."

"Aye, come, my son," spake the friar, low-voiced. "Tarry not, Belsaye is in the hand of God! Nay, what would you?"

"I must go back," said Beltane, loosening sword in

scabbard, "for needs must I this night have word with Gui of Allerdale."

"Nay," whispered the friar, with pleading hand on Beltane's arm, "'tis thing impossible —"

"Yet must I try, good brother —"

"Ah, dear my son, 'twill be thy death —"

"Why look you, gentle friar, I am in Belsaye, and Belsaye 'is in the hand of God!' So fear not for me, but go you all and wait for me beyond the river. And, if I come not within the hour, then press on with speed for Thrasfordham within Bourne, and say to Sir Benedict that, while *he* liveth to draw sword, so is there hope for Pentavalon. But now — quick! — where lodgeth Sir Gui?"

"Within the keep — there is a stair doth mount within the thickness of the wall — nay, I will be thy guide if go indeed thou must —"

"Not so, good friar, be it thy duty to lead these prisoners to freedom and to safety within Bourne."

"Then will I come," whispered Roger hoarse and eager, as the friar turned slow-footed to follow the others adown the slippery stair, "beseech thee, lord, thy man am I, twice sworn to thee till death, so suffer me beside thee."

"Nay," said Beltane, "Pentavalon's need of thee is greater e'en than mine, therefore will I adventure this thing alone. Go you with the friar, my Roger, and so farewell to each."

"God keep thee, noble son!" whispered the friar, his hand upraised in blessing: but Roger stood, chin on breast and spake no word.

Then Beltane turned him and sped away, soft-treading in the shadow of the great keep.

The waning moon cast shadows black and long, and in these shadows Beltane crept and so, betimes, came within the outer guard-room and to the room beyond; and here beheld a low-arched doorway whence steps led upward,— a narrow stair, gloomy and winding, whose velvet blackness was stabbed here and there by moonlight, flooding through some deep-set arrow-slit. Up he went, and up, pausing once with breath in check, fancying he heard the stealthy sound of one who climbed behind him in the black void below; thus stayed he a moment, with eyes that strove to pierce the gloom, and with naked dagger clenched to smite, yet heard nought, save the faint whisper of his own mail, and the soft tap of his long scabbard against the wall; wherefore he presently sped on again, climbing swiftly up the narrow stair. Thus, in a while, he beheld a door above: a small door, yet stout and strong, a door that stood ajar, whence came a beam of yellow light.

So, with sure and steady hand, Beltane set wide the door, that creaked faintly in the stillness, and beheld a small, square chamber where was a narrow window, and, in this window, a mail-clad man lolled, his unhelmed head thrust far without, to watch the glow that leapt against the northern sky.

Then Beltane sheathed his dagger and, in three long strides was close behind, and, stooping above the man, sought and found his hairy throat, and swung him, mighty-armed, that his head struck the wall; then Beltane, sighing, laid him upon the floor and turned toward a certain arras-hung arch: but, or ever his hand came upon this curtain, from beyond a voice hailed — a voice soft and musical.

"Hugo — O Hugo, spawn of hell, hither to me!"

Then Beltane, lifting the curtain, opened the door and, striding into the chamber beyond, closed and barred the door behind him, and so stood, tall and menacing, looking on one who sat at a table busied with pen and ink-horn. A slender man this, and richly habited: a sleepy-eyed man, pale of cheek, with long, down-curving nose, and mouth thin-lipped and masterful, who, presently lifting his head, stared up in amaze, sleepy-eyed no longer: for now, beholding Beltane the mighty, sheathed in mail from head to foot, the pen dropped from his fingers and his long pale hands slowly clenched themselves.

So, for a space, they fronted each other, speaking not, while eye met eye unswerving — the menacing blue and the challenging black, and, through the open casement near by came a ruddy glow that flickered on arras-hung wall and rugged roof-beam. Now raising his hand, Beltane pointed toward this glowing window.

"Sir Gui," quoth he, "Lord Seneschal of Belsaye town, thou hast good eyes — look now, and tell me what ye see."

"I see," said Sir Gui, stirring not, "I see a presumptuous knave — a dog who shall be flung headlong from the turret. Ha! Hugo!" he called, his black eyes yet unswerving, "O Hugo, son of the fiend, hither to me!"

"Trouble not, my lord," quoth Beltane gently, "behold, the door is barred: moreover, Hugo lieth without — pray God I have not killed him. But, as for thee — look yonder, use thine eyes and speak me what thou dost see."

But Sir Gui sat on, his thin lips upcurling to a smile, his black eyes unswerving: wherefore came Beltane and seized him in fierce hands and plucked him to his feet and so brought him to the window.

"Ha!" he cried, "look now and tell me what ye see. Speak! speak — for, God help me! now am I minded to kill thee here and now, unarmed though ye be, and cast thy carrion to the dogs — speak!"

Now, beholding the mail-clad face above him, the blue eyes aflame, the pale lips tight-drawn, Sir Gui, Seneschal of Belsaye, spake soft-voiced on this wise:

"I see my lord Duke's gallows go up in flame — wherefore men shall die!"

"Aye," sighed Beltane, "said I not thine eyes were good, Lord Seneschal? Now, use thine ears — hearken! 'Twas I and five others, men from beyond the marches, fired this night Black Ivo's gibbet, moreover, to-night also have we broke the dungeon that lieth beneath this thy keep, and set thy prisoners free — I and these five, all men from the north, mark me this well! This have we done for a sign and portent — ha! look!" and Beltane pointed of a sudden to where the great gallows, outlined against the night in seething flame, swayed to and fro, crumbled, and crashed to earth 'mid whirling sparks and flame, while, from the town below rose a murmur that swelled and swelled to a shout, and so was gone.

"Behold, lord Seneschal, Black Ivo's gallows to-night hath ceased to be: here is a sign, let those heed it that will. But for thee — this! To-night have I burned this gallows, to-night have I freed thy prisoners. Upon me therefore, and only me, be the penalty; for — mark me this, Seneschal! — spill but one drop of blood of these innocents of Belsaye, and, as God seeth me, so will I hunt thee down, and take thee and tear out thine eyes, and cut off thine hands, and drive thee forth to starve! And this do I swear by the honour of my father, Beltane the Strong, Duke of Pentavalon!"

But now, even as Sir Gui shrank back before the death in Beltane's look, amazed beyond all thought by his words, came a sudden shout, and thereafter a clash and ring of steel upon the stair without. And now, above the sudden din, hoarse and loud a battle-cry arose, at the sound of which Sir Gui's jaws hung agape, and he stood as one that doubts his ears; for 'twas a cry he had heard aforetime, long ago.

"Arise! Arise! I will arise!"

Then Beltane cast up the bar, and, plucking wide the door, beheld the broad, mail-clad back of one who held the narrow stair where flashed pike and gisarm.

"Roger!" he called, "Black Roger!"

"Aye, lord, 'tis I," cried Roger, parrying a pike-thrust, "make sure of thy work, master, I can hold these in check yet a while."

"My work is done, Roger. To me — to me, I say!"

So Roger, leaping back from the stair-head, turned about and ran to Beltane, stumbling and spattering blood as he came, whereupon Beltane clapped-to the door and barred it in the face of the pursuit. A while leaned Roger, panting, against the wall, then, beholding Sir Gui:

"How!" he cried, "lives the pale fox yet? Methought thy work was done, master!" So saying, he swung aloft his bloody sword, but, even as the Seneschal waited the

The Dungeon of Belsaye 109

blow, smiling of lip, Beltane caught Black Roger's wrist.

"Stay!" cried he, above the thunder of blows that shook the door, "would'st slay a man unarmed?"

"Aye, master, as he hath slain many a man ere now!" quoth Roger, striving to free his arm. "The door is giving, and there be many without: and, since to-night we must die, so let us slay the white fox first."

"Not so," said Beltane, "get you through the window — the river runs below: through the window — out, I say!" and, with the word, he stooped and bore Black Roger to the window.

"But, lord —"

"Jump!" cried Beltane, "jump, ere the door fall."

"But you, master —"

"Jump, I say: I will follow thee." So, groaning, Black Roger hurled his sword far out from the window, and leaping from the sill, was gone.

Then Beltane turned and looked upon Gui of Allerdale. "Seneschal," said he, "I who speak am he, who, an God so wills, shall be Duke of Pentavalon ere long: howbeit, I will keep my promise to thee, so aid me God!"

Thus saying, he mounted the window in his turn, and, even as the door splintered behind him, forced himself through, and, leaping wide, whirled over and over, down and down, and the sluggish river closed over him with a mighty splash; thereafter the placid waters went upon their way, bubbling here and there, and dimpling 'neath the waning moon.

CHAPTER XIV

HOW BELTANE CAME NIGH TO DEATH

Down went my Beltane, weighted in his heavy mail — down and ever down through a world of green that grew dark and ever more dark, until, within the pitchy gloom beneath him was a quaking slime that sucked viciously at foot and ankle. Desperately he fought and strove to rise, but ever the mud clung, and, lusty swimmer though he was, his triple mail bore him down.

And now his mighty muscles failed, lights flamed before his eyes, in his ears was a drone that grew to a rushing roar, his lungs seemed bursting, and the quaking ooze yearning to engulf him. Then my Beltane knew the bitter agony of coming death, and strove no more; but in that place of darkness and horror, a clammy something crawled upon his face, slipped down upon his helpless body, seized hold upon his belt and dragged at him fierce and strong; slowly, slowly the darkness thinned, grew lighter, and then — Ah, kind mercy of God! his staring eyes beheld the orbed moon, his famished lungs drank deep the sweet, cool air of night. And so he gasped, and gasping, strove feebly with arm and leg while ever the strong hand grasped at his girdle. And now he heard, faint and afar, a sound of voices, hands reached down and drew him up — up to good, firm earth, and there, face down among the grass, he lay awhile, content only to live and breathe. Gradually he became aware of another sound hard by, a sharp sound yet musical, and in a little, knew it for the " twang " of a swift-drawn bow-string. Now, glancing up, Beltane beheld an ancient tree near by, a tree warped and stunted wherein divers arrows stood, and behind the tree, Giles o' the Bow, who, as he watched, drew and loosed a shaft, which, flashing upward, was answered by a cry; whereon Giles laughed aloud.

"Six!" he cried, "six in seven shots: 'tis sweet archery methinks, and quicker than a noose, my Rogerkin, and more deadly than thy axe, my surly Walkyn. Let the rogues yonder but show themselves, and give me arrows enow, so will I slay all Gui's garrison ere the moon fail me quite."

But hereupon Beltane got him to his knees and made shift to stand, and, coming to the tree, leaned there, being faint and much spent.

"Aha, sweet lord," cried the archer, "a man after my very heart art thou. What wonders have we achieved this night — paladins in sooth we be, all four! By the blessed bones of St. Giles, all Pentavalon shall ring with our doings anon."

Said Beltane, faintly:

"Where is my good Roger?"

"Here, lord," a voice answered from the shade of a bush hard by: "'twas my comrade Walkyn dragged me up from death — even as he did thee."

"We thought you gone for good, master."

"Aye!" cried the archer, "so would ye all be dead, methinks, but for me and this my bow."

"Friends," said Beltane, "'tis by doings such as this that men do learn each other's worth: so shall the bonds betwixt us strengthen day by day, and join us in accord and brotherhood that shall outlast this puny life. So now let us begone and join the others."

So they turned their backs upon Belsaye town, and keeping to the brush, came at length to where upon the borders of the forest the white friar waited them, with the nine who yet remained of the prisoners; these, beholding Beltane, came hurrying to meet him, and falling upon their knees about him, strove with each other to kiss his hands and feet.

"Good fellows," said Beltane, "God hath this night brought ye out of death into life — how will ye use your lives hereafter? List now:— even as ye have suffered, others are suffering: as ye have endured the gloom of dungeon and fear of death, so, at this hour, others do the like by reason of misrule and tyranny. Now here stand I, together with Sir Benedict of Bourne who holdeth Thrasfordham Keep, pledged to live henceforth, sword in hand, until these evils are no more — since 'tis only by bitter strife and conflict that evil may be driven from our borders. Thus, Pentavalon needeth men, strong-armed and resolute: if such ye be, march ye this hour to Thrasfordham within Bourne, and say to Sir Benedict that God having given you new life, so now will ye give your lives to Pentavalon, that tyranny may cease and the Duchy be cleansed of evil. Who now among ye will draw sword for freedom and Pentavalon?"

Then sprang the squat man Osric to his feet, with clenched fist upraised and eyes ablaze 'neath his matted hair.

"That will I!" he cried. "And I! And I! And I!" cried the rest, grim-faced and eager. "Aye — give us but swords, and one to lead, and we will follow!"

Quoth Beltane:

"Go you then to Sir Benedict within Bourne and say to all men that Beltane the Duke hath this night burned down Black Ivo's shameful gibbet, for a sign that he is come at last and is at work, nor will he stay until he die, or Pentavalon be free!"

CHAPTER XV

HOW BELTANE HAD WORD WITH PERTOLEPE THE RED, AND HOW THEY LEFT HIM IN THE FOREST

> " Since all men breathing 'neath the sky
> Good or evil, soon must die,
> Ho! bring me wine, and what care I
>   For dying!"

IT was Giles Brabblecombe singing to himself as he knelt beside a fire of twigs, and Beltane, opening sleepy eyes, looked round upon a world all green and gold and dew-bespangled; a fair world and fragrant, whose balmy air breathed of hidden flowers and blooming thickets, whence came the joyous carolling of new-waked birds; and beholding all this and the glory of it, my Beltane must needs praise God he was alive.

"Hail and good morrow to thee, brother!" cried the bowman, seeing him astir. "The sun shineth, look you, I sit upon my hams and sing for that this roasting venison smelleth sweet, while yonder i' the leaves be a mavis and a merle a-mocking of me, pretty rogues: for each and ever of which, *Laus Deo, Amen!*"

"Why truly, God hath made a fair world, Giles, a good world to live in, and to live is to act — yet here have I lain most basely sleeping —"

"Like any paunched friar, brother. But a few days since, I met thee in the green, a very gentle, dove-like youth that yet became a very lion of fight and demi-god of battle! Heroes were we all, last night — nay, very Titans — four 'gainst an army! — whiles now, within this balmy-breathing morn you shall see Walkyn o' the Bloody Axe with grim Black Rogerkin, down at the brook yonder, a-sprawl upon their bellies busily a-tickling trout for breakfast, while I, whose good yew bow carrieth death in every twang, toasting deer-flesh on a twig, am mocked of wanton warblers i' the green: and thou, who art an Achilles, a Hector, an Ajax — a very Mars — do sleep and slumber, soft and sweet as full-fed friar — Heigho! Yet even a demi-god must nod betimes, and Titans eat, look ye."

Now looking from sun to earth and beholding the shortening of the shadows, Beltane leapt up. Quoth he:

"Sluggard that I am, 'tis late! And Roger was wounded last night, I mind —"

"Content you, brother, 'twas nought," said Giles bending above his cooking, "the kiss of a pike-head i' the thick o' the arm — no more."

"Yet it must be looked to —"

"I did it, brother, as I shoot — that is to say I did it most excellent well: 'twill be healed within the week."

"How then — art leech as well as bowman?"

"Quite as well, brother. When I was a monk I learned two good things, *videlicet:* never to argue with those in authority over me, and to heal the hurts of those that did. So, by my skill in herbs and leechcraft, Roger, having a hole in his arm, recks not of it — behold here he cometh, and Walkyn too, and *Laus Deo!* with a trout! Now shall we feast like any pampered prelate."

So when Beltane had stripped and bathed him in the brook, they presently sat down, all four together, and ate and talked and laughed right merrily, the while lark and thrush and blackbird carolled lustily far and near.

"Now eat, brothers," cried the bowman, full-mouthed, "eat and spare not, as I do, for to-day I smell the battle from afar: Ho! Ho! the noise of captains and the shouting! Yesterday were we heroes, to-day must we be gods — yet cautious gods, for, mark me, I have but twelve shafts remaining, and with twelve shafts can but promise ye a poor twelve lives."

But now came Roger wistful-eyed, and with belt a-swing in his hand.

"Master," quoth he, "last night did we four rescue twelve. Now I'm fain to know if for these twelve I may cut twelve notches from my belt, or must we share their lives betwixt us and I count but three?"

"Three?" laughed Giles, "Oho — out upon thee, Rogerkin! Our lord here claimeth six, since he the rescue planned, next, I claim three, since but for my goodly shooting ye all had died, then hath Walkyn two, since he saved thee from the fishes, which leaveth thee — one. *Quod erat demonstrandum!*"

But now, seeing Roger's downcast look, Giles snatched the belt and gave it unto Beltane, who forthwith cut therefrom twelve notches. And, in a while, having made an end of eating, Beltane rose and looked round upon the three.

"Good comrades all," quoth he, "well do I know ye to be staunch and trusty; yet to-day am I minded to speak with him men call Pertolepe the Red, lest he shed innocent blood for that we slew his foresters —"

"Twenty lusty fellows!" nodded Giles, with a morsel of venison on his dagger point.

"Nay, there one escaped!" quoth Roger.

"Yet he sore wounded!" said Walkyn.

"Ha! Sir Pertolepe is a terrible lord!" quoth Giles, eyeing the morsel of venison somewhat askance. "'Twill be a desperate adventure, methinks — and we but four."

"Yet each and all — gods!" quoth Walkyn, reaching for his axe.

"Aye," nodded Giles, frowning at the piece of venison, "yet are we but four gods."

"Not so," answered Beltane, "for in this thing shall we be but one. Go you three to Bourne, for I am minded to try this adventure alone."

"Alone, master!" cried Black Roger, starting to his feet.

"Alone!" growled Walkyn, clutching his axe.

"An death must come, better one should die than four," said Beltane, "howbeit I am minded to seek out Pertolepe this day."

"Then do I come also, master, since thy man am I."

"I, too," nodded Walkyn, "come death and welcome, so I but stand face to face with Pertolepe."

"Alack!" sighed Giles, "so needs must I come also, since I have twelve shafts yet unsped," and he swallowed the morsel of venison with mighty relish and gusto.

Then laughed Beltane for very gladness, and he looked on each with kindling eye.

"Good friends," quoth he, "as ye say, so let it be, and may God's hand be over us this day."

Now, as he spake with eyes uplift to heaven, he espied a faint, blue mist far away above the soft-stirring tree tops — a distant haze, that rose lazily into the balmy air, thickening ever as he watched.

"Ah!" he exclaimed, fierce-eyed of a sudden and pointing with rigid finger, "whence cometh that smoke, think ye?"

"Why," quoth Roger, frowning, "Wendonmere village lieth yonder!"

"Nay, 'tis nearer than Wendonmere," said Walkyn, shouldering his axe.

"See, the smoke thickens!" cried Beltane. "Now, God forgive me! the while I tarry here Red Pertolepe is busy, meseemeth!" So saying, he caught up his sword, and incontinent set off at speed toward where the soft blue haze stole upon the air of morning, growing denser and ever denser.

Fast and furious Beltane sped on, crashing through underbrush and crackling thicket, o'erleaping bush and brook and fallen tree, heedful of eye, and choosing his course with a forester's unerring instinct, praying fiercely beneath his breath, and with the three ever close behind.

"Would I had eaten less!" panted Giles.

"Would our legs were longer!" growled Walkyn.

"Would my belt bore fewer notches!" quoth Roger.

And so they ran together, sure-footed and swift, and ever as they ran the smoke grew denser, and ever Beltane's prayers more fervent. Now in a while they heard a sound,

How He Had Word with Pertolepe

faint and confused: a hum, that presently grew to a murmur — to a drone — to a low wailing of voices, pierced of a sudden by a shrill cry no man's lips could utter, that swelled high upon the air and died, lost amid the growing clamour.

"They've fired the ricks first!" panted Roger; "'tis ever Pertolepe's way!"

"They be torturing the women!" hissed Walkyn; "'tis ever so Red Pertolepe's pleasure!"

"And I have but twelve arrows left me!" groaned Giles.

But Beltane ran in silence, looking neither right nor left, until, above the hum of voices he heard one upraised in passionate supplication, followed by another — a loud voice and jovial — and thereafter, a burst of roaring laughter.

Soon Beltane beheld a stream that flowed athwart their way and, beyond the stream, a line of willows thick growing upon the marge; and again, beyond these clustering willows the straggling village lay. Then Beltane, motioning the others to caution, forded the stream and coming in the shade of the osiers, drew on his hood of mail, and so, unsheathing his long sword, peered through the leaves. And this is what he saw:

A wide road flanked by rows of scattered cottages, rude of wall and thatch; a dusty road, that led away east and west into the cool depths of the forest, and a cringing huddle of wretched village folk whose pallid faces were all set one way, where some score of men-at-arms lolled in their saddles watching a tall young maid who struggled fiercely in the grasp of two lusty fellows, her garments rent, her white flesh agleam in the sunlight. A comely maid, supple and strong, who ever as she strove 'gainst the clutching hands that held her, kept her blazing eyes turned upon one in knightly mail who sat upon a great war-horse hard by, watching her, big chin in big mailed fist, and with wide lips up-curling in a smile: a strong man this, heavy and broad of chest; his casque hung at his saddle-bow, and his mail-coif, thrown back upon his wide shoulders, showed his thick, red hair that fell a-down, framing his square-set, rugged face.

"Ha, Cuthbert," quoth he, turning to one who rode at his elbow — a slender youth who stared with evil eyes and sucked upon his finger, "Aha, by the fiend, 'tis a sweet armful, Sir Squire?"

"Aye, my lord Pertolepe, 'tis rarely shaped and delicately fleshed!" answered the esquire, and so fell to sucking his finger again.

"What, silly wench, will ye defy me still?" cried Sir Pertolepe, jovial of voice, "must ye to the whip in sooth? Ho, Ralph — Otho, strip me this stubborn jade — so! — Ha! verily Cuthbert, hast shrewd eyes, 'tis a dainty rogue. Come," said he smiling down into the girl's wide, fierce eyes, "save that fair body o' thine from the lash, now, and speak me where is thy father and brother that I may do justice on them, along with these other dogs, for the foul murder of my foresters yest're'en; their end shall be swift, look ye, and as for thyself — shalt find those to comfort thee anon — speak, wench!"

But now came a woman pale and worn, who threw herself on trembling knees at Sir Pertolepe's stirrup, and, bowed thus before him in the dust, raised a passionate outcry, supplicating his mercy with bitter tears and clasped hands lifted heavenwards.

"O good my lord Pertolepe," she wailed, "'twas not my husband, nor son, nor any man of our village wrought this thing; innocent are we, my lord —"

"O witch!" quoth he, "who bade thee speak?" So saying he drew mail-clad foot from stirrup and kicked her back into the dust. "Ho, whips!" he called, "lay on, and thereafter will we hang these vermin to their own roof-trees and fire their hovels for a warning."

But now, even as the struggling maid was dragged forward — even as Pertolepe, smiling, settled chin on fist to watch the lithe play of her writhing limbs, the willows behind him swayed and parted to a sudden panther-like leap, and a mail-clad arm was about Sir Pertolepe — a mighty arm that bore him from the saddle and hurled him headlong; and thereafter Sir Pertolepe, half stunned and staring up from the dust, beheld a great blade whose point pricked his naked throat, and, beyond this blade, a mail-clad face, pallid, fierce, grim-lipped, from whose blazing eyes death glared down at him.

"Dog!" panted Beltane.

"Ha! Cuthbert!" roared Red Pertolepe, writhing 'neath Beltane's grinding heel, "to me, Cuthbert — to me!"

But, as the esquire wheeled upon Beltane with sword uplifted, out from the green an arrow whistled, and Cuthbert, shrill-screaming, swayed in his saddle and thudded to earth, while his great war-horse, rearing affrighted, plunged among the men-at-arms, and all was shouting and confusion; while from amid the willows arrows whizzed and flew, 'neath whose cruel barbs horses snorted, stumbling and kicking, or crashed into the dust; and ever the confusion grew.

But now Sir Pertolepe, wriggling beneath Beltane's iron foot had unsheathed his dagger, yet, ere he could stab, down upon his red pate crashed the heavy pommel of Beltane's sword and Sir Pertolepe, sinking backward, lay outstretched in the dust very silent and very still. Then Beltane sheathed his sword and, stooping, caught Sir Pertolepe by the belt and dragged him into the shade of the willows, and being come to the stream, threw his captive down thereby and fell to splashing his bruised face with the cool water. And now, above the shouts and the trampling of hoofs upon the road, came the clash of steel on steel and the harsh roar of Walkyn and Black Roger as they plied axe and sword —"Arise! Ha, arise!" Then, as Beltane glanced up, the leaves near by were dashed aside and Giles came bounding through, his gay feather shorn away, his escalloped cape wrenched and torn, his broadsword a-swing in his hand.

"Ho, tall brother — a sweet affray!" he panted, "the fools give back already: they cry that Pertolepe is slain and the woods full of outlaws; they be falling back from the village — had I but a few shafts in my quiver, now —" but here, beholding the face of Beltane's captive, Giles let fall his sword, staring round-eyed.

"Holy St. Giles!" he gasped, "'tis the Red Pertolepe!" and so stood agape, what time a trumpet brayed a fitful blast from the road and was answered afar. Thereafter came Roger, stooping as he ran, and shouting:

"Archers! Archers! — run, lord!"

But Beltane stirred not, only he dashed the water in Sir Pertolepe's twitching face, wherefore came Roger and caught him by the arm, pleading:

"Master, O master!" he panted, "the forest is a-throng with lances, and there be archers also — let us make the woods ere we are beset!"

But Beltane, seeing the captive stir, shook off Black Roger's grasp; but now, one laughed, and Walkyn towered above him, white teeth agleam, who, staring down at Sir Pertolepe, whirled up his bloody axe to smite.

"Fool!" cried Beltane, and threw up his hand to stay the blow, and in that moment Sir Pertolepe oped his eyes.

"'Tis Pertolepe!" panted Walkyn, "'tis he that slew wife and child: so now will I slay him, since we, in this hour, must die!"

"Not so," quoth Beltane, "stand back — obey me — back, I say!" So, muttering, Walkyn lowered his axe, while Beltane, drawing his dagger, stooped above Sir Pertolepe and spake, swift and low in his ear, and with dagger at his throat. And, in a while, Beltane rose and Sir Pertolepe also, and side by side they stepped forth of the leaves out into the road, where, on the outskirts of the village, pikemen and men-at-arms, archer and knight, were halted in a surging throng, while above the jostling confusion rose the hoarse babel of their voices. But of a sudden the clamour died to silence, and thereafter from a hundred throats a shout went up:

"A Pertolepe! 'Tis Sir Pertolepe!"

Now in this moment Beltane laid his dagger-hand about

How He Had Word with Pertolepe 121

Sir Pertolepe's broad shoulders, and set the point of his dagger 'neath Sir Pertolepe's right ear.

"Speak!" quoth Beltane softly, and his dagger-point bit deeper, "speak now as I commanded thee!"

A while Sir Pertolepe bit savagely at his knuckle-bones, then, lifting his head, spake that all might hear:

"Ho, sirs!" he cried, "I am fain to bide awhile and hold talk with one Beltane, who styleth himself — Duke of Pentavalon. Hie ye back, therefore, one and all, and wait me in Garthlaxton; yet, an I come not by sunset, ride forth and seek me within the forest. Go!"

Hereupon from the disordered ranks a sound arose, a hoarse murmur that voiced their stark amaze, and, for a while, all eyes stared upon those two grim figures that yet stood so close and brotherly. But Sir Pertolepe quelled them with a gesture:

"Go!" he commanded.

So their disarray fell into rank and order, and wheeling about, they marched away along the forest road with helm agleam and pennons a-dance, the while Sir Pertolepe stared after them, wild of eye and with mailed hands clenched; once he made as if to call them back: but Beltane's hand was heavy on his shoulder, and the dagger pricked his throat. And thus stood they, side by side, until the tramp of feet was died away, until the last trembling villager had slunk from sight and the broad road was deserted, all save for Cuthbert the esquire, and divers horses that lay stiffly in the dust, silent and very still.

Then Beltane sighed and sheathed his dagger, and Sir Pertolepe faced him scrowling, fierce-eyed and arrogant.

"Ha, outlaw!" quoth he, "give back my sword and I will cope with thee — wolf's head though thou art — aye, and any two other rogues beside."

"Nay," answered Beltane, "I fight with such as thee but when I needs must. What — Roger!" he called, "go fetch hither a rope!"

"Dog — would ye murder me?"

"Not so," sighed Beltane, shaking his head, "have I not promised to leave thee alive within the greenwood? Yet I would see thee walk in bonds first."

"Ha, dare ye bind me, then? He that toucheth me, toucheth Duke Ivo — dare ye so do, rogue?"

"Aye, messire," nodded Beltane, "I dare so. Bring hither the rope, Roger." But when Roger was come nigh, Sir Pertolepe turned and stared upon him.

"What!" cried he, jovial of voice yet deadly-eyed, "is it my runaway hangman in very sooth. Did I not pay thee enough, thou black-avised knave? Did I not love thee for thy skill with the noose, thou traitorous rogue? Now, mark me, Roger: one day will I feed thee to my hounds and watch them tear thee, as they have certain other rogues — aha! — you mind them, belike?"

Pale of cheek and with trembling hands, Roger bound the arms of him that had been his over-lord, while Walkyn and Giles, silent and wide-eyed, watched it done.

"Whither would ye take me?" quoth Red Pertolepe, arrogant.

"That shalt thou know anon, messire."

"How an I defy thee?"

"Then must we carry thee, messire," answered Beltane, "yet thine own legs were better methinks — come, let us begone."

Thus, presently, having forded the brook, they struck into the forest; first went Walkyn, axe on shoulder, teeth agleam; next strode Sir Pertolepe, head high, 'twixt pale-faced Roger and silent Beltane, while the bowman followed after, calling upon St. Giles beneath his breath and crossing himself: and ever and anon Walkyn would turn to look upon their scowling captive with eyes that glared 'neath shaggy brows.

Now after they had gone some while, Sir Pertolepe brake silence and spake my Beltane, proud and fierce.

"Fellow," quoth he, "if 'tis for ransom ye hold me, summon hither thy rogues' company, and I will covenant for my release."

"I seek no ransom of thee, messire," answered Beltane, "and for my company —'tis here."

"Here? I see but three sorry knaves!"

"Yet with these same three did I o'ercome thy foresters, Sir Pertolepe."

"Rogue, thou liest —'tis thing impossible!"

"Moreover, with these three did I, last night, burn down Black Ivo's mighty gallows that stood without Belsaye town, and, thereafter set wide the dungeon of Belsaye and delivered thence certain woeful prisoners, and sent them abroad with word that I — Beltane, son of Beltane the Strong, Duke of Pentavalon, am come at last, bearing the sword of my father, that was wont to strike deep for liberty and justice: nor, having life, will I lay it by until oppression is no more."

Now indeed did Sir Pertolepe stare upon my Beltane in amaze and spake no word for wonder; then, of a sudden he laughed, scornful and loud.

"Ho! thou burner of gibbets!" quoth he, "take heed lest thy windy boasting bring thy lordly neck within a noose! Art lusty of arm, yet lustier of tongue — and as to thy father, whoe'er he be —"

"Messire?" Beltane's voice was soft, yet, meeting the calm serenity of his gaze, Sir Pertolepe checked the jeer upon his lip and stared upon Beltane as one new-waked; beheld in turn his high and noble look, the costly excellence of his armour, his great sword and belt of silver — and strode on thereafter with never a word, yet viewing Beltane askance 'neath brows close-knit in dark perplexity. So, at last, they came into a little clearing deep-hid among the denser green.

Beltane paused here, and lifting mailed hand, pointed to a certain tree. But hereupon, Sir Pertolepe, staring round about him and down upon his galling bonds, spake:

"Sir knight," said he, "who thou art I know not, yet, if indeed thou art of gentle blood, then know that I am Sir Pertolepe, Baron of Trenda, Seneschal of Garthlaxton, lord warden of the marches: moreover, friend and brother-in-arms am I to Duke Ivo —"

"Nay," said Beltane, " all this I know, for much of thee have I heard, messire: of thy dark doings, of the agony of men, the shame of women, and how that there be many desolate hearths and nameless graves of thy making, lord Pertolepe. Thou wert indeed of an high estate and strong, and these but lowly folk, and weak — yet mercy on them had ye none. I have this day heard thee doom the innocent to death and bitter shame, and, lord, as God seeth us, it is enough!"

Sir Pertolepe's ruddy cheek showed pale, but his blue eyes stared upon Beltane wide and fearless.

"Have ye then dragged me hither to die, messire?"

"Lord Pertolepe, all men must die, aye, e'en great lords such as thou, when they have sinned sufficiently: and thy sins, methinks, do reach high heaven. So have I brought thee hither into the wilderness that God's will may be wrought upon thee."

"How — wilt forswear thyself?" cried Sir Pertolepe, writhing in his bonds.

Quoth Beltane:

"Come Roger — Walkyn — bring me him to the tree, yonder."

"Ha! rogue — rogue," panted Sir Pertolepe, "would'st leave me to die in a noose, unshriven and unannealed, my soul dragged hell-wards weighted with my sins?"

Now, even as he spake, swift and sudden he leapt aside and would have fled; but Walkyn's fierce fingers dragged at his throat, and Roger's iron arms were close about him. Desperately he fought and struggled, but mighty though he was, his captors were mighty also, moreover his bonds galled him; wherefore, fighting yet, they dragged him to the tree, and to the tree Beltane fast bound him, whiles the forest rang and echoed with his panting cries until his great voice cracked and broke, and he hung 'gainst the tree, spent and breathless.

Then spake Beltane, grim-lipped yet soft of voice:

"Lord Pertolepe, fain would I hang thee as thou hast hanged many a man ere now — but this, methinks, is a better way: for here, unless some wanderer chance to find thee, must thou perish, an so God will it. Thus do we leave thee in the hands of God to grant thee life or death: and may he have mercy on thy guilty soul!"

Thus said Beltane, sombre of brow and pale of cheek; and so, beckoning to the others, turned away, despite Sir Pertolepe's passionate threats and prayers, and plunging into the dense underbrush, strode swift-footed from the place, with the captive's wild cries ringing in his ears.

Haphazard went Beltane, yet straining his ears to catch those mournful sounds that grew faint and fainter with distance till they were lost in the rustle of the leaves. But, of a sudden, he stayed his going and stood with his head aslant hearkening to a sound that seemed to have reached him from the solitudes behind; and presently it came again, a cry from afar — a scream of agony, hoarse and long drawn out, a hateful sound that checked the breath of him and brought the sweat out cold upon his brow; and now, turning about, he saw that his following was but two, for Walkyn had vanished quite. Now Giles, meeting Beltane's wide stare, must needs cough and fumble with his bow, whiles Roger stood with bowed head and fingers tight-clenched upon his quarter-staff: whereat, fierce-frowning, Beltane spake.

"Wait!" he commanded, "wait you here!" and forthwith turned and ran, and so running, came again at last to that obscure glade whence now came a sound of groans, mocked, thereafter, by fierce laughter. Now, bursting from the green, Beltane beheld Sir Pertolepe writhing in his bonds with Walkyn's fierce fingers twined in his red hair, and Walkyn's busy dagger at his upturned brow, where was a great, gory wound, a hideous cruciform blotch whence pulsed the blood that covered his writhen face like a scarlet vizard.

"Ah!" cried Beltane, "what hast thou done?"

Back fell Walkyn, fierce-eyed and grim yet with teeth agleam through the hair of his beard.

"Lord," quoth he, "this man hath slain wife, and child and brother, so do I know him thrice a murderer. Therefore have I set this mark of Cain upon him, that all men henceforth may see and know. But now, an it be so thy will, take this my dagger and slay me here and now — yet shall Red Pertolepe bear my mark upon him when I am dead."

Awhile stood Beltane in frowning thought, then pointed to the green.

"Go," said he, "the others wait thee!"

So Walkyn, obeying, turned and plunged into the green, while Beltane followed after, slow and heavy-footed. But now, even as he went, slow and ever slower, he lifted heavy head and turned about, for above the leafy stirrings rose the mournful lilting of a pipe, clear and very sweet, that drew nearer and louder until it was, of a sudden, drowned in a cry hoarse and woeful. Then Beltane, hasting back soft-treading, stood to peer through the leaves, and presently, his cock's-comb flaunting, his silver bells a-jingle, there stepped a mountebank into the clearing — that same jester with whom Beltane had talked aforetime.

"Beda!" cried Sir Pertolepe faintly, his bloody face uplifted, "and is it forsooth, thou, Beda? Come, free me of my bonds. Ha! why stay ye, I am Pertolepe — thy lord — know you me not, Beda?"

"Aye, full well I know thee, lord Pertolepe, thou art he who had me driven forth with blows and bitter stripes — thou art he who slew my father for an ill-timed jest — oho! well do I know thee, my lord Pertolepe." So saying, Beda the Jester set his pipe within his girdle, and, drawing his dagger, began to creep upon Sir Pertolepe, who shook the dripping blood from his eyes to watch him as he came. Quote he:

"Art a good fool, Beda, aye, a good fool. And for thy father, 'twas the wine, Beda — the wine, not I — come, free me of these my bonds — I loved thy father, e'en as I loved thee."

"Yet is my father dead, lord — and I am outcast!" said Beda, smiling and fingering his dagger.

"So then, will ye slay me, Beda — wilt murder thy lord? Why then, strike, fool, strike — here, i' the throat, and let thy steel be hard-driven. Come!"

Then Sir Pertolepe feebly raised his bloody head, proffering his throat to the steel and so stood faint in his bonds, yet watching the jester calm-eyed. Slowly, slowly the dagger was lifted for the stroke while Sir Pertolepe watched the glittering steel patient and unflinching; then, swift and sudden the dagger flashed and fell, and Sir Pertolepe staggered free, and so stood swaying. Then, looking down upon his severed bonds, he laughed hoarsely.

"How, 'twas but a jest, then, my Beda?" he whispered. "A jest — ha! and methinks, forsooth, the best wilt ever make!"

So saying, Sir Pertolepe stumbled forward a pace, groping before him like a blind man, then, groaning, fell, and lay a-swoon, his bloody face hidden in the grass.

And turning away, Beltane left him lying there with Beda the Jester kneeling above him.

CHAPTER XVI

OF THE RUEFUL KNIGHT OF THE BURNING HEART

SOUTHWARD marched Beltane hour after hour, tireless of stride, until the sun began to decline; on and on, thoughtful of brow and speaking not at all, wherefore the three were gloomy and silent also — even Giles had no mind to break in upon his solemn meditations. But at last came Roger and touched him on the shoulder.

"Master," said he, "the day groweth to a close, and we famish."

"Why, then — eat," said Beltane.

Now while they set about building a fire, Beltane went aside and wandering slow and thoughtful, presently came to a broad glade or ride, and stretching himself out 'neath a tree, lay there staring up at the leafy canopy, pondering upon Sir Pertolepe his sins, and the marvellous ways of God. Lying thus, he was aware of the slow, plodding hoof-strokes of a horse drawing near, of the twang of a lute, with a voice sweet and melodious intoning a chant; and the tune was plaintive and the words likewise, being these: —

> "Alack and woe
> That love is so
> Akin to pain!
> That to my heart
> The bitter smart
> Returns again,
> Alack and woe!"

Glancing up therefore, Beltane presently espied a knight who bestrode a great and goodly war-horse; a youthful knight and debonair, slender and shapely in his bright

The Knight of the Burning Heart

mail and surcoat of flame-coloured samite. His broad shield hung behind his shoulder, balanced by a long lance whose gay banderol fluttered wanton to the soft-breathing air; above his mail-coif he wore a small bright-polished bascinet, while, at his high-peaked saddle-bow his ponderons war-helm swung, together with broad-bladed battle-axe. Now as he paced along in this right gallant estate, his roving glance, by hap, lighted on Beltane, whereupon, checking his powerful horse, he plucked daintily at the strings of his lute, delicate-fingered, and brake into song anew:—

> "Ah, woe is me
> That I should be
> A lonely wight!
> That in mankind
> No joy I find
> By day or night,
> Ah, woe is me!"

Thereafter he sighed amain and smote his bosom, and smiling upon Beltane sad-eyed, spake:

"Most excellent, tall, and sweet young sir, I, who Love's lorn pilgrim am, do give thee woeful greeting and entreat now the courtesy of thy pity."

"And wherefore pity, sir?" quoth Beltane, sitting up.

"For reason of a lady's silver laughter. A notable reason this; for, mark me, ye lovers, an thy lady flout thee one hour, grieve not — she shall be kind the next; an she scorn thee to-day, despair nothing — she shall love thee to-morrow; but, an she laugh and laugh — ah, then poor lover, Venus pity thee! Then languish hope, and tender heart be rent, for love and laughter can ne'er be kin. Wherefore a woeful wight am I, foredone and all distraught for love. Behold here, the blazon on my shield—lo! a riven heart proper (direfully aflame) upon a field vert. The heart, methinks, is aptly wrought and popped, and the flame in sooth flame-like! Here beneath, behold my motto, 'Ardeo' which signifieth 'I burn.' Other device have I laid by for the nonce, what time my pilgrimage shall be accompt."

But Beltane looked not so much upon the shield as on the face of him that bore it, and beholding its high and fearless look, the clear, bright eyes and humorous mouth (albeit schooled to melancholy) he smiled, and got him to his feet.

"Now, well met, Sir Knight of the Burning Heart!" quoth he. "What would ye here, alone, within these solitudes?"

"Sigh, messire. I sing and sigh, and sigh and sing."

"'Tis a something empty life, methinks."

"Not so, messire," sighed the rueful knight, "for when I chance to meet a gentle youth, young and well beseen — as thou, bedight in goodly mail — as thou, with knightly sword on thigh, why then, messire, 'tis ever my wont to declare unto him that she I honour is fairer, nobler, and altogether more worthy and virtuous than any other she soever, and to maintain that same against him, on horse or afoot, with lance, battle-axe or sword. Thus, see you messire, even a love-lorn lover hath betimes his compensations, and the sward is soft underfoot, and level." Saying which, the knight cocked a delicate eyebrow in questioning fashion, and laid a slender finger to the pommel of his long sword.

"How," cried Beltane, "would'st fight with me?"

"Right gladly would I, messire — to break the monotony."

"I had rather hear thy song again."

"Ha, liked you it in sooth? 'Tis small thing of mine own."

"And 'tis brief!" nodded Beltane.

"Brief!" quoth the knight, "brief! not so, most notable youthful sir, for even as love is long enduring so is my song, it being of an hundred and seventy and eight cantos in all, dealing somewhat of the woes and ills of a heart sore smitten (which heart is mine own also). Within my song is much matter of hearts (in truth) and darts, of flames

The Knight of the Burning Heart 131

and shames, of yearnings and burnings, the which this poor heart must needs endure since it doth constant bleed and burn."

"Indeed, messire, I marvel that you be yet alive," said Beltane gravely, whereat the young knight did pause to view him, dubious-eyed. Quoth he:

"In sooth, most youthful and excellent sir, I have myself marvelled thereat betimes, but, since alive am I, now do I declare unto you that she for whom I sigh is the fairest, gentlest, noblest, most glorious and most womanly of all women in the world alive —"

"Save one!" said Beltane.

"Save none, messire!" said the young knight, eager-eyed.

"One!" said Beltane.

"None!" quoth the knight, as, casting aside ponderous lance he vaulted lightly from his saddle and drew his sword; but, seeing that Beltane bore no shield, paused to lay his own tenderly aside, and so faced him serene of brow and smiling of lip. "Sweet sir," said he gaily, "here methinks is fair cause for argument; let us then discuss the matter together for the comfort of our souls and to the glory of our ladies. As to my name —"

"'Tis Jocelyn," quoth Beltane.

"Ha!" exclaimed the knight, staring.

"That won a suit of triple mail at Dunismere joust, and wagered it 'gainst Black Ivo's roan stallion within Deepwold forest upon a time."

"Now, by Venus!" cried the knight, starting back, "here be manifest sorcery! Ha! by the sweet blind boy, 'tis black magic!" and he crossed himself devoutly. But Beltane, laughing, put back his hood of mail, that his long, fair hair fell a-down rippling to his shoulders.

"Know you me not, messire?" quoth he.

"Why," said Sir Jocelyn, knitting delicate brows, "surely thou art the forester that o'ercame Duke Ivo's wrestler; aye, by the silver feet of lovely Thetis, thou'rt Beltane the Smith!"

"Verily, messire," nodded Beltane, "and 'tis not meet that knight cross blade with lowly smith."

"Ha!" quoth Sir Jocelyn, rubbing at his smooth white chin, "yet art a goodly man withal — and lover to boot — methinks?"

"Aye," sighed Beltane, "ever and always."

"Why then, all's well," quoth Sir Jocelyn with eyes a-dance, "for since true love knoweth nought of distinctions, therefore being lovers are we peers, and, being peers, so may we fight together. So come, Sir Smith, here stand I sword in hand to maintain 'gainst thee and all men the fame and honour of her I worship, of all women alive, maid or wife or widow, the fairest, noblest, truest, and most love-worthy is —"

"Helen of Mortain!" quoth Beltane, sighing.

"Helen? — Helen? — thou too!" exclaimed Sir Jocelyn, and forthwith dropped his sword, staring in stark amaze. "How — dost thou love her also?"

"Aye," sighed Beltane, "to my sorrow!"

Then stooped Sir Jocelyn and, taking up his sword, slowly sheathed it. Quoth he, sad-eyed:

"Life, methinks, is full of disappointments; farewell to thee, Sir Smith," and sighing, he turned away; yet ere he had taken lance and shield, Beltane spake:

"Whither away, Sir Jocelyn?"

"To sigh, and sing, and seek adventure. 'Twas for this I left my goodly castle of Alain and journeyed, a lorn pilgrim, hither to Pentavalon, since when strange stories have I heard that whisper in the air, speeding from lip to lip, of a certain doughty knight-at-arms, valiant beyond thought, that beareth a sword whose mighty sweep none may abide, who, alone and unaided slew an hundred and twenty and four within the greenwood, and thereafter, did, 'neath the walls of Belsaye town burn down Duke Ivo's gibbet, who hath sworn to cut Duke Ivo into gobbets, look you, and feed him to the dogs; which is well, for I love not Duke Ivo. All this have I heard and much beside, idle tales mayhap, yet would I seek out this errant Mars and

The Knight of the Burning Heart 133

prove him, for mine own behoof, with stroke of sword."

"And how an he prove worthy?" questioned Beltane.

"Then will I ride with him, to share his deeds and glory mayhap, Sir Smith — I and all the ten-score lusty fellows that muster to my pennon, since in the air is whispered talk of war, and Sir Benedict lieth ready in Thrasfordham Keep."

"Two hundred men," quoth Beltane, his blue eyes agleam, "two hundred, say you?" and, speaking, he stepped forward, unsheathing his sword.

"How now," quoth Sir Jocelyn, "what would ye, sweet smith?"

"I would have thee prove me for thy behoof, Sir Jocelyn; for I am he that with aid of five good men burned down the gibbet without Belsaye."

"Thou!" cried Sir Jocelyn, "and thou art a smith! And yet needs must I credit thee, for thine eyes be truthful eyes. And did'st indeed slay so many in the green, forsooth?"

"Nay," answered Beltane, "there were but twenty; moreover I —"

"Enough!" cried Sir Jocelyn, gaily, "be thou smith or be thou demi-god, now will I make proof of thy might and valiance." And he drew sword.

So did these two youths face each other, smiling above their gleaming steel, and so the long blades rang together, and, thereafter, the air was full of a clashing din, in so much that Roger came running sword in hand, with Walkyn and Giles at his heels; but, seeing how matters stood, they sat them down on the sward, watching round-eyed and eager.

And now Sir Jocelyn (happy-eyed), his doleful heart forgot, did show himself a doughty knight, skipping lightly to and fro despite his heavy armour, and laying on right lustily while the three a-sprawl upon the grass shouted gleefully at each shrewd stroke or skilful parry; but, once Sir Jocelyn's blade clashed upon Beltane's mailed thigh, and straightway they fell silent; and once his point touched the links on Beltane's wide breast, and straightway their brows grew anxious and gloomy — yet none so gloomy as Roger. But now, on a sudden, was the flash and ring of hard smitten steel, and behold, Sir Jocelyn's sword sprang from his grasp and thudded to earth a good three yards away; whereupon the three roared amain — yet none so loud as Roger.

"Now by sweet Cupid his tender bow!" panted Sir Jocelyn — "by the cestus of lovely Venus — aye, by the ox-eyed Juno, I swear 'twas featly done, Sir Smith!"

Quoth Beltane, taking up the fallen sword:

"'Tis a trick I learned of that great and glorious knight, Sir Benedict of Bourne."

"Messire," said Sir Jocelyn, his cheek flushing, "an earl am I of thirty and two quarterings and divers goodly manors: yet thou art the better man, meseemeth, and as such do I salute thee, and swear myself thy brother-in-arms henceforth — an ye will."

Now hereupon Beltane turned, and looking upon the mighty three with kindling eye, beckoned them near.

"Lord Jocelyn," said he, "behold here my trusty comrades, valiant men all: — this, my faithful Roger, surnamed the Black: This, Giles Brabblecombe, who shooteth as ne'er did archer yet: and here, Walkyn — who hath known overmuch of sorrow and bitter wrong. Fain would we take thee for our comrade, Lord Jocelyn, for God knoweth Pentavalon hath need of true men these days, yet first, know this — that I, and these my three good comrades do stand pledged to the cause of the weak and woefully oppressed within this sorrowful Duchy; to smite evil, nor stay till we be dead, or Black Ivo driven hence."

"Ivo? — Ivo?" stammered Sir Jocelyn, in blank amaze, "'tis madness!"

"Thus," said Beltane, "is our cause, perchance, a little desperate, and he who companies with us must company with Death betimes."

"To defy Black Ivo — ha, here is madness so mad as

pleaseth me right well! A rebellion, forsooth! How many do ye muster?"

Answered Beltane:

"Thou seest — we be four —"

"Four!" cried Sir Jocelyn, "Four!"

"But Sir Benedict lieth within Thrasfordham Keep, and God is in heaven, messire."

"Aye, but heaven is far, methinks, and Duke Ivo is near, and hath an arm long and merciless. Art so weary of life, Sir Smith?"

"Nay," answered Beltane, "but to what end hath man life, save to spend it for the good of his fellows?"

"Art mad!" sighed Sir Jocelyn, "art surely mad! Heigho! — some day, mayhap, it shall be written how one Jocelyn Alain, a gentle, love-lorn knight, singing his woes within the greenwood, did meet four lovely madmen and straight fell mad likewise. So here, upon my sword, do I swear to take thee for my brother-in-arms, and these thy comrades for my comrades, and to spend my life, henceforth, to the good of my fellows!"

So saying, Sir Jocelyn smiled his quick bright smile and reached out his hand to my Beltane, and there, leaning upon their swords, their mailed fingers clasped and wrung each other. Thereafter he turned upon the three, but even as he did so, Walkyn uttered a fierce cry, and whirling about with axe aloft, sprang into the green, whence of a sudden rose a babel of voices, and the sound of fierce blows and, thereafter, the noise of pursuit. A flicker of steel amid the green — a score of fierce faces all about him, and Beltane was seized from behind, borne struggling to his knees, to his face, battered by unseen weapons, dragged at by unseen hands, choked, half-stunned, his arms twisted and bound by galling thongs. Now, as he lay thus, helpless, a mailed foot spurned him fiercely and looking up, half-swooning, he beheld Sir Pertolepe smiling down at him.

"Ha — thou fool!" he laughed jovially, "did'st think to escape me, then — thou fool, I have followed on thy tracks all day. By the eyes of God, I would have followed thee to hell! I want thee in Garthlaxton — there be gibbets for thee above the keep — also, there are my hounds — aye, I want thee, Messire Beltane who art Duke of Pentavalon! Ho! Arnulf — a halter for his ducal throat!" So, when they had cast a noose about his neck, they dragged Beltane, choking, to his feet, and led him away gasping and staggering through the green; and having eyes, he saw not, and having ears, he heard not, being very spent and sick.

Now, as they went, evening began to fall.

CHAPTER XVII

OF THE AMBUSHMENT NEAR THORNABY MILL

LITTLE by little, as he stumbled along, Beltane's brain began to clear; he became aware of the ring and clash of arms about him, and the trampling of horses. Gradually, the mist lifting, he saw long files of men-at-arms riding along very orderly, with archers and pike-men. Little by little, amid all these hostile forms, he seemed to recognise a certain pair of legs that went on just before: sturdy legs, that yet faltered now and then in their stride, and, looking higher, he saw a broad belt whose edges were notched and saw-like, and a wide, mail-clad back that yet bent weakly forward with every shambling step. Once this figure sank to its knees, but stumbled up again 'neath the vicious prick of a pike-head that left blood upon the bronzed skin, whereat Beltane uttered a hoarse cry.

"O Black Roger!" he groaned, "I grieve to have brought thee to this!"

"Nay, lord," quoth Roger, lifting high his drooping head, "'tis but my wound that bleeds afresh. But, bond or free, thy man am I, and able yet to strike a blow on thy behalf an heaven so please."

"Now God shield thee, brave Roger!" sighed Beltane.

"O sweet St. Giles — and what of me, brother?" spake a voice in his ear, and turning, Beltane beheld the archer smiling upon him with swollen, bloody lips.

"Thou here too, good Giles?"

"Even so, tall brother, in adversity lo! I am with thee — since I found no chance to run other-where, for that divers rogues constrained me to abide — notably yon knave with the scar, whose mailed fist I had perforce to kiss, brother, in whose dog's carcase I will yet feather me a shaft, sweet St. Giles aiding me — which is my patron saint, you'll mind. *Nil desperandum*, brother: bruised and beaten, bleeding and in bonds, yet I breathe, nothing desponding, for mark me, *a priori*, brother, Walkyn and the young knight won free, which is well; Walkyn hath long legs, which is better; Walkyn hath many friends i' the greenwood, which is best of all. So do I keep a merry heart — *dum spiro spero* — trusting to the good St. Giles, which, as methinks you know is my —"

The archer grew suddenly dumb, his comely face blanched, and glancing round, Beltane beheld Sir Pertolepe beside him, who leaned down from his great white horse to smile wry-mouthed, and smiling thus, put back the mail-coif from his pallid face and laid a finger to the linen clout that swathed his head above the brows.

"Messire," said he soft-voiced, "for this I might hang thee to a tree, or drag thee at a horse's tail, or hew thee in sunder with this great sword o' thine which shall be mine henceforth — but these be deaths unworthy of such as thou — my lord Duke! Now within Garthlaxton be divers ways and means, quaint fashions and devices strange and rare, messire. And when I'm done, Black Roger shall hang what's left of thee, ere he go to feed my hounds. That big body o' thine shall rot above my gate, and for that golden head — ha! I'll send it to Duke Ivo in quittance for his gallows! Yet first — O, first shalt thou sigh that death must needs be so long a-coming!"

But now, from where the van-ward marched, came galloping a tall esquire, who, reining in beside Sir Pertolepe, pointed down the hill.

"Lord Pertolepe," he cried joyously, "yonder, scarce a mile, flies the banner of Gilles of Brandonmere, his company few, his men scattered and heavy with plunder."

"Gilles!" quoth Sir Pertolepe. "Ha, is it forsooth Gilles of Brandonmere?"

"Himself, lord, and none other. I marked plain his banner with the three stooping falcons."

"And he hath booty, say you?"

"In truth, my lord — and there be women also, three horse litters —"

"Ah — women! Verily, good Fulk, hast ever a quick eye for the flutter of a kirtle. Now, mark me Fulk, Thornaby Mill lieth in our front, and beyond, the road windeth steep 'twixt high banks. Let archers line these banks east and west: let the pikemen be ambushed to the south, until we from the north have charged them with the horse — see 'tis done, Fulk, and silently — so peradventure, Sir Gilles shall trouble me no more. Pass the word — away!"

Off rode Sir Fulk, and straightway the pounding hoofs were still, the jingle of bridle and stirrup hushed, and in its place a vague stir of bustle and excitement; of pikemen wheeling right and left to vanish southwards into the green, and of archers stringing bows and unbuckling quiver-caps ere they too wheeled and vanished; yet now Sir Pertolepe stayed four lusty fellows, and beckoning them near, pointed to the prisoners.

"Good fellows," quoth he, nodding jovially upon the archers, "here be my three rogues, see you — who must with me to Garthlaxton: one to die by slow fire, one to be torn by my hounds, and one — this tall golden-haired youth — mark him well! — to die in slow and subtle fashion. Now these three do I put in charge of ye trusty four; guard them well, good fellows, for, an one escape, so shall ye all four die in his stead and in such fashion as he should have died. Ha! d'ye mark me well, my merry men?"

"Aye, lord!" nodded the four, scowling of brow yet pale-cheeked.

"Look to it I find them secure, therefore, and entreat them tenderly. March you at the rear and see they take no harm; choose ye some secure corner where they may lie safe from chance of stray shafts, for I would have them come hale and sound to Garthlaxton, since to die well, a man must be strong and hearty, look you. D'ye mark me well, good fellows?"

"Aye, lord!" growled the four.

Then Sir Pertolepe, fondling his great chin, smiled upon Beltane and lifted Beltane's glittering sword on high, "Advance my banner!" he cried, and rode forward among his men-at-arms. On went the company, grimly silent now save for the snort of a horse, the champing of curbing bits and the thud of slow trampling hoofs upon the tender grass, as the west flamed to sunset. Thus in a while they came to a place where the road, narrowing, ran 'twixt high banks clothed in gorse and underbrush; a shadowy road, the which, winding downwards, was lost in a sharp curve. Here the array was halted, and abode very still and silent, with helm and lance-point winking in the last red rays of sunset.

"O brother," whispered Giles, "ne'er saw I place sweeter or more apt for ambushment. Here shall be bloody doings anon, and we — helpless as babes! O me, the pity on't!" But now with blows and gibes the four archers dragged them unto a tall tree that stood beside the way, a tree of mighty girth whose far-flung branches cast a deep gloom. Within this gloom lay my Beltane, stirring not and speaking no word, being faint and sick with his hurts. But Giles the archer, sitting beside him, vented by turns bitter curses upon Sir Pertolepe and humble prayers to his patron saint, so fluent and so fast that prayers and curses became strangely blent and mingled, on this wise:

"May Red Pertolepe be thrice damned with a candle to the blessed Saint Giles that is my comfort and intercessor. May his bones rot within him with my gold chain to sweet Saint Giles. May his tongue wither at the roots — ah, good Saint Giles, save me from the fire. May he be cursed in life and may the flesh shrivel on his bones and his soul be eternally damned with another candle and fifty gold pieces to the altar of holy Saint Giles —"

But now hearing Roger groan, the archer paused to admonish him thus:

"Croak not, Roger, croak not," quoth he, "think not upon thy vile body — pray, man, pray — pray thyself speechless. Call reverently upon the blessed saints as I do, promise them candles, Roger, promise hard and pray harder lest we perish — I by fire and thou by Pertolepe's hounds. Ill deaths, look you, aye, 'tis a cruel death to be burnt alive, Roger!"

"To be torn by hounds is worse!" growled Roger.

"Nay, my Rogerkin, the fire is slower, methinks — I have watched good flesh sear and shrivel ere now — ha! by Saint Giles, 'tis an evil subject; let us rather think upon two others."

"As what, archer?"

"The long legs of our comrade Walkyn. Hist! hark ye to that bruit! Here cometh Gilles of Brandonmere, meseemeth!" And now from the road in front rose the sound of an approaching company, the tramp of weary horses climbing the ascent with the sound of cheery voices upraised in song; and ever the sinking sun glinted redly on helm and lance-point where sat Sir Pertolepe's mailed riders, grim and silent, while the cheery voices swelled near and more near, till, all at once, the song died to a hum of amaze that rose to a warning shout that was drowned in the blare of a piercing trumpet blast. Whereat down swept glittering lance-point, forward leaned shining bascinet, and the first rank of Sir Pertolepe's riders, striking spurs, thundered upon them down the hill; came thereafter the shock of meeting ranks, with shouts and cries that grew to a muffled roar. Up rose the dust, an eddying cloud wherein steel flickered and dim forms strove, horse to horse and man to man, while Sir Pertolepe, sitting his great white charger, nursed his big chin and, smiling, waited his chance. Presently, from the eddying cloud staggered the broken remnant of Sir Gilles' van-ward, whereon, laughing fierce and loud, Sir Pertolepe rose in his stirrups with Beltane's long sword lifted high, his trumpets brayed the charge, and down the hill thundered Sir Pertolepe and all his array; and the road near by was deserted, save for the prisoners and the four archers who stood together, their faces set down-hill, where the dust rose denser and denser, and the roar of the conflict fierce and loud.

But now, above the din and tumult of the fight below, shrill and high rose the notes of a horn winded from the woods in the east, that was answered — like an echo, out of the woods in the west; and, down the banks to right and left, behold Sir Pertolepe's archers came leaping and tumbling, pursued by a hissing arrow shower. Whereat up sprang Giles, despite his bonds, shouting amain:

",O, Walkyn o' the Long Legs — a rescue! To us! Arise, I will arise!" Now while he shouted thus, came one of the four archers, and Giles was smitten to his knees; but, as the archer whirled up his quarter-staff to strike again, an arrow took him full in the throat, and pitching upon his face, he lay awhile, coughing, in the dust.

Now as his comrades yet stared upon this man so suddenly dead, down from the bank above leapt one who bore a glittering axe, with divers wild and ragged fellows at his heels; came a sound of shouting and blows hard smitten, a rush of feet and, thereafter, silence, save for the din of battle afar. But, upon the silence, loud and sudden rose a high-pitched quavering laugh, and Giles spake, his voice yet shrill and unsteady.

" 'Twas Walkyn — ha, Saint Giles bless Walkyn's long legs! 'Twas Walkyn I saw — Walkyn hath brought down the outlaws — the woods be full of them. Oho! Sir Pertolepe's slow fire shall not roast me yet awhile, nor his dogs mumble thy carcase, my Rogerkin!"

"Aye," quoth Roger feebly, "but what of my lord, see how still he lieth!"

"Forsooth," exclaimed the archer, writhing in his bonds to stare upon Beltane, "forsooth, Roger, he took a dour ding upon his yellow pate, look ye; but for his mail-coif he were a dead man this hour —"

"He lieth very still," groaned Roger.

"Yet is he a mighty man and strong, my Rogerkin — never despond, man, for I tell thee — ha! — heard ye that outcry? The outlaws be at work at last, they have Sir Pertolepe out-flanked d'ye see — now might ye behold what well-sped shafts can do upon a close array — pretty work — sweet work! Would I knew where Walkyn lay!"

"Here, comrade!" said a voice from the shade of the great tree.

"How — what do ye there?" cried the archer.

"Wait for Red Pertolepe."

"Why then, sweet Walkyn, good Walkyn — come loose us of our bonds that we may wait with thee —"

"Nay," growled Walkyn, "ye are the bait. When the outlaws have slain enough of them, Pertolepe's men must flee this way: so will Red Pertolepe stay to take up his prisoners, and so shall I slay him in that moment with this mine axe. Ha! — said I not so? Hark! they break already! Peace now — wait and watch." So saying, Walkyn crouched behind the tree, axe poised, what time the dust and roar of battle rolled toward them up the hill. And presently, from out the rolling cloud, riderless horses burst and thundered past, and after them — a staggering rout, mounted and afoot, spurring and trampling each other 'neath the merciless arrow-shower that smote them from the banks above. Horse and foot they thundered by until at last, amid a ring of cowering men-at-arms, Sir Pertolepe galloped, his white horse bespattered with blood and foam, his battered helm a-swing upon its thongs; grim-lipped and pale he rode, while his eyes, aflame 'neath scowling brows, swept the road this way and that until, espying Beltane 'neath the tree, he swerved aside in his career and strove to check his followers' headlong flight.

"Stay," cried he striking right and left. "Halt, dogs, and take up the prisoners. Ha! will ye defy me — rogues, caitiffs! Fulk! Raoul! Denis! Ho, there!"

But no man might stay that maddened rush, wherefore, swearing a great oath, Sir Pertolepe spurred upon Beltane with Beltane's sword lifted for the blow. But, from the shade of the tree a mighty form uprose, and Sir Pertolepe was aware of a hoarse, glad cry, saw the whirling flash of a broad axe and wrenched hard at his bridle; round staggered the white horse, down came the heavy axe, and the great horse, death-smitten, reared up and up, back and back, and crashing over, was lost 'neath the dust of swift-trampling hoofs.

Now presently, Beltane was aware that his bonds cramped him no longer, found Roger's arm about him, and at his parched lips Roger's steel head-piece brimming with cool, sweet water; and gulping thirstily, soon felt the numbness lifted from his brain and the mist from his eyes; in so much that he sat up, and gazing about, beheld himself alone with Roger.

Quoth he, looking down at his swollen wrists:

"Do we go free then, Roger?"

"Aye, master — though ye had a woundy knock upon the head."

"And what of Giles?"

"He is away to get him arrows to fill his quiver, and to fill his purse with what he may, for the dead lie thick in the road yonder, and there is much plunder."

"And Walkyn?"

"Walkyn, master, having slain Sir Pertolepe's horse yonder, followeth Pertolepe, minded straight to slay him also."

"Yet dost thou remain, Roger."

"Aye, lord; and here is that which thou wilt need again, methinks; I found it hard by Sir Pertolepe's dead horse." So saying, Roger put Beltane's great sword into his hand. Then Beltane took hold upon the sword, and rising to his feet stretched wide his arms, and felt his strength renewed within him. Therefore he sheathed the sword and set his hand on Roger's broad, mail-clad shoulder.

"Roger," said he, "thou faithful Roger, God hath de-

The Ambushment

livered us from shameful death, wherefore, I hold, He hath yet need of these our bodies."

"As how, master?"

"As I went, nigh swooning in my bonds, methought I heard tell that Sir Gilles of Brandonmere had captive certain women; so now must we deliver them, thou and I, an it may be so."

"Lord," quoth Roger, "Sir Gilles marcheth with the remnant of his company, and we are but two. Let us therefore get with us divers of these outlaws."

"I have heard tell that to be a woman and captive to Sir Gilles or Pertolepe the Red is to be brought to swift and dire shame. So now let us deliver these women from shame, thou and I. Wilt go with me, Roger?"

"Aye lord, that will I: yet first pray thee aid me to bind a clout upon my arm, for my wound irketh me somewhat."

And in a while, when Beltane had laved and bound up Roger's wound, they went on down the darkening road together.

CHAPTER XVIII

HOW BELTANE MET SIR GILLES OF BRANDONMERE

It was a night of wind with a flying cloud-wrack overhead whence peeped the pallid moon betimes; a night of gloom and mystery. The woods about them were full of sounds and stealthy rustlings as they strode along the forest road, and so came to that dark defile where the fight had raged. Of what they saw and heard within that place of slaughter it bodeth not to tell, nor of those figures, wild and fierce, that crouched to strip the jumbled slain, or snarled and quarrelled over the work.

"Here is good plunder of weapons and armour," quoth Roger, "'tis seldom the outlaws come by such. Hark to that cry! There died some wounded wight under his plunderer's knife!"

"God rest his soul, Amen!" sighed Beltane. "Come, let us hence!" And forthwith he began to run. So in a little while they passed through that place of horror unseen, and so came out again upon the forest road. Ever and anon the moon sent down a feeble ray 'neath which the road lay a-glimmer 'twixt the gloom of the woods, whence came groans and wailings with every wind-gust, whereat Roger quailed, and fumbling at his sword-hilt, pressed closer upon Beltane.

"Master," he whispered, "'tis an evil night — methinks the souls of the dead be abroad — hark to those sounds! Master, I like it not! —"

"'Tis but the wind, Roger."

"'Tis like the cries of women wailing o'er their dead, I have heard such sounds ere now; I would my belt bore fewer notches, master!"

"They shall be fewer ere dawn, Roger, I pray God!"

"Master — an I am slain this night, think ye I must burn in hell-fire — remembering these same notches?"

"Nay, for surely God is a very merciful God, Roger. Hark!" quoth Beltane, and stopped of a sudden, and thus above the wailing of the wind they presently heard a feeble groaning hard by, and following the sound, beheld a blotch upon the glimmering road. Now as they drew near the moon peeped out, and showed a man huddled 'neath a bush beside the way, whose face gleamed pale amid the shadows.

"Ha!" cried Roger, stooping, "thou'rt of Brandonmere?"

"Aye — give me water — I was squire to Sir Gilles — God's love — give me — water!"

Then Beltane knelt, and saw this was but a youth, and bidding Roger bring water from a brook near by, took the heavy head upon his knee.

"Messire," said he, "I have heard that Sir Gilles beareth women captive."

"There is — but one, and she — a nun. But nuns are — holy women — so I withstood my lord in his — desire. And my lord — stabbed me — so must I die — of a nun, see you! — Ah — give me — water!"

"Where doth he ride this night, messire?"

"His men — few — very weary — Sir Pertolepe's — men-at-arms — caught us i' the sunken road — Sir Gilles — to Thornaby Mill — beside the ford — O God — water!"

"'Tis here!" quoth Roger, kneeling beside him; then Beltane set the water to the squire's eager lips, but, striving to drink he choked, and choking, fell back — dead.

So in a while they arose from their knees and went their way, while the dead youth lay with wide eyes that seemed to out-stare the pallid moon.

Now as they went on very silently together, of a sudden Black Roger caught Beltane by the arm and pointed into the gloom, where, far before them, small lights winked redly through the murk.

"Yon should be Sir Gilles' watch-fires!" he whispered.

"Aye," nodded Beltane, "so I think."

"Master — what would ye now?"

"Pray, Roger — I pray God Sir Gilles' men be few, and that they be sound sleepers. Howbeit we will go right warily none the less." So saying, Beltane turned aside from the road and led on through underbrush and thicket, through a gloom of leaves where a boisterous wind rioted; where great branches, dim seen, swayed groaning in every fierce gust, and all was piping stir and tumult. Twigs whipped them viciously, thorns dragged at them, while the wind went by them, moaning, in the dark. But, ever and anon as they stumbled forward, guiding themselves by instinct, the moon sent forth a pale beam from the whirling cloud-wrack — a phantom light that stole upon them, sudden and ghost-like, and, like a ghost, was gone again; what time Black Roger, following hard on Beltane's heel, crossed himself and muttered fragments of forgotten prayers. Thus at last they came to the river, that flowed before them vague in the half-light, whose sullen waters gurgled evilly among the willows that drooped upon the marge.

"Master," said Roger, wiping sweat from his face, "there's evil hereabouts — I've had a warning — a dead man touched me as we came through the brush yonder."

"Nay Roger, 'twas but some branch —"

"Lord, when knew ye a branch with — fingers — slimy and cold — upon my cheek here. 'Twas a warning, master — the dead hand! One of us twain goeth to his death this night!"

"Let not thine heart fail therefor, good Roger: man, being dead, liveth forever —"

"Nay, but — the dead hand, master — on my cheek, here — Ah! —" Crying thus, Black Roger sprang and caught Beltane's arm, gripping it fast, for on the air, borne upon the wind, yet louder than the wind, a shrill sound rang and echoed, the which, passing, seemed to have stricken the night to silence. Then Beltane brake from

Roger's clasp, and ran on beside the river, until, beyond the sullen waters the watch-fires flared before him, in whose red light the mill loomed up rugged and grim, its massy walls scarred and cracked, its great wheel fallen to ruin.

Now above the wheel was a gap in the masonry, an opening roughly square that had been a window, mayhap, whence shone a warm, mellow light.

"Master," panted Roger, "a God's name — what was it?"

"A woman screamed!" quoth Beltane, staring upon the lighted window. As he spake a man laughed sleepily beside the nearest watch-fire, scarce a bow-shot away.

"Look'ee, master," whispered Roger, "we may not cross by the ford because of the watch-fires — 'tis a fair light to shoot by, and the river is very deep hereabouts."

"Yet must we swim it, Roger."

"Lord, the water is in flood, and our armour heavy!"

"Then must we leave our armour behind," quoth Beltane, and throwing back his hood of mail, he began to unbuckle his broad belt, but of a sudden, stayed to point with outstretched finger. Then, looking whither he pointed, Roger saw a tree whose bole leaned far out across the stream, so that one far-flung branch well nigh scraped the broken roof of the mill.

"Yon lieth our way, Roger — come!" said he.

Being come to that side of the tree afar from the watch-fires, Beltane swung himself lightly and began to climb, but hearing a groan, paused.

"Roger," he whispered, "what ails thee, Roger?"

"Alas!" groaned Roger, "'tis my wound irketh me; O master, I cannot follow thee this way!"

"Nay, let me aid thee," whispered Beltane, reaching down to him. But, despite Beltane's strong hand, desperately though he tried, Black Roger fell back, groaning.

"Master," he pleaded, "O master, adventure not alone lest ill befall thee."

"Aye, but I must, Roger."

Then Roger leaned his head upon his sound arm, and wept full bitterly.

"O master,— O sweet lord," quoth he, "bethink thee now of the warning — the dead hand —"

"Yet must I go, my Roger."

"Then — an they kill thee, lord, so shall they kill me also; thy man am I, to live or die with thee —"

"Nay, Roger, sworn art thou to redeem Pentavalon: so now, in her name do I charge thee, haste to Sir Jocelyn, an he yet live — seek Giles and Walkyn and whoso else ye may, and bring them hither at speed. If ye find me not here, then hie ye all to Thrasfordham, for by to-morrow Sir Pertolepe and Gui of Allerdale will have raised the country against us. Go now, do even as I command, and may God keep thee, my faithful Roger." Then Beltane began to climb, but being come where the great branch forked, looked down to see Roger's upturned face, pale amid the gloom below.

"The holy angels have thee in their keeping, lord and master!" he sighed, and so turned with head a-droop and was gone. And now Beltane began to clamber out across the swirl of dark waters, while the tough bough swung and swayed beneath him in every gust of wind, wherefore his going was difficult and slow, and he took heed only to his hands and feet.

But, all at once, he heard a bitter, broken cry, and glancing up, it chanced that from his lofty perch he could look within the lighted window, and thus beheld a nun, whose slender, black-robed body writhed and twisted in the clasp of two leathern-clad arms; vicious arms, that bent her back and back across the rough table, until into Beltane's vision came the leathern-clad form of him that held her: a black-haired, shapely man, whose glowing eyes and eager mouth stooped ever nearer above the nun's white loveliness.

And thus it was that my Beltane first looked upon Sir Gilles of Brandonmere. He had laid sword and armour by, but as the nun yet struggled in his arms, her white hand came upon and drew the dagger at his girdle, yet, ere she could strike, Sir Gilles had seen and leapt back out of reach.

Then Beltane clambered on at speed, and with every yard their voices grew more loud — hers proud and disdainful, his low and soft, pierced, now and then, by an evil, lazy laugh.

Now ever as Beltane went, the branch swayed more dizzily, bending more and more beneath his weight, and ever as he drew nearer, between the wind-gusts came snatches of their talk.

"Be thou nun, or duchess, or strolling light-o'-love, art woman — by Venus! fair and passing fair! — captive art thou — aye, mine, I tell thee — yield thee — hast struggled long enough to save thy modesty — yield thee now, else will I throw thee to my lusty rogues without — make them sport —"

"O — beast — I fear thee not! For thy men — how shall they harm me, seeing I shall be dead!"

Down swayed the branch, low and lower, until Beltane's mailed foot, a-swing in mid air, found something beneath — slipped away — found it again, and thereupon, loosing the branch, down he came upon the ruined mill-wheel. Then, standing upon the wheel, his groping fingers found divers cracks in the worn masonry — moreover the ivy was thick; so, clinging with fingers and toes, up he went, higher and higher until his steel-mittened hands gripped the sill: thus, slowly and cautiously he drew himself up until his golden head rose above the sill and he could peer into the room.

Sir Gilles half stood, half sat upon the table, while the nun faced him, cold and proud and disdainful, the gleaming dagger clutched to her quick-heaving bosom; and Sir Gilles, assured and confident, laughed softly as he leaned so lazily, yet ever he watched that gleaming steel, waiting his chance to spring. Now as they stood fronting each other thus, the nun stirred beneath his close regard, turned her head, and on the instant Beltane knew that she had seen him; knew by the sudden tremor of her lips, the widening of her dark eyes, wherein he seemed to read wonder, joy, and a passionate entreaty; then, even as he thrilled to meet that look, down swept languorous lid and curling lash, and, sighing, she laid the dagger on the table. For a moment Sir Gilles stared in blank amaze, then laughed his lazy laugh.

"Ah, proud beauty! 'Tis surrender then?" said he, and speaking, reached for the dagger; but even as he did so, the nun seized the heavy table and thrust with sudden strength, so that Sir Gilles, taken unawares, staggered back and back — to the window. Then Beltane reached up into the room and, from behind, caught Sir Gilles by the throat and gripped him with iron fingers, strangling all outcry, and so, drawing himself over the sill and into the room, dragged Sir Gilles to the floor and choked him there until his eyes rolled upward and he lay like one dead. Then swiftly Beltane took off the belt of Sir Gilles and buckled it tight about the wrists and arms of Sir Gilles, and, rending strips from Sir Gilles' mantle that lay near, therewith fast gagged and bound him. Now it chanced that as he knelt thus, he espied the dagger where it lay, and taking it up, glanced from it to Sir Gilles lying motionless in his bonds. But as he hesitated, there came a sudden knocking on the door and a voice spake without:

"My lord! my lord —'tis I —'tis Lupo. My lord, our men be few and wearied, as ye know. Must I set a guard beyond the ford, think you, or will the four watch-fires suffice?"

Now, glancing up, scarce breathing, Beltane beheld the nun who crouched down against the wall, her staring eyes turned towards the door, her cheeks ashen, her lips a-quiver with deadly fear. Yet, even so, she spake. But that 'twas she indeed who uttered the words he scarce could credit, so soft and sweetly slumberous was her voice:

"My lord is a-weary and sleepeth. Hush you, and come again with the dawn." Now was a moment's breathless silence and thereafter an evil chuckle, and, so chuck-

How Beltane Met Sir Gilles 153

ling, the man Lupo went down the rickety stair without.

And when his step was died away, Beltane drew a deep breath, and together they arose, and so, speaking no word, they looked upon each other across the prostrate body of Sir Gilles of Brandonmere.

CHAPTER XIX

CONCERNING THE EYES OF A NUN

Eyes long, thick-lashed and darkly blue that looked up awhile into his and anon were hid 'neath languorous-drooping lids; a nose tenderly aquiline; lips, red and full, that parted but to meet again in sweet and luscious curves; a chin white, and round, and dimpled.

This Beltane saw 'twixt hood and wimple, by aid of the torch that flickered against the wall; and she, conscious of his look, stood with white hands demurely crossed upon her rounded bosom, with eyes abased and scarlet lips apart, as one who waits — expectant. Now hereupon my Beltane felt himself vaguely at loss, and finding he yet held the dagger, set it upon the table and spake, low-voiced.

"Reverend Mother —" he began, and stopped — for at the word her dark lashes lifted and she stared upon him curiously, while slowly her red lips quivered to a smile. And surely, surely this nun so sweet and saintly in veiling hood and wimple was yet a very woman, young and passing fair; and the eyes of her — how deep and tender and yet how passionate! Now beholding her eyes, memory stirred within him and he sighed, whereat she sighed also and meekly bowed her head, speaking him with all humility.

"Sweet son, speak on — thy reverend mother heareth."

Now did Beltane, my Innocent, rub his innocent chin and stand mumchance awhile, finding nought to say — then:

"Lady," he stammered, "lady — since I have found thee — let us go while yet we may."

"Messire," says she, with eyes still a-droop, "came you in sooth — in quest of me?"

"Yea, verily. I heard Sir Gilles had made captive of a nun, so came I to deliver her — an so it might be."

"E'en though she were old, and wrinkled, and toothless, messire?"

"Lady," says my Innocent, staring and rubbing his chin a little harder, "surely all nuns, young and old, be holy women, worthy a man's reverence and humble service. So would I now bear thee from this unhallowed place — we must be far hence ere dawn — come!"

"Aye, but whither?" she sighed, "death is all about us, messire — how may we escape it? And I fear death no whit — now, messire!"

"Aye, but I do so, lady, since I have other and greater works yet to achieve."

"How, messire, is it so small a thing to have saved a nun — even though she be neither old, nor wrinkled, nor toothless?" And behold, the nun's meek head was high and proud, her humility forgotten quite.

Then she frowned, and 'neath her sombre draperies her foot fell a-tapping; a small foot, dainty and slender in its gaily broidered shoe, so much at variance with her dolorous habit. But Beltane recked nought of this, for, espying a narrow window in the opposite wall, he came thither and thrusting his head without, looked down upon the sleeping camp. And thus he saw that Sir Gilles' men were few indeed, scarce three-score all told he counted as they lay huddled about the smouldering watch-fires, deep-slumbering as only men greatly wearied might. Even the sentinels nodded at their posts, and all was still save for the rush of a sudden wind-gust, or the snort and trampling of the horses. And leaning thus, Beltane marked well where the sentinels lolled upon their pikes, or marched drowsily to and fro betwixt the watch-fires, and long he gazed where the horses were tethered, two swaying, trampling lines dim-seen amid the further shadows. Now being busied measuring with his eye the distances 'twixt sentinel and sentinel, and noting where the shadows lay darkest, he was suddenly aware of the nun close beside him, of the feel of her, soft and warm against him, and starting at the contact, turned to find her hand, small and white, upon his mailed arm.

"Sweet son," said she soft-voiced, from the shadow of her sombre hood, "thy reverend mother now would chide thee, for that having but short while to live, thou dost stand thus mumchance, staring upon vacancy — for, with the dawn, we die."

Quoth Beltane, deeply conscious of the slender hand:

"To die, nay — nay — thou'rt too young and fair to die —"

Sighed she, with rueful smile:

"Thou too art neither old nor cold, nor bent with years, fair son. Come then, till death let us speak together and comfort each other. Lay by thy melancholy as I now lay by this hood and wimple, for the night is hot and close, methinks."

"Nay, lady, indeed 'tis cool, for there is much wind abroad," says Beltane, my Innocent. "Moreover, while standing here, methinks I have seen a way whereby we may win free —"

Now hereupon she turned and looked on him, quick-breathing and with eyes brim-full of fear.

"Messire!" she panted, "O messire, bethink thee. For death am I prepared — to live each moment fully till the dawn, then when they came to drag me down to — to shame, then should thy dagger free me quite — such death I'd smile to meet. But ah! should we strive to flee, and thou in the attempt be slain — and I alive — the sport of that vile rabblement below — O, Christ,— not that!" and cowering, she hid her face.

"Noble lady," said Beltane, looking on her gentle-eyed, "indeed I too had thought on that!" and, coming to the table, he took thence the dagger of Sir Gilles and would have put it in her hand, but lo! she shrank away.

"Not that, messire, not that," she sighed, "thy dagger let it be, since true knight art thou and honourable, I pray you give me thine. It is thy reverend mother asks," and smiling pale and wan, she reached out a white, imperious hand. So Beltane drew his dagger and gave it to her keeping; then, having set the other in his girdle, he crossed to the door and stood awhile to hearken.

"Lady," said he, "there is no way for us but this stair, and meseemeth 'tis a dangerous way, yet must we tread it together. Reach me now thy hand and set it here in my girdle, and, whatsoe'er befall, loose not thy hold." So saying, Beltane drew his sword and set wide the door. "Look to thy feet," he whispered, "and tread soft!" Then, with her trailing habit caught up in her left hand and with her right upon his belt, the nun followed Beltane out upon the narrow stair. Step by step they stole downwards into the dark, pausing with breath in check each time the timbers creaked, and hearkening with straining ears. Down they went amid the gloom until they spied an open door below, beyond which a dim light shone, and whence rose the snoring of wearied sleepers. Ever and anon a wind-gust smote the ancient mill and a broken shutter rattled near by, what time they crept a pace down the creaking stair until at last they stood upon the threshold of a square chamber upon whose broken hearth a waning fire burned, by whose uncertain light they espied divers vague forms that stirred now and then and groaned in their sleep as they sprawled upon the floor: and Beltane counted three who lay 'twixt him and the open doorway, for door was there none. Awhile stood Beltane, viewing the sleepers 'neath frowning brows, then, sheathing his sword, he turned and reached out his arms to the nun in the darkness and, in the dark, she gave herself, warm and yielding, into his embrace, her arms clung soft about him, and he felt her breath upon his cheek, as clasping his left arm about her, he lifted her high against his breast. And now, even as she trembled against him, so trembled Beltane also yet knew not why; therefore of a sudden he turned and stepped into the chamber. A man started up beside the hearth, muttering evilly; and Beltane, standing rigid, gripped his dagger to smite, but even then the muttering ceased, and falling back, the man rolled over and fell a-snoring again. So, lightly, swiftly, Beltane strode over the sprawling sleepers — out through the open doorway — out into the sweet, cool night beyond — out into the merry riot of the wind. Swift and sure of foot he sped, going ever where the shadows lay deepest, skirting beyond reach of the paling watch-fires, until he was come nigh where the horses stamped and snorted. Here he set the nun upon her feet, and bidding her stir not, crept towards the horses, quick-eyed and watchful. And thus he presently espied a man who leaned him upon a long pike, his face set toward the nearest watch-fire: and the man's eyes were closed, and he snored gently. Then Beltane shifted his dagger to his left hand, and being come within reach, drew back his mailed fist and smote the sleeper betwixt his closed eyes, and catching him as he fell, laid him gently on the grass.

Now swift and silent came Beltane to where the horses champed, and having made choice of a certain powerful beast, slipped off his chain mittens and rolled back sleeve of mail and, low-stooping in the shadow, sought and found the ropes whereto the halters were made fast, and straightway cut them in sunder. Then, having looked to girth and bridle, he vaulted to the saddle, and drawing sword, shouted his battle-cry fierce and loud: "Arise! Arise!" and, so shouting, smote the frighted horses to right and left with the flat of the long blade, so that they reared up whinnying, and set off a-galloping in all directions, filling the air with the thunder of their rushing hoofs.

And now came shouts and cries with a prodigious confusion and running to and fro about the dying watch-fires. Trumpets blared shrill, hoarse voices roared commands that passed unheeded in the growing din and tumult that swelled to a wild clamour of frenzied shouting:

"Fly! fly! Pertolepe is upon us! 'tis the Red Pertolepe!"

But Beltane, riding warily amid the gloom, came to that place where he had left the nun, yet found her not, and immediately was seized of a great dread. But as he stared wildly about him, he presently heard a muffled cry, and spurring thitherwards, beheld two dim figures that swayed to and fro in a fierce grapple. Riding close, Beltane saw the glint of mail, raised his sword for the blow, felt a shock — a searing smart, and knew himself wounded; but now she was at his stirrup, and stooping, he swung her up to the withers of his horse, and wheeling short about, spurred to a gallop; yet, as he rode, above the rush of wind and thud of hoofs, he heard a cry, hoarse and dolorous. On galloped Beltane all unheeding, until he came 'neath the leafy arches of the friendly woods, within whose gloom needs must he ride at a hand's pace. Thus, as they went, they could hear the uproar behind — a confused din that waxed and waned upon the wind.

But Beltane, riding slow and cautious within the green, heeded this not at all, nor the throb of his wounded arm, nor aught under heaven save the pressure of this slender body that lay so still, so warm and soft within his arm; and as he went, he began to wish for the moon that he might see her face.

Blue eyes, long and heavy-lashed! Surely blue eyes were fairest in a woman? And then the voice of her, liquid and soft like the call of merle or mavis. And she was a nun! How white and slim her hands, yet strong and resolute, as when she grasped the dagger 'gainst Sir Gilles; aye — resolute hands, like the spirit within her soft and shapely body. And then again — her lips; red and full, up-curving to sweet, slow smile, yet withal tinged with subtle mockery. With such eyes and such lips she might — aye, but she was a nun — a nun, forsooth!

"Messire!" Beltane started from his reverie. "Art cold, messire?"

"Cold!" stammered Beltane, "cold? Indeed no, lady."

"Yet dost thou tremble!"

"Nathless, I am not cold, lady."

"Then wherefore tremble?"

"Nay, I — I know not. In sooth, do I so, lady?"

"Verily, sir, and therewith sigh, frequent and O, most dolorous to hear!"

Now at this, my Beltane finding naught to say, straightway sighed again; and thus they rode awhile, speaking nothing.

"Think you we are safe, messire?" she questioned him at last.

"Tis so I pray, lady."

"Thou hast done right valiantly to-night on my behalf," says she. "How came you in at the window?"

"By means of a tree, lady."

"Art very strong, messire, and valiant beyond thought. Thou hast this night, with thy strong hand, lifted me up from shameful death: so, by right, should my life be thine henceforth." Herewith she sighed, leaning closer upon his breast, and Beltane's desire to see her face grew amain.

"Messire," said she, "methinks art cold indeed, or is it that I weary thee?"

"Nay, thou'rt wondrous easy to bear thus, lady."

"And whither do ye bear me, sir — north or south? And yet it mattereth nothing," says she, soft-voiced, "since we are safe — together!" Now hereafter, as Beltane rode, he turned his eyes full oft to heaven — yearning for the moon.

"What woods be these, messire?" she questioned.

"'Tis the wilderness that lieth betwixt Pentavalon and Mortain, lady."

"Know ye Mortain, sir?"

"Yea, verily," he answered, and sighed full deep. And as he sighed, lo, in that moment the moon peeped forth of a cloud-rift and he beheld the nun looking up at him with eyes deep and wistful, and, as she gazed, her lips curved in slow and tender smile ere her lashes drooped, and sighing, she hid her face against him in the folds of her mantle, while Beltane must needs bethink him of other eyes so very like, and yet so false, and straightway — sighed.

"Messire," she murmured, "pray now, wherefore do ye sigh so oft?"

"For that thine eyes do waken memory, lady."

"Of a woman?"

"Aye — of a woman."

"And thou dost — love her, messire?"

"Unto my dole, lady."

"Ah, can it be she doth not love thee, messire?"

"Indeed, 'tis most certain!"

"Hath she then told thee so — of herself?"

"Nay," sighed Beltane, "not in so many words, lady, and yet —"

"And yet," quoth the nun, suddenly erect, "thou must needs run away and leave her — poor sweet wretch — to mourn for thee, belike, and grieve — aye, and scorn thee too for a faint-heart!"

"Nay, lady, verily I —"

"O, indeed methinks she must contemn thee in her heart, poor, gentle soul — aye, scorn and despise thee woefully for running away; indeed, 'tis beyond all doubt, messire!"

"Lady," quoth Beltane, flushing in the dark, "you know naught of the matter —"

"Why then shalt thou tell me of it, messire — lo, I am listening." So saying, she settled herself more aptly within his encircling arm.

"First, then," said Beltane, when they had ridden awhile in silence, "she is a duchess, and very proud."

"Yet is she a woman, messire, and thou a man whose arms be very strong!"

"Of what avail strong arms, lady, 'gainst such as she?"

"Why, to carry her withal, messire."

"To — to carry her!" quoth Beltane in amaze.

"In very truth, messire. To lift her up and bear her away with thee —"

"Nay — nay, to — bear her away? O, 'twere thing impossible!"

"Is this duchess so heavy, messire?" sighed the nun, "is she a burden beyond even thy strength, sir knight?"

"Lady, she is the proud Helen, Duchess of Mortain!" quoth Beltane, frowning at the encompassing shadows. Now was the nun hushed awhile, and when at last she spake her voice was low and wondrous gentle.

"And is it indeed the wilful Helen that ye love, messire?"

"Even she, unto my sorrow."

"Thy sorrow? Why then, messire — forget her."

"Ah!" sighed Beltane, "would I might indeed, yet needs must I love her ever."

"Alack, and is it so forsooth," quoth the nun, sighing likewise. "Ah me, my poor, fond son, now doth thy reverend mother pity thee indeed, for thou'rt in direful case to be her lover, methinks."

Now did my Beltane frown the blacker by reason of bitter memory and the pain of his wound.

"Her lover, aye!" quoth he, bitterly, "and she hath a many lovers —"

"Lovers!" sighed the nun, "that hath she, the sad, sweet soul! Lovers! — O forsooth, she is sick of a very surfeit of lovers, — so hath she fled from them all!"

"Fled from them?" cried Beltane, his wound forgot, "fled from them — from Mortain? Nay, how mean you — how — fled?"

"She hath walked, see you, run — ridden — is riding — away from Mortain, from her lords, her counsellors, her varlets, her lovers and what not — in a word, messire, she is — gone!"

"Gone!" quoth Beltane, breathless and aghast, "gone — aye — but whither?"

"What matter for that so long as her grave counsellors be sufficiently vexed, and her lovers left a-sighing? O me, her counsellors! Bald-pates, see you, and grey-beards, who for their own ends would have her wed Duke Ivo — meek, unfortunate maid!"

"Know you then the Duchess, lady?"

"Aye, forsooth, and my heart doth grieve for her, poor, sweet wretch, for O, 'tis a sad thing to be a duchess with a multitude of suitors a-wooing in season and out, vaunting graces she hath not, and blind to the virtues she doth possess. Ah, messire, I give thee joy that, whatsoever ills may be thine, thou can ne'er be — a duchess!"

"And think you she will not wed with Ivo, lady — think you so in truth?"

"Never, while she is Helen."

"And — loveth — none of her lovers?"

"Why — indeed, messire — I think she doth —"

"Art sure? How know you this?"

"I was her bedfellow betimes, and oft within the night have heard her speak a name unto her pillow, as love-sick maids will."

Now once again was Beltane aware of the throb and sting of his wounded arm, yet 'twas not because of this he sighed so deep and oft.

"Spake she this name — often?" he questioned.

"Very oft, messire. Aye me, how chill the wind blows!"

"Some lord's name, belike?"

"Nay, 'twas no lord's name, messire. 'Tis very dark amid these trees!"

"Some knight, mayhap — or lowly squire?"

"Neither, messire. Heigho! methinks I now could sleep awhile." So she sighed deep yet happily, and nestled closer within his shielding arm.

But Beltane, my Innocent, rode stiff in the saddle, staring sad-eyed into the gloom, nor felt, nor heeded the yielding tenderness of the shapely young body he held, but plodded on through the dark, frowning blacker than the night. Now as he rode thus, little by little the pain of his wound grew less, a drowsiness crept upon him, and therewith, a growing faintness. Little by little his head drooped low and lower, and once the arm about the nun slipped its hold, whereat she sighed and stirred sleepily upon his breast. But on he rode, striving grimly against the growing faintness, his feet thrust far within the stirrups, his mailed hand tight clenched upon the reins. So, as dawn broke, he heard the pleasant sound of running water near by, and as the light grew, saw they were come to a grassy glade where ran a small brook — a goodly place, well-hidden and remote. So turned he thitherward, and lifting up heavy eyes, beheld the stars paling to the dawn, for the clouds were all passed away and the wind was gone long since. And, in a while, being come within the boskage of this green dell, feebly and as one a-dream, he checked the great horse that snuffed eagerly toward the murmuring brook, and as one a-dream saw that she who had slumbered on his breast was awake — fresh and sweet as the dawn.

"Lady," he stammered, "I — I fear — I can ride — no farther!"

And now, as one a-dream, he beheld her start and look at him with eyes wide and darkly blue — within whose depths was that which stirred within him a memory of other days — in so much he would have spoken, yet found the words unready and hard to come by.

"Lady,— thine eyes, methinks — are not — nun's eyes!"

But now behold of a sudden she cried out, soft and pitiful, for blood was upon him, upon his brow, upon his golden hair. And still as one a-dream he felt her slip from his failing clasp, felt her arms close about him, aiding him to earth.

"Thou'rt hurt!" she cried. "O, thou'rt wounded! And I never guessed!"

"'Tis but my arm — in sooth — and —"

But she hushed him with soft mother-cries and tender-spoke commands, and aiding him to the brook, laid him thereby to lave his hurt within the cool, sweet water; and, waking with the smart, Beltane sighed and turned to look up at her. Now did she, meeting his eyes, put up one white hand, setting back sombre hood and snowy wimple, and stooping tenderly above him, behold, in that moment down came the shining glory of her lustrous hair to fall about the glowing beauty of her face, touching his brow like a caress.

Then, at last, memory awoke within him, and lifting himself upon a feeble elbow, he stared upon her glowing loveliness with wide, glad eyes.

"Helen!" he sighed, "O — Helen!" And, so sighing, fell back, and lay there pale and wan within the dawn, but with a smile upon his pallid lips.

CHAPTER XX

HOW BELTANE PLIGHTED HIS TROTH IN THE GREEN

BELTANE yawned prodigiously, stretched mightily, and opening sleepy eyes looked about him. He lay 'neath shady willows within a leafy bower; before him a brook ran leaping to the sunshine and filling the warm, stilly air with its merry chatter and soft, laughing noises, while beyond the rippling water the bank sloped steeply upward to the green silence of the woods.

Now as Beltane lay thus 'twixt sleeping and waking, it seemed to him that in the night he had dreamed a wondrous dream, and fain he would have slept again. But now from an adjacent thicket a horse whinnied and Beltane, starting at the sound, felt his wound throb with sudden pain, and looking down, beheld his arm most aptly swathed in bandages of fair, soft linen. Now would he have sat up, but marvelled to find it so great a matter, and propping himself instead upon a weak elbow glanced about him expectantly. And lo, in that moment, one spake near by in voice rich and soft like the call of merle or mavis:

"Beltane," said the voice, "Beltane the Smith!"

With heart quick-beating, Beltane turned and beheld the Duchess Helen standing beside him, her glorious hair wrought into two long braids wherein flowers were cunningly entwined. Straightway he would have risen, but she forbade him with a gesture and, coming closer, sank beside him on her knees, and being there blushed and sighed, yet touched him not.

"Thou'rt hurt," said she, "so must we bide here awhile, thou to win thy strength again, and I to — minister unto thee."

Mutely awhile my Beltane gazed upon her shy, sweet loveliness, what time her bosom rose and fell tempestuous, and she bowed her head full low.

"Helen!" he whispered at last, "O, art thou indeed the Duchess Helen?"

"Not so," she murmured, "Helen was duchess whiles she was in Mortain, but I that speak with thee am a lonely maid — indeed a very lonely maid — who hath sighed for thee, and wept for thee, and for thee hath left her duchy of Mortain, Beltane."

"For me?" quoth Beltane, leaning near, "was it for me — ah, was it so in very sooth?"

"Beltane," said she, looking not toward him, "last night did'st thou bear a nun within thine arms, and, looking on her with love aflame within thine eyes, did yet vow to her you loved this duchess. Tell me, who am but a lonely maid, is this so?"

"Thou knowest I love her ever and always," he answered.

"And yet," quoth she, shaking her head and looking up with eyes of witchery, "thou did'st love this nun also? Though 'tis true thou did'st name her ' reverend mother'! O, wert very blind, Beltane! And yet thou did'st love her also, methinks?"

"Needs must I — ever and always!" he answered.

"Ah, Beltane, but I would have thee love this lonely maid dearest of all henceforth an it may be so, for that she is so very lonely and hath sought thee so long —"

"Sought me?" he murmured, gazing on her wide-eyed, "nay, how may this be, for with my kisses warm upon thy lips thou did'st bid me farewell long time since at Mortain, within the green."

"And thou," she sighed, "and thou did'st leave me, Beltane! O, would thou had kissed me once again and held me in thine arms, so might we have known less of sorrow. Indeed methinks 'twas cruel to leave me so, Beltane."

"Cruel!" says my Beltane, and thereafter fell silent

from sheer amaze the while she sighed again, and bowed her shapely head and plucked a daisy from the grass to turn it about and about in gentle fingers.

"So, Beltane," quoth she at last, "being young and cruel thou did'st leave the Duchess a lonely maid. Yet that same night did she, this tender maid, seek out thy lowly dwelling 'mid the green to yield herself joyfully unto thee thenceforth. But ah, Beltane! she found the place a ruin and thou wert gone, and O, methinks her heart came nigh to breaking. Then did she vow that no man might ever have her to his love — save only — thou. So, an thou love her not, Beltane, needs must she — die a maid!"

Now Beltane forgot his weakness and rose to his knees and lifted her bowed head until he might look deep within the yearning tenderness of her eyes. A while she met his look, then blushing, trembling, all in a moment she swayed toward him, hiding her face against him; and, trembling also, Beltane caught her close within his arms and held her to his heart.

"Dost thou love me so, indeed, my lady? Art thou mine own henceforth, Helen the Beautiful?"

"Ah, love," she murmured, "in all my days ne'er have I loved other man than thou, my Beltane. So now do I give myself to thee; in life and death, in joy and sorrow, thine will I be, beloved!"

Quoth Beltane:

"As thou art mine, so am I thine, henceforth and forever."

And thus, kneeling together within the wilderness did they plight their troth, low-voiced and tremulous, with arms that clasped and clung and eager lips that parted but to meet again.

"Beltane," she sighed, "ah, Beltane, hold me close! I've wearied for thee so long — so long; hold me close, beloved. See now, as thou dost hate the pomp and stir of cities, so, for thy sake have I fled hither to the wilderness, to live with thee amid these solitudes, to be thy love, thy stay and comfort. Here will we live for each other, and, hid within the green, forget the world and all things else — save only our great love!"

But now it chanced that, raising his head, Beltane beheld his long sword leaning against a tree hard by, and beholding it thus, he bethought him straightway of the Duke his father, of Pentavalon and of her grievous wrongs; and his clasping hands grew lax and fell away and, groaning, he bowed his head; whereat she started anxious-eyed, and questioned him, soft and piteous:

"Is it thy wound? I had forgot — ah, love, forgive me! See here a pillow for thy dear head —" But now again he caught her to him close and fierce, and kissed her oft; and holding her thus, spake:

"Thou knowest I do love thee, my Helen? Yet because I love thee greatly, love, alas, must wait awhile —"

"Wait?" she cried, "ah, no — am I not thine own?"

"'Tis so I would be worthy of thee, beloved," he sighed, "for know that I am pledged to rest not nor stay until my task be accomplished or I slain —"

"Slain! Thou?"

"O, Helen, 'tis a mighty task and desperate, and many perchance must die ere this my vow be accomplished —"

"Thy vow? But thou art a smith, my Beltane,— what hath humble smith to do with vows? Thou art my love — my Beltane the Smith!"

"Indeed," sighed Beltane, "smith was I aforetime, and therewithal content: yet am I also son of my father, and he —"

"Hark!" she whispered, white hand upon his lips, "some one comes—through the leaves yonder!" So saying she sprang lightly to her feet and stood above him straight and tall: and though she trembled, yet he saw her eyes were fearless and his dagger gleamed steady in her hands.

"Beltane, my love!" she said, "thou'rt so weak, yet am I strong to defend thee against them all."

But Beltane rose also and, swaying on unsteady feet,

kissed her once and so took his sword, marvelling to find it so heavy, and drew it from the scabbard. And ever upon the stilly air the rustle of leaves grew louder.

"Beltane!" she sighed, "they be very near! Hearken! Beltane — thine am I, in life, in death. An this be death — what matter, since we die together?"

But, leaning on his sword, Beltane watched her with eyes of love yet spake no word, hearkening to the growing stir amid the leaves, until, of a sudden, upon the bank above, the underbrush was parted and a man stood looking down at them; a tall man, whose linked mail glinted evilly and whose face was hid 'neath a vizored casque. Now of a sudden he put up his vizor and stepped toward them down the sloping bank.

Then the Duchess let fall the dagger and reached out her hands.

"Godric!" she sighed, "O Godric!"

CHAPTER XXI

OF THE TALE OF GODRIC THE HUNTSMAN

THUS came white-haired old Godric the huntsman, lusty despite his years, bright-eyed and garrulous with joy, to fall upon his knees before his lady and to kiss those outstretched hands.

"Godric!" she cried, "'tis my good Godric!" and laughed, though with lips a-tremble.

"O sweet mistress," quoth he, "now glory be to the kind Saint Martin that I do see thee again hale and well. These many days have I followed hard upon thy track, grieving for thee—"

"Yet here am I in sooth, my Godric, and joyful, see you!"

"Ah, dear my lady, thy wilfulness hath e'en now brought thee into dire perils and dangers. O rueful day!"

"Nay, Godric, my wilfulness hath brought me unto my heart's desire. O most joyful day!"

"Lady, I do tell thee here is an evil place for thee: they do say the devil is abroad and goeth up and down and to and fro begirt in mail, lady, doing such deeds as no man ever did. Pentavalon is rife with war and rumours of war, everywhere is whispered talk of war—death shall be busy within this evil Duchy ere long—aye, and even in Mortain, perchance—nay, hearken! Scarce was thy flight discovered when there came messengers hot-foot to thy guest, Duke Ivo, having word from Sir Gui of Allerdale that one hath arisen calling himself son of Beltane the Strong that once was Duke of Pentavalon, as ye know. And this is a mighty man, who hath, within the week, broke ope my lord Duke Ivo's dungeon of Belsaye, slain divers of my lord Duke's good and loyal subjects, and burnt down the great gallows of my lord Duke."

"Ah!" sighed the Duchess, her brows knit thoughtfully, "and what said Duke Ivo to this, Godric?"

"Smiled, lady, and begged instant speech with thee; and, when thou wert not to be found, then Duke Ivo smiled upon thy trembling counsellors. 'My lords,' said he, 'I ride south to hang certain rogues and fools. But, when I have seen them dead, I shall come hither again to woo and wed the Duchess Helen. See to it that ye find her, therefore, else will I myself seek her through the length and breadth of Mortain until I find her — aye, with lighted torches, if need be!'"

"And dare he threaten us?" cried the Duchess, white hands clenched.

"Aye, doth he, lady," nodded Godric, garrulous and grim. "Thereafter away he rode, he and all his company, and after them, I grieving and alone, to seek thee, dear my lady. And behold, I have found thee, the good Saint Martin be praised!"

"Verily thou hast found me, Godric!" sighed the Duchess, looking upon Beltane very wistfully.

"So now will I guide thee back to thine own fair duchy, gentle mistress, for I do tell thee here in Pentavalon shall be woeful days anon. Even as I came, with these two eyes did I behold the black ruin of Duke Ivo's goodly gallows — a woeful sight! And divers tales have I heard of this gallows-burner, how that he did, unaided and alone, seize and bear off upon his shoulders one Sir Pertolepe — called the 'Red'— Lord Warden of the Marches. So hath Duke Ivo put a price upon his head and decreed that he shall forthright be hunted down, and thereto hath sent runners far and near with his exact description, the which have I heard and can most faithfully repeat an you so desire?"

"Aye me!" sighed the Duchess, a little wearily.

"As thus, lady. Item: calleth himself Beltane, son of Beltane, Duke of Pentavalon that was: Item —"

The Tale of Godric the Huntsman

"Beltane!" said the Duchess, and started.

"Item: he is very tall and marvellous strong. Item: hath yellow hair —"

"Yellow hair!" said the Duchess, and turned to look upon Beltane.

"Item: goeth in chain-mail, and about his middle a broad belt of gold and silver. Item: beareth a great sword whereon is graven the legend — lady, dost thou attend? — Ha! Saint Martin aid us!" cried Godric, for now, following the Duchess's glance, he beheld Beltane leaning upon his long sword. Then, while Godric stared open-mouthed, the Duchess looked on Beltane, a new light in her eyes and with hands tight clasped, while Beltane looking upon her sighed amain.

"Helen!" he cried, "O Helen, 'tis true that I who am Beltane the Smith, am likewise son of Beltane, Duke of Pentavalon. Behold, the sword I bear is the sword of the Duke my father, nor must I lay it by until wrong is vanquished and oppression driven hence. Thus, see you, I may not stay to love, within my life it must not be — yet-a-while," and speaking, Beltane groaned and bowed his head. So came she to him and looked on him with eyes of yearning, yet touched him not.

"Dear my lord," said she, tender-voiced, "thou should'st make a noble duke, methinks: and yet alas! needs must I love my gentle Beltane the Smith. And I did love him so! Thou art a mighty man-at-arms, my lord, and terrible in war, meseemeth, O — methinks thou wilt make a goodly duke indeed!"

"Mayhap," he answered heavily, "mayhap, an God spare me long enough. But now must I leave thee —"

"Aye, but wherefore?"

"Thou hast heard — I am a hunted man with a price upon my head, by my side goeth death —"

"So will I go also," she murmured, "ever and always beside thee."

"Thou? Ah, not so, beloved. I must tread me this path alone. As for thee — haste, haste and get thee to

Mortain and safety, and there wait for me — pray for me, O my love!"

"Beltane — Beltane," she sighed, "dost love me indeed — and yet would send me from thee?"

"Aye," he groaned, "needs must it be so."

"Beltane," she murmured, "Beltane, thou shalt be Duke within the week, despite Black Ivo."

"Duke — I? Of Pentavalon?"

"Of Mortain!" she whispered, "an thou wilt wed me, my lord."

"Nay," stammered Beltane, "nay, outcast am I, my friends very few — to wed thee thus, therefore, were shame —"

"To wed me thus," said she, "should be my joy, and thy joy, and Pentavalon's salvation, mayhap. O, see you not, Beltane? Thou should'st be henceforth my lord, my knight-at-arms to lead my powers 'gainst Duke Ivo, teaching Mortain to cringe no more to a usurper — to free Pentavalon from her sorrows — ah, see you not, Beltane?"

"Helen!" he murmured, "O Helen, poor am I — a beggar —"

"Beltane," she whispered, "an thou wed this lonely maid within the forest, then will I be beggar with thee; but, an thou take to wife the Duchess, then shalt thou be my Duke, lord of me and of Mortain, with her ten thousand lances in thy train."

"Thou would'st give me so much," he sighed at last, "so much, my Helen?"

"Nay," said she, with red lips curved and tender, "for this wide world to me is naught without thee, Beltane. And I do need thy mighty arm — to shelter me, Beltane, since Ivo hath defied me, threatening Mortain with fire and sword. So when he cometh, instead of a woman he shall find a man to withstand him, whose sword is swift and strong to smite and who doeth such deeds as no man ever did; so shalt thou be my love, my lord, my champion. Wilt not refuse me the shelter of thy strength, Beltane?"

The Tale of Godric the Huntsman 175

Now of a sudden Beltane lifted his head and seized her in his arms and held her close.

Quoth he:

"So be it, my Helen. To wife will I take thee so soon as may be, to hold thee ever in love and reverence, to serve thee ever, to live for thee and for thee to die an needs be."

But now strode Godric forward, with hands outstretched in eager protest.

"Lady," he cried, "O dear lady bethink thee, now, bethink thee, thy choice is a perilous choice —"

"Yet is it my choice, Godric."

"But, O, dear my mistress —"

"O my faithful Godric, look now upon lord Beltane, my well-beloved who shall be Duke of Mortain ere the moon change. Salute thy lord, Godric!"

So, perforce, came old Godric to fall upon his knee before Beltane, to take his hand and swear the oath of fealty.

"Lord Beltane," said he, "son art thou of a mighty Duke; God send Mortain find in thee such another!"

"Amen!" said Beltane.

Thereafter Godric rose and pointed up to the zenith.

"Behold, my lady," said he, "it groweth to noon and there is danger hereabouts — more danger e'en than I had dreamed. Let us therefore haste over into Mortain — to thy Manor of Blaen."

"But Godric, see you not my lord is faint of his wound, and Blaen is far, methinks."

"Not so, lady, 'tis scarce six hours' journey to the north, nay, I do know of lonely bridle-paths that shall bring us sooner."

"To Blaen?" mused the Duchess. "Winfrida is there — and yet — and yet — aye, let us to Blaen, there will I nurse thee to thy strength again, my Beltane, and there shalt thou — wed with me — an it be so thy pleasure in sooth, my lord."

So, in a while, they set off through the forest, first

Godric to guide them, then Beltane astride the great warhorse with the Duchess before him, she very anxious for his wound, yet speaking oft of the future with flushing cheek and eyes a-dream.

Thus, as the sun declined, they came forth of the forestlands and beheld that broad sweep of hill and dale that was Mortain.

"O loved Mortain!" she sighed, "O dear Mortain! 'Tis here there lived a smith, my Beltane, who sang of and loved but birds and trees and flowers. 'Tis here there lived a Duchess, proud and most disdainful, who yearned for love yet knew naught of it until — upon a day, these twain looked within each other's eyes — O day most blissful! Ah, sweet Mortain!"

By pleasant ways they went, past smiling fields and sleepy villages bowered 'mid the green. They rode ever by sequestered paths, skirting shady wood and coppice where birds sang soft a drowsy lullaby, wooing the world to forgetfulness and rest; fording prattling brook and whispering stream whose placid waters flamed to the glory of sunset. And thus they came at last to Blaen, a cloistered hamlet beyond which rose the grey walls of the ancient manor itself.

Now as they drew near, being yet sheltered 'mid the green, old Godric halted in his stride and pointed to the highway that ran in the vale below.

"Lady," quoth he, "mine eyes be old, and yet methinks I should know yon horseman that rideth unhelmed so close beside the lady Winfrida — that breadth of shoulder! that length of limb! Lady, how think ye?"

"'Tis Duke Ivo!" she whispered.

"Aye," nodded Godric, "armed, see you, yet with but two esquires —"

"And with Winfrida!" said the Duchess, frowning. "Can it indeed be as I have thought, betimes? And Blaen is a very solitary place!"

"See!" whispered Godric, "the Duke leaveth her. Behold him kiss her hand! Ha, he summoneth his esquires.

The Tale of Godric the Huntsman 177

Hey now, see how they ride — sharp spur and loose bridle, 'tis ever Ivo's way!"

Now when the Duke and his esquires were vanished in the dusk and the sound of their galloping died away, the Duchess sprang lightly to the sward and bidding them wait until she summoned them, hasted on before.

Thus, in a while, as Winfrida the Fair paced slowly along upon her ambling palfrey, her blue eyes a-dream, she was suddenly aware of a rustling near by and, glancing swiftly up, beheld the Duchess Helen standing before her, tall and proud, her black brows wrinkled faintly, her eyes stern and challenging.

"Lady — dear my lady!" stammered Winfrida — "is it thou indeed —"

"Since when," quoth the Duchess, soft-voiced yet menacing, "since when doth Winfrida hold sly meeting with one that is enemy to me and to Mortain?"

"Enemy? — nay, whom mean you — indeed I — O Helen, in sooth 'twas but by chance —"

"Is this treason, my lady Winfrida, or only foolish amourette?"

"Sweet lady —'twas but chance — an you mean Duke Ivo — he came — I saw —"

"My lady Winfrida, I pray you go before, we will speak of this anon. Come, Godric!" she called.

Then the lady Winfrida, her beauteous head a-droop, rode on before, sighing deep and oft yet nothing speaking, with the Duchess proud and stern beside her while Beltane and Godric followed after.

And so it was they came to the Manor of Blaen.

CHAPTER XXII

CONCERNING THE WILES OF WINFRIDA THE FAIR

Now in these days did my Beltane know more of joy and come more nigh to happiness than ever in his life before. All day, from morn till eve, the Duchess was beside him; each hour her changing moods won him to deeper love, each day her glowing beauty enthralled him the more, so that as his strength grew so grew his love for her.

Oft would they sit together in her garden amid the flowers, and she, busied with her broidering needle, would question him of his doings, and betimes her breast would heave and her dexterous hand tremble and falter to hear of dangers past; or, talking of the future, her gracious head would droop with cheeks that flushed most maidenly, until Beltane, kneeling to her loveliness, would clasp her in his arms, while she, soft-voiced, would bid him beware her needle.

To him all tender sweetness, yet to all others within the manor was she the Duchess, proud and stately; moreover, when she met the lady Winfrida in hall or bower, her slender brows would wrinkle faintly and her voice sound cold and distant, whereat the fair Winfrida would bow her meek head, and sighing, wring her shapely fingers.

Now it befell upon a drowsy afternoon, that, waking from slumber within the garden, Beltane found himself alone. So he arose and walked amid the flowers thinking of many things, but of the Duchess Helen most of all. As he wandered slowly thus, his head bent and eyes a-dream, he came unto a certain shady arbour where fragrant herb and climbing blooms wrought a tender twilight apt to blissful musing. Now standing within this perfumed shade he heard of a sudden a light step behind him, and turning swift about, his eager arms closed upon a soft and yielding form, and behold — it was Winfrida! Then Beltane would have loosed his clasp, but her white hands reached up and clung upon his broad shoulders, yet when she spake her voice was low and humble.

"My lord Beltane," she sighed, "happy art thou to have won the love of our noble lady — aye, happy art thou! But as for me, alas! messire, meseemeth her heart is turned 'gainst me these days; I, who was her loved companion and childish play-fellow! So now am I very desolate, wherefore I pray you speak with her on my behalf and win her to forgiveness. Ah, messire, when thou shalt be Duke indeed, think kindly on the poor Winfrida, for as I most truly love the Duchess —" here needs must she sigh amain and turn aside her shapely head, and thereafter spake, clear and loud: "so will I love thee also!" Then, while he yet stood abashed by the touch of her and the look in her eyes, she caught his hand to her lips and fled away out of the arbour.

But now as he stood staring after her beyond all thought amazed, a white hand parted the leafy screen and the Duchess stood before him. And behold! her slender brows were wrinkled faintly, and when she spake her voice was cold and distant.

"Saw you the lady Winfrida, my lord?"

"Why truly," stammered Beltane, "truly I — she was here but now —"

"Here, my lord? Alone?"

"She besought me speak thee for her forgiveness; to remind thee of her love aforetime, to —"

"Would'st plead for her, in sooth?"

"I would but have thee do her justice, Helen —"

"Think you I am so unjust, my lord?"

"Not so indeed. But she is so young — so fair —"

"Aye, she is very fair, my lord — there be — others think the same."

"Helen?" said he, "O Helen!"

"And thou dost plead for her — and to me, my lord! And with her kisses yet burning thee!"

"She did but kiss my hand —"

"Thy hand, my lord! O aye, thy hand forsooth!"

"Aye, my hand, lady, and therewith named me 'Duke'!" quoth Beltane, beginning to frown. Whereat needs must the Duchess laugh, very soft and sweet yet with eyes aglow beneath her lashes.

"'Duke,' messire? She names thee so betimes, meseemeth. Thou art not Duke yet, nor can'st thou ever be but of my favour!"

"And the time flieth apace," sighed Beltane, "and I have mighty things to do. O, methinks I have tarried here overlong!"

"Ah — and would'st be going, messire?"

"'Tis so methinks my duty."

"Go you alone, messire — or goeth she with thee?"

"Ah, God! How dare ye so think?" cried Beltane, in anger so fierce and sudden that though she fronted him yet smiling, she drew back a pace. Whereat his anger fell from him and he reached out his hands.

"Helen!" said he, "O my Helen, what madness is this? Thou art she I love — doth not thine heart tell thee so?" and fain would he have caught her to him.

"Ah — touch me not!" she cried, and steel flickered in her hand.

"This — to me?" quoth he, and laughed short and bitter, and catching her wrist, shook the dagger from her grasp and set his foot upon it.

"And hath it come to this — 'twixt thee and me?" he sighed.

"O," she panted, "I have loved thee nor shamed to show thee my love. Yet because my love is so great, so, methinks, an need be I might hate thee more than any man!" Then, quick-breathing, flushed and trembling, she turned and sped away, leaving Beltane heavy-hearted, and with the dagger gleaming beneath his foot.

CHAPTER XXIII

OF THE HUMILITY OF HELEN THE PROUD

BELTANE, leaning forth of his lattice, stared upon the moon with doleful eyes, heavy with sense of wrong and big with self-pity.

"I have dreamed a wondrous fair dream," said he within himself, "but all dreams must end, so is my dream vanished quite and I awake, and being awake, now will I arise and go upon my duty!" Then turned he to his bed that stood beside the window and forthwith began to arm himself; but with every lace he drew, with every strap he buckled, he sighed amain and his self-pity waxed the mightier. He bethought him of his father's sayings anent the love of women, and in his mind condemned them all as fickle and light-minded. And in a while, being armed from head to foot, in glistening coif and hauberk and with sword girt about his middle, he came back to the lattice and leaned him there to stare again upon the moon, to wait until the manor should be wrapped in sleep and to grieve for himself with every breath he drew.

Being thus so profoundly occupied and, moreover, his head being thrust without the window, he heard nought of the tap upon his chamber door nor of the whispered sound of his name. Thus he started to feel a touch upon his arm, and turning, beheld the Duchess.

She wore a simple robe that fell about her body's round loveliness in sweetly revealing folds; her hair, all unbraided, was caught up 'neath a jewelled fillet in careless fashion, but — O surely, surely, never had she looked so fair, so sweet and tender, so soft and desirable as now, the tear-drops yet agleam upon her drooping lashes and her bosom yet heaving with recent grief.

"And — thou art armed, my lord?"

"I ride for Thrasfordham-within-Bourne this night, my lady."

"But I am come to thee — humbly — craving thy forgiveness, Beltane."

"Nought have I to forgive thee, lady — save that thou art woman!"

"Thou would'st not have me — a man, messire?"

"'Twould be less hard to leave thee."

"Thou art — leaving me then, Beltane?"

"Yea, indeed, my lady. The woes of Pentavalon call to me with a thousand tongues: I must away — pray God I have not tarried too long!"

"But art yet weak of thy wound, Beltane. I pray thee tarry — a little longer. Ah, my lord, let not two lives go empty because of the arts of a false friend, for well do I know that Winfrida, seeing me coming to thee in the garden, kissed thee of set purpose, that, beholding, I might grieve."

"Is this indeed so, my lady?"

"She did confess it but now."

"Said she so indeed?"

"Aye, my lord, after I had — pulled her hair — a little. But O, my Beltane, even when I thought thee base, I loved thee! Ah, go not from me, stay but until tomorrow, and then shalt thou wed me for thine own! Leave me not, Beltane, for indeed — I cannot live — without thee!"

So saying, she sank down upon his couch, hiding her face in the pillow.

Now came Beltane and leaned above her.

"Helen!" he whispered; and falling upon his knees, he set his arms about her. Then lifted she her tearful face and looked upon him in the moonlight; and lying thus, of a sudden reached out white arms to him: and in her eyes was love, and on her quivering lips and in all the yearning beauty of her, love called to him.

Close, close he caught her in his embrace, kissing her

hard and fierce, and her long hair came down to veil them in its glory. Then, trembling, he lifted her in his arms and bore her forth of his chamber out into the hall beyond, where lights flickered against arras-hung wall. There, falling upon his knees before her, he hid his face within the folds of her habit.

"O Helen!" he groaned, "thou art — so beautiful — so beautiful that I grow afraid of thee! Wed me this night or in mercy let me begone!"

And now did the Duchess look down upon him with eyes of wonder changing to a great and tender joy, and stooping, put back his mail coif with reverent hand and laid her cheek upon that bowed and golden head.

"Beltane," she whispered, "O Beltane of mine, now do I know thee indeed for a true man and noble knight! Such love as thine honoureth us both, so beloved, this night — within the hour, shalt thou wed with me, and I joy to hear thee call me — Wife!"

Therewith she turned and left him there upon his knees.

CHAPTER XXIV

OF WHAT BEFELL AT BLAEN

LATE though the hour, full soon the manor was astir; lights glimmered in the great hall where were gathered all the household of the Duchess, her ladies, her tire-women, the porters and serving men, even to the scullions — all were there, staring in wonderment upon the Duchess, who stood before them upon the dais in a rich habit of blue and silver and with her golden fillet on her brow.

"Good friends," said she, looking round upon them happy-eyed, "hither have I summoned ye, for that this night, here before you all, 'tis my intent to wed this noble knight Beltane, son of Beltane Duke of Pentavalon aforetime, who shall henceforth be lord of me and of Mortain."

Now did Winfrida the Fair start and therewith clench pink palms and look quick-eyed upon my Beltane, noting in turn his golden hair, his belt of silver and the great sword he bore: and, biting her red lip, she stooped her beauteous head, frowning as one in sudden perplexity.

"So now," spake on the Duchess, "let us to the chapel where good Father Angelo shall give us heaven's blessing upon this our union."

"Lady," said Godric, "Friar Angelo was summoned to the village this night, nor is he come again yet."

"Then go fetch him," sighed the Duchess, "and O, Godric, hasten!"

Thereafter turned she to the assemblage, gentle-eyed.

"Friends," said she, "since I am greatly happy this night, so would I have ye happy likewise. Therefore I decree that such as are serfs among ye shall go free henceforth, and to such as are free will I give grants of land that ye may come to bless this night and remember it ever."

But now, even as they fell on their knees, 'mid cries of gratitude and joyful acclaim, she, smiling and gracious, passed out of the hall: yet, as she went, beckoned the lady Winfrida to follow.

Being come into her chamber, all three, the Duchess sank down beside the open lattice and looked out upon the garden all bathed in the tender radiance of the moon. Anon she sighed and spake:

"My lady Winfrida, on this my wedding night a new life dawns for Mortain and for me, wherein old harms shall be forgiven and forgot, so come — kiss me, Winfrida."

Then swiftly came the beauteous Winfrida to kneel at her lady's feet, to clasp her lady's slender hand, to kiss it oft and bathe it in her tears.

"O sweet my lady, am I indeed forgiven?"

"Aye, most truly."

"Am I again thy loved companion and thy friend?"

"So shall it be, Winfrida."

"Then, O dear Helen, as sign all is forgot and we lovers again, let us pledge each other, here and now — to thy future happiness and glory."

"Aye, be it so," sighed the Duchess, "bring wine, for I am athirst."

Then turned she to the lattice again and Winfrida went lightly on her errand. Now, yet gazing upon the moon, the Duchess reached out and drew Beltane beside her.

"Dear my love," she whispered, "in but a little hour I shall be thine: art happy in the thought? Nay," she sighed, white hands against his mailed breast, "beloved, wait — kiss me not again until the hour be passed. Lean here thy golden head and look with me upon the splendour of the night. See the pale moon, how placid and serene, how fair and stately she doth ride —"

"So may thy life be in coming years!" said Beltane.

"And wilt love me ever, Beltane, no matter what betide?"

"Ever and always, so long as thou art Helen. Nay, why dost tremble?"

"O my lord — see yonder — that cloud, how black — see how it doth furtive creep upon the gentle moon —"

"'Tis a long way hence, my Helen!"

"Yet will it come. Ah, think you 'tis a portent? O would the gentle Angelo were here — and yet, an he were come — methinks I might wish him hence — for that, loving thee so, yet am I a maid, and foolish — ah, who is here — not Angelo so soon? What, 'tis thou, Winfrida? Welcome — bring hither the goblet."

So came Winfrida, and falling on her knee gave the goblet into her lady's hand, who, rising, turned to Beltane looking on him soft-eyed across the brimming chalice.

"Lord and husband," she breathed —" now do I drink to thy glory in arms, to our future, and to our abiding love!" So the Duchess raised the goblet to her lips. But lo! even as she drank, the thick, black cloud began to engulf the moon, quenching her radiant light in its murky gloom. So the Duchess drank, and handed the goblet to Beltane.

"To thee, my Helen, whom only shall I love until death and beyond!"

Then Beltane drank also, and gave the cup to Winfrida: but, even as he did so, the Duchess uttered a cry and pointed with hand a-tremble:

"O Beltane, the moon — the moon that was so bright and glorious —'tis gone, the cloud hath blotted it out! Ah, Beltane, what doth this portend? Why do I tremble thus because the moon is gone?"

"Nay, my beloved," quoth Beltane, kissing those slender fingers that trembled upon his lip and were so cold — so deadly cold, "dear Helen, it will shine forth again bright and radiant as ever."

"Yet why is my heart so cold, Beltane, and wherefore do I tremble?"

"The night grows chill, mayhap."

"Nay, this cold is from within. O, I would the moon would shine!"

"Nay, let us speak of our future, my Helen —"

"The future?" she sighed, "what doth it hold? Strife and bitter war for thee and a weary waiting for me, and should'st thou be slain — Ah, Beltane, forgive these fears and vain imaginings. Indeed, 'tis most unlike me to fear and tremble thus. I was ever accounted brave until now — is't love, think you, doth make me coward? 'Tis not death I fear — save for thy dear sake. Death? Nay, what have we to do with such, thou and I — this is our wedding night, and yet — I feel as if this night — I were leading thee — to thy — death —. O, am I mad, forsooth? Hold me close, beloved, comfort me, Beltane, I — I am afraid." Then Beltane lifted her in his arms and brought her to the hearth, and, setting her in the fire-glow, kneeled there, seeking to comfort her.

And now he saw her very pale, sighing deep and oft and with eyes dilated and heavy.

"Beltane," said she slowly, "I grow a-weary, 'tis — the fire, methinks." And smiling faintly she closed her eyes, yet sighed and gazed upon him as one new waked. "Did I sleep?" she questioned drowsily, "Beltane," she sighed, speaking low and thick —" I charge thee, whatsoe'er the future doth bring — yet love me alway — or I, methinks — shall — die!"

Awhile she lay against him breathing deep and slow, then started of a sudden, looking upon him vague-eyed.

"Beltane," she murmured, "art there, beloved? 'Tis dark, and my eyes — heavy. Methinks I — must sleep awhile. Take me — to my women. I must sleep — yet will I come to thee soon — soon, beloved." So Beltane brought her to the door, but as he came thither the broidered curtain was lifted and he beheld Winfrida, who ran to her mistress, kissing her oft and sighing over her.

"Winfrida," sighed the Duchess, slumberous of voice, "I grow a-weary — I must sleep awhile —"

"Aye, thou'rt overwrought, dear lady. Come, rest you until the holy Angelo be come, so shalt be thine own sweet self anon."

And when the Duchess was gone, Beltane sat and stared upon the fire and felt himself vaguely troubled, yet even so, as he watched the leaping flame, his head nodded and he slept, yet sleeping, dreamed he heard the Duchess calling him, and opening his eyes, found the fair Winfrida beside him:

"My lord Beltane," said she softly, "thy Duchess biddeth thee wait her in the chapel — follow me, messire!" Now being yet heavy with sleep, Beltane arose and followed her through an opening in the arras near by, and down a narrow stair, stumbling often as he went and walking as one in a dream. So by devious ways Winfrida brought him into a little chapel, where, upon the altar, was a crucifix with candles dim-burning in the gloom.

"Wait here, my lord," said Winfrida, "so will I go prepare my lady, Friar Angelo doth stay to do his holy office." So speaking, Winfrida turned and was gone. Then Beltane came unto the altar and, kneeling there, leaned his heavy head upon the fair white altar cloth, and kneeling thus, fell asleep.— The altar beneath him seemed of a sudden riven and split asunder and, while he gazed, behold the fair white altar cloth grew fouled and stained with blood — new blood, that splashed down red upon the white even as he watched. Then did Beltane seek to rise up from his knees, but a heavy weight bore him ever down, and hands huge and hairy gripped him fierce and strong. But beholding these merciless hands, a sudden mighty rage came upon Beltane, and struggling up, he stood upon his feet and drew sword; but the fierce hands had crept up to his naked throat, cutting off his breath, the sword was dashed from his loosening grasp, the weight about him grew too much for his strength, it bore him down and down into a pitchy gloom where all was very still. A wind, sweet and cool, breathed upon his cheek, grass was below and trees above him, shadowy trees beyond which a pallid moon rose high, very placid and serene. Now as Beltane stared heavenward the moon was blotted out, a huge and hairy face looked down in his, and hairy hands lifted him with mighty strength. Then Beltane thought to see the Duchess Helen standing by in her gown of blue and silver —

"Helen!" he whispered.

But she paid no heed, busied in fastening about her the nun's long cloak that veiled her down from head to foot. So the mighty arms that held Beltane bore him to a horse near by and across this horse he was flung; thereafter the monster mounted also, and they moved off amid the trees. Thus was Beltane borne from Blaen upon his wedding night — dazed, bleeding and helpless in his bonds. Yet even so, ever as they went he watched her who rode near by, now in moonlight, now in shadow, so youthful and shapely, but with hood drawn low as she had worn it when he bore her through the forest in his arms.

And ever as they went he watched the pale gleam of her hand upon the bridle, or her little foot in its embroidered shoe, or the fold of her blue gown with its silver needlework. And ever the trouble in his dazed brain grew the deeper; once, as they crossed a broad glade she rode up close beside him, and beneath her hood he saw a strand of her glorious hair, bright under the moon.

Then did he writhe and struggle in his bonds.

"Helen!" he cried, "O Helen!" . . .

But a great hand, coarse and hairy, came upon his mouth, stopping the cry and choking him to silence.

So they bore my Beltane southwards through the misty woods, on and ever on, till with the dawn they were come to a castle great and very strong, where battlement and tower frowned upon the paling stars.

But with the dawn, 'mid the gloom of the little chapel of Blaen, came one who stood, haggard and pallid as the dawn, to stare wild-eyed upon a great sword and upon a torn and blood-stained altar-cloth; and so gazing, she shrank away back and back, crouching down amid the gloom. When at last the sun arose, it glittered on a long broad blade, across which, upon the rough pavement, lay one very silent and very still, amid the tumbled glory of her hair.

CHAPTER XXV

HOW BELTANE BECAME CAPTIVE TO SIR PERTOLEPE

A HORN, lustily winded, waked my Beltane from his swoon, waked him to a glimmering world vague and unreal, where lights flared and voices sounded, hoarse and faint, in question and answer. Thereafter, down rattled drawbridge and up creaked portcullis, and so, riding 'neath a deep and gloomy arch they came out into a courtyard, where were many vague forms that flitted to and fro — and many more lights that glinted on steel bascinet and hauberk of mail.

Now as Beltane lay helpless in his bonds he felt a hand among his hair, a strong hand that lifted his heavy, drooping head and turned up his face to the glare of the torches.

"How now, Fool!" cried a gruff voice, "here's not thy meat — ha, what would ye — what would ye, Fool?"

"Look upon another fool, for fool, forsooth, is he methinks that cometh so into Garthlaxton Keep." Now hereupon, opening unwilling eyes, Beltane looked up into the face of Beda the Jester that bent above him with a ring of steel-begirt faces beyond.

"Aha!" quoth the jester, clapping Beltane's pale and bloody cheek, "here is a fool indeed — forsooth, a very foolish fool, hither come through folly, for being great of body and small of wit, look you, his folly hath hither brought him in shape of a hairy, ape-like fool —"

"Ape!" growled a voice, and the jester was seized in a hairy hand and shaken till his bells jingled; and now Beltane beheld his captor, a dwarf-like, gnarled and crooked creature, yet huge of head and with the mighty arms and shoulders of a giant; a fierce, hairy monster, whose hideousness was set off by the richness of his vesture. "Ape, quotha!" he growled. "Dare ye name Ulf the Strong ape, forsooth? Ha! so will I shake the flesh from thy bones!" But now, she who sat her horse near by so proud and stately, reached forth a white hand, touching Ulf the Strong upon the arm, and lo! in that moment, he loosed the breathless jester and spake with bowed head: "Dear my lady, I forgot!" Then turning to the grinning soldiery he scowled upon them. "Dogs," quoth he, "go to your master and say Helen, Duchess of Mortain bringeth a wedding gift to Ivo, called the Black. Behold here he that slew twenty within the green, that burned down Black Ivo's goodly gallows, that broke the dungeons of Belsaye and bore Red Pertolepe into the green, behold him ye seek — Beltane, son of Beltane the Strong, heretofore Duke of Pentavalon!"

Now hereupon arose a mighty turmoil and excitement, all men striving to behold Beltane, to touch him and look upon his drooping face, but Ulf's mighty hand held them back, one and all. And presently came hasting divers esquires and knights, who, beholding Beltane, his costly mail, his silver belt and golden hair, seized upon him right joyfully and bore him into an inner ward, and threw him down upon the floor, marvelling and rejoicing over him, while Beltane lay there fast bound and helpless, staring up with frowning brow as one that strives to think, yet cannot. Now suddenly the noise about him ceased, all voices were hushed, and he was aware of one who stood near by, a doleful figure swathed in bandages, who leaned upon the arm of a tall esquire. And looking upon this figure, he saw it was Sir Pertolepe the Red.

"Ha, by the eyes of God!" quoth Sir Pertolepe, "'tis he himself — O sweet sight — see, I grow better already! Who brought him, say you?"

"Lord, 'twas the Duchess Helen!" said one.

"Helen!" cried Sir Pertolepe, "Helen of Mortain?"

"Aye, lord, as her wedding gift to our lord Duke Ivo." Now hereupon Beltane's staring eyes closed, the great muscles of his body twitched and writhed and stood out gnarled and rigid awhile, then he sighed, a slow, hissing breath, and lay there staring up wide-eyed at the vaulted roof again.

"Came she herself, Raoul?"

"Aye, good my lord."

"Why, then — admit her. God's love, messires, would ye keep the glorious Helen without?"

"Lord, she is gone — she and her ape-man both."

"Gone? Gone, forsooth? 'Tis strange, and yet 'tis like the wilful Helen. Yet hath she left her wedding gift in my keeping. O a rare gift, a worthy gift and most acceptable. Strip me off his armour — yet no, as he came, so shall he bide until my lord Duke be come. Bring now shackles, strong and heavy, bring fetters and rivets, so will I sit here and see him trussed."

And presently came two armourers with hammers and rivets, and shackled Beltane with heavy chains, the while Sir Pertolepe, sitting near, laughed and spake him right jovially.

But Beltane suffered it all, uttering no word and staring ever straight before him with wide, vague eyes, knitting his brow ever and anon in troubled amaze like a child that suffers unjustly; wherefore Sir Pertolepe, fondling his big chin, frowned.

"Ha!" quoth he, "let our Duke that hath no duchy be lodged secure — to the dungeons, aye, he shall sleep with rats until my lord Duke Ivo come to see him die — yet stay! The dungeons be apt to sap a man's strength and spirit, and to a weak man death cometh over soon and easy. Let him lie soft, feed full and sleep sound — let him have air and light, so shall he wax fat and lusty against my lord Duke's coming. See to it, Tristan!"

So they led Beltane away jangling in his fetters, across divers courtyards and up a narrow, winding stair and thrust him within a chamber where was a bed and above it a loop-hole that looked out across a stretch of rolling, wooded country.. Now being come to the bed, Beltane sank down thereon, and setting elbow to knee, rested his heavy head upon his hand as one that fain would think.

"Helen!" he whispered, and so whispering, his strong fingers writhed and clenched themselves within his yellow hair. And thus sat he all that day, bowed forward upon his hand, his fingers tight-clenched within his hair, staring ever at the square flagstone beneath his foot, heedless alike of the coming and going of his gaoler or of the food set out upon the bench hard by. Day grew to evening and evening to night, yet still he sat there, mighty shoulders bowed forward, iron fingers clenched within his hair, like one that is dead; in so much that his gaoler, setting down food beside the other untasted dishes, looked upon him in amaze and touched him.

"Oho!" said he, "wake up. Here be food, look ye, and, by Saint Crispin, rich and dainty. And drink — good wine, wake and eat!"

Then Beltane's clutching fingers relaxed and he raised his head, blinking in the rays of the lanthorn; and looking upon his rumpled hair, the gaoler stared and peered more close.

Quoth he:

"Methought thou wert a golden man, yet art silver also, meseemeth."

"Fellow," said Beltane harsh-voiced and slow, "Troy town was burned, and here was great pity, methinks, for 'twas a fair city. Yet to weep o'er it these days were a fond madness. Come, let us eat!"

But as Beltane uprose in his jangling fetters, the gaoler, beholding his face, backed to the door, and slamming it shut, barred and fast bolted it, yet cast full many a glance behind as he hasted down the winding stair.

Then Beltane ate and drank, and thereafter threw himself upon his narrow couch, but his fetters jangled often in the dark. Thus as he lay, staring upwards into the gloom, he was aware of the opening of the iron-clamped door, and beheld his gaoler bearing a lanthorn and behind him Sir Pertolepe leaning on the arm of his favourite esquire, who, coming near, looked upon Beltane nodding right jovially.

"Messire Beltane," quoth he, "thou did'st dare set up thyself against Ivo our lord the Duke — O fool! 'Tis said thou hast sworn to drive him forth of Pentavalon — O mad fool! 'Tis said thou did'st woo the Duchess Helen, seeking her to wife, O fool of fools! Did'st think, presumptuous rogue, that she — the glorious Helen — that Helen the Beautiful, whom all men desire, would stoop to thee, an outcast — wolf's head and outlaw that thou art? Did'st dare think so, forsooth? To-morrow, belike, my lord Duke shall come, and mayhap shall bring the Duchess Helen in his train — to look upon the manner of thy dying —"

Now hereupon up started Beltane that his fetters clashed, and laughed so sudden, so fierce and harsh, that Raoul the esquire clapped hand to dagger and even Red Pertolepe started.

"Sweet lord," quoth Beltane, "noble messire Pertolepe, of thy boundless mercy — of thy tender ruth grant unto me this boon. When ye shall have done me to death — cut off this head of mine and send it to Helen — to Helen the beautiful, the wilful — in memory of what befell at Blaen."

CHAPTER XXVI

OF THE HORRORS OF GARTHLAXTON KEEP, AND HOW A DEVIL ENTERED INTO BELTANE

Six days came and went, and during all this time Beltane spake word to no man. Every evening came Sir Pertolepe leaning on the arm of Raoul the esquire, to view his prisoner with greedy eyes and ply him with jovial talk whiles Beltane would lie frowning up at the mighty roof-beams, or sit, elbows on knee, his fingers clenched upon that lock of hair that gleamed so strangely white amid the yellow.

Now upon the seventh evening as he sat thus, came Sir Pertolepe according to his wont, but to-night he leaned upon the shoulder of Beda the Jester, whose motley flared 'gainst rugged wall and dingy flagstone and whose bells rang loud and merry by contrast with the gloom.

Quoth Sir Pertolepe, seated upon the bench and smiling upon Beltane's grim figure:

"He groweth fat to the killing, seest thou, my Beda, a young man and hearty, very hale and strong — and therefore meet for death. So strong a man should be long time a-dying — an death be coaxed and managed well. And Tristan is more cunning and hath more love for his craft than ever had Black Roger. With care, Beda — I say with care, messire Beltane should die from dawn to sundown."

"Alack!" sighed the jester, "death shall take him over soon, as thou dost say — and there's the pity on't!"

"Soon, Fool — soon? Now out upon thee for a fool ingrain —"

"Forsooth, sweet lord, fool am I — mark these bells! Yet thou art a greater!"

"How, sirrah?"

"In that thou art a greater man, fair, sweet lord; greater in might, greater in body, and greater in folly."

"Ha, would'st mock me, knave?"

"For perceive me, fair and gentle lord, as this base body of ours being altogether thing material is also thing corruptible, so is it also a thing finite, and as it is a thing finite so are its sensations, be they of pleasure or pain, finite also — therefore soon must end. Now upon the other hand —"

"How now? What babbling folly is here?"

"As I say, most potent lord, upon the other hand — as the mind, being altogether thing transcendental, is also thing incorruptible, so is it also a thing infinite, and being a thing infinite so are its sensations infinite also — therefore everlasting."

"Ha, there's reason in thy folly, methinks. What more?"

"Bethink thee, lord, there be divers rogues who, having provoked thy potent anger, do lie even now awaiting thy lordly pleasure. E'en now irons be heating for them, moreover they are, by thy will, to suffer the grievous torment of the pulleys and the wheel, and these, as I do know, be sharp punishments and apt to cause prodigious outcry. Now, to hear one cry out beneath the torture is an evil thing for youthful ears — and one not soon forgot."

"Aye, aye, forsooth, I begin to see thy meaning, good Fool — yet say on."

"Let this thy prisoner be set within the cell above the torture chamber, so, lying within the dark he must needs hear them cry below, and in his mind shall he suffer as they suffer, every pang of racking wheel and searing iron. And, because the mind is thing infinite —"

"Enough — enough! O most excellent Beda, 'tis well bethought. O, rare Fool, so shall it be."

Forthwith Sir Pertolepe summoned certain of his guard, and, incontinent, Beltane was dragged a-down the winding stair and thereafter fast shut within a place of gloom, a narrow cell breathing an air close and heavy, and void of all light. Therefore Beltane sat him down on the floor, his back to the wall, staring upon the dark, chin on fist. Long he sat thus, stirring not, and in his heart a black void, deeper and more awful than the fetid gloom of any dungeon — a void wherein a new Beltane came into being.

Now presently, as he sat thus, upon the silence stole a sound, low and murmurous, that rose and fell yet never quite died away. And Beltane, knowing what sound this was, clenched his hands and bowed his face upon his knees. As he listened, this drone grew to a sudden squealing cry that rang and echoed from wall to wall, whiles Beltane, crouched in that place of horror, felt the sweat start out upon him, yet shivered as with deadly cold, and ever the cries thrilled within the dark or sank to whimpering moans and stifled supplications. And ever Beltane hearkened to these fell sounds, staring blindly into the gloom, and ever the new Beltane grew the stronger within him.

Hour after hour he crouched thus, so very silent, so very quiet, so very still, but long after the groans and wailings had died to silence, Beltane stared grim-eyed into the gloom and gnawed upon his fingers. Of a sudden he espied a glowing spark in the angle of the wall to the right — very small, yet very bright.

Now as he watched, behold the spark changed to a line of golden light, so that his eyes ached and he was fain to shade them in his shackled arm; and thus he beheld a flagstone that seemed to lift itself with infinite caution, and, thereafter, a voice breathed his name.

"Messire — messire Beltane!" And now through the hole in the floor behold a hand bearing a lanthorn — an arm — a shoulder — a shrouded head; thus slowly a tall, cloaked figure rose up through the floor, and, setting down the lanthorn, leaned toward Beltane, putting back the hood of his mantle, and Beltane beheld Beda the Jester.

"Art awake, messire Beltane?"

"Aye!" quoth Beltane, lifting his head. "And I have used mine ears! The wheel and the pulley are rare be-

Horrors of Garthlaxton Keep 199

getters of groans, as thou did'st foretell, Fool! 'Twas a good thought to drag me hither — it needed but this. Now am I steel, without and — within. O, 'tis a foul world!"

"Nay, messire —'tis a fair world wherein be foul things: they call them 'men.' As to me, I am but a fool — mark this motley — yet hither I caused thee to be dragged that I might save those limbs o' thine from wheel and pulley, from flame and gibbet, and set thee free within a world which I do hold a fair world. Yet first — those fetters — behold hammer and chisel! Oswin, thy gaoler, sleepeth as sweet as a babe, and wherefore? For that I decocted Lethe in his cup. Likewise the guard below. My father, that lived here before me (and died of a jest out of season), was skilled in herbs — and I am his son! My father (that bled out his life 'neath my lord's supper table) knew divers secret ways within the thickness of these walls — so do I know more of Pertolepe's castle than doth Pertolepe himself. Come, reach hither thy shackles and I will cut them off, a chisel is swifter than a file —"

"And why would'st give me life, Fool?"

"For that 'tis a useful thing, messire, and perchance as sweet to thee this night within thy dungeon as to me upon a certain day within the green that you may wot of?" So speaking, Beda the Jester cut asunder the chain that bound the fetters, and Beltane arose and stretched himself and the manacles gleamed on each wide-sundered wrist.

Quoth he:

"What now?"

Whereat the jester, sitting cross-legged upon the floor, looked up at him and spake on this wise:

"Two days agone as I walked me in the green, dreaming such foolish dreams as a fool may, there came, very suddenly, a sorry wight — a wild man, very ragged — who set me his ragged arm about my neck and a sharp dagger to my throat; and thus, looking him within the eyes, I knew him for that same Roger from whose hand thou did'st save me aforetime. 'Beda,' says he, 'I am he that hanged and tortured men at my lord's bidding: I am Roger, and my sins be many.' 'Then prithee,' says I, 'prithee, Roger, add not another to thy sins by cutting the throat of a fool.' 'Needs must I,' says he, dolorous of voice, 'unless thou dost answer me two questions.' 'Nay, I will answer thee two hundred an thou leave my throat unslit,' says I. 'But two,' says Roger, sighing. 'First, doth Pertolepe hold him I seek?' 'Him?' says I. 'Him they call Beltane?' says Roger, 'doth he lie prisoned within Garthlaxton?' 'He doth,' quoth I. Now for thine other question. ''Tis this,' says Roger, 'Wilt aid us to win him free?' 'Why look ye, Roger,' says I, ''Tis only a fool that seeketh aid of a fool — and fool am I.' 'Aye,' says Roger, 'but thou art a live fool; promise, therefore, or wilt be naught but a dead fool.' 'Roger,' says I, 'thou did'st once try to slay me in the green ere now.' 'Aye,' says Roger, 'and my lord Beltane saved thy carcass and my soul.' 'Aye,' quoth I, 'and e'en a fool can repay. So was I but now dreaming here within this boskage how I might perchance win this same Beltane to life without thy scurvy aid, Black Roger. Moreover, methinks I know a way — and thou spare me life to do it.' 'Aye, forsooth,' says Roger, putting away his dagger, 'thou wert ever a fool of thy word, Beda — so now do I spare thy life, and sparing it, I save it, and thus do I cut another accursed notch from my belt.' 'Why, then,' says I, 'to-morrow night be at the riven oak by Brankton Thicket an hour before dawn.' 'So be it, Beda,' says he, and so I left him cutting at his belt. And lo, am I here, and within an hour it should be dawn. Follow, messire!" So saying, Beda rose, and taking the lanthorn, began to descend through the floor, having first shown how the flagstone must be lowered in place. Thereafter, Beltane followed the jester down a narrow stair built in the thickness of the wall, and along a passage that ended abruptly, nor could Beltane see any sign of door in the solid masonry that barred their way. Here Beda paused, finger on lip, and extinguished the lanthorn. Then, in the dark a hinge creaked faintly, a quivering hand seized Beltane's manacled wrist, drawing him on and through a narrow opening that yawned suddenly before them. Thereafter the hinge creaked again and they stood side by side within a small chamber where was a doorway hung across with heavy curtains beyond which a light burned. Now even as Beltane looked thitherward, he heard the rattle of dice and a sleepy voice that cursed drowsily, and shaking off the clutching, desperate fingers that strove to stay him, he came, soft-treading, and peered through the curtains. Thus he beheld two men that faced each other across a table whereon was wine, with dice and store of money, and as they played, these men yawned, leaning heavily upon the table. Back swept the curtains and striding into the room Beltane stared upon these men, who, yet leaning upon the table, stared back at him open-mouthed. But, beholding the look in his blue eyes and the smile that curled his mouth, they stumbled to their feet and sought to draw weapon — then Beltane sprang and caught them each about the neck, and, swinging them wide-armed, smote their heads together; and together these men sank in his grasp and lay in a twisted huddle across the table among the spilled wine. A coin rang upon the stone floor, rolled into a distant corner and came to rest, the jester gasped in the shadow of the curtains; and so came silence, broke only by the soft drip, drip of the spilled wine.

"O, mercy of God!" whispered the jester hoarsely at last, "what need was there for this — they would have slept —"

"Aye," smiled Beltane, "but not so soundly as now, methinks. Come, let us go."

Silently the jester went on before, by narrow passageways that writhed and twisted in the thickness of the walls, up sudden flights of steps until at length they came out upon a parapet whose grim battlements scowled high in air. But as they hasted on, flitting soft-footed 'neath pallid moon, the jester of a sudden stopped, and turning, dragged Beltane into the shadows, for upon the silence came the sound of mailed feet pacing near. Now once again Beltane brake from the jester's clutching fingers and striding forward, came face to face with one that bare a pike on mailed shoulder, and who, beholding Beltane, halted to peer at him with head out-thrust; quoth he:

"Ha! stand! Stand, I say and speak me who thou art?"

Then Beltane laughed softly; said he:

"O fool, not to know — I am death!" and with the word, he leapt. Came a cry, muffled in a mighty hand, a grappling, fierce yet silent, and Beda, cowering back, beheld Beltane swing a writhing body high in air and hurl it far out over the battlements. Thereafter, above the soft rustle of the night-wind, a sound far below — a faint splash, and Beda the Jester, shivering in the soft-stirring night wind, shrank deeper into the gloom and made a swift motion as though, for all his folly, he had crossed himself.

Then came Beltane, the smile still twisting his mouth; quoth he:

"Forsooth, my strength is come back again; be there any more that I may deal withal, good Fool?"

"Lord," whispered the shivering jester, "methinks I smell the dawn — Come!"

So Beltane followed him from the battlements, down winding stairs, through halls that whispered in the dark; down more stairs, down and ever down 'twixt walls slimy to the touch, through a gloom heavy with mildew and decay. On sped the jester, staying not to light the lanthorn, nor once touching, nor once turning with helping hand to guide Beltane stumbling after in the dark. Then at last, deep in the clammy earth they reached a door, a small door whose rusted iron was banded with mighty clamps of rusted iron. Here the jester paused to fit key to lock, to strain and pant awhile ere bolts shrieked and turned, and the door yawned open. Then, stooping, he struck flint and steel and in a while had lit the lanthorn, and, looking upon Beltane with eyes that stared in the pallor of his face, he pointed toward the yawning tunnel.

"Messire," said he, "yonder lieth thy way to life and the world. As thou did'st give me life so do I give thee thine. Thou wert, as I remember thee, a very gentle, tender youth — to-night are three dead without reason —"

"Reason, good Fool," said Beltane, "thou did'st see me borne in a prisoner to Garthlaxton; now, tell me I pray, who was she that rode with us?"

"'Twas the Duchess Helen of Mortain, messire; I saw her hair, moreover —"

But lo, even as the jester spake, Beltane turned, and striding down the tunnel, was swallowed in the dark.

CHAPTER XXVII

HOW BELTANE TOOK TO THE WILD-WOOD

A FAINT glimmer growing ever brighter, a jagged patch of pale sky, a cleft in the rock o'er-grown with bush and creeping vines; this Beltane saw ere he stepped out into the cool, sweet air of dawn. A while he stood to stare up at the sky where yet a few stars showed paling to the day, and to drink in mighty breaths of the fragrant air. And thus, plain to his ears, stole the ripple of running water hard by, and going thitherward he stripped, and naked came down to the stream where was a misty pool and plunged him therein. Now as he bathed him thus, gasping somewhat because of the cold, yet glorying in the rush and tingle of his blood, behold, the leaves parted near by, and uprising in his naked might, Beltane beheld the face of one that watched him intently.

"Master!" cried a voice harsh but very joyful, "O dear, my lord!" And Roger sprang down the bank and heedless of the water, plunged in to catch Beltane's hands and kiss them. "Master!" he cried. And thus it was these two met again. And presently, having donned clothes and harness, Beltane sat down him beside the brook, head upon hand, staring at the swift-running water, whiles Roger, sitting near, watched him in a silent ecstasy.

"Whence come ye, Roger?"

"From Thrasfordham-within-Bourne, lord. Ho, a mighty place, great and strong as Sir Benedict himself. And within Thrasfordham be many lusty fighting men who wait thy coming,—for, master, Bourne, aye and all the Duchy, doth ring with tales of thy deeds."

"Hath Sir Benedict many men?"

Beltane Takes to the Wild-wood   205

"Aye — within Thrasfordham five hundred and more."

"So few, Roger?"

"And mayhap as many again in Bourne. But, for Sir Benedict — a right lusty knight in sooth, master! and he doth hunger for sight of thee. He hath had me, with Walkyn and the archer, speak full oft of how we fired the gibbet and roars mighty laughs to hear how thou didst bear off Sir Pertolepe in the green — aye, Sir Benedict doth love to hear tell of that."

"Aye; and what of Duke Ivo — where is he now, Roger?"

"He hath reinforced Belsaye garrison and all the coast towns and castles of the Marches, and lieth at Pentavalon, gathering his powers to attack Thrasfordham, so men say, and hath sworn to burn it within the year, and all therein save only Sir Benedict — him will he hang; 'tis so proclaimed far and wide."

"And do men yet come in to Sir Benedict?"

"Not so, master. Since Duke Ivo came they are afraid."

"Ha! And what of the outlaws — there be many wild men within the forests."

"The outlaws — hey, that doth mind me. I, with Giles and Walkyn and the young knight Sir Jocelyn brought down the outlaws upon Thornaby Mill. But when we found thee not, we burned it, and thereafter the outlaws vanished all within the wild-wood; Sir Jocelyn rode away a-singing mighty doleful, and we three came to Thrasfordham according to thy word. But when ye came not, master, by will of Sir Benedict we set out, all three, to find thee, and came to a cave of refuge Walkyn wots of: there do we sleep by night and by day search for thee. And behold, I have found thee, and so is my tale ended. But now, in an hour will be day, master, and with the day will be the hue and cry after thee. Come, let us haste over into Bourne, there shall we be safe so long as Thrasfordham stands."

"True," nodded Beltane and rose to his feet. "Go you

to Thrasfordham, Roger, Sir Benedict shall need such lusty men as thou, meseemeth."

"Aye — but what of thee, master?"

"I? O, I'm for the wild-wood, to a wild life and wilder doings, being myself a wild man, henceforth, lawful food for flame or gibbet, kin to every clapper-claw rogue and rascal 'twixt here and Mortain."

"Nay master, within Thrasfordham ye shall laugh at Black Ivo and all his powers — let us then to Thrasfordham, beseech thee!"

"Nay, I'm for the woods in faith, to seek me desperate rogues, wild men whose lives being forfeit, are void of all hope and fear. So, get thee to Sir Benedict and speak him this from me, to wit: that while he holdeth Ivo in check before Thrasfordham, I will arise indeed and bring with me flame and steel from out the wild-wood. When he shall see the night sky aflame, then shall he know I am at work, and when by day he heareth of death sudden and swift, then shall he know I am not idle. Bid him rede me this riddle: That bringing from chaos order, so from order will I bring chaos, that order peradventure shall remain. Haste you into Bourne, Roger, and so — fare thee well!"

Now as he spake, Beltane turned on his heel and strode along beside the brook, but even as he went, so went Roger, whereon Beltane turned frowning.

Quoth he:

"Roger — Thrasfordham lieth behind thee!"

"Aye, master, but death lieth before thee!"

"Why then, death will I face alone, Roger."

"Nay, master — not while Roger live. Thy man am I —"

"Ha — wilt withstand me, Black Roger?"

"Thy man am I, to follow thee in life and go down with thee in death —"

Now hereupon Beltane came close, and in the dim light Black Roger beheld the new Beltane glaring down at him fierce-eyed and with great mailed fist clenched to smite;

Beltane Takes to the Wild-wood 207

but even so Black Roger gave not back, only he drew dagger and strove to set it in Beltane's iron fingers.

"Take this," quoth he, "for, an ye would be free of Roger, first must ye slay him, master." So Beltane took the dagger and fumbled with it awhile then gave it back to Roger's hand.

"Roger!" muttered he, his hand upon his brow, "my faithful Roger! So, men can be faithful—" saying which he sighed — a long, hissing breath, and hid his face within his mittened hand, and turning, strode swiftly upon his way. Now in a while, they being come into the forest, Roger touched him on the arm.

"Master," said he, "whither do ye go?"

"Nay, it mattereth not so long as I can lie hid a while, for I must sleep, Roger."

"Then can I bring thee to a place where none shall ever find thee — Come, master!" So saying, Roger turned aside into the denser wood, bursting a way through a tangle of brush, plunging ever deeper into the wild until they came to a place where great rocks and boulders jutted up amid the green and the trees grew scant. Day was breaking, and before them in the pale light rose a steep cliff, whose jagged outline clothed here and there with brush and vines loomed up before them, barring their advance.

But at the foot of this cliff grew a tree, gnarled and stunted, the which, as Beltane watched, Black Roger began to climb, until, being some ten feet from the ground, he, reaching out and seizing a thick vine that grew upon the rock, stepped from the tree and vanished into the face of the cliff. But in a moment the leaves were parted and Roger looked forth, beckoning Beltane to follow. So, having climbed the tree, Beltane in turn seized hold upon the vine, and stumbling amid the leaves, found himself on his knees within a small cave, where Roger's hand met his. Thereafter Roger led him to the end of the cavern where was a winding passage very rough and narrow, that brought them to a second and larger cave, as Beltane judged, for in the dark his hands could feel nought but space. Here Roger halted and whistled three times, a melodious call that woke many a slumbering echo. And in a while, behold a glow that grew ever brighter, until, of a sudden, a man appeared bearing a flaming pine-torch, that showed a wide cave whose rugged roof and walls glistened here and there, and whose rocky floor ended abruptly in a yawning gulf from whose black depths came soft murmurs and ripplings of water far below. Now, halting on the opposite side of this chasm, the man lifted his flaming torch and lo! it was Walkyn, who, beholding Beltane in his mail, uttered a hoarse shout of welcome, and stooping, thrust a plank across the gulf. So Beltane crossed the plank and gave his hand to Walkyn's iron grip and thereafter followed him along winding, low-roofed passage-ways hollowed within the rock, until they came to a cavern where a fire blazed, whose red light danced upon battered bascinets and polished blades that hung against the wall, while in one corner, upon a bed of fern, Giles o' the Bow lay snoring right blissfully.

To him went Roger to shake him into groaning wakefulness and to point with eager finger to Beltane. Whereat up sprang Giles and came running with hands outstretched in welcome, yet of a sudden, paused and stood staring upon Beltane, as did the others also, for the place was very bright and moreover Beltane's mail-coif was fallen back. So they looked on him all three, yet spake no word. Therefore Beltane sat him down beside the fire and rested his head upon his hands as one that is weary. Sitting thus, he told them briefly what had chanced, but of the Duchess he said nothing. And in a while, lifting his head he saw them watching him all three, and all three incontinent glanced otherwhere.

Quoth Beltane:

"Wherefore do ye stare upon me?"

"Why, as to that, good brother," said the archer, "'tis but that — that we do think thee something — changed of aspect."

"Changed!" said Beltane, and laughed short and bitter, "aye, 'tis like I am."

"Lord," quoth Walkyn, clenching mighty fists, "have they tormented thee — was it the torture, lord?"

"Aye," nodded Beltane, "'twas the torture. So now good comrades, here will I sleep awhile. But first — go forth with the sun and question all ye may of Ivo and his doings — where he doth lie, and where his forces muster — hear all ye can and bring me word, for methinks we shall be busy again anon!" Then, throwing himself upon the bed of fern that Roger had re-made, Beltane presently fell asleep. And while he slept came the three, very silent and treading very soft, to look down upon his sleeping face and the manacles that gleamed upon his wrists; and behold, even as he slept, he groaned and writhed, his tender lips grown fierce, a relentless, down-curving line — his jaws grim set, and between his frowning brows a lock of silky hair that gleamed snow-white among the yellow.

"The torture!" growled Roger, and so, soft as they came, the three turned and left him to his slumber. But oft he moaned and once he spake a word, sudden and fierce, 'twixt clenched teeth.

And the word was:

"Helen!"

CHAPTER XXVIII

OF THE PLACE OF REFUGE WITHIN THE GREEN

It was toward evening that Beltane awoke, and sitting up, looked about him. He was in a chamber roughly square, a hollow within the rock part natural and part hewn by hand, a commodious chamber lighted by a jagged hole in the rock above, a fissure all o'er-grown with vines and creeping plants whose luxuriant foliage tempered the sun's rays to a tender green twilight very grateful and pleasant.

Now pendant from the opening was a ladder of cords, and upon this ladder, just beneath the cleft, Beltane beheld a pair of lusty, well-shaped legs in boots of untanned leather laced up with leathern thongs; as for their owner, he was hidden quite by reason of the leafy screen as he leaned forth of the fissure. Looking upon these legs, Beltane knew them by their very attitude for the legs of one who watched intently, but while he looked, they stirred, shifted, and growing lax, became the legs of one who lounged; then, slow and lazily, they began to descend lower and lower until the brown, comely face of Giles Brabblecombe o' the Hills smiled down upon Beltane with a gleam of white teeth. Cried he:

"Hail, noble brother, and likewise the good God bless thee! Hast slept well, it lacketh scarce an hour to sundown, and therefore should'st eat well. How say ye now to a toothsome haunch o' cold venison, in faith, cunningly cooked and sufficiently salted and seasoned — ha? And mark me! with a mouthful of malmsey, ripely rare? Oho, rich wine that I filched from a fatuous friar jig-jogging within the green! Forsooth, tall brother, 'tis a wondrous place, the greenwood, wherein a man shall come by all he

Of the Refuge Within the Green

doth need — an he seek far enough! Thus, an my purse be empty, your beefy burgher shall, by dint of gentle coaxing, haste to fill me it with good, broad pieces. But, an my emptiness be of the belly, then sweet Saint Giles send me some ambulating abbot or pensive-pacing prior; for your churchmen do ever ride with saddle-bags well lined, as I do know, having been bred a monk, and therefore with a rare lust to creature comforts."

Now while he spake thus, the archer was busily setting forth the viands upon a rough table that stood hard by, what time Beltane looked about him.

" 'Tis a wondrous hiding-place, this, Giles!" quoth he.

"Aye, verily, brother — a sweet place for hunted men such as we. Here be caves and caverns enow to hide an army, and rocky passage-ways, narrow and winding i' the dark, where we four might hold all Black Ivo's powers at bay from now till Gabriel's trump — an we had food enow!"

Quoth Beltane:

" 'Tis a fair thought that, and I've heard there be many outlaws in the woods hereabouts?"

"Yea, forsooth. And each and every a clapper-claw, a rogue in faith. O very lewd, bloody-minded knaves see ye now, that would have slain me three days agone but for my comrade Walkyn. Scurvy dogs, fit for the halter they be, in faith!"

"Ha!" quoth Beltane, thoughtful of brow. "They be wild men, meseemeth?"

"Desperate knaves, one and all; and look ye, they would have slain —"

"Aye?" nodded Beltane.

"All the off-scourings of town and village — and look ye, they would —"

"Aye," said Beltane.

"Thieves, rogues and murderers, branded felons, runaway serfs and villeins —"

" 'Tis well," said Beltane, " so shall they be my comrades henceforth."

"Thy comrades!" stammered the archer, staring in amaze —" thy comrades! These base knaves that would have hanged me — me, that am free-born like my father before me —"

"So, peradventure, Giles, will we make them free men also. Howbeit this day I seek them out —"

"Seek them — 'tis death!"

"Death let it be, 'tis none so fearful!"

"They will slay thee out of hand — a wild rabblement, lawless and disordered!"

"So would I bring order among them, Giles. And thou shalt aid me."

"I — aid thee? How — would'st have me company with such vile carrion? Not I, forsooth. I am a soldier, free-born, and no serf like Walkyn or villein like Roger. But sure you do but jest, brother, so will I laugh with thee —"

But now, very suddenly, Beltane reached out his long arm and seizing Giles in mighty hand, dragged him to his knees; and Giles, staring up in amaze, looked into the face of the new Beltane whose blue eyes glared 'neath frowning brows and whose lips curled back from gleaming teeth.

"Giles," said he softly, rocking the archer in his grasp, "O Giles Brabblecombe o' the Hills, did I not save thy roguish life for thee? Did not Walkyn and Roger preserve it to thee? So doth thy life belong to Walkyn and to Roger and to me. Four men are we together, four brothers in arms, vowed to each other in the fulfilment of a purpose — is it not so?"

"Yea, verily, lord. Good men and true are we all, but see you not, lord, these outlaws be lewd fellows — base-born —"

"See you not, Giles, these outlaws be men, even as we, who, like us, can laugh and weep, can bleed and die — who can use their lives to purpose good or evil, even as we. Therefore, since they are men, I will make of them our comrades also, an it may be."

Thus saying, Beltane loosed Giles and turning to the

Of the Refuge Within the Green

table, fell to eating again while the archer sat upon the floor nursing his bruised arm and staring open-mouthed.

Quoth Beltane at last:

"We will seek out and talk with these outlaws to-night, Giles!"

"Talk with a pack of — yea, forsooth!" nodded Giles, rubbing his arm.

"I am minded to strike such a blow as shall hearten Sir Benedict for the siege and shake Black Ivo's confidence."

"Aha!" cried Giles, springing up so that his link-mail jingled, "aha! a sweet thought, tall brother! Could we fire another gibbet now —"

"Know you where the outlaws lie hid, Giles?"

"Nay, lord, none save themselves and Walkyn know that. Walkyn methinks, was great among them once."

"And where is Walkyn?"

"So soon as ye slept, lord, he and Roger went forth according to thy word. As for me, I stayed here to watch. From the spy-hole yonder you may command the road a-wind in the valley, and unseen, see you, may see. But come, an thy hunger be allayed, reach me thy hand that I may file off those iron bracelets."

"Nay, let be, Giles. I will wear them henceforth until my vow be accomplished."

Hereupon Beltane arose, and, climbing the ladder, looked forth through a screen of leaves and underbrush and saw that from the fissure the ground sloped steeply down, a boulder-strewn hill thick with gorse and bramble, at whose base the road led away north and south until it was lost in the green of the forest. Now as Beltane stood thus, gazing down at the winding road whose white dust was already mellowing to evening, he beheld one who ran wondrous fleetly despite the ragged cloak that flapped about his long legs, and whose rough-shod feet spurned the dust beneath them so fast 'twas a marvel to behold; moreover as he ran, he bounded hither and thither, and with every bound an arrow sped by him from where, some distance behind, ran divers foresters bedight in a green livery

Beltane thought he recognized; but even as Beltane grasped the branches that screened him, minded to swing himself up to the fellow's aid, the fugitive turned aside from the road and came leaping up the slope, but, of a sudden, uttered a loud cry and throwing up his hands fell face down upon the ling and so lay, what time came up one of the pursuers that had outstripped his fellows, but as he paused, his sword shortened for the thrust, up sprang the fugitive, a great axe flashed and whirled and fell, nor need was there for further stroke. Then, while the rest of the pursuers were yet a great way off, Walkyn came leaping up the hill. Back from the ladder Beltane leapt and down through the fissure came Walkyn to fall cat-like upon his feet, to shake free the ladder after him, and thereafter to sit panting upon a stool, his bloody axe betwixt his knees.

"Pertolepe's wolves!" he panted, "two of them have I — slain — within the last mile," and grinning, he patted the haft of his axe.

"What news, Walkyn?"

"Death!" panted Walkyn, "there be five dead men a-swing from the bartizan tower above Garthlaxton Keep, and one that dieth under the torture e'en now, for I heard grievous outcry, and all by reason of thy escape, lord."

"Come you then from Garthlaxton?" quoth Beltane, frowning.

"Aye, lord. For, see you, 'twas market day, so went I to one I know that is a swineherd, a trusty fellow that bringeth hogs each week unto Garthlaxton. So did we change habits and went to Garthlaxton together, driving the hogs before us. Thereafter, while he was away chaffering, I sat me down in the outer bailey tending my beasts, yet with eyes and ears wide and with my hand upon mine axe 'neath my cloak lest haply I might chance within striking distance of Red Pertolepe. And, sitting thus, I heard tell that he had marched out with all his array to join Black Ivo's banner. Whereupon was I mightily cast down. But it chanced the wind lifted my cloak, and one

Of the Refuge Within the Green 215

of the warders, spying mine axe, must think to recognise me and gave the hue and cry; whereat I, incontinent, fled ere they could drop the portcullis — and divers rogues after me. Aha! then did I lead them a right merry dance by moor and moss, by briar and bog, and contrived to slay of them five in all. But as to Pertolepe, a malison on him! he is not yet to die, meseemeth. But, some day — aye, some day!" So saying he kissed the great axe and setting it by came to the table and fell to eating mightily while Giles sat hard by busied with certain arrows, yet betwixt whiles watching Beltane who, crossing to the bed of fern, laid him down thereon and closed his eyes. But of a sudden he raised his head, hearkening to a whistle, soft and melodious, near at hand.

"Aha!" exclaimed Giles, setting aside his arrows, " yonder should be Roger — a hungry Roger and therefore surly, and a surly Roger is rare sport to lighten a dull hour. Heaven send our Roger be surly!" So saying, the archer went forth and presently came hasting back with Roger at his heels scowling and in woeful plight. Torn and stained and besprent with mud, his rawhide knee-boots sodden and oozing water, he stood glowering at Giles beneath the bloody clout that swathed his head, his brawny fist upon his dagger.

"No food left, say ye, Giles, no food, and I a-famishing? You and Walkyn drunk up all the wine betwixt ye, and I a-perish — ha — so now will I let it out again —" and out flashed his dagger.

"Nay, 'tis but the archer's folly," quoth Walkyn — " sit, man, eat, drink, and speak us thy news."

"News," growled Roger, seating himself at table, " the woods be thick with Pertolepe's rogues seeking my master, rogues known to me each one, that ran to do my bidding aforetime — in especial one Ralpho — that was my assistant in the dungeons once. Thrice did they beset me close, and once did I escape by running, once by standing up to my neck in a pool, and once lay I hid in a tree whiles they, below, ate and drank like ravening swine — and I a-famishing. A murrain on 'em, one and all, say I — in especial Ralpho that was my comrade once — may he rot henceforth —"

"Content you, Roger, he doth so!" laughed grim Walkyn and pointed to his axe.

"Forsooth, and is it so?" growled Roger, his scowl relaxing —" now will I eat full and blithely, for Ralpho was an arrant knave."

Now when his hunger was somewhat assuaged, Roger turned and looked where Beltane lay.

"My master sleepeth?" said he, his voice grown gentle.

"Nay, Roger, I lie and wait thy news," spake Beltane, his eyes yet closed.

"Why then, 'tis war, master — battle and siege. The country is up as far as Winisfarne. Black Ivo lieth at Barham Broom with a great company — I have seen their tents and pavilions like a town, and yet they come, for Ivo hath summoned all his powers to march against Thrasfordham. 'Twixt here and Pentavalon city, folk do say the roads be a-throng with bows and lances — lords and barons, knights and esquires, their pennons flutter everywhere."

"'Tis well!" sighed Beltane.

"Well, master — nay, how mean you?"

"That being at Barham Broom, they cannot be otherwhere, Roger. Saw you Pertolepe's banner among all these?"

"Aye, master; they have set up his pavilion beside the Duke's."

"Tell me now," said Beltane, coming to his elbow, "how many men should be left within Garthlaxton for garrison, think you?".

"An hundred, belike!" said Walkyn.

"Less," quoth Roger; "Garthlaxton is so strong a score of men have held it ere now. 'Tis accounted the strongest castle in all the Duchy, save only Thrasfordham."

"Truly 'tis very strong!" said Beltane thoughtfully,

Of the Refuge Within the Green 217

and lying down again he closed his eyes and spake slow and drowsily — " Aye, 'tis so strong, its garrison, being secure, should sleep sound o' nights. So 'twould be no great matter to surprise and burn it ere the dawn, methinks! "

" Burn Garthlaxton! " cried the archer, and sprang up, scattering the arrows right and left.

" Master! " stammered Roger, " master —"

As for Walkyn, he, having his mouth full and striving to speak, choked instead.

" Lord — lord! " he gasped at last, " to see Garthlaxton go up in flame — O blessed sight! Its blood-soaked walls crumble to ruin — ah, sweet, rare sight! But alas! 'tis a mighty place and strong, and we but four —"

" There be outlaws in the wild-wood! " quoth Beltane.

" Ha! — the outlaws! " cried Giles, and clapped hand to thigh.

" Aye," nodded Beltane, " bring me to the outlaws."

" But bethink thee, tall brother — of what avail a thousand such poor, ragged, ill-armed rogues 'gainst the walls of Garthlaxton? They shall not tear you the stones with their finger-nails nor rend them with their teeth, see'st thou! "

" To burn Garthlaxton! " growled Walkyn, biting at his fingers. " Ha, to give it to the fire! But the walls be mighty and strong and the outlaws scattered. 'Twould take a week to muster enough to attempt a storm, nor have they engines for battery —"

" Enough! " said Beltane rising, his brows close drawn, " now hearken, and mark me well; the hole whereby one man came out may let a thousand in. Give me but an hundred men at my back and Garthlaxton shall be aflame ere dawn. So, come now, Walkyn — bring me to the outlaws."

" But lord, these be very wild men, obedient to no law save their own, and will follow none but their own; lawless men forsooth, governed only by the sword and made desperate by wrong and fear of the rope —"

"Then 'tis time one learned them other ways, Walkyn. So now I command thee, bring me to them —'tis said thou wert great among them once."

Hereupon Walkyn rose and taking up his mighty axe twirled it lightly in his hand. "Behold, lord," said he, "by virtue of this good axe am I free of the wild-wood; for, long since, when certain lords of Black Ivo burned our manor, and our mother and sister and father therein, my twin brother and I had fashioned two axes such as few men might wield — this and another — and thus armed, took to the green where other wronged men joined us till we counted many a score tall fellows, lusty fighters all. And many of Ivo's rogues we slew until of those knights and men-at-arms that burned our home there none remained save Red Pertolepe and Gui of Allerdale. But in the green — love came — even to me — so I laid by mine axe and vengeance likewise and came to know happiness until — upon a day — they hanged my brother, and thereafter they slew — her — my wife and child — e'en as ye saw. Then would I have joined the outlaws again. But in my place they had set up one Tostig, a sturdy rogue and foul, who ruleth by might of arm and liveth but for plunder — and worse. Him I would have fought, but upon that night I fell in with thee. Thus, see you, though I am free of the wild, power with these outlaws have I none. So, an I should bring thee into their secret lurking-place, Tostig would assuredly give thee to swift death, nor could I save thee —"

"Yet must I go," said Beltane, "since, while I live, vowed am I to free Pentavalon. And what, think you, is Pentavalon? 'Tis not her hills and valleys, her towns and cities, but the folk that dwell therein; they, each one, man and woman and child, the rich and poor, the high and low, the evil and the good, aye, all those that live in outlawry — these are Pentavalon. So now will I go unto these wild men, and once they follow my call, ne'er will I rest until they be free men every one. Each blow they strike, the wounds they suffer, shall win them back to

Of the Refuge Within the Green

honourable life, to hearth and home — and thus shall they be free indeed. So, Walkyn, bring me to the outlaws!"

Then stood Walkyn and looked upon Beltane 'neath heavy brows, nothing speaking, and turned him of a sudden and, striding forth of the cave, came back bearing another great axe.

"Lord," said he, " thy long sword is missing, methinks. Take now this axe in place of it —'twas my brother's once. See, I have kept it bright, for I loved him. He was a man. Yet man art thou also, worthy, methinks, and able to wield it. Take it therefore, lord Duke that art my brother-in-arms; mayhap it shall aid thee to bring order in the wild-wood and win Pentavalon to freedom. Howbeit, wheresoe'er thou dost go, e'en though it be to shame and failure, I am with thee!"

"And I!" cried Giles, reaching for his bow.

"And I also!" quoth Roger.

CHAPTER XXIX

HOW BELTANE SLEW TOSTIG AND SPAKE WITH THE WILD MEN

THE sun was down what time they left the hill country and came out upon a wide heath void of trees and desolate, where was a wind cold and clammy to chill the flesh, where rank-growing rush and reed stirred fitfully, filling the dark with stealthy rustlings.

"Master," quoth Roger, shivering and glancing about him, "here is Hangstone Waste, and yonder the swamps of Hundleby Fen — you can smell them from here! And 'tis an evil place, this, for 'tis said the souls of murdered folk do meet here betimes, and hold high revel when the moon be full. Here, on wild nights witches and warlocks ride shrieking upon the wind, with goblins damned —"

"Ha, say ye so, good Roger?" quoth the archer, "now the sweet Saint Giles go with us — amen!" and he crossed himself devoutly.

So went they in silence awhile until they were come where the sedge grew thick and high above whispering ooze, and where trees, stunted and misshapen, lifted knotted arms in the gloom.

"Lord," spake Walkyn, his voice low and awe-struck, "here is the marsh, a place of death for them that know it not, where, an a man tread awry, is a quaking slime to suck him under. Full many a man lieth 'neath the reeds yonder, for there is but one path, very narrow and winding — follow close then, and step where I shall step."

"Aye, master," whispered Roger, "and look ye touch no tree as ye go; 'tis said they do grow from the bones of perished men, so touch them not lest some foul goblin blast thee."

So went they, following a narrow track that wound betwixt slow-stirring sedge, past trees huddled and distorted that seemed to writhe and shiver in the clammy air until, beyond the swamp, they came to a place of rocks where ragged crags loomed high and vague before them. Now, all at once, Walkyn raised a warning hand, as from the shadow of those rocks, a hoarse voice challenged:

"Stand!" cried the voice, "who goes?"

"What, and is it thou, rogue Perkyn?" cried Walkyn, "art blind not to know me?"

"Aye," growled the voice, "but blind or no, I see others with thee."

"Good friends all!" quoth Walkyn.

"Stand forth that I may see these friends o' thine!" Drawing near, Beltane beheld a man in filthy rags who held a long bow in his hand with an arrow on the string, at sight of whom Roger muttered and Giles held his nose and spat.

"Aha," growled the man Perkyn, peering under his matted hair, "I like not the looks o' these friends o' thine—"

"Nor we thine, foul fellow," quoth Giles, and spat again whole-heartedly.

"How!" cried Walkyn fiercely, "d'ye dare bid Walkyn stand, thou dog's meat? Must I flesh mine axe on thy vile carcase?"

"Not till I feather a shaft in thee," growled Perkyn, "what would ye?"

"Speak with Eric o' the Noose."

"Aha, and what would ye with half-hung Eric, forsooth? Tostig's our chief, and Tostig's man am I. As for Eric—"

"Aye—aye, and what of Eric?" spake a third voice—a soft voice and liquid, and a man stepped forth of the rocks with two other men at his heels.

"Now well met, Eric o' the Noose," quoth Walkyn. "I bring promise of more booty, and mark this, Eric—I bring also him that you wot of."

Now hereupon the man Eric drew near, a broad-set man clad in skins and rusty mail who looked upon Beltane with head strangely askew, and touched a furtive hand to his battered head-piece.

"Ye come at an evil hour," said he, speaking low-voiced. "Tostig holdeth high feast and revel, for to-day we took a rich booty at the ford beyond Bassingthorp — merchants out of Winisfarne, with pack-horses well laden — and there were women also — in especial, one very fair. Her, Tostig bore hither. But a while since, when he bade them bring her to him, behold she had stabbed herself with her bodkin. So is she dead and Tostig raging. Thus I say, ye come in an evil hour."

"Not so," answered Beltane. "Methinks we come in good hour. I am fain to speak with Tostig — come!" and he stepped forward, but Eric caught him by the arm:

"Messire," said he soft-voiced, "yonder be over five score lusty fellows, fierce and doughty fighters all, that live but to do the will of Tostig and do proclaim him chief since he hath proved himself full oft mightiest of all —"

"Ah," nodded Beltane, "a strong man!"

"Beyond equal. A fierce man that knoweth not mercy, swift to anger and joyful to slay at all times —"

"Why, look you," sighed Beltane, "neither am I a lamb. Come, fain am I to speak with this Tostig."

A while stood Eric, head aslant, peering at Beltane, then, at a muttered word from Walkyn, he shook his head and beckoning the man Perkyn aside, led the way through a cleft in the rocks and up a precipitous path beyond; and as he went, Beltane saw him loosen sword in scabbard.

Ever as they clomb, the path grew more difficult, until at last they were come to a parapet or outwork with mantelets of osiers beyond, cunningly wrought, above which a pike-head glimmered and from beyond which a voice challenged them; but at a word from Eric the sentinel stood aside and behold, a narrow opening in the parapet through which they passed and so up another path defended by yet another parapet of osiers. Now of a sudden, having

How Beltane Slew Tostig

climbed the ascent, Beltane paused and stood leaning upon his axe, for, from where he now stood, he looked down into a great hollow, green and rock-begirt, whose steep sides were shaded by trees and dense-growing bushes. In the midst of this hollow a fire burned whose blaze showed many wild figures that sprawled round about in garments of leather and garments of skins; its ruddy light showed faces fierce and hairy; it glinted on rusty mail and flashed back from many a dinted head-piece and broad spear-head; and upon the air was the sound of noisy talk and boisterous laughter.

Through the midst of this great green hollow a stream wound that broadened out in one place into a still and sleepy pool upon whose placid surface stars seemed to float, a deep pool whereby was a tall tree. Now beneath this tree, far removed from the fire, sat a great swarthy fellow, chin on fist, scowling down at that which lay at his feet, and of a sudden he spurned this still and silent shape with savage foot.

"Oswin!" he cried, "Walcher! Throw me this useless carrion into the pool!" Hereupon came two sturdy rogues who, lifting the dead betwixt them, bore her to the edge of the silent pool. Once they swung and twice, and lo, the floating stars shivered to a sullen splash, and subsiding, rippled softly to the reedy banks.

Slowly the swarthy giant rose and stood upon his legs, and Beltane knew him for the tallest man he had ever seen.

"Oswin," quoth he, and beckoned with his finger, "Oswin, did I not bid thee keep watch upon yon dainty light o' love?" Now meeting the speaker's baleful eye, the man Oswin sprang back, striving to draw sword, but even so an iron hand was about his throat, he was lifted by a mighty arm that held him a while choking and kicking above the silent pool until he had gasped and kicked his life out 'midst shouts and gibes and hoarse laughter; thereafter again the sullen waters quivered, were still, and Tostig stood, empty-handed, frowning down at those floating stars.

Then Beltane leapt down into the hollow and strode swift-footed, nor stayed until he stood face to face with Tostig beside the sullen pool. But swift as he had come, Roger had followed, and now stood to his back, hand on sword.

"Aha!" quoth Tostig in staring amaze, and stood a while eying Beltane with hungry gaze. "By Thor!" said he, "but 'tis a good armour and should fit me well. Off with it — off, I am Tostig!" So saying, he drew a slow pace nearer, his teeth agleam, his great hands opening and shutting, whereat out leapt Roger's blade; but now the outlaws came running to throng about them, shouting and jostling one another, and brandishing their weapons yet striking no blow, waiting gleefully for what might befall; and ever Beltane looked upon Tostig, and Tostig, assured and confident, smiled grimly upon Beltane until the ragged throng about them, watching eager-eyed, grew hushed and still. Then Beltane spake:

"Put up thy sword, Roger," said he, "in very truth this Tostig is a foul thing and should not die by thy good steel — so put up thy sword, Roger."

And now, no man spake or moved, but all stood rigid and scarce breathing, waiting for the end. For Tostig, smiling no more, stood agape as one that doubts his senses, then laughed he loud and long, and turned as if to reach his sword that leaned against the tree and, in that instant, sprang straight for Beltane's throat, his griping hands outstretched; but swift as he, Beltane, letting fall his axe, slipped aside and smote with mailed fist, and as Tostig reeled from the blow, closed with and caught him in a deadly wrestling hold, for all men might see Beltane had locked one arm 'neath Tostig's bearded chin and that Tostig's shaggy head was bending slowly backwards. Then the outlaws surged closer, a dark, menacing ring where steel flickered; but lo! to Roger's right hand sprang Walkyn, gripping his axe, and upon his left came Giles, his long-bow poised, a shaft upon the string; so stood the three alert and watchful, eager for fight, what time the struggle waxed ever more fierce and deadly. To and fro the wrestlers swayed, locked in vicious grapple, grimly silent save for the dull trampling of their feet upon the moss and the gasp and hiss of panting breaths; writhing and twisting, stumbling and slipping, or suddenly still with feet that gripped the sod, with bulging muscles, swelled and rigid, that cracked beneath the strain, while eye glared death to eye. But Beltane's iron fingers were fast locked, and little by little, slow but sure, Tostig's swart head was tilting up and back, further and further, until his forked beard pointed upwards — until, of a sudden, there brake from his writhen lips a cry, loud and shrill that sank to groan and ended in a sound — a faint sound, soft and sudden. But now, behold, Tostig's head swayed loosely backwards behind his shoulders, his knees sagged, his great arms loosed their hold: then, or he could fall, Beltane stooped beneath and putting forth all his strength, raised him high above his head, and panting, groaning with the strain, turned and hurled dead Tostig down into the pool whose sullen waters leapt to a mighty splash, and presently subsiding, whispered softly in the reeds; and for a while no man stirred or spoke, only Beltane stood upon the marge and panted.

Then turned he to the outlaws, and catching up his axe therewith pointed downwards to that stilly pool whose placid waters seemed to hold nought but a glory of floating stars.

"Behold," he panted, "here was an evil man — a menace to well-being, wherefore is he dead. But as for ye, come tell me — how long will ye be slaves?"

Hereupon rose a hoarse murmur that grew and grew — a sound incoherent yet baleful; steel glittered again. Then stood the man Perkyn forward, and scowling, pointed at Beltane with his spear.

"Comrades!" he cried, "he hath slain Tostig! He hath murdered our leader — come now, let us slay him!" and speaking, he leapt at Beltane with levelled spear, but quick as he leapt, so leapt Walkyn, his long arms rose and fell, and thereafter, setting his foot upon Perkyn's body, he shook his bloody axe in the scowling faces of the outlaws.

"Back, fools!" he cried, "have ye no eyes? See ye not 'tis he of whom I spake — he that burned Belsaye gallows and brake ope the dungeon of Belsaye — that is friend to all distressed folk and broken men; know ye not Beltane the Duke? Hear him, ye fools, hear him!"

Hereupon the outlaws stared upon Beltane and upon each other, and fumbled with their weapons as men that knew not their own minds, while Beltane, wiping sweat from him, leaned upon his axe and panted, with the three at his elbow alert and watchful, eager for fight; but Perkyn lay where he had fallen, very still and with his face hidden in the grass.

Of a sudden, Beltane laid by his axe and reached out his hands.

"Brothers," said he, "how long will ye be slaves?"

"Slaves, forsooth?" cried one, "slaves are we to no man — here within the green none dare gainsay us — we be free men, one and all. Is't not so, comrades?"

"Aye! Aye!" roared a hundred voices.

"Free?" quoth Beltane, "free? Aye, free to wander hither and thither, hiding forever within the wilderness, living ever in awe and dread lest ye die in a noose. Free to go in rags, to live like beasts, to die unpitied and be thrown into a hole, or left to rot i' the sun — call ye this freedom, forsooth? Hath none among ye desire for hearth and home, for wife and child — are ye become so akin to beasts indeed?"

Now hereupon, divers muttered in their beards and others looked askance on one another. Then spake the man Eric, of the wry neck.

"Messire," quoth he, "all that you say is sooth, but what remedy can ye bring to such as we. Say now?"

Then spake Beltane on this wise:

"All ye that have suffered wrong, all ye that be broken men — hearken! Life is short and quick to escape a man, yet do all men cherish it, and to what end? What seek ye of life — is it arms, is it riches? Go with me and I will teach ye how they shall be come by. Are ye heavy-hearted by reason of your wrongs — of bitter shame wrought upon the weak and innocent? Seek ye vengeance? — would ye see tyrants die? — seek ye their blood, forsooth? Then follow me!"

Now at this the outlaws began to murmur among themselves, wagging their heads one to another and voicing their grievances thus:

"They cut off mine ears for resisting my lord's taxes, and for this I would have justice!"

"They burned me in the hand for striking my lord's hunting dog!"

"I had a wife once, and she was young and fair; so my lord's son took her and thereafter gave her for sport among his huntsmen, whereof she died — and for this would I have vengeance!"

"They burned my home, and therein wife and child — and for this would I have vengeance!"

"They cut off my brother's hands!"

"They put out my father's eyes!"

Quoth Eric:

"And me they sought to hang to mine own roof-tree! — behold this crooked neck o' mine — so am I Eric o' the Noose. Each one of us hath suffered wrong, great or little, so live we outlaws in the green, lawless men in lawless times, seeking ever vengeance for our wrongs. Who then shall bring us to our desire, how shall our grievous wrongs be righted? An we follow, whither would'st thou lead us?"

"By dangerous ways," answered Beltane, "through fire and battle. But by fire men are purged, and by battle wrongs may be done away. An ye follow, 'tis like some of us shall die, but by such death our brethren shall win to honour, and home, and happiness, for happiness is all men's birthright. Ye are but a wild, unordered rabble, yet are ye men! 'Tis true ye are ill-armed and ragged, yet is your cause a just one. Ye bear weapons and have arms to smite — why then lurk ye here within the wildwood? Will not fire burn? Will not steel cut? He that is not coward, let him follow me!"

"Aye," cried a score of harsh voices, "but whither — whither?"

Quoth Beltane:

"Be there many among ye that know Sir Pertolepe the Red?"

Now went there up a roar, deep-lunged and ominous; brawny fists were shaken and weapons flashed and glittered.

"Ah — we know him — the Red Wolf — we know him — ah!"

"Then tell me," said Beltane, "will not steel cut? Will not fire burn? Arise, I say, rise up and follow me. So will we smite Tyranny this night and ere the dawn Garthlaxton shall be ablaze!"

"Garthlaxton!" cried Eric, "Garthlaxton!" and thereafter all men stared on Beltane as one that is mad.

"Look now," said Beltane, "Sir Pertolepe hath ridden forth with all his company to join Black Ivo's banner. Thus, within Garthlaxton his men be few; moreover I know a secret way beneath the wall. Well, is't enough? Who among ye will follow, and smite for freedom and Pentavalon?"

"That will I!" cried Eric, falling upon his knee.

"And I! And I!" cried others, and so came they to crowd eagerly about Beltane, to touch his hand or the links of his bright mail.

"Lead us!" they cried, "come — lead us!"

"Nay first — hearken! From henceforth outlaws are ye none. Come now, one and all, draw, and swear me on your swords:— To make your strength a shelter to the weak; to smite henceforth but in honourable cause for freedom, for justice and Pentavalon — swear me upon your swords to abide by this oath, and to him that breaks it — Death. Swear!"

How Beltane Slew Tostig

So there upon their knees with gleaming swords uplifted, these wild men swore the oath. Then up sprang Walkyn, pointing to Beltane with his axe.

"Brothers!" he cried, "behold a man that doeth such deeds as no man ever did — that burned the gallows — burst ope the dungeon of Belsaye and slew Tostig the mighty with naked hands! Behold Beltane the Duke! Is he not worthy to be our leader — shall we not follow him?" Then came a roar of voices:

"Aye — let us follow — let us follow!"

"On, then!" cried Walkyn, his glittering axe aloft. "To Garthlaxton!"

Then from an hundred brawny throats a roar went up to heaven, a cry that hissed through clenched teeth and rang from eager lips, wilder, fiercer than before. And the cry was: —

"Garthlaxton!"

CHAPTER XXX

HOW THEY SMOTE GARTHLAXTON

It was in the cold, still hour 'twixt night and dawn that Beltane halted his wild company upon the edge of the forest where ran a water-brook gurgling softly in the dark; here did he set divers eager fellows to fell a tree and thereafter to lop away branch and twig, and so, bidding them wait, stole forward alone. Soon before him rose Garthlaxton, frowning blacker than the night, a gloom of tower and turret, of massy wall and battlement, its mighty keep rising stark and grim against a faint light of stars. Now as he stood to scan with purposeful eye donjon and bartizan, merlon and arrow-slit for gleam of light, for glint of mail or pike-head, he grew aware of a sound hard by, yet very faint and sweet, that came and went — a small and silvery chime he could by no means account for. So crept he near and nearer, quick-eyed and with ears on the stretch till he was stayed by the broad, sluggish waters of the moat; and thus, he presently espied something that moved in the gloom high above the great gateway, something that stirred, pendulous, in the cold-breathing air of coming dawn.

Now as he peered upward through the gloom, came the wind, colder, stronger than before — a chill and ghostly wind that flapped the heavy folds of his mantle, that sighed forlornly in the woods afar, and softly smote the misty, jingling thing above — swayed it — swung it out from the denser shadows of scowling battlement so that Beltane could see at last, and seeing — started back faint and sick, his flesh a-creep, his breath in check 'twixt pale and rigid lips. And beholding what manner of thing this was, he fell upon his knees with head bowed low yet spake no prayer, only his hands gripped fiercely upon his axe; while to and fro in the dark above, that awful shape turned and swung — its flaunting cock's-comb dreadfully awry, its motley stained and rent — a wretched thing, twisted and torn, a thing of blasting horror.

And ever as it swung upon the air, it rang a chime upon its little, silver bells; a merry chime and mocking, that seemed to gibe at coming day.

Now in a while, looking upon that awful, dim-seen shape, Beltane spake low-voiced.

"O Beda!" he whispered, "O manly heart hid 'neath a Fool's disguise! O Fool, that now art wiser than the wisest! Thy pains and sorrows have lifted thee to heaven, methinks, and freed now of thy foolish clay thou dost walk with angels and look within the face of God! But, by thine agonies endured, now do I swear this night to raise to thy poor Fool's body a pyre fit for the flesh of kings!"

Then Beltane arose and lifting high his axe, shook it against Garthlaxton's frowning might, where was neither glint of armour nor gleam of pike-head, and turning, hasted back to that dark and silent company which, at his word, rose up from brake and fern and thicket, and followed whither he led, a long line, soundless and phantom-like within a phantom world, where a grey mist swirled and drifted in the death-cold air of dawn. Swift and silent they followed him, these wild men, with fierce eyes and scowling faces all set toward that mighty keep that loomed high against the glimmering stars. Axe and bow, sword and pike and gisarm, in rusty mail, in rags of leather and skins, they crept from bush to bush, from tree to tree, till they were come to that little pool wherein Beltane had bathed him aforetime in the dawn. Here they halted what time Beltane sought to and fro along the bank of the stream, until at last, within a screen of leaves and vines he found the narrow opening he sought. Then turned he and beckoned those ghostly, silent shapes about him, and speaking quick and low, counselled them thus:

"Look now, this secret burrow leadeth under the foundations of the keep; thus, so soon as we be in, let Walkyn and Giles with fifty men haste to smite all within the gate-house, then up with portcullis and down with drawbridge and over into the barbican there to lie in ambush, what time Roger and I, with Eric here and the fifty and five, shall fire the keep and, hid within the dark, raise a mighty outcry, that those within the keep and they that garrison the castle, roused by the fire and our shout, shall issue out amazed. So will we fall upon them and they, taken by surprise, shall seek to escape us by the gate. Then, Walkyn, sally ye out of the barbican and smite them at the drawbridge, so shall we have them front and rear. How think you? Is it agreed?"

"Agreed! agreed!" came the gruff and whispered chorus.

"Then last — and mark this well each one — till that I give the word, let no man speak! Let death be swift, but let it be silent."

Then, having drawn his mail-hood about his face and laced it close, Beltane caught up his axe and stepped into the tunnel. There he kindled a torch of pine and stooping 'neath the low roof, went on before. One by one the others followed, Roger and Giles, Walkyn and Eric bearing the heavy log upon their shoulders, and behind them axe and bow, sword and pike and gisarm, a wild company in garments of leather and garments of skins, soft-treading and silent as ghosts — yet purposeful ghosts withal.

Soon came they to the iron door and Beltane stood aside, whereon the mighty four, bending brawny shoulders, swung the log crashing against the iron; thrice and four times smote they, might and main, ere rusted bolt and rivet gave beneath the battery and the door swung wide. Down went the log, and ready steel flashed as Beltane strode on, his torch aflare, 'twixt oozing walls, up steps of stone that yet were slimy to the tread, on and up by winding passage and steep-climbing stairway, until they came where was a parting of the ways — the first still ascending, the second leading off at a sharp angle. Here Beltane paused in doubt, and bidding the others halt, followed the second passage until he was come to a narrow flight of steps that rose to the stone roof above. But here, in the wall beside the steps, he beheld a rusty iron lever, and reaching up, he bore upon the lever and lo! the flagstone above the steps reared itself on end and showed a square of gloom beyond.

Then went Beltane and signalled to the others; so, one by one, they followed him up through the opening into that same gloomy chamber where he had lain in bonds and hearkened to wails of torment; but now the place was bare and empty and the door stood ajar. So came Beltane thither, bearing the torch, and stepped softly into the room beyond, a wide room, arras-hung .and richly furnished, and looking around upon the voluptuous luxury of gilded couch and wide, soft bed, Beltane frowned suddenly upon a woman's dainty, broidered shoe.

"Roger," he whispered, "what place is this?"

"'Tis Red Pertolepe's bed-chamber, master."

"Ah!" sighed Beltane, "'tis rank of him, methinks — lead on, Roger, go you and Walkyn before them in the dark, and wait for me in the bailey."

One by one, the wild company went by Beltane, fierce-eyed and stealthy, until there none remained save Giles, who, leaning upon his bow, looked with yearning eyes upon the costly splendour.

"Aha," he whispered, "a pretty nest, tall brother. I'll warrant ye full many a fair white dove hath beat her tender pinions —"

"Come!" said Beltane, and speaking, reached out his torch to bed-alcove and tapestried wall; and immediately silk and arras went up in a puff of flame — a leaping fire, yellow-tongued, that licked at gilded roof-beam and carven screen and panel.

"Brother!" whispered Giles, "O brother, 'tis a sin,

methinks, to lose so much good booty. That coffer, now — Ha!" With the cry the archer leapt out through the tapestried doorway. Came the ring of steel, a heavy fall, and thereafter a shriek that rang and echoed far and near ere it sank to a silence wherein a voice whispered:

"Quick, brother — the besotted fools stir at last — away!"

Then, o'erleaping that which sprawled behind the curtain, Beltane sped along a passage and down a winding stair, yet pausing, ever and anon, with flaring torch: and ever small fires waxed behind him. So came he at last to the sally-port and hurling the blazing torch behind him, closed the heavy door. And now, standing upon the platform, he looked down into the inner bailey. Dawn was at hand, a glimmering mist wherein vague forms moved, what time Walkyn, looming ghostly and gigantic in the mist, mustered his silent, ghostly company ere, lifting his axe, he turned and vanished, his fifty phantoms at his heels.

Now glancing upward at the rugged face of the keep, Beltane beheld thin wisps of smoke that curled from every arrow-slit, slow-wreathing spirals growing ever denser ere they vanished in the clammy mists of dawn, while from within a muffled clamour rose — low and inarticulate yet full of terror. Then Beltane strode down the zig-zag stair and came forthright upon Roger, pale and anxious, who yet greeted him in joyous whisper:

"Master, I began to fear for thee. What now?"

"To the arch of the parapet yonder. Let each man crouch there in the gloom, nor stir until I give word."

Now as they crouched thus, with weapons tight-gripped and eyes that glared upon the coming day, a sudden trumpet brayed alarm upon the battlements — shouts were heard far and near, and a running of mailed feet; steel clashed, the great castle, waking at last, was all astir about them and full of sudden bustle and tumult. And ever the clamour of voices waxed upon the misty air from hurrying groups dim-seen that flitted by, arming as they ran, and ever the fifty and five, crouching in the dark, impatient for the sign, watched Beltane — his firm-set lip, his frowning brow; and ever from belching arrow-slit the curling smoke-wreaths waxed blacker and more dense. Of a sudden, out from the narrow sally-port burst a huddle of choking men, whose gasping cries pierced high above the clamour:

"Fire! Fire! Sir Fulk is slain! Sir Fulk lieth death-smitten! Fire!"

From near and far men came running — men affrighted and dazed with sleep, a pushing, jostling, unordered throng, and the air hummed with the babel of their voices.

And now at last — up sprang Beltane, his mittened hand aloft.

"Arise!" he cried, "Arise and smite for Pentavalon!" And from the gloom behind him a hoarse roar went up: "Arise! Arise — Pentavalon!" Then, while yet the war-cry thundered in the air, they swept down on that disordered press, and the bailey rang and echoed with the fell sounds of a close-locked, reeling battle; a hateful din of hoarse shouting, of shrieks and cries and clashing steel.

Axe and spear, sword and pike and gisarm smote and thrust and swayed; stumbling feet spurned and trampled yielding forms that writhed, groaning, beneath the press; faces glared at faces haggard with the dawn, while to and fro, through swirling mist and acrid smoke, the battle rocked and swayed. But now the press thinned out, broke and yielded before Beltane's whirling axe, and turning, he found Roger beside him all a-sweat and direfully besplashed, his mailed breast heaving as he leaned gasping upon a broadsword red from point to hilt.

"Ha, master!" he panted,—"'tis done already — see, they break and fly!"

"On!" cried Beltane, "on — pursue! pursue! after them to the gate!"

With axe and spear, with sword and pike and gisarm they smote the fugitives across the wide space of the outer bailey, under the narrow arch of the gate-house and out upon the drawbridge beyond. But here, of a sudden, the fugitives checked their flight as out from the barbican Walkyn leapt, brandishing his axe, and with the fifty at his back. So there, upon the bridge, the fight raged fiercer than before; men smote and died, until of Sir Pertolepe's garrison there none remained save they that littered that narrow causeway.

"Now by the good Saint Giles — my patron saint," gasped Giles, wiping the sweat from him, "here was a good and sweet affray, tall brother — a very proper fight, *pugnus et calcibus* — while it lasted—"

"Aye," growled Walkyn, spurning a smitten wretch down into the moat, "'twas ended too soon! Be these all in faith, lord?"

But now upon the air rose shrill cries and piercing screams that seemed to split the dawn.

"O — women!" cried Giles, and forthwith cleansed and sheathed his sword and fell to twirling his beard.

"Aha, the women!" cried a ragged fellow, turning about, "'tis their turn — let us to the women —" But a strong hand caught and set him aside and Beltane strode on before them all, treading swift and light until he was come to the chapel that stood beside the banqueting hall. And here he beheld many women, young and fair for the most part, huddled about the high altar or struggling in the ragged arms that grasped them. Now did they (these poor souls) looking up, behold one in knightly mail stained and foul with battle, yet very young and comely of face, who leaned him upon a mighty, blood-stained axe and scowled 'neath frowning brows. Yet his frown was not for them, nor did his blue eyes pause at any one of them, whereat hope grew within them and with white hands outstretched they implored his pity.

"Men of Pentavalon," said he, "as men this night have ye fought in goodly cause. Will ye now forget your manhood and new-found honour, ye that did swear to me upon your swords? Come, loose me these women!"

"Not so," cried one, a great, red-headed rogue, "we

have fought to pleasure thee — now is our turn —"

"Loose me these women!" cried Beltane, his blue eyes fierce.

"Nay, these be our booty, and no man shall gainsay us. How think ye, comrades?"

Now Beltane smiled upon this red-haired knave and, smiling, drew a slow pace nearer, the great axe a-swing in his mailed hand.

"Fellow," quoth he, kind-voiced, "get thee out now, lest I slay thee!" Awhile the fellow glared upon Beltane, beheld his smiling look and deadly eye, and slowly loosing his trembling captive, turned and strode out, muttering as he went. Then spake Beltane to the shrinking women, yet even so his blue eyes looked upon none of them. Quoth he:

"Ye are free to go whither ye will. Take what ye will, none shall gainsay you, but get you gone within this hour, for in the hour Garthlaxton shall be no more."

Then beckoning Walkyn he bade him choose six men, and turning to the women —

"These honourable men shall bring you safe upon your way — haste you to be gone. And should any ask how Garthlaxton fell, say, 'twas by the hand of God, as a sure and certain sign that Pentavalon shall yet arise to smite evil from her borders. Say also that he that spake you this was one Beltane, son of Beltane the Strong, heretofore Duke of Pentavalon." Thus said Beltane unto these women, his brows knit, and with eyes that looked aside from each and every, and so went forth of the chapel.

CHAPTER XXXI

HOW GILES MADE A MERRY SONG

MORNING, young and fragrant, bedecked and brave with gems of dewy fire; a blithe morning, wherein trees stirred whispering and new-waked birds piped joyous welcome to the sun, whose level, far-flung beams filled the world with glory save where, far to the south, a pillar of smoke rose upon the stilly air, huge, awful, and black as sin — a writhing column shot with flame that went up high as heaven.

"O merry, aye merry, right merry I'll be,
To live and to love 'neath the merry green tree,
Nor the rain, nor the sleet,
Nor the cold, nor the heat,
I'll mind, if my love will come thither to me."

Sang Giles, a sprig of wild flowers a-dance in his new-gotten, gleaming bascinet, his long-bow upon his mailed shoulder, and, strapped to his wide back, a misshapen bundle that clinked melodiously with every swinging stride; and, while he sang, the ragged rogues about him ceased their noise and ribaldry to hearken in delight, and when he paused, cried out amain for more. Whereupon Giles, nothing loth, brake forth afresh:

"O when is the time a maid to kiss,
Tell me this, ah, tell me this?
'Tis when the day is new begun,
'Tis to the setting of the sun,
Is time for kissing ever done?
Tell me this, ah, tell me this?

Thus blithely sang Giles the Archer, above the tramp and jingle of the many pack-horses, until, being come to

How Giles Made a Merry Song

the top of a hill, he stood aside to let the ragged files swing by and stayed to look back at Garthlaxton Keep.

Now as he stood thus, beholding that mighty flame, Walkyn and Roger paused beside him, and stood to scowl upon the fire with never a word betwixt them.

"How now," cried Giles, "art in the doleful dumps forsooth on so blithe a morn, with two-score pack-horses heavy with booty — and Garthlaxton aflame yonder? Aha, 'tis a rare blaze yon, a fire shall warm the heart of many a sorry wretch, methinks."

"Truly," nodded Roger, "I have seen yon flaming keep hung round with hanged men ere now — and in the dungeons beneath — I have seen — God forgive me, what I have seen! Ha! Burn, accursed walls, burn! Full many shall rejoice in thy ruin, as I do — lorn women and fatherless children — fair women ravished of life and honour!"

"Aye," cried Giles, "and lovely ladies brought to shame! So, Garthlaxton — smoke!"

"And," quoth frowning Walkyn, "I would that Pertolepe's rank carcass smoked with thee!"

"Content you, my gentle Walkyn," nodded the archer, "hell-fire shall have him yet, and groweth ever hotter against the day — content you. So away with melancholy, be blithe and merry as I am and the sweet-voiced throstles yonder — the wanton rogues! Ha! by Saint Giles! See where our youthful, god-like brother rideth, his brow as gloomy as his hair is bright —"

"Ah," muttered Roger, "he grieveth yet for Beda the Jester — and he but a Fool!"

"Yet a man-like fool, methinks!" quoth the archer. "But for our tall brother now, he is changed these latter days: he groweth harsh, methinks, and something ungentle at times." And Giles thoughtfully touched his arm with tentative fingers.

"Why, the torment is apt to change a man," said Walkyn, grim-smiling. "I have tried it and I know."

Now hereupon Giles fell to whistling, Walkyn to silence and Roger to scowling; oft looking back, jealous-eyed, to where Beltane rode a black war-horse, his mail-coif thrown back, his chin upon his breast, his eyes gloomy and wistful; and as often as he looked, Roger sighed amain. Whereat at last the archer cried:

"Good lack, Roger, and wherefore puff ye so? Why glower ye, man, and snort?"

"Snort thyself!" growled Roger.

"Nay, I had rather talk."

"I had rather be silent."

"Excellent, Roger; so will I talk for thee and me. First will I show three excellent reasons for happiness — *videlicet*: the birds sing, I talk, and Garthlaxton burns."

"I would thou did'st burn with it," growled Roger. "But here is a deed shall live when thou and I are dust, archer!"

"Verily, good Roger, for here and now will I make a song on't for souls unborn to sing — a good song with a lilt to trip it lightly on the tongue, as thus:

> "How Beltane burned Garthlaxton low,
> With lusty Giles, whose good yew bow
> Sped many a caitiff rogue, I trow,
> *Dixit!*"

"How!" exclaimed Roger, "here be two whole lines to thy knavish self and but one to our master?"

"Aye," grumbled Walkyn, "and what of Roger? — what of me? — we were there also, methinks?"

"Nay, show patience," said Giles, "we will amend that in the next triplet, thus:

> "There Roger fought, and Walkyn too,
> And Giles that bare the bow of yew;
> O swift and strong his arrows flew,
> *Dixit!*"

"How think ye of that, now?"

"I think, here is too much Giles," said Roger.

"Forsooth, and say ye so indeed? Let us then **to another** verse:

> "Walkyn a mighty axe did sway,
> Black Roger's sword some few did slay,
> Yet Giles slew many more than they,
>   *Dixit!*"

"Here now, we have each one his line apiece, which is fair — and the lines trip it commendingly, how think ye?"

"I think it a lie!" growled Roger.

"Aye me!" sighed the archer, "thou'rt fasting, Rogerkin, and an empty belly ever giveth thee an ill tongue. Yet for thy behoof my song shall be ended, thus:

> "They gave Garthlaxton to the flame,
> Be glory to Duke Beltane's name,
> And unto lusty Giles the same,
>   *Dixit!*"

"*Par Dex!*" he broke off, "here is a right good song for thee, trolled forth upon this balmy-breathing morn sweet as any merle; a song for thee and me to sing to our children one day, mayhap — so come, rejoice, my rueful Rogerkin — smile, for to-day I sing and Garthlaxton is ablaze."

"And my master grieveth for a Fool!" growled sulky Roger, "and twenty and two good men slain."

"Why, see you, Roger, here is good cause for rejoicing also, for, our youthful Ajax grieving for a dead Fool, it standeth to reason he shall better love a live one — and thou wert ever a fool, Roger — so born and so bred. As for our comrades slain, take ye comfort in this, we shall divide their share of plunder, and in this thought is a world of solace. Remembering the which, I gathered unto myself divers pretty toys — you shall hear them sweetly a-jingle in my fardel here. As, item: a silver crucifix, very artificially wrought and set with divers gems — a pretty piece! Item: a golden girdle from the East — very sweet and rare. Item: four silver candlesticks — heavy, Roger! Item: a gold hilted dagger — a notable trinket. Item —"

A sudden shout from the vanward, a crashing in the underbrush beside the way, a shrill cry, and three or four of Eric's ragged rogues appeared dragging a woman betwixt them, at sight of whom the air was filled with fierce shouts and cries.

"The witch! Ha! 'Tis the witch of Hangstone Waste! To the water with the hag! Nay, burn her! Burn her!"

"Aye," cried Roger, pushing forward, "there's nought like the fire for your devils or demons!"

Quoth the archer:

"*In nomen Dominum* — Holy Saint Giles, 'tis a comely maid!"

"Foul daughter of an accursed dam!" quoth Roger, spitting and drawing a cross in the dust with his bow-stave.

"With the eyes of an angel!" said Giles, pushing nearer where stood a maid young and shapely, trembling in the close grasp of one Gurth, a ragged, red-haired giant, whose glowing eyes stared lustfully upon her ripe young beauty.

"'Tis Mellent!" cried the fellow. "'Tis the witch's daughter that hath escaped me thrice by deviltry and witchcraft —"

"Nay — nay," panted the maid 'twixt pallid lips, "nought am I but a poor maid gathering herbs and simples for my mother. Ah, show pity —"

"Witch!" roared a score of voices, "Witch!"

"Not so, in sooth — in very sooth," she gasped 'twixt sobs of terror, "nought but a poor maid am I — and the man thrice sought me out and would have shamed me but that I escaped, for that I am very swift of foot —"

"She lured me into the bog with devil-fires!" cried Gurth.

"And would thou had'st rotted there!" quoth Giles o' the Bow, edging nearer. Now hereupon the maid turned and looked at Giles through the silken curtain of her black and glossy hair, and beholding the entreaty of that

How Giles Made a Merry Song 243

look, the virginal purity of those wide blue eyes, the archer stood awed and silent, his comely face grew red, grew pale — then, out flashed his dagger and he crouched to spring on Gurth; but, of a sudden, Beltane rode in between, at whose coming a shout went up and thereafter a silence fell. But now at sight of Beltane, the witch-maid uttered a strange cry, and shrinking beneath his look, crouched upon her knees and spake in strange, hushed accents.

"Messire," she whispered, "mine eyes do tell me thou art the lord Beltane!"

"Aye, 'tis so."

"Ah!" she cried, "now glory be and thanks to God that I do see thee hale and well!" So saying, she shivered and covered her face. Now while Beltane yet stared, amazed by her saying, the bushes parted near by and a hooded figure stepped forth silent and soft of foot, at sight of whom all men gave back a pace, and Roger, trembling, drew a second cross in the dust with his bow-stave, what time a shout went up:

"Ha! — the Witch —'tis the witch of Hangstone Waste herself!"

Very still she stood, looking round upon them all with eyes that glittered 'neath the shadow of her hood; and when at last she spake, her voice was rich and sweet to hear.

"Liar!" she said, and pointed at Gurth a long, white finger, "unhand her, liar, lest thou wither, flesh and bone, body and soul!" Now here, once again, men gave back cowering 'neath her glance, while Roger crossed himself devoutly.

"The evil eye!" he muttered 'twixt chattering teeth, "cross thy fingers, Giles, lest she blast thee!" But Gurth shook his head and laughed aloud.

"Fools!" he cried, "do ye forget? No witch hath power i' the sun! She can work no evil i' the sunshine. Seize her! — 'tis an accursed hag — seize her! Bring her to the water and see an she can swim with a stone at her hag's neck. All witches are powerless by day. See, thus I spit upon and defy her!"

Now hereupon a roar of anger went up and, for that they had feared her before, so now grew they more fierce; a score of eager hands dragged at her, hands that rent her cloak, that grasped with cruel fingers at her long grey hair, bending her this way and that; but she uttered no groan nor complaint, only the maid cried aloud most pitiful to hear, whereat Giles, dagger in hand, pushed and strove to come at Gurth. Then Beltane alighted from his horse and parting the throng with mailed hands, stood within the circle and looking round upon them laughed, and his laugh was harsh and bitter.

"Forsooth, and must ye war with helpless women, O men of Pentavalon?" quoth he, and laughed again right scornfully; whereat those that held the witch relaxed their hold and fain would justify themselves.

"She is a witch — a cursed witch!" they cried.

"She is a woman," says Beltane.

"Aye — a devil-woman — a notable witch — we know her of old!"

"Verily," cried one, "'tis but a sennight since she plagued me with aching teeth —"

"And me with an ague!" cried another.

"She bewitched my shafts that they all flew wide o' the mark!" cried a third.

"She cast on me a spell whereby I nigh did perish i' the fen —"

"She is a hag — she's demon-rid and shall to the fire!" they shouted amain. "Ha! — witch! — witch!"

"That doeth no man harm by day," said Beltane, "so by day shall no man harm her —"

"Aye, lord," quoth Roger, "but how by night? 'tis by night she may work her spells and blast any that she will, or haunt them with goblins damned that they do run mad, or —"

"Enough!" cried Beltane frowning, "on me let her bewitchments fall; thus, see you, an I within this next week wither and languish 'neath her spells, then let her burn an ye will: but until this flesh doth shrivel on these my bones, no man shall do her hurt. So now let there be an end — free these women, let your ranks be ordered, and march —"

"Comrades all!" cried red-haired Gurth, "will ye be slaves henceforth to this girl-faced youth? We have arms now and rich booty. Let us back to the merry greenwood, where all men are equal — come, let us be gone, and take these witches with us to our sport —"

But in this moment Beltane turned.

"Girl-faced, quotha?" he cried; and beholding his look, Gurth of a sudden loosed the swooning maid and, drawing sword, leapt and smote at Beltane's golden head; but Beltane caught the blow in his mailed hand, and snapped the blade in sunder, and, seizing Gurth about the loins, whirled him high in air; then, while all men blenched and held their breath waiting the thud of his broken body in the dust, Beltane stayed and set him down upon his feet. And lo! Gurth's cheek was pale, his eye wide and vacant, and his soul sat numbed within him. So Beltane took him by the throat, and, laughing fierce, shook him to and fro.

"Beast!" said he, "unfit art thou to march with these my comrades. Now therefore do I cast thee out. Take thy life and go, and let any follow thee that will — Pentavalon needeth not thy kind. Get thee from among us, empty-handed as I found thee — thy share of treasure shall go to better men!"

Now even as Beltane spake, Gurth's red head sank until his face was hidden within his hands; strong hands, that slowly clenched themselves into anger-trembling fists. And ever as Beltane spake, the witch, tossing back her long grey hair, looked and looked on him with bright and eager eyes; a wondering look, quick to note his shape and goodly size, his wide blue eyes, his long and golden hair and the proud, high carriage of his head: and slowly, to her wonderment came awe and growing joy. But Beltane spake on unheeding:

"Thou dost know me for a hunted man with a price upon my head, but thou art thing so poor thy death can pleasure no man. So take thy life and get thee hence, but come not again, for in that same hour will I hang thee in a halter — go!" So, with drooping head, Gurth of the red hair turned him about, and plunging into the green, was gone; then Beltane looked awhile upon the others that stood shifting on their feet, and with never a word betwixt them.

"Comrades," quoth he, "mighty deeds do lie before us — such works as only true men may achieve. And what is a man? A man, methinks, is he, that, when he speaketh, speaketh ever from his heart; that, being quick to hate all evil actions, is quicker to forgive, and who, fearing neither ghost nor devil, spells nor witchcraft, dreadeth only dishonour, and thus, living without fear, he without fear may die. So now God send we all be men, my brothers. To your files there — pikes to the front and rear, bows to the flanks — forward!"

But now, as with a ring and clash and tramp of feet the ragged company fell into rank and order, the witch-woman came swiftly beside Beltane and, touching him not, spake softly in his ear.

"Beltane — Beltane, lord Duke of Pentavalon!" Now hereupon Beltane started, and turning, looked upon her grave-eyed.

"What would ye, woman?" he questioned.

"Born wert thou of a mother chaste as fair, true wife unto the Duke thy father — a woman sweet and holy who liveth but to the good of others: yet was brother slain by brother, and thou baptised in blood ere now!"

"Woman," quoth he, his strong hands a-tremble, "who art thou — what knowest thou of my — mother? Speak!"

"Not here, my lord — but, an thou would'st learn more, come unto Hangstone Waste at the full o' the moon, stand you where the death-stone stands, that some do call the White Morte-stone. There shalt thou learn many things,

How Giles Made a Merry Song 247

perchance. Thou hast this day saved a witch from cruel death and a lowly beggar-maid from shame. A witch! A beggar-maid! The times be out a joint, methinks. Yet, witch and beggar, do we thank thee, lord Duke. Fare thee well — until the full o' the moon!" So spake she, and clasping the young maid within her arm they passed into the brush and so were gone.

Now while Beltane stood yet pondering her words, came Roger to his side, to touch him humbly on the arm.

"Lord," said he, "be not beguiled by yon foul witches' arts: go not to Hangstone Waste lest she be-devil thee with goblins or transform thee to a loathly toad. Thou wilt not go, master?"

"At the full o' the moon, Roger!"

"Why then," muttered Roger gulping, and clenching trembling hands, "we must needs be plague-smitten, blasted and everlastingly damned, for needs must I go with thee."

Very soon pike and bow and gisarm fell into array; the pack-horses stumbled forward, the dust rose upon the warm, still air. Now as they strode along with ring and clash and the sound of voice and laughter, came Giles to walk at Beltane's stirrup; and oft he glanced back along the way and oft he sighed, a thing most rare in him; at last he spake, and dolefully:

"Witchcraft is forsooth a deadly sin, tall brother?"

"Verily, Giles, yet there be worse, methinks."

"Worse! Ha, 'tis true, 'tis very true!" nodded the archer. "And then, forsooth, shall the mother's sin cleave unto the daughter — and she so wondrous fair? The saints forbid." Now hereupon the archer's gloom was lifted and he strode along singing softly 'neath his breath; yet, in a while he frowned, sudden and fierce: "As for that foul knave Gurth — ha, methinks I had been wiser to slit his roguish weasand, for 'tis in my mind he may live to discover our hiding place to our foes, and perchance bring down Red Pertolepe to Hundleby Fen."

"In truth," said Beltane, slow and thoughtful, "so do I think; 'twas for this I spared his life."

Now here Giles the Archer turned and stared upon Beltane with jaws agape, and fain he would have questioned further, but Beltane's gloomy brow forbade; yet oft he looked askance at that golden head, and oft he sighed and shook his own, what time they marched out of the golden glare of morning into the dense green depths of the forest.

CHAPTER XXXII

HOW BELTANE MET WITH A YOUTHFUL KNIGHT

Now at this time the fame of Beltane's doing went throughout the Duchy, insomuch that divers and many were they that sought him out within the green; masterless men, serfs new-broke from thraldom, desperate fellows beyond the law, thieves and rogues in dire jeopardy of life or limb: off-scourings, these, of camp and town and village, hither come seeking shelter with Beltane in the wild wood, and eager for his service.

In very truth, a turbulent company this, prone to swift quarrel and deadly brawl; but, at these times, fiercer than any was Walkyn o' the Axe, grimmer than any was Roger the Black, whereas Giles was quick as his tongue and Eric calm and resolute: four mighty men were these, but mightier than all was Beltane. Wherefore at this time Beltane set himself to bring order from chaos and to teach these wild men the virtues of obedience; but here indeed was a hard matter, for these were lawless men and very fierce withal. But upon a morning, ere the sun had chased the rosy mists into marsh and fen, Beltane strode forth from the cave wherein he slept, and lifting the hunting horn he bare about his neck, sounded it fierce and shrill. Whereon rose a sudden uproar, and out from their caves, from sleeping-places hollowed within the rocks, stumbled his ragged following — an unordered rabblement, half-naked, unarmed, that ran hither and thither, shouting and rubbing sleep from their eyes, or stared fearfully upon the dawn. Anon Beltane sounded again, whereat they, beholding him, came thronging about him and questioned him eagerly on all sides, as thus:

"Master, are we attacked forsooth?"

"Is the Red Pertolepe upon us?"

"Lord, what shall we do —?"

"Lead us, master — lead us!"

Then, looking upon their wild disorder, Beltane laughed for scorn: —

"Rats!" quoth he, "O rats — is it thus ye throng to the slaughter, then? Were I in sooth Red Pertolepe with but a score at my back I had slain ye all ere sun-up! Where be your out-posts — where be your sentinels? Are ye so eager to kick within a hangman's noose?"

Now hereupon divers growled or muttered threateningly, while others, yawning, would have turned them back to sleep; but striding among them, Beltane stayed them with voice and hand — and voice was scornful and hand was heavy: moreover, beside him stood Roger and Giles, with Walkyn and Eric of the wry neck.

"Fools!" he cried, "for that Pentavalon doth need men, so now must I teach ye other ways. Fall to your ranks there — ha! scowl and ye will but use well your ears — mark me, now. But two nights ago we burned down my lord Duke's great castle of Garthlaxton: think you my lord Duke will not seek vengeance dire upon these our bodies therefore? Think ye the Red Pertolepe will not be eager for our blood? But yest're'en, when I might have slain yon knavish Gurth, I suffered him to go — and wherefore? For that Gurth, being at heart a traitor and rogue ingrain, might straightway hie him to the Duke at Barham Broom with offers to guide his powers hither. But when they be come, his chivalry and heavy armed foot here within the green, then will we fire the woods about them and from every point of vantage beset them with our arrows —"

"Ha! Bows — bows!" cried Giles, tossing up his bow-stave and catching it featly — "Oho! tall brother — fair lord Duke, here is a sweet and notable counsel. Ha, bows! Hey for bows and bills i' the merry greenwood!"

"So, perceive me," quoth Beltane, "thus shall the hunters peradventure become the hunted, for, an Duke Ivo

How Beltane Met With a Knight   251

come, 'tis like enough he ne'er shall win free of our ring of fire." Now from these long and ragged ranks a buzz arose that swelled and swelled to a fierce shout.

"The fire!" they cried. "Ha, to burn them i' the fire!"

"But so to do," quoth Beltane, "rats must become wolves. Valiant men ye are I know, yet are ye but a poor unordered rabblement, meet for slaughter. So now will I teach ye, how here within the wild-wood we may withstand Black Ivo and all his powers. Giles, bring now the book of clean parchment I took from Garthlaxton, together with pens and ink-horn, and it shall be henceforth a record of us every one, our names, our number, and the good or ill we each one do achieve."

So there and then, while the sun rose high and higher and the mists of dawn thinned and vanished, phantom-like, the record was begun. Two hundred and twenty and four they mustered, and the name of each and every Giles duly wrote down within the book in right fair and clerkly hand. Thereafter Beltane numbered them into four companies; over the first company he set Walkyn, over the second Giles, over the third Roger, and over the fourth Eric of the wry neck. Moreover he caused to be brought all the armour they had won, and ordered that all men should henceforth go armed from head to foot, yet many there were that needs must go short awhile.

Now he ordained these four companies should keep watch and watch day and night with sentinels and outposts in the green; and when they murmured at this he stared them into silence.

"Fools!" said he, "an ye would lie secure, so must ye watch constantly against surprise. And furthermore shall ye exercise daily how, at the spoke command, to address your pikes 'gainst charge of horse or foot, and to that company adjudged the best and stoutest will I, each week, give store of money from my share of booty. So now, Walkyn, summon ye your company and get to your ward."

Thus it was that slowly out of chaos came order, yet it

came not unopposed, for many and divers were they that growled against this new order of things; but Beltane's hand was swift and heavy, moreover, remembering how he had dealt with Tostig, they growled amain but hasted to obey. So, in place of idleness was work, and instead of quarrel and riot was peace among the wild men and a growing content. Insomuch that upon a certain balmy eve, Giles the Archer, lolling beside the fire looking upon Black Roger, who sat beside him furbishing his mail-shirt, spake his mind on this wise:

"Mark ye these lamb-like wolves of ours, sweet Roger? There hath been no blood-letting betwixt them these four days, and scarce a quarrel."

ROGER. "Aye, this comes of my lord. My master hath a wondrous tongue, Giles."

GILES. "My brother-in-arms hath a wondrous strong fist, Rogerkin—"

ROGER. "Thy brother-in-arms, archer? Thine, forsooth! Ha!"

GILES. "Snort not, my gentle Roger, for I fell in company with him ere he knew aught of thee—so thy snort availeth nothing, my Rogerkin. Howbeit, our snarling wolves do live like tender lambs these days, the which doth but go to prove how blessed a thing is a fist—a fist, mark you, strong to strike, big to buffet, and swift to smite: a capable fist, Roger, to strike, buffet and smite a man to the good of his soul."

ROGER. "In sooth my master is a noble knight, ne'er shall we see his equal. And yet, Giles, methinks he doth mope and grieve these days. He groweth pale-cheeked and careworn, harsh of speech and swift to anger. Behold him now!" and Roger pointed to where Beltane sat apart (as was become his wont of late) his axe betwixt his knees, square chin propped upon clenched fist, scowling into the fire that burned before his sleeping-cave.

"Whence cometh the so great change in him, think you, Giles?"

"For that, while I am I and he is himself, thou art but

what thou art, my Rogerkin — well enough after thy fashion, mayhap, but after all thou art only thyself."

"Ha!" growled Roger, "and what of thee, archer?"

"I am his brother-in-arms, Rogerkin, and so know him therefore as a wondrous lord, a noble knight, a goodly youth and a sweet lad. Some day, when I grow too old to bear arms, I will to pen and ink-horn and will make of him a ballade that shall, mayhap, outlive our time. A notable ballade, something on this wise: —

> "Of gentle Beltane I will tell,
> A knight who did all knights excel,
> Who loved of all men here below
> His faithful Giles that bare the bow;
> For Giles full strong and straight could shoot,
> A goodly man was Giles to boot.
> A lusty fighter sure was Giles
> In counsel sage and full of wiles.
> And Giles was handsome, Giles was young,
> And Giles he had a merry —

"How now, Roger, man — wherefore interrupt me?"

"For that there be too many of Giles hereabouts, and one Giles talketh enough for twenty. So will I to Walkyn that seldom talketh enough for one."

So saying Roger arose, donned his shirt of mail and, buckling his sword about him, strode incontinent away.

And in a while Beltane arose also, and climbing one of the many precipitous paths, answered the challenge of sentinel and outpost and went on slow-footed as one heavy in thought, yet with eyes quick to heed how thick was the underbrush hereabouts with dead wood and bracken apt to firing. Before him rose an upland crowned by a belt of mighty forest trees and beyond, a road, or rather track, that dipped and wound away into the haze of evening. Presently, as he walked beneath this leafy twilight, he heard the luring sound of running water, and turning thither, laid him down where was a small and placid pool, for he was athirst. But as he stooped to drink, he started, and thereafter hung above this pellucid mirror staring down at the face that stared up at him with eyes agleam 'neath lowering brows, above whose close-knit gloom a lock of hair gleamed snow-white amid the yellow. Long stayed he thus, to mark the fierce curve of nostril, the square grimness of jaw and chin, and the lips that met in a harsh line, down-trending and relentless. And gazing thus upon his image, he spake beneath his breath:

"O lady! O wilful Helen! thy soft white hand hath set its mark upon me; the love-sick youth is grown a man, meseemeth. Well, so be it!" Thus saying, he laughed harshly and stooping, drank his fill.

Now as he yet lay beside the brook hearkening to its pretty babel, he was aware of another sound drawing nearer — the slow plodding of a horse's hoofs upon the road below; and glancing whence it came he beheld a solitary knight whose mail gleamed 'neath a rich surcoat and whose shield flamed red with sunset. While Beltane yet watched this solitary rider, behold two figures that crouched in the underbrush growing beside the way; stealthy figures, that flitted from tree to tree and bush to bush, keeping pace with the slow-riding horseman; and as they came nearer, Beltane saw that these men who crouched and stole so swift and purposeful were Walkyn and Black Roger. Near and nearer they drew, the trackers and the tracked, till they were come to a place where the underbrush fell away and cover there was none: and here, very suddenly, forth leapt Roger with Walkyn at his heels; up reared the startled horse, and thereafter the knight was dragged from his saddle and Walkyn's terrible axe swung aloft for the blow, but Black Roger turned and caught Walkyn's arm and so they strove together furiously, what time the knight lay out-stretched upon the ling and stirred not.

"Ha! Fool!" raged Walkyn, "loose my arm — what would ye?"

"Shalt not slay him," cried Roger, "'tis a notch —'tis a notch from my accursed belt — shalt not slay him, I tell thee!"

How Beltane Met With a Knight

"Now out upon thee for a mad knave!" quoth Walkyn.

"Knave thyself!" roared Black Roger, and so they wrestled fiercely together; but, little by little, Walkyn's size and bull strength began to tell, whereupon back sprang nimble Roger, and as Walkyn's axe gleamed, so gleamed Roger's sword. But now as they circled warily about each other, seeking an opening for blow or thrust, there came a rush of feet, and Beltane leapt betwixt them, and bestriding the fallen knight, fronted them in black and bitter anger.

"Ha, rogues!" he cried, "art become thieves and murderers so soon, then? Would'st shed each other's blood for lust of booty like any other lawless knaves, forsooth? Shame — O shame on ye both!"

So saying, he stooped, and lifting the unconscious knight, flung him across his shoulder and strode off, leaving the twain to stare upon each other shame-faced.

Scowling and fierce-eyed Beltane descended into the hollow, whereupon up sprang Giles with divers others and would have looked upon and aided with the captive; but beholding Beltane's frown they stayed their questions and stood from his path. So came he to a certain cave hollowed within the hill-side — one of many such — but the rough walls of this cave Black Roger had adorned with a rich arras, and had prepared also a bed of costly furs; here Beltane laid the captive, and sitting within the mouth of the cave — beyond which a fire burned — fell to scowling at the flame. And presently as he sat thus came Roger and Walkyn, who fain would have made their peace, but Beltane fiercely bade them to begone.

"Lord," quoth Walkyn, fumbling with his axe, "we found this knight hard by, so, lest he should disclose the secret of this our haven — I would have slain him —"

"Master," said Roger, "'tis true I had a mind to his horse and armour, since we do such things lack, yet would I have saved him alive and cut from my belt another accursed notch —"

"So art thou a fool, Roger," quoth Walkyn, "for an this knight live, this our refuge is secret no longer."

"Ha!" sneered Beltane, "what matter for that an it shelter but murderers and thieving knaves —"

"Dost name me murderer?" growled Walkyn.

"And me a thief, master?" sighed Roger, "I that am thy man, that would but have borrowed —"

"Peace!" cried Beltane, "hence — begone, and leave me to my thoughts!" Hereupon Walkyn turned and strode away, twirling his axe, but Roger went slow-footed and with head a-droop what time Beltane frowned into the fire, his scowl blacker than ever. But as he sat thus, from the gloom of the cave behind him a voice spake — a soft voice and low, at sound whereof he started and turned him about.

"Meseemeth thy thoughts are evil, messire."

"Of a verity, sir knight: for needs must I think of women and the ways of women! To-night am I haunted of bitter memory."

Now of a sudden, the stranger knight beholding Beltane in the light of the fire, started up to his elbow to stare and stare; then quailing, shivering, shrank away, hiding his face within his mailed hands. Whereat spake Beltane in amaze:

"How now, sir knight — art sick in faith? Dost ail of some wound —?"

"Not so — ah, God! not so. Those fetters — upon thy wrists, messire —?"

"Alack, sir knight," laughed Beltane, "and is it my looks afflict thee so? 'Tis true we be wild rogues hereabout, evil company for gentle knights. Amongst us ye shall find men new broke from the gallows-foot and desperate knaves for whom the dungeon yawns. As for me, these gyves upon my wrists were riveted there by folly, for fool is he that trusteth to woman and the ways of woman. So will I wear them henceforth until my work be done to mind me of my folly and of one I loved so much I would that she had died ere that she slew my love for her."

How Beltane Met With a Knight

Thus spake Beltane staring ever into the fire, joying bitterly to voice his grief unto this strange knight who had risen softly and now stood upon the other side of the fire. And looking upon him in a while, Beltane saw that he was but a youth, slender and shapely in his rich surcoat and costly mail, the which, laced close about cheek and chin, showed little of his face below the gleaming bascinet, yet that little smooth-skinned and pale.

"Sir knight," said Beltane, "free art thou to go hence, nor shall any stay or spoil thee. Yet first, hear this: thou art perchance some roving knight seeking adventure to the glory and honour of some fair lady. O folly! choose you something more worthy — a horse is a noble beast, and dogs, they say, are faithful. But see you, a woman's love is a pitiful thing at best, while dogs and horses be a-plenty. Give not thine heart into a woman's hand lest she tear it in her soft, white fingers: set not thine honour beneath her shapely feet, lest she tread it into the shameful mire. So fare thee well, sir knight. God go with thee and keep thee ever from the love of woman!"

So saying Beltane rose, and lifting the bugle-horn he wore, sounded it; whereon came all and sundry, running and with weapons brandished — but Roger first of all.

To all of whom Beltane spake thus:

"Behold here this gentle knight our guest is for the nonce — entreat him courteously therefore; give him all that he doth lack and thereafter set him upon his way —"

But hereupon divers cast evil looks upon the knight, murmuring among themselves — and loudest of all Walkyn.

"He knoweth the secret of our hiding-place!"

"'Tis said he knoweth the causeway through the fen!"

"He will betray us!"

"Dogs!" said Beltane, clenching his hands, "will ye defy me then? I say this knight shall go hence and none withstand him. Make way, then — or must I?"

But now spake the youthful knight his gaze still bent

upon the flame, nor seemed he to heed the fierce faces and eager steel that girt him round.

"Nay, messire, for here methinks my quest is ended!"

"Thy quest, sir knight — how so?"

Then the knight turned and looked upon Beltane. Quoth he:

"By thy size and knightly gear, by thy — thy yellow hair, methinks thou art Beltane, son of Beltane the Strong?"

"Verily, 'tis so that I am called. What would you of me?"

"This, messire." Herewith the stranger knight loosed belt and surcoat and drew forth a long sword whose broad blade glittered in the firelight, and gave its massy hilt to Beltane's grasp. And, looking upon its shining blade, Beltane beheld the graven legend "Resurgam."

Now looking upon this, Beltane drew a deep, slow breath and turned upon the youthful knight with eyes grown suddenly fierce.

Quoth he softly:

"Whence had you this, sir knight?"

"From one that liveth but for thee."

"Ah!" said Beltane with scornful lip, "know ye such an one, in faith?"

"Aye, messire," spake the knight, low-voiced yet eager, "one that doth languish for thee, that hath sent me in quest of thee bearing this thy sword for a sign, and to bid thee to return since without thee life is an emptiness, and there is none so poor, so heart-sick and woeful as Helen of Mortain!"

"Ah — liar!" cried Beltane, and reaching out fierce hands crushed the speaker to his knees; but even so, the young knight spake on, soft-voiced and calm of eye:

"Greater than thine is her love for thee, methinks, since 'tis changeless and abiding — Slay me an thou wilt, but while I live I will declare her true to thee. Whate'er hath chanced, whate'er may chance, despite all doubts and enemies she doth love — love — love thee through life till death and beyond. O my lord Beltane —"

"Liar!" spake Beltane again. But now was he seized of a madness, a cold rage and a deadly.

"Liar!" said he, "thou art methinks one of her many wooers, so art thou greater fool. But Helen the Beautiful hath lovers a-plenty, and being what she is shall nothing miss thee: howbeit thou art surely liar, and surely will I slay thee!" So saying he swung aloft the great blade, but even so the young knight fronted the blow with eyes that quailed not: pale-lipped, yet smiling and serene; and then, or ever the stroke could fall — an arm, bronzed and hairy, came between, and Roger spake hoarse-voiced:

"Master," he cried, "for that thy man am I and love thee, shalt ne'er do this till hast first slain me. 'Tis thus thou did'st teach me — to show mercy to the weak and helpless, and this is a youth, unarmed. Bethink thee, master — O bethink thee!"

Slowly Beltane's arm sank, and looking upon the bright blade he let it fall upon the ling and covered his face within his two hands as if its glitter had blinded him. Thus did he stand awhile, the fetters agleam upon his wrists, and thereafter fell upon his knees and with his face yet hidden, spake:

"Walkyn," said he, "O Walkyn, but a little while since I named thee 'murderer'! Yet what, in sooth, am I? So now do I humbly ask thy pardon. As for thee, sir knight, grant thy pity to one that is abased. Had I tears, now might I shed them, but tears are not for me. Go you therefore to — to her that sent thee and say that Beltane died within the dungeons of Garthlaxton. Say that I who speak am but a sword for the hand of God henceforth, to smite and stay not until wrong shall be driven hence. Say that this was told thee by a sorry wight who, yearning for death, must needs cherish life until his vow be accomplished."

But as Beltane spake thus upon his knees, his head

bowed humbly before them all, the young knight came near with mailed hands outstretched, yet touched him not.

"Messire," said he, "thou hast craved of me a boon the which I do most full and freely grant. But now would I beg one of thee."

"'Tis thine," quoth Beltane, "who am I to gainsay thee?"

"Messire, 'tis this; that thou wilt take me to serve thee, to go beside thee, sharing thy woes and perils henceforth."

"So be it, sir knight," answered Beltane, "though mine shall be a hazardous service, mayhap. So, when ye will thou shalt be free of it."

Thus saying he arose and went aside and sat him down in the mouth of the cave. But in a while came Roger to him, his sword-belt a-swing in his hand, and looked upon his gloomy face with eyes full troubled. And presently he spake, yet halting in his speech and timid:

"Master," he said, "suffer me a question."

"Verily," quoth Beltane, looking up, "as many as thou wilt, my faithful Roger."

"Master," says Roger, twisting and turning the belt in hairy hands, "I would but ask thee if — if I might cut another notch from this my accursed belt — a notch, lord — I — the young knight —?"

"You mean him that I would have murdered, Roger? Reach me hither thy belt." So Beltane took the belt and with his dagger cut thence two notches, whereat quoth Roger, staring:

"Lord, I did but save one life — the young knight —"

"Thou did'st save two," answered Beltane, "for had I slain him, Roger — O, had I slain him, then on this night should'st have hanged me for a murderer. Here be two notches for thee — so take back thy belt and go, get thee to thy rest — and, Roger — pray for one that tasteth death in life."

So Roger took the belt, and turning softly, left Beltane crouched above the fire as one that is deadly cold.

CHAPTER XXXIII

HOW BELTANE HAD NEWS OF ONE THAT WAS A NOTABLE PARDONER

BELTANE awoke to the shrill notes of a horn and starting to sleepy elbow, heard the call and challenge of sentinel and outpost from the bank above. Thereafter presently appeared Giles (that chanced to be captain of the watch) very joyously haling along a little man placid and rotund. A plump little man whose sober habit, smacking of things ecclesiastic, was at odds with his face that beamed forth jovial and rubicund from the shade of his wide-eaved hat: a pilgrim-like hat, adorned with many small pewter images of divers saints. About his waist was a girdle where hung a goodly wallet, plump like himself and eke as well filled. A right buxom wight was he, comfortable and round, who, though hurried along in the archer's lusty grip, smiled placidly, and spake him sweetly thus:

"Hug me not so lovingly, good youth; abate — abate thy hold upon my tender nape lest, sweet lad, the holy Saint Amphibalus strike thee deaf, dumb, blind, and latterly, dead. Trot me not so hastily, lest the good Saint Alban cast thy poor soul into a hell seventy times heated, and 'twould be a sad — O me! a very sad thing that thou should'st sniff brimstone on my account."

"Why, Giles," quoth Beltane, blinking in the dawn, "what dost bring hither so early in the morning?"

"Lord, 'tis what they call a Pardoner, that dealeth in relics, mouldy bones and the like, see you, whereby they do pretend to divers miracles and wonders —"

"Verily, verily," nodded the little man placidly, "I have here in my wallet a twig from Moses' burning bush, with the great toe of Thomas a' Didymus, the thumb of the blessed Saint Alban—"

"Ha, rogue!" quoth Giles, "when I was a monk we had four thumbs of the good Saint Alban—"

"Why then, content you, fond youth," smiled the Pardoner, "my thumb is number one—"

"Oh, tall brother," quoth Giles, "'tis an irreverent knave, that maketh the monk in me arise, my very toes do twitch for to kick his lewd and sacrilegious carcase — and, lord, he would kick wondrous soft—"

"And therein, sweet and gentle lord," beamed the little buxom man, "therein lieth a recommendation of itself. Divers noble lords have kicked me very familiarly ere now, and finding me soft and tender have, forthwith, kicked again. I mind my lord Duke Ivo, did with his own Ducal foot kick me right heartily upon a time, and once did spit upon my cloak — I can show you the very place — and these things do breed and argue familiarity. Thus have I been familiar with divers noble lords — and there were ladies also, ladies fair and proud — O me!"

"Now, by the Rood!" says Beltane, sitting up and staring, "whence had you this, Giles?"

"My lord, 'twas found by the man Jenkyn snoring within the green, together with a mule — a sorry beast! a capon partly devoured, a pasty — well spiced! and a wine-skin — empty, alas! But for who it is, and whence it cometh—"

"Sweet, courteous lord,— resplendent, youthful sir, I come from north and south, from east and west, o'er land, o'er sea, from village green and market-square, but lately from the holy shrine of the blessed Saint Amphibalus. As to who I am and what — the universal want am I, for I do stand for health, fleshly and spiritual. I can cure your diseases of the soul, mind and body. In very sooth the Pardoner of Pardoners am I, with pardons and indulgences but now hot from the holy fist of His Holiness of Rome: moreover I have a rare charm and notable cure for the worms, together with divers salves, electuaries, medicaments and nostrums from the farthest Orient. I have also store of songs and ballades, grave and gay. Are ye melancholic? Then I have a ditty merry and mirthful. Would ye weep? Here's a lamentable lay of love and languishment infinite sad to ease you of your tears. Are ye a sinner vile and damnèd? Within my wallet lie pardons galore with powerful indulgences whereby a man may enjoy all the cardinal sins yet shall his soul be accounted innocent as a babe unborn and his flesh go without penance. Here behold my special indulgence! The which, to him that buyeth it, shall remit the following sins damned and deadly — to wit: Lechery, perjury, adultery, wizandry. Murders, rapes, thievings and slanders. Then follow the lesser sins, as —"

"Hold!" cried Beltane, "surely here be sins enough for any man."

"Not so, potent sir: for 'tis a right sinful world and breedeth new sins every day, since man hath a rare invention that way. Here is a grievous thing, alas! yet something natural: for, since men are human, and human 'tis to sin, so must all men be sinners and, being sinners, are they therefore inevitably damned!"

"Alas, for poor humanity!" sighed Beltane.

"Forsooth, alas indeed, messire, and likewise woe!" nodded the Pardoner, "for thou, my lord, thou art but human, after all."

"Indeed at times, 'twould almost seem so!" nodded Beltane gravely.

"And therefore," quoth the Pardoner, "and therefore, most noble, gentle lord, art thou most assuredly and inevitably —" The Pardoner sighed.

"Damned?" said Beltane.

"Damned!" sighed the Pardoner.

"Along with the rest of humanity!" nodded Beltane.

"All men be more prone to sin when youth doth riot in their veins," quoth the Pardoner, "and alas, thou art very young, messire, so do I tremble for thee."

"Yet with each hour do I grow older!"

"And behold in this hour come I, declaring to thee there is no sin so vile but that through me, Holy Church shall grant thee remission — at a price!"

"A price, good Pardoner?"

"Why, there be sins great and sins little. But, youthful sir, for thine own damnable doings, grieve not, mope not nor repine, since I, Lubbo Fitz-Lubbin, Past Pardoner of the Holy See, will e'en now unloose, assoil and remit them unto thee—"

"At a price!" nodded Beltane.

"Good my lord," spake Giles, viewing the Pardoner's plump person with a yearning eye, "pray thee bid me kick him hence!"

"Not so, Giles, since from all things may we learn — with patience. Here now is one that hath travelled and seen much and should be wise—"

"Forsooth, messire, I have been so accounted ere now," nodded the Pardoner.

"Dost hear, Giles? Thus, from his wisdom I may perchance grow wiser than I am. So get thee back to thy duty, Giles. Begone — thy presence doth distract us."

"Aye, base archer, begone!" nodded the Pardoner, seating himself upon the sward. "Thy visage dour accordeth not with deep-seated thought — take it hence!"

"There spake wisdom, Giles, and he is a fool that disobeys. So, Giles — begone!"

Hereupon Giles frowned upon the Pardoner, who lolling at his ease, snapped his fingers at Giles, whereat Giles scowled amain and scowling, strode away.

"Now, messire," quoth the Pardoner, opening his wallet, "now in the matter of sinning, messire, an thou hast some pet and peculiar vice — some little, pretty vanity, some secret, sweet transgression—"

"Nay, first," quoth Beltane, "'tis sure thou hast a tongue—"

"O infallibly, messire; a sweet tongue — a tongue attuned to cunning phrases. God gave to women beauty, to flowers perfume, and to me — a tongue!"

"Good Pardoner, a lonely wight am I, ignorant of the world and of its ways and doings. So for thy tongue will I barter base coin — what can'st tell me for this fair gold piece?"

"That fain would I have the spending on't, noble, generous sir."

"What more?"

"Anything ye will, messire: for since I am the want universal and gold the universal need, needs must want want need! And here is a rare-turned phrase, methinks?"

"So thus do I wed need with want," nodded Beltane, tossing him the coin. "Come now, discourse to me of worldly things — how men do trim their beards these days, what sins be most i' the fashion, if Duke Ivo sleepeth a-nights, whether Pentavalon city standeth yet?"

"Aha!" cried the Pardoner (coin safely pouched), "I can tell ye tales a-plenty: sly, merry tales of lovely ladies fair and gay. I can paint ye a tongue picture of one beyond all fair ladies fair — her soft, white body panting-warm for kisses, the lure of her mouth, the languorous passion of her eyes, the glorious mantle of her flame-like hair. I'll tell of how she, full of witching, wanton wiles, love-alluring, furtive fled fleet-footed from the day and — there amid the soft and slumberous silence of the tender trees did yield her love to one beyond all beings blest. Thus, sighing and a-swoon, did Helen fair, a Duchess proud —"

"Ah!" cried Beltane, clenching sudden fist, "what base and lying babble do ye speak? Helen, forsooth — dare ye name her, O Thing?"

Now before Beltane's swift and blazing anger the Pardoner's assurance wilted on the instant, and he cowered behind a lifted elbow.

"Nay, nay, most potent lord," he stammered, "spit on me an ye will — spit, I do implore thee, but strike me not. Beseech thee sir, in what do I offend? The story runs that the proud and wilful lady is fled away, none know wherefore, why, nor where. I do but read the riddle thus: wherefore should she flee but for love, and if for love, then with a man, and if with a man —"

"Enough of her!" quoth Beltane scowling, "woman and her wiles is of none account to me!"

"How — how?" gasped the Pardoner, "of no account —! Woman —! But thou'rt youthful — of no account —! Thou'rt a man very strong and lusty —! Of no account, forsooth? O, Venus, hear him! Woman, forsooth! She is man's aim, his beginning and oft-times his end. She is the everlasting cause. She is man's sweetest curse and eke salvation, his slave, his very tyrant. Without woman strife would cease, ambition languish, Venus pine to skin and bone (sweet soul!) and I never sell another pardon and starve for lack of custom; for while women are, so will be pardoners. But this very week I did good trade in fair Belsaye with divers women — three were but ordinary indulgences for certain small marital transgressions; but one, a tender maid and youthful, being put to the torment, had denounced her father and lover —"

"The torment?" quoth Beltane, starting. "The torment, say you?"

"Aye, messire! Belsaye setteth a rare new fashion in torments of late. Howbeit, the father and lover being denounced before Sir Gui's tribunal, they were forthwith hanged upon my lord Gui's new gibbets —"

"O — hanged?" quoth Beltane "hanged?"

"Aye, forsooth, by the neck as is the fashion. Now cometh this woeful wench to me vowing she heard their voices i' the night, and, to quiet these voices besought of me a pardon. But she had but two sorry silver pieces and pardons be costly things, and when she could get no pardon, she went home and that night killed herself — silly wench! Ha! my lord — good messire — my arm — holy saints! 'twill break!"

"Killed herself — and for lack of thy pitiful, accursed pardon! Heard you aught else in Belsaye — speak!" and Beltane's cruel grip tightened.

"Indeed — indeed that will I, good news, sweet news — O my lord, loose my arm!"

"Thine arm, good Pardoner — thine arm? Aye, take it back, it availeth me nothing — take it and cherish it. To part with a pardon for but two silver pieces were a grave folly! So pray you forgive now my ungentleness and speak my thy good, sweet tidings." But hereupon, the Pardoner feeling his arm solicitously, held his peace and glowered sullenly at Beltane, who had turned and was staring away into the distance. So the Pardoner sulked awhile and spake not, until, seeing Beltane's hand creep out towards him, he forthwith fell to volubility.

"'Tis told in Belsaye on right good authority that a certain vile knave, a lewd, seditious rogue hight Beltane that was aforetime a charcoal-burner and thereafter a burner of gibbets — as witness my lord Duke's tall, great and goodly gallows — that was beside a prison breaker and known traitor, hath been taken by the doughty Sir Pertolepe, lord Warden of the Marches, and by him very properly roasted and burned to death within his great Keep of Garthlaxton."

"Roasted, forsooth?" said Beltane, his gaze yet afar off; "and, forsooth, burned to ashes; then forsooth is he surely dead?"

"Aye, that is he; and his ashes scattered on a dung-hill."

"A dung-hill — ha?"

"He was but a charcoal-burning knave, 'tis said — a rogue base-born and a traitor. Now hereupon my lord, the good lord Sir Gui, my lord Duke's lord Seneschal of Belsaye —"

"Forsooth," sighed Beltane, "here be lords a-plenty in Pentavalon!"

"Hereupon the noble Sir Gui set a close watch upon the townsfolk whereby he apprehended divers suspected rogues, and putting them to the torture, found thereby proofs of their vile sedition, insomuch that though the women held their peace for the most part, certain men enduring not, did confess knowledge of a subterraneous passage 'neath the wall. Then did Sir Gui cause this passage to be stopped, and four gibbets to be set up within the market-place, and thereon at sunset every day did hang four men, whereto the towns folk were summoned by sound of tucket and drum: until upon a certain evening some six days since (myself standing by) came a white friar hight Friar Martin — well known in Belsaye, and bursting through the throng he did loud-voiced proclaim himself the traitor that had oped and shown the secret way into the dungeons unto that charcoal-rogue for whose misdeeds so many folk had suffered. So they took this rascal friar and scourged him and set him in the water-dungeons where rats do frolic, and to-night at sunset he dieth by slow fire as a warning to — Ah! sweet, noble, good my lord, what — what would ye —" for Beltane had risen and was looking down at the crouching Pardoner, suddenly haggard, pallid-lipped, and with eyes a-glare with awful menace; but now the Pardoner saw that those eyes looked through him and beyond — living eyes in a face of death.

"Messire — messire!" quavered the Pardoner on trembling knees; but Beltane, as one that is deaf and blind, strode forward and over him, and as he went set his bugle to his lips and sounded a rallying note. Forthwith came men that ran towards him at speed, but now was there no outcry or confusion and their mail gleamed in the early sun as they fell into their appointed rank and company.

Then Beltane set his hands unto his eyes and thereafter stared up to the heavens and round about upon the fair earth as one that wakes from a dream evil and hateful, and spake, sudden and harsh-voiced:

"Now hither to me Walkyn, Giles and Roger. Ye do remember how upon a time we met a white friar in the green that was a son of God — they call him Brother Martin? Ye do remember brave Friar Martin?"

"Aye, lord, we mind him!" quoth the three.

"Ye will remember how that we did, within the green,

aid him to bury a dead maid, young and fair and tender — yet done to shameful death?"

"Verily master — a noble lady!" growled Walkyn.

"And very young!" said Roger.

"And very comely, alas!" added Giles.

"So now do I tell thee that, as she died — snatched out of life by brutal hands — so, at this hour, even as we stand idle here, other maids do suffer and die within Belsaye town. To-day, as we stand here, good Friar Martin lieth within the noisome water-dungeons where rats do frolic —"

"Ha! the pale fox!" growled Walkyn. "Bloody Gui of Allerdale that I do live but to slay one day with Pertolepe the Red —"

"Thou dost remember, Roger, how, within the Keep at Belsaye I sware an oath unto Sir Gui? So now — this very hour — must we march on Belsaye that this my oath may be kept." But here a murmur arose that hummed from rank to rank; heads were shaken and gruff voices spake on this wise:

"Belsaye? 'Tis a long day's march to Belsaye —"

"'Tis a very strong city — very strongly guarded —"

"And we muster scarce two hundred —"

"The walls be high and we have no ladders, or engines for battery and storm —"

"Forsooth, and we have here much booty already —"

"Ha — booty!" cried Beltane, "there spake tall Orson, methinks!"

"Aye," cried another voice, loud and defiant, "and we be no soldiers, master, to march 'gainst walled cities; look'ee. Foresters are we, to live secure and free within the merry greenwood. Is't not so, good fellows?"

"And there spake Jenkyn o' the Ford!" quoth Beltane. "Stand forth Orson, and Jenkyn with thee — so. Now hearken again. Within Belsaye men — aye, and women too! have endured the torment, Orson. To-day, at sundown, a noble man doth burn, Jenkyn."

"Why, look'ee, master," spake Jenkyn, bold-voiced yet

blenching from Beltane's unswerving gaze, "look'ee, good master, here is no matter for honest woodsmen, look'ee —"

"Aye," nodded tall Orson, "'tis no matter of ours, so wherefore should us meddle?"

"And ye have swords, I see," quoth Beltane, "and thereto hands wherewith to fight, yet do ye speak, forsooth, of booty, and fain would lie hid secure within the green? So be it! Bring forth the record, Giles, and strike me out the names of Orson and Jenkyn, the which, being shaped like men, are yet no men. Give therefore unto each his share of booty and let him go hence." So saying, Beltane turned and looked upon the close-drawn ranks that murmured and muttered no more. Quoth he:

"Now, and there be any here among us so faint-hearted — so unworthy as this Orson and Jenkyn, that do hold treasure and safety above flesh and blood — if there be any here, who, regarding his own base body, will strike no blow for these distressed — why, let him now go forth of this our company. O men! O men of Pentavalon, do ye not hear them, these woeful ones — do ye not hear them crying to us from searing flame, from dungeon and gibbet — do ye not hear? Is there one, that, remembering the torments endured of groaning bodies, the dire wrongs of innocence shamed and trampled in the mire — lives there a man that will not adventure life and limb and all he doth possess that such things may be smitten hence and made an end of for all time? But if such there be, let him now stand forth with Orson here, and Jenkyn o' the Ford!"

Thus spake Beltane quick and passionate and thereafter paused, waiting their answer; but no man spake or moved, only from their grim ranks a growl went up ominous and deep, and eyes grown bright and fierce glared upon tall Orson and Jenkyn o' the Ford, who shuffled with their feet and fumbled with their hands and knew not where to look.

"'Tis well, 'tis well, good comrades all!" spake Beltane in a while, "this night, mayhap, shall we, each one, achieve great things. Go now, dig ye a pit and therein hide such treasure as ye will and thereafter arm ye at points, for in the hour we march. Eric, see each doth bear with him food, and Giles, look that their quivers be full."

So saying, Beltane turned and coming to his sleeping-place, forthwith began to don his armour. And presently he was aware of Orson and Jenkyn standing without the cave and each with look downcast; and eke they fumbled with their hands and shuffled with their feet and fain were to speak yet found no word. But at last spake Jenkyn humbly and on this wise:

"Master, here come I, look'ee, with Orson that is my comrade, look'ee —"

"Nay, go get thee to thy 'booty'!" says Beltane, busied with his armour.

"Nay, but look'ee master, we be —"

"No men!" quoth Beltane, "thus would I be free of ye both — so get you hence."

"But good master," spake Orson, "we do ha' changed our minds — it do be a direful thing to burn, and if they do ha' tormented maids —"

"'Tis no matter of thine," quoth Beltane. "So go thy ways and meddle not."

"But master, look'ee now, we be stout men, and look'ee, we be full of lust to fight — O master, let us go! Kneel, Orson, bend — bend thy long shanks, look'ee —" and forthwith on their knees fell Jenkyn and tall Orson with pleading eyes and eager hands outstretched.

"O master, look'ee, let us go!"

"Aye, we do ha' changed our minds, master!"

"Then be it so!" said Beltane, "and I pray ye be ever faithful to your minds!" Then took they Beltane's hand to kiss and thereafter up they sprang and went rejoicing to their company.

And within the hour, mail and bascinet agleam, the two hundred and twenty and four marched forth of the hollow with step blithe and free, and swung away through the green till the sound of voice and laughter, the ring and clash of their going was died away and none remained, save where, cross-legged upon the sward, his open wallet on his knee, the round and buxom Pardoner sat to cherish a bruised arm and to stare from earth to heaven and from heaven to earth with eyes wider and rounder even than was their wont and custom.

CHAPTER XXXIV

HOW THEY CAME TO BELSAYE

THROUGH broad glades deep-hid within the wild; by shady alleyway and leafy track they held their march south and by east, a close, well-ordered company striding long and free and waking the solitudes to a blithe babblement of laughing echoes. And who among them all so merry as Giles o' the Bow at the head of his sturdy archers? Oft trolling some merry stave or turning with some quip or jape upon his tongue, but with eyes quick to mark the rhythmic swing of broad, mail-clad shoulders, eyes critical, yet eyes of pride. Who so grimly eager as mighty Walkyn, his heavy axe lightly a-swing, his long legs schooling themselves to his comrade's slower time and pace? Who so utterly content as Black Roger, oft glancing from Beltane's figure in the van to the files of his pike-men, their slung shields agleam, their spears well sloped? And who so gloomy and thoughtful as Beltane, unmindful of the youthful knight who went beside him, and scarce heeding his soft-spoke words until his gaze by chance lighted upon the young knight's armour that gleamed in the sun 'neath rich surcoat; armour of the newest fashion of link, reinforced by plates of steel, gorget and breast, elbow and knee, and with cunningly jointed sollerets. Moreover, his shield was small and light according with the new fashion, and bare the blazon of two hands, tight clasped, and the legend: "Semper Fidelis."

Now viewing all this with a smith's knowledgful eye, quick to note the costly excellence of this equipment, Beltane forthwith brake silence:

"How do men name thee, sir knight?"

Hereupon, after some delay, the young knight made answer:

"Messire, the motto I bear upon my shield is a good motto methinks. So shalt call me Fidelis an ye will, my lord."

"So be it, Sir Faithful," saying which Beltane fell to deep thought again.

"I pray you, my lord," quoth Fidelis, "wherefore so sad, so full of gloom and thought?"

"I seek how we may win through the gates of Belsaye, Sir Fidelis, for they go strongly guarded night and day; yet this day, ere sunset, ope to us they must. But how — how?"

"My lord," spake Sir Fidelis, "I have heard say that few may go where many oft-times may not. Let first some two or three adventure it, hid 'neath some close disguise —"

"A disguise!" cried Beltane, "Ha — a disguise. 'Tis well bethought, good Fidelis. Forsooth, a disguise! And 'twill be market day!" Thereafter Beltane strode on, head bent in frowning thought, nor spake again for a space. And ever the files swung along behind in time to a marching song carolled blithe in the rich, sweet voice of Giles. At length Beltane raised his head and beholding the sun well-risen, halted his company beside a stream that flowed athwart their way, and sitting thereby, summoned to him the four — namely, Walkyn and Roger, Giles and Eric of the wry neck; and while they ate together, they held counsel on this wise:

BELTANE. "How think ye of this our adventure, comrades all?"

GILES. "Forsooth, as a man do I think well of it. Ho! for the twang of bowstrings! the whirr and whistle of well-sped shafts loosed from the ear! Ha! as an archer and a man 'tis an adventure that jumpeth with my desire. But — as a soldier, and one of much and varied experience, as one that hath stormed Belsaye ere now — with divers other towns, cities, keeps, and castles beyond number — as a soldier, I do think it but a gloomy business and foredoomed to failure —"

BELTANE. " And wherefore? "

GILES. " Method, tall brother, method precise and soldier-like. War is a very ancient profession — an honourable profession and therefore to be treated with due reverence. Now, without method, war would become but a scurvy, sorry, hole-and-corner business, unworthy your true soldier. So I, a soldier, loving my profession, do stand for method in all things. Thus, would I attack a city, I do it *modo et forma:* first, I set up my mantelets for my archers, and under cover of their swift shooting I set me up my mangonels, my trebuchets and balistae: then, pushing me up, assault the walls with cat, battering-ram and sap, and having made me a breach, would forthwith take me the place by sudden storm."

ROGER. " Ha, bowman! here is overmuch of thee, methinks! And dost speak like a very archer-like fool — and forsooth, a foolish archer to boot. Sure, well ye know that engines for the battery have we none —"

GILES. " Verily! So shall we none of Belsaye, methinks. Lacking engines, we lack for all — no method, no city! Remember that, dolt Rogerkin! "

ROGER. " Nay, I remember Garthlaxton aflame, the gallows aflare, and the empty dungeon. So, an we go up 'gainst Belsaye again, shall we surely take it. Remember these, long-winded Giles, and being a soldier, be ye also — a man."

BELTANE. " What think you, Walkyn? "

WALKYN. (patting his axe) " Of Gui of Allerdale, master."

BELTANE. " And you, Eric? "

ERIC. " That where thou dost go, messire, we follow."

BELTANE. " 'Tis well. Now here beside me sitteth Sir Fidelis, who though methinks the most youthful of us all, hath a head in council wiser than us all. For he hath spoke me that whereby though few in number and lacking engines for battery, Giles — we yet may win through the walls of Belsaye ere sun-down. Know you this country, Walkyn?"

WALKYN. "As my hand, lord."

BELTANE. "Is there a village hereabouts?"

WALKYN. "Aye, five miles west by south is Brand-le-Dene. But there is a mill scarce a mile down stream, I wot."

BELTANE. "A mill? 'Twill serve — go ye thither. Here is money — buy therewith four hats and smocks the like that millers wear, and likewise four meal-sacks well stuffed with straw."

WALKYN. (rising) "Smocks, master? Straw and meal-sacks?"

BELTANE. "And haste, Walkyn. We must be far hence within the hour."

Forthwith up rose Walkyn and summoning divers of his company strode away down stream, what time Giles, staring after him in wonderment, thereafter shook his head at Roger. Quoth he:

"Tall brother and lord, now do I see that our Roger burneth for knowledge, panteth for understanding, and fain would question thee but that his mouth is full-crammed of meat. Yet do his bulging eyes supplicate the wherefore of smocks, and his goodly large ears do twitch for the why of sacks. O impatient Rogerkin, bolt thy food, man, gulp — swallow, and ask and importune my lord thyself!"

"Not I — not I!" quoth Roger, "an my master lacketh for a smock or a sack, for me is no question of wherefore or why, so long as he doth get them!"

"But the straw, Roger," said Giles, glancing askew at Beltane, "an thou should'st plague my lord with questions, how think ye then he shall answer of this straw?"

"Thus, thou crafty Giles," answered Beltane. "Belsaye is strong, but strength may be, perchance, beguiled. So may a miller's smock hide a shirt of mail, and straw, I have heard, will burn."

"Oho, a wile!" cried Giles, "Aha! some notable wile! What more?"

"More shalt thou know, mayhap, in Belsaye market-place."

And when Beltane had handled the well-worn smocks, had viewed the bulging meal-sacks that Walkyn and his fellows brought him, he arose. At his word the company fell to their ranks and forthwith swung off again south and by east, what time Giles carolled blithely, and divers chorused lustily: while Roger whistled and even grim Walkyn (bethinking him of Gui of Allerdale) rumbled hoarsely in his hairy throat.

So the miles passed unheeded until, as the sun declined, they left the wild country behind; wherefore Beltane commanded all men to a strict silence and thus came they betimes to the edge of the woods, and halting within the green, beheld afar across the plain, the walls of fair Belsaye town.

"We are well to time," quoth Beltane, glancing from sinking sun to lengthening shadow, "we have yet an hour to sunset, but in this hour much have we to do! Hark ye now!" and drawing the four about him, he spake them thus: "Walkyn and Roger and Eric shall into the town with me in miller's guise, each bearing his sack of flour, what time you, Giles, with Sir Fidelis and all our power bide here well hid till such time as ye shall see a smoke within Belsaye. And when ye see this smoke, rise up and make you ready one and all, yet stir not from the green till that ye hear my bugle-horn sound our rallying-note. Then come ye on amain, and being within the city, charge ye where my horn shall sound. How now, is't agreed?"

"Aye, lord!" nodded Giles, "'tis an excellent strategy in faith, and yet 'twere wiser methinks to suffer me in Roger's place: for being guileful in war, so should I be a very beguiling miller, whereas Roger, an we plastered him with flour, would ne'er be other than Rogerkin the Black."

"Nay Giles, thy post is here. Let your bows be strung

and ready, but set your pikes to the fore — and Giles, watch! Walkyn, bring now the smocks."

So saying, Beltane tightened his belt, drew on his hood of mail and laced it close, and turning, found Sir Fidelis close by to aid him with the hooded smock; and Beltane wondered to see him so pale and his slender hands a-tremble.

So the smocks were donned, with straw about their legs bound by withies as was the custom, and taking the sacks upon their shoulders, they turned aside into the green and were gone.

CHAPTER XXXV

HOW GUI OF ALLERDALE CEASED FROM EVIL

SIR GUI of Allerdale, lord Seneschal of Belsaye town, rode hawk on fist at the head of divers noble knights and gentle esquires with verderers and falconers attendant. The dusty highway, that led across the plain to the frowning gates of Belsaye, was a-throng with country folk trudging on foot or seated in heavy carts whose clumsy wheels creaked and groaned city-wards; for though the sun was far declined, it was market-day: moreover a man was to die by the fire, and though such sights were a-plenty, yet 'twas seldom that any lord, seneschal, warden, castellan or — in fine, any potent lord dowered with right of pit and gallows — dared lay hand upon a son of the church, even of the lesser and poorer orders; but Sir Gui was a bold man and greatly daring. Wherefore it was that though the market-traffic was well nigh done, the road was yet a-swarm with folk all eager to behold and watch how a white friar could face death by the flame. So, on horse and afoot, in creaking cart and wain, they thronged toward the goodly city of Belsaye.

Sir Gui rode at a hand-pace, and as he rode the folk drew hastily aside to give him way, and bent the knee full humbly or stood with bowed heads uncovered to watch him pass; but 'neath bristling brows, full many an eye glared fiercely on his richly-habited, slender figure, marking his quick, dark glance, the down-curving, high-bridged nose of him with the thin lips and the long, pointed chin below.

Thus rode he, assured in his might and confident, heedless alike of the glory of day fast drawing into evening, of the green world whose every blade and leaf spake of life abundant, and of these trampling folk who bent so humbly at his passing, their cheeks aglow with health; thus, heeding but himself and his own most dear desires, how should he mark the four tall and dusty miller's men whose brawny backs were stooped each beneath its burden? And how should he, confident in his strength and might, hale and lusty in his body, come to think on death sharp and swift? Thus Sir Gui of Allerdale, lord Seneschal of Belsaye town, rode upon his way, with eyes that glowed with the love of life, and tongue that curled 'twixt smiling lips as one that savoured its sweetness or meditated coming joys. Perceiving the which, two youthful esquires that rode near by nudged elbows, and set their heads together.

"I know yon look — aha! 'tis the goldsmith's fair young wife. There have been lovers who loved love ere now — Pan, see you, and Jove himself they say: but Pan was coy, and Jove —"

"Hist, he beckons us!"

So came these young esquires beside Sir Gui who, tapping the dust from his habit with soft white hand, spake soft-voiced and sweet.

"Ride on, sirs, and bid our careful warden stay awhile the execution of this traitorous friar. Let the square be lined with pikes as is our custom: let the prisoner be chained unto his stake see you, but let all things stay until I be come. There will be many folk in Belsaye, meseemeth, well — let them wait, and stare, and whisper, and — wait, till I be come!"

Forward spurred the young esquires to do as was commanded, joyful to see the confusion that marked their swift career and making good play of their whips on the heads and shoulders of such as chanced to be within reach; in especial upon a mighty fellow in floured smock that bare a sack on his shoulder and who, stung with the blow, cried a curse on them in voice so harsh and bold that folk shrank from his neighbourhood, yet marvelled at his daring. Being come anon within the city Sir Gui dismounted beside the gate, and giving horse and falcon to an esquire, beckoned to him a grizzled man-at-arms; now as he did so, a tall miller passed him by, and stumbling wearily, set down his sack against the wall and panted.

"Bare you the letter as I commanded, Rolf?"

"Aye, my lord."

"What said she?"

"Wept, my lord."

"Spake she nought?"

"Nought, my lord."

"Lieth the goldsmith deep?"

"Above the water-dungeons, my lord."

"And she wept, say you? Methinks the goldsmith shall go free to-morrow!"

So saying, Sir Gui went on into the city, and as he went, his smile was back again, and his tongue curved red betwixt his lips. And presently the tall miller hoisted his burden and went on into the city also; turned aside down a narrow passage betwixt gloomy houses, and so at last out into the square that hummed with a clamour hushed and expectant. But my lord Seneschal, unheeding ever, came unto a certain quiet corner of the square remote and shady, being far removed from the stir and bustle of the place; here he paused at an open doorway and turned to look back into the square, ruddy with sunset — a careless glance that saw the blue of sky, the heavy-timbered houses bathed in the warm sunset glow, the which, falling athwart the square, shone red upon the smock of a miller, who stooping 'neath his burden, stumbled across the uneven cobble-stones hard by. All this saw Sir Gui in that one backward glance; then, unheeding as ever, went in at the doorway and up the dark and narrow stair. But now it chanced that the miller, coming also to this door, stood a while sack on shoulder, peering up into the gloom within; thereafter, having set down his burden in stealthy fashion, he also turned and glanced back with eyes that glittered in the shadow of his hat: then, setting one hand within his smock, he went in at the door and, soft-footed began to creep up that dark and narrow stair.

She sat in a great carven chair, her arms outstretched across the table before her, her face bowed low between, and the setting sun made a glory of her golden hair. Of a sudden she started, and lifting her head looked upon Sir Gui; her tears, slow-falling and bitter, staining the beauty of her face.

"My lord — ah, no!" she panted, and started to her feet.

"Dear and fair my lady — fear not. Strong am I, but very gentle — 'tis ever my way with beauty. I do but come for my answer." And he pointed to a crumpled parchment that lay upon the table.

"O, good my lord," she whispered, "I cannot! If thou art gentle indeed — then —"

"He lieth above the water-dungeons, lady!" sighed Sir Gui.

"Ah, the sweet Christ aid me!"

"To-morrow he goeth to death, or lieth in those round, white arms. Lady, the choice is thine: and I pray you show pity to thy husband who loveth thee well, 'tis said." Now hereupon she sobbed amain and fell upon her knees with arms outstretched in passionate appeal — but lo! she spake no word, her swimming eyes oped suddenly wide, and with arms yet outstretched she stared and stared beyond Sir Gui in so much that he turned and started back amazed — to behold one clad as a dusty miller, a mighty man whose battered hat touched the lintel and whose great bulk filled the doorway — a very silent man who looked and looked with neck out-thrust, yet moved not and uttered no word. Hereupon Sir Gui spake quick and passion-choked:

"Fool — fool! hence, thou blundering fool. For this shalt be flayed alive. Ha! — hence, thou dusty rogue!" But now this grim figure stirred, and lifting a great hand, spake hoarse and low:

"Peace, knight! Hold thy peace and look!" The wide-eaved hat was tossed to the floor and Sir Gui, clenching his hands, would have spoken but the harsh voice

How Sir Gui Ceased from Evil 283

drowned his words: "How, knight, thou that art Bloody Gui of Allerdale! Dost thou not know me, forsooth? I am Waldron, whose father and mother and sister ye slew. Aye, Waldron of Brand am I, though men do call me Walkyn o' the Dene these days. Brand was a fair manor, knight — a fair manor, but long since dust and ashes — ha! a merry blaze wherein father and mother and sister burned and screamed and died — in faith, a roguish blaze! Ha! d'ye blench? Dost know me, forsooth?"

Then Sir Gui stepped back, drawing his sword; but, even so, death leapt at him. A woman, wailing, fled from the chamber, a chair crashed to the floor; came a strange, quick tapping of feet upon the floor and thereafter rose a cry that swelled louder to a scream — louder to a bubbling shriek, and dying to a groaning hiss, was gone.

And, in a while, Walkyn, that had been Waldron of Brand, rose up from his knees, and running forth of the chamber, hasted down the dark and narrow stair.

CHAPTER XXXVI

HOW THE FOLK OF BELSAYE TOWN MADE THEM AN
END OF TYRANNY

THE market-place was full of the stir and hum of jostling crowds; here were pale-faced townsfolk, men and women and children who, cowed by suffering and bitter wrong, spake little, and that little below their breath; here were country folk from village and farmstead near and far, a motley company that talked amain, loud-voiced and eager, as they pushed and strove to see where, in the midst of the square beyond the serried ranks of pike-men, a post had been set up; a massy post, grim and solitary, whose heavy chains and iron girdle gleamed ominous and red in the last rays of sunset. Near by, upon a dais, they had set up a chair fairly gilded, wherein Sir Gui was wont to sit and watch justice done upon the writhing bodies of my lord Duke's enemies. Indeed, the citizens of Belsaye had beheld sights many and dire of late, wherefore now they blenched before this stark and grisly thing and looked askance; but to these country folk such things were something newer, wherefore they pushed and strove amid the press that they might view it nearer — in especial two in miller's hooded smocks, tall and lusty fellows these, who by dint of shoulder and elbow, won forward until they were stayed by the file of Sir Gui's heavy-armed pikemen. Thereupon spake one, close in his fellow's ear: —

"Where tarries Walkyn, think you?" said Beltane below his breath.

"Master, I know not — he vanished in the press but now —"

"And Eric?"

"He watcheth our meal-sacks. Shall I not go bid him

strike flint and steel? The time were fair, methinks?"

"Not so, wait you until Sir Gui be come and seated in his chair of state: then haste you to bold Eric and, the sacks ablaze, shout 'fire;' so will I here amid the press take up the cry, and in the rush join with ye at the gate. Patience, Roger."

And now of a sudden the throng stirred, swayed and was still; but from many a quivering lip a breath went up to heaven, a sigh — a whispered groan, as, through the shrinking populace, the prisoner was brought. A man of Belsaye he, a man strong and tender, whom many had loved full well. Half borne, half dragged betwixt his gaolers, he came on stumbling feet — a woeful shivering thing with languid head a-droop; a thing of noisome rags that told of nights and days in dungeon black and foul; a thing whose shrunken nakedness showed a multitude of small wounds, slow-bleeding, that spoke of teeth little yet vicious, bold with hunger in the dark; a miserable, tottering thing, haggard and pinched, that shivered and shook and stared upon all things with eyes vacant and wide.

And thus it was that Beltane beheld again Friar Martin, the white friar that had been a man once, a strong man and a gentle. They brought him to the great post, they clasped him fast within the iron band and so left him, shivering in his chains with head a-droop. Came the sound of muffled weeping from the crowd, while high above, in sky deepening to evening, a star twinkled. Now in a while the white friar raised his heavy head and looked round about, and lo! his eyes were vacant no longer, and as folk strove to come more nigh, he spake, hoarse-voiced and feeble.

"O children, grieve not for me, for though this body suffer a little, my soul doth sit serene. What though I stand in bonds, yet doth my soul go free. Though they burn my flesh to ashes yet doth my soul live on forever. So grieve not your hearts for me, my children, and, for yourselves, though ye be afflicted even as I — fear ye nothing — since I, that ye all do know for a truthful man, do tell ye 'tis none so hard to die if that our hearts be clean. What though ye suffer the grievous horror of a prison? Within the dark ye shall find God. Thus I amid the dreadful gloom of my deep dungeon did lie within the arms of God, nothing fearing. So, when the fire shall sear me, though this my flesh may groan, God shall reach down to me through smoke and flame and lift my soul beyond. O be ye therefore comforted, my children: though each must die, yet to the pure in heart death is none so hard —"

Thus spake Friar Martin, shivering in his bonds, what time the crowd rocked and swayed, sobbing aloud and groaning; whereat Sir Gui's pikemen made lusty play with their spear-shafts.

Then spake Beltane, whispering, to Roger, who, sweating with impatience, groaned and stared and gnawed upon his fingers:

"Away, Roger!" And on the instant Roger had turned, and with brawny shoulders stooped, drove through the swaying press and was gone.

Now with every moment the temper of the crowd grew more threatening; voices shouted, fists were clenched, and the scowling pike-men, plying vicious spear-butts, cursed, and questioned each other aloud: "Why tarries Sir Gui?"

Hereupon a country fellow hard by took up the question:

"Sir Gui!" he shouted, "Why cometh not Sir Gui?"

"Aye!" cried others, "where tarries Sir Gui?" "Why doth he keep us?" "Where tarries Sir Gui?"

"Here!" roared a voice deep and harsh, "Way — make way!" And suddenly high above the swaying crowd rose the head and shoulders of a man, a mighty man in the dusty habit of a miller, upon whose low-drawn hood and be-floured smock were great gouts and stains evil and dark; and now, beholding what manner of stains these were, all men fell silent and blenched from his path. Thus amid a lane of pallid faces that stared and shrank away, the tall miller came unto the wondering pike-men — burst their ranks and leapt upon the dais where stood the gilded chair.

"Ho! soldiers and men-at-arms — good people of Belsaye — call ye for Gui in sooth? hunger ye for sight of Bloody Gui of Allerdale in faith? Why then — behold!" and from under his be-dabbled smock he drew forth a head, pale as to cheek and hair, whose wide eyes stared blindly as it dangled in his hairy hand; and now, staring up at this awful, sightless thing — that brow at whose frown a city had trembled, those pallid lips that had smiled, and smiling, doomed men and women to torment and death — a hush fell on Belsaye and no man spoke or stirred.

Then, while all folk stood thus, rigid and at gaze, a wild cry was heard, shivering the stillness and smiting all hearts with sudden dread: —

"Fire! Fire!"

"Aye, fire!" roared the miller, "see yonder!" and he pointed where a column of thick smoke mounted slowly upon the windless air. But with the cry came tumult — a hurry of feet, shouts and yells and hoarse commands; armour clashed and pike-heads glittered, down-sweeping for the charge. Then Walkyn laughed, and hurling the pale head down at the nearest soldiery, drew from his smock his mighty axe and swung it, but lo! 'twixt him and the pike-men was a surging, ravening mob that closed, front and rear, upon knight and squire, upon pike-man and man-at-arms, men who leapt to grip mailed throats in naked hands, women who screamed and tore. And one by one, knight and squire, and man-at-arms, smiting, shrieking, groaning, were dragged down with merciless hands, to be wrenched at, torn, and trampled 'neath merciless feet, while high and clear above this fierce and dreadful clamour rose the shrill summons of a horn.

And lo! a shout — a roar — drowning the shrieks of dying men, the screams of vengeful women, "Arise — arise — Pentavalon!" Came a rush of feet, a shock, and thereafter a confused din that rose and fell and, gradually ceasing, was lost in a sudden clamour of bells, fierce-pealing in wild and joyous riot.

"Aha! 'tis done —'tis done!" panted Roger, stooping to cleanse his blade, "spite of all our lack of method, Giles —'tis done! Hark ye to those joy-bells! So doth fair Belsaye shout to all men she is free at last and clean of Gui and all his roguish garrison —"

"Clean?" quoth Giles. "Clean, forsooth? Roger — O Roger man, I have seen men die in many and divers ungentle ways ere now, but these men — these men of Gui's, look — look yonder! O sweet heaven keep me ever from the tearing hands of vengeful mothers and women wronged!" And turning his back on the littered market square, Giles shivered and leaned him upon his sword as one that is sick.

"Nay," said Black Roger, "Gui's black knaves being rent in pieces, Giles, we shall be saved the hanging of them — ha! there sounds my lord's horn, and 'tis the rallying-note — come away, Giles!"

Side by side they went, oft stepping across some shapeless horror, until in their going they chanced on one that knelt above a child, small and dead. And beholding the costly fashion of this man's armour, Roger stooped, and wondering, touched his bowed shoulder:

"Sir Fidelis," said he, "good young messire, and art thou hurt, forsooth?"

"Hurt?" sighed Sir Fidelis, staring up great-eyed, "hurt? Nay, behold this sweet babe — ah, gentle Christ — so innocent — and slain! A tender babe! And yonder — yonder, what dire sights lie yonder —" and sighing, the youthful knight sank back across Black Roger's arm and so lay speechless and a-swoon.

Quoth Roger, grim-smiling:

"What, Giles, here's one that loveth woman's finger-work no more than thou!" Thus saying, he stooped and lifting the young knight in his arms, bore him across the square, stumbling now and then on things dim-seen in the dark, for night was at hand.

So thus it was that the folk of fair Belsaye town, men and women with gnashing teeth and rending hands, made them an end of Tyranny, until with the night, there nothing remained of proud Sir Gui and all his lusty garrison, save shapeless blotches piled amid the gloom — and that which lay, forgotten quite, a cold and pallid thing, befouled with red and trampled mire; a thing of no account henceforth, that stared up with glazed and sightless eyes, where, remote within the sombre firmament of heaven, a great star glowed and trembled.

CHAPTER XXXVII

HOW THEY LEFT BELSAYE

LANTHORNS gleamed and torches flared in the great square of Belsaye where panting, shouting townsfolk thronged upon Beltane and his company with tears of joy, with laughter loud and high-pitched, with shouts and wild acclaim; many there were who knelt to kiss their sun-browned hands, their feet, the very links of their armour. And presently came Giles o' the Bow, debonair and smiling, a woman's scarf about his brawny throat, a dozen ribands and favours tied about each mailed arm.

"Lord," quoth he, "tall brother, I have been fairly kissed by full a score of buxom dames — the which is excellent good, for the women of Belsaye are of beauty renowned. But to kiss is a rare and notable science, and to kiss well a man should eat well, and forsooth, empty am I as any drum! Therefore prithee let us eat, that I may uphold my reputation, for, as the learned master Ovidius hath it, ' *osculos* '—"

But from the townsfolk a shout arose:

"Comes the Reeve! 'Tis good master Cuthbert! Way for the Reeve!"

Hereupon the crowd parting, a tall man appeared, his goodly apparel torn, his long white hair disordered, while in his hand he yet grasped a naked sword. Stern his face was, and lined beyond his years, moreover his broad shoulders were bowed with more than age; but his eye was bright and quick, and when he spake, his voice was strong and full.

"Which, I pray, is chiefest among ye?"

"That am I," quoth Beltane.

"Messire," said the Reeve, "who and what men ye are I know not, but in the name of these my fellow-citizens do I thank ye for our deliverance. But words be poor things, now therefore, an it be treasure ye do seek ye shall be satisfied. We have suffered much by extortion, but if gold be your desire, then whatsoever gold doth lie in our treasury, the half of it is freely thine."

"O most excellent Reeve!" cried Giles, "forsooth, a very proper spirit of gratitude."

"Good master," spake Beltane, quelling the archer with a look, "these my comrades hither came that a noble man should not perish, and that Sir Gui of Allerdale should cease from evil, and behold, 'tis done! So I pray you, give us food and shelter for the night, for with the dawn we march hence."

"But — O tall brother!" gasped Giles, "O sweet lord, there was mention made of treasure! A large-souled Reeve — a Reeve with bowels! 'Treasure' quoth he, and likewise 'gold!' And these be matters to excogitate upon. Moreover, *pecuniæ obediunt omnia*, brother."

"Money, forsooth!" quoth Beltane bitterly; "now out upon thee, Giles — how think ye money shall avail the like of us whose lives are forfeit each and every, whose foes be many and strong, who must ever be on our ward, quick to smite lest we be smitten — money, forsooth! So, good master Reeve, keep thy useless treasure, and, in its stead, give to us good steel — broadswords, sharp and well-tempered and stout link-mail — give of these to such as lack."

"But — O brother," says Giles, "with gold may we gain all these."

"Verily, Giles, but gaining all without gold we lack not for gold, nor have the added fear of losing it. He that would gain wealth must first win freedom, for without freedom the richest is but a sorry slave. So give us steel, good master Reeve."

Now from Giles' archers and divers others beside a growl went up, spreading from rank to rank, what time Beltane clenched his hands, frowning ever blacker. Then forth stepped Jenkyn o' the Ford with tall Orson, which last spake with voice uplift:

"Master," quoth he, "us do love gold — but fighting men us do be, and if ' steel ' says you —' steel ' says we!"

"Aye," nodded Jenkyn, " so look'ee master, here stands I wi' Orson my comrade look'ee, for witness that to-day we be better men than these growlers."

But here, of a sudden, rose the shrill bray of a trumpet without the walls, a long flourish, loud and imperious; and at the sound a silence fell, wherein divers of the townsfolk eyed each other in fear swift-born, and drew nearer to the white-haired Reeve who stood leaning heavily upon his sword, his head stooped upon his broad chest. And in the silence, Giles spake:

" Now, by the ever-blessed Saint Giles, there spake the summons of Robert of Hurstmanswyke — I know his challenge of old — ha, bows and bills!" So saying he bent and strung his bow.

" Aye," nodded Roger, loosening sword in sheath, " and Sir Robert is a dour fighter I've heard."

" So soon!" groaned the Reeve, " so very soon! Now God pity Belsaye!"

" Amen!" quoth Giles, fidgeting uneasily with his bow, " forsooth, Sir Robert is a very potent lord — God help us all, say I!"

" And Sir Robert likewise," quoth Roger, " for methinks an he come within Belsaye he is like to stay in Belsaye — mind ye Sir Gui, and mark ye my master's look!" And he pointed where Beltane stood near by, chin in fist, his eye bright and purposeful, his mouth grim-smiling; even as they watched he beckoned Walkyn and Eric to him and spake certain commands what time the trumpet brayed again in summons fierce and arrogant.

" Good master Reeve," quoth Beltane, as Walkyn and Eric, obedient to his word, moved into the square to right and left, each with his company, " there is one without that groweth impatient. Let us therefore parley with him from the battlement above the gate."

"Ah, messire," sighed the Reeve, "to what end? 'Tis Sir Robert's summons, and well I know he will demand speech with my lord Gui — alas for us and for Belsaye town!"

"Nay," answered Beltane, "be comforted. Answer as I shall direct and fear ye nothing. Come your ways."

Now when Roger turned and would have followed, Giles plucked him by the arm:

"Roger," quoth he, "Sir Robert will demand speech of Gui of Allerdale, mark ye that, my Rogerkin. Nor will he speak to any but Sir Gui — for a great lord and proud is Robert of Hurstmanswyke. Ha, what think ye, Roger?"

"I think perchance he must go dumb then — come, let us follow."

"Nay, but speak he must — since he may tell us much, aye, and speak he shall. So come, my Rogerkin, hither with me!"

"With thee, Giles? And wherefore?"

"A wile, sweet Roger, a notable wile — a wile of wiles. Hush! speak not, but come — for mark this:

> "In faith a cunning man is Giles
> In counsel sage and full of wiles!"

"So come, Rogerkin!" So saying, he gripped stout Roger's arm and plunged into the crowd.

Being come out upon the battlement above the gate, Beltane, with the Reeve beside him, peering down through the dark, beheld beyond the moat, a knight supported by four esquires, and beyond these Beltane counted thirty lances what time the Reeve, steadying his voice, challenged them.

Hereupon the knight spake:

"Ha! do ye stir at last, dogs! Open in the Duke's name —'tis I, Robert, lord of Hurstmanswyke, with message to the lord Seneschal, Sir Gui, and captives from Bourne!"

Then, grim-smiling in the dusk, Beltane spake:

"Now greeting and fair greeting to thee, my lord, and to thy captives. Hath Thrasfordham fallen so soon?"

"Thrasfordham, fool! 'tis not yet invested — these be divers of Benedict's spies out of Bourne, to grace thy gibbets. Come, unbar — down with the drawbridge; open I say — must I wait thy rogue's pleasure?"

"Not so, noble lord. Belsaye this night doth welcome thee with open arms — and ye be in sooth Sir Robert of Hurstmanswyke."

"Ha, do ye doubt me, knave? Dare ye keep me without? Set wide the gates, and instantly, or I will see thee in a noose hereafter. Open! Open! God's death! will ye defy me? gate ho!"

So Beltane, smiling yet, descended from the battlement and bade them set wide the gates. Down creaked drawbridge; bars fell, bolts groaned, the massy gates swung wide — and Sir Robert and his esquires, with his weary captives stumbling in their jangling chains, and his thirty men-at-arms riding two by two, paced into Belsaye market square; the drawbridge rose, creaking, while gates clashed and bar and chain rattled ominously behind them. But Sir Robert, nothing heeding, secure in his noble might, scowled about him 'neath lifted vizor, and summoned the Reeve to his stirrup with imperious hand:

"How now, master Reeve," quoth he, "I am in haste to be gone: where tarries Sir Gui? Have ye not warned him of my coming? Go, say I crave instant speech with him on matters of state, moreover, say I bring fifty and three for him to hang to-morrow — go!"

But now, while the Reeve yet stood, pale in the torchlight, finding nought to say, came Beltane beside him.

"My lord," quoth he, "fifty and three is a goodly number; must they all die to-morrow?"

"To-morrow? Aye — or whensoever Sir Gui wills."

"Ah, fair lord," says Beltane, "then, as I guess, these fifty and three shall assuredly live on awhile, since Sir Gui of Allerdale will hang men no more."

"Ha, dare ye mock me, knave?" cried Sir Robert, and

clenching iron hand he spurred upon Beltane, but checked as suddenly, and pointed where, midst the shrinking populace, strode one in knightly armour, whose embroidered surcoat bore the arms, and whose vizored helm the crest of Sir Gui of Allerdale. Now beholding this silent figure, a groan of fear went up, divers men sank crouching on their knees, the Reeve uttered a hoarse gasp and covered his face, while even Beltane, staring wide-eyed, felt his flesh a-creep. But now Sir Robert rode forward:

"Greeting, lord Seneschal!" said he, "you come betimes, messire, though not over hastily, methinks!"

"Forsooth," quoth the figure, his voice booming in his great war-helm, "forsooth and verily there be three things no man should leave in haste: *videlicit* and to wit: his prayers, his dinner and his lady. None the less came I hither to give thee greeting, good my lord."

"My lord Seneschal, what manner of men be these of thine?"

"O fair sir, they be ordinary men, rogues, see you, and fools — save one, a comely man this, an archer unequalled, hight Giles o' the Bow, a man of wit, very full of strategies and wiles."

"Aye, but what of yon tall knave, now," said Sir Robert, pointing at Beltane, "who is he?"

"Forsooth, a knave, my lord, an arrant knave with long legs."

"He will look well on a gibbet, methinks, Sir Gui."

"Indeed, my lord he might grace the gallows as well as you or I."

"The rogue telleth me that you will hang men no more."

"Ha, said he so forsooth? dared he so asperse mine honour? Ha, here is matter for red-hot irons, the pincers and the rack, anon. But come, Sir Robert — thou dost bear news, belike; come your ways and drink a goblet of wine."

"Nay, my lord, I thank thee, but I must hence this night to Barham Broom. But for my news, 'tis this: the outlaw men call Beltane, hath, by devilish arts, sacked and burned Garthlaxton Keep."

"Why, this I knew; there is a lewd song already made thereon, as thus:

> "They gave Garthlaxton to the flame,
> Be glory to Duke Beltane's name,
> And unto lusty Giles the same,
>   *Dixit!*"

"Forsooth, a naughty song, a very gallows' song, in faith. Pray you, what more?"

"There hath come unto the Duke one hight Gurth — a hang-dog rogue that doth profess to know the lurking-place of this vile outlaw, and to-morrow at sunset, Sir Pertolepe and I with goodly force march into the green. So now must I hence, leaving with thee these captives from Bourne that you shall hang above the walls for a warning to all such outlaws and traitors. Lastly, my lord Seneschal, drink not so deep a-nights, and so, fare thee well."

Now as he yet spake rose the shrill notes of a horn, and turning about, Sir Robert beheld men whose mail glistened in the torchlight and whose long pikes hemmed him in close and closer what time a fierce shout went up: "Kill!" "Kill!"

"Ho, treason!" he roared, and grasped at his sword hilt; but down came Roger's heavy broadsword upon Sir Robert's helm, beating him to earth where Walkyn's mighty foot crushed him down and his axe gleamed bright. Then, while the air rang with shouts and cries and the clatter of trampling hoofs, a white figure leapt and bestrode the fallen knight, and Walkyn glared down into the pale face of Friar Martin.

"Forbear, Walkyn, forbear!" he cried, and speaking, staggered for very weakness and would have fallen but Walkyn's long arm was about him. And ever the uproar grew; the grim ranks of archers and pikemen drew closer about Sir Robert's shrinking men-at-arms what time the townsfolk, brandishing their weapons, shouted amain, "Kill! Kill!"

Now Roger's blow had been full lusty and Sir Robert yet lay a-swoon, seeing which, divers of his company, casting down their arms, cried aloud for quarter; whereat the townsfolk shouted but the fiercer: "Slay them! Kill! Kill!" But now, high above this clamour, rose the shrill note of Beltane's horn bidding all men to silence. Hereupon there came to him the white friar, who, looking earnestly upon his mailed face, uttered a sudden glad cry and caught his hand and kissed it; then turned he to the surging concourse and spake loud and joyously:

"Stay, good people of Belsaye! O ye children of affliction, spill not the blood of these thine enemies, but look, rather, upon this man! For this is he of whom I told ye in the days of your tribulation, this is he who burned the shameful gallows, who brake open the dungeon and hath vowed his life to the cause of the oppressed and weak. Behold now the son of Beltane the Strong and Just! Behold Beltane, our rightful Duke!" Now went there up to heaven a great and wild acclaim; shouts of joy and the thunderous battle-cry "Arise! Arise! Pentavalon!" Then, while all eyes beheld and all ears hearkened, Beltane spake him, plain and to the point, as was his custom:

"Behold now, men of Belsaye, these our enemies do cry us mercy, and shall we not bestow it? Moreover one living hostage is better than two foemen slain. Entreat them gently, therefore, but let me see them lodged secure ere I march hence."

But hereupon came many of the townsfolk with divers counsellors and chief men of the city who, kneeling, most earnestly prayed Beltane to abide for their defence.

"Good my lord," quoth the Reeve, "bethink thee, when Duke Ivo shall hear of our doings he will seek bitter vengeance. Ah, my lord, 'twas but five years agone he stormed Belsaye and gave it up to pillage — and on that day — my wife — was slain! And when he had set up his great gallows and hanged it full with our men, he vowed that, should Belsaye anger him again, he would burn the city and all within it and, O my lord, my lord — I have yet a daughter — Ah, good my lord, leave us not to ravishment and death!"

"Aye, go not from us, my lord!" cried the others. "Be thou our leader henceforth!" and thereto they besought him with eager cries and with hands outstretched.

But Beltane shook his head; quoth he:

"Look now, as men are born into the world but for the good of man, so must I to my duty. And methinks, this is my duty: to do such deeds as shall ring throughout this sorrowful Duchy like a trumpet-blast, bidding all men arise and take hold upon their manhood. Garthlaxton is no more, but there be many castles yet to burn whose flames, perchance, shall light such a fire within the souls of men as shall ne'er be quenched until Wrong and Tyranny be done away. So must I back to the wild-wood to wild and desperate doings. But, as for ye — I have heard tell that the men of Belsaye are brave and resolute. Let now the memory of wrongs endured make ye trebly valiant to maintain your new-got liberty. If Duke Ivo come, then let your walls be manned, for 'tis better to die free men than trust again to his mercy."

"Verily, lord," said the Reeve, "but we do lack for leaders. Our provost and all our captains Duke Ivo hanged upon his gallows. Beseech thee, then, give to us a leader cunning in war."

"That will I," answered Beltane, "on this condition — that every able man shall muster under arms each day within the market-square."

"It shall be done, my lord."

Then summoned he Eric of the wry neck, together with Giles who came forthwith, being yet bedight in Sir Gui's harness.

"Eric, I have marked thee well; methinks thou art one long bred to arms and learned in war?"

"My lord Beltane, in other days I was the Duke thy father's High Constable of all the coast-wise towns."

"Ha — say'st thou so in sooth? Then now do I make thee lord Constable of Belsaye. As to thee, Giles, thou guileful rogue, hast full oft vaunted thyself a soldier of experience, so now am I minded to prove thee and thy methods. How if I give thee charge over the bowmen of Belsaye?"

"Why first, sweet, tall brother, first will I teach them to draw a bow, pluck a string, and speed a shaft as never townsman drew, plucked or sped — in fine, I will teach them to shoot: and, thereafter, devoutly pray the good Saint Giles (that is my patron saint) to send us Black Ivo and his dogs to shoot at!"

"So be it. Choose ye now each ten men of your companies that shall abide here with ye what time I am away — yet first mark this: In your hands do I leave this fair city, to your care I give the lives and well-being of all these men and women and children. Come now, lay here your hands upon my sword and swear me to maintain Belsaye to the last man 'gainst siege or storm, so long as life be in you!"

Now when they had sworn, Beltane turned him to the Reeve:

"Good sir," quoth he, "I pray you loose now the captives from their chains. Let your prisoners be secured, and for the rest, let us now eat and drink lest we famish."

Thus in a while, Sir Robert of Hurstmanswyke, dazed and bewildered, and his four esquires, together with his thirty men-at-arms, stripped of armour and weapons, were led away and lodged secure beneath the keep.

Now it chanced that as Beltane stood apart with head a-droop as one in thought, there came to him Sir Fidelis and touched him with gentle hand.

"My lord Beltane," said he softly, "of what think you?"

"Of Pentavalon, and how soonest her sorrows may be done away."

"Lovest thou Pentavalon indeed, messire?"

"Aye, truly, Fidelis."

"Then wherefore let her suffer longer?"

"Suffer? Aye, there it is — but how may I bring her woes to sudden end? I am too weak, her oppressors many, and my men but few —"

"Few?" quoth Sir Fidelis, speaking with head low-stooped. "Few, messire? Not so. Ten thousand lances might follow thee to-morrow an thou but spake the word —"

"Nay," sighed Beltane, "mock me not, good Fidelis, thou dost know me a lonely man and friendless — to whom should I speak?"

"To one that loveth thee now as ever, to one that yearneth for thee with heart nigh to breaking — to Helen —"

"Ah!" quoth Beltane, slow and bitter, "speak word to Helen the Beautiful — the Wilful — the Wanton? No, a thousand times! Rather would I perish, I and all my hopes, than seek aid of such as she —"

"Lovest thou Pentavalon indeed, messire? Nay, methinks better far thou dost love thy cold and cruel pride — so must Pentavalon endure her grievous wrongs, and so do I pity her, but — most of all — I pity thee, messire!"

Now would Beltane have answered but found no word, and therefore fell to black and bitter anger, and, turning on his heel, incontinent strode away into the council-hall where a banquet had been spread. Frowning, he ate and drank in haste, scarce heeding the words addressed to him, wherefore others grew silent also; and thereafter, his hunger assuaged, strode he out into the square and summoned his company.

"Men of Pentavalon," spake he loud and quick, "howso poor and humble ye be, henceforth ye shall go, each and every, equipped in knightly mail from foot to head, your man's flesh as secure as flesh of any potent lord or noble of them all. Henceforth each man of us must fight as valiantly as ten. Now, if any there be who know the manage of horse and lance, let him step forth." Hereupon divers stepped out of the ranks, and Beltane counted of these fifty and two.

"Master Reeve," spake Beltane, " give now for guerdon instead of gold, horses and equipment for these my comrades, stout lances and mail complete with goodly bascinets."

"It shall be done, my lord."

"Roger, in thy command I set these fifty lances. See now to their arming, let them be mounted and ready with speed, for in this hour we ride."

"Aye, master," cried Roger, his eyes a-dance, " that will I, moreover —"

"Walkyn, to thee I give the pikes henceforth. As for our archers — Giles, which now think you fittest to command?"

"Why truly, brother — my lord, if one there be can twang a lusty bow and hath a cool and soldier-like head 'tis Jenkyn o' the Ford, and after him Walcher, and after him —"

"Jenkyn, do you henceforth look to our archers. Are these matters heard and known among ye?"

"Aye!" came the thunderous answer.

"'Tis well, for mark me, we go out to desperate doings, wherein obedience must be instant, wherein all must love like brothers, and, like brothers, fight shoulder to shoulder!"

Now came there certain of the citizens to Beltane, leading a great and noble war-horse, richly caparisoned, meet for his acceptance. And thus, ere the moon rose, equipped with lance and shield and ponderous, vizored casque, Beltane, gloomy and silent, with Sir Fidelis mounted beside him, rode forth at the head of his grim array, at whose tramp and jingle the folk of Belsaye shouted joyful acclaim while the bells rang out right joyously.

CHAPTER XXXVIII

OF BELTANE'S BLACK AND EVIL MOOD, AND HOW HE FELL IN WITH THE WITCH OF HANGSTONE WASTE

It was very dark upon the forest road, where trees loomed gigantic against the pitchy gloom wherein dim-seen branches creaked and swayed, and leaves rustled faint and fitful in the stealthy night-wind; and through the gloom at the head of his silent company Beltane rode in frowning thought, his humour blacker than the night.

Now in a while, Sir Fidelis, riding ever at his elbow, ventured speech with him:

"Art very silent, messire. Have I angered thee, forsooth? Is aught amiss betwixt us?"

Quoth Beltane, shortly:

"Art over-young, sir knight, and therefore fond and foolish. Is a man a lover of self because he hateth dishonour? Art a presumptuous youth — and that's amiss!"

"Art thou so ancient, messire, and therefore so wise as to judge 'twixt thy hates and loves and the abiding sorrows of Pentavalon?" questioned Fidelis, low-voiced and gentle.

"Old enough am I to know that in all this world is no baser thing than the treachery of a faithless woman, and that he who seeketh aid of such, e'en though his cause be just, dishonoureth himself and eke his cause. So God keep me from all women henceforth — and as for thee, speak me no more the name of this light wanton."

"My lord," quoth Sir Fidelis, leaning near, "my lord — whom mean you?"

"Whom should I mean but Mortain Helen — Helen the Beautiful —"

Of Beltane's Black Mood

Now cried Sir Fidelis as one that feels a blow, and, in the dark, he seized Beltane in sudden griping fingers, and shook him fiercely.

"And dare ye name her 'wanton!'" he cried. "Ye shall not — I say ye shall not!" But, laughing, Beltane smote away the young knight's hold and laughed again.

"Is this light lady's fame so dear to thee, poor, youthful fool?" said he. "Aye me! doubt not her falsity shall break thy heart some day and teach thee wisdom —"

A shout among the woods upon their right, a twinkling light that came and went amid the underbrush, and Walkyn appeared, bearing a lighted brand.

"Lord," he growled, "here has been devil's work of late, for yonder a cottage lieth a heap of glowing ashes, and upon a tree hard by a dead man doth swing."

"Learned ye aught else, Walkyn?"

"Nothing, save that a large company passed here yesterday as I judge. Horse and foot — going south, see you," and he held his torch to the trampled road.

"Going south — aye, Walkyn, to Barham Broom, methinks. Here is another debt shall yet be paid in full, mayhap," quoth Beltane grimly. "Forward!"

The jingling column moved on again, yet had gone but a little way when Sir Fidelis, uttering a cry, swerved his horse suddenly and sprang to earth.

"What now?" questioned Beltane, staring into the murk.

"My lord — my lord, a woman lieth here, and — ah, messire — she is dead!"

"O, a woman?" quoth Beltane, "and dead, say you? Why then, the world shall know less of evil and treachery, methinks. Come — mount, sir knight, mount, I say, and let us on!"

But Sir Fidelis, on his knees beside that silent, dim-seen form, heeded him not at all, and with reverent, folded hands, and soft and tender voice, spake a prayer for the departed soul. Now hereupon Beltane knew sudden shame and swift remorse, and bowed his head also, and would have prayed — yet could not; wherefore his black mood deepened and his anger grew more bitter.

"Mount, mount, sir knight!" cried he harshly. "Better to seek vengeance dire than mumble on thy knees — mount, I say!"

Forthwith Sir Fidelis arose, nothing speaking, and being in the saddle, reined back and suffered Beltane to ride alone. But in a while, Beltane perceiving himself thus shunned, found therein a new grievance and fiercely summoned Sir Fidelis beside him.

"Wherefore slink ye behind me?" he demanded.

Then spake Sir Fidelis in voice full low and troubled:
"My lord Beltane, 'twas said thou wert a noble knight — very strong and very gentle —"

"Ha! dost think such report a lie, mayhap?"

"Alas!" sighed the young knight; and again "alas!" and therewith a great sob brake from him.

Of a sudden, from the gloom beside the way rose a woman's scream, and thereafter a great and fierce roar; and presently came Walkyn with his torch and divers of his men, dragging a woman in their midst, and lo! it was the witch of Hangstone Waste.

Now she, beholding Beltane's face beneath his lifted vizor, cried out for very joy:

"Now heaven bless thee, Duke Beltane! Ah, my lord — hear me!"

"What would ye? What seek ye of such as I?"

But hereupon Black Roger spurred beside Beltane, his eyes wide and fearful in the shadow of his helm, his strong, mailed hand a-tremble on Beltane's arm.

"Beware, my lord, beware!" he cried, "'tis nigh the midnight hour and she a noted witch — heed her not lest she blight thy fair body, lest she —"

"Peace, Roger! Now speak, woman — what would ye?"

"A life, my lord!"

"Ah, the blessed saints forfend — I feared so!" gasped Roger.

Of Beltane's Black Mood 305

But now the witch turned and looked on Roger, and he incontinent crossed himself and fell thenceforth to mumbling prayers beneath his breath.

"Lord Duke, for that I am but a woman poor and helpless, now would I beseech thine aid for —"

"Nay, tell me first, whence come ye?"

"From Barham Broom, messire. Ah! spare aid for one that lieth in peril of death — the maid Mellent — they do proclaim her witch — they will burn her —"

"O — a woman!" quoth Beltane, wrinkling his brows; and beholding Sir Fidelis watching him, straightway frowned the blacker.

"Nay, messire, hear me!" cried the witch, "ah, turn not away! This maid, indeed, is not of common blood — a lady is she of birth and wide demesnes —"

"Why then," said Beltane, heedful ever of the young knight's burning glance, "why then is she more apt for treachery and evil."

"Not so, my lord; weak is she and beset by cruel enemies. I found her, a stranger, wandering lonely in the green, and she, being sick of heart and brain, spake wild words of a great wrong, vainly done and suffered, and of an abiding remorse. And when I had nursed her into health she told me a wondrous tale. So, lord Beltane, do I know that in her hands thy happiness doth lie."

"Not so!" sighed Beltane. "Happiness and I are strangers henceforth —"

But here once again came a hoarse and angry roar with the sound of desperate struggling amid the leaves hard by, whence came Jenkyn and Orson with divers others, dragging a strange, hairy, dwarf-like creature, great and shaggy of head and with the arms and shoulders of a giant; smirched was he in blood from a great wound above the brow and his rich habit was mired and torn. Now looking upon this monstrous creature that writhed and struggled mightily with his captors, groaning and roaring betimes, Beltane felt his flesh a-creep with swift and pregnant memory, and straightway beset the witch with fierce question:

"Woman, what thing is this?"

"My lord, 'tis naught but poor Ulf, a natural, messire, very strong and faithful, that hath fought mightily and is nigh slain in our defence — see how he bleeds! Let them not harm him, my lord!"

"Yet have I seen him ere this, methinks."

"But for the maid Mellent — thou wilt not let her burn — and for thy deeds?"

"Mine, forsooth! How mean you?"

"'Twas yester-eve we were beset hereabouts by a lewd company, and brought unto their lord, Sir Gilles of Brandonmere — a man beyond all other men base and vile — who, beholding her so young and fair would have forced her to his will."

"Ha! — methinks Sir Gilles doth live too long!"

"So to save her from his violence, I discovered to him her name and high estate, whereupon at first he would fain have her wed with him. But, angered by her scorn, he bore her with him to Duke Ivo at Barham Broom, and me also. And there I heard her denounced as witch, by whose spells thou, lord Beltane, wert freed of thy duress and Garthlaxton utterly destroyed. Thus, to-morrow she must burn, unless one can be found to champion her cause and prove her innocent by trial of combat. So, when they had let me go I came seeking thee, my lord, since 'tis said thou art a very strong man and swift to aid the defenceless." Now glancing aside upon Sir Fidelis, Beltane beheld him leaning forward with his lips apart and slender hands tight-clasped; whereupon he frowned and shook his head.

"A woman!" quoth he, "nay, I had rather fight in a dog's cause."

"Forsooth!" cried Roger, "for rogue is he and fool that would champion a vile witch."

"Why, then, let us on, lord," growled Walkyn. "Why tarry we here?"

But now, as the witch sank upon the road with pleading hands uplifted, Sir Fidelis rode beside her and, stooping, caught her outstretched hands; quoth he:

"Of what avail to plead with such as these? So will I adventure me on behalf of this poor maid."

"Enough!" cried Beltane. "Walkyn, march ye one and all for Hundleby Fen — wait me there and let your watch be strict. But, an I come not within two days from now, then hie you each and every to reinforce Eric and Giles in Belsaye. As for Roger, he rideth with me to Barham Broom."

"Ha, lord! — wilt fight, then, in the witch's cause?" cried Walkyn.

"Aye, forsooth, though — forsooth I had rather fight in a dog's cause, for a dog, see you, is a faithful beast."

"To Barham Broom?" quoth Roger, staring. "Thou and I, master, to Black Ivo — alone?" And speaking, he loosened sword in scabbard.

"My lord Beltane," cried Sir Fidelis, beholding him with shining eyes, "an thou wilt do this noble thing, suffer me beside thee!"

"Not so, messire," answered Beltane, shaking his head, "art over young and tender, methinks — go, get thee back to her that sent thee — keep thou thy fond and foolish dream, and may thy gentle heart go unbroken. Come, Roger!"

So saying, Beltane wheeled about and rode away with Roger at his heels.

CHAPTER XXXIX

HOW BELTANE FOUGHT FOR ONE MELLENT THAT WAS A WITCH

BARHAM BROOM was gay with the stir of flags and streamers, where, above broidered pavilion and silken tent, pennons and banderoles, penoncels and gonfalons fluttered and flew, beyond which long lines of smaller tents stretched away north and south, east and west, and made up the camp of my lord Duke Ivo.

Beyond the confines of this great and goodly camp the lists had been formed, and here from earliest dawn a great concourse had been gathering; villein and vassal, serf and freedman from town and village: noble lords and ladies fair from castle hall and perfumed bower, all were here, for to-day a witch was to die — to-day, from her tortured flesh the flame was to drive forth and exorcize, once and for all, the demon who possessed her, by whose vile aid she wrought her charms and spells. So country wenches pushed and strove amid the throng, and dainty ladies leaned from canopied galleries to shudder with dread or trill soft laughter; but each and every stared at one who stood alone, 'twixt armed guards, so young and fair and pale within her bonds, oft turning piteous face to heaven or looking with quailing eye where stake and chain and faggot menaced her with awful doom. And ever the kindly sun rose high and higher, and ever the staring concourse grew.

Now, of a sudden the clarions rang out a point of war, and all voices were hushed, as, forth into the lists, upon his richly-caparisoned charger, my lord Duke Ivo rode, followed by his chiefest lords and barons; and as he rode, he smiled to himself full oft as one that meditates a hidden jest. Being come where the witch stood, her disordered garments rent by vicious handling, striving to veil her beauty in her long, dark hair, my lord Duke reined in his pawing steed to sit a while and look down at her 'neath sleepy lids; and, ever as he looked, his arching nostrils fluttered above curling lip, and ever he fingered his long, blue-shaven chin.

"Alack!" cried he at last, "'tis a comely wench, and full young, methinks, to die so soon! But witchcraft is a deadly sin, abhorred by man and hateful unto God —"

"My lord — my lord," spake the witch swift and passionate yet trembling 'neath his sleepy gaze, "thou knowest I am no witch indeed — thou knowest —"

"Nay, nay," quoth the Duke, shaking his head, and coming more near he stooped and spake her, low-voiced, "nay, she thou would'st name was a lady proud, soft and white, with hair bright and glorious as the sun — in sooth a fair lady — yet something too ambitious. But thou, though of her size and shape, art of a dark and swarthy hue and thy hair black, meseemeth. Of a verity thou art only the witch Mellent, and so, by reason of thy sun-browned skin and raven hair — aye, and for thy witchcraft — thou, alack! must die — unless thou find thee a champion. Verily I fear me no man will dare take up thy cause, for Sir Gilles is a lusty man and famous at the joust. Moreover — my will is known in the matter, so do I fear there none shall come to fight on thy behalf. Alack! that one should die so young!"

"Ah, my lord — my lord Ivo," she whispered, eager and breathless, "show me a little mercy. For that, to be thy Duchess, I denied thee thy desire in the past, let me now be prisoned all my days, an it be thy will — but give me not to the fire — ah, God — not the fire! Pity — pity me for what I did for thee — be merciful —"

"Did, wench — did?" quoth the Duke, gently. "Now when spake I with witch ere this? 'Tis true there was a lady — something of thy seeming — who, to gain much, promised much, and — achieved me nothing. So now do

I know thee for one Mellent, a notable witch, that shall this day instead of ducal crown, wear crown of flame. Alack! — and so, farewell!"

Thus speaking, my lord Duke rode on up the lists, where stood certain noble lords to hold his stirrup and aid him to earth; so mounted he to his place 'neath hroidered canopy, and many a fair cheek blanched, and many a stout knight faltered in his speech, beholding that slow-creeping, stealthy smile and the twitch of those thin nostrils.

Now once again the trumpet blew, and a herald stepped forth:

"God save ye, lord Duke," he cried, " ye noble lords and ladies fair — good people all, God save ye. Know that before you here assembled, hath been brought one Mellent — that hath been denounced a notable witch and sorceress, who, by her fiendish arts and by the aid of demons foul and damned, doth seek the hurt of our lord the Duke, whom God and the saints defend. Forasmuch as this witch, yclept Mellent, did, by her unhallowed spells and magic, compass and bring about the escape from close duress of one Beltane, a notable outlaw, malefactor and enemy to our lord the Duke; and whereas she did also by aid of charms, incantations and the like devilish practices, contrive the sack, burning and total destruction of my lord Duke's good and fair castle of Garthlaxton upon the March. Now therefore it is adjudged that she be taken and her body burned to ashes here before you. All of which charges have been set forth and sworn to by this right noble lord and gallant knight Sir Gilles of Brandonmere — behold him here in person."

Hereupon, while the trumpets brayed a flourish and fanfare, forth rode Sir Gilles upon a mighty charger, a grim and warlike figure in his shining mail and blazoned surcoat, his ponderous, crested war-helm closed, his long shield covering him from shoulder to stirrup, and his lance-point twinkling on high.

Then spake again the herald loud and clear:

"Good people all, behold Sir Gilles of Brandonmere, who cometh here before you prepared to maintain the truth and justice of the charges he hath made — unto the death, 'gainst any man soever, on horse or on foot, with lance, battle-axe or sword. Now if there be any here do know this witch Mellent for innocent, if there be any here dare adventure his body for her innocence and run the peril of mortal combat with Sir Gilles, let him now stand forth."

And immediately the trumpets sounded a challenge. Thereafter the herald paced slowly round the lists, and behind him rode Sir Gilles, his blazon of the three stooping falcons plain for all men to see, on gleaming shield and surcoat.

North and south, and east and west the challenge was repeated, and after each the trumpet sounded a warlike flourish, yet no horseman paced forth and no man leapt the barriers; and the witch Mellent drooped pale and trembling betwixt her warders. But, of a sudden she opened swooning eyes and lifted her heavy head; for, from the distant woods, faint as yet and far, a horn brayed hoarsely — three notes, thrice repeated, defiant and warlike. And now, among the swaying crowds rose a hum that grew and grew, while ever and anon the horn rang out, fiercely winded — and ever it sounded nearer: until, of a sudden, out from the trees afar, two horsemen galloped, their harness bright in the sunshine, helm and lance-point twinkling, who, spurring knee and knee, thundered over the ling; while every tongue grew hushed, and every eye turned to mark their swift career.

Tall were these men and lusty, bedight from head to foot in glistening mail, alike at all points save that one bare neither shield nor lance, and 'neath his open bascinet showed a face brown and comely, whereas his companion rode, his long shield flashing in the sun, his head and face hid by reason of his ponderous, close-shut casque. Swift they rode, the throng parting before them; knee and knee together they leapt the palisade, and reining in their horses, paced down the lists and halted before the pale and trembling captive. Then spake the knight, harsh-voiced behind his vizor:

"Sound, Roger!"

Forthwith the black-haired, ruddy man set a hunting horn to his lips, and blew thereon a flourish so loud and shrill as made the very welkin ring.

Now came pursuivants and the chief herald, which last made inquisition thus:

"Sir Knight, crest hast thou none, nor on thy shield device, so do I demand name and rank of thee, who thus in knightly guise doth give this bold defiance, and wherefore ye ride armed at points. Pronounce, messire!"

Then spake the tall knight loud and fierce, his voice deep-booming within the hollow of his closed casque.

"Name and rank have I laid by for the nonce, until I shall have achieved a certain vow, but of noble blood am I and kin unto the greatest — this do I swear by Holy Rood. To-day am I hither come in arms to do battle on behalf of yon innocent maid, and to maintain her innocence so long as strength abide. And furthermore, here before ye all and every, I do proclaim Sir Gilles of Brandonmere a shame and reproach unto his order. To all the world I do proclaim him rogue and thief and wilful liar, the which (God willing) I will here prove upon his vile body. So now let there be an end of words. Sound, Roger!"

Hereupon he of the ruddy cheek clapped horn to lip and blew amain until his cheek grew redder yet, what time the heralds and pursuivants and marshals of the field debated together if it were lawful for a nameless knight to couch lance 'gainst one of noble blood. But now came Sir Gilles himself, choking with rage, and fuming in his harness.

"Ha, thou nameless dog!" cried he, brandishing his heavy lance, "be thou serf or noble, art an arrant liar — so will I slay thee out of hand!" Thus saying, he reined round the great roan stallion he bestrode, and galloped to one end of the lists. Now spake Black Roger low-voiced, and his hand shook upon his bridle:

"Master, now do I fear for thee. Sir Gilles is a mighty jouster and skilled withal, moreover he rideth his famous horse Mars — a noble beast and fresh, while thine is something wearied. And then, master, direst of all, she thou would'st champion is a witch —"

"That worketh no evil by day, Roger. So do I charge thee, whatsoe'er betide, look to the maid, take her across thy saddle and strive to bring her to safety. As for me, I will now with might and main seek to make an end of Sir Gilles of Brandonmere."

So saying, Beltane rode to the opposite extremity of the lists.

And now, while the trumpets blared, the two knights took their ground, Sir Gilles resplendent in lofty crest and emblazoned surcoat, the three stooping falcons conspicuous on his shield, his mighty roan charger pawing the ling with impatient hoof; his opponent, a gleaming figure astride a tall black horse, his round-topped casque unadorned by plume or crest. So awhile they remained, very still and silent, what time a single trumpet spake, whereat — behold! the two long lances sank feutred to the charge, the broad shields flashed, glittered and were still again; and from that great concourse a sound went up — a hum, that swelled, and so was gone.

The maid Mellent had sunk upon her knees and was praying desperate prayers with face upturned to heaven; but none was there to mark her now amid that silent gathering — all eyes were strained to watch those grim and silent horsemen that fronted each other, the length of the lists between; even Duke Ivo, leaning on lazy elbow, looked with glowing eye and slow-flushing cheek, ere he let fall his truncheon.

And, on the instant, shrill and fierce the trumpets brayed, and on the instant each knight struck spurs, the powerful horses reared, plunged, and sprang away at speed. Fast and faster they galloped, their riders low-stooped above the high-peaked saddles, shields addressed and lances steady, with pounding hooves that sent the turves a-flying, with gleaming helms and deadly lance-points a-twinkle; fast and ever faster they thundered down upon each other, till, with a sudden direful crash, they met in full career with a splintering of well-aimed lances, a lashing of wild hooves, a rearing of powerful horses, staggering and reeling beneath the shock. And now a thunderous cry went up, for the tall black horse, plunging and snorting, went down rolling upon the sward. But his rider had leapt clear and, stumbling to his feet, stood swaying unsteadily, faint and dazed with the blow of Sir Gilles' lance that had borne down the great black horse and torn the heavy casque from his head. So stood Beltane, unhelmed, staring dazedly from heaving earth to reeling heaven; yet, of a sudden, shook aloft the fragment of his splintered lance and laughed fierce and loud, to behold, 'twixt reeling earth and sky, a great roan stallion that foamed upon his bit 'neath sharp-drawn rein, as, swaying sideways from the lofty saddle, Sir Gilles of Brandonmere crashed to earth, transfixed through shield and hauberk, through breast and back, upon the shaft of a broken lance. High over him leapt Beltane, to catch the roan's loose bridle, to swing himself up, and so, with stirrups flying and amid a sudden clamour of roaring voices, to thunder down the lists where Roger's heavy sword flashed, as smiting right and left, he stooped and swung the maid Mellent before him.

"Ride, Roger — ride! Spur — spur!" shouted Beltane above the gathering din, and shouting, drew his sword, for now before them, steel glittered and cries rang upon the air:

"'Tis Beltane the outlaw! Seize him — slay him! 'Tis the outlaw!"

But knee and knee, with loose rein and goading spur rode they, and nought could avail and none were quick enough to stay that headlong gallop; side by side they thundered over the ling, and knee and knee they leapt

How Beltane Fought for a Witch 315

the barrier, bursting through bewildered soldiery, scattering frighted country-folk, and so away, over gorse and heather and with arrows, drawn at a venture, whistling by them. Betimes they reached the shelter of the woods, and turning, Beltane beheld a confusion of armed men, a-horse and a-foot, what time borne upon the air came a sound hoarse and menacing, a sound dreadful to hear — the sound of the hue and cry.

CHAPTER XL

FURTHER CONCERNING THE MAID MELLENT; AND OF THE HUE AND CRY

Fast they galloped 'neath the trees, stooping ever and anon to avoid some low-swung branch; through grassy rides and sunny glades, until all sound of pursuit was died away. So, turning aside into the denser green, Beltane stayed, and sprang down to tighten the great roan's saddle-girths, strained in the encounter. Now as he was busied thus, came the maid Mellent, very pale 'neath her long black hair, and spake him low-voiced and humble:

"My lord Beltane, thou, at peril of thy body, hath saved to-day a sorrowful maid from the fiery torment. So to prove my gratitude and sorrow for past ill — now will I tell thee that in saving me, thou hast saved one that for ambition's sake, once did thee grievous wrong."

"Thou!" saith Beltane, staring in amaze, "ne'er hast thou seen me until this day!"

"Verily, messire — O messire, thou hast indeed seen me ere this and — to my bitter sorrow — for I who speak am the lady Winfrida —"

"Nay — nay —" stammered Beltane, "here is thing impossible — thy night-black hair —"

"'Tis but a wile that many women do know, messire, a device of the witch Jolette (that is no witch, but a noble woman) a device whereby I might lie hid awhile. O indeed, indeed I who speak to thee am the wicked Winfrida — Winfrida the Sorrowful!" Now herewith she sank before him on her knees and bowed her face within her hands, and Beltane saw that she trembled greatly. "My lord," she whispered, "now must I confess a thing beyond all words shameful, and though I fear death, I fear thy anger more.

If, therefore, when I have spoke thee all, thou wilt slay me, then — O my lord — I pray thee — let death come swift —"

"Master!" cried Roger of a sudden, "I hear horses — they be after us already! Mount — mount and let us ride — Hark! they come this way!"

"Aye!" nodded Beltane, drawing his sword, "yet here is but one methinks — list, Roger — leave him to me!" So waited they all three, what time the slow-pacing hoofs drew near and nearer, until, peering through the leaves, they beheld a knight, who rode low-stooping in his saddle, to mark their tracks plain upon the tender grass. Forth stepped Beltane, fierce and threatening, his long sword agleam, and so paused to scowl, for the knight raised his head of a sudden and lo! 'twas Sir Fidelis.

"Now what seek ye here, sir knight?" saith Beltane, nothing gentle.

"Thee, my lord," quoth Fidelis, meek of aspect, "to share thy perils according to thy word. Put up thy sword, messire, thou wilt not harm thy companion in arms?"

Now Beltane, finding nought to say, scowled sulkily to earth, and thus saw nothing of the eyes so deep and tender that watched him 'neath the shadow of the young knight's bascinet, nor the smile so sad and wistful that curled his ruddy lips, nor all the lithe and slender grace of him as he swayed to the impatient movements of the powerful animal he bestrode; but it chanced that Winfrida's eyes saw all this, and being a woman's eyes, beheld that which gave her breathing sudden pause — turned her red — turned her pale, until, with a gasp of fear she started, and uttering a cry, low and inarticulate, sped fleet-footed across the glade and was gone.

Quoth Beltane, staring:

"Now what aileth the maid, think ye? But 'tis no matter — we are well quit of her, meseemeth." So saying, he turned to behold Roger flat upon his belly and with his ear to the ground.

"Master," cried he, "master, there be horsemen i' the forest hereabouts — a great company!"

"Why then, do you mount, Roger, and hie thee with Sir Fidelis hot-foot to Walkyn at Hundleby Fen. Bid him set our bowmen in every place of vantage, and let every man stand to arms. So mayhap, Roger, will we this day make hunted men of them that hunt!" So saying, Beltane swung to saddle.

"Aye — aye — but what o' thee, master?"

"Mark ye this horse, Roger. Thou hast said 'twas of good speed and endurance, and methinks 'tis sooth. Howbeit, now shall he prove thy word, for here I wait the hunters, and to-day will I, keeping ever out of bow-shot, lead them through every quag, every bog and marsh 'twixt here and Hundleby Fen, and of those that follow still, thou and Walkyn and our merry men shall make an end, I pray God. So let all lie well hid, and watch for my coming. And now — farewell to thee, Roger."

"But, master," quoth Roger, waxing rueful, "in this thou must run dire perils and dangers, and I not with thee. So pray thee let Sir Fidelis — hard! — Ha! — now God aid us — hark to that! Master, they've loosed the dogs on us!"

Even as he spake, very faint and far as yet but plain to hear above the leafy stirring, the deep baying of a hound came down the wind.

"Hunting-dogs, master! Ride — ride!" quoth Roger, wiping sweat from him, "O sweet Christ forgive me, for I have hunted down poor rogues with such ere now —"

"Forsooth, Roger, and now is their turn to hunt thee, mayhap. Howbeit, ride you at speed, and you, sir knight also, get you gone, and whatsoever betide, Roger, wait you at Hundleby Fen for me. Go — obey me!" So, looking upon Beltane with eyes of yearning, Black Roger perforce wheeled and rode out into the glade, and striking spurs to his eager steed, galloped swiftly away. Now turned Beltane upon Sir Fidelis:

"How, messire — are ye not gone?"

Then answered Sir Fidelis, his drooping head averted:

"Thou seest, my lord — I go beside thee according to thy word —"

"Presumptuous youth, I want thee not!"

"The day will yet come, perchance, my lord — and I can be patient —"

"Ha — dost defy me?"

"Not so, my lord — nor do I fear thee. For I do know thee better than thyself, so do I pity thee — pity thee — thou that art so mighty and yet so weak. Thou art a babe weeping in a place of shadows, so will I go beside thee in the dark to soothe and comfort thee. Thou art a noble man, thy better self lost awhile 'neath sickly fancies — God send they soon may pass. Till then I can be very patient, my lord Beltane."

Now did Beltane stare with eyes of wonder upon Sir Fidelis who managed his fretting charger with a gracious ease, yet held his face ever averted. While, upon the stilly air, loud and more loud rose the fierce baying of the hounds.

Said Beltane at last:

"Messire, thou dost hear the hounds?"

"In faith, my lord, I tremble to be gone, but an thou dost tarry, so must I."

"Death shall follow hard after us this day, Sir Fidelis."

"Why then, an death o'ertake us — I must die, messire."

"Ha,— the hounds have winded us already, methinks! Hark! — Hark to them!" And in truth the air was full of their raving clamour, with, ever and anon, the shouts and cries of those that urged them on.

"Hast a noble horse, Sir Fidelis. Now God send he bear thee well this day, for 'twill be hard and cruel going. Come —'tis time, methinks!"

Thus speaking, Beltane gave his horse the rein and forth they rode together out into the broad and open glade, their armour glinting in the sun; and immediately the dogs gave tongue, louder, fiercer than before. Now looking back, Beltane beheld afar many mounted men who shouted amain, flourishing lance and sword, while divers others let slip the great dogs they held in leash; then, looking up the glade ahead, and noting its smooth level and goodly length, Beltane smiled grimly and drew sword.

"Sir Fidelis," said he, "hast a mace at thy saddle-bow: betake thee to it, 'tis a goodly weapon, and — smite hard. 'Twill be the dogs first. Now — spur!"

Forward bounded the two high-mettled steeds, gathering pace with every stride, but the great hounds came on amain, while beyond, distant as yet, the hunters rode — knight and squire, mounted bowman and man-at-arms they spurred and shouted, filling the air with fierce halloo. Slowly the hounds drew nearer — ten great beasts Beltane counted — that galloped two and two, whining and whimpering as they came.

Now of a sudden Beltane checked in his career, swerved, swung the plunging roan, and with long blade agleam, rode in upon the racing pack to meet their rush with deadly point and deep-biting edge; a slavering hound launched itself at his throat, its fangs clashing on the stout links of his camail, but as the great beast hung thus, striving to drag him from the saddle, down came the mace of Sir Fidelis and the snarling beast fell to be crushed 'neath the trampling hoofs of the war-horse Mars. And now did the mighty roan prove himself a very Mars indeed, for, beset round about by fierce, lean shapes that crouched and leapt with cruel, gleaming fangs, he stamped and reared and fought them off, neighing loud defiance. Thus, with lashing hoof, with whirling mace and darting sword fought they, until of the hounds there none remained save three that limped painfully to cover, licking their hurts as they went.

But other foes were near, for as Beltane reined his snorting steed about, he swayed in his stirrups 'neath the shock of a cross-bow bolt that glanced, whirring, from his bascinet, and in that moment Sir Fidelis cried aloud:

"My lord, my lord! alas, my poor horse is death-smitten!" Glancing round, Beltane beheld Sir Fidelis slip to earth as his charger, rearing high, crashed over, his throat transfixed by a cloth-yard shaft. Now did their many pursuers shout amain, fierce and joyful, goading their horses to swifter pace what time Beltane frowned from them to Sir Fidelis, who stood, mailed hands tight-clasped, watching Beltane eager and great-eyed.

"Ah!" cried Beltane, smiting hand to thigh in bitter anger, "now is my hope of ambush and surprise like to be marred by reason of thee, sir knight, for one horse may never carry us twain!"

"Why then, I can die here, my lord, an it be so thy will!" spake Sir Fidelis, his pale lips a-tremble, "yet is thy horse strong and — O in sooth I did yearn — for life. But, an thou wilt give me death —"

"Come!" cried Beltane hoarsely. "Come, wherefore tarry ye?"

Now leapt Sir Fidelis to the saddle of his fallen steed and snatched thence a wallet, whereat Beltane fell a-fuming, for bolts and arrows began to whirr and hum thick and fast. "Come — mount, sir knight — mount ye up behind me. Thy hand — quick! thy foot on my foot — so! Now set thy two arms fast about me and see thou loose me not, for now must we ride for the wild — brush and thicket, stock and stone, nought must let or stay us — so loose me not, sir knight!"

"Ah — not while life remain, messire Beltane!" said the young knight quick-breathing, and speaking, took Beltane within two mailed arms that clasped and clung full close. Then, wheeling sharp about, Beltane stooping low, struck sudden spurs and they plunged, crashing, into the denser green.

CHAPTER XLI

HOW THEY RODE INTO THE WILDERNESS

FAST galloped the good horse, bursting through underbrush and thicket with the roar of the pursuit following ever distant and more distant; and ever Beltane spurred deeper into those trackless wilds where few dare adventure them by reason of evil spirits that do haunt these solitudes (as they do say) and, moreover, of ravening beasts.

Strongly and well the good horse bore them, what time the sun waxed fierce and hot, filling the woods with a stifling heat, a close, windless air dank and heavy with the scent of leaves and bracken. The hue and cry had sunk long since, lost in distance, and nought broke the brooding silence but the stir of their going, as, checking their headlong pace, Beltane brought the powerful animal to slow and leisured gait. And presently, a gentle wind arose, that came and went, to fan brow and cheek and temper the sun's heat.

And now, as they rode through sunlight and shadow, Beltane felt his black mood slowly lifted from him and knew a sense of rest, a content unfelt this many a day; he looked, glad-eyed, upon the beauty of the world about him, from green earth to an azure heaven peeping through a fretted screen of branches; he marked the graceful, slender bracken stirring to the soft-breathing air, the mighty boles of stately trees that reached out sinuous boughs one to another, to touch and twine together amid a mystery of murmuring leaves. All this he saw, yet heeded not at all the round mailed arms that clasped him in their soft embrace, nor the slender hands that held upon his girdle.

So rode they through bosky dell and dingle, until the sun, having climbed the meridian, sank slowly westwards; and Sir Fidelis spake soft-voiced:

"Think you we are safe at last, my lord?"

"Fidelis," saith Beltane, "Yest're'en did'st thou name me selfish, to-day, a babe, and, moreover, by thy disobedience hast made my schemes of no avail — thus am I wroth with thee."

"Yet doth the sun shine, my lord," said Sir Fidelis, small of voice.

"Ha — think you my anger so light-a thing, forsooth?"

"Messire, I think of it not at all."

"By thy evil conduct are we fugitives in the wilderness!"

"Yet is it a wondrous fair place, messire, and we unharmed — which is well, and we are — together, which is — also well."

"And with but one beast to bear us twain!"

"Yet he beareth us strong and nobly, messire!"

"Fidelis, I would I ne'er had seen thee."

"Thou dost not see me — now, lord — content you, therefore," saith Fidelis softly, whereat Beltane must needs twist in the saddle, yet saw no more than a mailed arm and shoulder.

"Howbeit," quoth Beltane, "I would these arms o' thine clasped the middle of any other man than I."

"Forsooth, my lord? And do they crush thee so? Or is it thou dost pine for solitude?"

"Neither, youth: 'tis for thy youth's sake, for, though thou hast angered me full oft, art but a very youth —"

"Gramercy for my so much youthfulness, my lord. Methinks I shall be full long a-growing old —"

"Heed me, sir knight, 'tis a fell place this, where direful beasts do raven —"

"Nathless, messire, my youthfulness is but where it would be —"

"Aye, forsooth, and there it is! Where thou would'st be — thou, forsooth! Art indeed a wilful youth and very headstrong. And wherefore here?"

"To cheer thee in thy loneliness, my lord."

"How so?"

"Thou shalt reproach me for my youth and quarrel with me when thou wilt!"

"Am I of so ill humour, indeed?"

"Look within thyself, my lord."

Now here they rode a while in silence; but presently Beltane turned him again in the saddle and saw again only arm and shoulder. Quoth he:

"Fidelis, art a strange youth and a valiant — and yet, thy voice — thy voice hath betimes a — a something I love not — a note of softness that mindeth me of bitter days."

"Then heed it not, my lord; 'tis but that I grow a-weary, belike."

Here silence again, what time Beltane fell to frowning and Sir Fidelis, head a-slant, to watching him furtive-eyed, yet with lips that curved to wistful smile.

"Came you in sooth from — the Duchess Helen, Fidelis?"

"In truth, my lord."

"Dost love her — also?"

"Aye, my lord — also!"

"Then alas for thee, poor youthful fool, 'twere better I had left thee to thy death, methinks, for she — this wilful Helen —"

"My lord," cried Sir Fidelis, "nought will I hear to her defame!"

"Fidelis, art a gentle knight — but very young, art fond and foolish, so, loving this light lady, art doubly fool!"

"Wherein," saith Fidelis, "wherein, my lord, thou art likewise fool, meseemeth."

"Verily," nodded Beltane, "O verily fool am I, yet wise in this — that I do know my folly. So I, a fool, would counsel thee in thy folly thus — give not thy heart to Helen's faithless keeping — stoop not to her wanton lure — ha! what now?" For, lithe and swift, Sir Fidelis had sprung to earth and had seized the great roan's bridle, and checking him in his stride, faced Beltane with cheeks suffused and flaming eyes.

"Shame, messire — O shame!" he cried. "How vile is he that would, with lying tongue, smirch the spotless honour of any maid. And, as to Helen, I do name thee liar! — liar!"

"Would'st quarrel with me in matter so unworthy?"

"Enough!" quoth Fidelis, "unworthy art thou to take her name within thy lips — enough!" So saying Sir Fidelis stepped back a pace and drew his sword.

Now Beltane, yet astride the mighty roan that snuffed the fragrant air and stooped to crop the tender herbage, looked upon the youthful paladin 'neath wrinkled brow, and pulled his lip as one in doubt. Anon he sighed and therewith smiled and shook his head.

Quoth he:

"O Fidelis, now do I see that I must needs love thee some day. Fidelis, art a fool, but a right sweet fool, so do I humbly sue thy foolish pardon, and, as to Helen, may she prove worthy thy sweet faith and I thy love and friendship. So, fair knight, put up thy sword — come, mount and let us on. Sir Mars, methinks, doth snuff water afar, and I do yearn me for the cool of it."

So in a while they rode on again, yet presently Sir Fidelis, meek-voiced, preferred a sudden question, thus:

"Lord, fain would I know why thou dost contemn her so —"

"Nay," sighed Beltane, "here is a tale un-meet thy tender years. Speak we of other things — as thus, wherefore didst keep our lives in jeopardy to bring away the wallet that cumbereth thy hip?"

"For that within doth lie, first — our supper —"

"O foolish youth, these woods do teem with food!"

"A neat's tongue, delicately seasoned —"

"O!" said Beltane.

"'Twixt manchets of fair white bread —"

"Ah!" said Beltane.

"With a small skin of rare wine —"

"Enough!" quoth Beltane. "These be things forsooth worth a little risk. Now do I thirst and famish, yet knew it not."

"An thou wilt eat, my lord?"

"Nay, first will we find some freshet where we may bathe awhile. Ha, to plunge naked within some sweet pool — 'tis a sweet thought, Fidelis?"

But hereupon the young knight made answer none and fell into a reverie and Beltane also, what time they rode by murmuring rills, through swampy hollows, past brake and briar, until, as evening began to fall, they came unto a broad, slow-moving stream whose waters, aglow with sunset glory, split asunder the greeny gloom of trees, most pleasant to behold. Then, sighing for very gladness, Beltane checked his horse and spake right gleefully:

"Light down, light down, good Fidelis; ne'er saw I fairer haven for wearied travellers! We have ridden hard and far, so here will we tarry the night!" and down to earth he sprang, to stride up and down and stretch his cramped limbs, the while Sir Fidelis, loosing off the great, high-peaked saddle, led the foam-flecked war-horse down to the water.

Now because of the heat, Beltane laid by his bascinet, and, hearkening to the soft, cool ripple of the water, he straightway unbuckled his sword-belt and began to doff his heavy hauberk; perceiving the which, cometh Sir Fidelis to him something hastily.

"What do you, messire?" he questioned.

"Do, Fidelis? Forsooth, I would bathe me in yon cool, sweet water — list how it murmureth 'neath the bank yonder. Come then, strip as I do, youth, strip and let us swim together — pray you aid me with this lacing."

"My lord, I — indeed, I do think it unsafe —"

"Unsafe, boy?"

"An our foes should come upon us —"

"O content you," quoth Beltane, stooping to loose off his spurs, "our foes were lost hours since, nor shall any find us here in the wild, methinks — pray you, loose me this buckle. Come, list how the waters do woo us with their pretty babble."

"But, messire," quoth Fidelis, faint-voiced, and fumbling awkwardly with the buckle, "indeed I — I have no art in swimming."

"Then will I teach thee."

"Nay," spake the young knight hastily, his trouble growing, "I do dread the water!"

"Well, there be shallows 'neath the alders yonder."

"Aye, but the shallows will be muddy, and I —"

"Muddy?" cried Beltane, pausing with his hauberk half on, half off, to stare at Sir Fidelis in amaze, "muddy, forsooth! Art a dainty youth in faith, and over-nice, methinks. What matter for a little honest mud, prithee?"

"Why 'tis mud! And slimy under foot! And I love not mud! So will I none of the shallows!"

"Then verily must I chide thee, Fidelis, for —"

"Then verily will I unto yon boskage, messire, to prepare us a fire 'gainst the 'beasts that raven,' and our bracken beds. Howbeit, bathe me I — will — not, messire!"

"O luxurious youth, then will I, and shame thy nice luxuriousness!" quoth Beltane; and off came hauberk and quilted gambeson and away skipped Sir Fidelis into the green.

So, presently, Beltane plunged him into the stream, and swimming with powerful strokes, felt his youth and strength redoubled thereby, and rejoiced to be alive. Thereafter he leapt ashore, his blood aglow with ardent life, and, as he clothed him, felt a great and mighty hunger.

But scarce had he donned chausses and gambeson than he heard an outcry and sudden clamour within the green; whereupon, staying not for his armour, he caught up his sword and, unsheathing it as he ran, plunged in among the trees and there espied Sir Fidelis stoutly withstanding three foul knaves unwashed and ragged. Then shouted

Beltane, and fell upon them right joyously and smote them gleefully and laughed to see them reel and scatter before his sudden onset; whereon, beholding Sir Fidelis pale and scant of breath, he stayed to clap him on the shoulder.

"Blithely done, good Fidelis!" quoth he. "Rest thee awhile and catch thy wind, for fain am I to try a bout with yon tall rogues!" So saying, he advanced upon the scowling three, his eyes a-dance, his nimble feet light-poised for swift action — for lusty rogues were these, who, seeing him alone, forthwith met him point and edge, besetting him with many swashing blows, that, whistling, did but cleave the empty air or rang loud upon his swift-opposing blade. So hewed they, and smote amain until their brows shone moist and their breaths waxed short; whereat Beltane mocked them, saying:

"Ha — sweat ye, forsooth? Do ye puff so soon? This cometh of foul eating and fouler life. Off — off! ye beefy do-nothings! An ye would be worthy fighters, eat less and bathe ye more!" Then Beltane laid on with the flat of his heavy sword and soundly belaboured these hard-breathing knaves, insomuch that one, hard-smitten on the crown, stumbled and fell, whereupon his comrades, to save their bones, leapt forthwith a-down the steepy bank and, plunging into the stream, made across to the farther side, splashing prodigiously, and cursing consumedly, for the water they liked not at all.

Now as Beltane leaned him on his sword, watching their flounderings joyful-eyed, the weapon was dashed from his loosened hold, he staggered 'neath the bite of vicious steel, and, starting round, beheld the third rogue, his deadly sword swung high; but even as the blow fell, Sir Fidelis sprang between and took it upon his own slender body, and, staggering aside, fell, and lay with arms wide-tossed. Then, whiles the robber yet stared upon his sword, shivered by the blow, Beltane leapt, and ere he could flee, caught him about the loins, and whirling him aloft, dashed him out into the stream. Then, kneeling by Sir Fidelis, he took his heavy head upon his arm and beheld his cheeks pale and wan, his eyes fast shut, and saw his shining bascinet scored and deep-dinted by the blow.

"Fidelis!" he groaned, "O my brave Fidelis, and art thou slain — for my sake?" But in a while, what time Beltane kneeled and mourned over him full sore, the young knight stirred feebly, sighed, and spake.

"Beltane!" he whispered; and again, "Beltane!" Anon his white lids quivered, and, opening swooning eyes he spake again with voice grown stronger:

"My lord — my lord — what of thy wound?"

And lo! the voice was sweet to hear as note of merle or mavis; these eyes were long and deeply blue beneath their heavy lashes; eyes that looked up, brimful of tenderness, ere they closed slow and wearily; eyes so much at odds with grim bascinet and close-laced camail that Beltane must needs start and hold his breath and fall to sudden trembling what time Sir Fidelis lay there, pale and motionless, as one that is dead. Now great fear came upon Beltane, and he would have uttered desperate prayers, but could not; trembling yet, full gently he drew his arm from under that drooping head, and, stealing soft-footed to the river's marge, stood there staring down at the rippling waters, and his heart was rent with conflicting passions — amazement, fear, anger, joy, and a black despair. And of a sudden Beltane fell upon his knees and bowed him low and lower until his burning brow was hid in the cool, sweet grass — for of these passions, fiercest, strongest, wildest, was — despair.

CHAPTER XLII

HOW BELTANE DREAMED IN THE WILD-WOOD

Now in a while, he started to feel a hand among his hair, and the hand was wondrous light and very gentle; wherefore, wondering, he raised his head, but behold, the sun was gone and the shadows deepening to night. Yet even so, he stared and thrilled 'twixt wonder and fear to see Sir Fidelis bending over him.

"Fidelis!" he murmured, "and is it thee in truth,— or do I dream?"

"Dear my lord, 'tis I indeed. How long hast lain thus? I did but now wake from my swoon. Is it thy hurt?— suffer me to look."

"Nay, 'tis of none account, but I did dream thee— dead— Fidelis!"

"Ah, messire, thy hurt bleedeth apace— the steel hath gone deep! Sit you thus, thy back against the tree— so. Within my wallet I have a salve— wait you here." So, whiles Beltane stared dreamily upon the twilit river, Sir Fidelis hasted up the bank and was back again, the wallet by his side, whence he took a phial and goblet and mixed therein a draught which dreamy Beltane perforce must swallow, and thereafter the dreamy languor fell from him, what time Sir Fidelis fell to bathing and bandaging the ugly gash that showed beneath his knee. Now as he watched these busy, skilful fingers he knew a sudden, uneasy qualm, and forthwith spake his thought aloud:

"Thy hands are wondrous— small and slender, Sir Fidelis!"

"Belike, messire, they shall grow bigger some day."

"Yet are they wondrous fair— and soft— and white, Fidelis!"

"Mayhap, messire, they shall grow rough and brown and hairy anon — so content you."

"Yet wherefore are they so soft, Fidelis, and so — maid-like? And wherefore —"

"See you, my lord, thus must the bandage lie, fast-knotted — so. Nor must it slacken, lest the bleeding start afresh." So saying, Sir Fidelis arose, and taking the wallet in one hand and setting the other 'neath Beltane's arm, led him to where, deep-bowered under screening willows, a fire burned cheerily, whereby were two beds of scented bracken.

Dark and darker the shadows crept down, deepening to a night soft and warm and very still, whose quietude was unbroken save for the drowsy lap and murmur of the river and the sound the war-horse Mars made as he cropped the grass near by. Full of a languorous content lay Beltane, despite the smarting of his wound, what time Sir Fidelis came and went about the fire; and there, within this great and silent wilderness, they supped together, and, while they supped, Beltane looked oft upon Sir Fidelis, heedful of every trick of mail-girt feature and gesture of graceful hand as he ne'er had been ere now. Wherefore Sir Fidelis grew red, grew pale, was by turns talkative and silent, and was fain to withdraw into the shadows beyond the fire. And from there, seeing Beltane silent and full of thought, grew bold to question him.

"Dost meditate our course to-morrow, my lord Beltane?"

"Nay — I do but think — a strange thought — that I have seen thy face ere now, Fidelis. Yet art full young to bear arms a-field."

"Doth my youth plague thee still, messire? Believe me, I am — older than I seem."

"Thou, at peril of thy life, Fidelis, didst leap 'twixt me and death, so needs must I know thee for my friend, and yet —"

"And yet, messire?"

"Thou hast betimes the look and speech of one — of one beyond all traitors vile!"

"Ah," murmured Sir Fidelis, a sudden tremor in his voice, "thou dost mean —?"

"Helen of Mortain — poor Fidelis — whom thou dost love."

"Whom thou dost hate, Beltane! And O, I pray thee, wherefore is thy hate so bitter?"

"Fidelis, there lived a fool, that, for her beauty, loved her with a mighty love: that, for her seeming truth and purity, honoured her beyond all things: that, in the end, did find her beyond all things vile. Aye, there lived a fool — and I am he."

"Ah, beseech thee," cried Sir Fidelis, white hands outstretched, "how know you her thus false to thee, Beltane?"

"Know then, Sir Fidelis, that — upon our wedding-eve I was — by her command struck down — within the chapel — upon the very altar, and by her borne in bonds unto Garthlaxton Keep — a present to mine enemy, Duke Ivo —"

"O, 'tis a lie — O dear my lord — 'tis lie most foul — !"

"In witness whereof behold upon my wrists the shameful irons from my dungeon —"

"Alas! here was no work of Helen's — no thought, no will — Helen would have died to save thee this —"

"So, Fidelis, do I scorn all women that do live upon this earth henceforth — but, above all, Helen the Beautiful! the Wilful! who in her white bosom doth bear a heart more foul than Trojan Helen, that was a woman false and damned. So now, all's said."

Now fell Sir Fidelis upon his knees and spake quick and passionate:

"Nay, Beltane, hear me! For now do I swear that he who told thee 'twas Helen wrought thee this vile wrong — who told thee this doth lie — O, doth lie! Now do I swear that never by word or thought or deed, hath she been false to thee — I do swear she loveth thee — ah, spurn me not — O, believe —"

"Enough — enough, good Fidelis, perjure not thy sweet youth for one so much unworthy, for with these eyes did I behold her as they bore me in my bonds — and shall I not believe mine eyes?"

"Never — ah! never, when they do shew thee Helen false and cruel to thee! Here was some vile magic — witchcraft —"

"Enough, Fidelis, 'tis past and done. Here was a woman false — well, 'tis none so singular — there have been others — there will be others. So, God keep thee, sweet youth, from the ways of women. Nay, let us speak of this no more, for in sooth I grow a-weary and we must ride with the dawn to-morrow. So, betake thee to thy rest, nor grieve thee for my sorrows past and done — mayhap they shall be things to smile upon one day."

So saying, Beltane sighed, and laid him down among the bracken and thereafter Fidelis did the like; the fire sank and waned, and oft Sir Fidelis stirred restless in the shadows; the river murmured slumberously among the sedge, but Beltane, hearkening with drowsy ears, oft thought to hear another sound, very soft and repressed yet very dolorous, ere, worn and spent, and something weakened by wound and loss of blood, he sank at last to deep and gentle sleep.

But in his sleep he dreamed that one knelt above him in the dark, keeping watch upon his slumbers in the attitude of one in prayer — one whom he knew, yet knew not; it seemed to Beltane in his dream, that this silent, slender shape, stooped of a sudden, low and lower, to kiss the iron fetters that bound his wrists; then Beltane strove to wake yet could not wake, but in his slumber sighed a name, soft-breathed and gentle as the languorous murmur of the stream:

"Helen!"

CHAPTER XLIII

HOW BELTANE KNEW GREAT HUMILITY

THE rising sun, darting an inquisitive beam 'twixt a leafy opening, fell upon Beltane's wide, slow-heaving breast; crept upwards to his chin, his cheek, and finally strove to peep beneath his slumberous, close-shut lids; whereat Beltane stirred, yawned, threw wide and stretched his mighty arms, and thereafter, blinking drowsily, sat up, his golden hair be-tousled, and stared sleepily about him.

Birds piped joyously near and far; hid among the leaves near by, the war-horse Mars stamped eager hoof and snuffed the fragrant air of morning; but Sir Fidelis was nowhere to be seen. Thus in a while Beltane arose to find his leg very stiff and sore, and his throat be-parched with feverish thirst; wherefore, limping painfully, he turned where a little water-brook went singing o'er pebbly bed to join the slow-moving river; but, putting aside the leaves, he paused of a sudden, for there, beside the noisy streamlet he beheld Sir Fidelis, his bascinet upon the grass beside him, his mail-coif thrown back betwixt his shoulders, stooping to bathe his face in the sparkling water.

Now would he have called a greeting, but the words died upon his lips, his breath stayed, and he stared at something that had caught in the links of the young knight's mail-coif, something that stirred light and wanton, kissed by the breath of early morn — a lock of bright hair that glowed a wondrous red-gold in the new-risen sun. So stood Beltane awhile, and, beholding this, a trembling seized him and therewith sudden anger, and he strode forth of the leaves. And lo! on the instant, on went hood of mail and thereafter shining bascinet, and Sir Fidelis arose. But, ere he could turn, Beltane was beside him, had caught him within a powerful arm, and, setting a hand 'neath mailed chin, lifted the young knight's head and scowled down into his face.

Eyes long, black-lashed and darkly blue that looked up awhile into his, wide, yet fearless, and anon, were hid 'neath languorous-drooping lids; a nose tenderly aquiline, lips red and full that met in ripe and luscious curves. This Beltane saw, and straightway his anger grew.

"Ah!" cried he, hoarsely, "now, by the living God, who art thou, and — what?"

"Thy — comrade-in-arms, lord Beltane."

"Why hast thou the seeming of one beyond all women false? Why dost thou speak me betimes in her voice, look at me with her eyes, touch me with her soft, white, traitor's hands — answer me!"

"My lord, we are akin, she and I — of the same house and blood —"

"Then is thy blood foul with treachery!"

"Yet did I save thy life, Beltane!"

"Yet thy soft voice, thy red mouth and false eyes — thy very blood — all these do prove thee traitor — hence!" and Beltane threw him off.

"Nay my lord!" he cried, "prithee take care, Beltane, — see — thou hast displaced the bandage, thy wound bleedeth amain — so will I bind it up for thee —"

But Beltane, nothing heeding, turned and strode back into the green and there fell to donning his armour as swiftly as he might — albeit stealthily. Thereafter came he to the destrier Mars and, having saddled and bridled him with the same swift stealth, set foot in stirrup and would have mounted, yet found this a painful matter by reason of his wound; thus it befell, that, ere he could reach the saddle, the leaves parted close by and Sir Fidelis spake soft-voiced:

"My lord Beltane, why dost thou steal away thus? An it be thy will to leave me to perish alone here in the wilderness, first break thy fast, and suffer me to bind up thy hurt, so shalt thou ride hence in comfort."

Now stood Beltane motionless and silent, nor turned nor dared he look upon Sir Fidelis, but bowed his head in bitter shame, and, therewith, knew a great remorse.

"Ah, Fidelis," said he at last, "thy rebuke stingeth deep, for it is just, since I indeed did purpose thee a most vile thing! How vile a thing, then, am I —"

"Nay, Beltane — dear my lord, I would not have thee grieve, indeed 'twas but —"

"Once ere this I would have slain thee, Fidelis — murdered thee before my wild fellows — I — I, that did preach them mercy and gentleness! To-day I would have left thee to perish alone within this ravening wilderness — that do bear so honourable a name! O Beltane, my father! Yet, believe me, I did love honour once, and was accounted gentle. I did set forth to do great things, but now — now do I know myself unfit and most unworthy. Therefore, Sir Fidelis, do thou take the horse and what thou wilt beside and leave me here, for fain am I to end my days within these solitudes with no eye to see me more — save only the eye of God!" So saying, Beltane went aside, and sitting 'neath a tree beside the river, bowed his head upon his hands and groaned; then came Sir Fidelis full swift, and stooping, touched his bowed head with gentle hand, whereat he but groaned again.

"God pity me!" quoth he, "I am in sooth so changed, meseemeth some vile demon doth possess me betimes!" and, sighing deep, he gazed upon the rippling waters wide-eyed and fearful. And, as he sat thus, abashed and despairing, Sir Fidelis, speaking no word, bathed and bound up his wound, and, thereafter brought and spread forth their remaining viands.

"Eat," said he gently, "come, let us break our fast, mayhap thy sorrows shall grow less anon. Come, eat, I pray thee, Beltane, for none will I eat alone and, O, I famish!"

So they ate together, whiles the war-horse Mars, pawing impatient hoof, oft turned his great head to view them with round and wistful eye.

"Fidelis," quoth Beltane suddenly, "thou didst name me selfish, and verily, a selfish man am I — and to-day! O Fidelis, why dost not reproach me for the evil I purposed thee to-day?"

"For that I do most truly love thee, Beltane my lord!"

"Yet wherefore did ye so yesterday, and for lesser fault?"

"For that I did love thee, so would I see thee a strong man — yet gentle: a potent lord, yet humble: a noble man as — as thou wert said to be!"

"Alas, my Fidelis, harsh have I been, proud and unforgiving —"

"Aye, my lord — thou art unforgiving — a little!"

"So now, Fidelis, would I crave forgiveness of all men." Then came the young knight nearer yet, his face radiant with sudden joy, his white hands clasped.

"Lord!" he whispered, "O Beltane, could'st indeed forgive all — all harm done thee, howsoever great or small thy mind doth hold them — could'st forgive all!"

"Aye, I could forgive them all, Fidelis — all save Helen — who hath broke this heart of mine and made my soul a thing as black as she hath whited this my hair."

Now of a sudden Beltane heard a sound — a small sound 'twixt a sob and a moan, but when he raised his heavy head — lo! Sir Fidelis was gone.

CHAPTER XLIV

HOW A MADNESS CAME UPON BELTANE IN THE WILD-WOOD

THE sun rose high, yet still Beltane sat there beside the stream, staring down into the gurgling waters, grieving amain for his unworthiness.

Thus presently comes Sir Fidelis, and standing afar, spake in voice strange and bitter:

"What do ye there, my lord? Dost dream ever upon thy woes and ills? Wilt dream thy life away here amid the wild, forsooth?"

Quoth Beltane, very humbly:

"And wherefore not, Sir Fidelis? Unfit am I for great achievements. But, as to thee, take now the horse and ride you ever north and west —"

"Yea, but where is north, and where west — ?"

"The trees shall tell you this. Hearken now —"

"Nay, my lord, no forester am I to find my way through trackless wild. So, an thou stay, so, perforce, must I: and if thou stay then art thou deeply forsworn."

"How mean you, good sir?"

"I mean Belsaye — I mean all those brave souls that do wait and watch, pale-cheeked, 'gainst Ivo's threatened vengeance —"

"Ha — Belsaye!" quoth Beltane, lifting his head.

"Thou must save Belsaye from flame and ravishment, my lord!"

"Aye, forsooth," cried Beltane, clenching his hands, "though I be unworthy to stand in my noble father's place, yet Belsaye must be saved or I die in it. O Fidelis, friend art thou indeed and wise beyond thy years!" But as Beltane arose, Sir Fidelis incontinent turned away, and presently came back leading the great horse. So in a while they set out northwards; but now were no arms to clasp and cling, since Sir Fidelis found hold otherwise. Thus, after some going, Beltane questioned him:

"Art easy, Fidelis?"

"Aye, lord!"

"Wilt not take hold upon my belt, as yesterday?"

"Methinks I am better thus."

"Nay then, shalt have stirrups and saddle, for I am fain to walk."

"And re-open thy wound, messire? Nay, let be — I ride easily thus."

"Art angered with me, Fidelis?"

"Nay, lord, I do but pity thee!"

"And wherefore?"

"For thy so great loneliness — in all thy world is none but Beltane, and he is very woeful and dreameth ever of his wrongs —"

"Would'st call me selfish again, forsooth?"

"Nay, lord — a martyr. O, a very martyr that huggeth his chains and kisseth his wounds and joyeth in the recollection of his pain."

"Have I not suffered, Fidelis?"

"Thou hast known the jangling gloom of a dungeon — 'twas at Garthlaxton Keep, methinks?"

"Fetters!" cried Beltane, "a dungeon! These be things to smile at — my grief is of the mind — the deeper woe of high and noble ideals shattered — a holy altar blackened and profaned — a woman worshipped as divine, and proved baser than the basest!"

"And is this all, my lord?"

"All!" quoth Beltane amazed. "All!" saith he, turning to stare.

"So much of woe and tribulation for so little reason? Nay, hear me, for now will I make thee a prophecy, as thus: There shall dawn a day, lord Beltane, when thou shalt see at last and know Truth when she stands before thee. And, in that day thou shalt behold all things with new eyes: and in that day shalt thou sigh, and long, and yearn with all thy soul for these woeful hours wherein Self looms for thee so large thou art blind to aught else."

"Good Fidelis, thy prophecy is beyond my understanding."

"Aye, my lord, 'tis so I think, indeed!"

"Pray thee therefore rede and expound it unto me!"

"Nay, time mayhap shall teach it thee, and thou, methinks shalt passionately desire again the solitude of this wilderness."

"Aye, but wherefore?"

"For that it shall be beyond thy reach — and mine!" and Fidelis sighed in deep and troubled fashion and so fell to silence, what time Beltane, cunning in wood-lore, glancing hither and thither at knotted branch and writhen tree bole, viewing earth and heaven with a forester's quick eye, rode on into the trackless wilds of the forest-lands.

Now here, thinketh the historian, it booteth not to tell of all those minor haps and chances that befell them; how, despite all Beltane's wood-craft, they went astray full oft by reason of fordless rivers and quaking swamps: of how they snared game to their sustenance, or how, for all the care and skill of Sir Fidelis, Beltane's wound healed not, by reason of continual riding, for that each day he grew more restless and eager for knowledge of Belsaye, so that, because of his wound he knew small rest by day and a fevered sleep by night — yet, despite all, his love for Fidelis daily waxed and grew, what time he pressed on through the wild country, north-westerly.

Five weary days and nights wandered they, lost to sight and knowledge within the wild; days of heat and nights of pain and travail, until there came an evening when, racked with anguish and faint with thirst and weariness, Beltane drew rein within a place of rocks whereby was a shady pool deep-bowered in trees. Down sprang Fidelis to look anxiously on Beltane's face, pale and haggard in the light of a great moon.

Says Beltane, looking round about with knitted brow:

"Fidelis — O Fidelis, methinks I know this place —

How Madness Came Upon Beltane

these rocks — the pool yonder — there should be a road hereabout, the great road that leadeth to Mortain. Climb now the steep and tell me an you can see a road, running north and south."

Forthwith Sir Fidelis climbed the rocky eminence, and, being there, cried right joyously:

"Aye, lord —'tis the road — the road!" and so came hastily down, glad-eyed. "'Tis the end of this wilderness at last, my lord!"

"Aye!" sighed Beltane, "at last!" and groaning, he swayed in the saddle — for his pain was very sore — and would have fallen but for the ready arms of Sir Fidelis. Thereafter, with much labour, Beltane got him to earth, and Fidelis brought him where, beneath the steep, was a shallow cave carpeted with soft moss, very excellent suited to their need. Here Beltane laid him down, watching a little cataract that rippled o'er the rocky bank near by, where ferns and lichens grew; what time Sir Fidelis came and went, and, having set fire a-going whereby to cook their supper, brought an armful of fragrant heather to set 'neath Beltane's weary head. Then, having given him to drink of the cordial, fell to work bathing and bandaging his wound, sighing often to see it so swollen and angry.

"Fidelis," quoth Beltane, "methinks there is some magic in thy touch, for now is my pain abated — hast a wondrous gentle hand —"

"'Tis the cordial giveth thee respite, lord —"

"Nay, 'tis thy hand, methinks. Sure no man e'er was blest with truer friend than thou, my Fidelis; brave art thou, yet tender as any woman, and rather would I have thy love than the love of any man or woman soever, henceforth, dear my friend. Nay, wherefore hang thy head? without thee I had died many times ere this; without thy voice to cheer me in these solitudes, thy strength and skill to aid me, I had fallen into madness and death. Wherefore I do love thee, Fidelis, and fain would have thee go beside me ever — so great is become my need of thee."

"Ah, Beltane, thou dost know I will ne'er desert thee!"

"So henceforth am I content — and yet —"

"Well, my lord?"

"To-morrow, perchance, shall see the end of this our solitude and close comradeship — to-morrow we should reach Hundleby Fen. So, Fidelis, promise me, if thou, at any time hereafter should see me harsh, or proud, or selfish — do thou mind me of these days of our love and companionship. Wilt promise me?"

"Aye, lord!" spake Sir Fidelis, low-bending to his task; and thereafter sighed, and bowed him lower yet.

"Wherefore dost thou sigh?"

"For that I feel as if — ah, Beltane! — as if this night should be the end of our love and comradeship!"

"Nought but death shall do this, methinks."

"Why then," said Fidelis as he rose, "an it must be, fain would I have death."

But when Beltane would have questioned him further he smiled sad and wistful and went forth to the fire. Up rose the moon, a thing of glory filling the warm, stilly night with a soft and radiant splendour — a tender light, fraught with a subtle magic, whereby all things, rock and tree and leaping brook, found a new and added beauty.

And in some while comes Sir Fidelis to set out their viands, neat and orderly, as was ever his custom, and thereafter must needs chide Beltane, soft-voiced, for his lack of hunger, and cut dainty morsels, wooing him thereby to eat.

"Fidelis," says Beltane, "on so fair a night as this, methinks, the old fables and romances might well be true that tell of elves that dance on moony nights, and of shapely nymphs and lovely dryads that are the spirits of the trees. Aye, in the magic of so fair a night as this aught might happen — miracles and wonders."

"Save one thing, dear my lord."

"As what, my Fidelis?"

"That thou should'st dream Helen pure and faithful

How Madness Came Upon Beltane 343

and worthy to thy love — that, doubting thine own senses, thou should'st yearn and sigh to hold her once again, heart on heart —"

"Ah, Fidelis," quoth Beltane, sighing deep, "why wilt thou awake a sleeping sorrow? My love was dead long since, meseemeth, and buried in mine heart. O Fidelis, mine eyes, mine ears, my every sense do tell me she is false — so is an end of love for me henceforth."

"Dear my lord," spake Fidelis, and his voice thrilled strangely in Beltane's ears —"O, Beltane, my lord, could'st thou but doubt thyself a little — could'st thou, doubting thine own senses for love's sake, believe her now true — true as thou would'st have her, then Love indeed might work for thee a miracle this night and thou be loved as man of god-like faith."

"Nay, sweet Fidelis, I am but a man, apt to evil betimes and betimes seeking good. Howbeit, now am I a weary man that fain would sleep. Come then, lay you down here beside me where I may touch thee an I awake i' the night." And, lying down, Beltane beckoned Fidelis beside him.

So in a while the young knight came and did as Beltane bade, and side by side they lay within the shelter of the little cave; and in the dark, Beltane set his mighty arm about him and thereafter spake, wondering:

"Art not cold, Fidelis?"

"Nay, lord."

"Then why dost tremble?"

"Indeed I know not — mayhap I grieved that — the age of miracles — is passed away."

Now at this Beltane wondered the more and would fain have questioned him, but in that moment sighed, and fell to slumber. But in his sleep he dreamed that Fidelis was beset by foes and cried to him for aid, whereon he would have hasted to his deliverance yet could not for that unseen hands held him fast; then strove he amain against these griping hands, and so awaked in sudden terror and lay there trembling in the dark; and in the dark he reached out cautious hand further and further and so found himself alone — for the young knight was gone.

Now being very sick with the fever of his wound, dread came upon him, fear seized and shook him, and, trembling in the dark he called aloud "Fidelis! Fidelis!" But no sound heard he save the ripple of the brook near by. Groaning, he arose and, limping forth of the cave stood in the glory of the moon, voiceless now by reason of his ever-growing terror; conscious only of his passionate desire to find again the youth whose gentle voice had cheered him often in the dark, whose high courage and tender care had never failed. So, leaning upon his great sword, Beltane limped through light and shadow, heedless of direction, until he was stayed by the waters of the pool.

A faint splash, a rippling of the sleepy waters, and, out into the moonlight came one that swam the pool with long, easy strokes; one that presently leapt lightly ashore and stood there to shake down the unwetted glory of her hair. At first he thought this some enchanted pool and she the goddess of the place, but even then she turned, and thus at last — he knew. And in that moment also, she beheld him amid the leaves; tall and fair she stood, proud and maidenly, nor moved she, nor spake: only she shook about her loveliness the shining mantle of her hair. And beholding the reproachful sadness of those clear, virgin eyes, Beltane, abashed by her very beauty, bowed his head, and turning, stumbled away and thus presently finding himself within the cave, threw himself down and clasped his head within fierce hands. Yet, even so, needs must he behold the slim, white beauty of her, the rippling splendour of her hair, and the deep, shy sadness of her eyes, and, because of her beauty he trembled, and because of her falsity he groaned aloud.

Now as he lay thus, after some while he heard a swift, light footfall, the whisper of mail, and knew that she stood above him; yet he heeded not, wherefore at last she spake, sweet-voiced and gentle.

"Beltane — dear my lord, now dost thou know who is

Fidelis, and thou didst — love Fidelis!" But Beltane stirred not, and finding him silent, she spake on, yet faltering a little:

"When I waked from my swoon within the chapel at — at Blaen, and found thee gone, I, distraught with woeful fear and a most strange sickness, took thy sword and therewith horse and armour and in that same hour fled from Blaen, none knowing. Many days I rode seeking thee, until Love brought me to thee in the green. But, O Beltane, for those dire chances of our — wedding night, by what spells and witchcraft our happiness was changed to sorrow and dire amaze, I know no more than thou. Ah, Beltane — dear my lord — speak — speak to me!" And falling on her knees she would have lifted his head. But of a sudden he shrank away, and rose to his feet.

"Touch me not, I am but a man and thou — art woman, and there is evil in thee, so touch me not with thy false, alluring hands. O, thou hast deceived me now as ever — As Fidelis did I love thee above all men, but for what thou art, I do despise thee —"

But, with sudden gesture passionate and yearning, she reached out her white hands, and, kneeling thus, looked up at him with eyes a-swoon with love and supplication.

"Beltane!" she sighed, "Beltane! Is thy great love dead in very truth? nay, indeed I know it liveth yet even as mine, and shall live on forever. I know — I have seen it leap within thine eyes, heard it in thy voice — and wherefore did'st thou love Fidelis? Look at me, Beltane! I can be as brave, as faithful and tender as Fidelis! Look at me!"

But Beltane dared not look, and trembled because of her so great beauty, and fain would speak yet could not.

Whereat she, yet upon her knees, drew nearer.

"Beltane," she murmured, "trust me. Despite thyself, O, trust me — so shalt thou find happiness at last and Pentavalon an end to all her sorrows. Be thou my lord, my master — my dear love and husband — ride with me this night to my fair Mortain —"

"To Mortain?" cried Beltane wildly, "aye, to Blaen, belike — to silken wantonings and to — death! Tempt me not, O witch — aye, witch that weaveth spells of her beauty — tempt me not I say, lest I slay thee to mine own defence, for I know thee beyond all women fair, yet would I slay thee first —" But, groaning, Beltane cast aside his sword and covered burning eyes with burning palms, yet shook as with an ague fit.

The pleading hands fell, to clasp and wring each other; her proud head sank, and a great sob brake from her, what time Beltane watched her with eyes bright with fever and swayed upon his feet. Stumbling, he turned and left her, yet presently came back leading the war-horse Mars.

"To Mortain shalt thou ride to-night — I pray thee mount!" cried he, "Come — mount, I say!"

Standing tall and proud before him she sighed and spake deep-sorrowing:

"Then will I leave thee — an it must be so. But, in days to come, mayhap, thou shalt grieve for this hour, Beltane, nor shall all thy sighs nor all thy tears avail to bring it back again. Thou hast shamed me oft, yet for all thy bitter scorns I do forgive thee, aye, even the anguish of my breaking heart, for that my love doth rise beyond my pain; and so, dear my lord — fare thee well!"

So she mounted, whereat the mettled charger must needs rear, and Beltane, staggering aside, catch at a tree and lean there.

"Art sick, Beltane?" she cried in sudden fear —"how may I leave thee thus — art sick!"

"Aye, Helen, for thy beauty. The devil is here, and I am here, so here is no place for thee — so get thee gone, spur — spur! for despising thee in my heart yet would I have thee stay: yet, an thou stay needs must I slay thee ere the dawn and myself thereafter!"

Thus spake he, his voice loud, his speech quick and fevered.

"Indeed, thou'rt sick, my lord — nor do I fear thee, thou noble son of noble father!"

"My father! Forsooth he liveth in Holy Cross Thicket within Mortain; he bade me beware of women and the ways of women. So do I know thee witch, thou golden Helen. Ha! must Troy burn again — I loved thee once, but love is dead long since and turned corrupt — so get thee hence, Helen the Wilful!"

"O, God pity thee, my Beltane, for thou dost love me yet, even as I love thee — thou lonely man-child! God pity thee, and me also!" and, crying thus, forlorn and desolate, the Duchess Helen rode upon her solitary way.

Then turned Beltane and stumbled on he knew not whither, and betimes he laughed loud and high and betimes he was shaken by great and fierce sobs, yet found he never a tear. Thus, limping painfully, and stumbling anon as one smitten blind, he wandered awhile, and so at length found himself beside the little cave; and throwing himself down within its shadows, tore away the bandages her gentle hands had wrought.

And lying there, it seemed that Fidelis yet lay beneath his arm, the Fidelis who was no Fidelis; and in the shadows he laughed amain — wild laughter that died of a sudden, choked by awful sobs, what time he clenched his hands upon his throbbing ears; yet still, above the sounds of his own anguish, needs must he hear again that forlorn and desolate cry:

"O, God pity thee, Beltane!"

"And now followed long hours when demons vile racked him with anguish and mocked him with bitter gibes; a haunted darkness where was fear and doubt and terror of things unknown: yet, in the blackness, a light that grew to a glory wherein no evil thing might be, and in this glory SHE did stand, tall and fair and virginal. And from the depths of blackness, he cried to her in agony of remorse, and from the light she looked down on him with eyes brimful of yearning love and tenderness, for that a gulf divided them. But, across this hateful void she called to him —"O, God pity thee, my Beltane!"

CHAPTER XLV

HOW BLACK ROGER TAUGHT BELTANE GREAT WISDOM

A DARKNESS, full of a great quietude, a grateful stillness, slumberous and restful; yet, little by little, upon this all-pervading silence, a sound crept, soft, but distressful to one who fain would sleep; a sound that grew, a sharp noise and querulous. And now, in the blackness, a glimmer, a furtive gleam, a faint glow that grew brighter and yet more bright, hurtful to eyes long used to deeps of gloom; but, with the noise, ever this light grew — from gleam to glow and from glow to dazzling glare; and so, at last, Beltane opened unwilling eyes — eyes that blinked and smarted as they beheld a leaping flame where a fire of twigs crackled merrily against a purple void beyond; beholding all of which, Beltane forthwith shut his eyes again. But those soft deeps wherein he had found so sweet oblivion, that great and blessed quietude were altogether vanished and beyond him to regain; wherefore Beltane felt himself aggrieved and sorrowed within himself, and so, presently oped his reluctant eyes and fell to watching the play of wanton spark and flame. None the less he knew himself yet aggrieved, also he felt a sudden loneliness, wherefore (as was become his custom of late) he called on one ever heedful and swift to answer his call.

"Fidelis!" he called, "Fidelis!" Yet came there no one, and Beltane wondered vaguely why his voice should sound so thin and far away. So, troubling not to move, he called again:

"Fidelis — art sleeping, my Fidelis?"

Now of a sudden, one stirred amid the shadows beyond the fire, mail gleamed, and Black Roger bent over him.

"Master!" he cried joyfully, his eyes very bright, "O,

master, art awake at last? — dost know Roger — thy man, — dost know thy Roger, lord?"

"Aye, forsooth, I know thee, Roger," says Beltane, yet aggrieved and querulous, " but I called not thee. Send me Fidelis — where tarries Fidelis?"

"Master, I know not. He came to me within the Hollow six nights agone and gave to me his horse and bid me seek thee here. Thereafter went he afoot by the forest road, and I rode hither and found thee, according to his word."

Then would Beltane have risen, but could not, and stared at Black Roger's pitiful face with eyes of wonder.

"Why, Roger!" quoth he, "Why, Roger — ?"

"Thou hast been very nigh to death, master. A madman I found thee, in sooth — foaming, master, and crying in direful voice of spells and magic. Bewitched wert thou, master, in very sooth — and strove and fought with me, and wept as no man should weep, and all by reason of a vile enchantment which the sweet saints forfend. So here hast thou lain on the borders of death and here have I ministered to thee as Sir Fidelis did teach me; and, but for these medicaments, I had wept upon thy grave, for wert direly sick, lord, and —"

"Nay, here is no matter — tell me, tell me, where is Fidelis?"

"Dear master I know not, forsooth!"

"Went he by the forest road?"

"Aye, master, the forest road."

"Afoot?"

"Afoot, lord."

"Said he aught to thee of — of me, Roger?"

"Aye, 'twas all of thee and thy wound, and how to ease thy pain I must do this, forsooth, and that, forsooth, and to break the fever must mix and give thee certain cordials, the which I have done."

"Said he aught beside — aught else, Roger?"

"Aye, master, he bid me pray for thee, the which I have also done, though I had rather fight for thee; nathless the sweet saints have answered even my poor prayers, for behold, thou art alive and shall be well anon."

Now after this, Beltane lay with eyes fast shut and spake not; thus he lay so long, that Roger, thinking he slept again, would have moved away, but Beltane's feeble hand stayed him, and he spake, yet with eyes still closed.

"By the forest road, Roger!"

"Aye, master."

"Alone, Roger!"

"Aye, lord, alone."

"And — afoot, Roger!"

"Aye, lord, he bade me take his horse that I might come to thee the sooner."

"And — bid thee — pray for me — for me, Roger!"

"Verily, master. And pray I did, right lustily."

"So do I thank thee, Roger," said Beltane, speaking ever with closed eyes. "Yet I would that God had let me die, Roger." And behold, from these closed eyes, great tears, slow-oozing and painful, that rolled a-down the pallid cheek, very bright in the fire-glow, and glistening like the fairest gems.

"Master — O master!" cried Roger, "dost grieve thee for Sir Fidelis?"

"Forsooth, I must, Roger — he was a peerless friend, methinks!"

"Aye master, and — noble lady!"

"Roger — O Roger, how learned you this? Speak!"

"Lord, thou hast had visions and talked much within thy sickness. So do I know that thou dost love the Duchess Helen that men do call 'the Beautiful.' I do know that on thy marriage night thou wert snatched away to shameful prison. I do know that she, because her heart was as great as her love, did follow thee in knightly guise, and thou did most ungently drive her from thee. All this, and much beside, thou didst shout and whisper in thy fever."

Quoth Beltane, plucking at Roger with feeble hand:

"Roger — O Roger, since this thou knowest — tell me,

tell me, can faith and treachery lie thus within one woman's heart — and of all women — her's?"

"Master, can white be black? Can day be night? Can heaven be hell — or can truth lie? So, an Sir Fidelis be faithful (and faithful forsooth is he) so is the Duchess Helen faithful —"

"Nay, an she be true — O Roger, an she be true indeed, how think you of the treachery, of —"

"I think here was witchcraft, master, spells, see'st thou, and magic black and damned. As thou wert true to her, so was she true to thee, as true as — aye, as true as I am, and true am I, Saint Cuthbert knoweth that, who hath heard my prayers full oft of late, master."

"Now God bless thee, Roger — O, God bless thee!" So crying, of a sudden Beltane caught Black Roger's sunburned hand and kissed it, and thereafter turned him to the shadows. And, lying thus, Beltane wept, very bitterly yet very silent, until, like a grieving child he had wept himself to forgetfulness and sleep. So slept he, clasped within Roger's mailed arm. But full oft Black Roger lifted his bronzed right hand — the hand that had felt Beltane's sudden kiss — and needs must he view it with eyes of wonder, as if it had been indeed some holy thing, what time he kept his midnight vigil beside the fire.

CHAPTER XLVI

HOW BLACK ROGER PRAYED IN THE DAWN: AND HOW HIS PRAYERS WERE ANSWERED

"Holy Saint Cuthbert, art a very sweet and potent saint, and therefore hast good eyes — which is well; so canst thou see him for thyself, how weak he is and languid, that was a mighty man and lusty. Cherish him, I pray thee! A goodly youth thou dost know him, thou didst see him burn a gibbet, moreover I have told thee — and eke a knight of high degree. Yet doth he lie here direly sick of body. Cherish him, I pray! Moreover, sick is he of mind, for that he loveth one, a lady, methinks good and worthy — so bring them together, these twain, not above, as saints in heaven, but first as man and woman that shall beget such men as he, such noble dames as she, and make the world a better place therefor. See you to this matter, good Saint Cuthbert, and also the matter of his Dukedom. But when he shall be Duke indeed, and blest with her that is so fair a maid and apt to motherhood — I pray thee, Saint Cuthbert, let him not forget me whose soul he saved long since within the green in the matter of Beda that was a Jester — I pray thee let him have regard to Black Roger that am his man henceforth to the end. Amen. Holy Saint Cuthbert grant me this."

It was Black Roger, praying in the dawn, his broadsword set upright in the ling, his hands devoutly crossed and his black head stooped full low; thus he saw not Beltane's eyes upon him until his prayer was ended.

Quoth Beltane then:

"May heaven grant thee thy prayer, Roger —'twas a good prayer and I the better for it."

"Why, look now, master," says Roger, somewhat

abashed, " I am a something better pray-er than I was, and I pray in good Saxon English; thus do I call on Saint Cuthbert, that was a lusty Saxon ere that he was a saint."

" But, Roger, what need to supplicate lest I forget thee? Think you I should forget my faithful Roger? "

" Why, lord," says Roger, busily preparing wherewith to break their fast, " when a man marrieth, see you, and thereafter proceedeth forthwith to get him children, as the custom is —"

" Nay, dost talk folly, Roger! " quoth Beltane, his pale cheek flushing.

" Yet folly thou dost dream of, master, and she also — else wherefore love —"

" Nay, Roger, doth Belsaye lie secure yet? What of Walkyn and our comrades? Marched they to Belsaye as I did command? "

" Why, see you now, master, when our foes came not, and you came not, we sent word to Belsaye that, within two days we would march thither, according to thy word, and forthwith Giles sends word back that he was very well and wanted no long-legged Walkyn or surly Roger to share authority with him yet a while, and bid us twirl our thumbs within the green until he commanded our presence — with divers other ribald japes and wanton toys — whereon Walkyn and I waxed something wroth. Therefore, when ye came not, our comrades fell to factions and riot, whereat I, perforce, smote me one or two and Walkyn three or four and so brought peace among them. But when we would have tarried yet for thee, these rogue-fellows clamoured for Walkyn to lead them into the wild, back to their ancient outlawry; so loud they clamoured and so oft, that, in the end, Walkyn smiled — a strange thing in him, master — but he agreed, whereon we came nigh to cutting each other's throats, he and I. Howbeit, in the end he went, he and all the other rogues. So bided I alone in the Hollow, day and night, waiting thee, master, and at the last, cometh Sir Fidelis — and so all's said and behold thy breakfast — a coney, see you, lord, that I snared but yest're'en."

"Our company gone — outlaws, spending their lives to no purpose — here is evil news, Roger!"

"Here is tender meat, master, and delicate!"

"Back to outlawry! And Walkyn too!"

"Aye — but he smiled, master! Walkyn, methinks, is not a jovial soul, lord, and when he smileth it behoveth others to frown and — beware. So prithee eat hearty, lord, for, in a while the sun will stand above yon whin-bush, and then 'twill be the eleventh hour, and at the eleventh hour must I wash thy hurt and be-plaster it with this good ointment."

"What then?"

"Then shalt thou sleep, master, and I to the woods with my bow to get us meat — sweet juicy venison, an the saints be kind!"

"And wherefore at the eleventh hour?"

"For that — She did so command me, master."

"She?" sighed Beltane.

"Aye, forsooth, master. She that the good Saint Cuthbert shall give to thy close embracements one day."

"Think you so?" spake Beltane beneath his breath, and staring across the sunny glade with eyes of yearning, "think you so indeed, Roger?"

"Of a surety, lord," nodded Roger, "seeing that I do plague the good saint on the matter continually — for, master, when I pray, I do pray right lustily."

So, in a while, the meal done and crock and pannikin washed and set aside, Beltane's leg is bathed and dressed right skilfully with hands, for all their strength and hardness, wondrous light and gentle. Thereafter, stretched upon his bed of heather, Beltane watches Black Roger gird on belt and quiver, and, bow in hand, stride blithely into the green, and, ere he knows it, is asleep. And in his sleep, beholds one who bends to kiss him, white hands outstretched and all heaven in her eyes; and with her voice thrilling in his ears, wakes, to find the sun already westering and Black Roger near by, who, squatting before a rough table he has contrived set close beside the fire whereon a cooking pot seethes and bubbles, is busied with certain brewings, infusings and mixings in pipkin and pannikin, and all with brow of frowning portent.

Whereat says Beltane, wondering:

"What do ye, good Roger?"

"Master, I mix thee thy decoction as She did instruct — She is a learned youth, master — Sir Fidelis. In these dried herbs and simples, look you, lieth thy health and strength and Pentavalon's freedom — aye, a notable youth in faith, thy Duchess."

Hereupon Beltane, remembering his dream, must needs close his eyes that he may dream again, and is upon the portal of sleep when Roger's hand rouses him.

"What would'st, Roger?"

"Master — thy draught."

"Take it hence!"

"Nay, it must be swallowed, master."

"Then swallow it thyself!"

"Nay, lord, 'tis the hour for thy draught appointed by Sir Fidelis and She must be obeyed — come, master!" Forthwith, yet remembering his dream, Beltane opens unwilling eyes and more unwilling mouth and the draught is swallowed; whereupon comes languor and sleep, and therewith, more dreams.

Anon 'tis even-fall, and the stars, one by one, peep forth of the darkening heaven, shadows steal and lengthen and lo! 'tis night; a night wherein the placid moon, climbing apace, fills the silent world with the splendour of her advent. And ever and always Beltane lies deep-plunged in slumber; but in his sleep he groans full oft and oft doth call upon a name — a cry faint-voiced and weak, yet full of a passionate yearning; whereupon cometh sturdy Roger to behold him in the light of the fire, to stoop and soothe him with gentle hand; thus needs must he mark the glitter of a tear upon that pale and sunken cheek, wherefore Black Roger's own eyes must needs fall a-smarting and he to grieving amain. In so much that of a sudden he stealeth swiftly from the cave, and, drawing sword setteth it upright in the ling; then kneeling with bowed head and reverent hands, forthwith fell to his prayers, after this wise: —

"Sweet Cuthbert — gentle saint — behind me in the shadows lieth my master — a-weeping in his slumber. So needs must I weep also, since I do love him for that he is a man. Good Saint Cuthbert, I have wrought for him my best as thou hast seen — tended his hurt thrice daily and ministered the potion as I was commanded. I have worked for him — prayed for him — yet doth he weep great tears within his sleep. So now do I place him in thy care, good saint, for thou dost know me but poor rogue Roger, a rough man and all unlearned, yet, even so, I do most truly love him and, loving him, do fear — for meseemeth his hurt is deeper than hurt of body, he doth pine him and grieve for lack of his heart's desire — a young man, sweet saint, that doth yearn for a maid right fair and noble, *pars amours*, good saint, as is the custom. But alack, she is far hence and he lieth here sick and like to perish and I am but poor Roger — a very sinful man that knoweth not what to do. So do I call on thee, sweet saint — achieve me a miracle on his behalf, bring him to his heart's desire that he may wax hale and well and weep no more within his sleep. And this do I ask for his sake and his lady's sake and for the sake of Pentavalon Duchy — not forgetting poor Roger that doth plague thee thus for love of him. Amen!"

Now behold! even as the prayer was ended came a faint stir and rustle amid the leaves hard by, and, lifting startled head, Black Roger beheld a radiant vision standing in the pale glory of the moon, whereat he knew fear and a great awe.

"O, good Saint Cuthbert, and is it thou indeed?" he whispered, "Sweet saint, I thought not to win thee down from heaven thus, though forsooth I did pray right lustily. But, since thou art come —"

"Hush, good Roger!" spake a voice soft and wondrous sweet to hear; and, so speaking, the shining figure raised

How Roger Prayed in the Dawn

the vizor of its helm. "O hush thee, Roger, for he sleepeth. All day, unseen, have I watched over him, nor can I leave him until his strength be come again. And sleep is life to him, so wake him not. Come your ways, for I would speak thee many things — follow!"

As one that dreams, Roger stared into the eyes beneath the vizor, and as one that dreams he rose up from his knees, and, sheathing his sword, followed whither the gleaming vision led; yet betimes he blinked upon the moon, and once he shook his head and spake as to himself:

"Verily — aye, verily, a lusty pray-er, I!"

CHAPTER XLVII

HOW BELTANE SWARE AN OATH

SLOWLY the days sped, dewy dawn and tender eve, days of sun and shadow and gentle rain; golden days wherein Beltane lay 'twixt sleep and wake, and nights of silver wherein he slept full deep and dreamed wondrously of gentle hands that soothed him with their touch, and warm soft lips on cheek and brow that filled him with a great and deep content.

And in these days, who so cheery as Black Roger, full of a new-found gaiety, who laughed for small reason and ofttimes for none at all and was forever humming snatches of strange song as he stooped above pipkin and pannikin. Much given was he also to frequent comings and goings within the green to no apparent end, while Beltane, within the little cave, lay 'twixt sleep and waking; moreover, full oft as they ate their evening meal together, he would start, and falling to sudden silence, sit as one that hearkens to distant sounds. Yet withal was he ever heedful of Beltane's many wants, who, as health came, grew more eager to be gone, but finding himself too weak, straightway waxed moody and rebellious, whereat smiling Roger waxed firm, so needs must frowning Beltane be bathed and bandaged and swallow his draught — because of She who had so commanded.

Now it befell upon a certain evening as Roger bent to peer into the pot that seethed and bubbled upon the fire and to sniff its appetising savour, he presently fell a-singing to himself in a voice gruff yet musical withal; whereupon Beltane, turning languid head, fell to watching this new Roger, and thereafter spake on this wise:

BELTANE. "What do ye so oft within the green?"
ROGER. "Hunt, that we may eat, master."
BELTANE. "I have seen thee go full oft of late and leave thy bow behind, Roger."
ROGER. "Whereby I judge that though thine eyes be shut ye do not always slumber, master, and methinks our supper is done —"
BELTANE. "Nay — what do ye in the green?"
ROGER. "Master, thy horse Mars hath a proud spirit and snorteth against his bonds. So, lest he break thy slumber, have I made him a shelter of wattles in the green."
BELTANE. "Truly, Roger, thou art greatly changed, methinks."
ROGER (starting). "As how, master?"
BELTANE. "I have heard thee called Roger the grim, and Roger the surly, ere now."
ROGER (shaking woeful head). "Ere now, lord, I hanged men, conceiving it my duty."
BELTANE. "And to-day you sing — and wherefore?"
ROGER. "For joy in life, master."
BELTANE. "And thou dost laugh, surly Roger — ofttimes for little reason, meseemeth."
ROGER. "For that my heart is renewed within me, master. Happiness is my bedfellow and companion — here is good reason for laughter, methinks."
BELTANE. "And wherefore art thou happy, Roger?"
ROGER. "Item first: thou dost mend apace, lord. Item second: this mess of venison hath a savour most delectable. Item third: happiness is the birthright of every man. Moreover I have learned that behind the blackest cloud is a glory of sun, and beyond sorrow, joy. So do I rejoice that all is like to be well with thee."
BELTANE (bitterly). "Well with me, say you? Is Pentavalon free, Roger? Do I not lie here, weak and helpless — my company scattered? O, call you this well, forsooth?"
ROGER. "'Tis true thou art weak as yet, master, but thou shalt rise again stronger than aforetime — aye, thou

shalt arise indeed, and all Pentavalon with thee. So let thine heart rejoice and sing, as mine doth."

BELTANE (fiercely). "O evil day, that ere I gave my heart to woman's love, so do I lie here a useless thing — O day accursed!"

ROGER. "O day most blessed, since woman's love hath lifted thee from death and shall be thy glory and Pentavalon's salvation, master!"

BELTANE (eagerly). "Roger — Roger, speak you of the Duchess Helen? What mean you, man?"

ROGER. "There be signs and portents, master, the very air is full o' them. Whiles we tarry here, others be up and doing —"

BELTANE. "Others, Roger?"

ROGER. "Notably Walkyn o' the Axe, master!"

BELTANE. "Ha! and what of Walkyn?"

ROGER. "He smiled, master, as I told thee ere this, and when Walkyn smileth it behoveth others to be wary. So now do I tell thee that Walkyn hath taken and burned Duke Ivo's great Castle of Brandonmere, that Winisfarne city hath risen 'gainst the Duke and all the border villages likewise — aha! master, there be scythe-blades and good brown bills a-twinkle all along the marches eager to smite for freedom and Pentavalon when time is ripe!"

BELTANE (rising upon his knees). "Forsooth, is this so? O Roger, is this so in very truth?"

ROGER. "'Tis very truth, master. Upon my sword I swear it!"

BELTANE. "But whence had ye the wondrous news — how — when?"

ROGER. "Master, 'twas three nights agone, as I wrestled prodigiously in prayer on thy behalf, one came to me and spake me many things marvellous good to hear. Moreover, I have met divers folk within the greenwood and upon the forest-road yonder, and with all do I hold converse."

Then to Roger's amaze Beltane rose up, and standing square upon his feet lifted hands and eyes to heaven.

How Beltane Sware an Oath

"Now glory be to the living God," quoth he, "that hath heard the prayers of such as I. So now do I swear, come life, come death, to walk my appointed way sword in hand, henceforth, nor will I turn aside for man or woman, heeding not the lure of friendship or of love. I do swear never to look upon a woman to love —"

ROGER (fearfully). "Master — master!"

BELTANE. "Nor to suffer woman's love to come 'twixt me and my duty —"

ROGER (despairingly). "O master, swear it not — swear it not —"

BELTANE. "Nor shall aught let or stay me until Pentavalon win to freedom or my poor soul return whence it came. And this do I swear to the ears of God!"

Now turned he to Roger, bright-eyed and with hands tight-clenched.

"Roger," said he, "thou art witness to this my oath, an I do fail or falter henceforth, then in that same hour may sharp death be mine. So now bring to me sword and armour, for this night must I hence."

Now was Roger sore troubled and fain was to speak, but beholding his master's flashing eye, he presently did as he was commanded. So Beltane took hold upon the sword and drew it, and looked glad-eyed upon its broad and shining blade. But when he would have wielded it, behold! he scarce could lift it; with teeth fierce-clenched he strove against his weakness until his breath waxed short and the sweat ran from him, but ever the great blade grew the heavier. Then he groaned to find himself so feeble, and cried aloud an exceeding bitter cry, and cast the sword from him, and, staggering, fell into Roger's waiting arms. Forthwith Roger bare him to the cave and laid him down upon his bed.

"Master," quoth he, "O master, grieve not thyself, thou shalt be hale and strong anon, but the time is not yet. Comfort ye, comfort ye, my lord — ere long thou shalt be strong, aye, and mightier e'en than aforetime. So grieve not nor repine, my master!"

But Beltane lay heeding not, nor would he eat despite all Roger's wheedling arts; but being fevered and athirst, drank deep of the sleeping draught, and thereafter, falling to his black humour, turned his face to the shadows, and, lying thus, straightway fell to weeping, very silently, because of his so great weakness, until, like a child, he had wept himself to sleep.

Slowly the moon sank, the fire burned low and Roger snored blissfully hard by, but Beltane, blessed within his slumbers, dreamed again of one who stole, light of foot, to lie beside him watchful in the dark and with warm, soft arms set close about him like the sheltering arms of that mother he had never known.

Thus slept Beltane, like a weary child upon a mother's breast, and knew great peace and solace and a deep and utter content.

CHAPTER XLVIII

HOW BELTANE SET OUT FOR HANGSTONE WASTE

DAY by day Beltane waxed in health and strength, and daily, leaning upon Roger's trusty arm he walked further afield. And day by day, with growing strength, so grew his doubt, and therewith, by times, a black despond; for needs must he think ever of Helen the Beautiful, and fain was he to tear her from his heart yet could not; then fain he would have hated her, but in his ears her cry rang still —" God pity thee, my Beltane!"— wherefore he was wont to fall to sudden gloom and melancholy.

But upon a certain blithe evening Black Roger stood leaning on his bow-stave to watch where Beltane swam the pool with mighty strokes, who, laughing for very joy of it, presently sprang ashore, panting with his exertions, and fell to donning his garments.

"How think ye, Roger," he cried, "am I fit to adventure me the world again?"

"Forsooth, master, art well of thy wound and fever, and in a week or so mayhap thou shalt perchance be well enough —"

"A week, Roger! I tell thee, man, this very day will I hence!"

"But, master," says Roger, shaking cautious head, "thy world is a world of battles, and for battle art scarce yet strong enough —"

"Say ye so, Roger? Then here and now shalt make trial of me. Art a tall and lusty fellow — come, man, let us try a fall together. And mark this, Roger, an thou canst put me on my back shalt have thy will in the matter, but, an I down thee, then hey! for horse and armour and the forest-road this very night. Come, is't agreed?"

Now hereupon the wily Roger, noting the pallor of Beltane's sunken cheek and how his broad breast laboured yet, and moreover feeling himself aglow with lusty life and vigour, smiled grimly, nothing doubting the issue. Wherefore he nodded his head.

"So be it, master," said he, "only take thy wind first." So saying he set aside bow and quiver, loosed off his sword, and tightening his belt, stepped towards Beltane, his broad back stooped, his knotted arms advanced and fingers crooked to grapple. Once and twice he circled, seeking a hold, then leapt he swift and low; arms and fingers clenched and locked, and Beltane was bent, swayed, and borne from his feet; but even so, with a cunning twist he brake Black Roger's hold and staggered free. Quoth he:

"Art a very strong man, Roger, stronger than methought. Come again!"

Once more they circled heedfully, for Beltane had grown more wary: thrice he sought a certain hold and thrice Black Roger foiled him, ere, sudden and grim, he leapt and closed; and breast to breast they strove fiercely, mighty arms straining and tight-clenched, writhing, swaying, reeling, in fast-locked, desperate grapple. Now to Roger's strength and quickness Beltane opposed craft and cunning, but wily Roger met guile with guile nor was to be allured to slack or change his gripe. Therefore of a sudden Beltane put forth his strength, and wrestled mightily, seeking to break or weaken Roger's deadly hold. But Roger's iron arms gripped and held him fast, crushed him, checked him.

"Aha! master," panted Roger, "now I have thee!" and therewith heaved right lustily, felt Beltane yield and stagger, slacked his grip for the final hold, and, in that moment, his arms were burst asunder, he was whirled up, kicking, 'twixt earth and heaven, laid gently upon the sward and, sitting up, found Beltane lying breathless beside him.

"'Twas a trick, Roger!" he panted, "I beat thee — but by an artifice —"

"Yet beaten I am, master," quoth Roger, vastly rueful.

"And art mightier than I thought thee, Roger."

"Master, I have wrestled oft with Gefroi that was the Duke's wrestler."

"Then art a better man than he, meseemeth," quoth Beltane.

"Yet thou hast beaten me, master!"

"So within the hour we will begone to our duty, Roger!"

"Whither, lord?"

"First to Winisfarne, and thence south to Belsaye, with every lusty fellow we can muster. How think you?"

"I think the time is not yet, master."

"Wherefore?"

"For that though things go well with thee and thy cause, yet shall they go better anon."

"Nevertheless, Roger, within the hour we march. So come, first let us eat, for I do famish."

So, when they had caught their breath again, together they arose and, coming to the cave beneath the steep, they re-made the fire and set the pot thereon; which done, Roger brought forth his lord's armour, bright and newly polished, and in a while Beltane stood, a shining figure from golden spur to gleaming bascinet. Thereafter, Roger armed him likewise, and as two brothers-in-arms they sat together and ate their meal with mighty appetite and gusto. Now presently, as they sat thus, Beltane espied a thing that lay by Roger's knee, and, taking it up, behold! 'twas a wallet of fair-sewn leather, very artfully wrought, and, gazing upon it he must needs fall to sudden thought, whereto he sighed full deep and oft, till, finding Roger watching him, he forthwith checked his sighs and frowned instead.

"Roger," quoth he, "whence had ye this thing?"

"My lord, from — Her, the sweet knight Sir Fidelis, thy lady —"

"Why wilt thou call her my lady, Roger?"

"For that 'tis she you love and sigh for, she that doth

love thee and shall bear thee right fair and lusty children yet, so do I pray, and my prayers are potent these days, for the good Saint Cuthbert heedeth me regardfully. So do I know that she shall yet lie within thine arms and yield thee thine heart's desire, *pars* —"

"Art a fool, Roger — aye, a very fool, and talk arrant folly —"

"Yet, master, here is folly shall be thy joy and her joy and —"

"Enough, Roger! Hast forgot the oath I sware? And the ways of woman be crooked ways. And woman's love a light matter. Talk we of women no more."

"How!" quoth Roger, staring, "speak we no more of — Her?"

"No more!"

"Forsooth, so be it, master, then will we talk of Sir Fidelis his love —"

"Nor of Sir Fidelis."

"Ha!" growled Roger, scratching his head, "must we go mumchance then, master?"

"There be other matters for talk."

"Aye — there's witchcraft, master. For mark me, when thou wert sick and nigh to God and the holy saints, the evil spell could not come nigh thee, and thou didst yearn and cry continually for nought but — Her. But now — now that thou'rt hale and strong again —"

"I behold things with mind unclouded, Roger."

"Save by enchantments damned, master. Since that evil day we met yon accursed witch of Hangstone, hast never been thyself."

"Now do ye mind me how this woman did speak me of marvels and wonders, Roger —"

"Artifice, lord — devilish toys to lure thee to fouler bewitchments."

"Howbeit, I will seek her out."

"Nay, good master, here shall be perils dire and deadly. O bethink thee, lest she change thee into a swine, or black dog, aye, or even a small shrew-mouse — I've heard of such ere now — or blast thee with fire, or loathly disease, or —"

"None the less will I go."

"Never say so, master!"

"At the full o' the moon."

"Lord, now do I beseech thee —"

"And the moon will be full — to-night, Roger. Go you and saddle now the horse."

Forthwith went Roger, gloomy and nothing speaking, what time Beltane sat there staring down at the wallet on his knee, bethinking him of many things, and, for that he was alone, sighing deep and oft; and so, very suddenly, hung the wallet to his girdle and thereafter arose.

In a while cometh gloomy Roger leading the destrier Mars, whereon gloomy Beltane swung to saddle, and, looking round about him once and twice, rode slowly towards where, beyond the shade of trees, the forest road ran north and south.

But, as for Roger, needs must he pause upon the edge of the clearing to look back at the little cave beneath the steep, whereby the small water-brook flowed murmurously; a while he stood thus, to frown and shake gloomy head; then lifted he his hand on high, much as he had bid one sorrowful farewell, and, turning about, trudged away after his lord

CHAPTER XLIX

HOW BELTANE FOUND PEACE AND A GREAT SORROW

It had been an evening of cloud, but now the sky was clear and the moon shone bright and round as they reached that desolate, wind-swept heath that went by the name of Hangstone Waste, a solitary place at all times but more especially wild and awful 'neath the ghostly moon; wherefore Roger went wide-eyed and fearful, and kept fast hold of Beltane's stirrup.

"Ha — master, master!" cried he 'twixt chattering teeth, "did'st not hear it, master?"

"Nay," answered Beltane, checking his horse, "what was it? where away?"

"'Twas a cry, master — beyond the marsh yonder. 'Tis there again!"

"'Twas an owl, Roger."

"'Twas a soul, master; a poor damned soul and desolate! We shall see dire and dreadful sights on Hangstone Waste this night, master — holy Saint Cuthbert! What was yon?"

"Nought but a bat, Roger."

"A bat, lord? Never think so. Here was, belike, a noble knight or a lusty fellow be-devilled into a bat. Good master, let us go no further — if thou hast no thought for thyself, have a little heed for poor Roger."

"Why look ye, good Roger, canst go where thou wilt, but, as for me, I ride for the White Morte-stone."

"Nay then, an thou'rt blasted this night, master, needs must I be blasted with thee — yonder lieth the Morte-stone, across the waste. And now, may Saint Cuthbert and Saint Bede have us in their blessed care, Amen!"

So they began to cross the rolling desolation of the

heath and presently espied a great boulder, huge and solitary, gleaming white and ghostly 'neath the moon.

Being come very nigh, Beltane checked his horse and was about to dismount, when Roger, uttering a sudden gasping cry, cowered to his knees, for in the air about them was a sound very sweet to hear — the whisper of lute-strings softly plucked by skilled and cunning fingers, and thereafter a man's voice, rich and melodious, brake forth into tender singing: and the words were these: —

> "O moon! O gentle moon, to-night
> Unveil thy softest, tend'rest light
> Where feet I love, so small and white,
>   Do bear my love to me!"

"Stand up, Roger, here is nought to harm us, methinks," quoth Beltane softly, "stand up, and hold my bridle."

"But see now, master, there be devil-goblins a many that do pipe like very angels."

"Nathless here's one that I must speak with," said Beltane, slipping to earth and looking about him with wondering eyes, for the voice had seemed to come from the grass at his feet. And while he yet sought to and fro in frowning perplexity the melodious voice brake forth anew:

> "O little feet, more white than snow,
> If through the thorny brake ye go,
> My loving heart I'll set below
>   To take the hurt for thee."

Now as the voice sank and the lute-strings quivered to silence, Beltane, coming behind the great rock, beheld a glow, very faint and feeble, that shone through thick-clustering leaves; and, putting aside a whin-bush that grew against the rock, perceived a low and narrow alley or passage-way leading downwards into the earth, lighted by a soft, mellow beam that brightened as he advanced and presently showed him a fair-sized chamber cunningly hollowed within the rock and adorned with rich furs and skins.

And behold one who reclined upon a couch of skins, a slender, youthful figure with one foot wondrously bewrapped and swathed, who, beholding Beltane's gleaming mail, sprang up very nimbly and fronted him with naked sword advanced.

"Nay, hast forgot thy friend, Sir Jocelyn?"

Incontinent the sword was tossed aside, and with a joyous cry Sir Jocelyn sprang and caught him in close embrace.

"Now by sweet Venus her downy dove—'tis Beltane!" he cried. "Now welcome and thrice welcome, my lordly smith, thou mighty son of noble father. Ah, lord Duke, I loved thee that day thou didst outmatch Gefroi the wrestler in the green. Since then much have I learned of thee and thy valiant doings, more especially of Barham Broom — how thou didst slay the vile Sir Gilles 'neath the eyes of Ivo and all his powers and thereby didst snatch from shame and cruel death one that is become the very heart of me, so needs must I love and honour and cherish thee so long as I be Jocelyn and thou thy noble self. Come, sit ye — sit ye here, for fain am I to question thee —"

"But," said Beltane, wrinkling puzzled brow, "how came you hither — and art wounded, Jocelyn?"

"Aye, my lord, to desperation — O direly, Beltane. I do languish night and day, sleep doth bring me no surcease and music, alack, abatement none. Food — base food repelleth me and wine no savour hath. Verily, verily, wounded deep am I."

"Forsooth," said Beltane, "thy foot doth wear bandages a many, but —"

"Bandages?" cried Jocelyn, staring. "Foot? Nay, nay, my torment is not here," and he flourished his beswathed foot in an airy, dancing step. "Indeed, Beltane, herein do I confess me some small artifice, yet, mark me, to a sweet and worthy end. For my hurt lieth here,— sore smit am I within this heart o' mine."

"Thy heart again, Jocelyn?"

"Again?" said the young knight, wrinkling slender brows.

"Aye, thou did'st sing thy heart's woe to me not so long since — in an hundred and seventy and eight cantos, and I mind thy motto: 'Ardeo'."

"Nay, Beltane, in faith — indeed, these were folly and youthful folly, the tide hath ebbed full oft since then and I, being older, am wiser. Love hath found me out at last — man's love. List now, I pray thee and mark me, friend. Wounded was I at the ford you wot of beside the mill, and, thereafter, lost within the forest, a woeful wight! Whereon my charger, curst beast, did run off and leave me. So was I in unholy plight, when, whereas I lay sighful and distressed, there dawned upon my sight one beyond all beauty beautiful. Y-clad in ragged garb was she, yet by her loveliness her very rags were glorified. To me, shy as startled doe, came she and, with saintly pity sweet, did tend my hurt, which done, with much ado she did hither bring me. Each day, at morn and eve, came she with cates rare and delicate, and her gentle hands did woo my wound to health, the which indeed so swift grew well that I did feign divers pains betimes lest she should vanish from me quite — so grew my love. At the first loved I her something basely, for the beauty of her body fair, whereat she grieved and sorrowed and fled from my regard, and for an eternity of days came not again until yestere'en. And, Beltane, though base her birth, though friendless, poor and lonely, yet did my heart know her far 'bove my base self for worthiness. So did I, yestere'en, upon my knightly word, pledge her my troth, so shall she be henceforth my lady of Alain and chatelaine of divers goodly castles, manors, and demesnes. To-night she cometh to me in her rags, and to-night we set forth, she and I, to Mortain, hand in hand — nor shall my lips touch hers, Beltane, until Holy Church hath made us one. How think ye of my doing, friend?"

"I do think thee true and worthy knight, Sir Jocelyn, and moreover —"

But of a sudden, Roger's voice reached them from without, hoarse with terror.

"Master — O master, beware! 'Tis the witch, lord — O beware!"

And with the cry, lo! a hurry of feet running swift and light, a rustle of flying garments, and there, flushed and panting, stood the witch — the witch Mellent that was the lady Winfrida. Now, beholding Beltane, her eyes grew wide with swift and sudden fear — she quailed, and sank to her knees before him; and when Sir Jocelyn, smitten to mute wonder, would have raised her, she brake forth into bitter weeping and crouched away.

"Nay, touch me not my lord, lest thou repent hereafter — for now do I see that happiness is not for me — now must I say such words as shall slay thy love for me, so touch me not."

"Ha, never say so!" cried Sir Jocelyn, "not touch thee? art not mine own beloved Mellent?"

"Nay, I am the lady Winfrida —"

"Thou — Winfrida the rich and proud — in these rags? Thou, Winfrida the Fair? — thy raven hair —"

"O, my hair, my lord? 'twas gold, 'tis black and shall be gold again, but I am that same Winfrida."

"But — but I have seen Winfrida betimes in Mortain ere now."

"Nay, then, didst but look at her, my lord, for thine eyes saw only the noble Helen's beauty. Alas! that ever I was born, for that I am that Winfrida who, for ambition's sake and wicked pride, did a most vile thing — O my lord Beltane, as thou art strong, be pitiful — as thou art deeply wronged, be greatly merciful."

"How — how — mean you?" said Beltane, slow-speaking and breathing deep.

"Lord — 'twas I — O, how may I tell it? My lord Beltane, upon thy wedding night did I, with traitorous hand, infuse a potent drug within the loving-cup, whereby our lady Duchess fell into a swoon nigh unto death. And — while she lay thus, I took from her the marriage-robe — the gown of blue and silver. Thereafter came I, with my henchman Ulf the Strong and — found thee sleeping in the chapel. So Ulf — at my command — smote thee and — bound thee fast, and, ere the dawn, I brought thee — to Garthlaxton — O my lord!"

"Thou —? It was — thou?"

"I do confess it, my lord Beltane — traitor to thee, and base traitor to her —"

"Why, verily — here was treachery —" quoth Beltane speaking slow and soft, "truly here — methinks — was treachery — and wherefore?"

"O my lord, must I — tell this?"

"I do ask thee."

Then did Winfrida shrink within herself, and crouched yet further from Sir Jocelyn as though his eyes had hurt her.

"Lord," she whispered, "I was — jealous! Duke Ivo wooed me long ere he loved the Duchess Helen, so was I jealous. Yet was I proud also, for I would suffer not his love until he had made me wife. And, upon a day, he, laughing, bade me bring him captive this mighty man that defied his power — that burned gibbets and wrought such deeds as no other man dared, swearing that, an I did so, he would wed with me forthright. And I was young, and mad with jealousy and — in those days — I knew love not at all. But O, upon a day, I found a new world wherein Love came to me — a love so deep and high, so pure and noble, that fain would I have died amid the flame than thus speak forth my shame, slaying this wondrous love by my unworthiness. Yet have I told my shame, and love is dead, methinks, since I am known for false friend and traitor vile — a thing for scorn henceforth, that no honourable love may cleave to. So is love dead, and fain would I die also!"

Now, of a sudden, while yet Beltane frowned down upon her, came Sir Jocelyn, and kneeling beside Winfrida, spake with bent head:

"Messire Beltane, thou seest before thee two that are

one, henceforth. So do I beseech thee, forgive us our trespass against thee, an it may be so. But, if thy wrongs are beyond forgiveness, then will we die together."

"O Jocelyn!" cried Winfrida breathlessly, "O dear my lord — surely never man loved like thee! Lord Beltane, forgive — for this noble knight's sake — forgive the sinful Winfrida!"

"Forgive?" said Beltane, hoarsely, "forgive? — nay, rather would I humbly thank thee on my knees, for thou hast given back the noblest part of me. She that was lost is found again, the dead doth live. Helen is her noble self, and only I am vile that could have doubted her. The happiest man, the proudest, and the most woeful, I, in all the world, methinks. O kneel not to me — and pray you — speak on this matter no more. Rise, rise up and get ye to your joy. Lady, hast won a true and leal knight, and thou, Sir Jocelyn, a noble lady, who hath spoken truth at hazard of losing her love. And I do tell ye, love is a very blessed thing, greater than power, or honour, or riches, or aught in the world but love. Aye, surely Love is the greatest thing of all!" So saying, Beltane turned very suddenly, and strode out, where, beside the great horse Mars, stood Roger, very pale in the moonlight, and starting and staring at every rustling leaf and patch of shadow.

"Roger," said he, "thou art afraid of bats and owls, yet, forsooth, art a wiser man than I. Bring hither the horse."

In a while cometh Sir Jocelyn and the lady Winfrida, hand in hand, aglow with happiness, yet with eyes moistly bright under the moon.

"Good comrade-in-arms," quoth Beltane, "Mortain lieth far hence; now here is a goodly horse —"

"O!" cried Winfrida shrinking, "surely 'tis the horse that bore Sir Gilles of Brandonmere in the lists at Barham Broom —"

"So now, my lady Winfrida, shall it bear thee and thy love to Mortain and happiness — O loved Mortain! So mount, Jocelyn, mount! Haste to thy happiness, man, and in thy joy, forget not Pentavalon, for her need is great. And thou hast goodly men-at-arms! How think ye, messire?"

"Beltane," cried Sir Jocelyn gleefully, "Beltane, O dear my friend, doubt me not — I do tell thee we shall ride together yet, when the battle joins!" So saying, he sprang to saddle. Now turned Beltane to aid the lady Winfrida to Sir Jocelyn's hold; but, even then, she fell upon her knees, and catching his hand to her bosom, kissed it.

"Lord Beltane," said she, looking up 'neath glistening lashes —" as thou hast dealt with me, so may heaven deal with thee. May thy sore heart find solace until love find thee — and — dear my lord, I pray you where is — he — the young knight that rode with thee — for where he is, there also is — Helen —"

"And thou dost know, too?"

"I knew her that day in the forest when I fled away, for though I would have confessed my sin to thee, yet her cold scorn I could not have borne. Where is she now, my lord?"

"Safe within Mortain, I pray."

"Then come you to Mortain. Come with us this night — ah! come you to Mortain and — Helen!"

Now hereupon Beltane turned to look with yearning eyes towards the gloom of the forest beyond which lay the soft and peaceful valleys of fair Mortain, and she that called herself Fidelis, who had indeed been so faithful in all things, so patient and enduring; and, as his eyes yearned, so yearned the great passionate soul of him, insomuch that he must needs fall a-trembling, whereat Roger the watchful drew a soft pace nearer. So stood Beltane awhile, hands clenched, head bent, staring ever northwards, his blood aglow with eager love, his heart a-throb with passionate remorse.

"Come, my lord," breathed Winfrida, "O come — in Mortain is rest and solace — and love!"

"Rest?" said Beltane softly, "solace and love — O sweet thought! Yet I may not go hence, for here is sorrow and shame and suffering — sword and fire and battle. So must I bide here in Pentavalon — with my duty." So saying, he lifted Winfrida to Sir Jocelyn's ready clasp and thereafter spake with head downbent: "An thou chance to see — her — within Mortain, I pray you say that the blind doth see at last and is gone to his duty, that, peradventure, he may be, some day, more worthy her great love. And now fare ye well, good friends, God have ye ever in His tender care. Come, Roger!"

Then Beltane turned him suddenly away, and with broad back set towards Mortain, strode off across the desolate moor.

CHAPTER L

TELLETH HOW BELTANE WENT FORTH TO HIS DUTY

SILENT went Beltane, his lips firm-set, his wistful eyes staring ever before him, nor paused he once, nor once glanced back towards that happy Mortain which held for him all that was fair and sweet and noble; that pure and faithful heart wherein no evil could exist; that radiant body in whose soft, white loveliness lay all the joy, all the happiness the wide world might ever yield him.

And now, because of her proved innocence, he was uplifted by a great and mighty joy, and therewith his step was light and swift; anon, because of his base doubt of her, he writhed 'neath the sharp-gnawing tooth of bitter remorse, and therewith his step grew heavy and slow. Now was he proud of her so great love for him, and again, he knew a profound and deep humility because of his so great unworthiness. Thus went he, nothing speaking, now with flying feet, now with steps that dragged, insomuch that watchful Roger fell to solemn wonderment, to a furtive unease, and so, at last, to speech.

"Lord," quoth he in a voice of awe, but Beltane strode on unheeding, whereat Roger's eyes grew round and his ruddy cheek pale, and clenching his fist, he raised aloft his first and little fingers so that they formed two horns, and with the horns he touched Beltane lightly on the shoulder. "Master!" said he.

Then Beltane started, and turning, looked at Roger, whereupon Roger immediately crossed his fingers.

"Ha, Roger, I was deep in my thoughts, what would ye?"

"Master, hast ever a pricking in the hairs of thy head?"

"Not I."

"Dost ever feel a tingling in the soles of thy feet?"

"Not so, in truth."

"Why then a shivering, quaking o' the back-bone?"

"Roger, man, what troubles thee now?"

"I do fear thou'rt be-devilled and moon-struck, master!"

"Why so?"

"Betimes thou dost smile upon the moon — for no reason; scowl upon the earth — for no reason; work with thy lips yet speak no word, and therewith do bite thy fingers-ends, clench thy fists — and all for no reason. Moreover, thou'rt quick and slow in thy gait, sighing gustily off and on — so it is I do sweat for thee."

"And wherefore?"

"Master," quoth Roger, glancing furtively about, "in my youth I did see a goodly man be-devilled by horrid spells by an ancient hag that was a noted witch, and he acted thus — a poor wight that was thereafter damnably be-devilled into a small, black rabbit, see you —"

"Saw you all this indeed, Roger?"

"All but the be-devilling, master, for being young and sore frighted I ran away and hid myself. But afterwards saw I the old woman with the black rabbit in a cage — wherefore the vile hag was stoned to death, and the black rabbit, that was her familiar, also — and very properly. And, lord, because I do love thee, rather would I see thee dead than a rabbit or a toad or lewd cur — wherefore now I pray thee cross thy fingers and repeat after me —"

"Nay, my faithful Roger, never fear, here is no witchcraft. 'Tis but that within the hour the blind doth see, the fool hath got him some little wisdom."

"Master, how mean you?"

"This night, Roger, I have learned this great truth: that white can never be black, nor day night, nor truth lie — and here is great matter for thought, wherefore as I walk, I think."

Beltane Goes Forth to His Duty

Now hereupon Black Roger halted and looked upon Beltane glad-eyed.

"Lord," he cried, "is it that ye do know the very truth at last — of Sir Fidelis — that glorious lady, thy Duchess Helen?"

"Aye, the very truth at last, Roger."

"Ha! — 'tis so I petitioned the good Saint Cuthbert this very night!"

"And lo! he hath answered thy prayer, Roger."

"Verily he regardeth poor Roger these days, master, e'en though my belt doth yet bear many accursed notches."

"They shall be fewer anon, Roger; there be many poor souls for thee to save in woeful Pentavalon."

Hereafter went they a while in silence, until of a sudden Roger halted and clapped hand to thigh.

"Master, we go the wrong way, methinks."

"Not so, we be close upon the forest road, Roger."

"But thou dost know her faithful, master, pure and holy in mind and body — at sure of this at last!"

"Aye," sighed Beltane, "at last!"

"Why then, lord, let us incontinent seek her out."

"She is in for Mortain, Roger, moreover —"

"Nay, master, forsooth she is — hum! aye, she's in Mortain, mayhap, but 'tis none so far to Mortain for such legs as thine and mine. And belike we may — chance upon her by the way, or — or she with us, or both!"

"Even so, needs must I to my duty."

"Thy duty! — aye, master — thy duty is to woo her, wed her, take her to thy arms and —"

"I tell thee, Roger, ne'er will I speak word of love to her until I have proved myself in some sense fit and worthy. First will I free Pentavalon as I did swear —"

"Nay, master, wed first thy Duchess, so shall she aid thee in thy vows, and thereafter —"

"Enough!" cried Beltane, "think ye 'tis so easy to thus gainsay the love that burns me? But shame were it that I, beggared in fortune, my friends few, should wed her in my dire need, dragging thereby peaceful Mortain to mine, aid and the bloody arbitrament of battle. Moreover, hast forgot the oath I sware — that nought henceforth should let or stay me?"

"Master," sighed Roger, "there be times, methinks, thou dost swear over-many oaths. Art man and woman full of youth and love, wherefore not marry? Wherefore heed a vow here or there? Needs must I wrestle with the good Saint Cuthbert in the matter."

But here Beltane fell again to meditation and Roger likewise. So came they presently to the forest-road, and turning north towards Winisfarne they strode on, side by side, in silence profound and deep. And of a sudden upon this silence, rose a voice high-pitched and quavering:

"O ye that have eyes, have pity — show mercy on one that is maimed and helpless, and creepeth ever in the dark."

CHAPTER LI

HOW BLACK ROGER WON TO FULLER MANHOOD

FORTHWITH Beltane paused, and presently beheld one that sat by the wayside — a man who crouched 'neath a dusty cloak and kept his white head down-bent and who now reached out a hand to grope and grope for the staff that lay near; wherefore Beltane took hold upon this hand and raised the white-haired traveller, and thereafter put the cudgel in his grasp.

"Messire," said the blind man, "though I have no eyes I do know thee young, for thy clasp is strong and quick with life, yet wondrous gentle. God bless thee, youthful sir, for 'tis well to meet with gentleness within a world so cruel. Tell me, I pray, doth this road lead unto Belsaye town?"

"Verily," answered Beltane, "but 'tis a long day's march thither."

"Yet needs must I reach there, since I do bear a message. But, O young messire, when cruel men put out mine eyes, the good God, in His sweet clemency, made sharp mine ears. So do I know thy voice, methinks, for voice of one who, long months since, did cherish me in my need and hunger, and sent me unto the saintly Ambrose."

"Ha!" cried Beltane joyously, "and is it thou indeed? Tell me, how doth my father? — is he well? — what said he? — how looked he? O, I do yearn for word of him!"

"Thy father? How, young sir, is he indeed thy father? Then is thy name Beltane, for I have heard him name thee oft —"

"Forsooth, and did he so? But how came you here, and wherefore?"

"To seek thee, lord Beltane, according to thy saintly

father's word. And the manner of it, thus: As we sat together of a certain fair noon within Holy Cross Thicket, there came to us thither a woman, young, methinks, and fair, for her speech was soft and wondrous sweet in mine ears. And she did hail thy father 'Duke,' and thereafter spake thy name full oft, and so they fell to many words, walking together up and down before the hut. Anon, sudden and silent as she came, she was gone, and thy father walked full long, praying oft as one that rejoiceth greatly, and oft as one in deep perplexity. In a while cometh he to me and gave me scrip and therewith food and money, and bade me seek thee in Belsaye and speak thee thus: 'Tell Beltane, my well-beloved, that I, his father, have heard of his great and knightly deeds and that I do glory in them, praising God. Say that through him my youth and strength are renewed and my great sin made easier to bear. Tell him that the woes of Pentavalon draw to an end, and that ere long she shall arise above her sorrows. Bid him be of good courage yet a little longer, for the lion is waked at last, and the leopard also.' Behold now, messire, all's said." And the blind man stood with down-bent head, one hand grasping the staff, his other arm hid within his wide sleeve, what time Roger watched him furtive and askance, and moreover, his bow-stave shook and quivered in his grasp; as for Beltane, he stood as one lost in happy thought, upon his lips a smile ineffably tender. Smiling yet, he turned and touched the blind man's stooping shoulder. Quoth he:

"Greatly welcome is thy news and greatly would I thank thee. Pray you now, how may I show my gratitude?"

"Messire, fain would I shelter me in Belsaye, for there is fire and sword and battle on the marches. But the way is long, and on my road hither two rogues took from me purse and scrip. Give me, therefore, enough to bear me on my way."

"Aye, verily! Roger, thou dost bear the purse. Give him store of money and some of our food — see that he lacketh for nothing, Roger." So saying, Beltane turned him away and fell again to pondering his father's words.

Now at sound of Roger's name the blind man started round and fixed Roger with the horror of his eyeless sockets, and, therewith, flung up an arm as though fearing a blow; and behold! this arm was but a mutilated stump, for hand was there none.

"Roger!" he whispered, "not Roger the Black? No, no! There be a many Rogers. But who art thou dost bear such a name, and wherefore cower and gasp ye?"

Then stood the blind man with head out-thrust and awful arm upraised, before which Black Roger shrank and shrank to cower in the deeper shadow.

Of a sudden the blind man turned and coming beside Beltane, grasped him by the mantle.

"Lord," he questioned, "who is he that trembleth before the maimed and blind? — who is he that croucheth yonder?"

"Nay, fear ye nothing," said Beltane, "'tis none but my trusty Roger, my good comrade in arms — comfort ye!" Then he beckoned Roger and took the purse and gave to the blind man bounteously, saying:

"See now, when you shall come to Belsaye go you to Eric that hath command of the town and to Giles that is captain of the archers, and say that I, Beltane, will come to Belsaye within the week, and all our company with me, God willing. Bid them be vigilant and watch for our coming; let bows be strung and wall and turret manned night and day. So now fare thee well, and God's hand guide thy sightless going."

Then the blind man blessed Beltane, and turning, forthwith set out upon his way, and his staff tapped loud upon the forest-road. Right joyfully Beltane strode on again, his mind ever busied with thought of his father; but Roger's step was listless and heavy, so that Beltane must needs turn to look on him, and straightway marvelled to see how he hung his head, and that his ruddy cheek was grown wondrous pale and haggard.

"Roger?" quoth he, "art sick, Roger?"

"Sick, lord? nay — not sick, 'tis but that I — I —" But when he would have said more his voice failed him, his lip fell a-quivering, and even as Beltane stared in wonder, Black Roger groaned and flung himself upon his knees, and hid his face within his hands.

"Why Roger! What ails thee, Roger, man?" said Beltane and laid a hand upon his shoulder, whereat Roger groaned again and shrank away.

"Ah, lord, touch me not!" he cried, "unfit am I for hand of thine, unfit and all unworthy —"

"Nay, good friend —"

"Master — master!" groaned Roger, and therewith a great cry brake from him and he cast himself face downwards in the dust. "Unworthy am I to be thy man, so must I leave thee this night — aye, leave thee! For O my lord! yon poor blind man —'twas I — at the Red Pertolepe's command —'twas I — did burn out his eyes and — cut off his hand —'twas I — I — Black Roger! O Saint Cuthbert! O sweet Jesu! So all unworthy am I to be thy man!"

And now great sobs shook him, fierce sobs and bitter, and he writhed there in the dust, groaning in the agony of his remorse. Little by little his passion spent itself, but still he lay there, yearning mightily for sound of his master's voice or touch of his hand, yet dared he not look up because of his abasement.

At last, whenas his sobs had ceased, he lifted his wretched head and stared in wide-eyed wonder to see Beltane upon his knees, his mailed hands clasped and his lips moving in silent prayer; when, his prayer ended, he raised his head and straightway Roger's wonder grew, for behold! the eyes of Beltane were wondrous gentle, his mouth sweet-curved and tender, the old harsh lines of grim-curled lip and lowering brow had vanished quite; and thus at last Black Roger saw again the face of my Beltane that had smiled on him long since amid the green across the prostrate form of poor Beda the

Jester. So now, my Beltane smiled, and smiling, reached forth his hand.

"Roger," said he, "by shame and agony some men do win to new life and fuller manhood, and such a man, methinks, thou art. So hath God need of thee, and from this the dust of thy abasement, mayhap, shall lift thee, one day, high as heaven. Stand up, Roger, good my friend, stand up, O man, for he only is unworthy that ne'er hath wept remorseful in the dust for evil past and done."

Then Roger grasped that strong, uplifting hand, and stood upon his feet, yet spake he no word; and presently they went on along the road together.

And Roger's habit was stained with dust, and on his cheek the mark of bitter tears — but his head was high and manfully uplifted.

CHAPTER LII

HOW THEY HAD NEWS OF WALKYN

Now went they in silence again for that Beltane dreamed of many things while Roger marvelled within himself, oft turning to look on my Beltane's radiant face, while ever his wonder grew; so oft did he turn thus to gape and stare that Beltane, chancing to meet his look, smiled and questioned him, thus:

"Why gape ye on me so, Roger man?"

"For wonder, master."

"Wherefore?"

"To see thee so suddenly thyself again — truly Saint Cuthbert is a potent saint!"

"And thou a sturdy pray-er, good Roger."

"And most vile sinner, lord. Howbeit I have dared supplicate on thy behalf and behold! thou art indeed thyself again — that same sweet and gentle youth that smote me on my knavish mazzard with thy stout quarter-staff in Shevening Thicket in the matter of Beda, Red Pertolepe's fool — a dour ding, yon, master — forsooth, a woundy rap!"

Now fell they to thoughtful silence again, but oft Black Roger's stride waxed uneven, and oft he stumbled in his going, wherefore Beltane slackened his pace.

"What is it, Roger?"

"Naught but my legs, master. Heed 'em not."

"Thy legs?"

"They be shorter than thine, lord, and love not to wag so fast. An thou could'st abate thy speed a little — a very little, master, they shall thank thee dearly."

"Art so weary, Roger?"

"Master, I was afoot ere sunrise."

"Why truly, Roger. Yet do I, to mine own selfish ends, keep thee from thy slumber thus. Verily a selfish man, I!"

"Not so, master, indeed —"

"So now will we halt, and thou shalt to thy rest."

"Why then, lord, let us to the Hollow — it lieth scarce a mile through the brush yonder, and 'twas there I did appoint for Walkyn to meet with thee again — so shall we sleep secure; moreover I have a feeling — as it were one calling us thither, a wondrous strange feeling, master! Mayhap we shall come by news of Walkyn there —"

"'Tis well bethought, Roger. Come thy ways."

Forthwith turned they from the forest-road, and forcing their way through a leafy tangle, presently came out into a ride, or narrow glade; but they had gone only a very little distance when they espied the red glow of a fire within a thicket hard by, and therewith the sound of voices reached them:

"Three great bags, I tell thee!" cried one voice, high and querulous, "three great, fair and goodly bags full crammed of sweet gold pieces! All my lord Duke's revenue of Winisfarne and the villages adjacent thereunto! Taxes, see ye, my lord Duke's taxes — and all stolen, reft, and ravished from me, Guido, Steward and Bailiff of the northern Marches, by clapper-claws and raveners lewd and damned! Woe's me for my lord's good money-bags!"

"O, content thee!" spake another voice, sleepy and full-fed, "for, an these monies were the Duke's they were not thine, and if they were not thine thou wert not robbed, and, since thou wert not robbed, wherefore groan and glower ye on the moon? Moreover, thou hast yet certain monies thou didst — collect — from yon blind fellow, the which remindeth me I have not yet my share. So pray thee now disburse, good steward."

Hereupon, ere Beltane could stay him, Roger slipped, soft-treading, into the undergrowth; upon whose vanishing the air grew very suddenly full of shouts and cries, of scuffling sounds and woeful pleadings; and striding forward, Beltane beheld two men that crouched on bended knees, while Roger, fierce and threatening, stood betwixt, a hairy hand upon the throat of each. Now beholding Beltane, they (these gasping rogues) incontinent beset him with whimpering entreaties, beseeching of him their lives. Ragged knaves they seemed, and in woeful plight — the one a lank fellow and saturnine, with long, down-trending, hungry nose; the other a little man, plump and buxom, whose round eyes blinked woefully in his round and rosy face as he bent 'neath Roger's heavy hand. Yet spake he to Beltane in soft and soothing accents, on this wise:

"Resplendent sir, behold this thy most officious wight who doth my tender throat with hurtful hand encompass — doubtless to some wise and gracious end an he doth squeeze me thus at thy command. Yet, noble sir, humbly would I woo of thee the mercy of a little more air, lest this right noble youth do choke me quite!"

But hereupon the lank fellow cried out, bold and querulous:

"Take ye heed, for whoso dareth lay hand on me, toucheth the person of Duke Ivo's puissant self!"

"Ha — say ye so?" growled Roger, and forthwith squeezed him until he gasped again.

"Loose me, knave!" he panted, "Duke Ivo's Steward, I — Bailiff of the northern Marches with — towns and villages — adjacent thereunto —"

"Unhand them, Roger," said Beltane, "entreat them gently — in especial my lord Duke's Steward and Bailiff of the Marches, if so he be in very truth."

"Yea my lord, in very truth!" cried the Bailiff. "But two days since in ermined robe and chain of office, a notable man, I, courted by many, feared by more, right well be-seen by all, with goodly horse betwixt my knees and lusty men-at-arms at my beck and call. To-night, alas and woe! thou see'st me a ragged loon, a sorry wight the meanest rogue would scorn to bow to, and the very children jeer at — and all by reason of a lewd, black-avised clapper-claw that doth flourish him a mighty axe — O, a vile, seditious fellow ripe for the gallows."

"Ah! with an axe say'st thou, sir Bailiff?"

"O most infallibly an axe, messire — a ponderous axe with haft the length of this my leg. A vilely tall, base, and most unseemly dog that hath spoiled me of my lord's sweet money-bags, wherefore I yearn to see him wriggle in a noose. To the which end I journey in these my rags, unto my lord Duke on Barham Broom, with tale of wrong and outrage most abominable."

"And dared they rob thee indeed?" quoth Beltane, "and thou my lord Duke's High Steward and Bailiff of the Marches! Come, sit ye down and tell me of the matter — and Roger, methinks he shall talk the better an thou keep thy fingers farther from his wind-pipe."

So down sat they together round the fire, and, what time the little buxom man viewed Beltane 'twixt stealthy lids from golden spur to open bascinet, the Bailiff fell to his tale, as followeth:

"Know then, good and noble sir knight, that I sat me, but two days since, in right fair and goodly estate, my lackeys to hand, my men-at-arms at my back (twenty tall fellows). I sat me thus, I say, within the square at Winisfarne, whither, by sound of trumpet, I had summoned me the knavish townsfolk to pay into my hand my lord Duke's rightful dues and taxes, which folk it is my custom to call upon by name and one by one. When lo! of a sudden, and all uncalled, comes me a great, tall fellow, this same black-avised knave, and forthwith seized him one of my lord's great money-bags, and when I would have denied him, set me his axe beneath my very nose. Thereafter took he the bags all three and scattered (O hateful — hateful sight!) my lord's good monies among the base rabblement. And, when my lusty fellows sought to apprehend me this rogue, he smote them dolefully and roared in hideous fashion 'Arise — Pentavalon!' And straightway, at this lewd shout, forth of the crowd leapt many other rogues bedight as gentle knights in noble mail, cap-à-pie, and fell upon us and smote us dire, and stripped me of my goodly apparel, and drave me forth of the town with stripes and blows and laughter most ungentle. So here sit I, poor Guido, Steward and Bailiff of the Marches, in most vile estate, very full of woe yet, alack, empty of belly."

"But," says Beltane, shaking his head, "within thy pouch, methinks, a blind man's money."

"How — a blind man?" gasped the Bailiff, "a blind man's monies, say'st thou? Nay messire, in very truth."

"Search him, Roger."

Hereupon Roger, having straightway choked him to silence with the one hand full soon had found the money with the other, and thereafter, he loosed the Bailiff that he might get his breath again; the which he no sooner had done than he fell to prayers and humble entreaties:

"Sir knight — right noble sir, sure thou wilt not take thus from a woeful wight all that he hath."

"Nay," answered Beltane, "I take only from my lord Duke's Steward and Bailiff of the Marches. And now," said he, turning upon the small, round man, "thou hast marked me well, how say you, Pardoner?"

"First, most truly potent, wise, yet very youthful, noble sir, that for all the world and all the glory thereof I would not anger thee."

"Hast good eyes, Pardoner, and art quick to heed."

"Nay, dull am I, sweet lord, aye, dull forsooth and slow beyond belief."

"Would'st know me again? could'st bear my likeness in thy memory?"

"Never, lord. Never, O never! I swear it by the toe of the blessed Didymus, by the arm of Saint Amphibalus thrice blessed, by —"

"Why then, Pardoner, behold here my belt of silver, my good, long-bladed sword. And here — behold my yellow hair!" and off came bascinet, and back fell mail-coif, whereat the Bailiff started and caught his breath and stared on Beltane in sudden awe.

How They Had News of Walkyn 391

"Dost mark me well, Pardoner?"

"Aye, noble sir, verily and in truth do I. So, next time I think on thee thou wilt be a squat man, middle-aged and black-haired. For, my lord, a poor Pardoner I, but nought beside."

Then Beltane did on coif and bascinet and rose to his feet, whereat the Bailiff cried out in sudden fear and knelt with hands upraised:

"Slay me not, my lord! O messire Beltane, spare my life nor think I will betray thee, outlaw though thou art!"

"Fear not, sir Bailiff," answered Beltane, "thy life is safe from me. But, when thou dost name me to thy lord, Duke Ivo, tell him that I spake thee this: That, whiles I do lie within the green he shall not sleep o' nights but I will be at work with fire and steel, nor rest nor stay until he and the evil of him be purged from this my father's duchy of Pentavalon — say I bid him remember this upon his pillow. Tell him that whiles I do hold the woods my powers grow daily, and so will I storm and burn his castles, one by one, as I did burn Garthlaxton. Say I bid him to think upon these things what time he wooeth slumber in the night. As to thee, thou wily Pardoner, when thou shalt come to betray this our meeting, say that I told thee, that as Belsaye rose, and Winisfarne, so shall town and village rise until Ivo and his like are driven hence, or Beltane slain and made an end of. And so — fare ye well! Come, Roger!" Then Beltane strode away with grim Roger at his heels what time the Bailiff and the Pardoner stared in dumb amaze.

"Here," quoth the Pardoner at last, stroking his round chin, "here was a man, methinks, wherefore are we yet alive!"

"Here," quoth the Bailiff, scratching his long nose, "here was a fool, methinks, for that we are alive. A traitor, see ye, Pardoner, whose yellow head is worth its weight in gold! Truly, truly, here was a very fool!" So saying, he arose, albeit furtively, and slipping forthwith into the shadow, crept furtively away until the fire-glow was lost and hidden far behind him. Then, very suddenly, he betook him to his heels, and coming to the forest-road, fled southwards towards Duke Ivo's great camp that lay on Barham Broom.

CHAPTER LIII

OF JOLETTE, THAT WAS A WITCH

"LORD," said Roger, shaking his head, as they halted upon the edge of the Hollow, "lord, 'twere better thou hadst let me strangle them; those dogs will bay of thee to Black Ivo ere this time to-morrow!"

" 'Tis so I hope, Roger."

"Hope?"

"Could I but lure Black Ivo into the wild, Roger, where swamp and thicket should fight for us! Could I but draw him hither after me, of what avail the might of his heavy chivalry upon this narrow forest-road, his close-ranked foot-men a sure mark for the arrows of our war-wise foresters? Thus, our pikes in front, a charge in flank, his line once pierced needs must follow confusion and disorder. Then press we where his banner flieth, and, hemmed in by our pikes and gisarms and Giles's bowmen, he once our prisoner or slain, his great army would crumble and melt away, since they do serve but for base hire, whiles we, though few, do smite amain for home and children. O Roger man, could I but lure him into the green!"

"Yet methinks there is a surer way, master."

"How — as how, Roger?"

"Wed thou thy Duchess, and so bring down on him all the powers of Mortain!"

"Roger, dost well know my mind on this matter; prate ye no more!"

"Then will I pray, master — so I do warn thee! Forsooth, I will this night fall to work upon the good saint and plague him right prayerfully that thy Duchess may come and save thee and thy Duchy in despite of thee, and having made thee Duke of Pentavalon with her lances, thereafter make thee Duke of Mortain in her own sweet body, for as I do know —"

But Beltane was already descending the steep path leading down into the great green hollow that lay all silent and deserted 'neath the ghostly moon, where nought stirred in the windless air, where bush and tree cast shadows monstrous and distorted, and where no sound brake the brooding quiet save the murmurous ripple of the brook that flowed to lose itself in the gloomy waters of that deep and sullen pool.

Swift and sure-treading as only foresters might, they descended the steep, and lured by some elfin fancy, Beltane must needs come to stand beside the pool and to stare down into those silent waters, very dark by reason of that great tree 'neath whose writhen branches Tostig the outlaw had fought and died; so stood Beltane awhile lost in contemplation, what time Roger, drawing ever nearer his master's elbow, shivered and crossed himself full oft.

"Come away, master," said he at last, low-voiced, "I love not this pool at any time, more especially at the full o' the moon. On such nights ghosts do walk! Tostig was an ill man in life, but Tostig's ghost should be a thing to fright the boldest — prithee, come away."

"Go get thee to thy rest, Roger. As for me, I would fain think."

"But wherefore here?"

"For that I am so minded."

"So be it, master. God send thy thoughts be fair." So saying, Roger turned where, on the further side of the Hollow, lay those caves 'neath the rocky bank wherein the outlaws had been wont to sleep. But, of a sudden, Beltane heard a hoarse scream, a gasp of terror, and Roger was back beside him, his naked broad-sword all a-shake in his trembling hand, his eyes wide and rolling.

"Master — O master!" he whimpered, "ghosts! 'neath the tree — Tostig — the Dead Hand!"

"Nay, what folly is here, Roger?"

"Lord, 'twas the Dead Hand — touched me — on the

brow — in the shadow yonder! Aye — on the brow — 'neath the tree! O master, dead men are we, 'tis Tostig come to drag us back to hell with him!" And crouching on his knees, Roger fell to desperate prayers.

Then Beltane turned whither Roger's shaking finger had pointed, and strode beneath the great tree. And peering up through the dark, he presently espied a shadowy thing that moved amid a gloom of leaves and branches; and, beholding what it was, he drew sword and smote high above his head.

Something thudded heavily upon the grass and lay there, mute and rigid, while Beltane, leaning upon his sword, stared down at that fell shape, and breathing the noxious reek of it, was seized of trembling horror; nevertheless he stooped, and reaching out a hand of loathing in the dimness, found the cord whereby it had swung and dragged the rigid, weighty thing out into the radiance of the moon until he could see a pallid face twisted and distorted by sharp and cruel death. Now in this moment Roger sware a fierce, great oath, and forthwith kicked those stiffened limbs.

"Ha!" cried he, "methought 'twas Tostig his ghost come for to drag us down into yon accursed pool — and 'tis naught but the traitor-rogue Gurth!"

"And dead, Roger!"

"Forsooth, he's dead enough, master — faugh!"

"And it availeth nothing to kick a dead man, Roger."

"Yet was he an arrant knave, master."

"And hath paid for his knavery, methinks!"

"A very rogue! a traitor! a rogue of rogues, master!"

"Then hath he the more need of our prayers, Roger."

"Prayers! How, lord, would'st pray for — this?"

"Nay, Roger, but thou shalt, since thou art potent in prayer these days." So saying, Beltane knelt upon the sward and folded reverent hands; whereupon Roger, somewhat abashed, having set his sword upright in the ling as was his custom, presently knelt likewise, and clearing his throat, spake aloud in this fashion:

"Holy Saint Cuthbert, thou see'st here all that is left of one that in life was a filthy, lewd, and traitorous knave, insomuch that he hath, methinks, died of roguery. Now, most blessed saint, do thy best for the knavish soul of him, intercede on his behalf that he may suffer no more than he should. And this is the prayer of me, Black Roger, that has been a vile sinner as I have told thee, though traitor to no man, I praise God. But, most blessed and right potent saint, while I am at the ears of thee, fain would I crave thy aid on matter of vasty weight and import. To wit, good saint: let now Sir Fidelis, who, as ye well know, doth hide womanly beauties in ungentle steel — let now this brave and noble lady muster forthwith all the powers within her Duchy of Mortain — every lusty fellow, good saint — and hither march them to my master's aid. Let her smite and utterly confound Black Ivo, who (as oft I've told thee — moreover thine eyes are sharp), is but a rogue high-born, fitter for gallows than ducal crown, even as this most unsavoury Gurth was a rogue low-born. So when she hath saved my master despite himself, sweet saint, then do thou join them heart and body, give them joy abounding and happiness enduring, nor forget them in the matter of comely children. So bring to woeful Pentavalon and to us all and every, peace at last and prosperity — and to sorrowful Roger a belt wherein be no accursed notches and a soul made clean. *In nomen Dominum, Amen!*"

"Master," quoth he, yet upon his knees and viewing Beltane somewhat askance, "here is the best I can do for such as yon Gurth; will't suffice, think ye?"

"Aye, 'twill serve, Roger. But, for the other matter —"

"Why see you, master, a man may freely speak his dear desires within his prayers — more especially when his prayers are potent, as mine. Moreover I warned thee — I warned thee I would pray for thee — and pray for thee I have." Now hereupon Beltane rose somewhat hastily and turned his back, what time Roger sheathed his sword.

Of Jolette, That Was a Witch

Then spake Beltane, turning him to the pool again:

"We had store of tools and mattocks, I mind me. Go and look within the caves if there be ever a one left, for now must we bury this poor clay."

"Ha, must we pray for him — *and* bury him, master?"

"And bury him, Roger."

Then Roger sighed and shook his head and so left Beltane, who fell again to profound meditation; but of a sudden hearing a cry, he turned to behold Roger running very fleetly, who, coming near, caught him by the arm and sought to drag him away.

"Run!" he panted, "run, master — I ha' just seen a goblin — run, master!"

Now beholding the terror in Roger's eyes, Beltane unsheathed his sword. "Show me, Roger," said he.

"Nay, lord — of what avail? Let's away, this place is rank o' deviltries and witchcraft —"

"Show me, Roger — come!"

Perforce, Roger led the way, very heedful to avoid each patch of shadow, until they were come opposite that cave where aforetime Beltane had been customed to sleep. Here Roger paused.

"Master," he whispered, "there is a thing within that groaneth — goblin-groans, master. A thing very like unto a goblin, for I ha' seen it — a pale thing that creepeth — holy saints, 'tis here again — hark to it!"

And in very truth Beltane heard a sound the which, soft though it was, checked his breath and chilled his flesh; and, as he peered into the gloomy recesses of the cavern, there moved something vague amid the shadows, something that rose up slow and painfully.

Roger was down gasping on his knees, Beltane's hand was tight-clenched upon the hilt of his sword, as out into the moonlight crept one, very bent and feeble, shrouded in a long grey cloak; a pitiful figure, that, leaning a hand upon the rock, slowly raised a drooping head. Then Beltane saw that this was the witch Jolette.

A while she stood thus, one hand supporting her against

the rocky bank, the other hid within the folds of her long mantle.

"O my lord!" said she, low-voiced, "all day long my heart hath been calling — calling to thee; so art come at last — thanks be to God — O my lord Beltane!"

Now as she spake, she reached out a hand to him so that the shrouding mantle fell away; then, beholding what it had hid, Beltane let fall his sword, and leaping forward, caught her within his arm.

"Ah! — thou'rt hurt!" he cried.

"My lord, I — strove to bind it up — I am cunning in herbs and simples — but my hurt is too deep for any leech-craft. To-night — soon — I must die. Lay me down, I pray thee. Thine arms are strong, lord Beltane, and — very gentle. How, dost grieve for a witch, lord — for poor Jolette? Nay, comfort ye — my life has been none so sweet I should dread to lose it."

"How cometh this?" he questioned gently, on his knees beside her.

"'Twas the Red Pertolepe's men — nay, messire, they have but killed me. But O, my dear lord — heed me well. A week agone lord Pertolepe marched hither seeking thee with a great company led by yon Gurth. And when he found thee not he hanged Gurth, yet tarried here awhile. Then I, knowing a secret path hither that none else do know, came and hearkened to their councils. So do I know that he is marched for Winisfarne —"

"Ha, is this so!" cried Beltane, clenching his fist, "then will he hang and burn!"

"Aye, 'tis like enough, messire. But — O heed me! He goeth for a deeper purpose — list, Beltane — O list — he goeth to seize upon the noble and saintly Abbess Veronica — to bear her captive unto Pentavalon city, there to hold her hostage for — for thee, Beltane — for thee!"

"How mean you?"

"When he hath her safe, Duke Ivo, because he hath learned to fear thee at last, will send envoys to thee demanding thou shalt yield up to him the town of Belsaye

Of Jolette, That Was a Witch 399

and thy body to his mercy, or this fair and noble lady Abbess shall be shamed and dishonoured, and know a death most dire. And — ah! because thou art the man thou art, thou must needs yield thyself to Ivo's cruel hands, and Belsaye to flame and ravishment."

"Not so," answered Beltane, frowning, "within Belsaye are many women and children also, nor should these die that one might live, saintly abbess though she be."

Now hereupon the witch Jolette raised herself, and set her two hands passionately on Beltane's shoulders, and looked upon him great-eyed and fearful.

"Ah, Beltane — Beltane, my lord!" she panted, "but that I am under a vow, now could I tell thee a thing would fire thy soul to madness — but, O believe, believe, and know ye this — when Duke Ivo's embassy shall tell thee all, thou — shalt suffer them to take thee — thou shalt endure bonds and shame and death itself. So now thou shalt swear to a dying woman that thou wilt not rest nor stay until thou shalt free this lady Abbess, for on her safety doth hang thy life and the freedom of Pentavalon. Swear, O swear me this, my lord Beltane, so shall I die in peace. Swear — O swear!"

Now, looking within her glowing eyes, feeling the tremble of her passionate-pleading hands, Beltane bowed his head.

"I swear!" said he.

"So now may God hear — this thy oath, and I — die in peace —"

And saying this, Jolette sank in his arms and lay a while as one that swoons; but presently her heavy eyes unclosed and on her lips there dawned a smile right wondrous to behold, so marvellous tender was it.

"I pray thee, lord, unhelm — that I may see thee — once again — thy golden hair —"

Wondering, but nothing speaking, Beltane laid by his bascinet, threw back his mail-coif, and bent above her low and lower, until she might reach up and touch those golden curls with failing hand.

"Lord Beltane! — boy!" she whispered, "stoop lower,

mine eyes fail. Hearken, O my heart! Even as thy strong arms do cradle me, so — have these arms — held thee, O little Beltane, I — have borne thee oft upon my heart — ere now. Oft have hushed thee to rosy sleep — upon this bosom. 'Twas from — these arms Sir Benedict caught thee on — that woeful day. For I that die here — against thy heart, Beltane — am Jolette, thy foster-mother — wilt thou — kiss me — once?"

So Beltane stooped and kissed her, and, when he laid her down, Jolette the witch was dead.

Full long Beltane knelt, absorbed in prayer, and as he prayed, he wept. So long knelt he thus, that at last cometh Roger, treading soft and reverently, and touched him.

"Master!" he whispered,

Then Beltane arose as one that dreams and stood a while looking down upon that pale and placid face, on whose silent lips the wondrous smile still lingered. But of a sudden, Roger's fingers grasped his arm.

"Master!" he whispered again. Thereon Beltane turned and thus he saw that Roger looked neither on him nor on the dead and that he pointed with shaking finger. Now, glancing whither he pointed, Beltane beheld, high on the bank above them, a mounted knight armed cap-à-pie, who stared down at them through closed visor — a fierce and war-like figure looming gigantic athwart the splendour of the sinking moon. And even as they stared in wonder, a broad shield flashed, and knight and horse were gone.

CHAPTER LIV

HOW BELTANE FOUGHT WITH A DOUGHTY STRANGER

"Lord!" quoth Roger, wiping sweat from him, "yonder certes was Hob-gob! Forsooth ne'er saw I night the like o' this! How think ye of yon devilish things? Here was it one moment, and lo! in the twinkle of an eye it is not. How think ye, master?"

"I do think 'twas some roving knight."

"Nay but, lord — how shall honest flesh and blood go a-vanishing away into thin air whiles a man but blinketh an eye?"

"The ground hath sudden slope thereabouts, belike."

"Nay, yonder was some arch-wizard, master — the Man o' the Oak, or Hob-gob himself. Saint Cuthbert shield us, say I — yon was for sure a spirit damned —"

"Hark! Do spirits go in steel, Roger?" said Beltane, stooping for his sword; for indeed, plain and loud upon the prevailing quiet was the ring and clash of heavy armour, what time from the bushes that clothed the steep a tall figure strode, and the moon made a glory in polished shield, it gleamed upon close-vizored helm, it flashed upon brassart, vanbrace and plastron. Being come near, the grim and warlike figure halted, and leaning gauntleted hand upon long shield, stood silent a while seeming to stare on Beltane through the narrow slit of his great casque. But even as he viewed Beltane, so stared Beltane on him, on the fineness of his armour, chain and plate of the new fashion, on his breadth of shoulder and length of limb — from shining casque to gleaming shield, whereon was neither charge nor blazon; and so at last, spake my Beltane, very gentle and courteous:

"Messire, an thou be come in peace, now shalt thou be right welcome —"

"Peace!" quoth the knight loud and fierce, and his laughter rang hoarse within his helm. "Peace, forsooth! Thou art a tall and seemly youth, a youth fair spoken, and yet — ha! A belt of silver! And golden hair! And yet — so very youthful! Art thou in very truth this famous rogue whose desperate deeds do live on every tongue, who hath waked Duke Ivo from his long-time security, insomuch that he doth yearn him for that yellow head o' thine — art thou Beltane the Outlaw and Rebel?"

"'Tis so men do call me, messire."

"Verily, youth, methinks dost lie, for I have heard this outlaw is beyond all men wild and fierce and weaveth him demoniac spells and enchantments most accurst, whereby he maketh gate and door and mighty portcullis to ope and yield before his pointed finger, and bolt and bar and massy wall to give him passage when he will, as witness the great keep of Garthlaxton that he did burn with hellish fire. I have heard he doth commonly burn gibbets to warm him, and beareth off great lords beneath his arm as I might a small coney and slayeth him three or four with his every stroke. 'Tis said that he doth wax daily mightier and more fierce, since he doth drink hot blood and batteneth on flesh o' tender babes beneath the orbèd moon —"

"Messire," said Beltane beginning to frown, "within thy wild and foolish talk is this much truth, that I, with divers trusty comrades, did indeed burn down the shameful gallows of Belsaye, and bore captive a certain lordly knave. As for Garthlaxton, the thing was simple —"

"O boastful boy!" quoth the knight, tossing aside his shield, "O beardless one, since thou dost proclaim thyself this desperate rogue, here is reason just for some small debate betwixt us. Do on thy coif forthwith, for now will I strive to make an end of thee," and speaking, the knight unsheathed a long and ponderous sword.

"How an I fight thee not, sir knight?"

"Then must I needs belabour thee to the good of thy soul, sir outlaw. So on with thy coif, I say!"

Incontinent ran Roger to fetch his bascinet the which Beltane slowly fitted on above his hood of mail, and thereafter, albeit unwillingly, fronted this doughty knight, foot to foot and point to point. Now stepped they a moment about each other, light-treading for all their weighty armour, and with long blades advanced; then, of a sudden they closed, and immediately the air shivered to the ring and grind of flashing, whirling steel. To and fro, and up and down they fought upon the level sward what time Black Roger rubbed complacent hands, grim-smiling and confident; and ever as they fought the stranger knight laughed and gibed, harsh and loud, from behind his grimly casque.

"Ho! — fight, youth, fight!" cried he, "have done with love-taps! Sa-ha, have at thee — fight, I say!" A panther-like side-leap, a whirl of glimmering steel, and his long blade smote sparks from Beltane's bascinet, whereat Roger's smile, incontinent, vanished, and his face waxed suddenly anxious and long.

But fierce and fiercer the stranger knight beset my Beltane, the while he lashed him with mocking tongue:

"Call ye this fighting, sir youthful outlaw? Doth thine arm fail thee so soon? Tap not, I say, lest I grow angered and slay thee forthright!"

Then, blow for blow, did Beltane the mighty fall on right furiously, but ever blade met blade whiles Roger danced on anxious feet, praying for the end. Of a sudden, shouted he joyously, for, flashing high in air, down came Beltane's long blade strong and true upon the knight's helm — a fell, deep-dinting stroke that drave the stranger reeling back. Fierce and swift leapt Beltane to smite again — came a shock of clashing steel, a flurry of stroke and counter-stroke, and thereafter, a hoarse shout of dismay from Roger: for Beltane stood as one dazed, staring upon his empty right hand what time the knight boomed derisive laughter through his vizor. Then sprang grim Roger, dagger aloft, but swifter than he, the knight's sword swung; flat fell that long blade on Roger's bascinet, wielded by an arm so strong that Roger, staggering aside, rolled upon the ling, and thereafter, sat up, round-eyed and fearful:

"O master!" he panted, "here is none of — honest flesh and blood, 'tis — Hob-gob himself, as I did warn thee. May Saint Cuthbert, Saint Bede, Saint Edmund —"

"Go to — cease thy windy prattling, Roger Thickpate!" spake the knight, and letting fall his sword, he lifted his visor. And behold! a face lean and hawk-like, with eyes quick and bright, and a smiling mouth wry-twisted by reason of an ancient wound.

"Know ye me not, lord Beltane?" quoth he, with look right loving, "hast forgot me indeed, most loved lad?" But swift came my Beltane, glad-eyed and with arms outflung in eager welcome.

"Sir Benedict!" he cried, "hast come at last? Now do I joy to see thee!"

"My lord," says Benedict, wagging mailed finger. "Ha, Beltane, canst burn gibbets, storm mighty castles and out-face desperate odds, yet is old Benedict thy master at stroke of sword still — though, forsooth, hast dinted me my helm, methinks! O sweet lad, come to my arms, I've yearned for thee these many days." Herewith Sir Benedict caught Beltane within his close embrace, and patted him with gauntleted hands, and laughed for very gladness.

"O foolish youth — O youthful fool!" quoth he, "surely thou of all fools art greatest, a youthful, godlike fool! O mighty son of mighty father, how mighty hath thy folly been! O lovely lad that hath attempted deeds impossible, pitting thyself 'gainst Ivo and all his might! Verily, Beltane, thou'rt the loveliest fool that ever man did love —"

"Nay, but dear messire," says Beltane as Sir Benedict stayed for breath, "pray thee, where is thy meaning?"

"Sweet lad, I do but strive to tell thee thou'rt a fool, yet so glad am I of thy foolish company the words do stick somewhat, but my meaning shall be manifest — now mark me! Didst not carry off the Red Pertolepe 'neath the lances of his men-at-arms?"

"Aye, my lord."

"Didst not have thy hand on the throat of that cold, smiling rogue Sir Gui of Allerdale?"

"Verily, messire."

"And hold within thy grasp the life of that foul-living Gillés of Brandonmere, whose father I slew twelve years agone, I thank God!"

"'Tis true, good Benedict."

"And didst not suffer these arch-knaves to live on and work their pestilent wills, Beltane?"

"Sir, I did, but —"

"So art thrice a fool. When we see a foul and noxious worm, to tread it under foot is a virtuous act. So when a man doth constant sin 'gainst man and maid, to kill him —"

Quoth Beltane:

"Sir Gui and Gilles of Brandonmere have made an end of sinning, methinks."

"Why 'tis so I've heard of late, Beltane, and herein is some small comfort; but Red Pertolepe is yet to slay —"

"Truly!" cried Beltane, clenching his fists, "and he marcheth on Winisfarne, to burn and hang —"

"Content you, my lord Beltane, Waldron of Brand lieth in Winisfarne, and I am here —"

"So doth my heart rejoice for thee, Benedict, thou right trusty and doughty friend. But how came ye hither, and wherefore? Methought thee yet in Thrasfordham!"

"Aha, dear lad, so doth Ivo at this moment, I pray God. A week agone and, ere the investment was complete, wondrous news reached me from Waldron of Brand, whose sire bore my pennon in thy noble father's wars. And because I knew Waldron's word is ever less than his deed, and, belike, that I grow weary of sieges (seven have I withstood within these latter years) I, at dead of night, by devious and secret ways, stole forth of Thrasfordham — dight in this armour new-fashioned (the which, mark me! is more cumbrous than fair link-mail) howbeit, I got me clear, and my lord Beltane, here stand I to aid and abet thee in all thy desperate affrays, henceforth. Aha! methinks shall be great doings within the greenwood anon!"

"Aye, but what of Thrasfordham? An Duke Ivo besiege it —"

"He shall find five hundred and more right doughty fellows, with Sir Richard of Wark and Sir Brian of Shand (that were armour-bearers to thy knightly sire) to keep him in play."

"And what would ye here, Sir Benedict?"

"Fight, Beltane, fight! Methinks he shall lack nothing for hard smiting that rideth with thee — hey, boy, I do yearn amain for the shock of a charge!"

"My company is but small, alas!" sighed Beltane.

"'Tis so I've heard, my Beltane," quoth Sir Benedict, and smiling his wry smile, he took a small hunting-horn that hung about his neck, "let us therefore make it larger —"

"How so — how so, good Benedict? — Ha! mean you —"

"Watch now!"

So saying, Sir Benedict set the horn to his lip and winded it three times loud and shrill, and thereafter stood with hand upraised. And lo! upon the stillness a sound that grew and grew — a whisper, a rustling as of strong wind in trees, and presently upon the high banks to north and east and west a great company appeared, horse-men and footmen, whose armour flashed 'neath the moon, while high o'er bascinet and helm rose deadly pike and ponderous lance, rank upon rank, a very forest.

Quoth Sir Benedict loud-voiced, and pointing to the grim array:

"Behold, lord Duke, hither have I brought thee five hundred archers and pike-men, with three hundred knights and men-at-arms, and each and every a man well tried and chosen, all vowed to follow thee and smite in Pentavalon's cause even as I, their lord, that do love thee for thy noble father's sake and for thine own sweet and knightly worth!"

So saying, Sir Benedict fell upon his knee before that great assemblage and caught Beltane's hand and kissed it; whereon, from those gleaming ranks rose a deep and thunderous shout while lance and spear-head flashed again.

Now looking from this right goodly array to the proud and war-like figure that bent so humbly at his feet, Beltane's heart swelled amain and all things grew blurred and misty in his sight.

"Sir Benedict," said he hoarse-voiced, "thou good and noble knight — O Benedict, dear my friend, kneel not to me. For thy so great love, thy faith and loyalty, fain would I thank thee — yet words be so poor, and I — O, Benedict —"

"Lord," said Benedict, "our camp lieth scarce three miles westward, come, I pray thee —"

"Nay, first come ye, friend, and look upon a dead witch that was indeed a noble woman."

So Beltane brought Sir Benedict where lay the dead Jolette, smiling yet as though into the eyes of God. Now beholding her, Sir Benedict beckoned Roger and bid him summon certain of his company, forthwith; and when Roger hasted back with divers awestruck fellows at his heels, they stood staring, amazed to behold these two great knights humbly kneeling side by side to pray for the soul of her who, all her days, had been scorned of men as the witch Jolette.

CHAPTER LV

HOW THEY MARCHED FOR WINISFARNE

At peep of day the trumpets blew, and Beltane, starting up from slumber, found the great camp all astir about him; the smoke of a hundred watch-fires rose up into the stilly air of morning and made a fragrant mist amid the trees beneath which armour glinted as guard relieved guard and the new-waked companies mustered under arms. And ever as the sun rose the bustle waxed and grew, with a coming and going about the fires where the morning meal was preparing; here a mighty furbishing of arms and armour, yonder a prodigious hissing and so-ho-ing where chargers and pack-horses were picketed, line upon line — goodly beasts that stamped and snorted and whinnied joyously — and everywhere was noise and cheer of talk and laughter; yet everywhere was method and a strict orderliness in all things, wherefore Beltane's very heart sang within him.

Now as he stood thus, viewing all things keen-eyed and watchful, he was presently aware of Sir Benedict and Black Roger who walked together within a distant alley; and as they passed them to and fro Black Roger talked amain, what time Sir Benedict seemed to hearken right solemn and attentive, oft pausing to question him quick and eager, and oft to clap hand to Roger's brawny back; and sometimes laughed he blithe and joyous and sometimes hearkened with grizzled head a-droop, until a turn in the glade hid them from sight.

Little by little, above the resinous fragrance of the fires rose other scents more delectable to the nostrils of a hungry man, thus, waking from his meditations Beltane turned him wistfully towards where, above the nearest fire, a goodly cooking pot seethed and bubbled invitingly. But even now a hand slipped within his arm and holding him thus, Sir Benedict viewed him joyful-eyed and smiled on him his wry and twisted smile.

"Beltane," said he, wagging his head, "O Beltane, thou wilt mind how upon a time as I drank a bowl of milk with thee amid the green in Mortain, I did warn thee that she had red hair and was like to prove a spit-fire, therefore!"

Now hereupon my Beltane must needs catch his breath and flush to the ears of him, and therewith strive to look at his ease, like the very youth he was.

"How, messire, hath Roger babbled to thee?"

"Babbled?" quoth Sir Benedict, shaking his head, "nay, Roger is no babbler of secret matters, for many do ken of thy love, Beltane — and I am thy friend, so is thy happiness my happiness. Thus do I say God and the sweet saints bless thee in thy love, dear lad, for a right noble lady is Helen the Beautiful and meet to thine embracements. By her so great love, by her proved faithfulness shalt thou yet win to happiness —"

"Nay, dear my Benedict, first must Pentavalon win to peace."

"Aye, by Helen's noble love, for —"

"O Sir Benedict, I have sworn an oath!"

"Aye, sweet lad, but Roger hath prayed a prayer!"

"Hath he told thee so much, Benedict?"

"So much," quoth Sir Benedict, pressing his arm, "so much, O man, that hereafter needs must I love thee and honour thee the more. Since man art thou, my Beltane, for all thy so great youthfulness."

"Nay, Benedict, am none so youthful."

"Thy very speech doth prove thee so, yet, being boy, thou art forsooth a man to-day."

"And wherefore?"

"For that to-day I do know more of thee. 'Tis suffering, 'tis sorrow nobly borne doth make the man, Beltane."

"Suffering, messire?"

"Yon lock of hair showeth very white amid the gold, Beltane, but thou art better man therefore, methinks. The fetters of thy dungeon yet gleam upon thy wrists, Beltane. But truly I do think within thy prison was forged the sword shall avenge our woes and free Pentavalon at last."

"Think you indeed, thou wise Benedict, that we by grief and sorrow do rise to find our nobler selves?"

"Aye verily! 'Tis but by sorrow and suffering our strength or weakness groweth manifest, Beltane."

"Yet — O Benedict — I did doubt her — plied her with scornful tongue and — drave her lonely from me!"

"And dost grieve amain, and sorrow therefore, O youth!"

"Yea, indeed, indeed — sleeping and waking!"

"And do yearn to woo her to forgiveness on thy knees, to crush her in thine arms and kiss her breath away, O Lover?"

"Aye, dear Sir Benedict, in such sort and so greatly that my passion oft doth fright me, so fiercely do I yearn and long — yet tremble and grow faint at thought of it!"

"Yet art thou here, bedight in arms, O man — thy yearning body far removed from all temptation till thou hast proved thee worthy her embrace! And thus it is I know thee for a man, my Beltane!"

"And thou, Benedict, thou hast yearned and trembled with love ere now, thou hast been a lover once, methinks?" But here Sir Benedict fell to silence, walking with face averted and gaze bent towards the dewy grass, and quickened his steps until they were come nigh unto the camp. Then lifted he his head; quoth he:

"My lord Beltane, how think you of this thy new-found company?"

"Men — ha! men, good Benedict — soldiers born and bred!"

"Forsooth, and 'neath mine own eye, Beltane. There is not one but I have watched him in the stress of battle. Body o' me, but I have chosen heedfully, there is none but hath proved his worthiness! See you the little man yonder, in half-mail with sword as great as himself — he that pipeth shrill-voiced as a boy? 'Tis Prat who alone stood off a score what time I lay wounded and pinned beneath my charger. Mark ye yon lusty fellow beside him? 'Tis Cnut that, single-handed, hewed him a path through Ivo's battle and bare away his own banner, the which doth grace my hall at Thrasfordham e'en now. And yonder is Dirk that was a slave, yet fighteth like a paladin. And there again is Siward, that with his brother maintained the sally-port 'gainst Ivo's van what time they drave us from the outer bailey. And yonder Cedric — but so could I name them each and every — ha! there sounds the welcome tucket! Come, let us break our fast, and there be many knights and esquires and gentles of degree do wait to pay thee homage."

So presently came they into the midst of the camp, where, seated on the mossy ling, hungry and expectant, were many noble lords and gentle knights and esquires of degree, who, beholding Sir Benedict with Beltane, rose up with one accord. Young men were these for the most part, yet were there many grizzled heads and wrinkled brows among them — grim lords of the old Duke's following much versed in war, calm of judgment and wise in council; but one and all did they stare upon my Beltane in wonder at his youth because of his so famous deeds.

Now spake to them Sir Benedict, short and soldier-like:

"My lords, this is he of whom ye all have heard, Beltane hight, son of Beltane our Duke, for whom we together have held Thrasfordham so long and painfully. My lord Beltane, of all the knights and nobles of the Duke thy father's days, here do stand, sire or son, all that have withstood Black Ivo. Behold here Sir Bertrand, that was thy father's seneschal of Pentavalon City. Here, Sir John of Griswold whose sire bare thy father's banner, wherefore Griswold is ashes long since. Here Hubert of Erdington, that was thy father's marshal-of-the-field. Here, Hacon of Trant, that was wont to lead thy father's vanward, and here, Sir Brian of Hartismere, brother to Eric, called the Wry-neck. So now, all's said, my lord, wherefore I pray, let us eat."

Forthwith down they sat together on the grass, all and sundry, and ate and drank and laughed and talked, insomuch that in brake and thicket near and far the birds carolled and chattered in pretty mockery.

"Lord Beltane," quoth Sir Benedict when the meal was ended, "ere I met thee, 'twas my intent this hour to march on Winisfarne, according to my promise to Waldron of Brand, how say you?"

"Forsooth," nodded Beltane, "as soon as ye will."

Thus, within the hour, the trumpets brayed 'to horse' and all was seeming hurry and confusion; yet a confusion, this, governed by soldierly method, so that, ere long, horsemen were mounted and footmen in array what time Beltane, bedight in goodly vizored casque, with lance and shield borne behind him, came where stood Sir Benedict beside a great and noble war-horse.

Forthwith Beltane mounted, and forthwith from these well-ordered ranks a great shout arose:

"Beltane — the Duke — the Duke!"

Now, reining in his eager beast, Beltane looked upon that stern array, and as he looked his eye kindled and his heart swelled within him.

"O men!" said he, "I that ye do acclaim am but a man even as ye are men, to bear with ye the heat and labour of the day. What ye must endure that will I endure with you. Here stand I, ready to spill my blood that Wrong may cease. Even as ye, I am prepared to adventure me, life and limb, that Lust and Murder may cease to be and Innocence and Truth may walk again all unashamed. So shall I lead ye into battles and affrays desperate and bloody, where foes shall be a-many and we, few. But we do fight for hearth and home, and the thought of this, methinks, shall nerve us strong as giants. Yet is our way a perilous way, and some of us, belike, must die. But, by the blood of such, this our country is hallowed unto those that shall come after us, so shall our memories teach others how to die — and better — how to live that this our country may stand, hereafter, for all things great and noble. He that dieth for home and children shall, mayhap, from the floor of heaven, look down upon a great and happy people whose freedom he — by weary marches, by pain of wounds, by sharp and sudden death — he himself hath helped to purchase, and, in their peace and happiness, find an added joy.

"O men! who would not be a man to fight in such just cause? Who would not cherish life that he might lose it to such noble purpose?

"Now therefore, all ye that do love Pentavalon — follow!"

Thus saying, my Beltane wheeled his horse; and with rhythmic ring and clash, together, rank on rank, horsemen and footmen, they followed hard behind, a silent, grim array, with eyes that gleamed 'neath helm and bascinet, and purposeful hands that griped full strong on lance and spear-shaft, as, coming to the forest-road, they swung away northwards towards Winisfarne.

CHAPTER LVI

WHAT THEY FOUND AT WINISFARNE

Two and two they rode — for the way was oft-times narrow — their flanks well covered by light-armed archers who marched within the green, with mounted archers far in their van and others in their rear.

A glory of sun dappled their way with dancing shadows, flowers were a-bloom in bank and hedgerow, and birds carolled blithe in the fragrant air, what time Sir Benedict rode beside Beltane, his ponderous casque a-swing at saddle-bow; and oft he turned his grizzled head to view my thoughtful Beltane as one might look upon a son, new-found.

Now in a while Beltane turned and meeting his look reached out to him his hand.

"Dear Benedict," said he, "how much — how very much I owe to thee. Thou art methinks the greatest knight that e'er couched lance —"

"Save thy noble father!" quoth Sir Benedict with solemn nod.

"My father — you were his esquire and much-loved comrade, Benedict?"

"I was, Beltane."

"Knew you my mother well, also?"

"Thy mother? Why — aye, forsooth, I — knew thy mother — very well, Beltane."

"What manner of woman was she, I pray?"

"The fairest and noblest these eyes have e'er beheld!"

"The — noblest?"

"And purest! Hark ye, Beltane, and mark me well — there ne'er lived wife of so stainless honour as the noble woman that bare thee!"

"And yet," sighed Beltane, with wrinkled brow, "within the garden of Pentavalon — my father —"

"Thy father was a sick man, faint with wounds and spent with hardship. All that day, as we rode unto Pentavalon City, he and I, his mind oft wandered and he held wild talk in his fever. But hale was I, mind and body, and I do know the Duke thy father fell to strange and sudden madness upon that dreadful day, whereby came woe to Pentavalon, and bitter remorse to him. This do I swear, thy mother was noble wife and saintly woman!"

"Loved she my father?"

"Aye, verily — she was his wife! Thy father was a noble knight and peerless — and oft warring on the marches, but methinks — she was something lonely — at times, Beltane."

"Alas!" sighed Beltane, and again "Alas!" So fell they incontinent to deep thought and rode full long in silence. But ever and anon as they paced along together thus, Sir Benedict must needs lift his head to gaze upon my Beltane, and his grim lips curved to smile infinite tender, and in his eyes was growing wonder.

Quoth he at last:

"Beltane, d'ye mark this our silent company, not a stave have they carolled since we set forth! But how shall a man sing and jest whose heart is set on great emprise? Verily thy words have fired e'en this shrivelled heart o' mine till I, even as they, methinks, do burn to fight Pentavalon's cause, to shield her from woeful shame and — ha! — such vile sights as yon!"

Now looking where Sir Benedict pointed, Beltane beheld a thing, crookedly contorted, a-dangle from a knotted branch that jutted athwart the way, insomuch that the must needs stoop, cowering in his saddle, lest he touch the twisted feet of it.

"Dead three days I judge!" mused Sir Benedict. "Much is possible to the Red Pertolepe in three days. And he hath a great and powerful following, 'tis said!"

Quoth Beltane, pale-cheeked and frowning a little:

"So would I have it, Benedict — they shall be the more for us to smite!"

"I've heard he musters full three thousand, Beltane."

"What then, good Benedict? Yon poor, dead thing we passed but now was worth a score of men to us — and there will be others — Sir Pertolepe loveth to see men hang! So perchance, ere we come to Winisfarne, the strength of thousands shall lie within these arms of ours."

"'Tis a fair thought, lad — aye, 'tis a right fair thought! May all the poor souls done thus to sudden, cruel death, march within our slender ranks and smite with us, shoulder to shoulder, henceforth!"

And now as they went, came they on many and divers signs of the Red Pertolepe's passing; here a smouldering heap of ruin whereby lay pale, stiff shapes half hidden in the grass — yonder a little child outstretched as though asleep, save for wide eyes that looked so blindly on the sun: and there, beyond, upon the white dust of the road, great gouts and pools that had trickled from something sprawled among the underbrush.

And the soft wind crooned and whispered in the leaves — leaves that parting, showed other shapes swung high in air, whose pallid faces looked down on them, awful-eyed, from the tender green, faces drawn and haggard, with teeth agleam or open mouths whence screams had come, but very silent now until the Day of Judgment.

So rode they, with death above them and around, death in many hateful shapes; and oft Sir Benedict bowed his head as one that prayed, the while his strong hands knit themselves to iron fists; and oft from those grim ranks behind a sound went up to heaven, a sound ominous and low, that was like unto a moan.

Thus marched they, through heat and dust, through cool, green shadow, splashing through noisy brook and shallow ford, until, as the sun reached the zenith, they

What They Found at Winisfarne

came to the brow of a hill and saw afar the walls and roofs of the prosperous town of Winisfarne.

And ever as they drew nearer, Sir Benedict stared on it, his black brows close-knit, and fingered his square chin as one puzzled.

"Beltane," quoth he at last, "'tis full ten years since I saw Winisfarne, and yet — meseemeth — it looked not so! 'Tis as though I missed somewhat, and yet —"

But now came Roger, a dusty figure, spurring from the rear:

"Master," he cried, pointing with eager finger, "O master, the keep — where is the great keep that stood yonder?"

"Aye, verily — the keep!" nodded Sir Benedict, clapping mailed hand to thigh, "and 'twas a great and mighty hold as I do mind me!"

Now looked they gloomily on each other and halted their array what time Sir Benedict passed word for bows to be strung and every eye and every ear to be strained right heedfully; then moved they on again.

Betimes they reached the outskirts of the town, for defences it had none, but no man moved therein and no sound reached them but the noise of their own going. Thus, in a while, with hands tight-clenched and lips firm-set they rode into the desolation of the market-place befouled by signs of battle fierce and fell, while beyond, a mass of charred ruin, lay all that was left of Winisfarne's once great and famous keep.

Now above this ruin divers gibbets had been set up, and behold! these gibbets each bore a heavy burden. Then Beltane lighted from his horse, and going apart, laid by his casque and sat him down, his head bowed betwixt his hands as one that is direly sick. In a while as he sat thus, heedless of all things, cometh Roger.

"Master," said he, "saw ye the gibbets yonder?"

"I saw them, Roger."

"Upon those gibbets be divers of our good fellows, master. There is Diccon and Peter of my company of pikes, and Gregory that was a fair good bowman, and there be others also — and master, these be not hanged men!"

"Not hanged —?"

"No, master! All these our men died in battle, as their wounds do testify — they were dead men already when Pertolepe hanged them on his gibbets. And Walkyn is not here, wherefore, methinks, he liveth yet. And Pertolepe is not here, yet where Pertolepe is, there shall we surely find Walkyn, for Walkyn hath sworn full oft — ha! master — master, behold what cometh here — see, yonder!"

Then Beltane arose, and looking where Roger pointed, beheld a strange, misshapen thing, half beast, half man, that ran wondrous fleetly towards them, and, as it ran, flourished aloft a broken sword; now was he lost to sight behind some bush or quick-set, now he bounded high over stream or stone or fallen tree — nought was there could let or stay him — until he came where stood Sir Benedict's outposts, to whose conduct he yielded him forthwith and so was presently brought into the market-square.

A wild figure this, great and hairy of head and with the arms and shoulders of a very giant; bedight was he in good link-mail, yet foul with dirt and mire and spattered with blood from heel to head, and in one great hand he griped still the fragment of a reddened sword. All a-sweat was he, and bleeding from the hair, while his mighty chest heaved and laboured with his running.

So stood he betwixt his brawny captors what time he panted hoarse and loud, and stared about him fierce-eyed 'neath beetling brows. Thus, of a sudden he espied my Beltane standing bare-headed in his youthful might, whereon this monstrous man forthwith dashed aside his stalwart guards as they had been babes, and ran towards Beltane with hairy hands outstretched, whereon sprang Roger to front him, dagger a-gleam; but lo! Roger was caught up in those mighty arms and shaken helplessly.

"Fool!" cried this grim fellow, "think ye I would

harm Beltane that is my most loved lord henceforth? I am Ulf, called the Strong, and, as this my hateful body is strong, so is my love — lie there!" So saying, Ulf laid Roger upon his back, and coming to Beltane, fell upon his face before him and caught his mailed feet and kissed them.

"Lord Beltane," he cried, harsh-voiced, "thou seest I do love thee — yet 'twas I did bear thee captive to thy foe by command of one I love beyond all others. But thou, lord Beltane, thou at peril of thy life did save her from shame and fiery death when Ulf could not — so do I love thee, lord Beltane, and will be thy slave henceforth, to love and serve thee till I die — an thou wilt take me. Misshapen and unlovely ye behold me — a vile thing that men would jeer at but that they fear to die, for God who hath denied me all else, hath given me strength beyond all men. Yet do I hate myself and do hide me from the eyes of my fellows: but, an thou canst bear with me, canst suffer me beside thee and be not ashamed of my unloveliness, then will I front all eyes right boldly. Now lord, an thou wilt take Ulf for thy man, reach down to me thy hand."

Then Beltane reached down and took Ulf's hairy hand in his.

"Ulf," said he, "thou that God hath blessed with such noble strength, methinks 'neath thy grim shape thy heart is noble also, and thy soul, mayhap, straight and lovely. So will I make thee brother in arms to my faithful Roger, that ye two shall ride ever near me when the battle joins."

Now Ulf the strong stood up erect upon his feet, and on his swart cheeks great tears rolled, glistening.

"Lord!" said he, "O Beltane, my lord and master —" and bowed grim head with sudden sob, whereat Beltane questioned him full hastily, as thus:

"Art wounded, Ulf! And whence come ye in such guise?"

"Lord," says Ulf, wiping off his tears and choking upon a sob, "I came through Bloody Pertolepe's array."

"Through? — nay, how mean you?" questioned Beltane, the while Sir Benedict and many wondering knights and esquires pressed round them in a ring.

"I mean through, lord, for Walkyn's need is dire. So burst I through them — I had an axe but it brake in my hold, see you, even as this my sword — alack, there is no weapon that I do not break! Howbeit here am I, lord, hither come with word for one Sir Benedict of Bourne that did covenant to meet with Walkyn here at Winisfarne!"

"Behold us here — speak on!" quoth Sir Benedict.

"Thus, then, saith Walkyn o' the Dene: That scarce had he stormed and set fire to yonder prison-keep, than from the south cometh a great company, the which he at the first did take for ye. But, in a while, behold Sir Pertolepe's accursed Raven banner, the which giveth Walkyn much to think. Now cometh to him one beyond all women noble and gracious and holy (as I do know) the fair and stately Abbess Veronica, who, years agone, did build and endow yon great and goodly abbey, wherein all poor desolate souls should be cherished and comforted by her and her saintly nuns, and where the stricken fugitive might find sanctuary and peace and moreover be healed of his hurts. (All this know I since I was fugitive, hurt and very woeful and found me solace there.) So cometh this noble lady to Walkyn (and with her, I) and speaketh him calm and sweetly, thus: 'Yonder rideth Sir Pertolepe that is knight of noble birth, yet the rather would I trust myself and these my good sisters in thy hands, O man! So do I pray thee when thou goest hence, yield us the protection of thy strength, so shall heaven bless thee!' Hereon Walkyn frowned and plucked his beard awhile, but thereafter, came he to kneel and kiss her hand and swear to aid her the while life him lasted. Then summoned he his company (lusty fellows all) and called for thirty men that would remain to hold Red Pertolepe in play what time he seeketh place of greater vantage well beknown to him. Forthwith stood out one Tall Orson hight (a doughty fellow) and with him nine

What They Found at Winisfarne

and twenty other lusty fellows, right willing (and with them, I) and thereafter Walkyn formeth his company (the nuns in the midst) and marched in haste for Brand that is a lonely tower. Then did these thirty (and with them I) shoot arrows amain on Pertolepe's vanguard from every place of vantage hereabouts, and met them with right lusty hand-strokes and stayed thus their advance until of the thirty there none remained alive save seven (and of these, I). And, since we could do no more, I (that do know this country from my misshapen youth) brought these men by secret ways unto the Tower of Brand that is desolate and a ruin, yet strong withal. And there lay Walkyn (that is a notable fighter) keeping watch and ward within the tower what time he waited thy succour. Now who so skilful and tender with our wounded as this sweet and gracious lady Abbess! Next day, sure enough, cometh Pertolepe with brave show of horse and foot (above three thousand, lords) and straightway sendeth he a haughty fellow to demand incontinent surrender — a loud-voiced knight whom Walkyn forthwith shot and slew with his own hand. Whereat Sir Pertolepe waxed exceeding wroth and came on amain and beset the tower on all sides, whereby they lost others of their men, for Walkyn's fellows shot exceeding strong and true (and with them, I). Then, O my lords, in all that fierce debate, who so brave and calm, heartening wearied and wounded with gentle voice and gentler hand, than this same noble lady Abbess! For two days lay we besieged whereby our food and drink began to fail (for the well within the tower is well-nigh dried up) yet none did eat or drink so sparingly as this same holy Abbess. Now on this (the second day, lords) cometh Pertolepe himself (under flag of truce, lords) and demands we yield to him the body of this same lady Abbess (to our ransom) swearing on his knightly word he then will march away forthwith, and seek our hurt no more. And, to save our lives, fain would this brave lady have yielded her to Pertolepe's hands. But Walkyn (mindful of his oath, lords), leaning him from the battlement, spake Red Pertolepe defiantly, calling him knave and liar, and therewith spat upon him, very fairly. Whereat Pertolepe sware to hang us one and all and the battle joined again fiercer than before. Therefore, on this the third day, seeing no hope of succour, Walkyn made him ready to sally out (a right desperate venture because of the women). Then spake I before them all, saying I doubted not I might win through, and bring thee to their aid (an ye had kept the tryst) would they but ply their shafts amain to cover me. The which was so agreed. Then did this saintly lady Abbess set her white hand on this my hateful head and prayed the sweet Christ to shield this my monstrous body, and I thereafter being bedight in right good mail (as thou seest) issued suddenly out of the tower whiles our foemen sat at meat, and ran among them roaring dreadfully and smote amain full many until my axe brake and I betook me to my sword and smote them as I ran what time Walkyn's archers shot right furiously and well. Thus came I through Bloody Pertolepe's array, and thus, lords, ye do behold a something weary man and a mighty hungry one withal!"

Now came Sir Benedict to grasp Ulf's great hand.

"Forsooth, hast done a great and noble thing!" quoth he. "Thy twisted body doth hide a great and manly soul, meseemeth, so ne'er shalt lack for friend whiles Benedict doth live!"

And after Sir Benedict came many other knights and esquires of degree, to bring him of their own viands and press upon him rich and goodly wine. In so much that Ulf grew hot and awkward, and presently stole away to eat with Roger in a quiet corner.

But now within the market-place was sound of song, of jest and laughter, where bow-strings were looked to heedfully, sword-belts buckled tighter, mail-coifs laced the closer, stirrup-chain and saddle-girth carefully regarded, whiles ever and anon all eyes turned where Beltane sat among the older knights, Sir Benedict beside him, hearkening to their counsel. And presently he rose and lifted

What They Found at Winisfarne

his hand, whereat the trumpets blared and, thereafter, with ring of hoof and tramp of foot, marched they forth of Winisfarne, the sun bright on helm and shield, a right gallant array.

And at their head rode Ulf the Strong.

CHAPTER LVII

TELLETH OF THE ONFALL AT BRAND

By wild and lonely ways Ulf led them, through mazy thicket, o'er murmurous rill, through fragrant bracken that, sweeping to their saddle-girths, whispered as they passed; now rode they by darkling wood, now crossed they open heath; all unerring rode Ulf the Strong, now wheeling sharp and sudden to skirt treacherous marsh or swamp, now plunging into the gloom of desolate woods, on and on past lonely pools where doleful curlews piped, nor faltered he nor stayed until, as the sun grew low, they climbed a sloping upland crowned by mighty trees and thick with underbrush; here Ulf checked his horse and lifted long arm in warning, whereon the company halted, hard-breathing, yet very orderly and silent.

Forthwith down lighted Beltane with Sir Benedict and Ulf who pointed before them with his finger.

"Lords," said he, "beyond yon trees is a valley and in the valley the tower of Brand, the which you may see from the brush yonder — aha! and hear also, methinks!"

And indeed the air was full of a strange droning sound that rose and fell unceasing, a drowsy, ominous hum.

"Ah, Benedict," said Beltane, frowning a little, "I like not that sound! Summon we our wisest heads, for here is matter for thought and sudden action methinks!"

Hereupon Sir Benedict beckoned to his five chiefest knights and they together followed Ulf's broad back up the slope until they were come within the little wood; and ever as they advanced the strange hum grew louder, hoarser — a distant roar, pierced, ever and anon, by sharper sound, a confused din that was the voice of desperate conflict. Presently Ulf brought them to the edge of the little wood and, parting twig and leaf, they looked forth and down. And what they saw was this:

A little valley, wondrous green but very desolate-seeming, for here and there stood ruined walls and charred timbers that once had been fair dwellings; and in the midst of this small and ruined hamlet, a mighty tower uprose, hoary and weather-beaten, yet stark and grim against the sunset. All about this tower a great camp lay, set well out of bow-shot, and 'twixt camp and tower were many men whose armour flashed, rank on rank, and archers who, kneeling behind mantlets, shot amain at battlement and loophole. Against the tower were two great ladders, roughly fashioned and a-swarm with men; but ever as they strove to reach the battlement a mighty axe whirled and swung and a long sword flashed, and ever as they fell, so fell one of the besiegers.

"There stand Walkyn and Tall Orson!" quoth Ulf, biting his nails. "Ha!— they be dour fighters — would I stood with them!"

"We come in due season, methinks!" said Sir Benedict, stroking his square chin, "what is your counsel, my lords?"

Quoth young Sir John of Griswold:

"Let us to horse and sally out on them, the hill is with us and we shall —"

"Slay and be slain!" quoth Sir Benedict.

"Verily!" nodded grim Sir Bertrand, "dost speak like a very youth, John!"

"Here, methinks," said Sir Benedict, "is work for pike and bow-string. First break we their charge, then down on them in flank with shock and might of all our lances."

"Ha! 'tis well be-thought, Benedict!" growled old Hubert of Erdington, "so let me march with the pikes."

"Art silent, lord Beltane," quoth Sir Hacon, "dost agree?"

"Aye, truly," answered Beltane, rising, "but let our pikes march in V formation, our mightiest men at the point of the V, and with archers behind. Then, ere the foe do engage, let the V become an L, so shall we oppose them two faces. Now, when Sir Pertolepe's chivalry charge, let Sir Benedict with two hundred knights and men-at-arms spur in upon their flank, driving them confused upon their main battle, what time I, yet hid within the green, will sound my rallying note that Walkyn knoweth of old, whereat he shall sally out upon their further flank. Then will I, with my hundred horse, charge down upon their rear, so should we have them, methinks? How say you, my lords?"

"Truly," quoth Sir Bertrand, closing his vizor, "thy father liveth again in thee, methinks!"

Forthwith, pikemen and archers fell into array with Cnut at their head, while behind the spreading ranks of pikes Prat and his archers were ranged, bows strung and quivers slung before; and presently, at Beltane's word, they swung forth of the sheltering green, fierce-eyed, grim-lipped, bascinet and pike-head a-twinkle. Away they swung down the slope, a stalwart company swift-treading and light, and in their midst old Hubert of Erdington in his heavy armour, whose long sword flashed as he flourished his farewell.

With rhythmic step and swing of broad mailed shoulders they marched until they were come down into the valley. And now, as they advanced swift and steady, rose shouts from besieged and besiegers; Sir Pertolepe's trumpets brayed defiance and alarm, and of a sudden, forth of his camp mailed horsemen rode rank upon rank, pennons a-flutter and armour flashing in the sunset glare. But, as they mustered to the charge, as shields flashed and lances sank, Sir Benedict's pikemen wheeled, their ranks swung wide, and lo! the V was become an L. Now from this L bows twanged and arrows flew amain above the kneeling pikemen, what time Sir Pertolepe's trumpets blared the charge, and down upon those slender ranks his heavy-armed chivalry thundered; horses reared and fell, screaming, beneath the whistling arrow-shower, but on swept the charge; those thin ranks bent and swayed 'neath the shock as lance crossed pike, but these pike-butts rested on firm ground and upon their deadly points, horses, smitten low, reared transfixed, and above these rocking pikes steel flashed and flickered where the stout archers plied their heavy broadswords, while, loud above the din, Sir Hubert's voice boomed hoarse encouragement what time he thrust and smote above the kneeling pikemen.

Now out from the green Sir Benedict paced astride his great black charger, and behind him his two hundred steel-girt knights and men-at-arms, their vizors closed, their shields slung before, the points of their long and ponderous lances agleam high in air. Then turned Sir Benedict and looked on their grimly ranks, glad-eyed:

"O sirs," quoth he, "who would not be a man to fight in such just cause!"

So saying, he smiled his wry and twisted smile and closed his vizor: then, with shield addressed and feet thrust far within the stirrups he lightly feutred his deadly lance; and behold! down swept every lance behind him as, leaning low behind his shield, he shouted right joyously:

"Come ye, messires — lay on this day for Pentavalon!"

Forward bounded the great horses a-down the slope — away, away, gathering speed with every stride — away, away, across the level with flying rein and busy spur; and now a loud shouting and dire amaze among Sir Pertolepe's battle with desperate wheeling of ranks and spurring of rearing horses, while Sir Benedict's riders swept down on them, grim and voiceless, fast and faster. Came a roaring crash beneath whose dire shock Sir Pertolepe's ranks were riven and rent asunder, and over and through their red confusion Sir Benedict rode in thunderous, resistless might, straight for where, above their mid-most, close-set ranks, fluttered and flew Sir Pertolepe's Raven banner. Now, in hot haste, Sir Pertolepe launched another charge to check that furious onset, what time he reformed and strengthened his main battle; but, with speed unchecked, Sir Benedict's mighty ranks met them in full career — broke them, flung them reeling back on Sir Pertolepe's staggering van and all was wild disorder, above which roaring tumult the Raven banner reeled and swayed and the fray waxed ever fiercer.

Now ran Beltane where stood Roger to hold his horse, with Ulf who leaned upon a goodly axe and young Sir John of Griswold, who clenched and wrung his mailed hands and bit upon his boyish lip and stamped in his impatience.

"My lord," he cried, "my lord, suffer ns to charge — ah! see — our good Sir Benedict will be surrounded — cut off —"

"Nay, methinks he is too wise in war, he fighteth ever with calm head, Sir John."

"But, messire, do but see — his charge is checked — see — see, he yieldeth ground — he giveth back!"

"Aye, verily!" quoth Beltane, springing to saddle, "but behold how he orders his line! O lovely knight! O wise Benedict! See you not his wisdom now, Sir John? In his retreat he draweth Sir Pertolepe's main battle athwart our line of charge, their flank exposed and open — to horse, Sir John, to horse! Yet stir not until I give the word." Forthwith sprang Sir John to saddle and Roger and Ulf also, what time Beltane sat, his gaze upon the conflict, his bugle-horn in his hand; of a sudden he clapped it to lip and sounded the old fierce rallying note. High and shrill and loud it rang above the roar of battle, and lo! distant and far, like an answer to the call, from the grim and battered tower of Brand a mighty shout went up — "Arise! Arise! — Pentavalon!"

"Oho!" cried Roger, sitting close on Beltane's left, "list ye to that, now! And see — ha! there cometh our long-legged Walkyn, first of them all! See how they order their pikes — O master, they be sweet and doughty fellows! See how Jenkyn's archers shoot — each man to the ear!"

Awhile sat Beltane watching, wide-eyed, while Sir Benedict, fighting sword in hand, fell back and back before the furious onset of Sir Pertolepe's main battle until he had drawn the fight mid-way. Then, quick-breathing, my Beltane closed his vizor.

"Now!" cried he, "now, good comrades all, God willing, we have them. Let each man choose his foe and smite this day for Liberty and Justice!"

So saying, he levelled his lance, and a hundred lances sank behind him. Spurs struck deep, horses reared, plunged, and sped away. Before their galloping line rode Sir John of Griswold with Roger and Ulf: and before these, Beltane.

He felt the wind a-whistle through the eye-vents of his casque, heard the muffled thunder of the galloping hoofs behind mingled with the growing din of battle; heard a shout — a roar of anger and dismay, saw a confusion of rearing horses as Sir Pertolepe swung about to meet this new attack, steadied his aim, and with his hundred lances thundering close behind, drove in upon those bristling ranks to meet them shield to shield with desperate shock of onset — felt his tough lance go home with jarring crash — saw horses that reared high and were gone, lost beneath the trampling fray, and found his lance shivered to the very grip. Out flashed his sword, for all about him was a staggering press of horses that neighed and screamed, and men who smote, shouting, and were smitten; unseen blows battered him while he thrust and hewed, and wondered to see his long blade so dimmed and bloody. And ever as he fought, through the narrow vent of his casque he caught small and sudden visions of this close-locked, desperate fray; of Ulf standing in his stirrups to ply his whirling axe whose mighty, crashing blows no armour might withstand; of grim Roger, scowling and fierce, wielding ponderous broad-sword; of young Sir John of Griswold, reeling in his saddle, his helpless arms wide-flung.

So cut they bloody path through Pertolepe's deep array, on and forward with darting point and deep-biting edge, unheeding wounds or shock of blows, until Beltane beheld the press yield, thin out, and melt away, thereupon shouted he hoarse and loud, rode down a knight who sought to bar his way, unhorsed a second, and wheeling his snorting charger, wondered at the seeming quiet; then lifting his vizor, looked about him. And lo! wheresoever his glance fell were men that crawled groaning, or lay very mute and still amid a huddle of fallen horses, and, beyond these again, were other men, a-horse and a-foot, that galloped and ran amain for the shelter of the green. Sir Pertolepe's array was scattered up and down the valley — the battle was lost and won.

Now while he yet sat thus, dazed by the shock of blows and breathing deep of the sweet, cool air, he beheld one rise up from where the battle-wrack lay thickest, an awful figure that limped towards him, holding aloft the broken shaft of an axe.

"Aha, lord Beltane!" cried Ulf, wiping sweat and blood from him, "there be no more — left to smite, see you. The which — is well, for weapon — have I none. This axe was the third this day — broken, see you! Alas! there is no weapon I may use. Saw you Roger, lord, that is my comrade?"

"Nay, good Ulf — ha, what of him?"

"His horse was slain, lord. So fought he afoot, since when I saw him not."

"And where is Sir Benedict and Walkyn — O see you not Sir Benedict? mine eyes are dazzled with the sun."

But now Ulf uttered a joyful cry and pointed with his axe-shaft.

"Yonder cometh Roger, lord, and with him the little archer, but whom bring they?"

Very slowly they came, Roger and Prat the archer, up-bearing betwixt them good Sir Hubert of Erdington, his harness hacked and broken, his battered helm a-swing upon its thongs, his eyes a-swoon in the pallor of his face.

Down sprang Beltane and ran to greet him and to catch his nerveless hands:

"Lord Beltane," quoth he, faintly, "full oft have I shed my blood for — Pentavalon — to-day I die, messire. But, as thou didst say —'tis well to die — in cause so noble! My lord, farewell to thee!"

And with the word, even as he stood 'twixt Roger and the archer, the stout old knight was dead. So they laid Hubert of Erdington very reverently upon that trampled field he had maintained so well.

"A right noble knight, my lord," quoth Prat, shaking gloomy head, "but for him, methinks our pikemen would have broke to their third onset!"

"There is no man of you hath not fought like ten men this day!" said Beltane, leaning on his sword and with head a-droop. "Have we lost many, know ye?"

"A fair good number, master, as was to be expected," quoth Roger, cleansing his sword on a tuft of grass, "Sir John of Griswold fell beside me deep-smitten through the helm."

"And what of Sir Benedict?"

"See yonder — yonder he rides, my lord!" cried Prat, "though methinks you scarce shall know him." And he pointed where, on spent and weary charger, one rode, a drooping, languid figure, his bright armour bespattered and dim, his dinted casque smitten awry; slowly he rode before his weary company until of a sudden espying Beltane, he uttered a great and glad cry, his drooping shoulders straightened, and he rode forward with mailed arms outstretched.

"Beltane!" he cried, "praise be to God! One told me thou wert down — art well, sweet lad, and all unharmed? God is merciful!" And he patted Beltane's mailed shoulder, what time blood oozed from his steel gauntlet and his sobbing charger hung weary head and snorted purple foam. "O lad," quoth he, smiling his wry smile, "here was an hour worth living for — though Sir Bertrand is sore hurt and many do lie dead of my company."

"And here," sighed Beltane, "brave Hubert of Erdingtou — behold!"

"A gallant knight, Beltane! May I so valiantly die when that my time be come. Truly 'twas a sharp debate what time it lasted, there be many that will ride with us no more."

"And thou, my lord?" cried Beltane suddenly, "thy cheek so pale — thou'rt hurt, Benedict!"

"Nought to matter, lad, save that it is my sword-arm: nay indeed, my Beltane, 'twas but an axe bit through my vanbrace, 'twill heal within the week. But take now my horn and summon ye our scattered company, for I do lack the wind."

Knight and man-at-arms, limping and afoot, on horses weary and blown, they came at the summons — archer and pike-man they came, a blood be-spattered company; many were they that staggered, faint with wounds, and many that sank upon the trampled grass a-swoon with weariness, but in the eyes of each and every was the look of men that triumph.

Cnut was there, his bascinet gone, his fiery hair betousled: Tall Orson was there, leaning on a bent and battered pike, and there his comrade, Jenkyn o' the Ford, with many others that Beltane well remembered and others whose faces he knew not. So formed they their battle-scarred array what time Beltane viewed them with glowing eye and heart swelling within him.

"Master!" cried Tall Orson of a sudden, "O master, us do be clean men and goodly fighters as us did promise thee time 'gone i' the Hollow, master, ye'll mind us as did promise so to be — I and Jenkyn as be my comrade?"

"Aye, master!" cried Jenkyn o' the Ford, "aye, look'ee, we ha' kept our word to thee as we did promise, look'ee master! So now, speak word to us master, look'ee!"

"Ye men!" quoth Beltane, hoarse-voiced, "O my good comrades all, your deeds this day shall speak when we are dust, methinks! Your foes this day did muster three thousand strong, and ye do number scarce a thousand — yet have ye scattered them, for that your cause is just — 'tis thus ye shall lift Pentavalon from shame and give to her peace at last!"

Then Tall Orson shook aloft his battered pike and shouted amain, and on the instant, others took up the cry — a hoarse roar that rolled from rank to rank; lance and sword, axe and pike were flourished high in air, and from these men who had marched so grimly silent all the day a great and mighty shout went up:

"Arise, Pentavalon! Ha! Beltane — Pentavalon!"

Now even as they shouted, upon this thunderous roar there stole another sound, high and clear and very sweet, that rose and swelled upon the air like the voices of quiring angels; and of a sudden the shouting was hushed, as, forth of the tower's gloomy portal the lady Abbess came, tall and fair and saintly in her white habit, her nuns behind her, two and two, their hands clasped, their eyes upraised to heaven, chanting to God a hymn of praise and thanksgiving. Slow paced they thus, the stately Abbess with head low-bended and slim hands clasped upon her silver crucifix until, the chant being ended, she raised her head and beheld straightway Sir Benedict unhelmed and yet astride his great charger. The silver crucifix fell, the slim hands clasped themselves upon her bosom and the eyes of the tall, white Abbess grew suddenly wide and dark: and even as she gazed on him, so gazed Sir Benedict on her.

"Yolande!" said he, hoarse-voiced and low.

"Benedict!" she murmured.

Slowly Sir Benedict bowed his head, and turning, laid his hand on Beltane's mailed shoulder.

"Lady," said he, "behold here Beltane — that is son to Beltane heretofore Duke and Lord of Pentavalon!"

"Ah!" she whispered, "Beltane!" and of a sudden stretched out her arms in passionate yearning gesture, then, covering her face, sank upon her knees, "God pity me!" she sighed, "God pity me!" Thereafter she rose to her stately height and looked on Beltane, gentle and calm-eyed.

"My lord Beltane," said she, "I have heard tell thou art a noble knight, strong yet gentle — so should thy father be greatly blessed in thee — and thy — mother also. God have thee ever in His keeping — Beltane!"

Now as she spake the name her soft voice brake, and turning, she stood with head bowed upon her hands, and standing thus, spake again, deep-voiced and soft:

"Sir Benedict, we are come to minister to the hurt, all is prepared within the tower, let them be brought to us I pray, and — my lord, forget not the sacred oath thou didst swear me — long years agone!"

CHAPTER LVIII

HOW BELTANE HAD SPEECH WITH THE ABBESS

THEY found rich booty in Pertolepe's camp, with store of arms and armour and many goodly horses, and thither Sir Benedict's wearied followers betook them as night fell and knew blessed rest and sleep. But in the tower of Brand lights gleamed where the Abbess and her gentle nuns went to and fro among the wounded, ministering to their wants; and far beyond the camp, armour glinted ever and anon against the blackness of the surrounding woods, where outpost and sentinel kept vigilant watch and ward. Though late the hour Beltane sat wakeful, chin on fist, beside a glimmering watch-fire, oft turning his glance towards the massy, weather-beaten tower, bethinking him of the noble lady Abbess, of her strange looks and words, and so fell to brooding thought. High overhead the moon rode, obscured by flying clouds, a wild wrack up-whirling from the south: at fitful intervals was a wind that moaned drearily 'mid the gloom of distant woods, a desolate sound that sobbed upon the air, and dying to a wail, was gone. Now becoming aware of this, Beltane raised his head, and looked up at the ominous heavens and round about him. And thus he espied a light that hovered hither and thither above the distant battle-field, a small light whose red flame flashed back from cloven casque and riven shield, where eyes glared unseeing and mouths gaped mute and dumb from a dark confusion whence mailed arms stiffly rose with hands tight-clenched that seemed to menace heaven, and rigid feet whose spurred heels yet gored the flanks of rigid, fallen chargers; to and fro and up and down this small flame leaped merrily, dancing from dead face to dead face but staying never, a fiendish fire that seemed to mock the horror of wounds and gibe at solemn death.

Now as he watched this devilish light, Beltane arose and reaching for his sword went soft-footed to meet it, then paused, for the light was moving towards him. Near and nearer it came, until, into the glow of the fire, his betousled head wild and bare, his link-mail yet befouled with battle, Walkyn strode, and hurling his torch upon the grass, crushed it out 'neath his heel. Then came he to the fire and stood there, arms crossed, frowning down at the flame.

"Greeting to thee, Waldron of Brand!"

Swift turned Walkyn, his gloomy scowl relaxed at Beltane's voice, and stooping, he took and kissed my Beltane's hand.

"Whence come ye, Walkyn?"

"From going to and fro among the dead, seeking Pertolepe, master. Ha! they do lie thick yonder, five hundred and twenty and three I counted of Bloody Pertolepe's following. And in the woods do lie certain others, that I, with divers of our company, pursued and cut off."

"And what of their wounded?"

"I saw none, master — nor have I seen Pertolepe. I have viewed all the slain, but Pertolepe is not there, yet have I smitten and slain three Pertolepes this day — hawks, see you, in eagle's feathers! So is my work yet to do, and I grieve still for Pertolepe's head."

"Sit ye down, Walkyn, here with me beside the fire."

Forthwith Walkyn obeyed and stretching himself on the grass fell to toying with the haft of his axe and scowling at the fire again.

"This was, methinks, thy father's tower and demesne of Brand, Walkyn?"

"Aye, lord, here was I born — yon ruined walls did hear my father's groans — the screams of my mother and sister amid the flame. And Red Pertolepe was there, and Gui of Allerdale and Roger and young Gilles of Brandonmere — all were there with six other noble knights; but these six we slew long since, my brother and I. All these were here that day — and Sir Pertolepe — laughed — full loud, 'twas told me. So 'twere just he should have died here to-day, methinks? 'Twas for this I lured him hither — and he liveth yet!"

"But God is a just God, Walkyn! Now therefore leave him to God henceforth —!"

"To God!" cried Walkyn, his eyes wild, his hands tight-clenched, "to God! — ha! master, ye left him to God on a time and because of thee, I — I that had my dagger at his rogue's throat — I, yearning to slay him, did but mark him i' the brow — aye, forsooth, we left him to God and lo! to-day he burneth, he slayeth and hangeth as was ever his wont —"

"God's time is not ours, Walkyn, but for the evil wrought by Sir Pertolepe, Sir Pertolepe needs must answer when God so wills. So leave him to the vengeance of God — lest the fire of thy vengeance consume thee quite. Thou art strong, and few may cope with thee in fight, yet hath vengeance fettered and made thee bond-slave. Forego thy vengeance then, and be free, good comrade."

"Nay master, an I so do, what is left me?"

"The love of thy fellows, Walkyn. Thou art, forsooth, a man, so do I love thee, and perchance within a new Pentavalon thou may'st come to new fortune and honour. Thou shalt hold again thy father's lands —"

"To what end, lord? As ye do know, my wife and child do lie in nameless grave, done to cruel death by dogs of Pertolepe: my brother rotted in a noose — set there by Pertolepe. So am I a lonely man henceforth; one thing only seek I of life, master."

"And that, Walkyn?"

"The head of Bloody Pertolepe!" So saying, Walkyn rose, and stood scowling down at the fire again, whose glow shone ominous and red upon the broad blade of the mighty axe that lay on the grass at his feet.

Now of a sudden forth from the shadows, swift and silent on his long legs came crooked Ulf, and stooping, would have lifted the weapon, but in that moment Walkyn snarled, and set his foot upon it.

"Off!" he growled, "touch not mine axe, thou vile mannikin — lest I tread on thee!"

But scarce were the words spoken, than, with great back low-crouched, Ulf sprang, and whirling mighty Walkyn aloft, mailed feet on high, held him writhing above the fire: then, swinging about, hurled him, rolling over and over, upon the ling; so lay Walkyn awhile propped on an elbow, staring on Ulf with wide eyes and mouth agape what time, strung for sudden action, Beltane sat cross-legged upon the green, looking from one to the other.

"Mannikin?" roared Ulf, great hands opening and shutting, "unworthy to touch axe of thine, thou pestilent beast! Dare ye so say to one gently born, base fellow? Now will I break thee thine accursed axe — and thee thereafter, an ye will!"

So saying, Ulf the Mighty caught up the axe and wheeling it full-armed, smote and buried it in a young tree close by — wrenched it free and smote again. And lo! with prodigious crack and rending of fibres the tall tree swayed, crashing to earth. Now while Ulf yet stood to stare amazed upon this wondrous axe, upon its sharp-glittering, flawless edge, Walkyn had risen, dagger in hand; but even as he crouched to spring, a voice spake — a gentle voice but commanding; and in the fire-glow stood the white Abbess, tall and gracious, the silver crucifix agleam upon her bosom.

"Children!" she sighed; and looking from scowling Walkyn to frowning Ulf she reached a slim hand to each. "O children," said she, "lay by your steel and give to me your hands!"

Fumbling and awkward, Walkyn sheathed his dagger while Ulf laid the mighty axe upon the grass very tenderly, as it had been a sleeping child; so came they both, shame-faced, unto the lady Abbess and gave her each a hand. Holding them thus she looked with sad, sweet eyes from one grim face to the other, and drew them nearer the fire.

"Walkyn, son of God," said she, "behold here Ulf whose valiant heart and mighty strength have been our salvation! Ulf, child of Heaven, whom God hath made so mighty, behold here brave Walkyn who did protect the weak and helpless and fighteth for the right! Come then, as ye are children of God, go ye in brotherly love together henceforth, and may heaven bless ye, valiant sons!"

Thus saying, she set their hands one in another, and these hands gripped and held.

Quoth Ulf, sighing:

"Forsooth, I did but mean to try the balance of thine axe, Walkyn. And truly it is a mighty weapon and a peerless — one that even my strength cannot break!"

Quoth Walkyn, grim-smiling:

"There is in this world no axe like unto it save one that was my brother's — and shall be thine henceforth, Ulf the Strong. Come now, and I will give it unto thee." Then bent they reverently before the Abbess, saluted Beltane and, side by side, strode away together.

"Would all feuds might so end, sweet son," sighed the Abbess, her wistful eyes down-bent upon the fire.

"Would there were more sweet souls abroad to teach men reason!" quoth Beltane.

"Why sit you here, my son, wakeful and alone and the hour so late?"

"For that sleep doth fly my wooing, holy mother."

"Then fain would I share thy vigil awhile."

Forthwith Beltane brought her a stool, rough and rudely fashioned, and while she sat, he lay beside her in the firelight; and thus, despite her hood and wimple, he saw her face was of a calm and noble beauty, smooth and unwrinkled despite the silver hair that peeped forth of her loosened hood. A while they sat thus, nothing speaking, he viewing her, she gazing ever on the fire; at last:

"Thou'rt young, messire," she said wistfully, "yet in

thy life hath been much of strife, I've heard. Thou hast known much of hardship, my son, and sorrow methinks?"

"So do I live for that fair day when Peace shall come again, noble lady."

"Full oft have I heard tell of thee, my son, strange tales and marvellous. Some do liken thee to a demon joying in slaughter, and some to an archangel bearing the sword of God."

"And how think you, reverend mother?"

"I think of thee as a man, my son. I have heard thee named 'outlaw' and 'lawless ravener,' and some do call thee 'Beltane the Smith.' Now wherefore smith?"

"For that smith was I bred, lady."

"But thou'rt of noble blood, lord Beltane."

"Yet knew I nought of it until I was man grown."

"Thy youth — they tell me — hath been very lonely, my son — and desolate."

"Not desolate, for in my loneliness was the hermit Ambrose who taught me many things and most of all, how to love him. So lived I in the greenwood, happy and content, until on a day this saintly Ambrose told me a woeful tale — so did I know this humble hermit for the noble Duke, my father."

"Thy father! The Duke! A hermit! Told he of — all his sorrows, my son?"

"All, reverend mother, and thereafter bade me beware the falsity of women."

The pale cheek of the Abbess grew suddenly suffused, the slim hand clenched rigid upon the crucifix at her bosom, but she stirred not nor lifted her sad gaze from the fire.

"Liveth thy father yet, my son?"

"'Tis so I pray God, lady."

"And — thy mother?"

"'Tis so I've heard."

"Pray you not for — for her also?"

"I never knew my mother, lady."

"Alas! poor lonely mother! So doth she need thy

Has Speech With the Abbess 441

prayers the more. Ah, think you she hath not perchance yearned with breaking heart for her babe? To have kissed him into rosy slumber! To have cherished his boyish hurts and sorrows! To have gloried in his youthful might and manhood! O sure there is no sorrow like the loneliness of desolate motherhood. Would'st seek this unknown mother, lord Beltane?"

"Truly there be times when I do yearn to find her — and there be times when I do fear —"

"Fear, my lord?"

"Holy mother, I learned of her first as one false to her vows, light-minded and fickle from her youth —"

"O hath there been none to speak thee good of her — in all these years?"

"There was Jolette, that folk did call a witch, and there is Sir Benedict that doth paint her pure and noble as I would have her. Yet would I know for myself, fain would I be sure ere we do meet, if she is but the woman who bore me, or the proud and noble mother I fain would love.

"Could'st not love her first and judge her after, my son? Could not her very motherhood plead her cause with thee? Must she be weighed in the balance ere thou yield her a son's respect and love? So many weary years — 'tis something hard, methinks! Nay, heed me not, my lord — seek out thy mother, unbeknown — prove for thyself her worthiness or falsity, prove for thyself her honour or her shame — 'tis but just, aye, 'tis but just in very truth. But I, beholding things with woman's eyes, know only that a mother's love shrinketh not for any sin, but reacheth down through shame and evil with sheltering arms outstretched — a holy thing, fearless of sin, more lasting than shame and stronger than death itself."

So saying, the lady Abbess rose and turned to look up at the lights that burned within the tower.

"'Tis late, my lord," she sighed, "get thee now to thy rest, for I must begone to my duty till the dawn. There be many sick, and good Sir Bertrand lieth very nigh to death — he ne'er will see another dawn, methinks, so needs must I away. Good night, sweet son, and in thy prayers forget not thy — thy most unhappy mother!"

Then she lifted her hand and blessed him, and, ere he rose up from his knees she set that white hand upon his bowed head and touched his yellow hair — a light touch, furtive and shy, but a touch that was like to a caress.

Thereafter, Beltane, coming into his hut of woven wattle, rolled himself in his weather-worn mantle and presently fell to slumber.

CHAPTER LIX

TELLETH HOW SIR BENEDICT WENT A-FISHING

NEXT day Sir Bertrand died of his hurts, so they buried him beside young Sir John of Griswold and sturdy old Hubert of Erdington and a hundred and twenty and five others of their company who had fallen in that desperate affray; therefore tarried they a while what time their sick and wounded grew towards health and strength by reason of the skill and tender care of the lady Abbess and her nuns.

Now on the afternoon of this day, Sir Benedict being sick a-bed of his wound, Beltane sat in council among the oldest and wisest of the knights, and presently summoned Walkyn and Ulf, Roger and Jenkyn o' the Ford, speaking them on this wise:

"Good comrades, list ye now! These noble knights and I have hither summoned ye for that ye are of good and approved courage and moreover foresters born and cunning in wood-lore. As ye do know, 'tis our intent to march for Belsaye so soon as our wounded be fit. But first must we be 'ware if our road be open or no. Therefore, Walkyn, do ye and Ulf take ten men and haste to Winisfarne and the forest-road that runneth north and south: be ye wary of surprise and heedful of all things. You, Roger and Jenkyn, with other ten, shall seek the road that runneth east and west; marching due south you shall come to the northern road where ye shall wait two hours (but no longer) for Walkyn. Ye are woodsmen! Heed ye the brush and lower branches of the trees if any be broken, mark well the track in dusty places and seek ye the print of feet in marshy places, learn all ye may from whomsoever ye may and haste ye hot-foot back with tidings good or ill. Is it understood?"

"Aye, lord!" quoth the four.

"And look'ee master," said Jenkyn, "there be my comrade Orson the Tall, look'ee. His hurt is nigh healed and to go wi' us shall be his cure — now, look'ee lord, shall he go wi' us?"

"Nay, Roger shall answer thee this, Jenkyn. So now begone and God speed ye, good comrades all!" Hereupon the mighty four made their obeisance and hasted away, rejoicing.

Now Sir Benedict's hurt had proved an evil one and deep, wherefore the Abbess, in accent soft and tender, had, incontinent, ordered him to bed, and there, within the silken tent that had been Sir Pertolepe's, Beltane oft sat by, the while she, with slim and dexterous fingers, washed and anointed and bound the ugly wound: many times came she, soft-treading, gentle and gracious ever; and at such times Beltane noticed that full often he would find her deep, sad gaze bent upon him; he noticed also that though her voice was low and gentle, yet she spake ever as one 'customed to obedience. Thus it was, that Sir Benedict being ordered to his couch, obeyed the soft-spoke command, but being kept there all day, grumbled (albeit to Beltane): being kept there the second day he fell to muttered oaths and cursing (albeit to Beltane): but at sunset he became unruly, in so much that he ventured to remonstrate with the lady Abbess (albeit humbly), whereon she smiled, and bidding Beltane reach her cup and spoon, forthwith mixed a decoction and dosed Sir Benedict that he fell asleep and slumbered amain.

Thus, during this time, Beltane saw and talked much with the lady Abbess: oft went he to watch her among the sick and to aid her when he might; saw how fierce faces softened when she bent to touch fevered brow or speak them cheerily with smiling lip despite the deep and haunting sadness of her eyes; saw how eagerly rough hands were stretched forth to furtive touch her white habit as she passed; heard harsh voices grow sudden soft and all unfamiliar — voices that broke in murmurous gratitude. All this saw and heard he and failed not, morn and eve, to kneel him at her feet to hear her bless him and to feel that soft, shy touch among his hair.

So passed two days, but neither Roger, nor Walkyn, nor Ulf, nor indeed any of the twenty chosen men had yet returned or sent word or sign, wherefore Beltane began to wax moody and anxious. Thus it was that upon a sunny afternoon he wandered beside a little rivulet, bowered in alder and willow: here, a merry brook that prattled over pebbly bed and laughed among stones and mossy boulders, there a drowsy stream that, widening to dreamy pool, stayed its haste to woo down-bending branches with soft, kissing noises.

Now as Beltane walked beside the stream, head a-droop and very thoughtful, he paused of a sudden to behold one richly dight in gambeson of fair-wrought leather artificially quilted and pinked, who sat ensconced within this greeny bower, his back to a tree, one bandaged arm slung about his neck and in the other hand a long hazel-branch trimmed with infinite care, whereunto a line was tied.

" Sir Benedict! " cried Beltane, " methought thee asleep: what do ye so far from camp and bed? "

" I fish, lad, I fish — I ply a tentative angle. Nay — save thy breath, I have caught me nothing yet, save thoughts. Thoughts do flock a many, but as to fish — they do but sniff my bait and flirt it with their wanton tails, plague take 'em! But what o' fish? 'Tis not for fish alone that man fisheth, for fishing begetteth thought and thought, dreams — and to dream is oft-times sweet!"

" But — Benedict, what of the Abbess? "

" The Abbess? Ha, the Abbess, Beltane! Sweet soul, she sleepeth. At noon each day needs must she sleep since even she is mortal and mortals must sleep now and then. The Abbess? Come sit ye, lad, what time I tickle the noses of these pestilent fish. Sit ye here beside me and tell me, how think ye of this noble and most sweet lady?"

"That, for thy truancy, she will incontinent mix thee another sleeping draught, Benedict."

"Ha — then I'll never drink it!" quoth Sir Benedict, settling his shoulder against Beltane and frowning at his line. "Am I a babe, forsooth, to be dosed to slumber? Ha, by the foul fiend his black dam, ne'er will I drink it, lad!"

"Then will she smile on thee, sad-eyed, and set it to thy lip, and woo thee soft-voiced, so shalt thou swallow it every drop —"

"Not so — dear blood of all the saints! Must I be mewed up within an accursed bed on such a day and all by reason of a small axe-stroke? Malediction, no!"

"She is wondrous gentle with the sick, Benedict —"

"She is a very woman, Beltane, and therefore gentle, a noble lady sweet of soul and body! To die for such were joyful privilege, methinks, aye, verily!" and Sir Benedict, forgetful of his line, drooped his head and sighed.

"And thou didst know her well — long years agone, Benedict?"

"Aye, long — years — agone!"

"Very well, Benedict?"

"Very well."

"She was 'Yolande' then, Benedict?"

"Aye," quoth Sir Benedict, lifting his head with a start and looking at Beltane askance, "and to-day she is the lady Abbess Veronica!"

"That shall surely dose thee again and —"

"Ha! bones and body o' me, not so! For here sit I, and here angle I, fish or no fish, thunder o' God, yes! Aye, verily, here will I sit till I have caught me a fish, or weary and go o' my own free will — by Beelzebub I vow, by Bel and the Dragon I swear it! And furthermore —"

Sir Benedict paused, tilted his head and glancing up, beheld the lady Abbess within a yard of them. Gracious she stood in her long white habit and shook her stately head in grave rebuke, but beholding his abashed look and how the rod sagged in his loosened hold, her lips parted of a sudden and her teeth gleamed in a smile wondrous young and pleasant to see.

"O Benedict!" said she, "O child most disobedient! O sir knight! Is this thy chivalry, noble lord — to steal away for that a poor soul must needs sleep, being, alas! so very mortal?"

"Forsooth and indeed, dear my lady," quoth Sir Benedict, fumbling with his angle, " the sun did woo me forth — and the wind, see you — the wind —"

"Nay, I see it not, my lord, but I did hear something of thy fearsome, great oaths as I came hither."

"Oaths, lady?" said Sir Benedict, fingering his chin. "Forsooth and did I so? Mayhap 'twas by reason that the fish, see you, the pestilent fish — Ha! Saint Benedict! I have a bite!" Up sprang Sir Benedict, quite forgetting his wounded arm, capering lightly to and fro, now in the water, now out, with prodigious stir and splash and swearing oaths galore, until, his pallid cheek flushed and bright eyes a-dance, he had won the fish into the shallows and thence landed it right skilfully, where it thrashed and leapt, flashing in the sun.

"Ha, Yolande!" he cried, "in the golden days thou wert ever fond of a goodly trout fresh caught and broiled upon a fire of —"

"Benedict!" cried the Abbess, and, all forgetful of his hurt, caught him by his wounded arm, "O Sir Benedict!" Now, man of iron though he seemed, Sir Benedict must needs start and flinch beneath her hold and grow livid by reason of the sharp pain of it; whereat she loosed him of a sudden and fell away, white hands tight clasped together.

"Ah Benedict! — I have hurt thee — again!" she panted.

"Not so, 'twas when I landed the fish — my lady Abbess!" Now at this she turned away and standing thus awhile very silent, presently raised her hand, whereat came two of her gentle nuns.

"Dear my daughters," said she, "take now Sir Benedict unto the camp and look to his hurt, anoint it as ye have seen me do. Go!"

Nothing speaking, Sir Benedict bowed him humbly to the stately Abbess and went away between the two white-robed sisters and so was gone.

Slowly the Abbess turned to Beltane who had risen and was regarding her with a new and strange intensity, and meeting that look, her own glance wavered, sank, and she stood awhile gazing down into the murmurous waters; and as she stood thus, aware of his deep-searching eyes, into her pale cheek crept a flush that deepened and ever deepened.

"My lord," said she, very low and placid-seeming, "why dost thou look on me so?"

And for all her stately calm, her hand, which had clenched itself upon the silver crucifix, was woefully a-tremble. "What — is it — my lord Beltane?"

"A thought, noble lady."

"What is thy thought?"

"Lady, 'tis this — that, an I might find a mother such as thee, then would I pay her homage on my knees, and love her and honour her for what I do know her, praying God to make me worthy —!" So saying, he came a step towards her, faltered, stopped, and reached out appealing hands to her.

From red to white and from white to red again the colour flushed in cheek and brow while the Abbess hearkened to his words; then she looked on him with proud head uplifted and in her eyes a great and wondrous light, quick and passionate her slim hands came out to meet his —

A sudden clamour in the air! A clash of arms! A running of swift feet and Walkyn sprang betwixt them, his face grimed with dust and sweat, his armour gone, his great axe all bloody in his hand:

How Sir Benedict Went a-Fishing

"Master!" he cried, "in Winisfarne lieth Pertolepe with over a thousand of his company, I judge — and in the woods 'twixt here and Winisfarne is Rollo of Revelsthorne marching on us through the woods with full five thousand of Ivo's picked levies, new come from Barham Broom!"

CHAPTER LX

TELLETH HOW THEY MARCHED FROM THE VALLEY OF BRAND

WITHIN the camp was prodigious stir, a fanfare of trumpets and hoarse commands, where archers and pikemen, knights and men-at-arms were mustering; but nowhere was hurry or confusion, wherefore Beltane's heart rejoiced and he smiled glad-eyed as he came where, before Sir Benedict and the assembled council, stood Roger and Ulf with fifteen of their twenty men.

"Walkyn," said Sir Benedict, what time his esquire strapped and buckled him into his bright armour, "whereabouts do they hold their march?"

"Scarce twenty miles from here due west, lord."

"Ha, and they come through the forest, ye say?" questioned Sir Brian, "so shall they move more slowly, methinks."

"Why see you, messire," said Walkyn, "they march by way of Felindre that was once a fair town, and from Felindre is a road that leadeth through the wild unto this valley of Brand."

"So have we, I judge, 'twixt six and seven hours," quoth Hacon of Trant.

"Less, Hacon, less!" said Sir Benedict, beginning to stride up and down in his clanking armour, "Sir Rollo ever rideth with busy spur, and he will doubtless push on amain nor spare his men that he may take us unprepared. Put it at five hours, Hacon, mayhap less!"

"'Tis so I pray!" said Beltane, glancing towards the glowing west, " and in two hours it will be dark, my lords! Walkyn, thy company doth lack for five, meseemeth?"

March from the Valley of Brand 451

"Aye, master — for five; two fell in Winisfarne where I lay in bonds; other three were slain in the pursuit."

"Saw Sir Rollo aught of thee?"

"Nay, lord, we lay well hid."

"'Tis very well. Are they many?"

"Of horsemen I counted full three thousand, master."

"And I, lord," quoth Ulf, "did reckon over two thousand foot."

"'Tis a fairish company!" said Sir Brian.

"And I do lack my sword-arm!" sighed Sir Benedict, "but my left hath served me well ere now."

"And Sir Pertolepe lieth yet in Winisfarne!" said Beltane thoughtfully.

"Aye," nodded Sir Benedict, "and shall march south to cut off our retreat if haply any of us escape Sir Rollo's onfall."

"So should we strike camp and march forthright," said Sir Brian.

"March — aye, but whither?" questioned Sir Hacon. "We are threatened on two fronts and for the rest, we have the trackless wilderness! Whither would'st march, Brian?"

"South to Belsaye," answered Sir Benedict. "South through the wild until we strike the western road by Thornaby. I with certain others will form a rear-guard and hold Sir Rollo in play what time our main body presses on at speed."

"Ha!" quoth Sir Hacon, "and what of Red Pertolepe? Truly our case is desperate methinks, old comrade!"

"Why, 'tis not the first time we have out-faced desperate odds, Hacon!"

"Aye, verily, Benedict — thy cool head and cunning strategy have saved us from dungeon and death a score of times, but then were we a chosen company, swift at onfall or retreat, well mounted and equipped — to-night we go hampered with our wounded and these lady nuns. So is our case desperate, Benedict, and needeth desperate remedy —"

"And that, methinks, I've found, messire!" quoth Beltane, and rising up he looked upon them all, his eye bright with sudden purpose. "Hark ye, my lords! Great and valiant knights do I know ye, one and all — wise in experience of battle and much versed in warlike stratagem beyond my understanding; but this is the wild-wood where only wood-craft shall advantage us. Within these wilds your tactics shall avail nothing nor all your trampling chivalry — here must be foresters that may go silent and unseen amid the leaves, 'neath whose trained feet no twig shall snap, who smite unseen from brush and thicket and being wise in wood-craft thus make the forest their ally. And, lords, I am a forester; all my days the greenwood hath been my home, and in my loneliness I made the trees my friends. So, I pray you, let me with three hundred chosen foresters keep our rear to-night, and this night the forest shall fight for us and Sir Rollo rue the hour he dared adventure him within the green. Messires, how say you?"

"Why my lord, 'tis very well!" sighed Sir Benedict, glancing down at his wounded arm, "I, for one, do agree right heartily."

"And I!" nodded Sir Brian.

"And I also!" quoth Sir Hacon, "though 'tis a far cry to Belsaye and I love not to be pent within walls, and with Red Pertolepe threatening our flank 'tis a very parlous case, methinks."

"And thou art ever at thy best where danger is, Hacon," said Sir Benedict, "so will I give thee charge of our van-ward!" Now hereupon Sir Hacon's gloom vanished and rising up, he smiled and forthwith did on his great war-helm.

"Then it is agreed!" said Beltane and beckoned to Roger and Walkyn; quoth he:

"Good friends, go now and choose three hundred trusty fellows, skilled foresters all; look that each doth bear flint and steel for by yon clouds I judge 'twill be a dark night. Let every fire within the camp be quenched and the ground well cooled with water, that by the feel of it none may know how long we have removed — see you to this, Ulf."

Now when the mighty three were gone about the business, their fifteen lusty fellows at their heels, Beltane turned and pointed westward, and lo! the sun was set.

"Messires," said he, "you were wise, methinks, to mount and away ere the night fall. To-night, since the moon is hid, 'twill be very dark amid the trees, therefore let Orson guide you — he is forest-bred and well knoweth the way to Thornaby. Heaven prosper you, for in your valiant keeping is the safety of — of our noble lady Abbess — and her ladies. So mount, my lords, press on with what speed ye may, and God aid us this night each and every — fare ye well!"

Presently the trumpets sounded and forthwith armour was buckled on, horses saddled, while everywhere was stir and bustle of departure, what time, within his osier hut, my Beltane was busily doing on his armour, and, being in haste, making slow business of it; thrice he essayed to buckle a certain strap and thrice it escaped him, when lo! came a slim white hand to do it for him, and turning, he beheld the lady Abbess. And in her eyes was yet that soft and radiant look, but nought said she until Beltane stood armed from head to heel, until she had girt the great sword about him; then she set her hands upon his shoulders:

"Beltane," said she soft-voiced, "thou didst yearn for thy mother, so is she come to thee at last, dear son!" So saying, she drew him down into her embrace. "O Beltane, son of mine, long, long have I waited — aye, bitter, weary years, and oft-times in my sorrow I have dreamed of this hour — the arms about thee are thy mother's arms!"

Now fell Beltane upon his knees and caught those white and gentle hands and kissed them; quoth he:

"Mother — O dear my mother, ne'er did I know how deep had been my need of thee until now. And yet, all unknowing, I have yearned for thee; in my youth I did

love all sweet and gentle things in thy stead — the trees,
the tender flowers, the murmurous brooks — these did I
love in place of thee for that mine heart did yearn and
hunger for a mother's tender love —" Here needs must
she stoop, all soft whispers and tender mother-cries, to
kiss him oft, to lay her cheek upon his golden head and
murmur over him.

"And thou wilt love thy mother, Beltane — thou wilt
love thy unknown mother — now and always, for that she
is thy mother?"

"I will love her and honour her now and always, for
that my mother is a sweet and noble woman!"

"And thou didst need me, Beltane, in thy lonely child-
hood thou didst need me, and I — O God pity me — I
was far from thee! But, dear my son, because I could not
cherish thee within these arms I strove to love and cherish
all motherless children for thy dear sake and to grieve
for all sorrowing mothers. So builded I the nunnery at
Winisfarne and there sought to bring solace and comfort
to desolate hearts because my heart was so desolate for
thee, my babe, my Beltane. And I have prayed unceas-
ing unto God, and He, in His infinite mercy, hath given
thee to my arms again —"

A trumpet brayed harsh and loud near by, whereat
those tender mother-arms drew him closer yet within their
sheltering embrace.

"Sweet son," she sighed, "methinks death is very near
each one of us to-night — but I have held thee to my heart,
have felt thy kisses and heard thy loving words — now
if death come how shall it avail 'gainst such love as ours?
Sir Benedict telleth me thou hast chosen the post of
danger — 'tis so I would have it, dear my son, and thy
proud mother's prayers go with thee — God keep thee —
O God keep thee, my Beltane — ah, there sounds again the
clarion bidding me from thee! Kiss now thy mother fare-
well, for alas! I must be gone!"

So presently Beltane brought the Abbess where stood
Sir Benedict with an easy-paced jennet for her use and

his company formed up in column beyond the camp. Then Beltane lifted the lady Abbess to the saddle and with her hand yet clasped in his, reached the other to Sir Benedict.

"My lord of Bourne," said he, "dear my friend, to thy care I give this lady Abbess, Duchess of Pentavalon — my well-beloved and noble mother. O Benedict, no prouder son than I in all the world, methinks — nor one so humble! God send we meet again anon, but now — fare ye well!" Saying the which, Beltane caught his mother's hand to his lips, and turning him suddenly about, hasted to Roger and Walkyn and the chosen three hundred. And in a while, the nuns and wounded in their midst, Sir Benedict's steel-clad column moved forward up the slope. First rode Sir Hacon and his knights in the van and last Sir Benedict with his grim men-at-arms to form a rear-ward, while archers and pikemen marched upon their flanks. With ring of steel, with jingle of stirrup and bridle-chain they swung away up the slope and plunging into the gloom of the forest were gone; only Sir Benedict paused to turn in his saddle and lift unwounded arm in salutation ere he too vanished into the shadows of the wild-wood. Awhile stood Beltane before the three hundred, his head bowed as one in meditation until the sound of voices, the ring and clash of their companions' going was died away; then looked he at the cloudy sky already deepening to evening, and round about upon the encircling woods.

"The wind is from the south, methinks!" said he.

"Aye, master," nodded Walkyn.

"South-westerly!" quoth Roger.

Now came Beltane and looked upon his company, tall, lusty fellows they, whose bold, sun-tanned faces proclaimed them free men of the forest-lands; and beholding their hardy look Beltane's eye brightened.

"Comrades," quoth he, "we be foresters all, and the wild-wood our home and playground. But yonder from the west do march full five thousand of Duke Ivo's knights and soldiery men, they, of courts, of town and city, so now will we teach them 'tis an ill thing to adventure them 'gainst trained foresters within the green. List now — and mark me well, for, an our plan do fail, there shall few of us live to see to-morrow's sun."

Then Beltane spake them plain and to the point, insomuch that when all was said, these hardy foresters stood mute awhile, desperate fellows though they were; then laughed they fierce and loud, and flourished sword and bow-stave and so fell to clamourous talk.

Now did Beltane divide the three hundred into five companies of sixty; over the first company he set Walkyn, over the second, Roger, over the third, Ulf, over the fourth Jenkyn o' the Ford. Then spake he on this wise:

"Walkyn, take now these sixty good fellows and march you north-westerly yonder across the valley; let your men lie well hid a bow-shot within the forest, but do you stay upon the verge of the forest and watch for the coming of our foes. And when they be come, 'tis sure they will plant outposts and sentinels within the green, so be ye wary to smite outpost and sentinel suddenly and that none may hear within the camp nor take alarm; when 'tis done, cry you thrice like unto a curlew that we may know. Are all things understood?"

"Aye, lord!" they cried, one and all.

"Why then, be ye cautious each and every, for, an our foes do take alarm, so shall it be our death. March, Walkyn — away!"

Forthwith Walkyn lifted his axe and strode off up the slope until he and his sixty men had vanished quite into the glooming woods to the north-west.

"Jenkyn, didst hear my commands to Walkyn, so shalt thou do also — your post doth lie to the east, yonder."

"Aye, master, and look'ee now — my signal shall be three owl-hoots, master, look'ee!"

So saying, Jenkyn turned, his sixty at his heels, and

swung away until they were lost to sight in the woods to the east.

"Ulf the Strong, thy post doth lie south-westerly, and Roger's south-easterly; thus I, lying south, shall have ye on my left and right: go get ye to your places, watch ye, and wait in patience for the signals, and when time for action cometh, be swift and sure."

Away marched Roger and Ulf with their companies, and presently were gone, and there remained within the little valley only Beltane and his sixty men. Awhile he stood to look to the north and east and west but nought saw he save the dense gloom of forest growing dark and ever darker with evening. Then of a sudden turned he, and summoning his company, strode away into the forest to the south.

Thus, as night fell, the valley of Brand lay deserted quite, and no sound brake the pervading quiet save the wind that moaned feebly through those dark and solitary woods wherein Death lay hid, so very silent — so very patient, but Death in grim and awful shape.

CHAPTER LXI

HOW THE FOREST FOUGHT FOR THEM

A HUM upon the night-wind, lost, ever and anon, in wailing gust, yet a hum that never ceased; a sound that grew and grew, loud and·ever more loud until it seemed to fill the very night, a dreadful sound, ominous and threatening, a sound to shake the boldest heart — the ring and tramp of an armed, oncoming multitude.

Now, lying amid the leaves and fern with Cnut and the small man Prat beside him, Beltane presently espied certain figures moving in the valley below, stealthy figures that were men of Sir Rollo's van-ward. Soft-creeping they approached the deserted camp, soft-creeping they entered it; and suddenly their trumpets brayed loud and long, and, dying away, gave place to the ring and trampling thunder of the advancing host.

On they came, knights and men-at-arms, rank upon rank, company by company, until the valley seemed full of the dull gleam of their armour and the air rang loud with clash and jingle and the trample of countless hooves. Yet still they came, horsemen and foot-men, and ever the sound of them waxed upon the air, a harsh, confused din — and ever, from the glooming woods above, Death stared down on them.

And now the trumpets blew amain, lights flickered and flared, as one by one, fires were lighted whose red glow flashed back from many a helm and shield and breastplate, from broad gisarm and twinkling lance-point, what time, above the confused hum, above stamping hooves and clashing armour, voices shouted hoarse commands.

So, little by little, from chaos order was wrought, pack-horse and charger were led away to be watered and picketed and gleaming figures sank wearily about the many camp-fires where food was already preparing. In a while, from the stir of the camp, bright with its many watch-fires, divers small groups of men were detached, and, pike and gisarm on shoulder, began to mount toward the forest at varying points.

Hereupon, Beltane reached out in the dark and touched the small man Prat the Archer. Quoth he:

"Hither come their outposts, go now and bring up my company,— and bid them come silently!"

Forthwith Prat sank down among the fern and was gone, while Beltane watched, keen-eyed, where four men of Sir Rollo's outposts climbed the slope hard by. And one was singing, and one was cursing, and two were quarrelling, and all four, Beltane judged, were men aweary with long marching. Thus, singing, cursing, quarrelling, came they to keep their ward within these dark and silent woods, crashing through the underbrush careless of their going and all unheeding the sombre, stealthy forms that rose up so silently behind them and before from brush and brake and thicket, creeping figures that moved only when the night-wind moaned in the shivering leaves.

Beltane's dagger was out and he rose up from the fern, crouched and strung for action — but from the gloom near by rose a sudden, strange flurry amid the leaves, a whimpering sound evil to hear and swiftly ended, a groan, a cry choked to strangling gasp and thereafter — silence, save for the fitful wailing of the wind — a long, breathless pause; then, high and clear rose the cry of an owl thrice repeated, and presently small Prat was beside him in the fern again.

"Lord," said he softly, albeit panting a little, "these men were fools! We do but wait our comrades' signals now." And he fell to cleansing his dagger-blade carefully with a handful of bracken.

"Ha — list ye!" whispered Cnut, "there sounds Ulf's warning, methinks!"

And from the gloom on their left a frog croaked hoarsely.

A hundred watch-fires blazed in the valley below and around each fire armour glittered; little by little the great camp grew to silence and rest until nought was heard but the stamp and snorting of the many horses and the cries of the sentinels below. But ever dagger in hand Beltane strained eyes and ears northward across the valley, while big Cnut bit his nails and wriggled beside him in the bracken, and small Prat softly snapped his fingers; so waited they with ears on the stretch and eyes that glared ever to the north.

At last, faint and far across the valley, rose the doleful cry of a curlew thrice repeated, the which was answered from the east by the hooting of an owl, which again was caught up like an echo, and repeated thrice upon their right.

Then Beltane sheathed his dagger.

"Look," said he, "Cnut — Prat, look north and tell me what ye see!"

"Fire, my lord!" quoth Prat. "Ha! it burneth well — see, see how it spreads!"

"And there again — in the east," said Cnut, "Oho! Jenkyn is busy — look, master!"

"Aye, and Roger too!" said Beltane, grim-lipped, "our ring of fire is well-nigh complete — it lacketh but for us and Ulf — to work, then!"

Came the sound of flint meeting steel — a sound that spread along the ranks that lay unseen beyond Prat and Cnut. And behold — a spark! a glow! a little flame that died down, leapt up, caught upon dry grass and bracken, seized upon crackling twigs, flared up high and ever fiercer — a devouring flame, hungry and yellow-tongued that licked along the earth — a vengeful flame, pitiless and unrelenting — a host of fiery demons that leapt and danced with crackling laughter changing little by little to an angry roar that was the voice of awful doom.

How the Forest Fought for Them

Now of a sudden above the hiss of flame, from the valley of Brand a cry went up — a shout — a roar of fear and amaze and thereafter rose a wild clamour; a babel inarticulate, split, ever and anon, by frantic trumpet-blast. But ever the dreadful hubbub waxed and grew, shrieks and cries and the screaming of maddened horses with the awful, rolling thunder of their fierce-galloping hooves!

Within that valley of doom Death was abroad already, Death in many dire shapes. Proud knights, doughty archers and men-at-arms who had fronted death unmoved on many a stricken field, wept aloud and crouched upon their knees and screamed — but not so loud as those wild and maddened horses, that, bursting all bonds asunder, reared and leapt with lashing hooves, and, choked with rolling smoke-clouds, blinded by flame, plunged headlong through and over the doomed camp, wave upon wave of wild-flung heads and tossing manes. On they came, with nought to let or stay them, their wild hooves trampling down hut of osier and silken tent, spurning the trembling earth and filling the air with flying clods; and wheresoever they galloped there was flame to meet them, so swerved they, screaming their terror and fled round and round within the valley. So raced they blindly to and fro and back and forth, trampling down, maiming and mangling 'neath reddened, cruel hooves all and every that chanced to lie athwart their wild career: on and ever on they galloped until sobbing, panting, they fell, to be crushed 'neath the thundering hooves behind.

Within the little valley of Brand Death was rife in many and awful shapes that no eye might see, for the many watch-fires were scattered and trampled out; but up from that pit of doom rose shrieks and cries and many hateful sounds — sounds to pierce the brain and ring there everlastingly.

Thus Beltane, marching swift to the south at the head of his three hundred foresters, heard nought of their joyful acclaim, heeded not their triumph, saw nought of watchful Roger's troubled glances, but went with head bowed low, with pallid cheek and eyes wide-staring, for he saw yet again the fierce leap of those merciless flames and in his ears rang the screams and cries of Sir Rollo's proud chivalry.

CHAPTER LXII

HOW THEY CAME TO BELSAYE FOR THE THIRD TIME

THE sun was high as they came to the western road that led to the ford at Thornaby, but upon the edge of the forest Beltane stopped of a sudden to stare up at an adjacent tree.

"What is't, master?" questioned Roger, halting beside him.

"An arrow — and new-shot by the look of it!" said Beltane, gloomily.

"Aye master, and it hath travelled far — see, it hath scarce pierced the bark!"

"'Twas shot from the brush yonder, methinks," said Beltane, pointing to the dense underwood that skirted the opposite side of the dusty highway. "Reach me it down, Roger!" so saying Beltane stooped and hove Roger aloft until he could grasp and draw the arrow from the tree.

"Here is no woodsman's shaft, master!" quoth Roger, turning the missile over in his hand ere he gave it to Beltane, "no forester doth wing his shafts so."

"True!" nodded Beltane, frowning at the arrow. "Walkyn, Ulf! here hath been an ambushment, methinks — 'tis a likely place for such. Let our company scatter and search amid the fern hereabouts —"

But even as he spake came a cry, a clamour of voices, and Prat the archer came frowning and snapping his restless fingers.

"My lord," said he, "yonder doth lie my good comrade Martin and three other fellows of my archer-company that marched with Sir Benedict, and all dead, lord, slain by arrows all four."

"Show me!" said Beltane.

And when he had viewed and touched those stark and pallid forms that lay scattered here and there amid the bracken, his anxious frown deepened. "These have been dead men full six hours!" quoth he.

"Aye, lord," says Prat, "and 'tis unmeet such good fellows should lie here for beasts to tear; shall we bury them?"

"Not so!" answered Beltane, turning away. "Take their shafts and fall to your ranks — we must march forthright!"

Thus soon the three hundred were striding fast behind Beltane, keeping ever to the forest yet well within bow-shot of the road, and, though they travelled at speed they went very silently, as only foresters might.

In a while Beltane brought them to those high wooded banks betwixt which the road ran winding down to Thornaby Ford — that self-same hilly road where, upon a time, the Red Pertolepe had surprised the lawless company of Gilles of Brandonmere; and, now as then, the dark defile was littered with the wrack of fight, fallen charges that kicked and snorted in their pain or lay mute and still, men in battered harness that stared up from the dust, all unseeing, upon the new day. They lay thick within the sunken road but thicker beside the ford, and they dotted the white road beyond, grim signs of Sir Benedict's stubborn retreat. Hereupon Beltane halted his hard-breathing foresters and bidding them rest awhile and break their fast, hasted down into the roadway with Walkyn and Cnut and Black Roger.

"Aha!" cried Walkyn, pointing to divers of the slain that hampered their going, "these be Pertolepe's rogues —"

"Aye," quoth Roger, throwing back his mail-coif, "and yonder lie four, five — six of Sir Benedict's good fellows! It hath been a dour fight hereabouts — they have fought every yard of the way!"

"Forsooth," nodded Cnut, "Sir Benedict is ever most fierce when he retreats, look you."

To Belsaye for the Third Time 465

A while stood Beltane in that dark defile, the which, untouched as yet by the sun's level beams, struck dank and chill, a place of gloom and awful silence — so stood he, glancing from one still form to another, twice he knelt to look more closely on the dead and each time he rose thereafter, his brow was blacker and he shivered, despite his mantle.

" 'Tis strange," said he, "and passing strange that they should all lie dead — not a living man among them! How think you Roger?"

"I think, lord, others have been here afore us. See you this knight now, his gorget loosed off —"

"O messire!" said a faint voice hard by, "if ye have any pity save me from the crone — for the love of Christ let not the hag slay me as she hath so many — save me!"

Starting round, Beltane espied a pale face that glared up at him from a thick furze-bush beside the way, a youthful face albeit haggard and drawn.

"Fear not!" said Beltane, kneeling beside the wounded youth, "thy life is safe from us. But what mean you by talk of hag and crone?"

"Ah, messire, to-day, ere the dawn, we fell upon Sir Benedict of Bourne — a seditious lord who hath long withstood Duke Ivo. But though his men were few they fought hard and gained the ford ahead of us. And in the fight I, with many others as ye see, was smitten down and the fight rolled on and left us here in the dust. As I lay, striving to tend my hurt and hearkening to the sighs and groans of the stricken, I heard a scream, and looking about, beheld an ancient woman — busied with her knife — slaying — slaying and robbing the dead — ah, behold her — with the black-haired archer — yonder!"

And verily Roger stepped forth of the underwood that clothed the steep, dragging a thing of rags and tatters, a wretched creature, bent and wrinkled, that mopped and mowed with toothless chaps and clutched a misshapen bundle in yellow, talon-like fingers, and these yellow fingers were splotched horribly with dark stains even as were the rags that covered her. She whined and whimpered querulously, mouthing inarticulate plaints and prayers as Roger haled her along, with Cnut and Walkyn, fierce and scowling, behind. Having brought her to Beltane, Roger loosed her, and wrenching away her bundle, opened it, and lo! a yellow-gleaming hoard of golden neck-chains, of rings and armlets, of golden spurs and belt-buckles, the which he incontinent scattered at Beltane's feet; whereon the gibbering creature screamed in high-pitched, cracked and ancient voice, and, screeching, threw herself upon the gold and fell to scrabbling among the dust with her gnarled and bony fingers; and ever as she raked and raked, she screeched harsh and high — a hateful noise that ended, of a sudden, in a wheezing sob, and sinking down, she lay outstretched and silent, her wrinkled face in the dust and a cloth-yard shaft transfixing her yellow throat.

So swift had death been dealt that all men fell back a pace and were yet staring down at this awful dead thing when forth from the brush an archer crawled painfully, his bow yet in his hand, and so lay, panting loud and hoarse.

"Ha!" cried Cnut, "'tis lusty Siward of our archers! How now, Siward?"

"I'm sped, Cnut!" groaned Siward, "but yon hag lieth dead, so am I — content. I've watched her slay John that was my comrade, you'll mind — for his armlet. And — good Sir Hugh she stabbed, — yonder he lieth — him she slew for — spurs and chain. When I fell I — dropped my bow — in the brush, yonder — I have been two hours creeping — a dozen yards to — reach my bow but — I got it at last — Aha!" And Siward, feebly pointing to the ancient, dead woman, strove to laugh and so — died.

Then Beltane turned, and coming beside the wounded youth spake him tender and compassionate.

"Young sir, we must hence, but first can I do aught for thee?"

"O messire, an I might — come to the river — water!"

Saying no word, Beltane stooped and lifting the young knight very carefully, bore him down toward the ford.

"Messire," quoth the young knight, stifling his groans, "art very strong and wondrous gentle withal!" Presently Beltane brought him beside the river, and while the youth drank, laid bare an ugly wound above the knee and bathed it with his hand, and, thereafter, tearing a strip from his ragged cloak, he bound it tight above the hurt, (even as he had seen Sir Fidelis do) and thus stayed the bleeding. Now while this was a-doing, the young knight must needs talk.

"Ho!" cried he, "'twas a good fight, messire, and he who gave me this was none other than Benedict of Bourne himself — whom our good Duke doth fondly imagine pent up within Thrasfordham! O indeed 'twas Sir Benedict, I saw his hawk-face plain ere he closed his vizor, and he fought left-handed. Moreover, beside him I recognised the leaping dog blazoned on the shield of Hacon of Trant — Oho, this shall be wondrous news for Duke Ivo, methinks. But, faith, 'tis wonder how he escaped Sir Rollo, and as for the outlaw Beltane we saw nought of him — Sir Pertolepe vows he was not of this company — mayhap Sir Rollo hath him, 'tis so I pray — so, peradventure I shall see him hang yet! My grateful thanks, messire, for thy tender care of me. At home I have a mother that watcheth and prayeth for me — prithee tell me thy name that she may remember it in her prayers?"

"I am called Beltane the Outlaw, sir knight — and I charge thee to heed that thy bandage slip not, lest the bleeding start afresh — fare thee well!" So saying, Beltane turned and went on across the ford what time the young knight, propped upon weak elbow, stared after him wide of eye and mouth.

Forthwith Beltane, setting horn to lip, sounded the rally, and very soon the three hundred crossed the ford and swung off to the left into the green.

Thus, heartened and refreshed by food and rest, they pressed on amain southward through the forest with eyes and ears alert and on the strain; what time grim Sir Benedict, riding with his rearguard, peered through the dust of battle but saw only the threatening column of the foe upon the forest road behind, rank upon rank far as the eye could reach, and the dense green of the adjacent woods on either flank whence unseen arrows whizzed ever and anon to glance from his heavy armour.

"Ha, Benedict!" quoth Sir Brian, "they do know thee, methinks, 'spite thy plain armour —'tis the third shaft hath struck thee in as many minutes!"

"So needs must I stifle and sweat within closed casque!" Sir Benedict groaned. Upon his right hand Sir Brian rode and upon his left his chiefest esquire, and oft needs must they wheel their chargers to front the thunderous onset of Red Pertolepe's fierce van, at the which times Sir Benedict laughed and gibed through his vizor as he thrust and smote left-armed, parrying sword and lance-point right skilfully nevertheless, since shield he bare none. Time and again they beat back their assailants thus, until spent and short of wind they gave place to three fresh knights.

"By Our Lady of Hartismere!" panted Sir Brian, "but thy left arm serves thee well, Benedict!"

"'Tis fair, Brian, 'tis fair, God be thanked!" sighed Sir Benedict, eyeing his reeking blade, "though I missed my thrust 'neath yon gentle knight's gorget —"

"Yet shore clean through his helm, my lord!" quoth young Walter the esquire.

"Why truly, 'tis a good blade, this of mine," said Sir Benedict, and sighed again.

"Art doleful, Benedict?" questioned Sir Brian," 'tis not like thee when steel is ringing, man."

"In very sooth, Brian, I hanker for knowledge of our Beltane — ha, Walter!" he cried suddenly, "lower thy vizor, boy — down with it, I say!"

"Nay, dear my lord, fain would I breathe the sweet, cool air — but a moment and —"

The young esquire rose up stiffly in his stirrups, threw

To Belsaye for the Third Time 469

up gauntleted hands and swaying from the high saddle, pitched down crashing into the dust.

"Alas! there endeth my poor Walter!" sighed Sir Benedict.

"Aye, a shaft between the eyes, poor lad! A curse on these unseen archers!" quoth Sir Brian, beckoning a pikeman to lead forward the riderless horse. "Ha — look yonder, Benedict — we are beset in flank, and by dismounted knights from the underwood. See, as I live 'tis the nuns they make for!"

Nothing saying, Sir Benedict spurred forward beside his hard-pressed company; in the midst of the column was dire tumult and shouting, where, from the dense woods upon their left a body of knights sheathed in steel from head to foot were cutting their way toward the lady Abbess, who, conspicuous in her white habit, was soothing her frightened palfrey. All about her a shouting, reeling press of Sir Benedict's light-armed footmen were giving back and back before the swing of ponderous axe and mace and sword, were smitten down and trampled 'neath those resistless, steel-clad ranks.

"Ha! the Abbess!" they cried, "yield us the lady Abbess!" Into this close and desperate affray Sir Benedict spurred, striving with voice and hand to re-form his broken ranks, hewing him a path by dint of sword until he had won beside the Abbess.

"Yolande!" he shouted above the din, "keep thou beside me close — close, Yolande — stoop — ah, stoop thy head that I may cover thee — the debate waxeth a little sharp hereabouts!" Even as he spake he reeled 'neath the blow of a heavy mace, steadied himself, cut down his smiter, and thrust and smote amain until the grim, fierce-shouting ranks gave back before the sweep of that long sword.

"See, Yolande!" he panted, hard-breathing, "see yonder where my good Hacon spurs in to our relief — ha, mighty lance!"

"Ah, Benedict," cried the Abbess, pale-lipped but calm

of eye, "of what avail? 'Tis me they seek, though wherefore I know not, so — dear Benedict — let me go. Indeed, indeed 'tis best, so shall these fair lives be saved — ah, sweet Jesu, 'tis horrible! See — O see how fast they fall and die about us! I must go — I will go! My lord, let me pass — loose my bridle —"

A hunting horn fiercely winded among the woods hard by! A confused roar of harsh voices and forth of the green four terrible figures sprang, two that smote with long-shafted axes and two that plied ponderous broadswords; and behind these men were others, lean and brown-faced — the very woods seemed alive with them. And from these fierce ranks a mighty shout rent the air:

"Arise! Arise! Ha, Beltane — Pentavalon!"

Then did Sir Benedict, laughing loud and joyous, haste to re-form his swaying ranks, the bloody gap in his column closed up and Sir Pertolepe's knights, hemmed in thus, smote and were smitten and but scant few were they that won them free. And presently, through that red confusion brake Beltane with Roger and Ulf and Walkyn at his heels, and, sword in hand, he sprang and caught the Abbess in a close embrace.

"Mother!" he cried.

"Dear, dear son of mine — and thou art safe? Thanks be to God who hath heard the passion of thy mother's prayers!" Now Sir Benedict turned, and wheeling his horse, left them together and so beheld Sir Hacon near by, who, standing high in his stirrups, pointed to their rear.

"Benedict!" he panted, "ha, look — Brian is overborne! Ho! a rescue — a rescue to Sir Brian of Hartismere!" So shouting, he drave back into the confusion of the staggering rear-guard with Sir Benedict spurring behind. But, as Sir Benedict rode, pushing past the files of his halted company, he felt hands that gripped either stirrup and glancing down beheld Ulf the Strong on his one flank and grim Walkyn upon the other. So came they where the road broadened out and where the battle

To Belsaye for the Third Time

raged swaying and surging above the form of Sir Brian prostrate in the dust where horsemen and footmen strove together in desperate grapple, where knightly shields, aflare with proud devices, rang 'neath the blows of Beltane's lusty foresters and Sir Benedict's veteran pikemen.

Then of a sudden Walkyn shouted fierce and loud, and sprang forward with mighty axe whirled aloft.

"Ha — Pertolepe, turn!" he roared, "Ho, Bloody Pertolepe — turn, thou dog! 'Tis I — 'tis Waldron of Brand!" So cried he, and, plunging into the thick of the affray, smote aside all such as barred his way until he fronted Sir Pertolepe, who, astride a powerful mailed charger, wielded a bloody mace, and who, hearing that hoarse cry, turned and met the shearing axe with blazoned shield — and behold! the gorgeous shield was split in twain; but even so, he smote in turn and mighty Walkyn was beaten to his knee. Forth sprang Ulf, swift and eager, but Walkyn, bounding up, shouldered him aside — his axe whirled and fell once, and Sir Pertolepe's mace was dashed from his loosened hold — whirled and fell again, and Sir Pertolepe's great casque was beaten from his head and all men might see the ghastly, jagged cross that scarred his brow beneath his fiery hair — whirled again, but, ere it could fall, knights and esquires mounted and afoot, had burst 'twixt Walkyn and their reeling lord, and Walkyn was dashed aside, shouting, cursing, foaming with rage, what time Sir Pertolepe was borne out of the fight.

But the rear-guard was saved, and, with a hedge of bristling pikes behind, Sir Benedict's sore-battered company marched on along the forest-road and breathed again, the while their pursuers, staggered in their onset, paused to re-form ere they thundered down upon that devoted rear-guard once more. But Sir Benedict was there, loud-voiced and cheery still despite fatigue, and Sir Hacon was there, his wonted gloom forgotten quite, and Beltane was there, equipped with shield and vizored war-helm and astride a noble horse, and there, too, was Roger, grim and silent, and fierce Ulf, and Walkyn in black and evil temper; quoth he:

"Ha —'tis ever so, his life within my very grasp, yet doth he escape me! But one more blow and the Red Pertolepe had been in hell —"

"Yet, forsooth, didst save our rear-guard, comrade!" said Ulf.

"Aye — and what o' that? 'Twas Pertolepe's foul life I sought —"

"And there," quoth Beltane, "there spake Vengeance, and vengeance is ever a foul thing and very selfish!" Now hereupon Walkyn's scowl deepened, and, falling further to the rear, he spake no more.

"Beltane, dear my lad," said Sir Benedict as they rode together, "hast told me nought of thy doings last night — what of Sir Rollo?"

"Nay, Benedict, ask me not yet, only rest ye assured Sir Rollo shall not trouble us this side Belsaye. But pray, how doth our brave Sir Brian?"

"Well enough, Beltane; he lieth in a litter, being tended by thy noble lady mother. A small lance-thrust 'neath the gorget, see'st thou, 'twill be healed — Ha, they charge us again — stand firm, pikes!" So shouting, Sir Benedict wheeled his horse and Beltane with him, and once again the road echoed to the din of battle.

Thus all day long they fought their way south along the forest-road, as, time and again, Sir Pertolepe's heavy chivalry thundered down upon them, to check and break before that hedge of deadly pikes. So marched this valiant rear-guard, parched with thirst, choked with dust, grim with blood and wounds, until, as the sun sank westwards, the woods thinned away and they beheld at last, glad-eyed and joyful, the walls and towers of fair Belsaye town. Now just beyond the edge of the woods, Sir Benedict halted his shrunken column, his dusty pikemen drawn up across the narrow road with archers behind supported by his cavalry to hold Sir Pertolepe's powers in check amid the woods what time the nuns with the spent and wounded hasted on towards the city.

Hereupon Beltane raised his vizor and setting horn to lip, sounded the rally. And lo! from the city a glad and mighty shout went up, the while above the square and frowning keep a great standard arose and flapping out upon the soft air, discovered a red lion on a white field.

"Aha, Beltane!" quoth Sir Benedict, "yon is a rare-sweet sight — behold thy father's Lion banner that hath not felt the breeze this many a year —"

"Aye, lords," growled Walkyn," and yonder cometh yet another lion — a black lion on red!" and he pointed where, far to their left, a red standard flaunted above the distant glitter of a wide-flung battle line.

"Hast good eyes, Walkyn!" said Sir Benedict, peering 'neath his hand toward the advancing host, "aye, verily —'tis Ivo himself. Sir Pertolepe must have warned him of our coming."

"So are we like to be crushed 'twixt hammer and anvil," quoth Sir Hacon, tightening the lacing of his battered casque.

"So will I give thee charge of our knights and men-at-arms — what is left of them, alas! — to meet Black Ivo's banner, my doleful Hacon!" spake Sir Benedict.

"Nay, Benedict," said Sir Hacon, grim-smiling, "my dole is but caution!" So saying, he closed his vizor and rode away to muster his chivalry to meet their new assailants the while Sir Benedict fell to re-forming his scanty ranks of pikemen and archers. Meantime Beltane, sitting his weary charger, glanced from Sir Pertolepe's deep array of knights and men-at-arms that thronged and jostled each other in the narrow forest-road to the distant flash and glitter of Duke Ivo's mighty van-ward, and from these again to the walls of Belsaye. And as he looked thither he saw the great drawbridge fall, the portcullis raised, and the gates flung wide to admit the fugitives; even at that distance he thought to recognise the Abbess, who paused to turn and gaze towards him, as, last of all, she rode to safety into the city. Then my Beltane sighed, and, closing his vizor, turned to find Ulf beside him with Roger and Walkyn, who stood to watch the while Sir Benedict rode to and fro, ordering his company for their perilous retreat across the plain. Swift and silent his war-worn veterans fell to their appointed ranks; his trumpets blew and they began to fall back on Belsaye town. Grimly silent they marched, and ever Beltane gazed where, near and ever more near, flashed and flickered Duke Ivo's hard-riding van-ward.

And now from the forest-road Sir Pertolepe's company marched, and forming in the open, spurred down upon them.

"Stand firm, pikes!" roared Cnut.

"Aim low, archers!" squealed small Prat, and forthwith the battle joined.

The weary rear-guard rocked and swayed beneath the onset, but Prat and his archers shot amain, arrows whistled while pike and gisarm thrust and smote, as, encompassed now on three sides, they fell back and back towards the yawning gates of Belsaye; and ever as he fought, Beltane by times turned to watch where Duke Ivo's threatening van-ward galloped — a long line of gleaming shields and levelled lances gay with the glitter of pennon and banderol.

Back and back the rear-guard staggered, hewing and smiting; twice Beltane reeled 'neath unseen blows and with eyes a-swim beheld Roger and Ulf, who fought at either stirrup: heard of a sudden shrieks and cries and the thunder of galloping hooves; was aware of the flash of bright armour to his left, rank upon rank, where charged Duke Ivo's van-ward before whose furious onset Sir Benedict's weary pikemen were hurled back — their centre swayed, broke, and immediately all was dire uproar and confusion.

"Ah, Beltane — these be fresh men on fresh horses," cried Sir Benedict, "but hey — body o' me — all's not lost yet — malediction, no! And 'tis scarce half a mile to the gates. Ha — yonder rides lusty Hacon to stay their rush — in upon them, Beltane — Ho, Pentavalon!"

Shouting thus, Sir Benedict plunged headlong into the raging fury of the battle; but, as Beltane spurred in after him, his weary charger, smitten by an arrow, reared up, screaming, yet ere he fell, Beltane, kicking free of the stirrups, rolled clear; a mighty hand plucked him to his feet and Ulf, roaring in his ear, pointed with his dripping axe. And, looking whither he pointed, Beltane beheld Sir Benedict borne down beneath a press of knights, but as he lay, pinned beneath his squealing charger, Beltane leapt and bestrode him, sword in hand.

"Roger!" he shouted, "Ulf — Walkyn — to me!"

All about him was a swaying trample of horses and men, an iron ring that hemmed him in, blows dinted his long shield, they rang upon his helmet, they battered his triple mail, they split his shield in sunder; and 'neath this hail of blows Beltane staggered, thrice he was smitten to his knees and thrice he arose, and ever his long blade whirled and darted.

"Yield thee, sir knight — yield thee!" was the cry.

"Ho, Roger!" he shouted hoarsely, "Ulf — Walkyn, to me!"

An axe bit through his great helm, a sword bent against his stout mail, a knight spurred in upon him, blade levelled to thrust again, but Beltane's deadly point darted upward and the snorting charger plunged away — riderless.

But now, as he fought on with failing arm, came a joyous roar on his right where Ulf smote direly with bloody axe, upon his left hand a broad-sword flickered where Roger fought silent and grim, beyond him again, Walkyn's long arms rose and fell as he whirled his axe, and hard by Tall Orson plied goring pike. So fought these mighty four until the press thinned out and they had cleared them a space amid the battle, the while Beltane leaned him, spent and panting, upon his reeking sword.

Now, as he stood thus, from a tangle of the fallen near by a bent and battered helm was lifted and Sir Benedict spake, faint and short of breath:

"'Twas nobly done — sweet lad! 'Tis enough, methinks — there be few of us left, I fear me, so — get thee hence — with such as be alive — hence, Beltane, for — thy sweet mother's sake. Nay, heed not — old Benedict, I did my best and —'tis a fitting couch, this — farewell to thee, my Beltane —" So saying, Sir Benedict sank weakly to an elbow and from elbow upon his face, and lay there, very still and mute.

"Master — master!" cried Roger, "we shall win to Belsaye yet, see — see, Giles hath out-flanked them with his pikes and archers, and — ha! yonder good Eric o' the Noose chargeth them home!"

But Beltane leaned him upon his sword very spent and sick, and stared ever upon Sir Benedict's motionless form, his harness bent and hacked, his proud helm prone in the trampled ling. Slowly, and with fumbling hands, Beltane sheathed his sword, and stooping, raised Sir Benedict upon his shoulder and strove to bear him out of the fight, but twice he staggered in his going and would have fallen but for Roger's ready arm.

"Master," quoth he, "master, let me aid thee with him!" But nothing saying, Beltane stumbled on until they came where stood Ulf holding a riderless horse, on the which he made shift to mount with Roger's aid; thereafter Ulf lifted Sir Benedict to his hold.

"And, pray you," said Beltane, slow and blurred of speech, "pray you what of noble Sir Hacon?"

"Alack, lord," growled Ulf, "yonder is he where they lie so thick, and slain, methinks,— yet will I bring him off —"

"Aye, lord," cried Tall Orson, great tears furrowing the grime of his cheeks, "and little Prat do be killed — and lusty Cnut do be killed wi' him — and my good comrade Jenkyn do lie smitten to death — O there do be none of us left, methinks, lord!"

So, faint and heart-sick, with Sir Benedict limp across his saddle bow, Beltane rode from that place of death; beside him went Roger, stumbling and weary, and behind them strode mighty Ulf with Sir Hacon upon his shoulder. In a while, as they went thus, Beltane, glancing back at the fight, beheld stout Eric with the men of Belsaye, well mounted and equipped, at fierce grapple with Duke Ivo's van-ward, what time Giles and his archers supported by lusty pikemen, plied Sir Pertolepe's weary forces with whizzing shafts, drawing and loosing marvellous fast.

So came they at last unto the gates of Belsaye town that were already a-throng with many wounded and divers others of Sir Benedict's company that had won out of the affray; now upon the drawbridge Beltane paused and gave Sir Benedict and brave Hacon into kindly, eager hands, then, wheeling, with Ulf and Roger beside him, rode back toward the battle. And ever as they went came scattered groups of Sir Benedict's stout rear-guard, staggering with weariness and limping with wounds, the while, upon the plain beyond, Eric with his men-at-arms and Walkyn with the survivors of the foresters and Giles with his archers and pikemen, holding the foe in play, fell back upon the town, compact and orderly. Thus, they in turn began to cross the drawbridge, archers and pikemen, and last of all, the men-at-arms, until only Eric o' the Noose and a handful of his horsemen, with Beltane, Roger and Ulf remained beyond the drawbridge, whereon the enemy came on amain and 'neath their furious onset brave Eric was unhorsed; then Beltane drew sword and with Roger and Ulf running at either stirrup, spurred in to the rescue.

A shock of hard-smitten steel — a whirl and flurry of blows — a shout of triumph, and, reeling in his saddle, dazed and sick, Beltane found himself alone, fronting a bristling line of feutred lances; he heard Roger shout to him wild and fearful, heard Walkyn roar at him — felt a sudden shock, and was down, unhelmed, and pinned beneath his stricken charger. Half a-swoon he lay thus, seeing dimly the line of on-rushing lance-points, while on his failing senses a fierce cry smote:

"'Tis Beltane — the Outlaw! Slay him! Slay him!"

But now of a sudden and as one that dreamed, he beheld a tender face above him with sad-sweet eyes and lips that bent to kiss his brow, felt soft arms about him — tender arms that drew his weary head upon a gentle bosom to hide and pillow it there; felt that enfolding embrace tighten and tighten in sudden shuddering spasm, as, sighing, the lady Abbess's white-clad arms fell away and her proud head sank beside his in the dust.

And now was a rush and roar of fierce voices as over them sprang Roger and Giles with Ulf and Eric, and, amid the eddying dust, axe and sword swung and smote, while came hands strong yet tender, that bare Beltane into the city.

Now beyond the gate of the city was a well and beside the well they laid Beltane and bathed him with the sweet cool water, until at length the mist vanished from his sight and thus he beheld the White Abbess who lay upon a pile of cloaks hard by. And beholding the deadly pallor of lip and cheek, the awful stains that spotted her white robe and the fading light in those sad-sweet eyes, Beltane cried aloud — a great and bitter cry, and fell before her on his knees.

"Mother!" he groaned, "O my mother!"

"Dear my Beltane," she whispered faintly, striving to kiss his hand, "death is none so — painful, so grieve not thine heart for me, sweet son. And how may a mother — die better than for her own — beloved son? Beltane, if God — O if God in His infinite mercy — shall think me worthy — to be — one of His holy angels, then will I be ever near thee when thy way proveth dark — to comfort thee — to aid thee. O dear my son — I sought thee so long — so long —'tis a little hard to leave thee — so soon. But — God's will — fare thee well, I die — aye — this is death, methinks. Beltane, tell thy father that I — O — dear my — my Beltane —"

So died the gracious lady Abbess that had been the proud Yolande, Duchess of Pentavalon, wept and bemoaned by full many who had known her tender care; and, in due season, she was laid to rest within the fair Minster of Belsaye. And thereafter, Beltane took to his bed and abode there many days because of his wounds and by reason of his so great sorrow and heart-break.

But, that night, through the dark hours was strange stir and hum beyond the walls of Belsaye, and, when the dawn broke, many a stout heart quailed and many a cheek blanched to see a great camp whose fortified lines encompassed the city on all sides, where lay Ivo the Black Duke to besiege them.

CHAPTER LXIII

TELLETH SOMEWHAT OF THE WOES OF GILES O' THE BOW

SIX days and nights my Beltane kept his bed, seeing and speaking to no man; and it is like he would have died but for the fostering care of the good Friar Martin who came and went softly about him, who watched and tended and prayed over him long and silently but who, perceiving his heart-sickness, spake him not at all. Day in and day out Beltane lay there, heedless of all but his great sorrow, sleeping little and eating less, his face hid in his pillow or turned to the wall, and in all this time he uttered no word nor shed a single tear.

His wounds healed apace but his soul had taken a deeper hurt, and day and night he sorrowed fiercely for his noble mother, wherefore he lay thus, heeding nought but his great grief. But upon the seventh night, he dreamed she stood beside his couch, tall and fair and gracious, and looked down on him, the mother-love alight within her sweet, sad eyes. Now within her hand she bare his sword and showed him the legend graven upon the bright steel:

RESURGAM

And therewith she smiled wondrous tender and put the great weapon into his grasp; then stooped and kissed him, and, pointing upward with her finger, was gone.

And now within his sleep his anguished heart found solacement in slow and burning tears, and, sleeping yet, he wept full bitterly, insomuch that, sobbing, he awoke. And lo! beneath his right hand was the touch of cold steel and his fingers clenched tight upon the hilt of his great sword.

Then my Beltane arose forthwith, and finding his clothes near by, clad himself and did on his mail, and, soft-tread-

Of the Woes of Giles o' the Bow

ing, went forth of his narrow chamber. Thus came he where Friar Martin lay, deep-breathing in his slumber, and waking him not, he passed out into the dawn. And in the dawn was a gentle wind, very cool and grateful, that touched his burning brow and eyes like a caress; now looking up to heaven, where stars were paling to the dawn, Beltane raised the hilt of his sword and pressed it to his lips.

"O blessed mother!" he whispered, "God hath surely found thee worthy to be one of His holy angels, so hast thou stooped from heaven to teach to me my duty. Thus now will I set by my idle grieving for thee, sweet saint, and strive to live thy worthy son — O dear my mother, who, being dead, yet liveth!"

Then Beltane sheathed his sword and went softly up the narrow stair that led to the battlements.

It was a bleak dawn, full of a thick, low-lying mist beyond the walls, but within this mist, to north and south and east and west, was a faint stir, while, ever and anon, rose the distant cry of some sentinel within Duke Ivo's sleeping camp, a mighty camp whose unseen powers held the fair city in deadly grip. In Belsaye nothing stirred and none waked at this dead hour save where, high on the bartizan above the square and mighty keep, the watchman paced to and fro, while here and there from curtain wall and massy tower, spear-head and bascinet gleamed.

Slow and light of foot Beltane climbed the narrow stair that led up to one of the two square towers that flanked the main gate, but, being come thither, he paused to behold Giles, who chancing to be captain of the watch, sat upon a pile of great stones beside a powerful mangonel or catapult and stared him dolefully upon the lightening east: full oft sighed he, and therewith shook despondent head and even thus fell he to soft and doleful singing, groaning to himself 'twixt each verse, on this wise:

> "She will not heed her lover's moan,
> His mopèd tear, his deep-fetched groan,
> So doth he sit, and here alone
>   Sing willow!

("With three curses on this foul mist!")

"The little fishes, fishes woo,
Birds blithe on bough do bill and coo,
But lonely I, with sad ado
                    Sing willow!"

("And may Saint Anthony's fire consume Bernard, the merchant's round, plump son!)

"Tis sure a maid was made for man,
'Twas e'en so since the world began,
Yet doleful here, I only can
                    Sing willow!"

("And may the blessed saints have an eye upon her tender slumbers!")

Here Giles paused to sigh amain, to fold his arms, to cross his legs, to frown and shake gloomy head; having done the which, he took breath and sang again as followeth: —

"Alack-a-day, alas and woe!
Would that Genevra fair might know
'Tis for her love Giles of the Bow
                    Sings willow!"

But now, chancing to turn and espy Beltane, Giles fell suddenly abashed, his comely face grew ruddy 'neath its tan and he sprang very nimbly to his feet:

"Ha, tall brother — good brother," he stammered, "noble lord, God den to ye — hail and good morrow! Verily and in faith, by Saint Giles (my patron saint, brother) I do rejoice to see thee abroad again, as will our surly Rogerkin that doth gloom and glower for thee and hath hung about thy chamber door morn and noon and night, and our noble Sir Benedict and Walkyn — but none more unfeignedly than Giles that doth grow glad because of thee —"

"That is well," quoth Beltane, seating himself upon the battlement, "for verily thy song was vastly doleful, Giles!"

Of the Woes of Giles o' the Bow

"My song, lord, my song? Ha — hum! O verily, my song is a foolish song or the song of a fool, for fool am I, forsooth — a love-lorn fool; a doleful fool, a very fool of fools, that in my foolish folly hath set his foolish heart on thing beyond reach of such base fool as I. In a word, tall brother, I'm a fool, *videlicet* — a lover!"

"Truly, hast the speech and outward seeming of your approved lover, Giles," nodded Beltane.

"Aye, verily!" sighed Giles, "aye, verily — behold my beard, I have had no heart to trim it this sennight! Alack, I — I that was so point-de-vice am like to become a second Diogenes (a filthy fellow that never washed and lived in a foul tub!). As for food, I eat no more than the chameleon that doth fill its belly with air and nought else, foolish beast! I, that was wont to be a fair figure of a man do fall away to skin and bone, daily, hourly, minute by minute — behold this leg, tall brother!" And Giles thrust out a lusty, mailed limb. "Here was a leg once — a proper shapely leg to catch a woman's eye — see how it hath shrunk, nay, faith, 'tis hidden in mine armour! But verily, my shanks will soon be no thicker than my bow-stave! Lastly I — I that loved company and good cheer do find therein abomination these days, so do I creep, like moulting fowl, brother, to corners dark and dismal and there make much ado — and such is love, O me!"

"Doth the maid know of thy love?"

"Nay lord, good lack, how should she? — who am I to speak of it? She is a fair lady and noble, a peerless virgin, while I — I am only Giles — poor Giles o' the Bow, after all!"

"Truly, love is teaching thee wisdom, Giles," said Beltane, smiling.

"Indeed, my lord, my wisdom teacheth me this — that were I the proudest and noblest in the land yet should I be unworthy!" and Giles shook miserable head and sighed again full deep.

"Who is she, Giles?"

"She is Genevra, daughter to the Reeve! And the Reeve

is a great man in Belsaye and gently born, alas! And with coffers full of good broad pieces. O would she were a beggar-maid, the poorest, the meanest, then might I woo her for mine own. As it is, I can but look and sigh — for speak me her I dare not — ha, and there is a plump fellow!" Here Giles clenched bronzed fist. "A round and buxom fellow he, a rich merchant's son doth woo her boldly, may speak with her, may touch her hand! So do I ofttimes keep him shooting at the butts by the hour together and therein do make me some small amend. Yet daily do I mope and pine, and pine and mope — O tall brother, a most accursed thing is this love — and dearer than my life, heigho!"

"Nay, pluck up thy heart, thou'rt a man, Giles."

"Aye, verily, but she is a maid, brother, therein lieth vasty difference, and therefore do I fear her for her very sweetness and purity — fear her? Faith, my knees do knock at sound of her voice, her very step doth set me direly a-tremble. For she is so fair — so pure and nigh the angels, that I — alack! I have ever been a something light fellow in matters of love — forget not I was bred a monk, noble brother! Thus, brother, a moping owl, I — a very curst fellow, gloomy and silent as the grave, saving my breath for sighs and groans and curses fell, wherefore I have builded me a 'mockery' above the wall and therefrom do curse our foes, as only a churchman may, brother."

"Nay, how mean you, Giles?" questioned Beltane, staring.

"Follow me, lord, and I will show thee!" So saying, Giles led the way down to the battlement above the great gates, where was a thing like unto a rough pulpit, builded of massy timbers, very stout and strong, and in these timbers stood many arrows and cross-bow bolts.

"Here, lord," quoth Giles, "behold my 'mockery' wherefrom it is my wont and custom to curse our foes thrice daily. The which is a right good strategy, brother, in that my amorous anguish findeth easement and I do draw

Of the Woes of Giles o' the Bow

the enemy's shafts, for there is no man that heareth my contumacious dictums but he forthwith falleth into rageful fury, and an angry fellow shooteth ever wide o' the mark, brother. Thus, thrice daily do we gather a full sheaf of their ill-sped shafts, whereby we shall not lack for arrows an they besiege us till Gabriel's trump — heigho! Thus do I live by curses, for, an I could not curse, then would my surcharged heart assuredly in sunder burst — aye me!"

Now whiles they sat thus in talk, up rose the sun, before whose joyous beams the stealthy mists slunk away little by little, until Beltane beheld Duke Ivo's mighty camp — long lines of tents gay with fluttering pennon and gonfalon, of huts and booths set well out of bowshot behind the works of contravallation — stout palisades and barriers with earthworks very goodly and strong. And presently from among these booths and tents was the gleam and glitter of armour, what time from the waking host a hum and stir arose, with blare and fanfare of trumpet to usher in the day: and in a while from the midst of the camp came the faint ring and tap of many hammers.

Now as the mists cleared, looking thitherward, Beltane stared wide-eyed to behold wooden towers in course of building, with the grim shapes of many powerful war-engines whose mighty flying-beams and massy supporting-timbers filled him with great awe and wonderment.

"Ha!" quoth Giles, "they work apace yonder, and by Saint Giles they lack not for engines; verily Black Ivo is a master of siege tactics — but so is Giles, brother! See where he setteth up his mangonels, trebuchets, perriers and balistæ, with bossons or rams, towers and cats, in the use of the which he is right cunning — but so also is Giles, brother! And verily, though your mangonels and trebuchets are well enough, yet for defence the balista is weapon more apt, methinks, as being more accurate in the shooting and therefore more deadly — how think you, lord?"

"Indeed Giles, being a forester I could scarce tell you one from another."

"Ha — then you'll know nought of their nature and use, lord?"

"Nought, Giles. Ne'er have I seen their like until now."

"Say ye so, brother?" cried Giles full eager, his brown eyes a-kindle, "say ye so in very truth? Then — an it be so thy wish — I might instruct thee vastly, for there is no man in the world to-day shall discourse you more fluent and learned upon siege-craft, engines and various tormenta than I. So — an it be thy wish, lord —?"

"It is my wish: say on, Giles."

"Why then firstly, lord, firstly we have the great Mangon or mangonel, *fundis fundibula*, that some do also term *catapultum*, the which worketh by torsion and shall heave you great stones of the bigness of a man fully two hundred yards an it be dry weather; next is the Trebuchet, like to the mangon save that it swingeth by counterpoise; next cometh the Balista or Springald that worketh by tension — a pretty weapon! and shall shoot you dart or javelin so strong as shall transpierce you six lusty fellows at a time, hauberk and shield, like so many fowl upon a spit — very sweet to behold, brother! Then have we the Bore or Cat that some again do name *musculus* or mouse for that it gnaweth through thick walls — and some do call this hog, sow, *scrofa* or *sus*, brother, and some again, *vulpes*. And this Cat is a massy pole that beareth a great and sharp steel point, the which, being mounted within a pent-house, swingeth merrily to and fro, much like to a ram, brother, and shall blithely pick you a hole through stone and mortar very pleasing to behold. Then we have the Ram, *cancer testudo*, that battereth; next we have the Tower or Beffroi that goeth on wheels — yonder you shall see them a-building. And these towers, moving forward against your city, shall o'ertop the walls and from them archers and cross-bowmen may shoot into your town what time their comrades fill up and dam your moat until the tower may come close unto your walls. And these towers, being come against the wall, do let fall drawbridges over which the besiegers may rush amain and carry your walls by assault. Lastly, there be Mantlets — stakes wattled together and covered with raw-hide — by the which means the besiegers make their first approaches. Then might I descant at goodly length upon the Mine and Furnace, with divers and sundry other stratagems, devices, engines and tormenta, but methinks this shall mayhap suffice thee for the nonce?"

"Aye, verily — 'twill suffice!" said Beltane, rising. " Truly war is even more terrible than I had thought."

"Why lord, 'tis an art — a notable art and — ha! this doth mind me of my heart, heigho! And of all terrible things, of all the woes and ills man-hearts may know is — love. O me, alack and woe!"

"When doth thy watch end, Giles?"

"It ended an hour agone, but to what end? Being a lover I sleep little and pine much, and this is a fair good place and solitary, so will I pine awhile and likewise mope and languish, alack!"

So presently, as Beltane descended the stair, he heard the archer break forth again in doleful song.

Across the wide market-square went Beltane, with brow o'ercast and head low-bowed until he came to one of the many doors of the great minster; there paused he to remove bascinet and mail-coif, and thus bareheaded, entered the cathedral's echoing dimness. The new-risen sun made a glory of the great east window, and with his eyes uplifted to this many-coloured glory, Beltane, soft-treading, crossed dim aisle and whispering transept; but, as he mounted the broad steps of the sanctuary he paused with breath in check, for he heard a sound — a soft sound like the flutter of wings or the rustle of silken draperies. Now as he stood thus, his broad, mail-clad shoulders and golden hair bathed in the refulgence of the great window, it seemed to him that from somewhere near there breathed a sigh, tremulous and very soft, and thereafter was the quick, light tread of feet, and silence.

A while stood Beltane scarce breathing, then, slow and

reverent, he approached the high altar; and ever as he went was a fragrance, wonder-sweet, that grew stronger and stronger until he was come behind the high altar where was his mother's grave. And lo! upon that long, white stone lay flowers a-bloom, roses and lilies whose dewy loveliness filled the place with their pure and fragrant sweetness. So looked he round about and upon these flowers with grateful wonder, and sinking to his knees, bowed his head and folded his hands in prayer.

But presently, as he knelt thus, he was roused by the clank of steel and a shuffling step, wherefore he arose and crossing to the shadows of the choir, sat him down within the deeper gloom to wait until his disturber should be gone. Slowly these halting steps advanced, feet that stumbled oft; near they came and nearer, until Beltane perceived a tall figure whose armour gleamed dully and whose shoulders were bowed like one that is feeble or very weary.

"Yolande!" said a voice, a hoarse voice but very tender, "Yolande, beloved!" And on the word the voice broke and ended upon a great sob, swift followed by another and yet another, the fierce sobbing of a man.

Then Beltane clenched his hands and rose up, for behold! this man was Sir Benedict. But now, and very suddenly, Sir Benedict was upon his knees, and bent and kissed that white, smooth stone whereon as yet was no inscription.

"Yolande!" he whispered, "now thou art one among the holy angels, O forget not thy most unworthy Benedict. God — O God! Father to whom all hearts are open, Thou dost know how as child and maid I loved her, how as a wife I loved her still — how, in my madness, I spake my love — and she, being saint and woman, bade me to my duty. So, by her purity, kept she my honour unstained —".

Beltane's long scabbard struck the carven panelling, a soft blow that yet echoed and re-echoed in vaulted arch and dim roof, and, glancing swiftly up, Sir Benedict beheld him.

And kneeling thus beside the grave of the woman he had

loved, Sir Benedict looked up into Beltane's face with eyes wide, eyes unflinching but dimmed with great grief and pain.

Quoth he, firm-voiced:

"My lord, thou hast learned my life's secret, but, ere thou dost judge me, hear this! Long ere thy princely father met thy mother, we loved, she and I, and in our love grew up together. Then came the Duke thy father, a mighty lord; and her mother was ambitious and very guileful — and she — but a maid. Thus was she wed. Then rode I to the foreign wars seeking death — but death took me not. So, the wars ended, came I home again, burning ever with my love, and sought her out, and beholding the sadness in her eyes I spake my love; and forgetful of honour and all save her sweet soul and the glory of her beauty, I tempted her — aye, many times! — tempted her in fashion merciless and cruel insomuch that she wept many bitter tears, and, upon a day, spake me thus: 'Benedict, 'tis true I loved thee, for thou wert a noble knight — but now, an thy love for me be so small that thou canst bring me to this shame, then — take me where thou wilt — but — ne'er shall all thy love nor all my tears thereafter cleanse us from the shame of it.' Thus went I from her, nor have I looked on woman since. So followed I thy father in all his warring and all my days have I fought much — fierce foes within me and without, and lived — a very solitary life. And to-day she lieth dead — and I am here, old and worn, a lonely man and sinful, to be judged of as ye will."

Then came Beltane and looked down into Sir Benedict's pale, sad face. And beholding him thus in his abasement, haggard with wounds and bowed with grief, needs must Beltane kneel also and thereafter spake thus:

"Sir Benedict, who am I, to judge of such as thou?"

"I tempted her — I wooed her to shame, I that loved her beyond life — did cause her many bitter tears — alas!"

"Yet in the end, Sir Benedict, because thy love was a

great and noble love, thou didst triumph over base self. So do I honour thee and pray that I, in like case, may act as nobly."

"And now — she lieth dead! So for me is life ended also, methinks!"

"She is a saint in heaven, Benedict, living forever. As to thee, on whose skill and valiance the safety of this fair city doth hang — so hath God need of thee here, methinks. So now for thy sake and for her sake needs must I love thee ever and always, thou noble knight. She, being dead, yet liveth and shall go betwixt us henceforth, drawing us together in closer bonds of love and amity — is it not so, dear my friend?" And speaking, Beltane reached out his hands across his mother's narrow grave, and straightway came Sir Benedict's hands, swift and eager, to meet and clasp them.

For a while knelt they thus, hand clasping hand above that long, white stone whence stole to them the mingled fragrance of the flowers, like a silent benediction. And presently, together they arose and went their way; but now, seeing how Sir Benedict limped by reason of his wounds, Beltane set an arm about him. So came they together out of the shadows into the glory of the morning.

Now as they came forth of the minster, the tocsin rang loud in sudden alarm.

CHAPTER LXIV

HOW GILES CURSED BELSAYE OUT OF HER FEAR

WITHIN the market-place all was dire confusion; men hasted hither and thither, buckling on armour as they went, women wept and children wailed, while ever the bell clashed out its fierce summons.

Presently, through the populace cometh Sir Brian of Hartismere, equipped in his armour and leaning on the mailed arm of his brother Eric of the wry neck, but perceiving Sir Benedict and Beltane, they turned and came up forthwith.

"Eric — Brian, what meaneth the tumult?" questioned Sir Benedict, his eye kindling, "are we attacked — so soon?"

"Not so," answered Sir Brian, "at the least — not by Ivo's men."

"'Tis worse than that," sighed Eric, shaking his head, "yonder cometh a churchman, borne on the shoulders of his monks, and with choristers and acolytes attendant."

"Ha!" said Sir Benedict, frowning and rubbing his chin, "I had dreaded this! The citizens do shake and shiver already, I'll warrant me! There is nought like a cowl with bell, book and candle to sap the courage of your citizen soldier. Let us to the walls!"

In a corner hard by the main gate they beheld Giles, holding forth to Roger and Walkyn and Ulf, but perceiving Sir Benedict he ceased abruptly, and advancing, saluted the noble company each in turn, but addressed himself to Sir Benedict.

"My lord," quoth he, eyes a-dance, "yonder cometh a pompous prior that was, not very long since, nought but massy monk that did upon a time (though by dint of some small persuasion) bestow on me a goodly ass. My lord, I was bred a monk, so do I know, by divers signs and portents, he cometh here to ban the city with book, bell and candle, wherefore the townsfolk, fearing greatly, do shiver and shake, especially the women and maids — sweet souls! And, lord, by reason of the matter of the ass, I do know this priest prolific of damnatory pronouncements and curses contumacious (O verily). Yet I, messire (having been bred a monk) shall blithely him out-curse, an the joy be permitted me, thus turning tears to laughter and gloomy fear to loud-voiced merriment — my lord, messires, how say you?"

" 'Tis blasphemy unheard!" quoth Sir Brian.

"Save in the greenwood where men do breathe God's sweet air and live free!" said wry-necked Eric.

"And," spake Sir Benedict, stroking his square chin, "there is a fear can be quelled but by ridicule, so may thy wit, sir archer, avail more than our wisdom — an thou canst make these pale-cheeked townsfolk laugh indeed. How think you, my Beltane?"

"That being the wise and valiant knight thou art, Sir Benedict, thy will during the siege is law in Belsaye, henceforth."

Now hereupon Giles made his obeisance, and together with Roger and Walkyn and Ulf, hasted up to the battlement above the gateway.

"Benedict," said Sir Brian as they climbed the turret stair, "blasphemy is a dread and awful thing. We shall be excommunicate one and all — better methinks to let the populace yield up the city and die the death, than perish everlastingly!"

"Brian," quoth Sir Benedict pausing, something breathless by reason of his recent sickness, "I tell thee fire and pillage and ravishment of women is a thing more dread and awful — better, methinks, to keep Innocence pure and unspotted while we may, and leave hereafter in the hands of God and His holy angels!"

Upon the tower there met them the Reeve, anxious of

Belsaye Cursed Out of Her Fear

brow, who pointed where the townsfolk talked together in fearful undertones or clustered, mute and trembling, while every eye was turned where, in the open, 'twixt town and camp, a procession of black-robed priests advanced, chanting very solemn and sweet.

"My lords," said the Reeve, looking round with haggard eyes, "an these priests do come to pronounce the Church's awful malediction upon the city — then woe betide! Already there be many — aye, some of our chiefest citizens do fear the curse of Holy Church more than the rapine of Ivo's vile soldiery, fair women shamed, O Christ! Lords — ha, messires, there is talk afoot of seizing the gates, of opening to this churchman and praying his intercession to Ivo's mercy — to Ivo the Black, that knoweth nought of mercy. Alas, my lords, once they do ope the gates —"

"That can they in nowise do!" said Sir Benedict gently, but with face grim and hawk-like. "Every gate is held by stout fellows of my own following, moreover I have good hope yon churchman may leave us yet uncursed." And Sir Benedict smiled his wry and twisted smile. "Be you our tongue, good Reeve, and speak this churchman as thy bold heart dictateth."

Solemn and sweet rose the chanting voices growing ever more loud, where paced the black-robed priests. First came acolytes swinging censers, and next, others bearing divers symbolic flags and standards, and after these again, in goodly chair borne on the shoulders of brawny monks, a portly figure rode, bedight in full canonicals, a very solid cleric he, and mightily round; moreover his nose was bulbous and he had a drooping lip.

Slow and solemn the procession advanced, and ever as they came the choristers chanted full melodiously what time the white-robed acolytes swung their censers to and fro; and ever as they came, the folk of Belsaye, from wall and turret, eyed these slow-pacing, sweet-singing monks with fearful looks and hearts cold and full of dire misgiving.

Beyond the moat over against the main gate, the procession halted, the chair with its portly burden was set down, and lifting up a white, be-ringed hand, the haughty cleric spake thus, in voice high-pitched, mellifluous and sweet:

"Whereas it hath pleased ye, O rebellious people of Belsaye, to deny, to cast off and wantonly repudiate your rightful allegiance to your most just, most merciful and most august lord — Ivo, Duke of Pentavalon (whom God and the saints defend — amen!) and whereas ye have moreover made captive and most barbarously entreated certain of your lord Duke his ambassadors unto you sent; now therefore — and let all ears be opened to my pronouncements, since Holy Church doth speak ye, one and all, each and every through humble avenue of these my lips — list, list, O list, rebellious people, and mark me well. For inasmuch as I, Prior of Holy Cross within Pentavalon City, do voice unto ye, one and all, each and every, the most sacred charge of Holy Church, her strict command or enactment, mandate or caveat, her holy decree, *senatus consultum*, her writ, edict, precept or decretal, namely and to wit: That ye shall one and all, each and every, return to your rightful allegiance, bowing humbly, each and every, to the will of your lawful lord the Duke (whom God and the saints defend) and shall forthwith make full and instant surrender of this his ancient city of Belsaye unto your lord the Duke (whom God and the saints defend — amen!) Failing the which, I, in the name of Holy Church, by power of papal bull new come from Rome — will, here and now, pronounce this most rebellious city (and all that therein be) damned and excommunicate!"

Now hereupon, from all the townsfolk crowding wall and turret a groan went up and full many a ruddy cheek grew pale at this dire threat. Whereupon the Prior, having drawn breath, spake on in voice more stern and more peremptory:

"Let now your gates unbar! Yield ye unto your lord Duke his mercy! Let the gates unbar, I say, lest I blast this wicked city with the most dread and awful ban and curse of Holy Church — woe, woe in this life, and, in the life to come, torment and everlasting fire! Let the gates unbar!"

Now once again the men of Belsaye sighed and groaned and trembled in their armour, while from crowded street and market-square rose buzz of fearful voices. Then spake the Reeve in troubled tones, his white head low-stooped above the battlement.

"Good Prior, I pray you an we unbar, what surety have we that this our city shall not be given over to fire and pillage and ravishment?"

Quoth the Prior:

"Your lives are your lord's, in his hand resteth life and death, justice and mercy. So for the last time I charge ye — set wide your rebellious gates!"

"Not so!" cried the Reeve, "in the name of Justice and Mercy ne'er will we yield this our city until in Belsaye no man is left to strike for maid and wife and child!"

At the which bold words some few men shouted in acclaim, but for the most part the citizens were mumchance, their hearts cold within them, while all eyes stared fearfully upon the Prior, who, lifting white hand again, rose up from cushioned chair and spake him loud and clear:

"Then, upon this rebellious city and all that therein is, on babe, on child, on youth, on maid, on man, on wife, on the hale, the sick, the stricken in years, on beast, on bird, and on all that hath life and being I do pronounce the church's dread curse and awful ban: — ex —"

The Prior's mellifluous voice was of a sudden lost and drowned in another, a rich voice, strong and full and merry:

"Quit — quit thy foolish babblement, thou fat and naughty friar; too plump art thou, too round and buxom to curse a curse as curses should be cursed, so shall thy curses avail nothing, for who doth heed the fatuous fulminations of a fat man? But as to me, I could have outcursed thee in my cradle, thou big-bellied thing of emptiness — go to for a sounding brass and tinkling cymbal!"

Thus, from his "mockery" perched high above the battlement, spake Giles, with many and divers knowing gestures of arm, waggings of the head, rollings of the eyes and the like, what time Roger and Walkyn and Ulf, their heads bent close together, busied themselves above a great and bulging wine-skin.

And now on wall and tower and market-square a great silence had fallen, yet a silence broken now and then by sound of stifled laughter, while the Prior, staring in wonder and amaze, suddenly clenched white fist, and, albeit very red and fiery of visage, strove whole-heartedly to curse on:

"Ha — now upon the lewd populace of this most accursed and rebellious city do I call down the —"

"Upon thy round and barrel-like paunch," cried Giles, "do I pronounce this dire and dreadful ban, *videlicet*, Sir Fatness, *nota bene* and to wit: may the fiend rend it with gruesome gripings — aye, rend it with claws and beak, *unguibus et rostro*, most mountainous monk!"

Here, once again came sounds of stifled merriment, what time the Prior, puffing out his fat cheeks, fell to his curses full-tongued:

"Upon this evil city be the malison of Holy Church, her maledictions bitter, her imprecation and anathema. I do pronounce all within this city ex —"

"Abate thee, friar, abate!" roared Giles, "cease thy rumbling, thou empty wine-butt. An thou must deal in curses, leave them to one more apt and better schooled — to Giles, in faith, who shall forthwith curse thee sweet and trippingly as thus — now mark me, monk! Aroint, aroint thee to Acheron dark and dismal, there may the foul fiend seize and plague thee with seven and seventy plaguey sorrows! May Saint Anthony's fire frizzle and fry thee — woe, woe betide thee everlastingly — (bate thy babble, Prior, I am not ended yet!) In life may thou be accursed from heel to head, within thee and without — (save thy wind, Prior, no man doth hear or heed thee!) Be thou accursed in father and in mother, in sister and in brother, in oxen and in asses — especially in asses! Be thou accursed in sleeping and in waking, eating and drinking, standing, sitting, lying — O be thou accursed completely and consumedly! Here now, methinks, Sir Monkish Tunbelly, is cursing as it should be cursed. But now — (hush thy vain babbling, heed and mark me well!) — now will I to dictums contumacious, from cursing thee I will to song of thee, of thy plump and pertinacious person — a song wherein shall pleasant mention be o' thy round and goodly paunch, a song that shall be sung, mayhap, when thee and it are dusty dust, O shaveling — to wit:

"O frater fat and flatulent, full foolish, fatuous Friar
A prime plump priest in passion seen, such pleasure doth inspire,
That sober souls, 'spite sorrows sad, shall sudden shout and sing
Because thy belly big belittleth baleful ban ye bring.
Wherefore with wondrous wit withal, with waggish wanton wiles,
I joyful chant to glorify the just and gentle Giles."

And now behold! fear and dread were forgotten quite, and wheresoever Beltane looked were men who bent and contorted themselves in their merriment, and who held their laughter yet in check to catch the archer's final words.

"Thus, thou poor and pitiful Prior, for thy rude speech and curses canonical we do requite thee with song sweet-sung and of notable rhyme and metre. Curse, and Belsaye shall out-curse thee; laugh, and Belsaye laugheth at thee —"

"Sacrilege!" gasped the Prior, "O 'tis base sacrilege! 'Tis a vile, unhallowed city and shall go up in flame —"

"And thou," cried Giles, "thou art a fiery churchman and shall be cooled. Ho, Rogerkin — loose off!"

Came the thudding crash of a powerful mangonel, whose mighty beam, swinging high, hurled aloft the bulging wine-skin, the which, bursting in mid-air, deluged with water all below — prior and monk, acolyte and chorister; whereat from all Belsaye a shout went up, that swelled to peal on peal of mighty laughter, the while, in stumbling haste, the dripping Prior was borne by dripping monks back to Duke Ivo's mighty camp. And lo! from this great camp another sound arose, a roar of anger, fierce and terrible to hear, that smote Belsaye to silence. But, out upon the battlement, plain for all folk to see, sprang Giles flourishing his six-foot bow.

"Archers!" he cried, "archers, ye hear the dogs bay yonder — fling back their challenge!

> "Ho, archers! shout and rend the skies,
> Bold archers shout amain,
> Belsaye, Belsaye — arise, arise!
> Pentavalon — Beltane!"

Then from tower and turret, from wall and keep and market-square a great and joyous shout was raised — a cry fierce and loud and very purposeful, that rolled afar:

"Arise, arise! — ha, Beltane — Pentavalon!"

"Beltane," quoth Sir Benedict, smiling his wry smile as he turned to descend the tower, "methinks yon roguish archer's wit hath served us better than all our wisdom. Belsaye hath frighted away fear with laughter, and her men, methinks, will fight marvellous well!"

CHAPTER LXV

TELLETH OF ROSES

A FAIR and strong city was Belsaye, for (as hath been said) to north and east of it the river flowed, a broad stream and deep, while south and west it was fortified by a goodly moat; wherefore it was to south and west that the besiegers mustered their chief force and set up their mightiest engines and towers. Day in, day out, mangonel, trebuchet and balista whirred and crashed from keep and tower and curtain-wall, while from every loophole and crenelle long-bows twanged and arrows flew; yet with each succeeding dawn the besiegers' fence-works crept nearer, closing in upon the city until, within close bowshot of the walls, they set up earthworks and stockades and from these strong barriers plied the defenders with cloth-yard shaft and cross-bow bolt what time their mighty engines advanced, perriers and rams wherewith to batter and breach the city's massy walls.

So day in, day out, Eric's chosen men plied trebuchet and balista, and Beltane, beholding the dire havoc wrought by heavy stone and whizzing javelin among the dense ranks of the besiegers despite their mantlets and stout palisades, grew sick at times and was fain to look otherwhere. But the besiegers were many and Duke Ivo had sworn swift destruction on Belsaye; thus, heedless of all else, he pushed on the attack until, despite their heavy losses, his men were firmly established close beyond the moat; wherefore my Beltane waxed full anxious and was for sallying out to destroy their works: at the which, gloomy Sir Hacon, limping in his many bandages, grew suddenly jovial and fain was to call for horse and lance forthwith.

Quoth Sir Benedict placidly:

"Nay, let them come, messires; they are a sea, but Belsaye is a rock. Duke Ivo is cunning in war, but is, mark me! a passionate man, and he who fighteth in blind anger, fighteth ill. So let them come, I say the time for us to beware is when Ivo's hot temper shall have cooled. Ha, look yonder!" and Sir Benedict pointed where a great wooden tower, urged forward by rope and pulley and winch, was creeping near and nearer the walls, now stopping jerkily, now advancing, its massy timbers protected from fire by raw hides, its summit bristling with archers and cross-bow men, who from their lofty post began to sweep wall and turret with their whizzing shafts.

"Now mark yon tower," said Sir Benedict, closing his vizor, "here shall be good sport for Eric's perriers — watch now!" and he nodded where on the battlement below, crouched Eric with Walkyn and Roger who laboured at the winches of a great trebuchet hard by. To left and right on wall and turret, Eric glanced, then blew a blast upon the horn he carried; and immediately, from wall and turret mangonels, trebuchets and balistæ unknown of until now crashed and whirred, and the tall tower shook and quivered 'neath the shock of great stones and heavy bolts, its massy timbers were split and rent, insomuch that it was fain to be withdrawn.

Thereafter the besiegers brought up a long pent-house or cat unto the edge of the moat, and sheltered within this cat were many men who fell to work filling up the moat with bags of earth and stone werewith to form a causeway across which they might assault the wall with bore and ram; and because this cat was builded very strong, Eric's engines battered it in vain, wherefore he presently desisted; thus, hour by hour the causeway grew and lengthened. So needs must Beltane seek Sir Benedict and point this out with anxious finger.

"Let them come, Beltane!" quoth Sir Benedict, placid as was his wont, "once they are close against the wall with ram a-swing, I will make their labour of no avail; you shall see me burn them with a devil's brew I learned of in the foreign wars. So, let them come, Beltane!"

Thus, day in, day out, was roar of conflict about the walls of Belsaye town, and ever Sir Benedict, with Beltane beside him, went to and fro, quick of eye and hand, swift to foresee and counteract the tactics of the besiegers, meeting cunning artifice with crafty strategem; wheresoever was panic or pressing need there was Sir Benedict, calm-voiced and serene. And Beltane, watching him thus, came to understand why this man had withstood the powers of Duke Ivo all these years, and why all men trusted to his judgment.

Thus, all day was rage of battle, but with the night peace came, since in the dark men might not see to aim and slay each other. And by night the folk of Belsaye made good their battered walls what time the besiegers prepared fresh devices of attack. Every morning at sunrise it was Beltane's custom to steal to the great minster and, soft-treading despite his armour, come to his mother's grave to hold communion with her in his prayers. And lo! upon that hallowed stone there always he found fragrant flowers, roses and lilies, new-gathered, upon whose sweet petals the dew yet sparkled, and ever his wonder grew.

More than once he had thought to hear again that indefinable stir and whisper the which had thrilled him on that first morning, and, starting up, he would peer into the vague shadows. Twice he had thought to see a draped figure bending above that long, white stone, a veiled figure slender and graceful, that upon his approach, soft though it was, flitted swiftly into the dark recesses of the choir. Once he had followed, and stood amazed to see it vanish through the carven panelling, though door could he find none. Therefore was he sore perplexed and oft would touch the dewy flowers as half expecting they should vanish also. Now upon a certain dawn he had hid himself within the shadows and waited with bated breath and heart strangely a-throb. And with the day-spring she came

again, tall and gracious in her clinging draperies and long
green veil. Then, even as she bent to lay the flowers upon
the grave came Beltane, soft of foot, and spake ere she
was 'ware of him.

"Lady —!" now though his voice was very low and
gentle she started, the flowers fell from her loosened clasp,
and, after a moment, she turned and fronted him, proud
head up-flung beneath her veil. So stood they within that
place of silence, while high above, the great window grew
luminous with coming day.

"Lady," said he again, "for thy sweet flowers, for
thy sweeter thought for one that is — gone, fain would I
thank thee, for she who lieth here I found, and loved, and
have lost again a while. She did love all fair things, so
loved she the flowers, methinks; yet I, who have grieved
for my noble mother, ne'er thought to bring her flowers —
this did need a woman's gentle soul. So, for thy flowers,
I do most truly thank thee."

Very still she stood, nor spake nor moved, save for the
sweet hurry of her breathing; and beholding her thus, of
a sudden Beltane's heart leapt and he fell a-trembling
though wherefore he knew not, only yearned he mightily
to look beneath her veil. And now it seemed to him that,
in the stillness, she must needs hear the passionate throbbing of his heart; twice would he have spoken yet could
not; at last:

"Beseech thee," he whispered, "O beseech thee unveil,
that I may behold the face of one so tender to her that
was my dear-loved mother — O beseech thee!"

As he spake, he drew a swift pace nearer, hand outstretched in supplication, but, because this hand shook and
quivered so, he clenched it, whereat the unknown shrank
back and back and, turning swift and sudden, was gone.

A while stood my Beltane, his head a-droop, and fell to
wonderment because of the so painful throbbing of his
heart. Then knelt he above his mother's grave with
hands tight-clasped.

"Dear mother in heaven," he sighed, "being an angel,

thou dost know all my heart, its hopes and fears — thou hast seen me tremble — thou dost know wherefore this my heart doth yearn so bitterly. O sweet mother with God, plead thou on my behalf that I may be worthy her love — meet to her embracements — fit for so great happiness. Angel of God, thou dost know how great is my desire — how empty life without her — O mother — aid me!"

In a while he arose and immediately beheld that which lay beyond his mother's grave full in the radiance of the great east window — a thing small and slender and daintily wrought; and stooping, he picked up a little shoe. Of soft leather it was fashioned, cunningly pinked, and sewn, here and there, with coloured silks; and as he stared down at it, so small-seeming in his mailed hand, his heart leapt again, and again his strong hand fell a-trembling. Of a sudden he raised his eyes to heaven, then, coming to his mother's grave, very reverently took thence a single great bloom and thrusting the shoe in the wallet at his girdle (that same wallet Sir Fidelis had borne) went out into the golden dawn.

Like one in a dream went Beltane, heedless of his going; by silent street and lane where none stirred at this early hour, thus he wandered on until he was stayed by a high wall wherein was set a small, green door.

As he stood, staring down at the rose he held and lost in pleasant dream, he was aroused by a scrambling sound near by, and, glancing up, beheld a mailed head and shoulders rise suddenly above the wall and so looked into the face of Giles o' the Bow. Now in his teeth Giles bare a great red rose — even as that which Beltane held.

"Giles," quoth he, sharp and stern, "whence had ye that flower?"

For answer, Giles, straddling the wall, laid finger to lip, then dropping cat-like to his feet, drew Beltane down an adjacent lane.

"Lord," said he, "yonder is the Reeve's garden and in the Reeve's garden cometh the Reeve to taste the sweet dawn, wherefore Giles doth incontinent vanish him over the Reeve's wall because of the Reeve; nevertheless needs must I bless the Reeve because of the Reeve's daughter — though verily, both in my speech and in the Reeve's garden is too much Reeve, methinks. As to this rose, now — ha!"

"How came you by the rose, Giles?"

"Why, in the first place, tall brother, I stole it —"

"Stole it!" repeated Beltane, and behold! his frown was gone completely.

"But, in the second place, brother, 'twas given to me —"

"Given to thee — by whom?" and immediately Beltane's frown was back again.

"And therefore, in the third place, brother, Giles this day would not change skins with any lord, duke, archduke, pope or potentate that e'er went in skin —"

"Who gave it thee? — speak, man!"

"Faith, lord, I had it from one as pure, as fair, as —"

"Aye, but what like is she?"

"Like unto this flower for sweetness, lord, and — ha, saints and martyrs! whence had ye that bloom, tall brother — speak!" and Giles pointed to the rose in Beltane's fingers.

"What like is she — answer me!"

"Alack!" sighed Giles, shaking gloomy head, "she is very like a woman, after all, methinks —"

"Mean ye the Reeve's daughter?"

"Even so, lord!"

"Doth she wear ever a — a green veil, Giles?"

"Verily, lord, and with a most sweet grace —"

"And her shoes —"

"Her shoes, tall brother, O methinks her sweet shoe doth kiss the earth so sweet and light poor earth must needs love and languish as doth poor Giles! Her shoe —"

"Is it aught like to this, Giles?" and forthwith Beltane took out the little shoe.

"Aye, 'tis her very own, master!" groaned Giles. "Ah, woe is me, for if she hath given to thee rose and therewith her pretty shoe — thou hast, belike, her heart also, and with her heart —"

"Nay, take it, Giles,— take it!" quoth Beltane, sighing. "I did but find it in my going, and this rose — I found also, but this will I keep. Methinks thy love is what thy heart telleth thee — a maid very gentle and sweet — so God prosper thy wooing, Giles!"

So saying, Beltane thrust the shoe upon bewildered Giles and, turning swiftly about, hasted away. But even then, while the archer yet stared after him, Beltane turned and came striding back.

"Giles," quoth he, "how tall is the Reeve's daughter?"

"Lord, she is better than tall —"

"Ha — is she short of stature, good Giles?"

"Messire, God hath shaped her lovely body no higher and no lower than my heart. Small is she and slender, yet in her sweet and slender shapeliness is all the beauty of all the women that all men have ever loved —"

"Small, say you, Giles — small? Then give me back yon lovely thing!"

Saying the which, Beltane caught the shoe from Giles's hold and strode away blithe and debonair, leaving the garrulous archer dumb for once and beyond all words amazed.

Now as Beltane went very deep in thought there met him Friar Martin, who bore upon his arm a great basket full of green vegetables and sweet herbs. Quoth Beltane:

"Good friar, what do ye abroad so early?"

"Sweet son, I praise the good God for His mercies and pant by reason of this my weighty basket."

"Indeed 'tis a something well-laden basket," said Beltane, relieving the friar of his burden with gentle force.

"Why, verily, my children are hungry children and clamour to be filled. And see you, my son, I have a secret of a certain broth whereof these lentils and these sweet herbs do so tickle their palates that to satisfy them is a hard matter — more especially Orson and Jenkyn — who being nigh cured of their hurts do eat like four men and vaunt my cooking full-mouthed, insomuch that I must needs grow heedful of vain pride."

"Fain would I see these children of thine an I may, good friar, so will I bear thy burden for thee."

"Verily they shall rejoice to see thee," quoth the friar, "but for my basket, methinks 'tis better suited to my habit than thy knightly mail —"

For answer Beltane slipped the basket on his arm and they went on together talking whole-heartedly of many things. Thus the gentle friar brought him at last to a low-arched portal within a narrow lane, and pushing open the door, ushered him into the great refectory of the abbey, where Beltane set down the basket, and Friar Martin, rolling up his sleeves, brought pot and pannikin but paused to smile and shake his head, as from a stone-flagged passage hard by came the sound of voices raised in altercation.

"My children do grow a little fractious at times," quoth he, "as is but natural, methinks. Yonder you shall hear Orson and Jenkyn, who having saved each other's life in battle and loving like brothers, do oft contend together with tongues most ungentle; go you, my son, and quiet me the naughty rogues."

So saying, Friar Martin fell to washing and preparing his herbs and vegetables whiles Beltane, hasting down the passage, opened a certain door and entered a cool and airy dormitory, where upon pallets neat and orderly lay divers fellows whose hurts were swathed in fair white linen, and who, despite their bandages, started up on hand or elbow to greet Beltane right gladly. And behold! beside each man's couch was a bowl wherein roses bloomed.

"Master," quoth Tall Orson, "us do be glad to see thee — in especial me — and Jenkyn that I did save the carcase of and as do be a liar as do say my roses do be a-fading, master, and as his roses do bloom fairer than my roses and —"

"And look'ee master, so they be, for I ha' watered mine wi' Orson's drinking-water, while he snored, look'ee —"

"So Jenkyn do be thief as well, master —"

"Nay," said Beltane smiling, and seating himself on Orson's bed, "stint now your angers and tell me who gave ye flowers so fair?"

"Master, she do be an angel!"

"Heed him not, lord, for look'ee, she is a fair and lovely woman, and look'ee, a good woman is better than an angel, look'ee!"

"And what like is she?" questioned Beltane.

"She do be like to a stag for grace o' body, and wi' the eyes of a stag —"

"Nay, master, her eyes do be maid's eyes, look'ee, very soft and sweet, and her hair, look'ee —"

"Her hair do be like a forest-pool brim-full o' sunset —"

"Not so, master, her hair is red, look'ee —"

"And each day she do bring us flowers, master —"

"And suckets, look'ee, very sweet and delicate, master."

In a while Beltane arose and going from bed to bed spake with each and every, and went his way, leaving Orson and Jenkyn to their recriminations.

Being come back into the refectory, he found Friar Martin yet busied with the preparations of his cooking, and seating himself upon the great table hard by, fell to a profound meditation, watched ever and anon by the friar's kindly eyes: so very silent and thoughtful was he that the friar presently looked up from slicing and cutting his vegetables and spake with smile wondrous tender:

"Wherefore so pensive, my son?"

"Good father, I think and dream of — red roses!"

Friar Martin cut and trimmed a leek with great care, yet surely here was no reason for his eyes to twinkle within the shadow of his white cowl.

"A sweet and fragrant thought, my son!" quoth he.

"As sweet, methinks, holy father, as pure and fragrant as she herself!"

"'She,' my son?"

"As Helen, good friar, as Helen the Beautiful, Duchess of Mortain!"

"Ah!" sighed the friar, and forthwith popped the leek into the pot. "I prithee, noble son, reach me the salt-box yonder!"

CHAPTER LXVI

CONCERNING A BLUE CAMLET CLOAK

NEXT morning, ere the sun was up, came Beltane into the minster and hiding within the deeper gloom of the choir, sat there hushing his breath to listen, trembling in eager anticipation. Slowly amid the dimness above came a glimmer from the great window, a pale beam that grew with dawn until up rose the sun and the window glowed in many-hued splendour.

And in a while to Beltane's straining senses came the faint creak of a door, a soft rustle, the swift light tread of feet, and starting forth of his lurking place he stepped forward with yearning arms outstretched — then paused of a sudden beholding her who stood at gaze, one slender foot advanced and white hands full of roses and lilies, one as fair, as sweet and pure as the fragrant blooms she bore. Small was she and slender, and of a radiant loveliness, red of lip and grey-eyed: now beholding Beltane thus suddenly, she shrank and uttered a soft cry.

"Nay," quoth he, "fear me not, sweet maid, methought thee other than thou art — I grieve that I did fright thee — forgive me, I pray," so saying, he sighed and bowing full humbly, turned, but even so paused again: "Thou art methinks the Reeve's fair daughter — thou art the lady Genevra?" he questioned.

"Aye, my lord."

"Then, an thou dost love, gentle maid, heaven send thee happier in thy love than I." At the which Genevra's gentle eyes grew softer yet and her sweet mouth full pitiful and tender.

"Art thou so unhappy, lord Beltane?"

"Aye, truly!" he sighed, and drooped mournful head.

"Ah, messire, then fain would I aid thee an I might!" said she, soft-voiced.

"Then where, I pray you, is she that came here yesterday?"

"Nay, lord, how may I tell thee this? There be many women in Belsaye town."

"For me," quoth Beltane, "in all the world there is but one and to this one, alas! thou canst not aid me, yet for thy kind intent I thank thee, and so farewell, sweet maid." Thus saying, he took three steps away from her, then turning, came back in two. "Stay," quoth he, slipping hand in wallet, "know you this shoe?"

Now beholding this, Genevra's red lips quivered roguishly, and she bowed her little, shapely head:

"Indeed, my lord, 'tis mine!" said she.

"Then pray you, who was she did wear it yesterday —?"

"Aye, messire, 'twas yesterday I — missed it, wilt not give it me therefore? One shoe can avail thee nothing and — and 'tis too small for thee to wear methinks —"

"Did she — she that lost this yesterday, send thee to-day in her stead?"

"Wilt not give a poor maid her shoe again, messire?"

"O Genevra, beseech thee, who was she did wear it yesterday — speak!"

"Nay, this — this I may not tell thee, lord Beltane."

"And wherefore?"

"For that I did so promise — and yet — what seek you of her, my lord?"

"Forgiveness," said Beltane, hot and eager, "I would woo her sweet clemency on one that hath wrought her grievous wrong. O sweet Genevra, wilt not say where I may find her?"

A while stood the maid Genevra with bowed head as one in doubt, then looked on him with sweet maiden eyes and of a sudden smiled compassionate and tender.

"Ah, messire," said she, "surely thine are the eyes of one who loveth greatly and well! And I do so love her that fain would I have her greatly loved — so will I tell thee despite my word — hearken!" And drawing him near she laid white finger to rosy lip and thereafter spake in whispers. "Go you to the green door where yesterday thou didst meet with Gi — with the captain of the archers — O verily we — she and I, my lord, did see and hear all that passed betwixt you — and upon this door knock you softly three times. Go — yet, O prithee say not 'twas Genevra told thee this!" and again she laid white finger to roguish, pouting lip.

Then Beltane stooped, and catching that little hand kissed it, and thereafter hasted blithely on his way.

Swift of foot went he and with eyes a-dance, nor paused in his long stride until he was come to a certain high wall wherein was set the small, green door, whereon he knocked three times. And presently he heard the bar softly raised, the door was opened slow and cautiously, and stooping, Beltane stepped beneath the lintel and stood suddenly still, staring into the face of Black Roger. And even as Beltane stared thus amazed, so stared Roger.

"Why, master —" quoth he, pushing back his mail-coif to rumple his black hair, "why, master, you — you be early abroad — though forsooth 'tis a fair morning and —"

"Roger," quoth Beltane, looking round upon a fair garden a-bloom with flowers, "Roger, where is the Duchess Helen?"

"Ha, so ye do know, master — who hath discovered it —?"

"Where is she, Roger?"

"Lord," quoth Roger, giving a sudden sideways jerk of his head, "how should Roger tell thee this?" Now even as he spake, Roger must needs gesture again with his head and therewith close one bright, black eye, and with stealthy finger point to a certain tall hedge hard by; all of which was seen by one who stood beyond the hedge, watching Beltane with eyes that missed nought of him, from golden spur to golden head; quick to note his flushing cheek, his parted lips and the eager light of his blue eyes; one who perceiving him turn whither Roger's sly finger pointed, gathered up her flowing robe in both white hands that she might flee the faster, and who, speeding swift and light, came to a certain leafy bower where stood a tambour frame, and sitting there, with draperies well ordered, caught up silk and needle, yet paused to close her eyes and set one hand upon rounded bosom what time a quick, firm step drew near and ever nearer with clash and ring of heavy mail until Beltane stood before her. And how was he to know of the eyes that had watched him through the hedge, or that the hand that held the needle had paused lest he should see how direfully it trembled: how should my Beltane know all this, who was but a very man?

A while stood he, viewing her with eyes aglow with yearning tenderness, and she, knowing this, kept her face down-bent, therefore. Now beholding all the beauty of her, because of her gracious loveliness, his breath caught, then hurried thick and fast, insomuch that when he would have spoken he could not; thus he worshipped her in a look and she, content to be so worshipped, sat with head down-bent, as sweetly demure, as proud and stately as if — as if she ne'er in all her days had fled with hampering draperies caught up so high!

So Beltane stood worshipping her as she had been some young goddess in whose immortal beauty all beauty was embodied.

At last he spake, hoarse and low and passionate:

"Helen!" said he, "O Helen!"

Slowly, slowly the Duchess lifted stately head and looked on him: but now, behold! her glance was high and proud, her scarlet mouth firm-set like the white and dimpled chin below, and her eyes swept him with look calm and most dispassionate.

"Ah, my lord Beltane," she said, sweet-voiced, "what do you here within the privacy of Genevra's garden?"

Now because of the sweet serenity of her speech, because

of the calm, unswerving directness of her gaze, my Beltane felt at sudden loss, his outstretched arms sank helplessly and he fell a-stammering.

"Helen, I — I — O Helen, I have dreamed of, yearned for this hour! To see thee again — to hear thy voice, and yet — and yet —"

"Well, my lord?"

Now stood Beltane very still, staring on her in dumb amaze, and the pain in his eyes smote her, insomuch that she bent to her embroidery and sewed three stitches woefully askew.

"O surely, surely I am mad," quoth he wondering, "or I do dream. For she I seek is a woman, gentle and prone to forgiveness, one beyond all women fair and brave and noble, in whose pure heart can nothing evil be, in whose gentle eyes her gentle soul lieth mirrored, whose tender lips be apt and swift to speak mercy and forgiveness. Even as her soft, kind hands did bind up my wounds, so methought she with gentle sayings might heal my grieving heart — and now — now —"

"O my lord," she sighed, bending over idle fingers, "methinks you came seeking an angel of heaven and find here — only a woman."

"Yet 'tis this woman I do love and ever must —'tis this woman I did know as Fidelis —"

"Alas!" she sighed again, "alas, poor Fidelis, thou didst drive him from thee into the solitary wild-wood. So is poor Fidelis lost to thee, methinks —"

"Nay, Helen — O Helen, be just to me — thou dost know I loved Fidelis —"

"Yet thou didst spurn and name him traitor and drave him from thee!"

Now of a sudden he strode towards her, and as he came her bosom swelled, her lashes drooped, for it seemed he meant to clasp her to his heart. But lo! being only man, my Beltane paused and trembled, and dared not touch her, and sinking before her on his knees, spake very humbly and with head low-bowed.

"Helen — show me a little mercy!" he pleaded. "Would'st that I abase myself? Then here — here behold me at thy feet, fearing thee because of my unworthiness. But O believe — believe, for every base doubt of thee this heart hath known, now doth it grieve remorseful. For every harsh and bitter word this tongue hath spoke thee, now doth it humbly crave thy pitiful forgiveness! But know you this, that from the evil hour I drave thee from me, I have known abiding sorrow and remorse, for without thee life is indeed but an empty thing and I a creature lost and desolate — O Helen, pity me!"

Thus spake he, humble and broken, and she, beholding him thus, sighed (though wondrous softly) and 'neath her long lashes tears glittered (though swift dashed away) but — slowly, very slowly, one white hand came out to him, faltered, stopped, and glancing up she rose in haste and shrank away. Now Beltane, perceiving only this last gesture, sprang up, fierce-eyed:

"How?" quoth he, "am I then become a thing so base my presence doth offend thee — then, as God liveth, ne'er shalt see me more until thou thyself do summon me!"

Even as he spake thus, swift and passionate, Giles clambered the adjacent wall and dropping softly within the garden, stared to behold Beltane striding towards him fierce-eyed, who, catching him by the arm yet viewing him not, spun him from his path, and coming to the green door, sped out and away.

Now as Giles stood to rub his arm and gape in wonderment, he started to find the Duchess beside him; and her eyes were very bright and her cheeks very red, and, meeting her look, poor Giles fell suddenly abashed.

"Noble lady —" he faltered.

"Foolish Giles!" said she, "go, summon me my faithful Roger." But as she spake, behold Roger himself hasting to her through the roses.

"Roger," said she, frowning a little, "saw you my lord go but now?"

"Aye, verily, dear my lady," quoth he, ruffling up his hair, "but wherefore —"

"And I," said Giles, cherishing his arm, "both saw and felt him —"

"Ha," quoth Roger, "would'st have him back, sweet mistress?"

"Why truly I would, Roger —"

"Then forsooth will I go fetch him."

"Nay — rather would I die, Roger."

"But — dear lady — an thou dost want him —"

"I will bring him by other means!" said the Duchess, "aye, he shall come despite himself," and her red lips curved to sudden roguish smile, as smiling thus, she brought them to a certain arbour very shady and remote, and, seating herself, looked from one tanned face to the other and spake them certain matters, whereat the archer's merry eyes grew merrier yet, but Roger sighed and shook his head; said he:

"Lady, here is tale shall wring his noble heart, methinks, wherefore the telling shall wring mine also —"

"Then speak not of it, Roger. Be this Giles's mission."

"Aye, Rogerkin, leave it to me. In faith, noble lady, I will with suggestion soft and subtle, with knowing look and wily wag of head, so work upon my lord that he shall hither hot-foot haste —"

"At moonrise," said the Duchess softly, "this evening at moonrise!"

"Verily, lady, at moonrise! And a blue camlet cloak, say you?"

"Come, Giles, and I will give it thee."

Meanwhile, Beltane, hurt and angry, betook him to the walls where bow and perrier had already begun their deadly morning's work; and coming to a quiet corner of the battlement, he leaned him there to watch where the besiegers, under cover of the cat that hourly crept more nigh, worked amain to dam the moat.

Now as he leaned thus, a hand slipped within his arm, and turning, he beheld Sir Benedict.

"A right fair morning, my Beltane," quoth he.

"Aye, truly, Benedict," sighed Beltane, "though there be clouds to the west. And the causeway across the moat groweth apace; I have watched yon cat creep a full yard —"

"Aye, verily, by mid-day, Beltane, 'twill reach our wall, then will they advance their ram to the battery, methinks."

"And what then, Benedict?"

"Then shall we destroy their ram forthwith with devil-fire, dear lad!"

"Aye, and how then, Benedict?"

"Then, belike will they plant ladders on the causeway and attempt the wall by storm, so shall we come to handstrokes at last and beset them with pitch and boiling oil and hew their ladders in sunder."

"And after, Benedict?"

"Hey-day, Beltane, here be a many questions —"

"Aye, Benedict, 'tis that I do look into the future. And what future can there be? Though we maintain our walls a year, or two, or three, yet in the end Belsaye must fall."

"And I tell thee, Beltane, were Ivo twice as strong Belsaye should yet withstand him. So gloom not, lad, Belsaye is safe, the sun shineth and behold my arm —'tis well-nigh healed, thanks to — to skilful nursing —"

"Of the Duchess Helen, Benedict?"

"Ha — so hast found it out — at last, lad —"

"Knew you she was here?"

"Aye, verily."

"And told me not?"

"For that she did so command, Beltane."

"And wherefore came she hither?"

"For thy dear sake in the first place, and —"

"Nay, mock me not, friend, for I do know myself of none account."

"And in the second place, Beltane, to save this fair city of Belsaye."

"Nay, how mean you?"

"I mean that Belsaye cannot fall whiles it holdeth Helen the Proud. And the reason this — now mark me, Beltane! Since her father's death Duke Ivo hath had his glutton eye on fair Mortain, whereof her counsellors did ken, yet, being old men and averse to war, would fain have had her wed with him. Now upon a day word reached me in Thrasfordham bidding me come to her and Waldron of Brand at Winisfarne. So, as thou dost know, stole I from my goodly castle and marched north. But on the way she came to me bedight in mail, and she and I took counsel together. Wherefore came she hither to Belsaye and sent speedy messengers to Sir Jocelyn of Alain and others of her greatest lords and knights, bidding them come down with all their powers — nay, why shake ye gloomy head, fond boy? Body o' me, Beltane, I tell thee this — to-day she —"

"To-day," sighed Beltane, frowning, "to-day she spurneth me! Kneeling at her feet e'en as I was she shrank away as I had leprous been!"

"Aye, lad, and then — didst woo as well as kneel to her, didst clasp her to thee, lift her proud head that needs must she give to thine her eyes — she is in sooth very woman — did you this, my Beltane?"

"Ah, dear Benedict, she that I love was not wont to shrink from me thus! 'Tis true I am unworthy — and yet, she spurned me — so is her love dead, methinks!"

"So art thou but youth, and foolish youth, and belike, foolish, hungry youth — so come, let us break our fast together."

"Not I, Benedict, for if love be dead, no mind have I to food."

"O lad — lad!" sighed Sir Benedict, "would I had one as fair and noble to love me in such sort!" And turning, he gazed sad-eyed towards Belsaye's great minster, and sighing, went his way.

And presently, as Beltane leaned thus, grieving and alone, cometh Giles that way, who, pausing beside him, peered down where the besiegers, but ill-sheltered by battered mantlet and palisades, strove amain to bring up one of their rams, since the causeway across the moat was well-nigh complete.

"Holy saints!" quoth Giles, "the rogues grow bold and venturesome, methinks!" So saying, he strung his powerful bow, and laying arrows to his hand fell to drawing and loosing amain. So swift shot he and with aim so true, that in a while the enemy gave over their attempt and betook them to cover what time their archers and cross-bowmen plied the wall with a storm of shafts and bolts.

Upon this Giles, laying by his bow, seated himself in corner well screened from harm, beckoning Beltane to do the like, since the enemy's missiles whizzed and whistled perilously near. But sighing, Beltane closed his vizor and heedless of flying bolt and arrow strode to the narrow stair that led up to the gate-tower and being come there sat him down beside the great mangonel. But lo! very soon Giles was there also and even as Beltane sighed, so sighed Giles.

"Heigho — a sorry world, brother!" quoth he, "a sorry world!" and forthwith fell to his archery, yet now, though his aim was true as ever, he sighed and murmured plaintively 'twixt every shot: "Alack, a sorry world!" So deep and oft were his sighs, so plaintive his groans, that Beltane, though plunged in bitter thought, must needs at length take heed of him.

"Giles," quoth he, looking up, "a heaven's name, what aileth thee, man?"

"'Tis my eyes, lord."

"Thine eyes are well enough, Giles, and see wondrous well to judge by thy shooting."

"Wondrous well — aye, there it is, tall brother, mine eyes do see wondrous well, mine eyes do see so much, see you, that they do see over-much, over-much, aye — too,

too much. Alack, 'tis a sorry and woeful world, brother! beshrew my eyes, I say!"

"And wherefore, Giles?"

"For that these eyes do see what other eyes see not — thine, methinks, saw nought of a fine, lusty and up-standing fellow in a camlet cloak within the Reeve's garden this morning, I'll warrant me now? A tall, shapely rogue, well be-seen, see you, soft-voiced and very debonair?"

"Nay, not I," said Beltane, and sighing he arose and descended to the battlement above the gates. And presently, behold Giles was there also!

"Brother," quoth he, selecting an arrow with portentous care, "'tis an ill thing to be cursed with eyes such as mine, I tell thee!"

"Aye, and wherefore, Giles?" said Beltane, yet intent on his own thoughts.

"For that they do see more than is good for this heart o' mine — as this fellow in the blue camlet cloak —"

"What fellow, Giles?"

"The buxom fellow that was in the Reeve's garden this morning."

"Why then," quoth Beltane, turning away, "go you not to the Reeve's garden, Giles."

All day long Beltane kept the wall, eating not at all, wherefore his gloom waxed the more profound; so spake he to few men and oft exposed himself to shaft and missile. And so, all day long, wheresoever he came, on tower or keep, in corners most remote, there sure was Giles to come also, sighing amain and with brow of heavy portent, who, so oft as he met Beltane's gloomy eye, would shake his head in sad yet knowing fashion. Thus, as evening fell, Beltane finding him at his elbow yet despondent, betook him to speech at last; quoth he:

"Giles, art thou sick?"

"Aye, lord, by reason of this fellow in the blue camlet —"

"What fellow?"

"The tall and buxom fellow in the Reeve's garden."

"Ha!" quoth Beltane, frowning. "In the garden, say you — what manner of man is this?"

"O brother — a shapely man, a comely man — a man of words and cunning phrases — a man shall sing you sweet and melodious as any bird — why, I myself can sing no sweeter!"

"Cometh he there often, Giles?"

"Why lord, he cometh and he goeth — I saw him there this morning!"

"What doeth he there?"

"Nay, who shall say — Genevra is wondrous fair, yet so is she that is Genevra's friend, so do I hope belike 'tis she —"

"Hold thy peace, Giles!"

Now beholding Beltane's fierce eye and how his strong hands clenched themselves, Giles incontinent moved further off and spake in accents soft and soothing:

"And yet, tall brother, and yet 'tis belike but some gentle troubadour that singeth songs to their delectation, and 'tis meet to hark to songs sweet-sung — at moonrise, lord!"

"And wherefore at moonrise?"

"'Tis at this sweet hour your minstrel singeth best. Aye me, and to-night there is a moon!" Hereupon Beltane must needs turn to scowl upon the moon just topping the distant woods. Now as they sat thus, cometh Roger with bread and meat for his lord's acceptance; but Beltane, setting it aside, stared on Roger with baleful eye.

"Roger," said he, "wherefore hast avoided me this day?"

"Avoided thee, master — I?"

"And what did you this morning in the Reeve's garden?"

"Master, in this big world are two beings that I do truly love, and thou art one and the other Sir Fidelis thy right sweet and noble lady — so is it my joy to serve her when I may, thus daily do I go aid her with the sick."

"And what of him that singeth; saw you this troubadour within the garden?"

"Troubadour?" quoth Roger, staring.

"Why verily," nodded Giles, "my lord meaneth the tall and goodly fellow in the cloak of blue camlet, Roger."

"Ne'er have I seen one in blue cloak!" said Roger, "and this do I swear!"

"None the less," said Beltane, rising, "I will seek him there myself."

"At moonrise, lord?" questioned Giles.

"Aye," said Beltane grimly; "at moonrise!" and scowling he turned away.

"Aha!" quoth Giles, nudging Roger with roguish elbow, "it worketh, Roger, it worketh!"

"Aye, Giles, it worketh so well that an my master get his hands on this singing fellow — then woe betide this singing fellow, say I."

CHAPTER LXVII

TELLETH WHAT BEFELL IN THE REEVE'S GARDEN

THE moon was already filling the night with her soft splendour when Beltane, coming to a certain wall, swung himself up, and, being there, paused to breathe the sweet perfume of the flowers whose languorous fragrance wrought in him a yearning deep and passionate, and ever as love-longing grew, bitterness and anger were forgot. Very still was it within this sheltered garden, where, fraught by the moon's soft magic, all things did seem to find them added beauties.

But, even as he paused thus, he heard a step approaching, a man's tread, quick and light yet assured, and he beheld one shrouded in a long cloak of blue, a tall figure that hasted through the garden and vanished behind the tall yew hedge.

Down sprang Beltane fierce-eyed, trampling the tender flowers under cruel feet, and as he in turn passed behind the hedge the moon glittered evilly on his dagger blade. Quick and soft of foot went he until, beholding a faint light amid the leaves, he paused, then hasted on and thus came to an arbour bowered in eglantine.

She sat at a table where burned a rushlight that glowed among the splendour of her hair, for her head was bowed above the letter she was writing.

Now as he stood regarding her 'neath frowning brows, she spake, yet lifted not her shapely head.

"Well, my lord?"

"Helen, where is he that came here but now?"

Slowly she lifted her head, and setting white hands 'neath dimpled chin, met his frown with eyes of gentleness.

"Nay, first put up thy dagger, my lord."

"Helen," said he again, grim-lipped, "whom dost wait for?"

"Nay, first put up thy dagger, messire."

Frowning he obeyed, and came a pace nearer.

"What do you here with pen and ink-horn?"

"My lord, I write."

"To whom?"

"To such as it pleaseth me."

"I pray you — show me."

"Nay, for that doth not please me, messire."

"I pray you, who was he that came hither but now — a tall man in a long blue cloak?"

"I saw him not, my lord."

"So needs must I see thy letter."

"Nay, that thou shalt not, my lord," said she, and rose to her stately height.

"Aye, but I shall!" quoth Beltane softly, and came a pace yet nearer.

Now because of the grim and masterful look of him, her heart fell a-fluttering, yet she fronted him scornful-eyed, and curled her red lip at him.

"Messire," said she, "methinks you do forget I am the Duchess, and slave to no man, I thank God!"

"I remember thou art woman and thy name — Helen!"

Now at this laughed she softly and thereafter falleth to singing very sweet and blithe and merry withal.

"The letter!" said he, "give me thy letter!"

Hereupon she took up the letter, and, yet singing, crumpled it up within white fingers.

Then Beltane set by the table and reaching out sudden arms, caught her up 'neath waist and knee, and lifting her high, crushed her upon his breast.

"Helen!" said he, low-voiced and fierce, "mine art thou as I am thine, forever, 'twas so we plighted our troth within the green. Now for thy beauty I do greatly love thee, but for thy sweet soul and purity of heart I do reverence and worship thee — but an thou slay my reverent worship then this night shalt thou die and I with thee — for mine art thou and shalt be mine forever. Give me thy letter!"

But now her eyes quailed 'neath his, her white lids drooped, and sighing, she spake small-voiced:

"O my lord, thine arms are so — so tyrannous that I do fear thee — almost! And how may a poor maid, so crushed and helpless thus, gainsay thee? So prithee, O prithee take my poor letter an thou wilt ravish it from one so defenceless — O beseech thee, take it!"

So she gave the crumpled parchment into his hand, yet while he read it, nestled closer in his arms and hid her face against him; for what he read was this:

"Beloved, art thou angered, or sorrowful, or humble in thy foolish jealousy? If angered, then must I woo thee. If sorrowful, cherish thee. But being Beltane, needs must I love thee ever — so write I this, bidding thee come, my Beltane the Smith, for I —"

The crumpled letter fell to the ground.

"Helen!" he whispered, "Beloved, I am all of this, so do I need thy comfort, thy cherishing, and all thy dear love — turn thy head — O Helen, how red is thy sweet mouth!" Then stooped he, and so they kissed each other, such kisses as they ne'er had known, until she sighed and trembled and lay all breathless in his arms.

"O my lord," she whispered, "have mercy, I pray! Dear Beltane, loose me for I — I have much to tell thee."

And because of her pleading eyes he loosed her, and she, sinking upon the bench, leaned there all flushed and tremulous, and looking on him, sighed, and sighing, put up her hands and hid her face from his regard.

"Beltane," she whispered, "how wondrous a thing is this our love, so great and fierce it frighteth me — see how I tremble!" and she held out to him her hands.

Then came he and knelt before her, and kissed those slender fingers amain.

"Dear hands of Fidelis," said he, "but for their tender skill and gentle care I had not lived to know this night — O brave, small hands of Fidelis!"

"Poor Fidelis!" she sighed, "but indeed it wrung my heart to see thy woeful face when I did tell thee Fidelis was lost to thee — Nay, Beltane, stay — O prithee let me speak —"

Quoth Beltane 'twixt his kisses:

"Wherefore wert so cold and strange to me but yesterday?"

"Dear my heart," she murmured, "I needs must make thee suffer a little — just a very little, for that I had known so much of pain and heartache because of thee. But I was glad to see thee bear the wallet of poor Fidelis — and O, 'twas foolish in thee to grieve for him, for he being gone, thy Helen doth remain — unless, forsooth, thou had rather I came to thee bedight again in steel — that did so chafe me, Beltane — indeed, my tender skin did suffer much on thy account —"

"Then soon with my kisses will I seek —" But a cool, soft hand schooled his hot lips to silence and the while he kissed those sweet arresting fingers, she spake 'twixt smiling lips: "Prithee where is my shoe that was Genevra's? Indeed, 'twas hard matter to slip it off for thee, Beltane, for Genevra's foot is something smaller than mine — a very little! Nay, crush me not, messire, but tell me, what of him ye came hither seeking — the man in the long cloak — what of him?"

"Nought!" answered Beltane, "the world to-night doth hold but thee and me —"

"Aye, my Beltane, as when sick of thy wound within the little cave I nursed thee, all unknown. O love, in all thy sickness I was with thee, to care for thee. Teaching good Roger to tend thee and — to drug thee to gentle sleep that I might hold thee to me in the dark and — kiss thy sleeping lips —"

"Ah!" he sighed, "and methought 'twas but a dream! O Helen, sure none ever loved as we?"

"Nay, 'twere thing impossible, Beltane."

"And thou art truly mine?"

"Beltane — thou dost know this! Ah, love — what would you?" For of a sudden his mighty arms were close about her, and rising, he lifted her upon his breast. "What would'st do with me, Beltane?"

"Do?" quoth he, "do? This night, this very hour thou shalt wed me —"

"Nay, dear my lord — bethink thee —"

"It hath been my thought — my dearest dream since first I saw thee within the woods at Mortain — so now shalt wed me —"

"But, Beltane —"

"Shalt wed me!"

"Nay, love, I — I — thou art so sudden!"

"Aye, within this hour shalt call me 'husband'!"

"Wilt force me, my lord?"

"Aye, verily," said Beltane, "as God sees me, I will!"

"Why then," she sighed, "how may I gainsay thee!" and she hid her face against him once more. But, as he turned to leave the arbour, she stayed him:

"I prithee, now, whither dost take me, Beltane?"

"To the minster — anywhere, so that I find good Friar Martin."

"Nay, prithee, Beltane, prithee set me down!"

"What would'st, my Helen?"

"Loose me and shalt see."

So Beltane, sighing, let her go, whereupon she took a small silver whistle that hung at her girdle and sounded it.

"Ah — what do you?" he questioned.

"Wait!" said she, roguish-eyed.

And in a while came the sound of steps from the outer garden, and looking thither, Beltane beheld a tall man in cloak of blue camlet, and when this man drew near, behold! it was Giles.

"Giles!" quoth he, "thou wily rogue —"

"Giles," spake the Duchess softly, "I pray you let them come!"

Then Giles bowed him low, and smiling, hasted joyously away.

"Beltane, dear my lord," said the Duchess a little breathlessly, "because thou art true man and thy love is a noble love, I did lure thee hither to-night that I might give myself to thee in God's holy sight — an so it be thy will, my lord. O Beltane, yonder Giles and Roger do bring — Friar Martin to make me — thy wife — wherefore I do grow something fearful. 'Tis foolish in me to fear thee and yet — I do — a little, Beltane!" So saying, she looked on him with eyes full sweet and troubled, wherefore he would have kissed her, but steps drew nigh and lo! without the arbour stood the white friar with Giles and Roger in the shadows behind.

Now came Beltane and took the friar's hand.

"Holy father," said he, "O good Friar Martin, though I am but what I am, yet hath this sweet and noble lady raised me up to be what I have dreamed to be. To-night, into my care she giveth her sweet body and fair fame, of which God make me worthy."

"Sweet children," spake the friar, "this world is ofttimes a hard and cruel world, but God is a gentle God and merciful, wherefore as he hath given to man the blessed sun and the sweet and tender flowers, so hath he given him love. And when two there be who love with soul as well as body, with mind as well as heart, then methinks for them this world may be a paradise. And, my children, because I do love thee for thy sweet lives and noble works, so do I joy now to bind ye one to another."

Then hand in hand, the Duchess and my Beltane knelt together, and because he had no ring, needs must she give to him one of hers; so were they wed.

As one that dreamed, Beltane knelt there murmuring the responses, and thus knelt he so long that he started to feel a soft touch upon his cheek, and looking up, behold! they were alone.

"Dost dream, my lord?" she questioned, tender-voiced.

"Aye, verily," he answered, "of the wonder of our love

and thee, beloved, as I did see thee first within the thicket at Mortain, beautiful as now, though then was thy glorious hair unbound. I dream of thine eyes beneath thy nun's veil when I did bear thee in my arms from Thornaby — but most do I dream of thee as Fidelis, and the clasp of thy dear arms within the dark."

"But thou didst leave me in Mortain thicket despite my hair, Beltane! And thou didst tell me mine eyes were not — a nun's eyes, Beltane —"

"Wherefore this night do I thank God!" said he, drawing her close beside him on the bench.

"And for my arms, Beltane, thou didst think them man's arms — because they went bedight in mail, forsooth!"

"So this night shall they go bedight in kisses of my mouth! loose me this sleeve, I pray —"

"Nay, Beltane,— I do beseech thee —"

"Art not my wife?"

"Aye, my lord."

"Then loose me thy sleeve, Helen."

So blushing, trembling, needs must she obey and yield her soft arms to his caresses and hide her face because of their round, white nakedness.

But in a while she spake, low and very humble.

"Dear my lord, the moon doth set already, methinks!"

"Aye, but there is no cloud to dim her glory to-night, Helen!"

"But the hour waxeth — very late, my lord and I — must away."

"Aye, beloved, let us go."

"Nay my lord, I — O dear Beltane —"

"Wife!" said he, "dear my love and wife, have I not waited long enough?"

Hand in hand they walked amid the flowers with eyes that met but seldom and lips that spake not at all; so came they to a stair and up the stair to a chamber, rich with silk and arras and sweet with spicy odours, a chamber dim-lighted by a silver lamp pendent from carven roof-beam, whose soft glow filled the place with shadow. Yet even in this tender dimness, or because of it, her colour ebbed and flowed, her breath came apace and she stood before him voiceless and very still save for the sweet tumult of her bosom.

Then Beltane loosed off his sword and laid it upon the silken couch, but perceiving how she trembled, he set his arm about her and drew her to the open lattice where the moon made a pool of glory at their feet.

"Dost fear me, Helen?"

"Nay, my lord, I — think not."

"Then wherefore dost tremble?"

"Ah, Beltane, thou methinks dost — tremble also?"

Then Beltane knelt him at her feet and looked upon her loveliness with yearning eyes, yet touched her not:

"O beloved maid!" said he, "this is, methinks, because of thy sweet virgin eyes! For I do so love thee, Helen, that, an it be thy will, e'en now will I leave thee until thy heart doth call me!"

Now stooped she and set her white arms about him and her soft cheek to his hot brow.

"Dear my lord and — husband," she whispered, "'tis for this so sweet tenderness in thee that I do love thee best, methinks!"

"And fear me no more?"

"Aye, my lord, I do fear thee when — when thou dost look on me so, but — when thou dost look on me so — 'tis then I do love thee most, my Beltane!"

Up to his feet sprang Beltane and caught her to him, breast to breast and lip to lip.

The great sword clattered to the floor; but now, even as she sank in his embrace, she held him off to stare with eyes of sudden terror as, upon the stilly night broke a thunderous rumble, a shock, and thereafter sudden roar and outcry from afar, that swelled to a wild hubbub of distant voices and cries, lost, all at once, in the raving clamour of the tocsin.

Locked thus within each other's arms, eye questioned

eye, while ever the bell beat out its fierce alarm. And presently, within the garden below, was the sound of running feet and, coming to the casement, Beltane beheld a light that hovered to and fro, growing ever nearer and brighter, until he saw that he who bore it was Black Roger; and Roger's face shone with sweat and his breath laboured with his running.

"Master!" he panted, "O master — a mine! a mine! They have breached the wall beside the gate — hark, where they storm the city! Come, master, O come ere it be too late!"

Now Beltane clenched his fists and scowled on pale-faced Roger and from him to the radiant sky, yet when he spake his voice was low and even:

"I thank thee, faithful Roger! Go you and summon such of our foresters as ye may, muster them in the market-square, there will I come to thee."

Now when Roger's flickering light had vanished he turned, and found Helen close beside him; her cheeks were pale, but in her hand she held his sword.

"'Tis well thou wert not all unarmed, my lord!" she sighed, and forthwith belted the weapon about him. "Kneel down, I prithee, that I may lace for thee thy hood of mail." And when it was done she knelt also, and taking his hand pressed it to her throbbing heart, and holding him thus fell to prayer:

"O God of mercy, have in care those that fight in our defence this night, in especial guard and shield this man of mine that I do love beyond all men — O God of mercy, hear us!"

So they arose, and as he looked on her so looked she on him, and of a sudden clasped him in close and passionate embrace:

"Beltane — Beltane!" she sobbed, "God knoweth I do so love thee that thy dear flesh is mine, methinks, and the steel that woundeth thee shall hurt me also. And — O love — an thou should'st die to-night, then surely will this heart of mine die with thee — no man shall have my love other than thou — so to my grave will I go thy virgin wife for thy dear sake. Fare thee well Beltane, O dear my husband, fare thee well. Tarry no longer, lest I pray thee on my knees to go not to the battle."

So Beltane kissed her once and went forth of the chamber, looking not back. She heard the ring of his armour a-down the stair, the quick tread of his feet, and leaning from the casement watched him go; and he, knowing her there, looked not up, but with teeth hard shut and iron hands clenched, strode fast upon his way.

And now, since he looked not up, it seemed to her she was out of his thoughts already, for his face was stern and set, and in his eyes was the fierce light of battle.

And she, kneeling alone in the failing glory of the moon, hid her face within yearning, desolate arms and wept long and bitterly.

CHAPTER LXVIII

FRIAR MARTIN'S DYING PROPHECY

Now as Beltane hasted along he heard the tread of mailed feet, and looking round beheld the white friar, and 'neath his white frock mail gleamed, while in his hand he grasped a heavy sword. Close on his heels came many men, old men these for the most part, grey of beard and white of head, and their armour, even as they, was ancient and rusty; but the faces that stared from casque and mailhood were grim and sorrow-lined, stern faces and purposeful, and the eyes that gleamed 'neath shaggy brows ere now had looked on sons and brothers done to death by fire and gallows, and wives and daughters shamed and ravished. And ever as they came Friar Martin smote, sword in hand, on door and shuttered window, and cried hoarse and loud:

"Ye men of Belsaye — fathers and husbands, arm ye, arm ye! Ye greybeards that have seen Duke Ivo's mercy, arm ye! Your foes be in, to burn, to loot again and ravish! O ye husbands and fathers, arise, arise — arm, arm and follow me to smite for wife and children!"

So cried the tall white friar, pallid of cheek but dauntless of eye, and ever as he cried, smote he upon door and shutter with his sword, and ever his company grew.

Within the square was Roger, hoarse-voiced, with Beltane's battered war-helm on a pike whereto the foresters mustered — hardy and brown-faced men, fitting on bascinet and buckling belt, yet very quiet and orderly. And beside Roger, Ulf the Mighty leaned him upon his axe, and in the ranks despite their bandages stood Orson the Tall and Jenkyn o' the Ford, even yet in wordy disputation.

Quoth Beltane:

"How many muster ye, Roger?"

"One hundred and nine, master."

"And where is Walkyn — where Giles?"

"With Sir Benedict, hard by the gate, master. My lord, come take thy helm — come take it, master, 'twill be a close and bitter fight — and thou art no longer thine own man — bethink thee of thy sweet wife, Sir Fidelis, master!"

So Beltane did on the great casque and even now came Sir Brian beside whom Sir Hacon limped, yet with sword bloody.

"Ha, my lord," he cried, "mine eyes do joy to see thee and these goodly fellows —'tis hard and fierce business where Benedict and his pikes do hold the gate —"

"Aye, forsooth," quoth Sir Brian, "they press their attack amain, for one that falleth, two do fill his place."

"Verily, and what fighting man could ask more of any foe? And we be fighting men, praise be to Saint Cuthbert —"

"Aye," quoth Roger, crossing himself, "Saint Cuthbert be our aid this night."

Forthwith Beltane formed his column and with Ulf and Roger beside him marched from the square. By narrow streets went they, 'neath dim-lighted casements where pale faces looked down to pray heaven's aid on them.

So came they where torch and lanthorn smoked and gleamed, by whose fitful light they beheld a barricade, rough and hastily contrived, whence Sir Benedict fought and Walkyn smote, with divers of their stout company and lusty fellows from the town. Above, upon the great flanking tower of the gate, was Giles with many archers who plied their whizzing shafts amain where, 'twixt outer and inner wall, the assailants sought to storm the barricade; but the place was narrow, and moreover, beyond the breach stout Eric, backed by his fierce townsmen, fought in desperate battle: thus, though the besiegers' ranks were constantly swelled by way of the breach, yet in that confined space their very numbers hampered them, while from sheltered wall and gate-tower Giles and his archers showered them with whistling shafts very fast and furious; so in that narrow place death was rife and in the fitful torch-glare was a sea of tossing steel and faces fierce and wild, and ever the clamour grew, shouts and screams and cries dreadful to be heard.

Now as Beltane stood to watch this, grim-lipped, for it needed but few to man the barricade, so narrow was it, Roger caught his arm and pointed to the housetops above them; and what he saw, others saw also, and a cry went up of wonder and amaze. For, high upon the roof, his mail agleam, his white robe whiter in the torch-glare, stood Friar Martin, while crouched behind him to left and right were many men in ancient and rusty armour, men grey-bearded and white of head, at sight of whom the roar of battle died down from sheer amaze until all men might hear the friar's words:

"Come, ye men of Belsaye!" he cried, "all ye that do love wife or daughter or little child — all ye that would maintain them innocent and pure — follow me!"

As he ended, his sword flashed, and, even as he sprang, so sprang all those behind him — down, down they leapt upon the close-ranked foemen below, so swift, so sudden and unexpected, that ere they could be met with pike or sword the thing was done. And now from that narrow way, dim-lit by lanthorn and torch-glare, there rose a sound more awful to hear than roar of battle, a hoarse and vicious sound like to the worrying snarl of many great and fierce hounds.

With ancient swords, with axe and dagger and fierce-rending teeth they fought, those fathers of Belsaye; thick and fast they fell, yet never alone, while ever they raved on, a company of madmen, behind the friar's white robe. Back and back the besiegers reeled before that raging fury — twice the white friar was smitten down yet twice he arose, smiting the fiercer, wherefore, because of his religious habit, the deathly pallor of his sunken cheek and the glare of his eyes, panic came, and all men shrank from the red sweep of his sword.

Then Sir Benedict sounded his horn, and sword in hand leapt over the barricade, and behind him Beltane with Roger and Ulf and Walkyn and their serried pikemen, while Sir Brian and Sir Hacon limped in their rear.

"The breach!" cried Sir Benedict, "seize we now the breach!"

"The breach! The breach!" roared a hundred voices. And now within the gloom steel rasped steel, groping hands seized and griped with merciless fingers; figures, dim-seen, sank smitten, groaning beneath the press. But on they fought, slipping and stumbling, hewing and thrusting, up and up over ruined masonry, over forms that groaned beneath cruel feet — on and ever on until within the narrow breach Beltane's long sword darted and thrust and Ulf's axe whirled and fell, while hard by Walkyn's hoarse shout went up in roaring triumph.

So within this narrow gap, where shapeless things stirred and whimpered in the dark, Beltane leaned breathless upon his sword and looked down upon the watch-fires of Duke Ivo's great camp. But, even as he gazed, these fires were blotted out where dark figures mounted fresh to the assault, and once again sword and axes fell to their dire work.

And ever as he fought Beltane bethought him of her whose pure lips voiced prayers for him, and his mighty arm grew mightier yet, and he smote and thrust untiring, while Walkyn raged upon his left, roaring amain for Red Pertolepe, and Ulf the strong saved his breath to ply his axe the faster.

Now presently as they fought thus, because the breach was grown very slippery, Beltane tripped and fell, but in that instant two lusty mailed legs bestrode him, and from the dimness above Roger's voice hailed:

"Get thee back, master — I pray thee get back and take thy rest awhile, my arm is fresh and my steel scarce bloodied, so get thee to thy rest — moreover thou art a notch, lord — another accursed notch from my belt!"

Wherefore Beltane presently crept down from the breach and thus beheld many men who laboured amain beneath Sir Benedict's watchful eye to build a defence work very high and strong where they might command the breach. And as Beltane sat thus, finding himself very spent and weary, cometh Giles beside him.

"Lord," said he, leaning him on his bow, "the attack doth languish, methinks, wherefore I do praise the good God, for had they won the town — ah, when I do think on — her — she that is so pure and sweet — and Ivo's base soldiery — O sweet Jesu!" and Giles shivered.

"Forsooth, thou didst see fair Belsaye sacked — five years agone, Giles?"

"Aye, God forgive me master, for I — I — O, God forgive me!"

"Thou once did show me a goodly chain, I mind me, Giles."

"Aye, but I lost it — I lost it, master!" he cried eagerly, "O verily I did lose it, so did it avail me nothing."

"Moreover, Giles, thou didst with knowing laugh, vaunt that the women of Belsaye town were marvellous fair — and methinks didst speak truly, Giles!"

Now at this Giles bowed his head and turning him about, went heavily upon his way. Then, sighing, Beltane arose and came where stood Sir Benedict who forthwith hailed him blithely:

"Can we but hold them until the dawn, Beltane — and mark me, we can, here is a work shall make us strong 'gainst all attacks," and he pointed to the growing barricade. "But what of our noble Friar Martin? But for him, Beltane, but for him and his ancient company we had been hard put to it, lad. Ha, 'neath that white gown is saint and friar, and, what is better — a man! Now God be praised, yonder cometh the dawn at last! Though forsooth this hath been a sorry wedding-night for thee, dear lad — and for her, sweet maid —"

"Thou dost know then, Benedict?"

"Think ye not good Roger hasted to tell me, knowing thy joy is my joy — ha! list ye to those blessed joy-bells! glory be to God, there doth trusty Eric tell us he hath made an end of such as stormed the breach. But who cometh here? And by this hand, in tears!"

Already in the east was a roseate glory by whose soft light Beltane beheld Tall Orson, who grasped a bloody sword in one hand and wiped away his tears with the other. He, perceiving Beltane and Sir Benedict, limped to them forthwith and spake, albeit hoarse and brokenly.

"Lords, I do be bid hither to bring ye where he lieth a-dying — the noblest as do be in this world alive — his white robe all bloodied, lords, yet his face do be an angel's face!"

"Ah," sighed Beltane rising, "is it the noble Friar Martin, Orson?"

"Aye, lord, it do be he — as blessed me wi' his poor hand as do be so faint and feeble."

So saying, Orson brought them to a house beside the wall, wherein, upon a pallet, the white friar lay with Jenkyn beside him, and the white-haired Reeve and many other of the sturdy townsfolk about him.

Now came Beltane to kneel beside the friar, who, opening swooning eyes, smiled and spake faint-voiced:

"My lord Beltane — noble son, my work on earth is ended, methinks — so doth God call me hence — and I do go right gladly. These dying eyes grow dim — but with the deathless eyes of the soul I do see many things most plainly — so, dear and valiant children, hear ye this! The woes of Belsaye are past and done — behold, thy deliverance is at hand! I see one that rideth from the north — and this I give thee for a sign — he is tall, this man, bedight in sable armour and mounted upon a great white horse. And behind him marcheth a mighty following — the woods be bright with the gleam of armour! O ye valiant men — O children of Belsaye that I have loved so well, let now your hearts be glad! O Belsaye town, thy shames and sorrows be passed away forever. I see thee through the years a rich city and a happy, thy gates ever open to the woeful and distressed! Rejoice, rejoice — thy sorrows are past and done — even as mine. Ah, list — list ye to those bells! Hear ye not their joyful clamour — hearken!"

But indeed, silence had fallen upon Belsaye, and no sound brake the quiet save the distant hum and stir of conflict upon the broken wall. Nevertheless the friar's dying face waxed bright with a wondrous happiness.

"O blessed — blessed sound!" he whispered. Of a sudden he rose up from his pillow with radiant eyes uplifted, and stretched up arms in eager welcome.

"Sweet Jesu!" he whispered. Slowly his arms sank, the thin hands strove to fold themselves — fell apart, and, sighing rapturously, Friar Martin sank back upon his pillows like one that is weary, and, with the sigh, was dead. And lo! in that same moment, from tower and belfry near and far, rose a sudden wild and gladsome clamour of bells ringing out peal on peal of rapturous joy, insomuch that those who knelt beside that couch of death lifted bowed heads — eye questioning eye in a wonder beyond words.

And now, all at once was the ring and tramp of mailed feet coming swiftly, and in the doorway stood Roger, his riven mail befouled with battle.

"Lords!" he panted, "rejoice — rejoice! our woes and sorrows be past and done — hark ye to the bells! Our deliverance cometh from the north — you shall see the woods alight with — the gleam of their armour!"

Nothing saying, Beltane arose and went soft-treading from the chamber, past the blood and horror of the breach, and climbing the flanking tower beside the gate, looked to the north. And there he beheld a mighty company that marched forth of the woods, rank upon rank, whose armour, flashing in the early sun, made a dazzling splendour against the green. Company by company they mustered on the plain, knights and men-at-arms with footmen and archers beyond count.

And presently, before this deep array, two standards were advanced — a white banner whereon was a red lion and a banner on whose blue ground black leopards were enwrought.

Now as Beltane gazed upon this glorious host he felt a gentle hand touch him and turning, beheld the Duchess Helen, and her cheek showed pale with her long night vigil.

"My Beltane," said she, flushing 'neath his regard, " lord Duke of Mortain, behold yonder thy goodly powers of Mortain that shall do thy bidding henceforth — look yonder, my lord Duke!"

"Duke!" quoth Beltane, "Duke of Mortain — forsooth, and am I so indeed? I had forgot this quite, in thy beauty, my Helen, and did but know that I had to wife one that I do love beyond all created things. And now, beloved, thy sweet eyes do tell me thy night was sleepless."

"Mine eyes — ah, look not on them, Beltane, for well I know these poor eyes be all red and swollen with weeping for thee — though indeed I bathed them ere I sought thee —"

"Sweet eyes of love!" said he, setting his arm about her, "come let me kiss them!"

"Ah, no, Beltane, look yonder — behold where salvation cometh —"

"I had rather look where my salvation lieth, within these dear eyes — nay, abase them not. And didst weep for me, and wake for me, my Helen?"

"I was so — so fearful for thee, my lord."

"Aye, and what more?"

"And very sorrowful —"

"Aye, and what more?"

"And — heartsick —"

"Aye, sweet my wife — but what more?"

"And — very lonely, Beltane —"

Then my Beltane caught her close and kissed her full long, until she struggled in his embrace and slipping from him, stood all flushed and breathless and shy-eyed. But of a sudden she caught his hand and pointed where, before the glittering ranks of Mortain's chivalry, a herald advanced.

"Look, Beltane," she said, "oh, look and tell me who rideth yonder!"

Now behind this herald two knights advanced, the one in glittering armour whose shield was resplendent with many quarterings, but beholding his companion, Beltane stared in wondering awe; for lo! he saw a tall man bedight in sable armour who bore a naked sword that flashed in the sun and who bestrode a great, white charger. And because of Friar Martin's dying words, Beltane stood awed and full of amaze.

Nearer and nearer they came until all men might read the cognizance upon the first knight's resplendent shield and know him for one Sir Jocelyn, lord of Alain, but his companion they knew not, since neither charge nor blazon bore he of any sort. Of a sudden the herald set clarion to lip and blew a challenge that was taken up and answered from within the camp, and forth came Duke Ivo, bareheaded in his armour and with knights attendant, who, silencing the heralds with a gesture, spake loud and fierce.

"Sir Jocelyn, lord of Alain, why come ye against me in arms and so ungently arrayed, wherefore come ye in such force, and for what?"

Then answered Sir Jocelyn:

"My lord Ivo, thou wert upon a time our honoured guest within Mortain, thou didst with honeyed word and tender phrase woo our fair young Duchess to wife. But — and heed this, my lord! — when Helen the Beautiful, the Proud, did thy will gainsay, thou didst in hearing of divers of her lords and counsellors vow and swear to come one day and seek her with flaming brands. So here today stand I and divers other gentles of Mortain — in especial this right noble lord — to tell thee that so long as we be men ne'er shalt set foot across our marches. Lastly, we are hither come to demand the safe conduct from Belsaye of our lady Duchess Helen, and such of the citizens as may choose to follow her."

"So!" quoth Duke Ivo, smiling and fingering his long, blue chin, "'tis war ye do force on me, my lord of Alain?"

"Nay, messire," answered Sir Jocelyn, "that must be asked of this sable knight — for he is greater than I, and leadeth where I do but follow."

Now hereupon the black knight paced slowly forward upon his great, white horse nor stayed until he came close beside Duke Ivo. Then reining in his charger, he lifted his vizor and spake in voice deep and strong.

"O thou that men call Ivo the Duke, look upon this face — behold these white hairs, this lined brow! Bethink thee of the innocent done to cruel death by thy will, the fair cities given to ravishment and flame — and judge if this be just and sufficient cause for war, and bitter war, betwixt us!"

Now beholding the face of the speaker, his proud and noble bearing, his bold eyes fierce and bright and the grim line of nose and chin, Duke Ivo blenched and drew back, the smile fled from his lip, and he stared wide of eye and breathless.

"Beltane!" quoth he at last, "Beltane — ha! methought thee dusty bones these many years — so it is war, I judge?"

For answer Duke Beltane lifted on high the long sword he bore.

"Ivo," said he, "the cries and groans of my sorrowful and distressed people have waked me from my selfish griefs at last — so am I come for vengeance on their innocent blood, their griefs and wrongs so long endured of thee. This do I swear thee, that this steel shall go unsheathed until I meet thee in mortal combat — and ere this sun be set one of us twain shall be no more."

"Be it so," answered Black Ivo, "this night belike I

shall hang thee above the ruins of Belsaye yonder, and thy son with thee!" So saying, he turned about and chin on fist rode into his camp, where was mounting and mustering in hot haste.

"Beltane," spake the Duchess, clasping Beltane's hand, "dost know at last?"

"Aye," answered he with eyes aglow, "But how cometh my noble father yonder?"

"I sought him out in Holy Cross Thicket, Beltane. I told him of thy valiant doings and of thy need of instant aid, and besought him to take up arms for thee and for me and for dear Mortain, and to lead my army 'gainst —"

But Beltane, falling before her on his knee spake quick and passionate:

"O Helen — Helen the Beautiful! without thee I had been nought, and less than nought! Without thee, Pentavalon had groaned yet 'neath cruel wrong! Without thee — O without thee, my Helen, I were a thing lost and helpless in very truth!"

Now hereupon, being first and foremost a woman, young and loving and passionate, needs must she weep over him a little and stoop to cherish his golden head on her bosom, and holding it thus sweetly pillowed, to kiss him full oft and thereafter loose him and blush and sigh and turn from his regard, all sweet and shy demureness like the very maid she was.

Whereat Beltane, forgetful of all but her loveliness, heedful of nought in the world but her warm young beauty, rose up from his knees and, trembling-mute with love, would have caught her to his eager arms; but of a sudden cometh Giles, breathless — basting up the narrow stair and, all heedless of his lord, runneth to fling himself upon his knees before the Duchess, to catch her robe and kiss it oft.

"O dear and gracious lady!" he cried, "Genevra hath told me! And is it true thou hast promised me a place within thy court at fair Mortain — is it true thou wilt lift me up that I may wed with one so much o'er me in

station — is it true thou wilt give me my Genevra, my heart's desire — all unworthy though I be — I — O —"
And behold! Giles's ready tongue faltered for very gratitude and on each tanned cheek were bright, quick-falling tears.

"Giles," said she, "thou wert true and faithful to my lord when his friends were few, so methinks thou should'st be faithful and true to thy sweet Genevra — so will I make thee Steward and Bailiff of Mortain an my lord is in accord —"

"Lord," quoth Giles brokenly, "ere thou dost speak, beseech thee hear this. I have thought on thy saying regarding my past days — and grieved sorely therefore. Now an ye do think my shameful past beyond redemption, if these arms be too vile to clasp her as my wife, if my love shall bring her sorrow or shame hereafter, then — because I do truly love her — I will see her no more; I will — leave her to love one more worthy than I. And this I do swear thee, master — on the cross!"

Quoth Beltane:

"Giles, he that knoweth himself unworthy, if that his love be a true love, shall by that love make himself, mayhap, worthier than most. He that loveth so greatly that in his love base self is forgot — such a man, methinks, doth love in God-like fashion. So shall it be as my lady hath said."

Then Giles arose, and wiping off his tears strove to speak his thanks but choked upon a sob instead, and turning, hasted down the turret stair.

Now presently within the city Sir Benedict's trumpets blew, and looking from the battlement Beltane beheld Sir Hacon mustering their stout company, knights and men-at-arms, what time Roger and Walkyn and Ulf ordered what remained of their pikemen and archers.

"Beloved!" sighed Beltane, drawing his Duchess within his arm, "see yonder, 'tis horse and saddle — soon must I leave thee again."

Now did she sigh amain, and cling to him and droop her

lovely head, yet when she spake her words were brave:

"My Beltane, this love of mine is such that I would not have thee fail in duty e'en though this my heart should break — but ah! husband, stay yet a little longer, I — I have been a something lonely wife hitherto, and I — do hate loneliness, Beltane —" A mailed foot sounded upon the stone stair and, turning about, they beheld a knight in resplendent armour, blazoned shield slung before.

"Greeting to thee, my lord Duke of Mortain, and to thy lovely lady wife," spake a cheery voice, and the speaker, lifting his vizor, behold! it was Sir Benedict. "I go in mine own armour to-day, Beltane, that haply thy noble father shall know me in the press. Ha, see where he ordereth his line, 'twas ever so his custom, I mind me — in four columns with archers betwixt. Mark me now lad, I have brought thee here a helm graced with these foolish feathers as is the new fashion — white feathers, see you — that my lady's sweet eyes may follow thee in the affray."

"For that, dear Benedict," cried she, "for that shalt kiss me, so off with thy great helm!" Forthwith Sir Benedict did off his casque, and stooping, kissed her full-lipped, and meeting Beltane's eye, flushed and laughed and was solemn all in a moment.

"Ah, Beltane, dear lad," quoth he, "I envy thee and grieve for thee! To possess such a maid to wife — and to leave her — so soon! May God bring thee safe again to her white arms. Ah, youth is very sweet, lad, and love — true love is youth's fair paradise and — body o' me, there sound our tuckets! See where Ivo formeth his main battle — and yonder he posteth a goodly company to shut us up within the city. So must we wait a while until the battle joins — thy noble father is wondrous wise in war — O verily he hath seen, behold how he altereth his array! O wise Beltane!"

Now Duke Ivo threw out a screen of archers and horsemen to harass the powers of Mortain what time he formed his battle in three great companies, a deep and formidable array of knights and men-at-arms whose tall lances rose, a very forest, with pennons and banderols a-flutter in the gentle wind of morning. Far on the left showed the banner of his marshal Sir Bors; above his right battle flew the Raven banner of Sir Pertolepe the Red, and above his main battle rose his own standard — a black lion on a red field. So mustered he his powers of Pentavalon, gay with stir of pennons and rich trappings; the sun flashed back from ponderous casques and bascinets innumerable and flamed on blazoned shields. And beholding their might and confident bearing, Beltane clenched nervous hands and his mouth grew hard and grim, so turned he from this formidable host to where, just beyond the woods, his father's banner flew beside the leopards of Mortain. Conspicuous upon his white charger he beheld Duke Beltane, a proud and warlike figure, who sat his stamping war-horse deep in converse with Sir Jocelyn, while behind were the dense ranks of Mortain. Suddenly, Sir Jocelyn wheeled his charger and galloped along Mortain's front, his rich armour glittering, until he halted at the head of that knightly company posted upon the left.

Meantime, Black Ivo's archers advancing, fell into arrow formation and began to ply the Mortain ranks with clouds of shafts and bolts 'neath which divers men and horses fell — what time Black Ivo's massed columns moved slowly forward to the attack — yet Duke Beltane, sitting among his knights, stirred not, and the army of Mortain abode very silent and still. But of a sudden Duke Beltane wheeled his horse, his sword flashed on high, whereat trumpets brayed and on the instant Sir Jocelyn wheeled off to the left, he and all his company, and gathering speed began to skirt Duke Ivo's advanced pikemen and archers, and so rode down upon those men of Pentavalon who were drawn up against Belsaye. Hereupon Black Ivo would have launched a counter-charge to check Sir Jocelyn's attack, but his advanced lines of cross-bowmen and archers hampered him. Once again Duke Beltane's sword flashed up, the first line of Mortain's great array leapt forward and with levelled lances thundered down upon Black Ivo's ranks, scattering and trampling down his archers; but as they checked before the serried pikes behind, forth galloped Duke Beltane's second line and after this a third — o'erwhelming Ivo's pikemen by their numbers, and bursting over and through their torn ranks, reformed, and, spurring hard, met Ivo's rank with crashing shock in full career. And, behind this raging battle, Duke Beltane rode at the head of his reserves, keen-eyed and watchful, what time Sir Jocelyn was hotly engaged upon the left, nigh unto the town itself.

"Ah, Beltane!" sighed the Duchess, shivering and covering her face —"'tis horrible, horrible — see how they fall!"

"Nay, my brave Fidelis, heed rather how valiant Sir Jocelyn and his knights drive in their advanced lines — ha! Benedict, see how he breaks their array — an he can but turn their flank —"

"Nay, Beltane — yonder cometh the Raven banner where Pertolepe spurreth in support —"

"Aye, but yonder doth my father launch yet another charge — ha! Benedict, let us out and aid them — the way lieth open beyond the drawbridge an we can but turn Ivo's flank!" quoth Beltane looking ever upon the battle, "O, methinks the time is now, Benedict!"

With Helen's soft hand a-tremble in his, Beltane hasted down from the tower and Sir Benedict followed, until they were come to the square where, amid the joyful acclaim of the populace, their small and hardy following were drawn up; and, as they came, from townsfolk and soldiery a shout arose:

"Beltane — the Duke — the Duke!"

"My lord Duke of Mortain," quoth Sir Benedict, "I and thy company do wait thee to lead us."

But Beltane smiled and shook his head.

"Not so, my lord of Bourne, thou art so cunning in war and hast led us so valiantly and well — shalt lead us to this battle, the which I pray God shall be our last! As for me, this day will I march with the foresters — so mount, my lord."

Hereupon, from foresters, from knights and men-at-arms another shout arose what time Sir Benedict, having knelt to kiss the Duchess Helen's white hand, found it woefully a-tremble.

"Alas, my lady Helen," said he, "methinks thine is the harder part this day. God strengthen thy wifely heart, for God, methinks, shall yet bring him to thine embrace!" So saying, Sir Benedict mounted and rode to the head of his lances, where flew his banner. "Unbar the gates!" he cried. And presently the great gates of Belsaye town swung wide, the portcullis clanked up, the drawbridge fell, and thus afar off they beheld where, 'mid swirling dust-cloud the battle raged fierce and fell.

And behold a sorry wight who hobbled toward them on a crutch, so begirt and bandaged that little was to see of him but bright eyes.

"O Sir Hacon!" cried the Duchess, "did I not bid thee to thy bed?"

"Why truly, dear my lady, but since I may not go forth myself, fain would I see my good comrades ride into the battle — faith, methinks I might yet couch a lance but for fear of this thy noble lady, my lord Beltane — aye me, this shall be a dismal day for me, methinks!"

"Nay, then I will keep thee company, good Sir Hacon!" smiled the Duchess a little tremulously, "shalt watch with me from the bartizan and tell me how the day goeth with us."

And now Sir Benedict lifted aloft his lance, the trumpet sounded, and with ring and tramp he with his six hundred knights and men-at-arms rode forth of the market-square, clattering through the narrow street, thundering over the drawbridge, and, forming in the open, spurred away into the battle.

Then Beltane sighed, and kneeling, kissed his lady's white hands:

"Beloved," spake he low-voiced, "e'en now must I go

from thee, but howsoever fortune tend — thine am I through life — aye, and beyond."

"Beltane," she whispered 'twixt quivering lips, "O loved Beltane, take heed to thy dear body, cover thee well with thy shield since thy hurts are my hurts henceforth and with thee thou dost bear my heart — O risk not my heart to death without good cause!" So she bent and kissed him on the brow: but when he would have risen, stayed him. "Wait, my lord!" she whispered and turning, beckoned to one behind her, and lo! Genevra came forward bearing a blue banner.

"My lord," said the Duchess, "behold here thy banner that we have wrought for thee, Genevra and I."

So saying, she took the banner and gave it into Beltane's mailed hand. But as he arose, and while pale-cheeked Genevra, hands clasped upon the green scarf at her bosom, looked wet-eyed where the archers stood ranked, forth stepped Giles and spake quick and eager.

"Lord!" said he, "to-day methinks will be more hard smiting than chance for good archery, wherefore I do pray let me bear thy standard in the fight — ne'er shall foeman touch it whiles that I do live — lord, I pray thee!"

"Be it so, Giles!" So Giles took the banner whiles Beltane fitted on his great, plumed helm; thereafter comes Roger with his shield and Ulf leading his charger whereon he mounted forthwith, and wheeling, put himself at the head of his pikemen and archers, with Roger and Ulf mounted on either flank and Giles bestriding another horse behind.

Yet now needs must he turn to look his last upon the Duchess standing forlorn, and beholding the tender passion of her tearless eyes he yearned mightily to kiss them, and sighed full deep, then, giving the word, rode out and away, the blue standard a-dance upon the breeze; but his heart sank to hear the clash and clang of gate and portcullis, shutting away from him her that was more to him than life itself.

Now when they had gone some way needs must he look

Friar Martin's Dying Prophecy

back at Belsaye, its battered walls, its mighty towers; and high upon the bartizan he beheld two figures, the one beswathed in many bandages, and one he knew who prayed for him, even then; and all at once wall and towers and distant figures swam in a mist of tears wherefore he closed his bascinet, yet not before Giles had seen — Giles, whose merry face was grim now and hard-set, and from whose bright bascinet a green veil floated.

"Lord," said he, blinking bright eyes, "we have fought well ere now, but to-day methinks we shall fight as ne'er we fought in all our days."

"Aye," nodded Beltane, "verily, Giles, methinks we shall!"

Thus saying, he turned and looked upon the rolling battle-dust and settling his feet within the stirrups, clenched iron fingers upon his long sword.

CHAPTER LXIX

HOW AT LAST THEY CAME TO PENTAVALON CITY

ALL day long the din and thunder of battle had roared upon the plain; all day the Duchess Helen with Sir Hacon at her side had watched the eddying dust-clouds rolling now this way, now that, straining anxious eyes to catch the gleam of a white plume or the flutter of the blue banner amid that dark confusion. And oft she heard Sir Hacon mutter oaths half-stifled, and oft Sir Hacon had heard snatches of her breathless prayers as the tide of battle swung to and fro, a desperate fray whence distant shouts and cries mingled in awful din. But now, as the sun grew low, the close-locked fray began to roll southwards fast and ever faster, a mighty storm of eddying dust wherein armour gleamed and steel glimmered back and forth, as Duke Ivo and his proud array fell back and back on their last stronghold of Pentavalon City. Whereupon Sir Hacon, upon the bartizan, cursed no more, but forgetful of his many wounds, waxed jubilant instead.

"Now, by Holy Rood!" he cried, "see, lady — they break — they break! 'Twas that last flanking onset! None but Beltane the Strong could have marshalled that last charge — drawing on Black Ivo to attempt his centre, see you, and crushing in his flanks — so needs must their main battle fall back or meet attack on two sides! Oho, a wondrous crafty leader is Duke Beltane the Strong! See — ha, see now how fast he driveth them — and southward — southward on Pentavalon town!"

"So do I thank God, but see how many — O how many do lie fallen by the way!"

"Why, in battle, most gentle lady, in battle men must

needs fall or wherefore should battles be? Much have I seen of wars, lady, but ne'er saw eyes sterner fray than this —"

"And I pray God," spake the Duchess, shivering, "these eyes may ne'er look upon another! O 'tis hateful sight — see — look yonder!" and she pointed where from the awful battle-wrack reeled men faint with wounds while others dragged themselves painfully across the trampled ground.

"Why, 'twas a bloody business!" quoth the knight, shaking his bandaged head.

"Sir Hacon," said the Duchess, frowning and pale, "I pray you summon me the Reeve, yonder." And when the Reeve was come, she spake him very soft and sweet:

"Messire, I pray you let us out and aid the poor, stricken souls yonder."

"But lady, the battle is not yet won — to open our gates were unwise, methinks."

"Good Reeve, one died but lately whom all men loved, but dying, Friar Martin spake these words —'I see Belsaye rich and happy, her gates ever open to the woeful and distressed.' Come, ope the gates and let us out to cherish these afflicted."

Thus presently forth from Belsaye rode the Duchess Helen, with Sir Hacon beside her and many of the townsfolk, hasting pale-cheeked and trembling to minister unto the hurt and dying, and many there were that day who sighed out their lives in blessings on her head.

But meantime the battle roared, fierce and furious as ever, where Black Ivo's stubborn ranks, beset now on three sides, gave back sullenly, fighting step by step.

And amid the blood and dust, in the forefront of that raging tumult, a torn and tattered blue banner rocked and swayed, where Beltane with Giles at his right hand led on his grim foresters, their ranks woefully thinned and with never a horse among them. But Roger was there, his face besmeared with blood that oozed 'neath his dinted bascinet, and Ulf was there, foul with slaughter, and there was

Walkyn fierce and grim, while side by side amid the trampling pikemen behind, Jenkyn and Tall Orson fought. And presently to Beltane came Walkyn, pointing eagerly to their left.

"Master," he cried, "yonder flaunteth Pertolepe's banner, beseech thee let us make thitherward —"

"Not so," quoth Beltane, stooping 'neath the swing of a gisarm, "O forget thy selfish vengeance, man, and smite but for Pentavalon this day — her foes be many enow, God wot! Ho!" he roared, "they yield! they yield! Close up pikes — in, in — follow me!" Forward leapt he with Roger beside him and the blue banner close behind, and forward leapt those hardy foresters where the enemy's reeling line strove desperately to stand and re-form. So waxed the fight closer, fiercer; griping hands fumbled at mailed throats and men, locked in desperate grapple, fell and were lost 'neath the press; but forward went the tattered banner, on and on until, checking, it reeled dizzily, dipped, swayed and vanished; but Roger had seen and sprang in with darting point.

"Up, man," he panted, covering the prostrate archer with his shield, "up, Giles, an ye can — we're close beset —"

"But we be here, look'ee Roger — 'tis we, look'ee!" cried a voice behind.

"Aye, it do be us!" roared another voice, and Roger's assailants were borne back by a line of vicious-thrusting pikes.

"Art hurt, Giles?"

"Nay," quoth the archer, getting to unsteady legs, "but they've spoiled me Genevra's veil, methinks — and our flag is something smirched, but, as for me, I'll sing ye many a song yet!"

"Then here's twice I've saved thee, Giles, so art two accursed notches from my —"

A mace beat Roger to his knees, but, ere his assailant could strike again, Giles's broadsword rose and fell.

"So are we quits, good Roger!" he cried, "Ha, see

— they break! On, pikes, on! Bows and bills, sa-ha!"

Up rose the dust, forward swept the battle as Black Ivo's hosts gave back before the might of Mortain; forward the blue banner reeled and staggered where fought Beltane fierce and untiring, his long shield hacked and dinted, his white plumes shorn away, while ever his hardy foresters smote and thrust on flank and rear. Twice Black Roger fell and twice Giles leapt 'twixt him and death, and perceiving his haggard eyes and the pallor of his grimed and bloody cheek, roared at him in fierce anxiety:

"Fall out, Roger, fall out and rest ye, man!"

"Not whiles I can stand, archer!"

"Art a fool, Roger."

"Belike I am, Giles —"

"And therefore do I love thee, Rogerkin! Ha, bear up man, yonder is water — a muddy brook —"

"O blessed Saint Cuthbert!" panted Roger.

Now before them was a water-brook and beyond this brook Black Ivo's harassed columns made a fierce and desperate rally what time they strove to re-form their hard-pressed ranks; but from Duke Beltane's midmost battle the trumpets brayed fierce and loud, whereat from a thousand parched throats a hoarse cry rose, and chivalry and foot, the men of Mortain charged with levelled lance, with goring pike, with whirling axe and sword, and over and through and beyond the brook the battle raged, sweeping ever southwards.

Presently before them the ground sloped sharply down, and while Beltane shouted warning to those behind, his voice was drowned in sudden trumpet-blast, and glancing to his left, he beheld at last all those knights and men-at-arms who had ridden with his father in their reserve all day — a glittering column, rank on rank, at whose head, his sable armour agleam, his great, white charger leaping 'neath the spur, Duke Beltane rode. Swift and sure the column wheeled and with lances couched thundered down upon Black Ivo's reeling flank.

A crash, a sudden roaring clamour, and where had marched Black Ivo's reserve of archers and pikemen was nought but a scattered rout. But on rode Duke Beltane, his lion banner a-flutter, in and through the enemy's staggering columns, and ever as he charged thus upon their left, so charged Sir Jocelyn upon their right. Then Beltane leaned him on his sword, and looking down upon the battle, bowed his head.

"Now praise be to God and his holy saints!" quoth he, "yonder is victory at last!"

"Aye, master," said Roger hoarsely, "and yonder as the dust clears you shall see the walls and towers of Pentavalon City!"

"And lord — lord," cried Walkyn, "yonder — in their rear — you shall see Red Pertolepe's accursed Raven banner! Why tarry we here, lord? See, their ranks break everywhere — 'twill be hot-foot now for the city gates — ha, let us on, master!"

"Aye, verily," quoth Beltane, looking westward, "it groweth to sunset and the city is yet to storm. To your ranks, there — forward!"

Now as they advanced, Beltane beheld at last where, high above embattled walls and towers, rose Pentavalon's mighty keep wherein he had been born; and, remembering his proud and gentle mother, he drooped his head and grieved; and bethinking him of his proud and gentle Helen, he took fresh grip upon his sword, and lengthening his stride, looked where Black Ivo's broken columns, weary with battle, grim with blood and wounds, already began to ride 'neath the city's frowning gateway, while hard upon their straggling rearguard Duke Beltane's lion banner fluttered. A desperate hewing and thrusting in the narrow gateway, and Black Ivo's shattered following were driven in and the narrow streets and alleys of the town full of battle and slaughter. Street by street the town was won until before them loomed the mighty keep of Pentavalon's ducal stronghold. Outer and inner bailey were stormed and so at last came they, a desperate, close-

How They Came to the City

fighting company, into the great tilt-yard before the castle.

Now of a sudden a shout went up and thereafter was a great quiet — a silence wherein friend and foe, panting and weary, stood alike at gaze. And amid this expectant hush the two Dukes of Pentavalon fronted each other. No word said they, but, while all eyes watched them, each took lance and riding to the extremity of the courtyard, wheeled, and couching their lances, spurred fiercely against each other. And now men held their breath to behold these two great knights, who, crouched low in their saddles, met midway in full career with crash and splintering shock of desperate onset. Duke Beltane reeled in his stirrups, recovered, and leaning forward stared down upon his enemy, who, prostrate on his back, slowly lifted gauntleted hand that, falling weakly, clashed upon the stones — a small sound, yet plain to be heard by reason of that breathless hush.

Slow and stiffly Duke Beltane dismounted, and reeling in his gait, came and knelt beside Black Ivo and loosed off his riven helm. Thereafter, slow and painfully, he arose, and looking round upon all men, spake faint-voiced.

"God — hath judged — betwixt us this day!" said he, "and to-day — methinks — He doth summon me — to judgment —" Even as he spake he lifted his hands, struggling with the lacing of his helmet, staggered, and would have fallen, wherefore Beltane sprang forward. Yet one there was quicker than he, one whose goodly armour, smirched and battered, yet showed the blazon of Bourne.

"Benedict!" quoth Duke Beltane feebly, "faithful wert thou to the last! O Benedict, where is my noble son!"

"Father!" cried Beltane, "thou hast this day won Pentavalon from her shame and misery!" But the Duke lay very still in their arms and spake no word.

So, when they had uncovered his white head, they bore him tenderly into the great banqueting hall and laid him on goodly couch and cherished him with water and wine, wherefore, in a while, he opened swooning eyes.

"Beltane!" he whispered, "dear and noble son — thy

manhood — hath belike won thy father's soul to God's mercy. So do I leave thee to cherish all those that — have known wrong and woe — by reason of my selfish life! Dear son, bury me with thy — noble mother, but let me lie — at her feet, Beltane. O had I been less selfish — in my sorrow! But God is merciful! Benedict — kiss me — and thou, my Beltane — God calleth me — to rest. *In manus tuas — Domine!*" Then Duke Beltane, that had been the Hermit Ambrose, clasped his mailed hands and smiling wondrous glad and tender, yielded his soul to God.

In a while Beltane came forth into the courtyard and beheld Sir Jocelyn mustering their knightly prisoners in the ward below, for, with Black Ivo's death, all resistance was ended. And now the trumpets blared, rallying their various companies, but Beltane abode very full of sorrowful thoughts. To him presently cometh Giles yet grasping the blue standard befouled with dust and blood, the which he laid reverently at Beltane's feet.

"Lord," said he, "my trust is ended. See, yonder standeth our company of foresters!" and he pointed where a single rank of grimed and weary men lay upon the hard flag-stones or leaned on their battered weapons.

"Giles — O Giles, is this all?"

"Aye, lord, we muster but seventy and one all told, and of these Tall Orson lieth dead yonder in Jenkyn's arms, and Roger — poor Roger is a-dying, methinks — and Ulf and Walkyn are not."

But even as he spake he turned and started, for, from the ward below a hunting horn brayed feebly.

"'Tis our forester's rally, master!" quoth he, "and see — Jesu, what men are these?" For into the courtyard, followed by many who gaped and stared in wonderment, six men staggered, men hideously stained and besplashed from head to foot, and foremost came two. And Walkyn was one and Ulf the Strong the other.

Now as he came Walkyn stared in strange, wild fashion, and choked often in his breathing, and his mailed feet dragged feebly, insomuch that he would have fallen but for Ulf's mighty arm. Being come where Beltane stood with Sir Benedict and many other wondering knights and nobles, Walkyn halted and strove to speak but choked again instead. In one hand bare he his great axe, and in the other a torn and stained war-cloak.

"Lord," quoth he in sobbing breaths, " a good day for thee — this — lord Duke — a good day for Pentavalon — a joyous day — blessed day for me — You'll mind they slew mother and father and sister, lord — brother and wife and child? Empty-hearted was I and desolate therefore, but — to-day, ha, to-day I die also, methinks. So, an ye will, lord Duke — keep thou mine axe in memory — of Walkyn — 'tis a goodly axe — hath served me well to-day — behold!"

Now as he spake he loosed a corner of the war-cloak, and from its grimed and ghastly folds there rolled forth into the red light of the cleanly sun a thing that trundled softly across the pavement and stopping, shewed a pallid face crowned with red hair, 'neath which upon the brow, betwixt the staring eyes, was a jagged scar like to a cross.

Now while all men stared upon this direful thing, holding their breaths, Walkyn laughed loud and high, and breaking from Ulf's clasp, staggered to where it lay and pointed thereto with shaking finger.

"Behold!" he cried, "behold the head of Bloody Pertolepe!" Therewith he laughed, and strove to kick it with feeble foot — but staggered instead, and, loosing his axe, stretched wide his long arms and fell, face downward.

"Bloody Pertolepe — is dead!" he cried, and choked; and choking — died.

CHAPTER LXX

WHICH SPEAKETH FOR ITSELF

It was not the piping of throstle or sweet-throated merle that had waked my Beltane, who with slumberous eyes stared up at carven canopy, round him upon rich arras, and down upon embroidered bed-covering and silken pillow, while through the narrow lattice the young sun played upon gilded roof-beam and polished floor. So lay Beltane, blinking sleepy eyes and hearkening to a soft and melodious whistling from the little garden below his casement.

Being thus heavy with sleep, he wondered drowsily what great content was this that filled him, and wherefore? Wondering yet, he sighed, and because of the sun's radiance, closed slumberous eyes again and would have slept; but, of a sudden the whistling ceased, and a rich, sweet voice fell to gentle singing.

> "Hark! in the whisper of the wind
> Love calleth thee away,
> Each leaf a small, soft voice doth find,
> Each pretty bird doth cry in kind,
> O heart, haste north to-day."

Beltane sat up broad awake, for Blaen lay to the north, and in Blaen — But Giles was singing on:

> "Youth is quick to speed away,
> But love abideth ever.
> Fortune, though she smile to-day,
> Fickle is and will not stay,
> But true-love changeth never.
>
> "The world doth change, as change it must,
> But true-love changeth never.
> Proud ambition is but dust,

> The bow doth break, the sword doth rust,
> But love abideth ever."

Beltane was leaning half out of the casement, of the which fact who so unconscious as Giles, busily furbishing armour and bascinet.

"Giles!" he cried, "O Giles — rouse ye, man!"

"How, lord — art awake so early?" questioned Giles, looking up innocent of eye.

"Was it not for this thou didst sing, rogue Giles? Go now, bid Roger have three horses saddled, for within the hour we ride hence."

"To Mortain, lord?" questioned Giles eagerly.

"Aye, Giles, to Mortain — north to Blaen; where else should we ride to-day?"

So saying, Beltane turned back into his sumptuous chamber and fell to donning, not his habiliments of state, but those well-worn garments, all frayed by his heavy mail. Swift dressed he and almost stealthily, oft pausing to glance into the empty garden below, and oft staying to listen to some sound within the massy building. And thus it was he started to hear a soft knocking at the door, and turning, beheld Sir Benedict.

"Forsooth, art up betimes, my lord Duke," quoth he, bright eyes a-twinkle, "and verily I do commend this so great zeal in thee since there be many and divers matters do need thy ducal attention — matters of state and moment —"

"Matters of state?" saith Beltane, something troubled.

"There be many noble and illustrious lords come in to pay thee homage and swear to thee divers fealty oaths —"

"Then must they wait, Benedict."

"Wait, my lord — men so illustrious! Then this day a deputation waiteth on thee, merchants and what not —"

"These must wait also, Benedict —" saith Beltane, his trouble growing.

"Moreover there is high festival at the minster with much chanting and glorification in thy behalf — and 'tis intended to make for thee a triumphal pageant — fair maidens to strow flowers beneath thy horse's feet, musiciaus to pleasure thee with pipe and tabor — and —"

"Enough, enough, Benedict. Prithee why must I needs endure this?"

"Such things do wait upon success, Beltane, and moreover thou'rt Duke! Aye, verily thou'rt Duke! The which mindeth me that, being Duke, it behoveth thee —"

"And yet, Benedict, I do tell thee that all things must wait awhile, methinks, or better — do you attend them for me —"

"Nay — I am no Duke!" quoth Sir Benedict hastily.

"Yet thou art my chiefest counsellor and lord Seneschal of Pentavalon. So to thy wise judgment I do entrust all matters soever —"

"But I have no warranty, thou cunning boy, and —"

"Shalt have my bond, my ducal ring, nay, the very crown itself, howbeit this day —"

"Wilt ride for Mortain, O lover?" said Sir Benedict, smiling his wry smile.

"Aye, verily, dear Benedict, nor shall aught under heaven let or stay me — yet how knew ye this, Benedict?"

"For that 'tis so my heart would have prompted had I been so blessed as thou art, dear my Beltane. And knowing thou needs must to thy beauteous Helen, I have a meal prepared within my chamber, come your ways and let us eat together."

So came they to a handsome chamber hard by where was spread a goodly repast whereto they did full justice, though talking much the while, until one tapped lightly upon the door, and Roger entered bearing Beltane's newburnished mail.

"Nay, good Roger," said Beltane, smiling, "need for that is done methinks; we ride light to-day!" But Sir Benedict shook wise head.

"My lord 'tis true our wars be ended I thank God, and we may sheathe our swords at last, but the woods be full of Black Ivo's scattered soldiery, with outlaws and other masterless men."

"Ha, verily, lords," quoth Roger, "there shall many turn outlaw, methinks —"

"Then must we end outlawry!" said Beltane, frowning.

"And how would'st do it, Beltane?"

"Make an end of the game laws, Benedict — throw wide the forests to all who will —"

"But master, thus shall every clapper-claw rogue be free to kill for his base sport thy goodly deer, or belike a hart of ten, fit for sport of kings —"

"Well, let them in this thing be kings. But I do hold a man's life dearer than a stag's. So henceforth in Pentavalon the woods are free — I pray you let this be proclaimed forthwith, my lord."

Quoth Sir Benedict, as with Roger's aid Beltane did on his armour:

"There is a postern beyond the pleasaunce yonder shall bring you forth of the city and no man the wiser."

"Why, then, bring ye the horses thither, Roger, and haste ye!"

Now when Roger was gone, Sir Benedict arose and setting his hands on Beltane's shoulders questioned him full serious:

"Mean ye forsooth to make the forests free, Beltane?"

"Aye, verily, Benedict."

"This shall cause much discontent among the lords —"

"Well, we wear swords, Benedict! But this I swear, whiles I am Duke, never again shall a man hang for killing of my deer. Moreover, 'tis my intent forthwith to lower all taxes, more especially in the market towns, to extend their charters and grant them new privileges."

"Beltane, I fear thy years shall be full of discord."

"What matter, an my people prosper? But thou art older and much wiser than I, Benedict, bethink thee of these things then, I pray, and judge how best such changes may be 'stablished, for a week hence, God willing, I summon my first council. But now, dear Benedict, I go to find my happiness."

"Farewell, my lord — God speed thee, my Beltane! O

lad, lad, the heart of Benedict goeth with thee, methinks!" and Sir Benedict turned suddenly away. Then Beltane took and clasped those strong and able hands.

"Benedict," said he, "truer friend man never had than thou, and for this I do love thee — and thou art wise and valiant and great-hearted, and thou didst love my noble mother with a noble love, and for this do I love thee best of all, dear friend."

Then Benedict lifted his head, and like father and son they kissed each other, and together went forth into the sweet, cool-breathing morn.

Beyond the postern were Giles and Black Roger with the horses, and Giles sang blithe beneath his breath, but Roger sighed oft and deep.

Now being mounted, Beltane reined close beside Sir Benedict and smiled full·joyous and spake him thus, low-voiced:

"Dear Benedict, to-day one that loveth thee doth ride away, but in a week two that love thee shall return. And needs must these two love thee ever and always, very greatly, Benedict, since but for thee they had not come to their joy." So saying, he touched spur to flank and bounded away, with Giles and Roger spurring behind.

Soon were they free of the city and reaching that rolling down where the battle had raged so lately, Beltane set his horse to a stretching gallop, and away they raced, over upland and lowland until they beheld afar to their right the walls and towers of Belsaye. But on they rode toward the green of the woods, and ever as they rode Giles sang full blithely to himself whiles Roger gloomed and sighed; wherefore at last the archer turned to clap him on the shoulder.

"What aileth thee, my Rogerkin?" quoth he.

"Ha," growled Roger, "the world waggeth well with thee, Giles, these days, but as for me — poor Roger lacketh. Saint Cuthbert knoweth I have striven and likewise plagued him sore upon the matter, and yet my belt — my accursed belt yet beareth a notch — behold!"

"Why, 'tis but a single notch, Roger."

"Yet a notch it is, forsooth, and how shall my heart go light and my soul clean until I have a belt with notches not one?"

"Belike thou hast forgot some of the lives thou didst save, Roger — mine thou didst save four times within the battle, I mind me —"

"Nay, 'twas but twice, Giles."

"Why, then 'twas thrice, Roger — the banner hampered me and —"

"'Twas but twice, alack!" sighed Roger, "Saint Cuthbert knoweth 'twas but twice and being a very watchful saint may not be cheated, Giles."

"Why then, Roger, do ye beset him in prayer, so, while thou dost hold him in play thus, I will snick away thy solitary notch so sweetly he shall never know —"

"Alack, 'twill not avail, Giles. I must needs bear this notch with me unto the grave, belike."

"Nay, Roger, I will to artifice and subtle stratagem on thy behalf as — mark me! I do know a pool beside the way! Now if I slip within the pool and thou should'st pull me from the pool — how then? Ha — 'tis well bethought, let's do't!"

"Were it any but Saint Cuthbert!" sighed Roger, "but I do thank thee for thy kindly thought, Giles."

Now after this went they some way in silence, Beltane riding ahead very full of thought, and his companions behind, the one smiling and debonair, the other frowning and sad.

"Forsooth," quoth Giles at last, "as thou sayest, Roger, the world waggeth well with me. Hast heard, belike, our lady Duchess hath been pleased to —"

"Aye, I've heard, my lord Bailiff — who hath not?"

"Nay, I did but mention it to two or three," quoth Giles. "Moreover our lord doth smile on me these days, though forsooth he hath been familiar with me since first I found him within the green — long ere he found thee, Rogerkin! I rode a white ass, I mind me, and my lord walked beside me very fair and soft-spoken, whereupon I called him — Sir Dove! O me — a dove, mark you! Since when, as ye know, we have been comrades, he and I, nay, brothers-in-arms, rather! Very close in his counsels I — very near to all his thoughts and actions. All of the which cometh of possessing a tongue as ready as my wit, Rogerkin!"

Now as he hearkened, Roger's frown grew blacker and his powerful hand clenched upon the bridle.

"And yet," quoth Giles, "as I am in my lord's dear friendship, so art thou in mine, Roger, man, nor in my vaulting fortunes will I e'er forget thee. Belike within Mortain shalt aid me in my new duties, or shall I speak my lord on thy behalf?"

"Ha!" cried Roger suddenly, "first tell me this, my lord Steward and high Bailiff of Mortain, did the Duke my master chance ever to take thy hand, to wet it with his tears and — kiss it?"

"Art mad, Roger! Wherefore should my lord do this?"

"Aye," nodded Roger, "wherefore?"

And when Giles had whistled awhile and Roger had scowled awhile, the archer spake again:

"Hast never been in love, Roger?"

"Never, Saint Cuthbert be praised!"

"Then canst know nought of the joy and wonder of it. So will I make for thee a song of love, as thus: open thine ears and hearken:

"So fair, so sweet, so pure is she
I do thank God;
Her love an armour is to me
'Gainst sorrow and adversity,
So in my song right joyfully
I do thank God for love.

"Her love a cloak is, round me cast,
I do thank God;
To cherish me 'gainst fortunes blast.

Her love, forgetting evils past,
Shall lift me up to heaven at last,
So I thank God for love."

"Here is a fair song, methinks; dost not wonder at love now, Roger, and the glory of it?"

"I wonder," quoth Roger, "how long thou shalt believe all this when thou art wed. I wonder how long thou wilt live true to her when she is thy wife!"

Now hereupon the archer's comely face grew red, grew pale, his bronzed hands flew to his belt and leapt on high, gripping his dagger; but Roger had seen, his fingers closed on the descending wrist and they grappled, swaying in their saddles.

Grim and silent they slipped to earth and strove together on the ling. But Roger had Giles in a cruel wrestling-hold, wrenched him, bent him, and bearing him to earth, wrested away the dagger and raised it above the archer's naked throat. And Giles, lying powerless beneath, looked up into Roger's fierce scowling face and seeing no pity there, his pale cheek grew paler and in his eyes came an agony of broken hopes; but his gaze quailed not and when he spake, his voice was firm.

"Strike true, comrade!" said he.

The hand above him wavered; the dagger was dashed aside and covering his face, Black Roger crouched there, his broad shoulders and powerful figure quaking and shivering. Then Giles arose and stepping to his dagger, came back with it grasped in his hand.

"Roger!" said he.

Quoth Roger, his face still hidden:

"My throat is bare also, archer!"

"Roger — comrade, give to me thy belt!"

Now at this Roger looked up, wondering.

"My belt?" quoth he, "what would ye, Giles?"

"Cut away thy last notch, Roger — thy belt shall go smooth-edged henceforth and thy soul clean, methinks."

"But I meant to slay thee, Giles."

"But spared me, Roger, spared me to life and — love, my Rogerkin. O friend, give me thy belt!"

So Roger gave him the belt, wherefrom Giles forthwith cut the last notch, which done, they together, like mischievous lads, turned to look where their lord rode far ahead; and beholding him all unconscious and lost in thought, they sighed their relief and mounting, went on together.

Now did Roger oft glance at Giles who kept his face averted and held his peace, whereat Roger grew uneasy, fidgeted in his saddle, fumbled with the reins, and at last spake:

"Giles!"

"Aye, Roger!"

"Forgive me!"

But Giles neither turned nor spake, wherefore contrite Roger must needs set an arm about him and turn him about, and behold, the archer's eyes were brimming with great tears!

"O Giles!" gasped Roger, "O Giles!"

"Roger, I — I do love her, man — I do love her, heart and soul! Is this so hard to believe, Roger, or dost think me rogue so base that true love is beyond me? 'Tis true I am unworthy, and yet — I do verily love her, Roger!"

"Wilt forgive me — can'st forgive me, Giles?"

"Aye, Roger, for truly we have saved each other's lives so oft we must needs be friends, thou and I. Only thy words did — did hurt me, friend — for indeed this love of mine hath in it much of heaven, Roger. And — there be times when I do dream of mayhap — teaching — a little Giles — to loose a straight shaft — some day. O sweet Jesu, make me worthy, amen!"

And now Beltane glancing up and finding the sun high, summoned Giles and Roger beside him.

"Friends," said he, "we have journeyed farther than methought. Now let us turn into the boskage yonder and eat."

So in a while, the horses tethered, behold them within a

Which Speaketh for Itself 567

leafy bower eating and drinking and laughing like the blithe foresters they were, until, their hunger assuaged, they made ready to mount. But of a sudden the bushes parted near by and a man stepped forth; a small man he, plump and buxom, whose quick, bright eyes twinkled 'neath his wide-eaved hat as he saluted Beltane with obeisance very humble and lowly. Quoth he:

"Right noble and most resplendent lord Duke Beltane, I do most humbly greet thee, I — Lubbo Fitz-Lubbin, past Pardoner of the Holy See — who but a poor plain soul am, do offer thee my very insignificant, yet most sincere, felicitous good wishes."

"My thanks are thine, Pardoner. What more would you?"

"Breath, lord methinks," said Giles, "wind, my lord, after periods so profound and sonorous!"

"Lord Duke, right puissant and most potential, I would but tell thee this, to wit, that I did keep faith with thee, that I, by means of this unworthy hand, did set thee beyond care, lift thee above sorrow, and gave to thee the heaven of thy most warm and earnest desires."

"How mean you, Pardoner?"

"Lord Duke, when thou didst bestow life on two poor rogues upon a time, when one rogue stole away minded to betray thee to thine enemy, the second rogue did steal upon the first rogue, and this second rogue bare a small knife whereof the first rogue suddenly died. And thus Duke Ivo, thine enemy, came not before Belsaye until thou and thy company were safe within its walls. So by reason of this poor second rogue, Pentavalon doth rejoice in freedom. To-day is singing on every village green — happiness is in the very air, for 'tis Pentavalon's Beltane, and Beltane is a sweet season; so doth this poor second rogue find him recompense. Verily art well named, lord Beltane, since in thee Pentavalon's winter is passed away and spring is come — O happy season of Beltane, O season of new beginnings and new hopes! So, my lord Beltane, may it ever be Beltane with thee, may it be sweet spring ever within thy noble heart. God keep thee and farewell."

So saying the Pardoner turned about, and plunging into the dense green, was gone.

"A pestilent wordy fellow, lord," quoth Giles, "one of your windy talkers that talketh that no other talker may talk — now give me a good listener, say I."

"And yet," said Beltane, swinging to saddle, "spake he truly I wonder? Had Ivo been a little sooner we had not been here, methinks!"

On they rode, through sun and shadow, knee and knee, beneath leafy arches and along green glades, talking and laughing together or plunged in happy thought.

Quoth Beltane of a sudden:

"Roger, hast heard how Giles waxeth in fortune these days?"

"And methinks no man is more worthy, master. Giles is for sure a man of parts."

"Aye — more especially of tongue, Roger."

"As when he did curse the folk of Belsaye out o' their fears, master. Moreover he is a notable archer and —"

"Art not envious, then, Roger?"

"Not I, master!"

"What would'st that I give unto thee?"

"Thy love, master."

"'Tis thine already, my faithful Roger."

"And therewithal am I content, master."

"Seek ye nought beside?"

"Lord, what is there? Moreover I am not learned like Giles, nor ready of tongue, nor —"

"Art wondrous skilled in wood-lore, my Rogerkin!" quoth Giles. "Forsooth, lord, there is no man knoweth more of forestry than my good comrade Roger!"

"So will I make of him my chiefest huntsman, Giles —"

"Master — O master!" gasped Roger.

"And set thee over all my foresters of Pentavalon, Roger."

"Why master, I — forsooth I do love the greenwood —

but lord, I am only Roger, and — and how may I thank thee —"

"Come!" cried Beltane, and spurred to a gallop.

Thus rode they through the leafy by-ways, avoiding town and village; yet oft from afar they heard the joyous throb of bells upon the air, or the sound of merry voices and happy laughter from village commons where folk rejoiced together that Ivo's iron yoke was lifted from them at last. But Beltane kept ever to the woods and by-ways, lest, being recognised, he should be stayed longer from her of whom he dreamed, bethinking him ever of the deep, shy passion of her eyes, the soft tones of her voice, the clinging warmth of her caress, and all the sweet, warm beauty of her. Betimes they crossed the marches into Mortain, but it was late evening ere they saw at last the sleepy manor of Blaen, its white walls and steepy roofs dominated by its one square watch-tower, above which a standard, stirring lazily in the gentle air, discovered the red lion of Pentavalon.

And now Beltane's breath grew short and thick, his strong hand trembled on the bridle, and he grew alternate hot and cold. So rode they into the echoing courtyard whither hasted old Godric to welcome them, and divers servants to take their horses. Being ushered forthwith into the garden, now who so silent and awkward as my Beltane, what time his lady Duchess made known to him her gentle ladies, among whom sweet Genevra, flushed of cheek, gazed breathless upon Giles even as Giles gazed upon her — who so mumchance as Beltane, I say, who saw and heard and was conscious only of one among them all. And who so stately, so calm-voiced and dignified as this one until — aye, until they stood alone together, and then —

To see her sway to his fierce arms, all clinging, yearning womanhood, her state and dignity forgotten quite! To hear her voice soft and low and all a-thrill with love, broken with sighs and sinking to passionate-whispered questioning:

"And thou art come back to me at last, Beltane! Hast brought to me my heart unharmed from the battle, beloved! And thou didst take no hurt — no hurt, my Beltane? And art glad to see — thy — wife, Beltane? And dost love me — as much as ever, Beltane? O wilt never, never leave me desolate again, my lord — art thou mine — mine henceforth as I am thine, Beltane? And wilt desire me ever near thee, my lord?"

"Helen," said he, "O my 'Helen the Beautiful'— our wars be ended, our time of waiting is done, I thank God! So am I here to claim thee, beloved. Art glad to be in mine arms — glad I am come to — make thee mine own at last, Helen?"

"I had died without thee, Beltane — I would not live without thee now, my Beltane. See, my lord, I — O how may I speak if thus you seal my lips, Beltane? And prithee how may I show thee this gown I wear for thee if thou wilt hold me so — so very close, Beltane?"

And in a while as the moon rose she brought him into that bower he well remembered and bade him admire the beauty of her many flowers, and he, viewing her loveliness alway, praised the flowers exceeding much yet beheld them not at all, wherefore she chid him, and yet chiding, yielded him her scarlet mouth. Thus walked they in the fragrant garden until Genevra found them and sweet-voiced bid them in to sup. But the Duchess took Genevra's slender hands and looked within her shy, sweet eyes.

"Art happy, sweet maid?" she questioned.

"O dear my lady, methinks in all this big world is none more happy than thy grateful Genevra."

"Then haste thee back to thy happiness, dear Genevra, to-morrow we will see thee wed."

And presently came they within a small chamber and here Beltane did off his armour, and here they supped together, though now the lady Helen spake little and ate less, and oft her swift-flushing cheek rebuked the worshipping passion of his eyes; insomuch that presently she arose and going into the great chamber beyond, came back, and kneeling at his feet, showed him a file.

"Beltane," said she, "thou didst, upon a time, tell poor Fidelis wherefore thy shameful fetters yet bound thy wrists — so now will thy wife loose them from thee."

Then, while Beltane, speaking not, watched her down-bent head and busy hands, she filed off his fetters one by one, and kissing them, set them aside.

But when she would have risen he prevented her, and with reverent fingers touched the coiled and braided glory of her hair.

"O Helen," he whispered, "loose me down thy hair."

"Nay, dear Beltane —"

"My hands are so big and clumsy —"

"Thy hands are my hands!" and she caught and kissed them.

"Let down for me thy hair, beloved, I pray thee!"

"Forsooth my lord and so I will — but — not yet."

"But the — the hour groweth late, Helen!"

"Nay — indeed —'tis early yet, my lord — nay, as thou wilt, my Beltane, only suffer that I — I leave thee a while, I pray."

"Must I bide here alone, sweet wife?"

"But indeed I will — call thee anon, my lord."

"Nay, first — look at me, my Helen!"

Slowly, slowly she lifted her head and looked on him all sweet and languorous-eyed.

"Aye, truly — truly thine eyes are not — a nun's eyes, Helen. So will I wait thy bidding." So he loosed her and she, looking on him no more, turned and hasted into the further chamber.

And after some while she called to him very soft and sweet, and he, trembling, arose and entered the chamber, dim-lighted and fragrant.

But now, beholding wherefore she had left him, his breath caught and he stood as one entranced, nor moved, nor spake he a while.

"O Helen!" he murmured at last, "thou art glorious so — and with thy long hair —"

But now, even as he came to her, the Duchess Helen put out the little silver lamp. But in the moonlit dusk she gave her lips to his, and her tender arms were close about him.

"Beltane," she whispered 'neath his kiss, "dear my lord and husband, here is an end at last of sorrow and heart-break, I pray."

"Here — my Helen, beginneth — the fulness of life, methinks!"

Now presently upon the stillness, from the court below, stole the notes of a lute and therewith a rich voice upraised in singing:

> "O when is the time a maid to kiss?
> Tell me this, now tell me this.
> 'Tis when the day is scarce begun,
> 'Tis from the setting of the sun.
> Is time for kissing ever done,
> Tell me this, now tell me this."

THE END

CPSIA information can be obtained
at www.ICGtesting.com
Printed in the USA
BVHW090946271118
534105BV00017B/226/P